The Sea in World History

The Sea in World History

EXPLORATION, TRAVEL, AND TRADE

Volume 1: Ancient Egypt through the First Global Age

Stephen K. Stein, Editor

An Imprint of ABC-CLIO, LLC

Santa Barbara, California • Denver, Colorado

Library of Congress Cataloging-in-Publication Data

Names: Stein, Stephen K., editor.
Title: The sea in world history : exploration, travel, and trade / Stephen K. Stein, editor.
Description: Santa Barbara, California : ABC-CLIO, 2017. | Includes bibliographical
    references and index.
Identifiers: LCCN 2016040878 (print) | LCCN 2016059925 (ebook) |
    ISBN 9781440835506 (set : alk. paper) | ISBN 9781440847868 (volume 1 : alk. paper) |
    ISBN 9781440847875 (volume 2 : alk. paper) | ISBN 9781440835513 (ebook)
Subjects: LCSH: Discoveries in geography—History. | Voyages and travels—History. |
    Ocean travel—History. | Commerce—History. | Trade routes—History. | Navigation—History.
Classification: LCC G80 .S39 2017 (print) | LCC G80 (ebook) | DDC 909/.0962—dc23
LC record available at https://lccn.loc.gov/2016040878

ISBN: 978-1-4408-3550-6 (Set)
ISBN: 978-1-4408-4786-8 (Volume 1)
ISBN: 978-1-4408-4787-5 (Volume 2)
EISBN: 978-1-4408-3551-3

21 20 19 18 17   1 2 3 4 5

This book is also available as an eBook.

ABC-CLIO
An Imprint of ABC-CLIO, LLC

ABC-CLIO, LLC
130 Cremona Drive, P.O. Box 1911
Santa Barbara, California 93116-1911
www.abc-clio.com

This book is printed on acid-free paper ∞
Manufactured in the United States of America

Contents

VOLUME 2. A WORLD OF REVOLUTIONS THROUGH THE PRESENT

Preface

The Sea in World History is a two-volume encyclopedia that introduces under-graduate students and general readers to the sea's influence on world history from antiquity to the present. It offers a cross-cultural survey of maritime history that emphasizes the sea as a place of connection among diverse peoples. The sea plays a pivotal role in shaping world history. From ancient times to the present, the sea facilitated diplomacy, trade, and travel. It was a site of exploration and of war. Sailing and navigating the world's oceans stimulated scientific and technological advances and captured people's imaginations, stimulating artistic and literary en-deavors. Examining the human use of the sea provides unique insights in world history. Until the mid-20th century, water voyages offered the fastest way to travel long distances and the only way to move large volumes of goods. Even today, more than 90 percent of world trade moves by sea. Long before the era of great explorers or the globalization of the modern age, the sea connected diverse peoples, and fostered trade and the exchange of ideas. Without discounting the importance of the great era of European overseas exploration and expansion, this work seeks to put that effort into a larger context and provide a broad discussion of maritime activity around the world—from ancient Egypt and Mesopotamia to the modern era. Understanding human involvement with the sea is fundamental to understanding the human experience.

This reference is organized into eight chronological chapters. Each chapter opens with a timeline and general overview of the era's important maritime devel-opments. Next are essays on that era's important seafaring cultures and nations, which explore their interactions with the sea, how it shaped their development, and how the ways people use and see the sea have changed over time. Accompanying these are shorter entries on important topics including explorers, inventors, major events, ports, shipbuilders, ships, and technologies. Although military topics are addressed, the focus of the work is on the major themes of trade, travel, and exploration.

Sidebars accompany many of the longer entries and provide additional insights on particular technologies, ships, people, events, and problems. Each chapter concludes with primary documents that provide contemporary examples of seafaring and enhance the text by highlighting the observations of explorers, traders, travelers, and warriors from different eras, as well as sea literature from diverse cultures and times. The book is arranged by nation or culture, which enables readers to explore specific regions and peoples in detail, following nations through history, rather than hopping from topic to topic as in a reference arranged alphabetically by topic. This continuity facilitates deep learning.

Covering roughly 5,000 years of maritime history, the book is written to be understandable and accessible to undergraduate students and general audiences. It presents a multinational and multicultural perspective on the history of the human use of the sea. Extensive bibliographic resources—including an annotated bibliography at the end of the book—point readers to books and other resources that can further expand their knowledge of topics covered in this work.

Acknowledgments

A project such as this is as much a creation of the writers of individual entries as it is its editor, and I am deeply indebted to them. The writers hail from around the world and include leading scholars in their fields. Many of them contributed beyond my expectations. Kris Alexanderson, Courtney Luckhardt, and Edward Melillo made important suggestions and helped me create and finalize the list of topics. Pearce Paul Creaseman provided important advice on shaping the sections on Egypt and helped connect me with his fellow Egyptologists. Several people provided, suggested, or advised me on primary sources, including Pearce Paul Creaseman, Kevin Dawson, Jeffery Emanuel, Stephan Köhler, Julia Leiken, Courtney Luckhardt, Joy McCann, Tyler Parry, and Felix Schürmann. Others wrote additional entries at the last minute that allowed this book's timely completion, including Torsten Arnold, Brian Becker, Jill Church, Sarah Davis-Secord, Karen Garvin, Samantha Haines, Michael Laver, Edward Melillo, Karl Petruso, Adwita Rai, Birgit Tremml-Werner, and Emma Zuroski. Patrick Hall, my editor at ABC-CLIO, was particularly helpful in guiding this project along smoothly. The students in my 2015 graduate seminar in maritime history, some of whose work appears in this book, helped shape my conception of the project. Finally, my wife Carolyn, apart from her usual unstinting support, stepped in to help at the last minute to help with the manuscript's final preparation.

Introduction

When people first built boats and took to the sea remains uncertain. More than 5,000 years ago, when the first urban civilizations formed in China, Egypt, India, and Mesopotamia, people were already accomplished seafarers, and seafaring facilitated their travels as they spread across the globe. As Plato remarked in the *Phaedo*, people spread along bodies of water, living on islands and coastal areas, such as the Aegean and Mediterranean, like "frogs around a pond" (Plato, *Phaedo* 109b), and this has made the sea a place of trade, travel, exploration, and conflict. The world's seas and oceans—which account for 70 percent of the world's surface—are places of connection that linked diverse cultures and facilitated the spread not only of people, but also plants, animals, ideas, and technologies. It also, though, helped bring diseases to new lands, often with devastating consequences. Until the development of railroads in the 19th century, water transport offered the fastest way to cover distances of hundreds of miles and the only effective way to transport large cargoes over long distances. Even today, the majority of the world's goods move by sea.

Some of our earliest historical documents record travel by river and sea, and the sea figures in our earliest tales of adventure, such as the voyages of Odysseus in the *Iliad,* or the earlier tales of Egyptian sailors. Whether they were factual accounts of travelers such as Marco Polo and Ibn Battuta, epic poems celebrating Viking heroes, tales of Polynesian navigators passed down through the generations, or the fictional adventures of Sinbad the Sailor and Captain Ahab, tales of the sea found a ready audience. Long before Europe's great voyages of exploration, bookended by the voyages of Christopher Columbus and James Cook, people marveled at Phoenicians, who might have circumnavigated Africa, and Pytheas of Massalia, who sailed north from the British Isles. In the 19th century, returning Arctic explorers spoke to rapt audiences, and deep-sea explorers such as Jacques Cousteau attracted similar attention in the immediate decades after World War II.

Too often, maritime history has been a western tale that begins with voyages of Christopher Columbus. It is hoped that this book will help redress that imbalance by highlighting the long history of seafaring by diverse cultures around the world.

The Indian Ocean, in particular, was a place of intense maritime activity long before the Portuguese arrived there in 1498. Polynesians traveled vast distances across the Pacific, settling islands thousands of miles apart, and Arab mariners reached Southeast Asia and Indonesia, where they spread their faith. Africans, who too often appear in maritime histories only as the cargo of slavers, developed their own maritime traditions and sustained them despite the disruptions of the slave trade and colonialism.

The importance of the sea to diverse human societies was such that people invested time and resources in building ships of increasing sophistication and learning to navigate across ever-longer distances. The Nile River linked ancient Egyptians and facilitated their development of a nation-state. Egypt traded with the Levant for wood to build ships, sought to conquer it to secure shipbuilding resources, and then faced invasion from "Sea Peoples" who invaded Egypt from the Levant. Ancient civilizations in China, India, and Mesopotamia similarly took to the water, expanded along rivers and coastlines, and traded by sea with distant peoples. Overseas trade helped these and later societies flourish, while the collapse of trade, as occurred in the Mediterranean and Mesopotamia around 1200 BCE, invariably hurt local economies and even contributed to the collapse of great nations and empires. Sea trade funded the fifth century BCE golden age of Athens, and underpinned the growth of nations and empires across Asia, Europe, and Africa. By the beginning of the Common Era, sea trade linked communities from northern Europe through the Mediterranean, into the Indian Ocean, and from there to Southeast Asia and China. No single ship could have a voyage from Britain to China in these years, but goods—particularly silk, gold, spices, and other luxuries—regularly moved across the sea, and between empires as distant as Rome and China.

It would be false to present human activity at sea as one of steady progress. Nonetheless, people learned to construct larger and larger ships, eventually straining the practical limits of wooden-ship construction in the great ships built in China in the 15th century and Europe in the 18th century. Empires fell, but trade persisted; for example as it did in the Indian Ocean despite the collapse of the Han and Roman empires. In addition to the goods and passengers they carried, sailors spread a host of faiths to new lands and the sea became a route for Buddhist, Christian, and Muslim pilgrims. Muslim traders in particular became active in the Indian Ocean and developed trade networks that reached from East Africa through India and on to Southeast Asia and China. These networks endured despite the 16th century arrival of Europeans in the region, who displaced indigenous traders—often violently.

The development of the full-rigged ship in Western Europe resulted from a long process of maritime improvement in which diverse cultures learned from one another and shared and transmitted a host of technologies ranging from the compass and sternpost rudder, to styles of sails and rigging, and construction techniques.

People also developed a succession of navigational instruments that enabled European captains to sail these great ships around the world and into its most dangerous seas. Thanks to these technologies, European nations came to dominate world trade, which grew in succeeding centuries. Its benefits, though, flowed disproportionately to Europe whose nations launched a succession of colonial and imperial ventures into the late-19th century.

The introduction of steamships in the 19th century increased the volume of trade that flowed by sea as well as the number of passengers—millions of whom immigrated to the Americas. A global economy developed, but centered mostly on Europe and later the United States whose factories consumed resources from around the world and produced goods of increasing quantity and technical sophistication. Both World Wars disrupted world trade and weakened Europe's colonial empires. Airplanes, introduced as practical weapons in the First World War, dominated the Second World War and revolutionized travel in its aftermath. The millions of passengers who crossed the Atlantic Ocean by boat during the first decade of the 20th century, then traveled by plane in the last decades of the century. Over the same period, ships became larger and more efficient and more and more of them were built in shipyards in Asia rather than Europe or the United States. The roughly four centuries of European maritime dominance ended, and world oceans became, again, trafficked by ships and peoples from diverse regions and nations. Although ships carried a growing amount of cargo—especially after the container revolution of the 1990s that created an integrated system of truck, rail, and sea transport—fewer and fewer people worked at sea. Yet, more people than ever before, especially in the developed world, took to the sea for leisure aboard cruise ships, or small boats or yachts of their own. They also became increasingly concerned about the damage of human activity to marine environments, fueling the growth of environmental organizations.

Over more than 5,000 years, improvements in sea travel strengthened connections among diverse peoples and widened the scope of international commerce. In the late-20th century, these helped produce what people recently have labeled "globalization," a complex intertwining of finance, labor, production, transport, and markets that spans the world. Globalization would be impossible without air travel and a host of communications technologies, but the movement of goods by sea—more than 90 percent of cargo volume—is the backbone of the global economy. This volume to some extent is a chronicle of the growing use of the sea by diverse peoples, but it also illustrates the many ways in which people have envisioned the sea, its appearance in art and literature, and the continuing importance of the sea to the human experience.

■ CHAPTER 1
Early Civilizations, 4000 BCE to 1000 BCE

INTRODUCTION

Mobility is, perhaps, rooted in human nature. Our distant ancestors traveled vast distances by land and the invention of watercraft accelerated this mobility. Their first water voyages were undoubtedly along rivers and small lakes. When people first took to the sea remains unknown. What is certain, though, is that they did so long before recorded history. More than 50,000 years ago, people began spreading across the islands of Southeast Asia. Between 60,000 and 10,000 years ago, during the last great ice age, sea levels were lower than they are today and it was possible to sail substantial distances among the islands of Southeast Asia without ever leaving sight of land. People reached New Guinea by 50,000 BCE and spread among the islands, both large and small. They arrived in Australia more than 40,000 years ago and in Japan about 30,000 years ago. Roughly 13,000 years ago humans reached Manus Island, 150 miles northeast of New Guinea. Parts of that voyage would have been beyond the sight of land, which indicates that these seafarers had confidence in both their navigational abilities and their boats. People similarly sailed the coasts of the Indian Ocean and Mediterranean Sea and settled nearby islands, such as those of the Aegean, which boasted substantial settlements by the fifth millennium BCE.

The first boats were probably simple logs. Later people lashed together logs or bundles of reeds to make rafts. Over time they learned to shape the hulls of their craft and developed three types of boats: dugout canoes, sewn-bark or hide canoes, and reed boats. Later they developed techniques to cut logs into planks and built boats from these.

The simplest dugout canoes are little more than hollowed-out tree trunks. Necessarily long and narrow, they can be swamped easily and have limited cargo capacity. People solved their stability issues using outriggers or double hulls and these supported platforms that improved the canoe's carrying capacity. The Polynesians later built voyaging canoes capable of traveling vast stretches of the Pacific Ocean, and the indigenous peoples of the northwest coast of North America built canoes as much as 40 feet long and seven feet wide from which they fished and hunted whales. Archeologists have discovered remnants of dugout canoes around the world. The oldest, found in the Netherlands, dates to 6300 BCE.

An alternative to log canoes is to fasten hide, bark, or other material around a wooden frame. Among the best known of these is the kayak, which facilitated human migration across the Arctic. The Thule people used seal or walrus hide over a framework of whalebone and sinew to build kayaks and larger umiaks, using them spread across the Arctic from the Aleutians to Greenland. The peoples of Ireland built similar boats, called "curraghs," as did those of Scandinavia, where rock carvings indicate their use by 10,000 BCE. To the south, wood, which was plentiful, was the preferred construction material. Native Americans peeled bark from trees, particularly the birch, sewed the pieces together and attached them to a wooden frame. They waterproofed these bark canoes with gums and resins extracted from trees. Remarkably light and maneuverable, these canoes facilitated the development of trade along American rivers.

Other ancient peoples turned to reeds for boat building, particularly the Egyptians, who built reed boats of increasing sophistication. Reeds offer a number of advantages over other materials. They make light boats that are easily carried ashore, and bundles of reeds are much easier to shape than are logs, which allowed builders to narrow the bow and craft a streamlined hull. Reeds sag, however, which limits the length of reed boats; they also become waterlogged and must be dried out after a few days of use. Cheap to make, reed boats are still in use by coastal fishers in Vietnam and Peru.

Wherever wood was available people eventually adopted it for boat building. At first, they raised the sides of dugout canoes with planks. As they improved their tools and craftsmanship, they built boats entirely from wooden planks, a technique used in Mesopotamia by 3500 BCE, and a few centuries later in Egypt. These early ships were "hollow," as Homer notes in his epic poems, but builders soon covered their ships with decks, which facilitated their sailing and sheltered crew and cargo. Two ships built for Pharaoh Khufu in about 2650 BCE and buried near his tomb reveal the remarkable craftsmanship of Egypt's ancient builders. Built shell first, the planks were sewn together with rope to produce strong yet flexible hulls. The cedar used to build both ships, and probably most Egyptian ships, came from Lebanon, and it was to secure this timber and other valuable materials that Egyptians increasingly took to the sea.

People propelled the first boats with paddles. Oars—long paddles slipped through a rowlock or secured by tholepins—enable rowers, through leverage, to exert more force and were adopted by Egyptian shipbuilders in the third millennium BCE and by Minoan shipbuilders in the second millennium. Sails, however, became the primary means of propulsion for most ancient ships. The date of their invention remains uncertain, but they were in use in the Mediterranean Sea and

Indian Ocean by the end of fourth millennium BCE and appear in Egyptian artwork dating to 3100 BCE. The invention of the sail revolutionized sea travel, allowing for smaller crews and greater cargoes, which facilitated trade. People also developed rudders to help steer these ships and anchors to secure them.

One of the most important events of the Bronze Age was the development of sustained contact and trading networks among different civilizations. Although we know very little about some of these—such as the Harrapan civilization centered on the Indus River Valley—other civilizations have left more substantial records of their seafaring, and underwater archaeology has added much to this with the exploration of numerous sunken ships in recent decades. The wrecks of ancient ships, such as the Uluburun ship, demonstrate the existence of trading networks that spanned the eastern Mediterranean and Middle East, and most of this trade flowed by sea. Transporting goods by ship was substantially easier and cheaper than moving the same goods over land. A draft horse can carry about two hundred pounds on its back. Well-harnessed, hitched to a wagon, and travelling a reasonably good road—all rarities in antiquity—a horse can pull about 4,000 pounds. In contrast, ships could carry cargoes weighing dozens of tons. Trade flourished and by the second millennium BCE networks of trade linked the peoples of the eastern Mediterranean. Similar trading networks developed in the Persian Gulf and the Indian Ocean.

Tin and copper, needed to make bronze, were central to Mediterranean trade. In addition to other goods, the Uluburun ship carried a ton of tin and 10 tons of copper, enough to equip 300 warriors with arms and armor. Egyptians regularly traded for timber and some of our earliest records of ancient commerce describe these voyages to secure cedar logs from Byblos and other cities in the Levant. Grain, animals, slaves, spices, gemstones, metals, and timber moved by sea, as did a growing amount of manufactured goods, particularly textiles and pottery. Particular regions became associated with particular goods: Cyprus for copper, Sicily for grain, and the Black Sea for fish. Some goods, including olives, olive oil, fish, and wine, were transported in amphora (tall, narrow-necked clay containers with handles on the side). Stacked aboard ships in rows, they were likely mounted in wooden racks and secured with ropes passed through their handles.

For most of this period ships followed the coast and sailed close to land. Ships from the Aegean, for example, sailed from Crete along the coast to Cyprus and then to Syria. From there, they followed the coast down to Egypt. Successful navigation requires the continuous calculation of distance and direction travelled, and little is known about the skills of ancient navigators. Apart from sounding weights, secured to lines to measure the depth of water, no ancient navigational instruments have been found. Yet, by 1700 BCE, the Minoans sailed directly to Egypt across the Mediterranean, an impressive achievement that indicates significant navigational capability. In Homer's epic poem, Odysseus navigates by the stars, and it is likely the Minoans did so, as well.

As sea trade flourished, sophisticated ports developed. Archaeologists have found the remnant of wharves in Lothal, India, dating to the third millennium BCE. By 2000 BCE, the Harrapan civilization, which spread along the Indus River valley and India's northwest coast, was a center of maritime trade. Thus far, no remnants of Harrapan ships have been discovered, but port facilities at Bharuch, Dvaraka, Lothal, and Sopara were extensive, and Harrapan goods have been found throughout the Persian Gulf, indicating extensive trade. Mesopotamian seafarers traveled to Western India and Eastern Arabia, a trade described in cuneiform tablets found at Ur, and port cities such as Dilmun—noted in ancient Sumeria for its wealth—flourished.

Ships facilitated the growth of the first empires and became important for warfare, supporting the advance of armies. Egypt launched regular campaigns into the Levant and supply ships accompanied Egyptian armies as they marched along the coast of what are today Israel and Lebanon. Around 2450 BCE, Pharaoh Sahure used ships to ferry troops to the Levant for one of his campaigns. The earliest recorded naval battles date from this era. Like the 12th century BCE battle between the Egyptians and the Sea Peoples, they generally were fought near shore or in rivers and featured close combat and attempts to board and capture enemy ships. As evidenced by its repeated mention in Homer and other sources, piracy became a serious problem in the Mediterranean. Egypt's New Kingdom rulers erected fortresses to protect the Nile delta from seaborne raiders and conducted campaigns against pirates. Because catching pirates at sea was rarely possible, anti-piracy campaigns focused on capturing or destroying pirate bases and the communities that supported them.

Over time, ships developed into specialized types: long, sleek warships propelled by oars; rounder, deeper cargo ships that relied primarily on sails; and light fishing craft. Larger, slower ships carried bulk cargoes, such as timber and grain, and smaller, sleeker ships carried luxury or perishable goods including wine and gold and other precious materials. Ships reflected local conditions, including the available building materials, sea and wind conditions, depth of water, and trading networks. These, in turn, influenced the types of cargoes available for merchants. Warships remained relatively rare before 1200 BCE. Most ships were designed and built for fishing or to carry cargo.

In the Mediterranean and Mesopotamia, a series of cataclysms, invasions, and mass migrations beginning about 1200 BCE overwhelmed most of the region's major states. The "Sea Peoples" launched devastating raids along the Syrian coast and invaded Egypt. Trade collapsed and piracy flourished. Egypt narrowly avoided destruction, and the Minoans, Mycenaeans, Hittites, and others were overwhelmed. The collapse of these great kingdoms, however, allowed smaller polities to flourish, particularly the Phoenician city-states of the Syrian coast whose sailors soon traded throughout the Mediterranean.

Stephen K. Stein

Further Reading

Adney, Tappan, and Howard Chapelle. 1964. *The Bark Canoes and Skin Boats of North America*. Washington: Smithsonian.

Cline, Eric H. 2014. *1177 B.C.: The Year Civilization Collapsed*. Princeton: Princeton University Press.

Fabre, David. 2004. *Seafaring in Ancient Egypt*. London: Periplus.

Fagan, Brian. 2012. *Beyond the Blue Horizon: How the Earliest Mariners Unlocked the Secrets of the Oceans*. New York: Bloomsbury Press.

McGrail, Sean. 2001. *Boats of the World from the Stone Age to Medieval Times*. Oxford: Oxford University Press.

Wachsmann, Shelley. 1998. *Seagoing Ships and Seamanship in the Bronze Age Levant*. College Station: Texas A&M University.

CHRONOLOGY

Chronology: Early Civilizations, 4000 to 1000 BCE

ca. 50,000 BCE	People begin settling the islands of Southeast Asia.
ca. 14,000 BCE	Settlement of the Americas.
ca. 3500 BCE	Plank boats built in Mesopotamia.
ca. 3400 BCE	Development of sails.
ca. 3100 BCE	Sails appear in Mesopotamian art.
ca. 3050 BCE	Unification of Egypt under Narmer, who founds the First Dynasty.
2750 BCE	Legendary foundation of Tyre on the Mediterranean Coast.
ca. 2640 BCE	Egyptians begin construction of the first pyramid.
ca. 2600 BCE	Pharaoh Snefru imports timber from Lebanon for shipbuilding.
ca. 2600–1900 BCE	Harrapan civilization flourishes in India and trades with Mesopotamia.
ca. 2580–2560	Great Pyramid of Giza constructed.
ca. 2575	Construction of Khufu ships, the oldest surviving ships.
ca. 2450 BCE	First trade documents between Dilmun and Sumerian cities.
ca. 2100 BCE	*Epic of Gilgamesh* written.
ca. 2000 BCE	Emergence of Knossos and other Minoan palace centers. Minoan overseas trade flourishes.

ca. 2000–1650 BCE	Middle Kingdom Egypt. *Tale of the Shipwrecked Sailor* written.
ca. 1700 BCE	Minoans begin sailing directly to Egypt.
ca. 1500 BCE	Eruption of Thera and the decline of Minoan civilization.
ca. 1500–1200 BCE	*Rig Veda* composed.
ca. 1470 BCE	Queen Hatshepsut dispatches expeditions to Punt.
1379–1362 BCE	Akhenaten rules in Egypt and attempts religious reform.
ca. 1325 BCE	Uluburun ship sinks.
1279–1213 BCE	Reign of Ramses II in Egypt.
ca. 1200 BCE	First Sea Peoples arrive in Egypt.
ca. 1180 BCE	Mycenaean city of Pylos destroyed. Mycenaean civilization declines.
ca. 1175 BCE	Battle of the Delta. Ramses III defeats the Sea Peoples.
ca. 1050 BCE	*The Report of Wenamun* composed.
ca. 950–750 BCE	Homer's *Iliad* and *Odyssey* composed.

EGYPT, 4000 TO 1000 BCE

The material world of the ancient Egyptians encompassed three major bodies of water, the Nile River, the Mediterranean Sea, and the Red Sea. Each provided a flow of traffic with peoples, products, and ideas that resulted in the grandeur that became pharaonic Egypt. These waters were equally important in the spiritual world—one creation myth envisioned the world as an island floating in the primordial waters of eternity. That the Egyptians conceived of their world as an island is a powerful recognition that they were subjects of the seas. It is little wonder that boat imagery or even boat burials were ubiquitous in temples and tombs throughout the pharaonic period.

From about 5300 to 3500 BCE, the monsoonal rains that kept the prehistoric eastern Sahara green shifted. The new, harsher conditions forced the prehistoric populations living there to move toward the resource-rich Nile River Valley. Over the next 500 years, rapid social and technological adaptations to the new environment laid the foundations for the complex society known as pharaonic Egypt, which thrived for nearly 3,000 years.

The importance of the maritime world to the Egyptians is evidenced from the earliest era in which an "Egyptian" identity can be discerned. The early Egyptians clearly recognized their essential connection to the water and their need to navigate upon it. Boats make regular appearances in the art of the Predynastic Period (ca. 4000–3100 BCE), notably in ceramics and petroglyphs, and boats are the most prominent subject in the only known tomb painting from the time. Not long thereafter, what might be the world's first naval battle was carved into an ivory knife handle.

Egypt's early maritime mastery was initiated from within. The Egyptians' ability to harness the river evolved prior to (or perhaps in tandem with) development of the state. Creation of a unified Egyptian state required any hopeful king to bring together disparate communities spread out along 700 miles of river from the first Nile cataract (an area of rapids) at Aswan to the Nile Delta. Rapid transport of people (e.g., soldiers, administrators, laborers), supplies, and information was a requirement for governing such a vast expanse. Watercraft feature in the earliest iconography related to state formation; for example, a ship appears above rows of decapitated prisoners on the Narmer Palette (ca. 3000 BCE), one of the earliest records of a king in control of both Upper (southern) and Lower (northern) Egypt.

By the beginning of the Early Dynastic period (ca. 3100–2700 BCE), the Egyptians had developed the sail. This was a monumental advance. Because the prevailing winds in the Nile Valley blow southward, the sail facilitated upstream travel. Mastering the elements on the comparatively calm river was a prerequisite for seafaring.

Painted ceramic jar with boats: Egypt, Naqada II Period, 3500–3150 BCE. (Los Angeles County Museum of Art)

Wooden watercraft not only served as essential tools for the unification and administration of Egypt but also supported the export of royal power, in the form of armies and messengers, beyond Egypt's borders. With the country unified, the first kings (ca. 3000–2800 BCE) looked beyond their borders. The degree to which early trade between Egypt and its nearest Asian neighbor, Canaan, was maritime in nature is difficult to judge. A sea route might have helped support Egyptian trading colonies established (and subsequently abandoned) there, but no shipwrecks (for any culture) of this period are known. Nor does any direct archaeological evidence indicate that the Egyptians or their neighbors were yet capable of taking to the open seas. Nonetheless, Egyptian and Levantine pottery dating to the Early Dynastic Period has been found in waters off the coast of Israel. More definitively, the presence of a contemporary harbor at Tel Ashkelon (Israel) indicates the existence of a maritime trade network. Whether the Egyptians were involved directly at this time remains unclear.

It is not until the Old Kingdom (ca. 2700–2150 BCE) that Egyptian seafaring can be confirmed. Royal annals recorded on the Palermo Stone relate that during the reign of the Fourth Dynasty King Sneferu, "40 ships filled [with] coniferous wood" arrived in Egypt (Breasted, 66). The source of cedar closest to Egypt was modern Lebanon, suggesting importation by sea. Two boats buried beside the Great Pyramid at Giza, belonging to Sneferu's son and successor Khufu (ca. 2575 BCE), were each built from more than 30 tons of cedar.

The oldest known direct evidence of Egyptian seafaring dates to Khufu's reign. Remains of Egyptian activities on the Red Sea are preserved at Wadi el Jarf, a site on the Gulf of Suez (northern end of the Red Sea). Finds there include galleries cut into the hillsides for storage, evidence of timber repair and ship construction, stone anchors, and a breakwater built out into the sea. At least one similar site from the Old Kingdom is now known on the Gulf of Suez, at Ayn Soukhna. Both were likely involved in the transport of copper ores from mines in the Sinai Peninsula on the opposite shore.

Egyptian seafaring continued through the Fifth Dynasty probably with regularity. Reliefs from a temple at the pyramid of the Fifth Dynasty king Sahure depict robust boats with new technologies designed to help withstand the rigors of sea travel. Iconography from Fifth and Sixth Dynasty tombs suggests that riverboats also underwent changes in construction and technology, most notably in the sail and steering gear, which would appear on later seagoing ships.

In the Sahure reliefs, Egyptian ships are depicted on their return carrying western Asian men, women, and children. During this time Egypt participated in a regular trade route with the harbor city of Byblos (modern Jubayl, Lebanon), with which it formed a close relationship that persisted through much of the pharaonic period.

Sahure also launched the earliest known long-range ventures on the Red Sea, coincident with the first known mention of the land of Punt. From Punt, a region

---

Anchor

Used to prevent the movement of a ship, anchors are tethered to a ship by rope or chain and are lowered to rest on the bed of a body of water. Present incarnations of anchors are made of metal and usually have hooks. These hooks, or "flukes," enable the anchor to dig into the bed. Prehistoric peoples used stones tied with flax rope to anchor their canoes or rafts. During the later Bronze Age, baskets filled with stones, hollowed logs filled with lead, bags filled with sand, and other heavy items were used as anchors. Although these objects did not dig into the bed of the body of water, they did cause friction, which was useful for slowing down drifting. Large boulders were—and still are—used as permanent anchors or moorings. Too heavy to move from one place to the next, boulders were useful for anchoring ships close to the shore or in a harbor with no chance of the ship drifting away. As shipbuilding became more sophisticated, the classical Greeks and other civilizations developed metal anchors having one or two teeth, much like the anchors used today.

Matthew Blake Strickland

---

located somewhere along the southern end of the Red Sea, the Egyptians obtained exotic goods, especially aromatic resins necessary for temple rituals. The arduous voyage required substantial resources, making it the exclusive purview of the king. Sahure's pyramid complex featured a relief depicting a returning fleet and incense trees, which might reflect the arrival of a large quantity of goods from Punt during his reign as recorded on the Palermo Stone.

At the height of the Old Kingdom, the Egyptians were travelling farther and more often to new places in both of its neighboring seas. But the Old Kingdom ended (ca. 2150 BCE) as the result of a complex combination of events that led to decentralized state control. For the next approximately 150 years, known as the First Intermediate Period, no single king ruled all of Egypt, and little is known about Egypt's maritime activities.

The First Intermediate Period came to an end with Mentuhotep II's reunification of Upper and Lower Egypt, during the Eleventh Dynasty. First king of the Middle Kingdom (ca. 2000–1650 BCE), Mentuhotep II began his rule from Thebes in Upper Egypt (modern Luxor), where geography provided him with a tactical advantage against the rival dynasty in the north. Transportation of men and materiel to conquer a foe is much easier downstream than upstream. The (re)unification (or conquest) of Egypt originating from the south was a trend throughout pharaonic history.

Seafaring ventures seem to reappear only at the apex of the Middle Kingdom, the Twelfth Dynasty. The *Tale of the Shipwrecked Sailor*, perhaps the best-known literary composition from the period, tells of an ill-fated fictional voyage to the

"Island of the Soul" ruled by a serpent who calls himself "Lord of Punt." Numerous historical inscriptions indicate launches of expeditions to Punt. What is likely the primary Middle Kingdom harbor for voyages to and from Punt has been located at a Red Sea site called "Mersa/Wadi Gawasis." The names of most kings of the Twelfth Dynasty have been found here.

Although the Middle Kingdom renewed its international trade network with Byblos as well, the Egyptians did not prioritize Mediterranean exploration and navigation. They did have contact with the Aegean world, but its nature—beyond being maritime—remains unclear. With a reliable and regular connection to the Mediterranean and Near Eastern worlds via Byblos, the Egyptians directed their attention elsewhere.

The Middle Kingdom was a period of significant geographic expansion for Egypt, with most efforts concentrated on reopening mines in Sinai and extending the southern border into Nubia (modern Sudan). Fleets supported both missions. To facilitate the voyage to and through Nubia, the Egyptians improved the river's navigability with canals and slipways that bypassed difficult stretches of the Nile.

Despite the economic growth and expansion of a bureaucratic "middle class" during the Middle Kingdom and the resulting expansion of material culture and texts, direct evidence for maritime activities is paltry. International trade continued to grow, as demonstrated by the use of Lebanese cedar for boats and coffins, the presence of Asiatic and Aegean goods dispersed along the length of the Nile, and Egyptian exports in those locations. The extremely Egyptocentric nature of the Egyptian worldview most likely accounts for the relative scarcity of textual and, especially, iconographic evidence for sea-based foreign engagement.

The Middle Kingdom ended with a series of weakened rulers and the emergence of an independent kingdom of Asiatics in the eastern Nile Delta. The result was the Second Intermediate Period in which, for about a century (ca. 1650–1550 BCE), competing cultures ruled various parts of the former Egyptian kingdom: Hyksos (Asiatics) in the north, Egyptians in the middle, and Kushites (Nubians) in the south. Little indication of Egyptian maritime endeavors remains from this period, as they were effectively landlocked by the Hyksos (who themselves engaged in a dynamic Mediterranean-based trade network). Walking through the Eastern Desert to the Red Sea remained the Egyptian's only potential access to maritime traffic, but no evidence of Red Sea travel at this time has been recovered, likely because Egypt lacked the strong centralized institutions and resources needed to support inherently risky seafaring ventures.

Once again a dynasty of regional kings based in Thebes (Upper Egypt) used geography to its advantage to reunify the country, establishing the New Kingdom (ca. 1550–1075 BCE). Having expelled the Kushites and Hyksos from Egypt's traditional borders in campaigns that relied on ships to transport infantry and engage in naval combat, the Theban kings were determined to expand Egypt's reach farther than ever. With access to the Mediterranean secured, for the first time Egypt looked to control lands far beyond the Nile.

Records of Egyptian seafaring at this time are the most plentiful in all of pharaonic history. Expeditions to Punt via the Red Sea played a significant role in New Kingdom politics. At the time Punt voyages were reinitiated by Hatshepsut (near the beginning of the Eighteenth Dynasty), her co-regent and stepson Thutmose III was actively engaged in military exploits in the Mediterranean region, from the Sinai to as far north as modern Turkey, and far inland past the Euphrates River (in Syria today). Thutmose III used ships during most of these campaigns, including those captured in enemy harbors. It was under Thutmose III, with his robust navy, that Egypt's boarders reached their greatest extent.

A dynamic, multicultural maritime network existed in the Mediterranean during the New Kingdom. Egypt was a significant participant both as supplier (especially of gold and grain) and consumer (of almost everything). The Uluburun shipwreck (ca. 1325 BCE) provides the clearest example of the complexity of maritime trade networks of this time.

Egyptian participation in the Mediterranean trade system with Egyptian ships and crews probably climaxed in the mid- to late-Eighteenth Dynasty (ca. 1350 BCE), in the reigns of Amenhotep III and his heir, Akhenaten. Akhenaten's ill-fated

An Old Kingdom Egyptian ship from the mastaba-tomb of Ty in Saqqara. Ty was High Priest of Ptah in Memphis during the time of Eighteenth Dynasty reign of Tutankhamen and/or Ay. (P.P. Creasman)

attempt to overhaul Egypt's religious and political institutions funneled all available resources to the task. After his death, reversion to the prior tradition consumed even more. This process appears to have contributed to an unintentional loss of Egypt's maritime prowess: Egypt focused on internal matters, and the world beyond carried on with its vibrant maritime trade with others filling the role that Egypt once played. These circumstances combined with an untimely Egyptian failure to adopt certain shipbuilding technologies that enabled more efficient trade voyages (e.g., mortise-and-tenon construction), resulted in waning Egyptian maritime control of the Mediterranean.

New Kingdom Egypt's Mediterranean network primarily was based on trade with the Syro-Canaanite coast (modern Lebanon and Syria) and the Aegean. Because Egypt often was at war with Syro-Canaanite societies, the Aegean connection became increasingly important. It appears that the Aegean cultures and Egypt established regular, direct trade by the early Eighteenth Dynasty (ca. 1550 BCE). This led to increased cultural and technological diffusion between the two regions, well evidenced by archaeological finds in both areas. The Egyptians hired Aegeans as mercenaries and provided them with significant access to trade within Egypt. Several private tombs of Egyptians in Egypt depict Aegeans (Minoans and Mycenaeans) and their goods.

One of the best preserved graves of the early Eighteenth Dynasty, Paheri's grave was decorated with reliefs such as this one, which shows bags being loaded onto one of the moored boats. Shown in a typical Egyptian abridgment, it is also raising anchor to sail north (since its mast is folded back), either towards another provincial storage place, or perhaps the capital, Memphis. (Library of Congress)

When not hostile with Egypt, Syro-Canaanites likewise were allowed substantial access to the Nile for trade. They, too, are depicted in tombs conducting ship-based trade in the heart of Egypt. An Egyptian governor was installed in Byblos to oversee Egyptian interests there. By the Nineteenth Dynasty (ca. 1300–1190 BCE), the Egyptian presence there was so entrenched that Egyptian-style temples and forts were built.

After a brief resurgence in the Nineteenth Dynasty, Egyptian maritime prowess waned through the Twentieth Dynasty (ca. 1190–1075 BCE), the last of the New Kingdom. Texts and temple reliefs from Medinet Habu dating to the eighth year of Ramesses III's reign depict a great naval battle in the Nile Delta. A band of foreign tribes the Egyptians called the "Sea Peoples" attempted to invade but were defeated.

A literary composition known as *The Report of Wenamun* provides further evidence of the disintegration of Egyptian maritime prowess. Set just after the end of the New Kingdom, in the very early Third Intermediate Period (ca. 1050 BCE), the work purports to be an account written by a high-ranking Egyptian who meets with robbery and disrespect on a mission to Byblos to obtain timbers for a sacred boat. His treatment at the hands of local rulers suggests that Egypt poses no credible threat. Later in that period, with the aid of Greek mercenaries and shipbuilding technology, the Egyptian navy became a power in the Mediterranean once again,

Image of the Egyptian creative myth from the Papyrus of Anhai, showing Shu (the god of air) supporting the boat of Khefri (the scarab-headed god of creation) and the sun disk being received by Nut (the goddess of the sky). (CM Dixon/Print Collector/ Getty Images)

but ultimately it could not stave off foreign invasions from both Asia and Nubia that would eclipse the native Egyptian kings.

Pearce Paul Creasman

Further Reading

Breasted, James H. 1906. *Ancient Records of Egypt*, Vol. 1. Chicago: University of Chicago Press.

Creasman, Pearce Paul, ed. 2013. *Seafaring and Maritime Interconnections*. Tucson: Journal of Ancient Egyptian Interconnections.

Creasman, Pearce Paul, and Noreen Doyle. 2015. "From Pit to Procession: The Diminution of Ritual Boats and the Development of Royal Burial Practices in Pharaonic Egypt." *Studien zur Altägyptischen Kultur* 44: 83–101, pl. 8–11.

Redford, Donald B. 1992. *Egypt, Canaan, and Israel in Ancient Times*. Princeton: Princeton University Press.

Vinson, Steven. 2009. "Seafaring." In *UCLA Encyclopedia of Egyptology*, edited by Elizabeth Frood and Willeke Wendrich, 1–10. Los Angeles: University of California, Los Angeles.

Wachsmann, Shelley. 1998. *Seagoing Ships and Seamanship in the Bronze Age Levant*. College Station: Texas A&M University Press. 1993

Delta, Battle of, ca. 1175 BCE

Famous for being the first nautical battle ever recorded in both texts and reliefs, the battle was fought at the Nile Delta around 1175 BCE. The Egyptian king, Ramesses III, recorded his victorious campaign against a coalition of foreign nations, referred to in modern scholarship as the "Sea Peoples." The reliefs and inscriptions commemorating this victory were carved on the walls of Ramesses III's mortuary temple at Medinet Habu in western Thebes (present day Luxor).

The battle scene depicts four Egyptian warships equipped with long oars, rigged sails, and Egyptian soldiers, and five ships manned by Sea Peoples, one of which had capsized. The water is littered with the bodies of the fallen Sea Peoples who are falling into complete chaos and disarray in the face of the well-organized Egyptian forces. The king himself stands with his guards on the riverbank shooting arrows towards the helpless Sea Peoples.

The long inscriptions that accompany these reliefs record the events of the fifth and eighth regal years of Ramesses III. The Pharaoh narrates the trap he has laid down for the aggressors saying, "Those who entered the Nile-mouths were like birds ensnared in the net," and their subsequent total annihilation, "Their arms and their hearts removed, taken away, no longer in their bodies. Their leaders were taken and slain; they were prostrate and made into pinioned [ones]."

This of course is an ideological representation of the battle, meant for the glorification of the Egyptian king and not necessarily a realistic rendering of the events. Nevertheless, historians have drawn some significant conclusions from these depictions. The first appearance of the rigged sail is ascribed to this scene, being a technological advancement with considerable effect on the duration and speed of seafaring. This is also the first glimpse of the strategies of naval warfare in history. The texts and the reliefs imply that the Sea Peoples' ships were allowed to enter the rivermouths only to be ambushed by the Egyptian ships that closed on them from the sea to prevent their escape, and from the riverbanks to prevent their safe mooring.

The actual outcome of the battle is debatable. According to the ancient Egyptian sources the "Sea Peoples" were defeated and the survivors were integrated as conscript soldiers in the Egyptian forts. Shortly thereafter, however, Egyptian control over the southern Levant collapsed and Egypt never recovered its former strength.

Shirly Ben-Dor Evian

Further Reading

Nelson, H. H. 1943. "The Naval Battle Pictured at Medinet Habu." *Journal of Near Eastern Studies* 2: 40–55.

Spalinger, A. J. 2005. *War in Ancient Egypt*. Oxford: Wiley.

Wachsmann, S. 2000. "To the Sea of the Philistines." In *The Sea Peoples and Their World: A Reassessment*. Edited by Oren, 103–43. University Museum Monograph 108. Philadelphia: University Museum Symposium Series 11.

The Khufu Vessels

Two large watercraft buried beside the Great Pyramid at Giza, Egypt, have redefined our understanding of ancient Egyptian shipbuilding and nautical capabilities since their discovery in 1954. Known today as "Khufu I" and "Khufu II," each was found dismantled in a sealed, rock-cut pit beside the tomb built for King Khufu (Fourth Dynasty; 26th century BCE). The Khufu I—excavated from 1954–1957—stands as the world's oldest and grandest surviving example of a complex ship or boat. Between 1957 and 1974, the Egyptian archaeological service reconstructed its approximately 38 tons of Lebanese cedar (*Cedrus libani*) into a vessel roughly 140 feet in length, 18.5 feet in beam (width), and 6 feet in depth. Approximately 700 tenons (wooden joinery pieces) and three miles of rope fastened its 651 timbers.

Scholars have debated whether Khufu I was structurally capable of plying the Nile. It was not, however, a vessel of the open seas. Nonetheless, Khufu I has given context to several records of ancient Egyptian seafaring and shipbuilding. Ancient royal records mention ships 100 cubits (about 171 feet) in length during the reign of Khufu's father, Sneferu. This size was considered an exaggeration by scholars

The reconstructed funerary boat of Khufu, about 2500 BCE. The boat was found near the Great Pyramid at Giza. (Paula Stanley/Dreamstime)

until the reconstruction of Khufu I confirmed it was possible. In what is perhaps the earliest reference to seafaring in Egypt and the Mediterranean world, these records also note 40 ships "bringing" coniferous wood to Egypt during the same reign. The Khufu boat timbers reflect such international maritime trade in the Mediterranean.

Khufu II remained unexcavated for nearly 50 years after its discovery. It is now undergoing excavation and conservation by a joint Egyptian (Ministry of Antiquities) and Japanese (Institute of Egyptology, Waseda University) team, led by Professor Sakuji Yoshimura.

Sakuji Yoshimura
Pearce Paul Creasman

Further Reading

Lipke, Paul. 1984. *The Royal Ship of Cheops*. Oxford: BAR International Series 225.

Mark, Samuel. 2009. "The Construction of the Khufu I Vessel (c. 2566 BC): A Re-Evaluation." *International Journal of Nautical Archaeology* 38.1: 133–52.

Nour, M. Z., Z. Y. Iskandar, M. S. Osman, and A. Y. Moustafa. 1960. *The Cheops Boat, Part I*. Cairo: Egyptian Government Press.

Vinson, Steven. 2009. "Seafaring," http://www.escholarship.org/uc/item/9d93885v. Accessed September 16, 2016.

Punt, Expeditions to

Among the many foreign lands known to the ancient Egyptians was a region they referred to as "Punt." This name first appears in an inscription describing the arrival of precious cargo during the reign of the Fifth Dynasty king Sahure (ca. 2450 BCE). The goods included a large quantity of an aromatic resin called "*antyw*," commonly thought to be myrrh. Reliefs associated with Sahure's pyramid at Abusir show an Egyptian naval expedition returned from Punt with trees that produce this resin, an ingredient vital to Egyptian temple rituals. The Egyptians also obtained ebony, gold, dogs, monkeys, and many other "exotics" from Punt, including Puntites themselves.

The location of Punt has been much debated and has not yet been resolved. It seems likely that "Punt" was located south and east of Egypt, with boundaries fluctuating according to political relationships. At the very least, Punt referred to the African coast of the southern Red Sea and adjacent regions (modern Eritrea and eastern Sudan). As the two coasts of the Red Sea had long been active trading partners, Punt—at least on occasion—likely included modern Yemen and neighboring areas.

Trade between Egypt and Punt took place by two routes. One (probably the older) was via the Nile corridor, through Egypt's southern neighbor, Nubia (modern Sudan). The other was via the Red Sea. The Red Sea presents challenges of wind and reef to a sailing fleet, particularly during the northbound return. The ancient Egyptians might have favored the arduous marine voyages particularly during times when the Nubians were powerful enough to dominate the old land-and-river route.

Launching fleets to Punt always was a privilege of kings who could muster the requisite resources in men and material. Fashioned at workshops on the Nile, ship timbers and other naval equipment and supplies were brought across the desert to temporary encampments along the sea. Here shipwrights assembled the vessels. These locations (which included, in the north, Wadi el-Jarf and Ayn Soukhna, and in the south, Mersa/Wadi Gawasis) featured long, narrow galleries (caves) dug into adjacent hills that provided shelter and long-term storage. Expedition personnel, who could number in the thousands, often included men for mining and quarrying in Egypt's Eastern Desert while the ships were away. When a fleet returned from Punt, the hulls were dismantled and damaged areas of the timbers were trimmed away. What the Egyptians did not bring back to the Nile they stored in the galleries, along with other equipment, for future expeditions.

Many kings of the Twelfth Dynasty (ca. 2000–1800 BCE) dispatched expeditions to Punt, but the most famous was commissioned by Queen Hatshepsut of the Eighteenth Dynasty (ca. 1470 BCE). Undertaken to strengthen her claim to the throne, hers potentially was the first voyage after a lapse of 200 or 300 years. Mention of and trade with Punt waned with the New Kingdom. The last definite sea voyage was recorded in the reign of Ramesses III (ca. 1175 BCE).

Pearce Paul Creasman

Noreen Doyle

Further Reading

Bard, Kathryn A., and Rudolfo Fattovich, eds. 2007. *Harbor of the Pharaohs to the Land of Punt: Archaeological Investigations at Mersa/Wadi Gawasis, Egypt, 2001–2005*. Naples: Università degli Studi di Napoli "L'Orientale."

Creasman, Pearce Paul. 2014. "Hatshepsut and the Politics of Punt." *African Archaeological Review* 31(3): 366–405.

Fattovich, Rudolfo. 2012. "Egypt's Trade with Punt: New Discoveries on the Red Sea Coast." *British Museum Studies in Ancient Egypt and Sudan* 18: 1–59.

Kitchen, K. A. 1993. "The Land of Punt." In *The Archaeology of Africa: Food, Metals, and Towns*, edited by Thurston Shaw, 587–608. London: Routledge.

Manzo, Andrea. 2012. "From the Sea to the Deserts and Back: New Research in Eastern Sudan." *British Museum Studies in Ancient Egypt and Sudan* 18: 75–106.

Sea Peoples

The "Sea Peoples" are best known from Egyptian records of the 13th and 12th centuries BCE, where they are portrayed as foreign invaders who laid waste to empires across the Near East in the years surrounding the tumultuous transition from the Late Bronze Age to the Iron Age. The groups who collectively comprise the Sea Peoples, rendered in Egyptian as "*Denyen*," "*Ekwesh*," "*Lukka*," "*Peleset*" (the biblical Philistines), "*Shekelesh*," "*Sherden*," "*Sikils*" (or "*Tjekker*"), "*Teresh*," and "*Weshesh*," primarily appear individually and in various combinations in the records of the pharaohs Ramesses II (ruled 1279–1213 BCE), Merneptah (1213–1203 BCE), and Ramesses III (1183–1153 BCE), as well as in multiple texts from the Syrian trading emporium of Ugarit.

The term derives from an Egyptian inscription referring to participants in an invasion of the Nile Delta from neighboring Libya (1207 BCE) as being "of the foreign countries of the sea." The most famous description comes from the mortuary temple of Ramesses III at Medinet Habu, where monumental reliefs depicting land and sea battles between Egyptians and Sea Peoples are accompanied by a bombastic inscription declaring that "no land could stand before their arms" and listing polities from Anatolia to the Levant that the coalition is credited with having destroyed.

Records from Egypt and Ugarit attest to the nautical affinities and piratical nature of some Sea Peoples groups. Ramesses II, for example, references "*Sherden* . . . who came in warships from the midst of the sea" early in the pharaoh's reign. An even earlier text refers to the "*Lukka*" conducting maritime raids on the coasts of both Cyprus and Egypt. Also, questions about the "*Sikils*" "who live on ships" appear in a letter from the great king of the Hittites to the prefect of Ugarit (Emmanuel 2014, 35). Textual references provide little information about the types of vessels that the Sea Peoples sailed; however, those shown at Medinet Habu are modeled after the Helladic oared galley, a type of Aegean vessel well-suited to raiding and warfare. This connection is reinforced by a small wooden model of a galley discovered in a tomb in Middle Egypt, an area inhabited by "*Sherden*" who might have been rewarded with land in exchange for military service.

Though likely of diverse origin (archaeological and linguistic connections, sometimes questionable, have been made to Mycenaean Greece, Cyprus, Sardinia, and western Anatolia, among other locations), the Aegean affinities of at least some Sea Peoples are further demonstrated by the appearance, just after 1200 BCE, of Aegean-style material culture and domestic practices at several sites on the coasts of Turkey and the Levant. The most well-known of these sites are the cities of the "Philistine pentapolis" on the southern coastal plain of Canaan.

After their dramatic appearance in the Egyptian records, most of the Sea Peoples seem to have become assimilated into local Anatolian, Levantine, or Egyptian society. Brief references to the *Sherden*, *Sikils*, and *Peleset* persist in later Egyptian texts, including the *Onomasticon of Amenope*, the *Tale of Wen-Amon*, and the monumental Wilbour Papyrus, which lists several *Sherden* as landowners in Middle Egypt, and the *Peleset* also play a prominent role in the Hebrew Bible as the primary adversary of the Israelites. Though the region ceased to be Philistine in any meaningful sense early in the first millennium BCE, the toponym *Palestine* (Roman *Palaestina*) remains as a lasting testament to the arrival and impact of at least one Sea Peoples group.

Jeffrey P. Emanuel

Further Reading

Cline, Eric H. 2014. *1177 BC: The Year Civilization Collapsed*. Princeton: Princeton University Press.

Emanuel, Jeffrey P. 2013. "Šrdn from the Sea: The Arrival, Integration, and Acculturation of a Sea People." *Journal of Ancient Egyptian Interconnections* 4.1: 14–27.

Emanuel, Jeffrey P. 2014. "The Sea Peoples, Egypt, and the Aegean: Transference of Maritime Technology in the Late Bronze–Early Iron Transition (LH IIIB–C)." *Aegean Studies* 1: 21–56.

Sandars, Nancy K. 1985. *The Sea Peoples: Warriors of the Ancient Mediterranean*. London: Thames & Hudson.

Stager, Lawrence E. 1995. "The Impact of the Sea Peoples in Canaan (1185–1050 BCE)." In *The Archaeology of Society in the Holy Land*, edited by Thomas E. Levy. London: Facts on File, 332–48.

Wachsmann, Shelley. 2013. *The Gurob Ship-Cart Model and Its Mediterranean Context*. College Station: Texas A&M Press.

The Uluburun Shipwreck

Lost in the second half of the 14th century BCE (ca. 1340–1305), the Uluburun ship is the world's oldest excavated shipwreck. Found off the southwestern coast of Turkey near the town of Kaş in 1982 by sponge diver Mehmet Çakır, study of the ship and its cargo has redefined our understanding of the Mediterranean world during the Late Bronze Age.

The Uluburun promontory was surveyed by the Institute of Nautical Archaeology in 1983 and excavation began the next year under the direction of nautical archaeology pioneer George F. Bass. Cemal Pulak directed the subsequent 10 years of underwater excavation (totaling more than 22,000 dives) and more than three decades of study, which is ongoing. Through methodical excavation, conservation, and study, this site has revealed complex interconnections between the eastern Mediterranean world, North Africa, and Europe during the Late Bronze Age.

The approximately 49-foot-long ship wrecked with a full cargo hold, containing thousands of items from Cyprus, Egypt, Greece, Syria-Palestine, and other regions from as far as northern Europe. The ship appears to have been a royal dispatch headed from the Carmel Coast (northern Israel) to a single but unknown destination, carrying a rich cargo of both raw and manufactured goods. Exotic raw materials aboard included glass ingots, ostrich eggshells, faience, and hippopotamus tusks. The small, but significant, manufactured luxury cargo included gold jewelry (for example, a scarab naming Egypt's Queen Nefertiti), worked ivory, and semiprecious stones. Bulk cargo included more common items such copper (10 tons) and tin (1 ton), likely intended for bronze production, as well as Cypriot pottery and various foodstuffs. The entire cargo appears to have been under the escort of two armed Mycenaeans, likely aboard to see the ship to harbor somewhere in the Aegean Sea.

Pearce Paul Creasman

Gold items excavated from the Uluburun Bronze Age Wreck, the oldest shipwreck ever found, Bodrum Underwater Archaeology Museum, Turkey. (Images & Stories/Alamy Stock Photo)

Further Reading

Pulak, Cemal. 2005. "Discovering a Royal Ship from the Age of King Tut: Uluburun, Turkey." In *Beneath the Seven Seas: Adventures with the Institute of Nautical Archaeology*. Edited by G. F. Bass, 34–47. London: Thames and Hudson.

Pulak, Cemal. 2008. "The Uluburun Shipwreck and Late Bronze Age Trade." In *Beyond Babylon: Art, Trade, and Diplomacy in the Second Millennium B.C.* Edited by J. Aruz, K. Benzel, and J. M. Evans, 288–305. New York: The Metropolitan Museum of Art.

Pulak, Cemal. 2010. "Uluburun Shipwreck." In *The Oxford Handbook of the Bronze Age Aegean (ca. 3000–1000 BC)*. Edited by E. H. Cline, 862–76. Oxford: Oxford University Press.

THE AEGEAN SEA, 4000 TO 1000 BCE

The Aegean Sea and its surrounding regions lie between Greece and Turkey, bounded on the north by Macedonia and Thrace, and on the south by Crete, which is the fifth-largest island in the Mediterranean. The Aegean Sea is home to the Cycladic archipelago, including some three-dozen habitable islands that are mostly of low elevation, arid and exposed, with thin, rocky soil. Sailing and navigating in the Cyclades is relatively straightforward because ships rarely are out of sight of land. This is conducive to exploration, contact, and trade.

During the final centuries of the Stone Age, circa 4000 BCE, through the end of the Bronze Age, circa 1100 BCE, this small area was characterized by significant regional variation in architecture, art, and social and political organization. New excavations in the islands and new interpretations have demonstrated the tremendous complexity of Aegean cultural evolution over this period.

Although sporadic stone tool finds attest to hominin presence in the Greek mainland by 250,000 years ago (Lower Paleolithic), the archaeological evidence for a human presence in the Aegean islands comes much later. Quartzite Acheulean–type hand axes embedded in geologically datable deposits recently found in Crete suggest the island saw habitation as early as 130,000 years ago. Inasmuch as Crete has been separated from all mainland bodies for some five million years, human occupation of the island presupposes arrival by sea. Thereafter there is an apparent gap in human occupation until about 7000 BCE.

Although Crete always was an island, this was not true of many of the Cyclades. In the four major phases of the Pleistocene (Ice Ages), the surface of the Mediterranean was 400 feet lower than it is today, thus exposing vast coastal plains on the land masses of what are today Greece and Turkey. During these cold spells, the areas of the Cycladic islands would have been much larger, and some would have been close or connected to the nearby mainland.

The main source of evidence for the next chapter in the story of Aegean seagoing comes from the Franchthi Cave in southern Greece, occupied approximately 38,000 to 5,000 years ago, as the earth was emerging from the final phase of the Pleistocene. The Franchthi stratigraphic sequence captures the transition from an economy based on hunting and gathering in the Upper Paleolithic period to one based on mixed agriculture (ca. 7000 BCE) in the Neolithic. The site enables historians to speak with confidence about the first sustained seafaring in the region. By 11,000 years ago, there appear in the deposits chipped stone tools made from grayish-black obsidian (a volcanic glass), which holds a sharp edge and is superior to local flints. There are no volcanoes on the Greek mainland; the nearest one (and the source of the Franchthi obsidian) is on the island of Melos, more than 100 kilometers distant in the central Cyclades. The amount of obsidian increases through the Neolithic, suggesting that desire for this material compelled regular voyages to

Melos. No remains survive of the boats that made these voyages (dugouts and rafts being the most likely craft); but a growing familiarity with the sea as a food resource is evident in the Franchthi Cave in the form of bones of both small and large saltwater fish (including tuna and, occasionally, large cetaceans). Methods of netting, angling, and gaffing (using a pole with a sharp hook) were all used to catch fish.

Curiously, the actual settlement of the Cyclades came only toward the end of the Neolithic (fifth through fourth millennia BCE), perhaps due to a demand for more agricultural land than was available on the mainland of Greece. The ensuing Early Bronze Age (EBA) in the Cyclades (ca. 3100–2000 BCE) was a period of remarkable cultural efflorescence, most evident in the striking works of sculpture and vessels carved from marble (a resource that was plentiful in the western islands) as well as ceramics and tools and weapons of copper and bronze. By the middle of the EBA (the phase labeled Early Cycladic II, ca. 2700–2200 BCE) representations of boats incised and painted on local ceramics, as well as a few clay models of boats appear. Two vessel types are attested: canoes (likely dugouts) and "longboats"— essentially elongated craft which, like the canoes, also were paddled.

The austere and simple renderings suggest that these vessels were propelled by some two dozen hands. They could have served to move cargo (livestock, foodstuffs, raw materials such as obsidian and ores, and finished goods of copper, bronze, and occasionally silver and gold) within the Aegean and beyond. The longboats likely also functioned as instruments of raiding and symbols of power. Indeed, the fifth-century BCE historian Thucydides transmits the tradition that in bygone days the navy of Minos, legendary sea-king of Crete, made the Aegean safe from pirates (Thucydides, 1.4). This suggests that piracy was a common phenomenon—perhaps an occupation—in those early seafaring days. It can be no coincidence that depictions of longboats appeared at the same time as other innovations in the archaeological record of the Aegean, notably substantial fortification walls surrounding settlements and a variety of bronze weaponry. The EBA II period was characterized by scholars half a century ago as a cosmopolitan, even international period with respect to contact, exchange, trade, and the movement of ideas, and there is ample evidence for these phenomena for the first time in the archaeological record of the Aegean.

The distinctive Aegean geography, combined with the islands' suboptimal agricultural land (and hence relatively low population) inspired the development of a culture with an outward orientation. Islanders with technical skills in shipwrighting and sailing—as well as those who were inclined toward raiding and trading— likely enjoyed enhanced status. By the EBA II period, the Cyclades were nodes on a marine network: the Aegean Sea had become a highway. More than ever before, it connected rather than divided people. With the next technological achievement—namely the harnessing of wind to propel watercraft—the Aegean world would be enlarged considerably, and would establish increasingly regular interaction with distant foreign neighbors.

The Aegean Middle Bronze Age (MBA) gave birth to the first high civilization of Europe, and the island of Crete was its birthplace. Just after 2000 BCE, four sprawling architectural complexes worthy of the name "palace" rise in the island, most notably Knossos. The society labeled "Minoan" by archaeologist Sir Arthur Evans (1851–1941 CE), early in the 20th century was stratified, complex, and sophisticated. The palaces were centers of administrative control, served by a *sui generis* script incised into clay tablets now known as Linear A (although not yet deciphered, it was not Greek). Minoan palatial art is well-known for the bright colors, liveliness, and detail in frescoes, especially those depicting women of the court in high fashion. Minoan elites were in touch with their counterparts to the east and south of the Mediterranean. The small and remote palace at Kato Zakros near the eastern tip of Crete served as an entrepôt for high-value goods and materials trafficked between the Aegean and the Syro-Palestinian coast.

The Thucydidean passage mentioned above crediting King Minos with clearing pirates from the Aegean introduces the notion of "*thalassocracy*" (literally "rule of the sea"). Scholars have long debated the existence, nature, and ramifications of this notion for the Aegean during this era; but these palaces are recognized as centers of royalty, art, and industry, as well as of management, storage, and distribution of agricultural produce. Surely Crete was serving its turn as master of the Aegean.

It is to the Aegean MBA that we attribute depictions (on engraved Cretan sealstones) of boats displaying masts and sails, thus clearly anticipating a new era. The most precisely rendered and most fascinating boat depictions, however, were excavated at the site of Akrotiri on the island of Santorini (Thera) in the southern Cyclades, some 60 miles (100 kilometers) due north of Crete, dating to an early phase of the Late Bronze Age (LBA) (ca. 1600 BCE). Frescoes recovered from an upper-class house at the site perhaps add another dimension to the understanding of the term "thalassocracy." The frescoes show an extraordinary ceremonial procession of a flotilla of eight ships, including a flagship. These vessels were carefully drawn and elaborately fitted out; although small in size (they constitute the major scene of the so-called "Miniature Fresco"), they were painted in exacting detail. They are piloted by steersmen, and passengers (marines?) are shown sitting primly on their decks. Seven of the ships are propelled by paddlers, as many as 21 rows of them leaning into their work. The eighth ship is in full sail. The men on these boats provide good evidence for scale and size of the vessels, not to mention full profile views. No waterline is drawn, as if to emphasize the boats' graceful hydrodynamic profiles, and thus their potential for speed.

This extraordinary mural has inspired dozens of articles and books that aim to explicate and interpret this stately and very complex scene. It is clear that by the mid-second millennium BCE, mariners on the Aegean had harnessed the power of

Eruption of Thera

The catastrophic volcanic eruption of the island of Thera (modern Santorini) occurred around 1500 BCE, and generally is believed to be the catalyst that initiated the decline of Minoan society.

The eruption had four phases which lasted over several years. A series of earthquakes followed by the initial eruption rendered the island uninhabitable for a time. Pyroclastic flows—clouds of superheated gas and volcanic material—rapidly burned the island, and 20 feet of ash and pumice buried the island and surrounding sea. The second phase of the eruption, about 20 years later, was characterized by blasts of steam and ash that created mudflows almost 40-feet thick. The third phase closely followed the second, and was the most destructive. Seawater likely entered the magma chamber, and the resulting blasts left deposits up to 200 feet deep and deposited ash as far away as the Nile Delta. Tsunamis generated by the blast devastated northern Crete and ash buried farmland.

Artifacts found above the ash layer on Crete and other nearby islands demonstrate that the eruption did not immediately cause the downfall of the Minoan civilization. In fact, the lack of artifacts on Thera indicates that the Minoans probably evacuated the island before the eruption. Nonetheless, the eruption and tsunamis likely devastated Minoan shipping, which they depended upon for their livelihood and left the Minoans vulnerable to advancing Greeks.

Jill M. Church

wind, and with it a technology of propulsion that would not be substantially improved until the age of steam, nearly three and a half millennia later.

In the Late Bronze Age (ca. 1100 BCE) the Mycenaeans rose to prominence in the Aegean from palace complexes of their own on the Greek mainland, notably at Mycenae and Tiryns in the Argolid, Pylos in southwestern Greece, Thebes in central Greece, and Athens. The Mycenaean rulers admired the conventions of iconography and the imaginative minor arts of the Minoans; moreover, Minoan Linear A inspired them to develop their own script—Linear B—now known to be the Greek language. The late MBA and LBA clearly were times of close contact between these two peoples, but the mainlanders expressed a heightened interest in territorial expansion accompanied by a proclivity for combat, to judge from the fresco and relief scenes that survive in their major and minor arts. In contrast to their Minoan parallels, most Mycenaean palaces were protected by impressive citadel walls that demonstrate sophisticated military design, every bit as formidable as older and contemporary military fortifications of Anatolia, Syro-Palestine, and Mesopotamia.

A sustained and vigorous trade with the Near East and Egypt (and to a lesser extent the central Mediterranean) existed in both exotic materials (e.g., ivory, gemstones, precious metals) and finished objects exchanged by the elites of the period, as well as fine ceramics and—most notably—ingots of copper, tin, and their alloy, bronze, which have been excavated in considerable numbers at LBA sites from Syria to Sardinia. Doubtless sail technology facilitated the movement of these materials and goods and, as painted representations of watercraft demonstrate, the repertoire of boats and ships had become increasingly specialized. Two LBA merchantmen whose homeports are believed to have been in Syria have been excavated off southern Turkey at Gelidonya and Uluburun, and several painted examples of warships are known. The commercial and militaristic foci here are quite consistent with the ambitions of several other LBA polities in the eastern Mediterranean.

One other line of evidence is relevant in this context, one that portends the chaotic end of the LBA in the Aegean. The largest Linear B archive, excavated at the Mycenaean palace at Pylos, has yielded a series of five tablets prefaced, "Thus the watchers are guarding the coastal areas," followed by a list of contingents numbering some 800 men and their 10 commanders (Chadwick 1976, 175). These tablets are among the last ones written by Pylian scribes. Many scholars believe that this passage reflected anxiety about attack from the sea, perhaps by marauders known from Egyptian reliefs as the "Sea Peoples." In the end, the palace at Pylos in fact burned violently and was abandoned around 1180 BCE. It is perhaps relevant that this palace was apparently without circuit fortifications, and thus was unlike the other citadels of mainland Greece. The coast watchers of the tablets might have constituted the only system of defense, then, and the absence of archaeological evidence of a slaughter at Pylos might suggest that the coast guard performed its duty well, successfully evacuating the complex before the end came.

The next four centuries in this region are poorly attested archaeologically. Several centuries of entrenchment and introspection follow—a period known as the Greek Dark Ages—during which technological innovations leave little trace. By tradition, in the 11th century the Aegean Sea resumed its function as a highway with the Ionian migrations to coastal Anatolia, and shortly afterward to Italy and other points west. A vibrant Hellenic presence was to characterize the Aegean for another millennium before the absorption of Greece by Rome in the second century BCE.

Karl M. Petruso

Further Reading

Barrett, John C., and Paul Halstead (eds.). 2004. *The Emergence of Civilisation Revisited*. Oxford: Oxbow Books.

Broodbank, Cyprian. 2000. *An Island Archaeology of the Early Cyclades*. Cambridge: Cambridge University Press.

Chadwick, John. 1976. *The Mycenaean World*. Cambridge: Cambridge University Press.

Cline, Eric. 1994. *Sailing the Wine-Dark Sea: International Trade and the Late Bronze Age Aegean*. British Archaeological Reports Series, no. 591. Oxford: Tempus Reparatum.

Cline, Eric, ed. 2010. *The Oxford Handbook of the Aegean Bronze Age*. Oxford: Oxford University Press.

Renfrew, Colin. 1972. *The Emergence of Civilisation: The Cyclades and the Aegean in the Third Millennium BC*. London: Methuen.

Runnels, Curtis. 2014. "Early Palaeolithic on the Greek Islands?" *Journal of Mediterranean Archaeology* 27(2): 211–30.

Shelmerdine, Cynthia, ed. 2008. *The Cambridge Companion to the Aegean Bronze Age*. Cambridge: Cambridge University Press.

Simmons, Alan H. 2014. *Stone Age Sailors: Paleolithic Seafaring in the Mediterranean*. Walnut Creek, CA: Left Coast Press.

Tartaron, Thomas. 2013. *Maritime Networks in the Mycenaean World*. Cambridge: Cambridge University Press.

Homer

Homer is the name given to a Greek figure credited with composing the epic poems *Iliad* and *Odyssey*—monumental works that ancient Greeks viewed as cornerstones of their civilization. The identity, date, and very existence of an individual named Homer are no more clearly understood or agreed upon by modern scholars than they were by the ancients. Homeric poetry or Homeric epic is a product of lengthy oral tradition, and elements of the epics variously reflect periods from the Bronze Age to the Archaic period of ancient Greece—a span of several centuries between the 13th century and the eighth century BCE.

The sea (primarily *hals, pontos,* and *thalassa*) plays multiple roles in Homeric epic: It is a canvas upon which many events take place; a vehicle for connecting people and places within the narrative; and a source for the vivid metaphors and metonymies that characterize the oral tradition of which these poems are a part. The *Iliad* and *Odyssey* depict seafaring as integral to civilization, a fact that reflects the role of the sea in the Late Bronze Age and from the Archaic period onward, when interconnected civilizations and non-state actors plied the Mediterranean for the purposes of travel, trade, colonization, piracy, and warfare.

Ships in the epics are propelled by both oars and sails, are used for both combat and transport, and are skillfully navigated across long distances during both the day and night (e.g., *Il*. VII 4–6, *Od*. II 434, IV 634–637, X 28, XV 476). They are described as "swift," "curved," and "hollow," as well as "black" and "dark-prowed," a reference to dark pitch used to coat the hull planking (e.g., *Il*. XV 694, 715–716, *Od*. XIII 83). Odysseus's ships also are referred to as "red-cheeked" and "purple-cheeked," an allusion to the band of pigment sometimes applied just

Odysseus and the Sirens, a mosaic scene from Homer's *Odyssey* in the Bardo Museum in Tunis, Tunisia. (Fotokon/Dreamstime.com)

below the caprail and above the oarports of a vessel (*Il.* II 637, *Od.* IX 125, XI 124, XXIII 271). The standard ship size was a "*pentaconter*," manned by 50 rowers, although Homer also mentions ships with crews as small as 20 and as large as 100 or more (*Il.* I 309, II 509–510, 719, XVI 170, XX 247; *Od.* I 280, IV 669).

Sounding Line

The act of "sounding" means to measure water depth. A sounding line, or lead line, is a marked rope with a weight attached to one end. These are lowered from ships, and depth is measured using the marks on the rope. Mentioned in Homer and in other ancient Greek and Roman sources, sounding lines are among the oldest shipboard instruments and are critical for navigating ships through shallow waters. Initially, the wet portion was hauled aboard and measured. Later, scraps of leather or other material were tied to the line to act as measurement markings. The weighted end allows for the rope to travel to the bottom of a body of water and remain relatively straight. The weight also can be used to sample material from seabed, giving experienced captains important information about their locations.

Matthew Blake Strickland

The Achaean flotilla to conquer Troy and retrieve Helen is the largest movement of ships recorded in Homeric poetry (*Il*. II). Seafaring activity takes many forms in the epics, however, including raids, such as those of Heracles, Achilles, and Odysseus (e.g., *Il*. V 638–642, XI 327–330; *Od*. IX 38–46, XIV 245–284); flight from danger or into exile (*Il*. II 664–666); and migrations, such as King Nausithoös's forced resettlement of the Cyclopes (*Od*. VI 6–8). Other examples include trading voyages (e.g., *Il*. VII 470–475; *Od*. I 184), ferrying of travelers and livestock (*Od*. XXIV 419); and trafficking in stolen goods and people (e.g., *Od*. IX 39–41, XIV 229–233). A passing mention of naval warfare can be found in references to pikes kept on ships "for use in a sea-fight" (*cf. Il*. XV 388–389 with VI 319 and XV 674–678), although combat on the water generally resulted from ambush, as seen in the trap the suitors set for Telemachus in *Odyssey* IV.

The dual nature of the sea is emphasized in the Homeric epics: She is a fertile and life-giving resource, providing a means of transportation, communication, and sustenance to the people of the Eastern Mediterranean world (e.g., *Od*. II 416–III 12, XV 283–300, 495–500; XIX 113–114); but also is a harsh mistress, who can "weaken even a strong man" (*Od*. VIII 138–139). For those who travel on the water, the risk of storms and shipwrecks is ever-present (e.g., *Od*. V 313–332, VII 270–279, IX 282–286, XII 66–68, 403–425, XIV 301–303, XXIII 233–235; *Il*. XV 381–383, 624–628). The sea itself is treated with cautious respect in Homeric poetry—it is "surging," "dark," "dangerous," "barren," and "loud-sounding," and similes invoking storms and shipwrecks frequently are utilized, particularly when describing the movements of people and the intense combat scenes of the *Iliad* (e.g., *Il*. II 144, VII 63–64, XV 381–383, 624–628, XXIII 60–62; *Od*. II 370, VI 205). Other Homeric similes demonstrate a detailed knowledge of roles within a ship's crew and the labor-intensive process of resource procurement and shipbuilding (e.g., *Il*. XIII 389–391, XVII 742–744, XXIII 316–317).

Jeffrey P. Emanuel

Further Reading

Crielaard, Jan P. 1998. "Surfing on the Mediterranean Web: Cypriot Long-Distance Communications During the Eleventh and Tenth Centuries B.C." In *Proceedings of the International Symposium "Eastern Mediterranean: Cyprus-Dodecanese-Crete 16th–6th Cent. B.C.,"* edited by V. Karageorghis and N. Stampolidis, 187–206. Athens: A. G. Leventis Foundation.

Davis, Dan. 2013. "Ship Colors in the Homeric Poems." In S. Wachsmann, *The Gurob Ship–Cart Model and Its Mediterranean Context*, 219–224. College Station: Texas A&M.

Emanuel, Jeffrey P. 2014. "Odysseus' Boat? Bringing the Homeric Epics to Life with New Mycenaean Evidence from Ramesside Egypt." *Discovery of the Classical World: An Interdisciplinary Workshop on Ancient Societies Hosted by the Departments of History and the Classics at Harvard University, 2014–15.* Cambridge, MA. http://www.aca demia.edu/6928217/Odysseus_Boat_Bringing_Homers_Epics_to_Life_with_New _Mycenaean_Evidence_from_Ramesside_Egypt_DCW_Lecture_. Accessed September 16, 2016.

Mark, Samuel. 2005. *Homeric Seafaring.* College Station: Texas A&M University Press.

McGrail, Sean. 1996. "Navigational Techniques in Homer's Odyssey." In *TROPIS IV: 4th International Symposium on Ship Construction in Antiquity, Athens 1991*, edited by H. Tzalas, 311–320. Athens: Hellenic Institute for the Preservation of Nautical Tradition.

Nagy, Gregory. 2013. *The Ancient Greek Hero in 24 Hours.* Cambridge: Harvard University Press.

Knossos

Inhabited for many centuries, Knossos became the largest and most prosperous Minoan palace complex. Situated on a knoll at the confluence of two streams, about five miles inland from the northern coast of Crete, it became a crossroads of trade among southern Europe, Egypt, and the Levant during the Bronze Age.

The palace complex of Knossos served as the ceremonial, political, and economic center of Minoan culture. The first palace was built at the beginning of the Middle Minoan period, roughly 2000 BCE. Damaged and rebuilt several times over its history, Knossos contained more than 1,300 rooms, including those that served as residences; storage magazines; workrooms for processing grain, wine, and olives; ceremonial rooms; and sanctuaries. The palace was architecturally advanced—some portions were up to five stories tall. Knossos also had porticos and airshafts to catch and direct the sea breezes for ventilation, and had superior water-management systems. Paved roads led to other towns on Crete, with the Royal Road connecting directly to its ports at Amnisos and Katsamba. At its peak, circa 1700 BCE, Knossos had about 100,000 inhabitants, making it twice as large as the next biggest Minoan palace complex.

Later Greek traditions spoke of King Minos of Knossos having great fleets of ships that suppressed piracy in the Aegean, and the Minoans established trading posts as far away as the Nile Delta. Artifacts found at Knossos support the existence of extensive Minoan trading. These include ivory; faience; alabaster; obsidian from Melos; stoneware from Egypt and Syria; and a wide variety of bronze, copper, and tin objects from the Near East. Minoan artifacts—particularly pottery—in turn have been found throughout Asia Minor, Greece, Egypt, Syria, Cyprus, and the Levant. Egyptian texts mention Amnisos and Cretan traders. Mycenaean Greeks invaded Crete in the 15th century BCE, and Knossos was abandoned about a century later. English archeologist Arthur Evans discovered the ruins of Knossos in 1878 and later excavated the city.

Jill M. Church

Further Reading

Abulafia, David. 2011. *The Great Sea: A Human History of the Mediterranean*. New York: Oxford University Press, Inc.

The British School at Athens. "The Palace at Knossos: A 3-D Virtual Tour." http://www.bsa.ac.uk/knossos/vrtour/. Accessed March 1, 2015.

Castleden, Rodney. 1990. *The Knossos Labyrinth: A New View of the "Palace of Minos" at Knossos*. London & New York: Routledge.

Castleden, Rodney. 1993. *Minoans: Life in Bronze Age Crete*. London, New York: Routledge.

MESOPOTAMIA, 4000 TO 1000 BCE

Southern Mesopotamia lacked basic resources such as timber, stone, and metal ores, but—due to the waters from the Tigris and Euphrates rivers—it was wealthy in agricultural products, such as grains and cattle. By 3000 BCE, city-states including al Ubaid, Eridu, Uruk, and Ur existed on these rivers. Timber, stone, and metals were brought downstream on rafts of inflated cow skins held together with wooden frames and in large circular boats woven from plant material or made from hides and sealed with bitumen. Donkey caravans brought imports from Iran. Imports also were shipped to these cities through the Persian Gulf. As cities became wealthier, exotic imports came via caravans from as far away as China, and came by ship from the Persian Gulf, eastern Africa, and India. The volume of trade became so great that some cities, such as Ur, developed into international entrepôts.

The precise period that Mesopotamians first sailed on the sea is unknown, but the earliest seafarers probably were fishermen sailing on rafts built with bundles of reeds tied together and sealed with bitumen, and also possibly in hide boats. The former were commonly used in southern Mesopotamia and often are depicted on clay seals, and clay models of the latter also have been found. The earliest proposed evidence for long-distance seafaring, however, dates to approximately 5000 to 3800 BCE, during the Ubaid period, and is based on the distribution of Ubaid pottery—most of which came from al Ubaid, Eridu, and Ur. These pots have been found at as many as 50 sites, as far north as Kuwait and as far south as Oman with most being found along the coast of Saudi Arabia north of the Island of Bahrain. No evidence exists for permanent structures or trade at these sites; most were small and occupied for short periods and at widely different times. Moreover, these pots frequently were mended and other characteristic Ubaid artifacts are rare. No evidence therefore exists for large-scale trade or seasonal fishing or pearling villages used by Ubaid traders or fishermen. Three other possibilities include local fishermen taking their catch to Ubaid cities to trade for grain, textiles, and a few pots; or that trade was carried by donkey caravans rather than seaborne; or a combination of all. Because most of these trade goods consisted of materials that do not survive in the archaeological record, there presently is no way to definitively conclude how these pots were distributed around the Persian Gulf.

After the period from approximately 3500 to 3200 BCE, it has been proposed that Mesopotamian seafarers sailed in large reed vessels around Arabia, and up the Red Sea to Egypt where they traded such goods as pottery, stone seals, and lapis lazuli for raw materials, especially gold. This is unlikely for two reasons. First, the southern Mesopotamian colony of Habuba Kabira (in present-day northern Syria) was about 100 miles from the Mediterranean Sea. Furthermore, this colony traded with Anatolian mining settlements to the north for copper, lead, and silver deposits, which were collected at Habuba Kabira and sent downriver to southern Mesopotamia. Thus, Habuba Kabira was a likely intermediary for trade between Mesopotamia and Egypt possibly via Ras Shamera. The only other evidence for long-distance seafaring to Egypt around Arabia is boat depictions that are found in a number of wadis in Egypt, such as the Wadi Hammamat. Depictions of Egyptian and Mesopotamian boats show them as being very similar in shape—both are double-ended vessels with high curving ends. These similarities, however, are more likely due to the inherent structural characteristics of reed, which appears to be a common boatbuilding material used in both places. Due to the structural limitations of reed only a few raft shapes can be made. This is why reed rafts in Peru look

Inscriptions showing an early ship at Wadi Hammamat, Eastern Desert, Red Sea Hills, Egypt. (Mike P Shepherd/Alamy Stock Photo)

so similar to ancient Egyptian reed rafts, and not because of direct contact. In effect, no evidence exists to suggest that Mesopotamians were making long-distance voyages before 3000 BCE or anytime afterwards.

At roughly the same time, approximately 3600 to 3100 BCE, trade did become significant in southern Mesopotamia, but most evidence for it is indirect. For example, pre-monetary Mesopotamian equivalency standards were created to use for making business transactions. Surviving records of land sales note that transactions were undertaken in units of wool, oil, copper, and silver, and that several other materials commonly were used for transactions—including barley, lead, copper, tin, silver, and gold—suggesting that metals were readily available in southern Mesopotamia at the time. Because all metals had to be imported, there must have been a well-developed trade network, but how much came by land, river, and sea is not clear.

According to inscriptions, southern Mesopotamian cities had three seaborne trade partners, Dilmun, Meluhha, and Magan. The earliest mentioned is Dilmun, dating to late in the fourth millennium BCE in a document from Uruk. The name Dilmun then becomes increasingly common in documents in the early third millennium BCE. Scholars originally believed Dilmun was the island of Bahrain, but archaeological data suggest that it encompassed a larger area, including the island of Bahrain as well as part of the surrounding mainland. Much of this same area coincides with where most of the earlier Ubaid pottery was found.

Dilmun not only exported its own goods, but much of its wealth might have come from functioning as a transshipment site between southern-Mesopotamian cities and ports to the south such as Magan and Meluhha. In approximately 2450 BCE, for example, Ur-Nanshe of Lagash described on a stone tablet that Dilmun ships brought timber from foreign lands. For most of the third millennium, Dilmun was Mesopotamia's most important seaborne trading partner, especially for copper, for which the Mesopotamians traded wool, fat, silver, and various milk and cereal products.

Meluhha—which is believed to have been the Harappan culture in northwest India—was a source of raw materials such as timber; copper; gold; ivory; semiprecious stones, including lapis lazuli and etched carnelian beads; and animals such as monkeys, dogs, and cats. No details are given of Meluhha, but the listed imports—especially the etched carnelian beads—are consistent with cargoes from India. Meluhha disappears from written accounts shortly after 2000 BCE, which is close to the date usually cited for the end of the Harappan civilization.

Magan is believed to have been located in the region including present-day Oman, possibly the surrounding region, and possibly the land on the opposite shore of the Persian Gulf. On the Oman peninsula, evidence for a Mesopotamian influence is found in the early centuries of the third millennium BCE. Based on the archaeological data, one possible reason is that Oman was a major copper producer from about 2500 to 2000 BCE (which is called the Umm an-Nar period). Copper was mined and smelted, and arsenic and tin were imported to make bronze. Magan also was noted as a source of timber, especially for boatbuilding; but timber and other goods probably came directly from India via the sea and then were transshipped to either Dilmun or southern Mesopotamia—Harappan and Harappa-related goods are more numerous in the Oman peninsula than in the Dilmun region. Thus, Magan seemed to have been the preferred port. This trade probably began around 2500 BCE and ended shortly after about 2000 BCE, at roughly the same time that the Harappan period ends.

Although Dilmun and Magan were important transshipment points for Meluhha, some ships from India did bypass both of them and sailed directly to southern Mesopotamia. Sargon of Akkad (ca. 2334–2279 BCE), who was from north of Sumer, conquered the Sumerian cities and established his capital of Akkad near where Babylon later was established. Sargon boasted that ships from Meluhha, Magan, and Dilmun tied-up along the quays of Akkad. This statement has been interpreted to mean that all three were under his rule, but now that Meluhha has almost certainly been identified as the Harappan society in northwest India, that interpretation must be incorrect. Instead, Sargon probably meant that because the three greatest seaborne international traders were traveling upriver to his capital instead of stopping farther south as in previous times, his capital city had achieved the status of an international city of trade.

Around 2250 BCE, relations between Mesopotamia and Magan became hostile, but by 2100 BCE references to Dilmun decrease and those to Magan increase, suggesting Magan had replaced Dilmun as southern Mesopotamia's primary trade partner. In return for the imports from Magan, Mesopotamian cities gave raw wool, finished garments, sesame oil, hides, and plant products. The Mesopotamians still might have had a contentious relationship with the people of Magan because, unlike Dilmun, they make note that they sent to the Magan people only their inferior wool and garments.

Shortly after 2000 BCE, Dilmun once again becomes Mesopotamia's primary seaborne trade partner. This change coincides with the end of the copper-producing period in Magan and the demise of the Harappan culture in India. Indian artifacts have been found in Mesopotamian contexts from about 2000 to 1760 BCE, and imports might have continued to be shipped via Dilmun, suggesting that it continued to be the transshipment point for Mesopotamia's overseas trade. This relationship does not appear to change until the reign of the Assyrian king Sargon II (ca. 721–705 BCE). One of the kings who brought tribute to him was Uperi, king of Dilmun, and he gave Sargon lapis lazuli, heaps of stones, linen garments, plants, gold, silver, bronze, and iron. Whether this was actual tribute or imports that were called tribute to increase the status of Sargon II is unknown, but Dilmun continued to be an important transshipment and trade center.

A review of the textual evidence concerning ancient Mesopotamian sea trade suggests that all trade was conducted by ships from Dilmun, Magan, and Meluhha, with no mention of Mesopotamian ships. Moreover, no tradition of building wooden ships is known from Mesopotamia at this time in either representations or the archaeological record. Thus, they might never have built and sailed their own ships. Two reasons were because southern Mesopotamia had little timber suitable for boatbuilding or shipbuilding, and it was located inland. Boats can be built from the date palm tree, which is common, but dates were a valuable export. Thus these trees were too important to use as a consistent source of shipbuilding timber. Texts from the temple at Bau in Lagash (ca. 2370 BCE) do record two local trees that were used for boatbuilding, but they might not have been suitable or plentiful enough to build and maintain a fleet of seagoing ships. Furthermore, shipworms quickly devour most indigenous timbers from this region.

Timber was imported to Mesopotamia from India at least as early as circa 2450 BCE. Other texts describe ships from Dilmun and Magan bringing timber and Meluhha bringing two different species of timber. It is believed that these timbers—especially teak from India—would be prohibitively expensive to use to build anything but royal riverboats. Although teak would have been very expensive, cost-effective merchant ships could have been built by either the government or private merchants. Indian teak was a favored wood of Omani shipwrights in the 19th century because teak ships, if properly maintained, would sail for one or two centuries. Such a long sailing life made high initial costs quite affordable. Thus, although the evidence suggests that southern Mesopotamians were landlubbers, it is possible that at least some Mesopotamian cities sent out merchant ships during this long period.

Samuel Mark

Further Reading

Mark, Samuel. 2006. *From Egypt to Mesopotamia: A Study of Predynastic Trade Routes*. College Station, TX: Texas A&M University Press.

McGrail, Séan. 2001. *Boats of the World: From the Stone Age to Medieval Times*. Oxford: Oxford University Press.

Ray, Himanshu Prabha. 2003. *The Archaeology of Seafaring in Ancient South Asia*. Cambridge: Cambridge University Press.

Dilmun

Dilmun is a Sumerian term designating an eponymous Ancient Near Eastern civilization of eastern Arabia and certain islands of the Arabian Gulf, which flourished from the mid-third to the mid-first millennium BCE. Dilmun became a key transshipment point, the hub of trade networks that connected the civilizations of Arabia, Mesopotamia, and the Indus River valley. The complexity and sophistication of this network was truly one of the most significant achievements of Old World internationalism at a surprisingly early date.

The name "*Dilmun*" appears first in a very early clay tablet of the late fourth millennium BCE. It is named in cuneiform documents (later Akkadian *Tilmun*) down to about 2500 BCE from the Gulf and as far afield as Syria. Scholars today generally accept that Dilmun is to be identified primarily with the large Gulf island of Bahrain. Singularly blessed with sweet water from an Arabian aquifer, Bahrain's date palms had a high reputation in Mesopotamia. Archaeological research conducted over more than a century has brought to light several cities on the island and, significantly, some 175,000 tombs of the period when Dilmun flourished. Some scholars have argued that many of the tombs' inhabitants were from mainland Arabia and Mesopotamia, and others—emphasizing the relative rarity of off-island grave goods—suggest that these sprawling cemeteries were simply the resting places of dozens of generations of native Dilmunites.

Dilmun's economy flourished, in part, due to the aforementioned natural resources, but also because of the activities of its sailors, and especially its merchants. Sumer (southern Iraq) in antiquity was a vast area of flat, low-lying marshland, thick with sturdy reeds from which houses—including impressively large and elaborate ones—were constructed. The reeds inevitably inspired the building of boats, and their voyages on the Euphrates and Tigris systems, carrying cargo and people, were an engine of the first urban civilization. It could be inferred that increasingly common communication by watercraft and overland caravan—for purposes both peaceful and not peaceful—led to exploration and then development of economic relationships far afield, within and outside of the Gulf.

Indeed, archaeological and epigraphic evidence for the geographical reach of Dilmun's merchants, beginning perhaps as early as the fifth millennium, is the most noteworthy feature of this culture. Clay tablets and distinctive Dilmunite sealstones found over a wide area paint a picture of a far-flung import-export network. Among the materials and goods attested in the texts of the third and second millennia were copper, tin, silver, and lapis lazuli; textiles; timber; and dates, breads, cheeses, and other foodstuffs. The commercial network over sea, river, and land encompassed northern Mesopotamia; coastal Arabia to Oman; Iran and Afghanistan; and the sprawling early cities of the Indus Valley in Pakistan. Dilmun was a transshipment node, an entrepôt perfectly situated and resourced to both serve and gain from its direct and indirect connections over this enormous region.

Karl M. Petruso

Further Reading

Bibby, Geoffrey. 1969. *Looking for Dilmun*. New York: Knopf.

Crawford, Harriet. 1998. *Dilmun and Its Gulf Neighbours*. Cambridge: Cambridge University Press.

Khalifa, Shaikha, and Michael Rice (eds.). 1986. *Bahrain Through the Ages: The Archaeology*. London: Routledge.

Potts, Daniel T. 1990. *The Arabian Gulf in Antiquity*, vol. I: *From Prehistory to the Fall of the Achaemenid Empire*. Oxford: Clarendon Press.

Rice, Michael. 1994. *The Archaeology of the Arabian Gulf, ca. 5000–323 BC*. London: Routledge.

The Epic of Gilgamesh

The Epic of Gilgamesh, one of the earliest stories composed during the Sumerian Period in the third millennium BCE, parses important Mesopotamian themes such as love, friendship, heroism, kingship, destiny, and immortality. There are three versions of the text in both Sumerian and Akkadian, written on 12 tablets. The Sumerian story, written as a serial, likely began as oral tradition and later was transcribed into various short stories about Gilgamesh and his cohort Enkidu. The story discusses the semi-divine Gilgamesh (two-thirds god, one-third man), the King of Uruk, "[w]ho crossed the ocean, the broad seas, as far as sunrise" (Tablet I.1). The figure of Gilgamesh might have been loosely based on a historical king, as the *Epic* notes his relationship with known and attested Sumerian rulers. The Sumerian stories include: Gilgamesh and the *Halub*-Tree; Gilgamesh and Huwawa/Humbaba; Gilgamesh and the Bull of Heaven; the Death of Gilgamesh; the Flood; the Descent of Inanna/Ishtar into the Underworld; and Gilgamesh and Agga. The standard version, written in Akkadian during the Old Babylonian Period (ca. 2000–1600 BCE), amends and expands many of the Sumerian stories, and might have been composed as a single saga.

The most famous episode of the standard version, the flood narrative (Tablet XI), parallels the earlier Mesopotamian creation myth of Atrahasis, the later biblical story of Noah (Genesis 6–9), and three Classical stories about Deucalion and Pyrrha. In this installment, Utnapishtim (Sumerian Ziasudra) receives instructions from Ea (Sumerian Enki), the god of intelligence, creation, and water, to build an ark and thus survive the divine deluge created to destroy mankind. Utnapishtim is later granted immortality for his obedience and pious acts towards the gods. Though the plots of the stories are similar, each culture describes the hero's boat according to its societal norms: the round Mesopotamian arks, the elliptical biblical ark, and a small boat (Ovid, *Metamorphoses*, Bk 1.319) or a chest (Apollodorus, *The Library*, 1.7.2) in the Classical stories. The last Classical account, part of a compilation by Hyginus, does not describe a boat and instead states that Deucalion fled to Mt. Etna (*Fabulae*, Fabula 153).

The Epic of Gilgamesh, especially the flood narrative, indicates the large-scale trade networks and exchange of ideas within the Mediterranean Ocean Basin. Its legacy can be found in many cultures and in numerous versions, spanning both space and time.

Rachel J. Mittelman

Further Reading

Lendering, Jona. 2007. "The Great Flood: The Story from the Bible." http://www.livius.org/fa-fn/flood/flood1.html. Accessed December 20, 2014.

Ovid. 2005. *Metamorphoses: A New Translation*. Charles Martin (trans.). New York: W.W. Norton & Company, Inc.

Pritchard, J. B. (ed.). 2011. *The Ancient Near East: An Anthology of Texts and Pictures*. Princeton: Princeton University Press.

Smith, R. Scott, and Stephen Trzaskoma (trans.). 2007. *Apollodorus' Library and Hyginus' Fabulae: Two Handbooks of Greek Mythology*. Indianapolis: Hackett Publishing Company, Inc.

PRIMARY DOCUMENTS

Epic of Gilgamesh, Tablet XI, ca. 2100 BCE

Many cultures have flood stories. In the following—which appears in the "Epic of Gilgamesh," a series of Sumerian poems dating to roughly 2100 BCE—Utnapishtim tells Gilgamesh, a legendary king of Uruk, how he built an enormous ark, stocked it with food and animals, and survived a massive flood. Although the tale is more legend than fact, it sheds light on ancient shipbuilding.

Utnapishtim saith to him, even to Gilgamesh
Let me unfold to thee, Gilgamesh, a secret story,
And the decree of the gods let me tell thee!
Shurippak, a city thou knowest,—
On the bank of Euphrates it lieth;
That city was very old, and the gods within it—
To make a flood their heart urged them, even the mighty gods.
. . .Their father was Anu.
Their counseller the warrior Enlil.
Their messenger Ninib,
Their prince Ennugi.

Nin-igi-azag, the god Ea, sat in counsel with them
And their word he repeated to the reed-house:
"Reed-house, Reed-house! Wall, Wall!
Man of Shurippak, son of Ubara-Tutu,
Pull down thy house, build a ship!

Leave wealth, seek life!
Property forsake, and life preserve!
Cause seed of life of every sort to go up into the ship!
The ship which thou shalt build,
Let her proportions be [well] measured!
Its breadth and length correspond!
On the ocean launch it!
I understood, and said unto Ea, my lord:—
"The command, my lord, which thou spakest thus,
I honour, I will execute,
But what shall I say to the city, the people and the elders?"
Ea opened his mouth, and spake.
He said unto me his servant:—
"Thou shalt thus say unto them:—
'Enlil hateth me, and
I may no longer dwell in your city, and towards Enlil's ground no longer may I turn my face,
I will go down to the ocean, and with Ea, my lord, will I dwell!'
Upon you will he then rain fullness!
[A catch] of birds, a catch of fish
. . . Shall rain upon you a mighty rain-storm."

. . .

On the fifth day, I drew its design.
In its [plan] 120 cubits high on each of its sides.
By 120 cubits it corresponded on each edge of its roof.
I laid down its form, I enclosed it.
I constructed it in six stories,
Dividing it into seven parts.
Its interior I divided into nine parts,
Water-plugs I fastened within it.
I prepared the rudder, and supplied what was necessary.
Three *sars* of bitumen I poured over the outside,
Three *sars* of bitumen I poured over the inside,
While the basket-bearers were carrying three *sars* of oil aboard,
Besides a *sar* of oil which men use as a libation,
The skipper stowed away two *sars* of oil. . . .

For the . . . I slaughtered oxen;
I slew lambs every day.
Of must, sesame-wine, oil and wine,
I gave the people to drink like water from the river
A feast [I made], like that of a festival day.

I opened a box of ointment; I put it in my hand.
[At the rising] of the great Shamash, the ship was completed. . . .
With all that I had, I freighted it.
With all that I had of silver, I freighted it.
With all that I had of gold, I freighted it.
With all that I had of living things, I freighted it.
I put on board all my family and relatives,
The cattle of the field, the beasts of the field,
Craftsmen all of them, I put on board.

A fixed time had Shamash appointed [saying]:
"When the ruler of darkness sends a heavy rain in the evening,
Then enter into the ship, and shut thy door."

The appointed time arrived,
The ruler of darkness at eventide sent a heavy rain.
The appearance of the weather I observed,
I feared to behold the weather,
I entered the ship and shut my door.
To the ship's master, to Puzur-Amurri, the sailor,
The great building I handed over with its goods.

When the first light of dawn appeared
There came up from the horizon a black cloud,
Adad in the midst thereof thundered,
While Nabu and Sharru went before
They passed like messengers over mountain and plain,
Nergal tore away the anchor-cable,
Ninib goes on, the storm he makes to descend,
The Anunnaki lifted up their torches,
And with their brightness they lit up the land.
The raging of Adad reached into heaven,
All light was turned into darkness.
It [flooded] the land like . . .

One day the tempest . . .
Hard it blew and . . .
Like an onslaught in battle it rushed in on the people.
No man beheld his fellow,
No longer could men know each other. In heaven
The gods were dismayed at the flood. . . .

For six days and nights
The wind blew, the flood, the tempest overwhelmed the land.

When the seventh day drew near, the tempest, the flood, ceased from the battle in which it had fought like a host.

Then the sea rested and was still, and the wind-storm and the flood ceased.

When I looked upon the sea, the uproar had ceased,

And all mankind was turned to clay.

The tilled land was become like a swamp,

I opened the window and daylight fell upon my face,

I bowed myself down and sat a-weeping;

Over my face flowed my tears.

I gazed upon the quarters [of the world]—terrible was the sea.

After twelve days, an island arose,

To the land of Nisir the ship took its course,

The mountain of the land of Nisir held fast the ship, and suffered it not to stir.

Source: Handcock, Percy (ed.). 1921. *Babylonian Flood Stories.* New York: The MacMillan Co., pp. 10–14.

"The Shipwrecked Sailor," ca. 2000–1650 BCE

Three centuries after its initial publication, Daniel Defoe's Robinson Crusoe *(1719) continues to captivate readers and has been repeatedly adapted for plays and movies. Our oldest story of an island castaway, however, dates to Egypt's Middle Kingdom (ca. 2000–1650 BCE). This tale, "The Shipwrecked Sailor," is about a high Egyptian official returning from an apparently unsuccessful voyage, and is encouraged by one of his sailors who, after reminding of their safe return, tells him about one of his past adventures. The sailor's ship was wrecked and he was stranded on an island. Unlike Robinson Crusoe, however, the Egyptian sailor was cared for by a benevolent snake that gave him rich trade goods to take home to appease the Pharaoh.*

The wise servant said, "Let thy heart be satisfied, my lord, for we have come back to the country; after we have been long on board, and rowed much, the prow has at last touched land. All the people rejoice and embrace us one after another. Moreover, we have come back in good health, and not a man is lacking; although we have been to the ends of Wawat, and gone through the land of Senmut, we have returned in peace, and our land—behold, we have come back to it. Hear me, my lord; I have no other refuge. Wash thee, and turn the water over thy fingers; then go and tell the tale to the majesty."

. . . "Now I shall tell what happened to me . . . I was going to the mines of Pharaoh, and I went down on the sea in a ship one hundred and twenty cubits long and forty cubits wide, with one hundred and twenty sailors of the best of Egypt, who had seen heaven and earth, and whose hearts were stronger than lions. They had said that the wind would not be contrary, or that there would be none. But as we approached the land, the wind arose, and threw up waves eight cubits high. As for me, I seized a piece of wood; but those who were in the vessel perished, without one remaining. A wave threw me on an island, after that I had been three days alone, without a companion beside my own heart. I laid me in a thicket, and the shadow covered me. Then stretched I my limbs to try to find something for my mouth. I found there figs and grain, melons of all kinds, fishes, and birds. Nothing was lacking. And I satisfied myself; and left on the ground that which was over, of what my arms had been filled withal. I dug a pit, I lighted a fire, and I made a burnt offering unto the gods.

"Suddenly I heard . . . thunder, which I thought to be that of a wave of the sea. The trees shook, and the earth moved. I uncovered my face, and I saw that a serpent drew near. He was thirty cubits long, and his beard greater than two cubits; his body was overlaid with gold, and his color was that of true lazuli. He coiled himself before me.

"Then he opened his mouth . . . and said to me, 'What has brought thee? . . . If thou sayest not speedily what has brought thee to this isle, I will make thee know thyself; as a flame thou shalt vanish, if thou tellest me not something I have not heard, or which I knew not, before thee.'

"Then he took me in his mouth and carried me to his resting-place, and laid me down without any hurt. I was whole and sound, and nothing was gone from me. Then he opened his mouth against me, while that I lay on my face before him, and he said, 'What has brought thee, what has brought thee, little one, what has brought thee to this isle which is in the sea, and of which the shores are in the midst of the waves?'

[The sailor repeats his story of shipwreck and concludes]: "I was brought to this isle by a wave of the sea."

"Then said he to me, 'Fear not, fear not, little one, and make not thy face sad. If thou hast come to me, it is God who has let thee live. For it is He who has brought thee to this isle of the blest, where nothing is lacking, and which is filled with all good things. See now, thou shalt pass one month after another, until thou shalt be four months in this isle. Then a ship shall come from thy land with sailors, and thou shalt leave with them and go to thy country, and thou shalt die in thy town.'

. . .

"Then I bowed, in my obeisance, and I touched the ground before him. 'Behold now that which I have told thee before. I shall tell of thy presence unto Pharaoh, I shall make him to know of thy greatness, and I will bring to thee of the sacred oils and perfumes, and of incense of the temples with which all gods are honored.' "

. . .

"And behold, when the ship drew near, according to all that he had told me before, I got up into a high tree, to strive to see those who were within it. Then I came and told to him this matter, but it was already known unto him before. Then he said to me, 'Farewell, farewell, go to thy house, little one, see again thy children, and let thy name be good in thy town; these are my wishes for thee.'"

"Then I bowed myself before him, and held my arms low before him, and he, he gave me gifts of precious perfumes, of cassia, of sweet woods, of kohl, of cypress, an abundance of incense, of ivory tusks, of baboons, of apes, and all kinds of precious things. I embarked all in the ship, which was come, and bowing myself, I prayed God for him."

. . .

Source: Eva March Tappan (ed.). 1914. *The World's Story: A History of the World in Story, Song and Art.* Vol. III "Egypt, Africa, and Arabia." Boston: Houghton Mifflin, pp. 41–45.

"Great Inscription of Year 8" and "Inscription Accompanying the Naval Battle," from Ramesses III's Mortuary Temple at Medinet Habu, ca. 1175 BCE

The "Sea Peoples" invaded Egypt in the 12th and 13th centuries. In roughly 1175 BCE, Pharaoh Ramses III (r. 1186–1155 BCE) trapped a large group of the Sea Peoples' ships in one of the branches of the Nile Delta and utterly destroyed the ships. Descriptions of the battle appear in two inscriptions Ramesses III's mortuary temple at Medinet Habu, and are provided below. They are the oldest known records of a naval battle.

Great Inscription of Year 8

Year 8 under the majesty of [Ramesses III]. . . . The foreign countries made a conspiracy in their islands. All at once the lands were removed and scattered in the fray. No land could stand before their arms, from Hatti, Kode, Carcemish, Arzawa, and Alashiya on, being cut off at [one time]. A camp [was set up] in one place in Amor [Amurru]. They desolated its people, and its land was like that which has never come into being. They were coming forward toward Egypt, while the flame was being prepared before them. Their confederation was the Philistines, Tjeker, Shekelesh, Denye[n], and Weshesh, lands united. They laid their hands upon the lands as far as the circuit of the earth, their hearts confident and trusting: "Our plans will succeed!"

Now the heart of this god, the Lord of the Gods, was prepared and ready to ensnare them like birds. . . . I organized my frontier in Djahi, prepared before them:—princes, commanders of garrisons, and *maryanu*. I have the river-mouths prepared like a strong wall, with warships, galleys, and coasters, [fully] equipped, for they were manned completely from bow to stern with valiant warriors carrying their weapons. The troops consisted of every picked man of Egypt. They were like lions roaring upon the mountain tops. The chariotry consisted of runners of picked men, of every good and capable chariot-warrior. The horses were quivering in every part of their bodies, prepared to crush the foreign countries under their hoofs. I was the valiant Montu, standing fast at their head, so that they might gaze upon the capturing of their hands. . . .

Those who reached my frontier, their seed is not, their heart and their soul are finished forever and ever. Those who came forward together on the sea, the full flame was in front of them at the river-mouths, while a stockade of lances surrounded them on the shore. They were dragged in, enclosed, and prostrated on the beach, killed, and made into heaps from tail to head. Their ships and their goods were as if fallen into the water.

Inscription Accompanying the Naval Battle

Now then, the northern countries, which were in their islands, were quivering in their bodies. They penetrated the channels of the river-mouths. Their nostrils have ceased (to function, so) their desire is to breathe the breath. His majesty has gone forth like a whirlwind against them, fighting on the battlefield like a runner. The dread of him and the terror of him have entered into their bodies. They are capsized and overwhelmed where they are. Their heart is taken away, their soul is flown away. Their weapons are scattered upon the sea. His arrow pierces whom of them he may have wished, and the fugitive is become one fallen into the water.

Source: William F. Edgerton and John Wilson. 1936. *Historical Records of Ramesses II.* Chicago: University of Chicago Press, pp. 41, 49–50.

The Report of Wenamun, ca. 1189–1077 BCE

Egypt depended on Lebanon for timber for ship construction. During the New Kingdom (ca. 1550–1075 BCE) Egypt regularly fought to gain or maintain control of Lebanon. "The Report of Wenamun," dating to Egypt's Twentieth Dynasty (1189–1077 BCE), is the tale of a priest called Wenamun, who was sent by the Pharaoh—possibly Ramses XI (r. 1107–1077 BCE)—to the Lebanese city of Byblos to secure timber for a ship. Along the way Wenamun is robbed and then has trouble convincing the Prince of Byblos, nominally a subject of the Pharaoh, to compensate him for his loss and supply the needed timber.

Year 5, third month of the third season, day 16, the day of departure of Wenamun, the Eldest of the [temple] of Amon, Lord of Thrones-of-the-Two-Lands, to bring timber for the great and august barge of Amen Re, King of Gods, which is upon the river and [is called] Userhet of Amon.

On the day of my arrival at Tanis, at the place of abode or Nesubenebded and Tentamon, I gave them the writings [dispatches] of Amon-Re, King of Gods, which they caused to be read in their presence; and they said "I will do [it]. I will do . . . as Amon-Re, King of Gods, our lord saith."

I abode until the fourth month of the third season [summer] in Tanis. Then Nesubenebded and Tentamon sent me off with the ship-captain Mengebet, and I descended into the great Syrian Sea. . . . I arrived at Dor, a city of Thekel, and Bedel, its prince, caused to be brought for me much bread, a jar of wine, and a joint of beef. Then a man of my ship fled, having stolen a vessel of gold worth 5 *deben,* four vessels of silver worth 20 *deben,* and a sack of 11 *deben* of silver. . . .

In the morning I went to the abode of the prince, and I said to him: "I have been robbed in thy harbor. Since thou art the king of this land, thou art therefore its investigator, who should search for my money. For the money belongs to Amon-Re, king of gods. . . ." He said to me: "To thy honor and thy excellence! But, behold, I know nothing of this complaint, which thou hast lodged with me. If the thief belonged to my land, he who went on board thy ship, that he might steal thy treasure, I would repay it to thee from my treasury till they . . . but the thief who robbed thee belongs to thy ship. Tarry a few days here with me, and I will seek him."

When I had spent nine days, moored in his harbor, I went to him, and said to him: "Behold, thou hast not found my money." [Let me depart] with the ship-captain, and with those who go to sea."

. . .

[After departing, Wenamun's ship attacks a passing a ship and seizes 30 *deben* of silver, which he says he will keep until his stolen money is returned. Dropped off by his ship, Wenamun pitched] a tent on the shore of the sea in the harbor of Byblos [and made a hiding place for] Amon-of-the-Road [a protective statue of his god] and placed his possessions in it. Then the prince of Byblos sent to me saying: "Betake thyself away from my harbor!" . . . I spent nineteen days in his harbor, and he continually sent to me daily saying: "Betake thyself away from my harbor!"

. . . I found a ship bound for Egypt, and I loaded all my belongings into it. I waited for the darkness, saying: "When it descends I will embark the god also, in order that no other eye may see him."

The harbor-master came to me, saying: "Remain until morning [says] the prince." I said to him: "Art not thou he who continually came to me daily, saying: 'Betake thyself away from my harbor'?"

When morning came . . . I found [the prince] sitting in his upper chamber. . . . He said to me: "How long is it until this day since thou camest from the abode of Amon?" I said: "Five months and one day until now."

. . .

[After some back-and-forth banter, he asked Wenamun]:

"On what business hast thou come hither?" I said to him: "I have come after the timber for the great and august barge of Amon-Re, king of gods. Thy father [supplied] it, thy grandfather did it, and thou wilt also do it." . . . He said to me: "They did it, truly. If thou give me something for doing it, I will do it. . . ."

[The king claims independence from the Pharaoh and demands payment, to which Wenamun responds]: O guilty one! I am not on a foolish journey. There is no ship upon the river, which Amon does not own. For his is the sea, and his is Lebanon of which thou sayest, "It is mine." . . . behold, thou hast let "this great god wait twenty-nine days . . . Amon-Re, king of gods, he is the lord of life and health, and he was the lord of thy fathers, who spent their lifetime offering to Amon. And thou also, thou art the servant of Amon. If thou sayest to Amon, 'I will do [it], I will do [it],' and thou executest his command, thou shalt live, and thou shalt be prosperous, and thou shalt be healthy, and thou shalt be pleasant to thy whole land and thy people. . . ."

"Let my scribe be brought to me, that I may send him to Nesubenebded and Tentamon . . . and they will send all that of which I shall write to them, saying: 'Let it be brought'; until I return to the South and send thee all, all thy trifles again."

He placed my letter in the hand of his messenger; and he loaded the keel, the prow-piece, and the stern-piece, together with four other hewn logs, seven in all and sent them to Egypt. . . .

Source: J. H. Breasted. 1906. *Ancient Records of Egypt, Volume 4.* Chicago: University of Chicago Press, pp. 278–84.

Homer, *Odyssey*, Book 5, lines 244–330, ca. 750–650 BCE

The Odyssey *is one of two epic poems attributed to Homer. The other, the* Iliad, *describes the events of the Trojan War in which Greek and Trojan heroes fought one another. The* Odyssey *traces the long voyage home of one of these Greek heroes, Odysseus, who outwits a succession of foes including the Cyclops*

Polyphemus—son of Poseidon, god of the sea—whom Odysseus blinds, incurring the wrath of Poseidon. A great tale of nautical adventure, the Odyssey *inspired a host of similar tales down through the centuries, including those of Sinbad. In the passage below, Odysseus, having lost his crew and been shipwrecked, builds a boat to continue his voyage home. Although called a "raft" in the text, it is clearly more elaborate than any raft and the text details Greek construction techniques including the mortice and tenon joints they used to hold together planks.*

Then she [Calypso] led the way to the borders of the island where the tall trees were standing, alder and poplar and fir, reaching to the skies, long dry and well-seasoned, which would float for him lightly. But when she had shown him where the tall trees grew, Calypso, the beautiful goddess returned homewards, but he [Odysseus] fell to cutting timbers, and his work went forward apace. Twenty trees in all did he fell, and trimmed them with the axe; then he cunningly smoothed them all and made them straight to the line. Meanwhile Calypso, the beautiful goddess, brought him augers; and he bored all the pieces and fitted them to one another, and with pegs and morticings did he hammer it together. Wide as a man well-skilled in carpentry marks out the curve of the hull of a freight-ship, broad of beam, even so wide did Odysseus make his raft. And he set up the deck-beams, bolting them to the close set ribs, and labored on; and he finished the raft with long gunwales. In it he set a mast and a yard-arm, fitted to it, and furthermore made him a steering-oar, wherewith to steer. Then he fenced in the whole from stem to stern with willow withes to be a defense against wave, and strewed much brush thereon. Meanwhile Calypso, the beautiful goddess, brought him cloth to make him a sail, and he fashioned that too with skill. And he made fast in the raft braces and halyards and sheets, and then with levers forced it down into the bright sea.

Now on the fourth day came and all his work was done. And on the fifth day the beautiful Calypso sent him [Odysseus] on his way from the island after she had bathed him and clothed him in fragrant raiment. On the raft the goddess put a skin of dark wine, and another, a great one, of water, and provisions, too, in a wallet. Therein she put abundance of dainties to satisfy his heart, and she sent forth a gentle wind and warm. Gladly then did goodly Odysseus spread his sail to the breeze; and he sat and guided his raft skillfully with the steering-oar, nor did sleep fall upon his eyelids, as he watched the Pleiads, and late-setting Bootes, and the Bear, which men also call the Wain, which ever circles where it is and watches Orion. . . . For this star Calypso, the beautiful goddess, had bidden him to keep on the left hand as he sailed over the sea. For seventeen days then he sailed over the sea, and on the eighteenth appeared the shadowy mountains of the land of the Phaeacians, where it lay nearest to him; and it showed like onto a shield in the misty deep.

But the glorious Earth-shaker [Poseidon] . . . beheld him from afar, from the mountains of the Solymi . . . and he waxed the more wroth in spirit, and shook his head, and thus he spoke to his own heart: ". . . I shall drive him to surfeit of evil."

So saying, he [Poseidon] gathered the clouds, and seizing his trident in hands troubled the sea, and roused all blasts of all manner of winds, and hid with clouds land and sea alike; and night rushed down from heaven. Together the East Wind and the South Wind clashed, and the fierce-blowing West Wind and the North Wind, born in the bright heaven, rolling before him a mighty wave. Then were the knees of Odysseus loosened and his heart melted, and deeply moved he spoke to his own mighty spirit:

Ah me, wretched that I am! What is to befall me at the last? . . . [W]ould that I had died and met my fate on that day when the throngs of the Trojans hurled upon me bronze-tipped spears, fighting around the body of the dead son of Peleus [Achilles]. Then should I have got funeral rites, and the Achaeans would have spread my fame, but now a miserable death was it appointed me to be cut off.

Even as he spoke, the great wave smote him from on high, rushing upon him with terrible might, and around it whirled his raft. Far from the raft he fell, and let fall the steering-oar from his hand, but his mast was broken in the midst by the fierce blast of tumultuous winds that came upon it, and far in the sea sail and yardarm fell. As for him, long time did the wave hold him in the depths, nor could he rise at once from beneath the onrush of the mighty wave, for the garments which beautiful Calypso had given him weighed him down. At length, however, he came up, and spat forth from his mouth the bitter brine, which flowed in streams from his head. Yet even so he did not forget his raft, in evil case though he was, but sprang after it amid the waves, and laid hold of it, and sat down in the midst of it, seeking to escape the doom of death; and a great wave bore him this way and that along its course. . . .

Source: Homer. A. T. Murray (trans.). 1919. *The Odyssey.* New York: G.P. Putnam's Sons, pp. 187–95.

■ CHAPTER 2
The Ancient World, 1000 BCE to 300 CE

INTRODUCTION

Long-distance trade recovered quickly in the Mediterranean and Middle East after the disruptions of the 12th century BCE. The Phoenicians, in particular, sailed far from their home cities along the coast of modern Lebanon. Trade similarly blossomed in the Indian Ocean, linking the diverse cultures of East Africa, the Persian Gulf, India, Southeast Asia, and eventually China. Greek traders operating from Egypt began sailing to India in the second century BCE and the Roman Empire later established diplomatic relations with Han China. The Lapita people, ancestors of the Polynesians, sailed into the Pacific and began settling increasingly distant islands as they sailed east. Shipbuilding techniques improved and both the mortise and tenon joinery favored by the Greeks and Phoenicians and the sewn-hull techniques favored in the Indian Ocean produced stout ships capable of long voyages. Seafarers from Greece to India improved their astronomical and navigational knowledge and produced guidebooks for common routes. Several states, particularly in the Mediterranean, developed specialized warships and maintained standing navies.

The Phoenicians developed a reputation as master navigators and exceptional merchants. They sailed throughout the Mediterranean and established trading outposts and colony cities in North Africa and southern Europe. Although scholars still debate the breadth of their achievements and the distances they traveled, there is little doubt that the Phoenicians sailed beyond the Strait of Gibraltar and began exploring the Atlantic coasts of both Africa and Europe. Though the Phoenicians' home cities were absorbed into larger empires, including that of the Assyrians, Egyptians, and Persians, they were valued for their seafaring skills. Assyrian king Senacherib (705–681 BCE) brought Phoenician shipbuilders and sailors, along with timber and other supplies, to his capital at Nineveh to build ships, which they sailed down the Euphrates to the Persian Gulf where they embarked troops to invade northeastern Arabia. Egypt's Pharaoh Necho II (ca. 610 BCE to ca. 595 BCE), who sought to build a canal linking the Nile River to the Red Sea, dispatched Phoenician sailors on voyages of exploration and trade to the west and south. The

Persians, too, relied on Phoenician warships to support the advance of their armies, and many of the ships that fought the Greeks at Salamis and other battles of the Persian Wars were Phoenician.

The Greeks took to the sea long before Salamis, establishing colony cities throughout southern Europe, particularly in southern Italy and Sicily. The victory at Salamis inspired the citizens of Athens, which expanded its fleet and maritime connections and prospered, inaugurating a golden age of both art and culture and imperial expansion. Alexander the Great (356–323 BCE), relied on the Athenian fleet to invade Persia, and Alexandria, the city he founded in Egypt, became a center of learning. In addition to other subjects, scholars there studied geography and astronomy and advanced the science of navigation. Greeks developed the idea of parallels of latitude and meridians of longitude to show distance and aid navigation and used them in their maps. Eratosthenes (276–196 BCE), a renowned mathematician and geographer, calculated the circumference of the earth within 200 miles of the correct figure. Many Greeks, such as the historian Herodotus (484–425 BCE), traveled widely and wrote of their travels, expanding Greeks' understanding of the world. Later Greeks compiled detailed guides to sailing and trade ("*periploi*"), among them the *Periplus of the Erythraean Sea*, a guide to navigation and trade between Egypt, East Africa, the Persian Gulf, and India.

Scholars in India similarly documented and expanded on a sophisticated body of navigational knowledge that included information on winds, currents, and stars that could be used as navigational reference points. In the Pacific Ocean, the Laipta people mastered latitude navigation, which involves sailing north or south to reach a target's latitude and then sailing straight east or west to the target destination, ensuring that sailors did not miss it. Following the stars, they settled a series of islands, reaching Samoa and Tonga by about 800 BCE.

As Rome conquered Greek cities and states and built an empire, its people benefited from Greek maritime knowledge and trade. The city of Rome itself came to depend on regular shipments of grain from Sicily and Egypt. These grain ships were enormous for their day, as much as 180 feet long and weighing 1,200 tons. According to Lucian (ca. 125–180 CE), one of them carried enough grain to feed the people of Athens for several months. More than 1,000 years would pass until ships of their size again sailed the Mediterranean, and most Mediterranean freighters of the Greek and Roman era were between 100 to 250 tons. Larger Athenian freighters could hold 100 to 150 tons of wine or oil and returned with their holds filled with grain. Freighters capable of carrying 250 tons also sailed for Athens. Although the Roman Empire became justifiably famous for the roads that linked its cities, moving goods by sea at less than a tenth the cost compared to traveling on the best roads of the day, and Rome's maritime links across the Mediterranean sustained the empire. At its peak Rome benefited from trading networks that stretched from Britain and Spain to Egypt, and from there to India, Southeast Asia, and China.

During the Han Dynasty (206 BCE to 220 CE), China developed extensive trading networks. Chinese silk, in particular, was in great demand. Exported to Southeast Asian ports, cargoes of silk passed through the hands of several merchants who carried it across the Indian Ocean and then the Red Sea and through Egypt, taking about 18 months to travel from China to Rome. By the Song era (960–1279 CE), some Chinese merchants sailed as far as Arabia.

Numerous small cargo ships sailed from port to port in the Mediterranean Sea and Indian Ocean, buying and selling cargoes as they moved along the coast. These tramp freighters probably carried the majority of goods that moved by sea. Though derided by land-owning aristocrats in many societies, professional merchants emerged in the major port cities and conducted most of the long-distance trade, particularly in high-value goods such as silk and spices. Phoenician traders used their ships as collateral to borrow funds to purchase cargoes, paying off the loans after selling the cargo. Loans such as these became the basis for systems of maritime insurance, which covered ships or cargoes or both, and the ability to insure cargoes facilitated long-distance trade in an era when ships at sea faced dangers ranging from storms to pirates. Most states strictly regulated their ports and trade, charging ships fees to dock and unload.

Shipworm

"Shipworm" applies to several species of wood-boring saltwater clams, a scourge of seafarers for millennia. The tiny, free-swimming larvae affix themselves to submerged wood. There they develop a wormlike body covered only in small part by a helmet-like shell, which they use to bore deep tunnels into the wood where they live out their lives.

Where the most common species of shipworm, *Teredo navalis* (hence another general name, "teredo worm") (*T. navalis*), originated is unknown, but it breeds most prolifically in the tropics. More tolerant of lower salinities than other species, *T. navalis* now is found in salty and brackish waters worldwide, including colder latitudes (e.g., the Baltic Sea).

Considered an invasive species, *T. navalis* poses significant risks to wooden structures built in or operating on saltwater. Its boring can dangerously weaken hulls, as well as piles supporting wharves, bridges, and buildings. Shipworms have destroyed entire harbors (e.g., the U.S. Navy base in San Francisco Bay, 1919–1920). Likewise at risk are timbers of shipwrecks and other sunken archaeological wood if not covered by sediment.

Historic measures taken against shipworm have included using stone or concrete in construction, sheathing wood with metal, and painting or pressure-treating wood with substances such as creosote.

Noreen Doyle
Pearce Paul Creasman

By 500 BCE, specialized warships had emerged in the Mediterranean. Sleek, oared galleys armed with rams, they became increasingly larger over the next few centuries as builders added a second and then third line of oars, as well as fighting platforms and towers for soldiers and a deck to protect oarsmen. The 50-oared galleys (pentekonters) described by Homer were displaced by biremes, with two rows of oarsmen, and then triremes with 170 oarsmen split among three rows. Ships fought by ramming or boarding the enemy ships, and the Greeks developed elaborate naval tactics to outmaneuver enemy ships. Generally, the more experienced sailors preferred to ram, and those with less maritime experience preferred to close and board. Small, crowded ships with crews of 200 men or more who fought at close quarters made naval battles bloody affairs, with death tolls in larger battles often numbering in the thousands.

Triremes were displaced in the fourth century BCE by larger quadriremes (fours) and quinqueremes (fives), built by Carthage, the Hellenistic states, and the Roman Republic. Unable to add yet another bank of rowers, these fours and fives had two men pull some oars. Larger galleys could mount catapults and the Romans developed the corvus, a boarding bridge that helped them quickly overwhelm enemy ships. Yet, these oared galleys could take to the sea only in good weather and calm seas. Controlling the sea, a phrase popularized by Alfred Thayer Mahan (1840–1914) in the late 19th century, was beyond their capabilities, though the Athenian navy proved capable of dominating maritime chokepoints, such as the narrow entrances to the Black Sea. Following Rome's conquest of the Mediterranean, large warships became rare as the fleet was reduced to a police force that exterminated pirates and protected the convoys that carried Egyptian grain to Rome.

People improved on numerous maritime technologies in these years. The Greeks protected many of their ships from shipworms with lead sheathing, though not warships, which needed to be fast and maneuverable. Port facilities improved in size and quality and added features to aid in navigation, such as the lighthouse of Alexandria. Built circa 250 BCE, it was at the time the world's tallest structure. Ship builders improved rigging, making it easier to handle sails, and introduced the lateen sail—a triangular sail that enables ships to sail closer to the wind, sometime before the first century BCE. Smaller ships, in particular, found the lateen sail advantageous.

Many of the enduring characteristics of maritime activity emerged in this era. Ships became increasingly specialized for particular tasks, from sleek warships to bulk freighters. Nations maintained standing navies, both to fight rival states and to suppress piracy, and collected customs duties, which helped fund port improvements and other projects. Few, if any, merchants sailed the entire distance from Italy to China, but gold, silk, and other goods regularly made that journey, creating the foundations of a global economy.

Stephen K. Stein

Further Reading

Casson, Lionel. 1991. *The Ancient Mariners*. Princeton: Princeton University Press.

Casson, Lionel. 1995. *Ships and Seamanship in the Ancient World*. Baltimore: Johns Hopkins University Press.

Casson, Lionel. 1998. *The Periplus Maris Erythraei: Text with Introduction, Translation, and Commentary*. Princeton: Princeton University Press.

McGrail, Sean. 2004. *Boats of the World: From the Stone Age to Medieval Times*. Oxford: Oxford University Press.

Miller, J. Innes. 1969. *The Spice Trade of the Roman Empire: 29 BC to AD 641*. Oxford: Clarendon.

CHRONOLOGY

Chronology: The Ancient World, 1000 BCE to 300 CE

ca. 950 BCE	Reign of King Solomon in Israel. Phoenicians supply him with timber to build a fleet.
800s BCE	Phoenicians establish several colonies in North Africa.
814 BCE	Phoenicians found Carthage.
ca. 800 BCE	The Lapita people, ancestors of the Polynesians, arrive in Samoa. Greeks begin colonizing southern Italy and Sicily.
	Development of the first Mediterranean warships armed with rams.
760s BCE	Phoenician trade along Spain's Atlantic coast.
753 BCE	Legendary foundation of Rome.
ca. 700 BCE	Development of the bireme.
600s BCE	Development of the trireme.
590 BCE	Athens institutes Solon's reforms, marking the beginning of democracy.
ca. 563 BCE	Birth of Guatama Buddha.
559 BCE	Cyrus the Great defeats the Babylonians and establishes the Achaemenid Dynasty, beginning the expansion of the Persian Empire.
525 BCE	Persian conquest of Egypt.
ca. 500 BCE	Hanno the Navigator explores West Africa for Carthage.
ca. 496 BCE	Under Persian rule, Egyptians finish construction of a canal linking the Nile River to the Red Sea.

494 BCE	Persian forces defeat the Greek fleet at Miletus and crush the revolt of the Ionian (eastern) Greeks.
490 BCE	Persian expedition to punish Athens for supporting the Ionian Revolt defeated at the Battle of Marathon by the Athenians.
484–425 BCE	Life of Greek historian Herodotus.
483/2 BCE	Athenians vote to use newfound silver deposits to fund naval construction and begin building the world's largest fleet.
480 BCE	Led by Themistocles, the Greek fleet wins the Battle of Salamis, halting the second Persian invasion of mainland Greece.
479 BCE	Chinese philosopher Confucius dies.
460/59 BCE	Athenian admiral Themistocles dies.
450s BCE	Consolidation of the Athenian maritime empire.
447 BCE	Athens begins constructing the Parthenon.
431 BCE	The Peloponnesian War between Athens and Sparta and their respective allies begins.
405 BCE	Spartan admiral Lysander surprises Athenian fleet while it is beached at Aegospotami and destroys it.
404 BCE	Athens surrenders to Sparta, ending the Peloponnesian War.
334 BCE	A Greek fleet transports Alexander the Great's army to Asia Minor, and he begins his conquest of the Persian Empire.
323 BCE	Alexander the Great dies shortly after returning from India.
ca. 320 BCE	Pytheas of Massalia explores northern European waters.
264–241 BCE	First Punic War between Carthage and Rome.
200s BCE	Chinese deploy *louchuan* tower warships.
ca. 250 BCE	Lighthouse of Alexandria built.
ca. 240 BCE	Archimedes helps design and build the *Syracusia*, one of the ancient world's largest ships.
260–210 BCE	Qin Shi Huangdi unites and rules China as its first emperor.
232 BCE	Death of Indian King Ashoka.
218–201 BCE	Second Punic War between Carthage and Rome. Hannibal invades Italy.
210 BCE	Xu Fu sails on his second expedition from China.

ca. 120s BCE	Eudoxus of Cyzicus travels to India.
146 BCE	Rome defeats and destroys Carthage in the Third Punic War.
67 BCE	Pompey the Great suppresses Mediterranean piracy.
56 BCE	Julius Caesar defeats the Veneti in Gaul.
49 BCE	Julius Caesar crosses the Rubicon, beginning a Roman civil war.
44 BCE	Julius Caesar is assassinated.
31 BCE	Octavian (soon known as Augustus) defeats Marc Antony at the Battle of Actium.
1st century CE	*Periplus of the Erythraean Sea*, a Greek manual describing Indian Ocean trade and navigation, is published.
ca. 100–170 CE	Life of Roman geographer Claudius Ptolemy.
117–138 CE	Reign of Roman Emperor Hadrian.
166 CE	Arrival of Roman delegation in China.
220 CE	Fall of the Han Dynasty in China.

CHINA, 1000 BCE TO 300 CE

The Chinese often have viewed the sea as a barrier—like the Great Wall—that provided China with a secure eastern border. Nevertheless, the fact that even the seas were "*Tian Xia*" ("all under heaven") put them implicitly under the emperor's control and helped produce "a complex psychic relation to the vast ocean: longing but disdaining" (Sun, 2010: 327). The topography of China was a key factor for developing its inner river routes through its two largest rivers, the Yellow River (Huanghe) and the Yangzi River. China's natural system of interior waterways was crucial to ensure field irrigation, trade, and communication, and also to move and supply armies during war. Successive emperors and governments funded the construction of a great network of canals to connect these waterways, which became a fundamental instrument to administer and control the growing Chinese empire. Chinese shipbuilding developed first on the rivers, and even ocean-going craft retained the flat bottoms common to riverboats. Although later Chinese rulers focused more attention on the sea, China's interior waterways always were paramount in their thought.

Peoples along China's coast—such as the Yin, who occupied part of the Shandong peninsula and Hubei province and later founded the Shang Dynasty (1558–1046 BCE)—had long maritime traditions, fishing in coastal waters and perhaps trading along the coast. Evidence for this though, is sparse, and it is not until the Spring and Autumn Period (770–476 BCE) that more detailed accounts of maritime activity are found. The southern kingdoms of Wu (Zhejiang, Shanghai, and Jiangsu) and Yue (at the mouth of the Yangtze River), for example, developed a fruitful coastal trade with Chinese cities. Yue, in particular, emerged as a significant naval power. It maintained warships and in the fifth century BCE dispatched a naval expedition to the Shandong Peninsula. For a time, its naval power allowed it to survive and even thrive in the tumultuous Warring States Era (476–221 BCE) as lesser kingdoms jockeyed for power and fought to unite China under their rule.

It was the Qin, though, who unified China. Qin Shi Huangdi (260–210 BCE) established the short-lived Qin Dynasty (221–206 BCE), which controlled a large Chinese state and the entire coastline from Manchuria south almost to Zhejiang. Qin Shi Huangdi devoted more attention to maritime affairs than past rulers had, and led his armies south to conquer Yue and seize control of the coastal territories of Zhejiang, Fujian, Guangdong, and Tonkin (North Vietnam). These territories—rich from rice cultivation and maritime trade with Southeast Asia—were attractive targets. The port of Canton, for example, already was known for imported luxuries, including rhinoceros horn, pearls, tortoise shells, metals, and medical plants. Qin Shi Huangdi dispatched five successive military expeditions that steadily conquered these lands, finally defeating the Yue in 214 BCE. Divided into four territories, each one with its own governor and military garrison, they became the center of Chinese maritime activity and foreign trade.

According to legend, Qin Shi Huangdi sent a Daoist monk, Xu Fu, to the three mythical islands of the immortals (Penglai, Fangzhang, and Yangzhou) to find herbs that granted immortality. Xu Fu failed to find them and failed to return from his third voyage. The emperor died in 210 BCE, ending, for a time, China's southern expansion. Early rulers of the succeeding—and long-lasting—Han Dynasty (206 BCE to 220 CE) reputedly dispatched Li Shaochun, a magician, on a similar overseas quest for herbs of immortality, but he, too, failed to return.

Under the Han, China built a variety of specialized warships, often in government-operated shipyards, and shipbuilding techniques improved markedly as builders—located mostly in the southern coastal provinces of Guangdong, Fujian, and Zhejiang—experimented with a variety of materials and techniques. A 1974 archaeological expedition discovered and excavated a shipyard in Guangzhou. Dated to the third century BCE, it contained facilities for building ships up to 100 feet long. The Chinese built junks in a variety of styles and dimensions according to their use and the geographical characteristics of the sea or rivers. The Han's professional navy aided in the conquest of the northern half of the Korean Peninsula in 108 BCE. Naval tactics focused on boarding and capturing enemy ships, for which the Han used heavily protected "tower ships" ("*louchuan*") and also "bridge ships" ("*qiao chuan*"), special junks with platforms that allowed men and horses to fight as if they were on land.

Louchuan

The Louchuan ("tower ship") was a military vessel used in China as early as the Qin and Han Dynasties (221 BCE to 220 CE). These awe-inspiring ships were described as floating castles that served as command ships within a flotilla. What set the Louchuan apart from other ships were its three vertically layered decks. Each deck was protected by wooden walls. Running the length of the walls were regularly spaced openings that provided cover for crossbowmen and lancers. The defensive barriers of the Louchuan were covered with leather and felt to protect the vessel from incendiary attacks.

On the Louchuan's uppermost deck trebuchets—a type of catapult—were installed. From these war machines large stones or molten iron contained in specially treated containers could be launched at enemy forces. An example of the enormous size of the Louchuan is seen in a surviving description of one built by an admiral of the Qin Dynasty whose vessel was so large that horse-drawn chariots could maneuver on it. Although impressive, the lumbering Louchuan eventually was regarded as an impractical naval vessel because of its lack of maneuverability and its inability to withstand rough waters during a storm. The Louchuan continued to appear in fleets, however, serving as a psychological tactic to intimidate adversaries.

Zachary N. Reddick

In the south, the powerful ruler Guangdong (Nan Yue)—the southernmost part of modern China—was awarded feudal status in the expectation that he would submit to imperial authority. When a palace coup deposed members of the royal family favoring annexation by Han China, Emperor Han Wudi (156–87 BCE) invaded. Once again, Chinese army and naval forces cooperated well and cemented victory, pursuing and capturing the rebel leaders. Han Wudi similarly subdued the Min Yue in Fujian and established firm control over China's maritime provinces. Even at its peak, the Han navy was not a high-seas fleet. Designed to operate on rivers and in coastal waters, it supported the advance of Han armies and maintained control of coastal waters.

Several coastal cities engaged in long-distance trade, particularly after the conquests noted above, as well as that of northern Vietnam in the late second century BCE. Trade with Southeast Asia increased, and Han merchants travelled into the Indian Ocean. *The Records of the Grand Historian* (Shiji) written by the Grand Astronomer Sima Qian (145–86 BCE) indicate that Han sailors were sophisticated navigators who learned and mastered the pattern of the monsoons, essential knowledge for sailing in the Indian Ocean. Dating to the first century BCE, the Han Shu (*Book of the Han*) describes maritime trade in detail and the countries to which the Chinese travelled, including Japan. The Emperor Han Ping (1 BCE to 5 CE) dispatched a tribute expedition to Huang-chi, possibly a kingdom in southern India or Ceylon, which returned with live rhinoceros. Voyages like these government expeditions to collect tribute from and bestow gifts upon favored states became the norm for the Chinese court.

The Chinese Annals report that in 166 CE a group of men reportedly from "Da Qin" (Great China) reached China via the Indian Ocean, probably as passengers aboard Indian ships. It is likely that Da Qin (Ta-ch'in) identified the Roman Empire. The exact circumstances of this visit remain uncertain. They might have been formal ambassadors from the Roman Empire, or perhaps were simple traders. Presently, a lack of documents—either Chinese or Roman—prevents understanding the exact nature of diplomatic relations between Han China and the Roman Empire. The leaders of each were certainly aware of each other and conducted some long-distance trade. Silk, in particular, was in high demand in Rome, which it reached through a series of intermediary traders, passing through the Strait of Malacca, through South East Asia, across the Indian Ocean, and into the Red Sea—the so-called "Maritime Silk Road." Few of these ships were Chinese, and instead were Indian and later Persian and Arab.

The last century BCE and early first century CE marked the apex of Han southern expansion. Increasingly, sea trade became cause for concern within an imperial administration shaped around Confucian beliefs and an agrarian view of the society and the Empire. Increasingly, members of the Han court feared the rising power of the merchant class and their entry into the imperial administration. Han administrators in the maritime south generally were northerners, and tensions between rulers and ruled increased over time. Han governors put down several rebellions forcefully, as local populations resisted the process of assimilation into Han China. As rebellions against Han authority increased, the court reacted with increasingly conservative policies that emphasized China's agrarian traditions over maritime trade. Han naval power—which peaked circa 42 CE following a victory over Annan, a maritime kingdom on Taiwan—declined in the second century CE, as did Han power in general.

The fall of the Han Dynasty in 220 CE opened a turbulent period during which three kingdoms fought among each other. Among them, the Eastern Wu (222–280 CE) had a powerful navy and controlled the territories south of the Yangzi River. In 242 CE, it successfully attacked the island of Hainan and supported armies that advanced into northern Vietnam. The Western Jin (265–316 CE), centered in the north, assembled a powerful fleet of "tower ships" ("*louchuan*") and slowly gained control of China's major rivers. Often, they connected these to form floating fortresses that closed rivers to navigation and blockaded cities, a strategy that finally overwhelmed the Eastern Wu in 280 CE. Following three centuries of disunity, China was unified first under the Sui Dynasty (581–617 CE) and then the Tang Dynasty (618–907 CE). Both revived the Han Dynasty's expansion into Vietnam in the south and Korea and Manchuria in the north. Increasing contact with the rest of the world brought Buddhism to China and in the fifth century Buddhist monks began sailing back and forth between China and India, often visiting the growing number of monasteries and temples that sprang up along this route.

The first Chinese emperor, Shi Huangdi (260–210 BCE), who unified China for the first time (221 BCE), wanted to become immortal. He therefore charged Xu Fu to sail to Japan to find the elixir of long life. Born in the state of Qi, Xu Fu (255 to ca. 210 BCE) is a legendary figure who was an expert on Chinese medicine. Xu Fu led two expeditions to Japan that included 50 ships, 5,000 crew members and around 3,000 children. *The Records of History* written by the historian Sima Qian (145–87 BCE) reports that these expeditions aimed to reach three legendary mountains, Penglai, Fangzhang, and Yingzhou. Reportedly the home of the immortals, the expeditions were to collect medical herbs that would promote immortality. The first expedition failed to locate these sites and returned to China. Xu Fu's second naval expedition departed in 210, but never returned home. That same year, Emperor Shi Huangdi died, thus eliminating the necessity of these expeditions.

According to ancient Chinese tradition, Xu Fu successfully reached Japan and named the island the "rising sun country." Hence, he was the first Chinese person to establish direct contact with Japan. He also might have brought Taoism to Japan along with other Chinese traditions and farming techniques, contributing to the dramatic changes in Japanese society in the third century BCE. Lee K. Choy and other historians speculate that Xu Fu became the first Japanese emperor, a figure about whom only legends remain. The first to have raised such a possibility was a Chinese historian, Wei Tingshen (1890–1977) who pioneered the studies on Xu Fu in his published works in the 1950s. His theory attracted supporters in Japan during the 1970s when his books were translated into Japanese.

Claudia Zanardi

Further Reading

Choy, Lee K. 1995. "Xu Fu and the Bittersweet Sino-Japanese Relations." In *Japan—Between Myth and Reality*. Singapore: World Scientific Publishing, 7–18.

Leather, Louise. 1994. *When China Ruled the Seas. The Treasure Fleet of the Dragon Throne*. Oxford: Oxford University Press.

Li, Qingxin. 2006. *Maritime Silk Road*. William W. Wang (trans.). Beijing: China Intercontinental Press, 7–12.

Ng, Wai-ming. 2010. "Sino-Japanese Studies in Hong Kong: History, Characteristics and Problems." *Sino-Japanese Studies* 17, article 3, 20–21.

Schottenhammer, Angela. 2012. "The 'China Seas' in World History: A General Outline of the Role of Chinese and East Asian Maritime Space from Its Origins to c.1800." *Journal of Marine & Island Culture* 1(2): 63–86.

Sun, Lixin. 2010. "Chinese Maritime Concepts." *Asia Europe Journal* 8(3): 327–38.

Wang Gungwu. 2003. *The Nanhai Trade. Early Chinese Trade in the South China Sea.* Singapore: Eastern Universities Press.

Yu, Yingshi. 1967. *Trade and Expansion in Han China: A Study in the Structure of Sino-Barbarian Economic Relations.* Berkeley: California University Press.

EGYPT, 1000 BCE TO 300 CE

Egypt entered this era riven by internal political disputes. Following a brief recovery and resurgence in the fifth and sixth centuries, Egypt faced a succession of foreign enemies and was conquered, in turn, by Persians, Greeks, and Romans. Whether independent or under foreign rule, however, Egypt remained an important commercial center that linked the Mediterranean Sea and Indian Ocean.

During the Third Intermediate Period (1069–664 BCE, Twenty-First to Twenty-Fifth Dynasties), Egypt experienced a prolonged period of political instability. The country lost its integrity and fell under the domination of rulers of Libyan and Nubian origins. The "Story of Wenamun"—probably rewritten during the Twenty-Second Dynasty (945–715 BCE)—unfolds in the reign of Ramses XI (1099–1069 BCE) and illustrates the state of Egypt's weakened foreign influence during this period. Wenamun, a priest of Amun at Karnak, was sent to Lebanon to buy the cedar necessary to build the divine bark (a small ship). The many indignities he had to suffer in the course of his mission reflect Egypt's loss of power and prestige abroad. During the Twenty-Fourth Dynasty a major naval encounter occurred at the siege of Memphis (ca. 727 BCE) by King Piye (formerly "Piankhi") (747–716 BCE). The shipyard and the important port of *Prw-nfr* in Memphis was functioning since the reign of Thutmose III (1479–1425 BCE) at least, and it probably remained equally significant until the Late Period (Ray 1988, 270). As for iconography, ship representations are very rare in the Third Intermediate and Late Periods (664–332 BCE). The so-called "blocs of Piankhi" dated to the reign of Psammetichus I (664–610 BCE) contain the best-preserved images of Nilotic boats that generally follow the traditional line of Egyptian shipbuilding.

With the beginning of the Twenty-Sixth Dynasty (also called Saite Period, 664–525 BCE) Egyptian maritime policy revived. According to Herodotus, Pharaoh Necho II (610–595 BCE) started the construction of a canal linking the Nile to the Red Sea (probably through Wadi Tumilat) and built fleets of triremes on the Mediterranean Sea and the Red Sea, although a Greek or Phoenician origin for the construction of these ships is still debated (Herodotus 1920, 2.158, 2.159). This pharaoh is reported to have sent a crew of Phoenician sailors to circumnavigate Africa, a task that took three years to complete. Pharaoh Apries (589–570 BCE) had victorious sea battles with Phoenicia and Cyprus, and Amasis II (570–526 BCE) might have conquered the island (Herodotus 2.161; Diodorus 1933, 1.68). The latter also established a Greek merchant colony in Naucratis in the western Nile Delta.

The city of Thonis-Heracleion, discovered by underwater archaeologists in 2000, was located in the Bay of Abukir and settled since the eighth century BCE. Foreign ships coming to Egypt were obliged to call at the border city, customs station, and emporion. Sixty-four shipwrecks were discovered at Thonis-Heracleion— the majority of them dating between the sixth and the second centuries BCE—and form the largest collection of ancient ships in the world. Many of them were identified as belonging to a local Egyptian river-faring type called "*baris*," described by Herodotus (2.96), and partly paralleled by the boat of Mataria discovered at Heliopolis in the 1980s (Belov 2014). More than 700 stone anchors, imported amphorae, sculptures, and various foreign items attest to the great activity of these "Sea Gates" of Egypt (Goddio 2007). Two twin-stelae dating to the reign of Nectanebo I (380 BCE) from Naucratis and Thonis-Heracleion bear witness to the importance of these cities and to the close link that existed between them.

The strong maritime policy of the pharaohs of the Twenty-Sixth Dynasty allowed for extending trade and strengthening the diplomatic influence of Egypt, but not for long. Egypt fell to Persia in 525 BCE, following the defeat at Pelusium.

A large statue of the god Hapi, foreground, and two other unidentified statues lay on the deck of a boat in Alexandria, Egypt, on June 7, 2001, after a French underwater archaeological team raised them to the surface along with other precious items that were hidden in the murky depths. (AP Photo/Amr Nabil)

Darius I resumed the construction of the Nile–Red Sea canal, which became operational in 497–496 BCE. The Egyptian navy came under the command of a satrap. An Egyptian squadron fought successfully as part of the Persian fleet at Artemisium and Salamis (480 BCE). Several native revolts happened at the end of the first Persian domination (Twenty-Seventh Dynasty, 525–404 BCE). One of the insurgencies—led by Inaros in 463–462 BCE—was supported by an Athenian fleet of 200 ships that sailed up the Nile and seized the larger part of Memphis (Thucydides 1.104). The Athenians and the rebels were completely defeated in approximately 454 BCE. Much of our information on Egypt at that time including its naval history (mainly Books 2 and 3 of *Histories*) comes from Herodotus, who visited the country around 450 BCE. The papyrus palimpsest of Elephantine (ca. 473–402 BCE) in Aramaic, which at that time was the international language for trade and commerce, contains a range of information on the types, tonnage, and cargo of the foreign ships coming into Egypt. This proves the vigor and intensity of commercial seafaring at the time and the prevalence of imported goods. Papyrus Cowley 26 (412 BCE) contains an inventory for a boat built of cedar and numerous bronze nails, which probably were used to attach the frames to the planking. This suggests that some Nilotic ships were built in a Syro-Caananite style with a well-developed internal structure, and others followed the traditional Egyptian line and made of local timber.

Lateen Sail

One of the most significant pre-modern naval technologies, the lateen sail, is the subject of intense scholarly debate. The origin of this triangular sail with fore and aft rigging is still uncertain. It was once believed to have been a Muslim introduction from the Indian Ocean into the Mediterranean, where it was later adopted by Christians. The name comes from "Latin-rig," due to the later prevalence of Latin European ships with such sails. Today, however, most agree that triangular sails were an ancient development, arising independently in the Mediterranean (common by at latest the fifth century CE) and Southeast Asia (in evidence from the eighth century CE), before being popularized by later medieval sailors. Square sails nonetheless remained in use on Mediterranean merchant vessels and Northern European cogs until the 14th century.

The benefit of the lateen sail is that it allows more precise maneuvering and navigation, making it ideal for sailing against the wind or in low wind: it can sail upwind by tacking a zigzag course (beating to windward). This was especially useful in the monsoon winds of the Indian Ocean, for pulling into or out of harbors, or for coastal exploring. Square sails were more stable and powerful and thus preferred for voyages across the Mediterranean and, later, across the Atlantic, with lateen sails used for auxiliary power.

Sarah Davis-Secord

Egypt regained its independence from Persia with the advent of the Twenty-Eighth Dynasty in 404 BCE. Egypt's foreign policy in relation to Persia varied from material support of foreign rebels to open military confrontation. In 396 BCE, Nepherites I sent to Sparta the equipment for 100 triremes and 500,000 measures of corn to support the Greeks against Persia (Diodorus 14.79). The Egyptian pharaohs Achoris (393–380 BCE) and Tachos (362–360 BCE) confronted Persians on the battlefield. Persia responded with at least four attempts to re-conquer Egypt, the first of which occurred in 374–373 BCE. The naval forces at the disposal of Pharnabazus, the Persian commander during this assault, included 300 triremes and 200 triaconters. Pharaoh Nectanebo I (380–362 BCE) strengthened fortifications at all of the mouths of the Nile—already difficult to access in times of peace—and this invasion failed (Diodorus 15.42). Other attempts by Persians to recapture Egypt followed in 354 BCE, and in 351 BCE, but these failed. Finally, after a well-conceived operation with an active participation of the navy, Artaxerxes III (343–338 BCE) successfully invaded Egypt in 343 BCE.

Within 10 years, the Persians were superseded by the Greeks, and the Ptolemaic Period began (332–330 BCE). Alexander the Great founded his eponymous city on the site of the village of Rhâkotis. After the death of Alexander, his general—Ptolemy—founded a dynasty that ruled Egypt for 300 years based on a concept of sea power ("*thalassocracy*"). An extensive harbor network and a strong fleet were essential to the existence of the Ptolemaic Empire, and lasted until the death of Ptolemy VI in 145 BCE. Ptolemaic ships plied the Mediterranean, the Black Sea, and the Red Sea and, starting from 116 BCE, the Indian Ocean (Strabo 1928, 2.3.4–5). The League of Islanders founded by the first Ptolemies and their friendly policy towards Rhodes helped protect the sea routes in the Mediterranean. Syria, Phoenicia, and Cyprus were of strategic value as sources of shipbuilding timber of prime quality. The Ptolemaic imperial possessions in the Mediterranean also included Cyrenaica, the islands of the Aegean, the ports of Maronea and Aenus on the north coast of the Aegean, and the coast of Asia Minor to the Hellespont.

The city of Ptolemais was founded on the Nile some 400 miles up the river from its Delta and the ports of Berenice and of Myos Hormos served the Red Sea and Indian trade. Ptolemy II Philadelphus (309–246 BCE) reopened the canal leading from Heliopolis to Suez. From the Red Sea came African exotica: elephants for the army (transported in special "*elephantegos*" ships), ivory, frankincense, and myrrh. Spices, cotton, and other rare items were brought from India.

The foundation of the Ptolemaic state was secured by its important grain production and exportation (both wheat and barley). Alexandria *ad Aegyptum* (Alexandria near Egypt), conceived as a Greek city, soon became "the largest emporium of the inhabited world" (Strabo 1928, 17.1.13). Due to the advantageous position of the new capital, the trade was diverted from Thonis-Heracleion leading to its gradual abandonment. The well-conceived and interconnected harbors of

Alexandria (*Megas Limen, Eunostos, Kibotos,* and a lake port) were protected by the island of Pharos with the famous lighthouse—the seventh wonder of the Ancient World—built between 297 and 283 BCE and standing 400–460 feet tall (Pfrommer 1999, 11). Alexandria became a center of maritime knowledge and technology. Important residents included the admiral of Ptolemy II Timosthenes, who wrote 10 books *On Harbours*; Eratosthenes (ca. 276–194 BCE), who created the first map of the world with parallels and meridians; and Claudius Ptolemy (ca. 90–168 CE) who wrote the most important work on the Roman Empire's geography. It is possible that many innovations such as the lateen sail, caulking technology, and the frame-based type of ship construction were invented in Alexandria during the first centuries CE.

The division of Alexander's empire gave rise to a real arms race between the rival navies of the Diadochi (*Successors*). The Egyptian fleet under Ptolemy II Philadelphus is estimated to have included about 400 warships (Rauh 2003: 82–83). According to Athenaeus (second through third century CE), who reports a tenfold number of vessels—one and a half thousand ships—belonged to the "class" of "fives" or higher, including two "thirties" and one "twenty." It has been suggested that the warship "class" corresponded to the total number of rowers on one board working on three superimposed benches at the maximum. The culmination of this trend is a monstrous "forty" ("*tesseraconteres*") built by Ptolemy IV Philopator (221–204 BCE). This vessel was constructed as a showpiece and could barely move. She was probably a catamaran, 407 feet in length that could accommodate 4,000 oarsmen, 400 other sailors, and 3,000 soldiers. An enormous floating palace that was 340 feet long also was built on the Nile by this king (Athenaeus 5.203–206).

During the Wars of the Diadochi (322–275 BCE) and the subsequent Syrian wars (274–168 BCE), the Ptolemaic fleet participated in a number of important sea battles. Following the Battle of Salamis in Cyprus (306 BCE), lost by Ptolemy I Soter (367–283 BCE) to Antigonus Monophtalmos, Cyprus temporarily fell out of Egypt's control. The fleet of Ptolemy II was later defeated by Antigonus II at the Battle of Cos (262–256 BCE). Despite these losses, the Ptolemaic fleet was constantly present in the Mediterranean and efficiently protected the sea routes. The sea power of Ptolemaic Egypt manifested itself in maritime cults and queen Arsinoe—identified with Aphrodite—became the patron deity of the maritime empire. The Nile was considered an extension of the sea (Arnaud 2015). River navigation remained always intense with prevailing volumes of shipments of grain (mainly to Alexandria but also to Memphis and other centers). Among numerous types of Nile transport ships the largest was the *kerkouros,* with a capacity of up to 450 metric tons. It seems that indigenous Egyptian ship types coexisted with Greek ones referred to as "*ploion hellenikon*" in papyri.

Ptolemaic supremacy in the Mediterranean came to an end in the middle of the second century BCE and the later Ptolemies, torn apart by rivalry, experienced growing Roman intervention in Egypt's affairs. The struggle between Ptolemy XIII Theos Philopator and his sister and wife Cleopatra VII (69–30 BCE), supported by Julius Caesar (100–44 BCE), led to naval encounters in the harbors of Alexandria and on the Nile in 48–47 BCE. After Caesar's assassination, Cleopatra entered into an alliance with Marc Antony, and in 31 BCE the Egyptian fleet was defeated by Augustus in a sea battle in the Gulf of Actium (Adriatic Sea).

Egypt became a Roman province and its major granary. Large ships shuttled Egyptian grain to Rome. In the heyday of Roman Empire, about 32 loaded ships sailed from Alexandria weekly (Haas 1994, 42). One of the Roman trade ships was recently excavated in the Magnus Portus of Alexandria (Sandrin et al. 2013). An eyewitness description of Roman Egypt and Alexandria was left by Strabo (64 BCE to 24 CE) in book 17 of his *Geography*. Following the division of the Roman Empire in 285 CE, Egypt became a part of the Eastern (Byzantine) Empire.

Alexander Belov

Further Reading

Arnaud, P. 2015. "La batellerie de fret nilotique d'après la documentation papyrologique (300 av. J.-C. – 400 apr. J.-C.)." In *La Batellerie égyptienne. Archéologie, Histoire, Ethnographie. Actes du colloque international du Centre d'Etudes Alexandrines, 25–27 juin 2010, Alexandrie*, edited by P. Pomey. Alexandrie: Centre des Etudes Alexandrines.

Basch, L. 1977. "Triéres grecques, phéniciennes et égyptiennes." *Journal of Hellenic Studies* 97: 1–10.

Belov, A. 2014. "A New Type of Construction Evidenced by Ship 17 of Heracleion-Thonis." *International Journal of Nautical Archaeology* 43.2: 314–29.

Diodorus Siculus. 1933. *Library of History*. Translated by C. H. Oldfather. Cambridge: Harvard University Press.

Edwards, I. E. S. 1982. "Egypt: From the Twenty-Second to the Twenty-Fourth Dynasty." In *The Cambridge Ancient History, 3.1 The Prehistory of the Balkans, the Middle East and the Aegean World, Tenth to Eighth Centuries BC,* edited by J. Boardman. Cambridge: 534–81.

Empereur, J.-Y. 1998. *Alexandria Rediscovered*. London: British Museum Press.

Fraser, P. M. 1972. *Ptolemaic Alexandria*. Oxford: Oxford University Press.

Goddio, F. 2007. *The Topography and the Excavation of Heracleion-Thonis and East Canopus (1996–2006)*. Oxford: Oxford Centre for Maritime Archaeology.

Goddio, F. (ed.). 1998. *Alexandria. The Submerged Royal Quarters*. London: Periplus Publishing.

Haas, C. J. 1994. *Alexandria in Late Antiquity: Topography and Social Conflict*. Baltimore: The Johns Hopkins University Press.

Herodotus. 1920. *The Persian Wars*. Cambridge: Harvard University Press. Translated by A. D. Godley.

Lloyd, A. B. 1994. "Egypt, 404–332 B.C." In *The Cambridge Ancient History, 6. The Fourth Century B.C.*, edited by D. M. Lewis. Cambridge, 337–60.

Pfrommer, M. 1999. *Alexandria: Im Schatten der Pyramiden*. Mainz.

Rauh, N. K. 2003. *Merchants, Sailors and Pirates in the Roman World*. Stroud: Tempus.

Ray, J. D. 1988. "Egypt: 525–404 B.C." In *The Cambridge Ancient History, 4. Persia, Greece and the Western Mediterranean c.525 to 479 B.C.*, edited by J. Boardman, J. Cambridge, 254–86.

Sandrin, P., A. Belov, and D. Fabre. 2013. "The Roman Shipwreck of Antirhodos Island in the Portus Magnus of Alexandria, Egypt." *International Journal of Nautical Archaeology* 42.1: 44–59.

Strabo. 1928. *Geography*. Translated by Horace Leonard Jones. Cambridge: Harvard University Press.

Alexandria

The port city of Alexandria, Egypt—one of at least 20 cities named for their founder Alexander the Great—became the center of Hellenistic learning and the capital of Ptolemaic (332–331/330 BCE) and Roman Egypt (331/330 BCE to 641 CE). Though he never visited Alexandria after its completion, Alexander originally was interred in this prosperous maritime city.

The metropolis, located on the westernmost Nile branch of the Delta and close to the Aegean, was a prime location for trade. The small island near the Egyptian coastline, Pharos, had been a Bronze Age port (third millennium BCE) for trading with Cyprus and Crete. Upon entering Egypt, Alexander decided to build a city incorporating both the Delta and Pharos. Mythology states that the architects ran out of chalk while mapping the city's streets; undeterred, they continued by using grain. A flock of birds descended and ate the grain, however; an omen of the city's success, which was soon proven true (Strabo 1928, Book 17.6).

At its height, Alexandria exemplified Alexander's goal of cultural unity. The city attracted Greek, Roman, and Near Eastern traders and scholars and boasted large Egyptian and Jewish quarters. Goods and ideas flowed throughout the city, which linked Nile and Mediterranean Sea trade.

The exchange of information among Mediterranean scholars led to groundbreaking ideas, studies, and inventions including the understanding of the circulatory, nervous, and respiratory systems (Galen); the invention of the steam engine (Hero); the calculation of the earth's circumference (Erosthanes); the concept of a heliocentric solar system (Aristarchus); the development of geometry (Euclid); and the hypothesis that all matter was created from tiny particles (atomism). Major epics such as *Jason and the Argonauts* (Appolonius) and the Septuagint (the Greek version of the Hebrew Bible) were also composed and translated, respectively, in Alexandria. All treatises were held in the Library (attached to the Museum), which housed more than three-quarters of a million scrolls, including earlier works (Homer, Pythagoras, and Plato, for example) and essays from distant countries such as India.

The culmination of this research and discussion was the Lighthouse, designed by Sostratus and built on Pharos. The 400-foot limestone, granite, and marble building was divided into three sections: the square bottom section housed the lighthouse workers; the octagonal middle section functioned as an observation deck; and the circular highest section contained a polished brass reflector. A statue of Poseidon was placed on top. The lighthouse operated by reflecting the sun by day and bonfire by night. Surviving several earthquakes and tsunamis, the lighthouse collapsed in the 14th century CE. Today, Qaitbey Fort (built in the 1480s CE by Sultan Qaitbey) sits on the same site. The Library, Alexandria's iconic center of learning, suffered several attacks in its long history, including by Julius Caesar whose troops might have accidentally burned part of it when besieging Alexandria (48 BCE). It suffered again when Emperor Theodosius ordered all pagan temples and learning centers closed (391 CE), and in the Muslim conquest of Egypt (641 CE).

An important source of the grain that fed Rome, Alexandria declined following the collapse of the Roman Empire. By the time Napoleon travelled to Egypt in

One of the Seven Wonders of the Ancient World, the Pharos lighthouse guided ships into the busy port of Alexandria during the Ptolemaic Dynasty. One of the tallest structures of the time, it became the model for many later lighthouses. (George Bailey/Dreamstime.com)

1798, it was once again a small fishing village. After the construction of the Suez Canal (1869), Alexandria flourished anew, reclaiming its status as an important port, center of learning, and vacation destination.

Rachel J. Mittelman

Further Reading

Empereur, Yean-Yves. 2002. *Alexandria: Past, Present and Future*. London: Thames and Hudson Ltd.

Finneran, Niall. 2005. *Alexandria: A City and Myth*. Gloucestershire: Tempus Publications.

Jones, Horace. 1949. Strabo, *Geography, Book VIII*. Loeb Classical Library 267. Massachusetts: Cambridge University Press.

Pollard, Justin, and Howard Reid. 2006. *The Rise and Fall of Alexandria: The Birthplace of the Modern Mind*. New York: Viking Press.

Strabo. 1928. *Geography*. Cambridge: Harvard University Press. Translated by Horace Leonard Jones.

Eudoxus of Cyzicus

In the late second century BCE, Eudoxus of Cyzicus made the earliest recorded voyages in European history to reach India via an open-ocean route and to attempt the circumnavigation of Africa. (A fleet purported to have sailed around Africa during the reign of Necho II of Egypt [610–595 BCE] is likely fictitious.) Eudoxus's near contemporary, the scholar Posidonius (second to first century BCE), recorded his story, but the original text is lost. Portions survive in Strabo's *Geographica*, written about a century later.

To announce a religious festival held in Cyzicus, a Greek colony on the Sea of Marmara, Eudoxus visited the court of the Egyptian king, Ptolemy VIII (r. 145–116 BCE). During his stay, soldiers presented an Indian sailor who claimed to have shipwrecked while sailing from India. The man promised to reveal the route. Although not described in the text, this route took advantage of monsoon winds to run across the Indian Ocean. Such knowledge—then a secret of Indian and Arabian sailors—gave Egypt direct access to trade with India, which intermediaries had previously monopolized. Noted for his geographical curiosity, Eudoxus joined the crew and returned from India with precious cargo. Perhaps because this was a royal expedition, Ptolemy VIII claimed it all, bitterly disappointing Eudoxus.

Commissioned by the king's widow, Cleopatra III, Eudoxus sailed again to India with a larger fleet. During its homebound voyage, this fleet wrecked on the East African coast. Here Eudoxus found a distinctive prow from another shipwreck. Upon his return to Egypt, the Egyptians foiled Eudoxus's attempt to appropriate some of the cargo, but he kept the timber. Learning that it was from a fishing vessel from Gades (Cádiz, Spain), Eudoxus realized that sailing around Africa from a western port was possible. This could provide a route to India from which he might finally benefit.

Having set sail from Gades, Eudoxus's fleet quickly met shipwreck and misadventure in northwest Africa. Undaunted, Eudoxus planned a more elaborate expedition. Posidonius did not know Eudoxus's fate, but he probably died during this attempt.

Strabo discredited the entire story Posidonius told, and a first century CE Red Sea sailing manual claims that a Greek named Hippalus discovered the monsoon route. Nonetheless, Hippalus is very likely a fiction devised to explain the name of a westerly Indian Ocean wind ("*hypalus*"). Despite embroidery of some details in Posidonius's account, credit for these navigational feats appears due to Eudoxus.

Noreen Doyle
Pearce Paul Creasman

Further Reading

Buraseilis, Kostas, Mary Stephanou, and Dorothy J. Thompson (eds.). 2013. *The Ptolemies, the Sea and the Nile: Studies in Waterborne Power*. Cambridge: Cambridge University Press.

Kidd, I. G. (trans.). 1999. *Posidonius* vol. 3, "The Translation of the Fragments." Cambridge: Cambridge University Press.

Thiel, J. H. 1967. *Eudoxus of Cyzicus: A Chapter in the History of the Sea-Route to India and the Route Round the Cape in Ancient Times*. Groningen: J. B. Wolters.

Ptolemy, Claudius, ca. 100–170 CE

Greek mathematician, astronomer, and cartographer, Claudius Ptolemy was a polymath whose curiosity, precision, and respect for empirical observation were uncommonly modern. He lived in Egypt and carried out his research in the Library of Alexandria. He was not related to the Ptolemaic ruling dynasty of Hellenistic Egypt. Little more is known about his life.

His major works were *The Almagest*, a prodigious treatise on geometry and its applications in celestial mechanics; and *The Geography*, which survives in some 50 Greek manuscripts (none of which is older than the 13th century) and in Latin translations. There is no scholarly consensus on the question whether Ptolemy's original edition included maps drawn by the author (or by others with his oversight), or if they were introduced much later in the copying and printing of subsequent editions.

Despite the fact that Ptolemy considered Earth to be the center of the universe, his *Geography* was nonetheless of enduring significance in applied science. Its authority prevailed until the Age of Discovery—some 13 centuries later—when voyages by the great explorers drew attention to its errors and inconsistencies. Ptolemy regarded latitude and longitude (introduced by the earlier Greek geographer Eratosthenes) and the plotting of loci in a coordinate system as key to any endeavor to describe the world. He divided the sphere of the earth into 360 degrees along the polar axis, and introduced further precision in both meridians and parallels with minutes (Latin "*partes minutae primae*") and seconds (Latin "*partes minutae, secundae*"). The *Geography*—essentially a series of rosters of places alongside their coordinates—lists more than 8,000 cities, towns, and natural features of the then-known world from the Isles of the Blest (i.e., the Canaries, off Morocco) to Kattigara (on the east coast of Vietnam); and from Thule (perhaps the Shetland Islands) to the equator (where human habitation was assumed but not confirmed). In a 1466 edition (*Codex Ebnerianus*), the rosters were supplemented by 26 regional maps representing Europe (including the British Isles), Asia, and North Africa; hence it has the feel of a modern atlas and gazetteer.

Ptolemy occupied himself with the difficult matter of projection—how best to render in two dimensions the spherical surface of the earth without sacrificing accuracy in measuring distance. He developed three approaches to projection, each superior to the simple grid system invoked by his predecessors and yet none entirely satisfactory.

The oceans and seas (and, for that matter, the unpopulated lands of his day) presented significant challenges in a work focusing on the location of points in the *oikouméne*. Ptolemy and other ancient geographers sought out the experience of long-distance sailors and merchants regarding distances at sea—for which voyage durations, being subject to winds and currents, make poor proxies. The least reliable sectors of his regional maps, not surprisingly, are the oceans and *terrae incognitae* of the largest landmasses.

In the end, the *Geography* deserves its reputation as one of the great founding books in the history of science. It is worth noting in passing that the farthest-flung reaches of our globe would not be mapped adequately until the 20th century—and that descriptive geography in the modern era has increasingly served military, economic, and imperialistic ends. This is a far cry from the scientific curiosity that so thoroughly animated Claudius Ptolemy.

Karl M. Petruso

Further Reading

Berggren, J. Lennart, and Alexander Jones. 2000. *Ptolemy's Geography: An Annotated Translation of the Theoretical Chapters*. Princeton: Princeton University Press.

Dilke, Oswald A. W. 1985. *Greek and Roman Maps*. Ithaca, New York: Cornell University Press.

Dilke, Oswald A.W. 1987. "The Culmination of Greek Cartography in Ptolemy," Chapter 11. In *The History of Cartography,* vol. I: *Cartography in Prehistoric, Ancient, and Medieval Europe and the Mediterranean,* edited by J. B. Harley and David Woodward, 177–200. Chicago: University of Chicago Press.

Wilford, John Noble. 1981. *The Mapmakers: The Story of the Great Pioneers in Cartography from Antiquity to the Space Age.* New York: Random House.

GREECE, 1000 BCE TO 300 CE

Between 1000 BCE and 300 CE, Greeks took to the sea for a wide range of reasons: migration and colonization, raiding and trading, naval warfare against foreign powers or other Greeks, and sacred missions to PanHellenic sanctuaries. Small craft were used by ferryboat men, fishermen, and the divers who braved shark-infested waters in quest of pearls, sponges, and treasure salvaged from sunken ships. During these centuries, the ancient Greeks were truly a "people of the sea" just as much as the later Vikings and Polynesians. Maritime matters penetrated every element of Greek civilization, from art and poetry to science and politics. Moreover, between the historic naval battles of Salamis in 480 BCE and Actium in 31 BCE, Greek city-states and kingdoms were the dominant sea powers of the Aegean, Mediterranean, and Black Sea regions.

In 1000 BCE, the Greeks still were suffering from the crisis of depopulation, cultural impoverishment, and economic collapse that followed the fall of the Bronze Age Mycenaean civilization. Early in the Iron Age, however, Greeks began to leave their old homeland in wave after wave of maritime migrations to Aegean islands and the coastlands of Asia Minor. These ventures were made in "*makra ploia*" or "long ships" propelled by 20, 30, or 50 rowers, all of them fighting men who could take up arms to protect the colonizing mission from attack. Thus, the revival of Greek culture began not in the old homeland but in the new overseas communities.

During this period, Greek poets kept the memories of their heroic past alive in tales handed down from their ancestors of the Bronze Age. Judging from the myths, early Greeks explored distant seas in quest of precious metals, especially gold. Jason and the Argonauts crossed the Black Sea to gain a Golden Fleece, while Heracles ventured to the edge of the Atlantic Ocean for the golden apples of the Hesperides. Homer's *Iliad* and *Odyssey,* tales of the Trojan War, were also epics of the "wine-dark sea." The *Iliad* included a "Catalogue of Ships" that enumerated the hundreds of "swift ships" that conveyed the Greek to Troy, and the *Odyssey* recounted the mythical homeward voyage of the hero-king Odysseus, apparently including landfalls in Libya, Sicily, Italy, and southern Spain.

From about 900 to 730 BCE, a second wave of migrations carried Greeks from the Aegean islands and Asia Minor to more distant destinations. New settlements such as Byzantium cropped up along the route to the Black Sea, via the Hellespont and Bosporus. In the west, Greeks founded Marseilles and "Neapolis" (Naples). The Homeric *Hymn to Apollo* described the annual reunion festival of the widely scattered Ionian Greeks, who voyaged to the holy island of Delos early each spring. During this age of expansion, the Greeks found themselves in continuous competition with Phoenicians from the Near Eastern city-states of Tyre and Sidon (modern Lebanon), who spread their own colonies along the coasts of North Africa and Iberia. From these sea-going Canaanites the Greeks borrowed the alphabet and the trireme, which was a large triple-tiered galley well adapted to either colonizing missions or naval warfare. They also might have borrowed the concept of the "*polis*" or city-state, which became the defining feature of classical Greek civilization.

A new age of organized sea-raiding began in 732 BCE, when heavily armored Greek soldiers known as "hoplites" attacked coastal cities of the Assyrian Empire. The overseas exploits of these Viking-like marauders were celebrated by the poets of the Archaic Age. Their successes also began to pump vast quantities of precious metals and artwork into Greek temples, households, and markets. Eventually Near-Eastern kings and Egyptian pharaohs began to hire large numbers of Greek hoplites as mercenary troops: the Egyptian royal fort of Daphnae accommodated tens of thousands of hoplites from all over the Greek world. Greek merchants followed in the wake of the raiding parties, and established emporia in the Nile delta. Through many generations, these seafaring merchants and soldiers of fortune enriched Greek culture with new religious concepts, scientific ideas, and technological advances. During this period the poet Hesiod composed his epic *Works and Days*, a "farmer's almanac" that included nature's signs for the start and close of the seafaring season, and advice on protecting one's watercraft during the stormy months of winter.

As fleets of longships from the Greek city-states began to dominate the seas and suppress piracy, the old Bronze Age tradition of "round ships" was revived. More secure conditions allowed for valuable cargoes to be carried in big vessels propelled not by oars but by a single large square sail. In addition to the captains and steersmen, only a few mariners were needed to sail these heavily ballasted and often fully laden merchant ships. Longships and round ships found it difficult to voyage in mixed convoys, because the brisk winds that filled the sails of the big merchant vessels made for choppy seas that impeded the rowing of the triremes and other galleys with their narrow hulls and low freeboard.

In 660 BCE, the tradition of naval warfare between Greek city-states was launched with a battle between the Corinthians (who controlled an overland shipway or "*diolkos*" that linked the Aegean Sea to the Ionian and Adriatic) and their own colonists from the western island of Corcyra (modern Corfu). By this time, Greek warships were fitted with bronze rams on their prows so that the steersmen and rowing crews could disable or break open the wooden hulls of enemy vessels. On deck, archers and hoplites fought for victory using a barrage of missiles or boarding actions. Following these early contests, trireme fleets dominated Mediterranean naval warfare for the next three centuries.

A perilous new involvement with eastern powers began in about 545 BCE, when Cyrus king of Persia sent generals to conquer the Greek city-states of Asia Minor. The ensuing decades of conflict were recorded by the Greek historian Herodotus, who had been born a Persian subject in the Greek port city of Halicarnassus (modern Bodrum, Turkey). In 494 BCE, the naval forces of King Darius of Persia defeated the Ionian Greeks at Lade near Miletus. In 480 BCE, however, the fleets of the Athenians and other mainland Greeks withstood the attacks of Darius's son

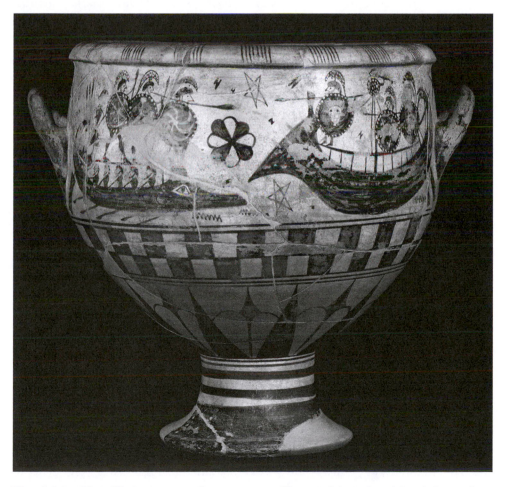

The Aristonothos Krater, a seventh-century BCE illustrated pot signed by Aristonothos, shows an early sea battle. (Leemage/UIG via Getty Images)

Xerxes, first at Artemisium and then at Salamis near Athens. An Athenian poet named Aeschylus, who had fought the Persians in 490 BCE at the battle of Marathon, gave an eyewitness account of the Greek naval victory at Salamis in his tragedy *Persians*—the world's oldest surviving dramatic work.

In 479 BCE, the victorious Greek fleet of triremes crossed the Aegean and defeated the remnant of the Persian forces at Mycale in Asia Minor. The Spartans then returned home, followed by most of the Greek allies, but the Athenians undertook the mission of liberating all the Greek city-states from Persian rule, and protecting them from future foreign aggressors. By about 450 BCE this new alliance had evolved into an Athenian maritime empire, with about 150 Greek islands and city-states paying annual tribute to support the seemingly unbeatable Athenian navy. Thus the concept of "thalassocracy" or "sea-power" came to dominate Greek ideas about history.

Athenian rule of the sea and investment in ships and naval installations ultimately led to the birth of the world's first radical democracy. In Greek warships the rowers were considered to be combatants, and because Athenian rowing crews traditionally were drawn from working-class citizens known as "thetes," their new status as warriors on maritime missions led to demands for political equality on the home front. Much as women won the vote in the 20th century in part due to their services in time of war, the masses of low-income, non–land owning citizens suddenly became a major force in Athenian government.

Modern accounts of ancient sea battles often have assumed that the oars were pulled by slaves, as was the case in Medieval and Renaissance galleys. In classical Greece, however, it was considered an honor and a mark of citizenship to row in a warship. When manpower was short and slaves had to be recruited as crew members, they were given their freedom before joining in the war effort. Thus in Athens, and perhaps in other Greek city-states, naval power was a powerful force for progressive social and political change.

Although Athenian thalassocracy was challenged continually, first by Spartans in the Peloponnesian War (431–404 BCE) (recorded by the general-turned-historian, Thucydides) and later by the Macedonians, it was widely recognized that the Golden Age of Athens was entirely an outgrowth of Athenian rule of the sea. The Parthenon itself was built with money drawn from the naval tribute, as was the famous marble temple of the sea-god Poseidon at Cape Sounion. To house the triremes ashore, huge complexes of ship-sheds were constructed around the harbors of the Piraeus. The Athenian philosopher Plato was one of many who believed that sea power corrupted the ancestral values of Greek tradition. In his *Critias* and *Timaeus*, Plato created an enduring allegory on the dangers of thalassocracy in his myth of Atlantis. By contrast, Plato's successor Aristotle explored the properties of masts and oars in his *Mechanics*, and wrote detailed descriptions of marine life in his biological treatises.

On the commercial front, the popularity of Greek wines led to the building of large sailing vessels as freighters for ceramic wine containers called "amphoras." Shipwrecks investigated by underwater archaeologists from Kyrenia on Cyprus to Gela on the southern coast of Sicily provide an invaluable record of Greek ship designs and cargoes on both merchant freighters and colonizing missions.

Starting in 336 BCE, Athenian sea power was eclipsed by the rise of Macedon under Philip II and his son Alexander the Great. From this time onward, Greek naval history merges with that of the wider Mediterranean. The ensuing Hellenistic period was an age of gigantic galleys, with sea-rule passing to Greek dynasties in Rhodes, Ptolemaic Egypt, and Syracuse in Sicily. These larger, heavier warships had immense crews, with multiple rowers pulling each long, heavy oar. There were never more than three tiers of oars, just as on the old triremes, but in this new age the warships were classed according to how many rowers worked the oars in each rowing unit. The "penteres" or (to use the Roman term) "quinquereme" replaced the trireme as the new ship of the line in naval combat.

The name of the great Greek scientist Archimedes is linked to this final period of Greek naval warfare. Based in Syracuse, he developed the famous "Archimedes

Antikythera Mechanism

The Antikythera Mechanism is the name given to a complex mechanical computer, fragments of which were discovered in a large Roman shipwreck found near the Greek island of Antikythera at the western edge of the Aegean Sea.

The ship, which might have been sailing to Rome, sank between 76 and 67 BCE, but the mechanism itself appears to date from about 205 BCE. The sophisticated mechanism could for any particular date indicate the positions of the sun, the moon, and the five extraterrestrial planets known to the ancients. Once thought to be a navigational device, the Antikythera Mechanism probably was used to aid astronomical observations. It could, for example, compute the dates of solar eclipses. The three larger fragments of the mechanism are displayed in the National Archaeological Museum in Athens, Greece.

The Antikythera Mechanism was recovered by sponge divers in 1900–1901, but it was only in 2006 that computed tomography (CT) scans revealed at least 30 bronze gears within its fragments. Although the mechanism's inventor presumably was Greek and might have been working on the Aegean island of Rhodes, he is thought to have drawn upon Babylonian mathematical principles. Similar devices would not be built again until the 14th century CE. A five-year project to investigate the site of the Antikythera shipwreck more thoroughly using an Exosuit pressurized diving system was announced in 2015.

Grove Koger

screw" to clear water from the bilges of the new, super-sized naval galleys, though the invention was later adapted to irrigate raised fields. The largest Hellenistic ships, some of which were catamarans, were used to maneuver siege engines such as battering rams against the walls of cities built by the sea. To combat such attacks at Syracuse, Archimedes devised a lifting device that could snare the prow of an enemy ship and then capsize the entire vessel. Legend also attributes to Archimedes the invention of large mirrors or lenses that could focus sunlight on enemy ships and set them on fire.

The rise of Rome, an Italian city-state on the Tiber River, ultimately put an end to the Greek sea powers of the Hellenistic Age. When Octavian of Rome (the future Caesar Augustus) defeated the fleet of Cleopatra and Anthony at Actium in western Greece in 31 BCE, the entire Greek world became subservient to Roman imperial rule. More than three centuries would pass before a new generation of Greek naval vessels—now based at Byzantium on the Bosporus—would spark a revival in the tradition of Greek sea power.

John R. Hale

Further Reading

Casson, L. 1971. *Ships and Seamanship in the Ancient World*. Princeton University Press, Princeton.

Fox, Robin Lane. 2009. *Travelling Heroes in the Age of Homer*. Alfred A. Knopf, New York.

Graham, A. J. 1983. *Colony and Mother City in Ancient Greece*. Ares Publishers, Chicago.

Hale, J. R. 2009. *Lords of the Sea: The Epic Story of the Athenian Navy and the Birth of Democracy*. Viking Penguin, New York.

Johnston, P. F. 1985. *Ship and Boat Models in Ancient Greece*. Naval Institute Press, Annapolis.

Kaltsas, N., E. Vlachogianni, and P. Bouyia. 2012. *The Antikythera Shipwreck: The Ship, the Treasures, and the Mechanism*. National Archaeological Museum, Athens.

Leroi, A. M. 2014. *The Lagoon: How Aristotle Invented Science*. Viking Penguin, New York.

Levi, P. 1984. *Atlas of the Greek World*. Facts on File, New York.

Loven, B., and M. Schaldemose. 2011. *The Ancient Harbours of the Piraeus*. The Danish Institute, Athens.

Malkin, I. 2011. *A Small Greek World: Networks in the Ancient Mediterranean*. Oxford University Press.

Miller, H. H. 1967. *Bridge to Asia: The Greeks in the Eastern Mediterranean*. Charles Scribner's Sons, New York.

Miller, M. 1971. *The Thalassocracies*. State University of New York Press, Albany.

Morrison, J. 1980. *Long Ships and Round Ships: Warfare and Trade in the Mediterranean, 3000 BC–500 AD*. National Maritime Museum, London.

Morrison, J. S., and R. T. Williams. 1968. *Greek Oared Ships 900–322 B.C.* Cambridge University Press, Cambridge.

Tandy, D. W. 1997. *Warriors into Traders: The Power of the Market in Early Greece*. University of California Press, Berkeley.

Van Wees, H. 2013. *Ships and Silver, Taxes and Tribute*. I. B. Tauris, London.

Wood, A. K. 2012. *Warships of the Ancient World, 3000–500 BC*. Osprey Publishing, Oxford.

Herodotus, ca. 484–425 BCE

Herodotus, called the "Father of History" by the Roman philosopher Cicero, was an ancient Greek historian, explorer, and geographer. Herodotus also was the first writer (that we know of) to conduct historical research in an attempt to discover and explain the past. Much of his life remains uncertain. It is believed that he was born around 484 BCE in Halicarnassus (modern Bodrum, Turkey), a city in southwest Asia Minor then under Persian rule. He probably died around 425 BCE in Athens where he had migrated. During his life, Herodotus traveled throughout the Mediterranean and Middle East, visiting most of the places known to Ancient Greece. He also constructed his own maps. Influenced by Homer, as well as his birth as a Persian subject, he decided to produce the first known narrative history, the subject of which is the Greco-Persian Wars (499–479 BCE).

Two or three centuries after his death, Herodotus's *Histories* were divided by Alexandrian philosophers into nine books, *Herodotus' Muses* (I–IX), which they named after the nine Muses of Greek mythology: *Clio, Euterpe, Thalia, Melpomene, Terpsichori, Erato, Polyhymnia, Urania*, and *Calliope*. The first four books describe the background to the wars between the Greeks and the Persians; the rest contain the history of the wars themselves. Herodotus's *Histories* discuss the expansion of the Archaemenid Empire progressing from King Darius I the Great and his defeat at Marathon to King Xerxes' expeditions against the Greeks and the great battles at Thermopylae, Artemesium, Salamis, Plataea, and Mycale. Herodotus offers vivid descriptions of these battles, particularly those at sea, and his work remains an important source for modern scholars.

Herodotus visited and explored numerous places and his eyewitness accounts give unique information on how the world around ancient Greece was shaped from a geographic, topographic, and ethnographic perspective. A characteristic example is the construction of Herodotus's World Map (Book IV) where he shows how Greeks understood the world during the fifth century BCE, particularly the maritime area of the eastern Mediterranean, the Black Sea, the Red Sea, the Nile, and the

Often called the first historian, Herodotus traveled throughout the eastern Mediterranean and Near East, collecting stories from the region's diverse peoples, which he incorporated into his history of the Persian War. This statue is in the U.S. Library of Congress. (Library of Congress)

Indian Ocean. Additionally, Herodotus, with much talent, integrated a host of digressions into his narratives, which he called lectures ("*logoi*"). Many of these offer amazing insights into the cultures he visited, and present additional information about Herodotus's sea voyages, Greek and Egyptian trade, international relations, and local customs and legends.

By turning from the main subject Herodotus gives readers the opportunity to know more about his voyages in the sea, the ancient Greek and Egyptian and their neighbors' overseas trade, the different trading routes, the goods carried, and the relations among different nations. In the introduction of Book III, for example, Herodotus discusses Greek merchants and argues that their courage, maritime knowledge, maritime tradition, and seamanship allowed them to gain commercial advantage in even the most remote, "barbaric" places. Yet, he also praised the Phoenicians as accomplished sailors and navigators.

Gina Balta

Further Reading

De Selincourt, Aubrey. 2001. *The World of Herodotus*. USA: Phoenix.

Evans, James Allan. 2006. *The Beginnings of History: Herodotus and the Persian Wars*. Campbellville, Ontario: Edgar Kent.

Lateiner, Donald. 1989. *The Historical Method of Herodotus*. Toronto: Toronto University Press.

Momigliano, Arnaldo. 1990. *The Classical Foundations of Modern Historiography*. Berkeley: University of California Press.

Thomas, Rosalind. 2000. *Herodotus in Context: Ethnography, Science and the Art of Persuasion*. Cambridge: Cambridge University Press.

Piraeus

The Piraeus has been the main port of Athens since the fifth century BCE up to the present day. It is situated seven miles southwest of the city of Athens and consists of three harbors: Zea, Munychia, and Cantharus.

Prior to the sixth century BCE, the Athenians had little interest in the Piraeus as a port; instead they used the nearby Bay of Phaleron. The first to take notice of the Piraeus was the tyrant Hippias, who fortified the Munychia hill in 511–10 BCE. Major fortification works began in 493–92 BCE under the direction of the Athenian statesman Themistocles, who later persuaded the Athenians to build a fleet of triremes, thus rendering Athens a major naval force. In 458–57 BCE, with the construction of the so-called "Long Walls," the Piraeus was connected to the city of Athens. The walls were intended to make Athens impregnable if it were under siege, as long as the city maintained access to the sea.

By the middle of the fifth century BCE, the Piraeus had become the most important commercial port in the eastern Mediterranean, and it attracted large numbers of foreign merchants and businessmen. The commercial quarter, known as the Emporion, was located on the eastern and northern sides of Cantharus. It was during this time that Pericles, the leader of the Athenians, invited the architect Hippodamus of Miletus to develop a city plan for the Piraeus, which he did using a grid pattern.

In 431 BCE, the Peloponnesian War broke out between Athens and Sparta. The war ended in 404 BCE, with the victorious Spartans destroying both the Long Walls and the fortifications of the Piraeus, and demanding that the Athenians destroy the vast majority of their fleet. In 394 BCE, the Athenian Conon revitalized the port by rebuilding and expanding major portions of the fortifications, and in 330 BCE the so-called "Arsenal of Philon" was constructed. Epigraphical sources indicate that by the late 330s BCE, the three harbors of the Piraeus could house 372 triremes (196 at Zea, 94 at Cantharus, and 82 at Munychia).

During the Macedonian occupation of Greece, the Piraeus hosted a Macedonian garrison from 322 to 229 BCE, and in 200 BCE the port served as winter quarters for 30 Roman warships. In 88 BCE, Mithridates VI Eupator of Pontus challenged Roman supremacy in the eastern Mediterranean, and Athens sided with him. In 86 BCE, and after a one-year siege, the Roman general Sulla captured and completely destroyed the port of Piraeus.

The Piraeus did not play a major role during the Middle Ages and the Ottoman occupation of Greece. It was not until the mid-19th century, after the liberation of Greece from the Ottomans, that the Piraeus was thoroughly rebuilt and once again became the main port of Greece. Today, nearly 20 million passengers pass through the port every year, making it one of the world's busiest passenger ports.

Ioannis Georganas

Further Reading

Garland, Robert. 2001. *The Piraeus: From the Fifth to the First Century B.C.* 2nd ed. London: Duckworth.

Lovén, Bjørn. 2011. *The Ancient Harbours of the Piraeus*. Monographs of the Danish Institute at Athens, Vol. 15, 1. Gylling: Narayana Press.

Steinhauer, Georgios, Matina Malikouti, and Bassias Tsokopoulos (eds.). 2000. *Piraeus: Centre of Shipping and Culture*. Athens: Ephesus Publishing.

Pytheas of Massalia, ca. 350 BCE to ca. 285 BCE

Pytheas of Massalia was an ancient Greek astronomer, geographer, and author known for his exploration of the Atlantic Ocean off the coast of northwest Europe, around 320 BCE.

A native of Massalia, a Greek colony on the southern coast of France (modern Marseille), Pytheas traveled as a private citizen (i.e., not acting as an agent of his city). His book *On the Ocean* described voyages that took him to many fascinating places in the Atlantic. The book does not survive except in a dozen or so scattered quotations by subsequent ancient authors, including Strabo and Polybius, who doubted its more exotic passages.

Perhaps the first educated person from the classical Mediterranean to travel to northern Europe, Pytheas determined that climate was in part a function of latitude. His careful scientific observation of the stars enabled him to take precise readings of latitude that enabled him to plot his journeys. He suggested that the earth rotated about a fixed axis. Upon reaching the Atlantic, he observed that tides—inconsequential in the closed Mediterranean Sea—correlated with the phases of the moon.

Because our few ancient sources for Pytheas are fragmentary, contradictory, and biased, it is impossible to map out his peregrinations with precision. He spent about a year in Britain and commented extensively on the tin-mining industry in Cornwall, for which Massalia was a major destination. He circumnavigated the island, determined it was triangular in shape, and calculated the length of its coastline. He was likely familiar with the Orkney and Hebrides island groups.

It is his voyage from Britain to Thule, however, that has most fascinated subsequent scholars. Pytheas described Thule as six days' sailing north from Britain; modern scholars have variously identified it as Iceland, Norway, and Shetland. He described the sea in the vicinity of Thule as "congealed," today referred to as "sludge ice"; and a day's sailing farther north, frozen. The gray north Atlantic in a fog, with no visible line dividing sea and sky, evoked an enigmatic, even primeval, elemental unity to Pytheas. Such un-Mediterranean imagery doubtless contributed to the scorn with which some contemporaries greeted his exploits—perhaps understandably so, because remote Thule was popularly regarded as a fantastic or imaginary place. The last leg of his great journey took Pytheas to an island called Abalus, where amber was collected. Although the exact location of Abalus is uncertain (perhaps Gotland or Helgoland), Pytheas was certainly in the Baltic region—the source of this coveted substance for the Mediterranean since the Bronze Age.

Long-distance travel in ancient times, whether on land among potentially hostile people or in open watercraft braving the volatile north Atlantic, always was a dangerous proposition. Although his surviving writings are few, disparate, and problematic, there is no doubt that Pytheas was one of the most intrepid travelers of antiquity.

Karl M. Petruso

Further Reading

Cunliffe, Barry. 2002. *The Extraordinary Voyage of Pytheas the Greek*. NY: Walker Publishing Company.

Hawkes, Christopher. 1977. *Pytheas: Europe and the Greek Explorers*. The Eighth J.L. Myres Memorial Lecture. Oxford: Blackwell Publishing.

Roller, Duane W. 2006. *Through the Pillars of Herakles: Greco-Roman Exploration of the Atlantic*. New York: Routledge.

Roseman, Christina. 1994. *Pytheas of Massalia: On the Ocean. Text, Translation and Commentary*. Chicago: Ares Publishers.

Whitaker, Ian. 1981–82. "The Problem of Pytheas' Thule." *Classical Journal* 77:2: 148–64.

Salamis, Battle of

The Battle of Salamis occurred in September 480 BCE, and was the climactic naval battle of the Greco-Persian Wars between the Greek alliance and Persian Empire that was fought in the strait between the west coast of Attica and Salamis, the largest island in the Saronic Gulf. The decisive Greek victory expelled the Persian armada from Greece and paved the way for Greek victory in the war the following year and the establishment of Athenian naval hegemony (thalassocracy) in the Aegean that lasted for the next 75 years.

The main textual sources, all Greek (primarily Aeschylus *Persae*; Herodotus 7.141–43, 8.40–96, and later Diodorus Siculus 11.15–19; Plutarch, *Themistocles*), do not provide wholly consistent accounts of the battle. The size of the fleets, tactics employed, and the exact sequence of events remain a matter for conjecture and debate among scholars.

After the Persian victory at Thermopylae and the indecisive naval engagement at Artemisium, Persian King Xerxes I (519–465 BCE) led his large army into central Greece. Athenians, convinced by Themistocles's interpretation of the Delphic oracle's mysterious phrases "wooden wall" and "divine Salamis" as a prognosis of Greek naval victory in Salamis, evacuated Attica. Contemporaneously, the Greek fleet, estimated at 380 to 400 ships (mostly triremes, predominantly Athenian) and led by Themistocles (but nominally by the Spartan Eurybiades), located itself on the eastern coast of Salamis, where the strait provided topographical and meteorological advantages for Greek triremes and restricted the number of Persian vessels (estimated to be as much as 1,207) that could enter and maneuver in the narrow mile-wide channel.

Following Xerxes's capture of Athens and burning of the Acropolis, panic spread among the Greek alliance, leading the majority of its admirals to favor retreating to defend the narrow Isthmus of Corinth. Ancient sources recount Themistocles's determination to prevent this and force an engagement with Xerxes's fleet, which he lured into the Salamis strait with a false message indicating the Greek alliance had fractured.

The battle was fought from dawn to sunset. The Persians ships' quantitative advantage and their overloaded vessels proved detrimental. They found it difficult to maneuver in the restricted waters, particularly under the heavy cross-channel swell. Confusion spread through the fleet as ships collided with one another. Tightly packed together, they proved vulnerable to Greek ramming and were unable to retreat. Xerxes, sitting on his golden throne on shore, witnessed the crushing destruction of his fleet, which lost upwards of 200 ships and suffered heavy casualties. After the battle, he retreated home to Persia with his fleet and two-thirds of his army. A Greek army defeated Xerxes's remaining troops the following year at the Battle of Plataea.

For Athens, which contributed substantially to the victory, the battle proved a milestone in its emergence as a predominant naval power. Athenians, understanding their military virtue as the outcome of their democratic regime, exploited Salamis as an integral part of their civic identity and political ideology. Aeschylus, in his tragedy, *The Persians* (472 BCE)—the earliest extant European drama—commemorated the battle as a democratic triumph, shaping the Salamis legend.

Saving European Greece from Persian subjugation enabled classical Greek civilization to flourish. The narrative of Salamis became a symbol of freedom and "the rise of the West," and figured canonically from antiquity to the present in scholarly works and in various literary and artistic genres as a seminal event in human history.

Fayah Haussker

Further Reading

Green, P. 1996. *The Greco-Persian Wars*. Berkeley and Los Angeles: University of California Press.

Hanson, V. D. 2001. *Carnage and Culture: Landmark Battles in the Rise of Western Power*. New York: Doubleday.

Strauss, B. 2004. *The Battle of Salamis: The Naval Encounter That Saved Greece—and Western Civilization*. New York: Simon and Schuster.

Syracusia

The *Syracusia* was a third-century BCE Greek ship, generally considered to be the largest transport/cargo ship of antiquity, measuring some 360 feet in length. Commissioned around 240 BCE by the tyrant of Syracuse, Hieron II, *Syracusia* was designed by Archias of Corinth and built by Phileas under the supervision of Archimedes. Construction lasted a year and required enough timber to build 60 quadriremes (warships with 4 banks of oars). *Syracusia* had 3 decks, 3 masts, and 12 anchors. The upper deck was equipped with 8 towers, each carrying 2 archers and 4 soldiers. On the bow was a giant catapult, made by Archimedes; he also was responsible for the ship's water-pumping device, which could be operated by a single man. A special coating of horsehair and pitch protected the hull from shipworms.

In addition to its large cargo hold, the ship boasted 30 cabins, 10 stables, gardens, indoor hot baths, a library, gymnasium, fish tank, freshwater tank, ovens for the preparation of food, and a shrine dedicated to Aphrodite. The ship's lavish decorations included ivory and marble statuary and mosaics depicting scenes from the *Iliad*. According to ancient sources, *Syracusia* could carry 1,942 passengers and a cargo of nearly 2,000 tons. Expensive to operate, the ship sailed only once, from Syracuse to Alexandria in Egypt, where it was presented as a gift to king Ptolemy III Euergetes who renamed *Alexandris*.

Ioannis Georganas

Further Reading

Casson, Lionel. 1971. *Sea and Seamanship in the Ancient World*. Princeton, NJ: Princeton University Press.

Meijer, Fik, and André Wegener Sleeswyk. 1996. "On the Construction of the 'Syracusia' (Athenaeus V. 207 A-B)." *The Classical Quarterly* 46.2: 575–78.

Turfa, Jean Macintosh, and Alwin G. Steinmayer Jr. 1999. "The Syracusia As a Giant Cargo Vessel." *The International Journal of Nautical Archaeology* 28.2: 105–25.

Themistocles, ca. 524–23 to 460–59 BCE

Themistocles, the architect of the Greek victory in the Battle of Salamis (480 BCE), was an Athenian general (*strategos*) and leading statesman during the Greco-Persian Wars. His far-reaching naval policy led to Athens's transformation into a maritime hegemony (thalassocracy) over the fifth century. Ancient historians, primarily Herodotus, Thucydides, and Plutarch, attest to his sagacity, diplomatic wisdom, and strategic ingenuity. He remains a controversial figure, both in ancient tradition and modern scholarship, admired as an outstanding leader, yet criticized as a corrupt and power-hungry demagogue.

Themistocles was the son of Neocles, a native Athenian from an ancient Lycomid clan, and probably of a non-Athenian mother. As archon (493–92 BCE), he oversaw the development and fortification of Athens's harbor at Piraeus. He might have fought at Marathon (490 BCE). By the late 480s, he became prominent in Athenian politics, and persuaded the Athenians in 483–82 to divert funds from a rich silver find at Laureum to expand the Athenian fleet with an additional 100 triremes. Intended for use against longtime rival Aegina, they provided the foundation for Athenian naval supremacy and proved decisive against the Persians at Salamis.

Themistocles reached his pinnacle while commanding Athenian forces on land and sea during the Persian invasion of Greece (480–79 BCE). Adhering to his interpretation of the Delphic oracle forecasting a Greek victory at Salamis, he initiated the evacuation of Athens and prepared the Greek fleet for battle against the Persians in the narrow waters off Salamis.

In 478, following the war, Themistocles directed the refortification of Athens and completed work on the Piraeus. In the late 470s, he fell from favor and was ostracized from Athens by conservative political rivals. He found refuge in Argos, and from there he pursued his anti-Spartan policy. Following Spartan accusations of treasonable correspondence with the Persian king, Themistocles was forced to flee Greece. After 465 BCE Artaxerxes I, the new Persian king, awarded Themistocles the governance of the province Magnesia on the Maeander on the southwest coast of Asia Minor, where he died shortly afterwards, probably of natural causes.

Themistocles's naval policy, a cornerstone of his political career, had an ongoing effect on fifth-century Athens's socio-politics. Maritime power relied on the city's lower class, the *"thetes,"* who served in the fleet as rowers and became increasingly important in Athenian politics after gaining the right to vote. As much as leaders like Themistocles, they helped build Athens's sea empire and promote democracy in the maritime cities of Greece.

Posthumously, Themistocles's reputation was restored, reestablishing him as a savior of Athens and Greece, canonically commemorated in classical historiography, oratory, and drama, and inspiring scholarly writings and popular culture in Western civilization, from antiquity to the present.

Fayah Haussker

Further Reading

Frost, F. J. 1980. *Plutarch's Themistocles, an Historical Commentary*. Princeton: Princeton University Press.

Hammond, N. G. L. 1982. "The Narrative of Herodotus VII and the Decree of Themistocles at Troezen." *Journal of Hellenic Studies* 102: 75–93.

Lenardon, R. J. 1982. *The Saga of Themistocles*. London: Thames and Hudson.

Marr, J. L. 1998. *Plutarch: Life of Themistocles*. Warminster: Aris and Phillips.

Trireme

Just as biremes (which deployed their rowers in two banks) displaced single-banked oared warships, triremes displaced biremes. Introduced in the late seventh century BCE, perhaps by the Greek city-state Corinth, triremes ("*trieres*" in Greek, meaning "three-fitted") became the premier Mediterranean warships by the fifth century. They made up the bulk of the Greek and Persian fleets in the Persian War (480–477 BCE), as well as the Athenian and Spartan fleets in the Peloponnesian War (431–404 BCE).

Archaeologists have yet to unearth a trireme, so our understanding of them is based on ancient texts, art, and material remnants, such as the Piraeus ship sheds. Careful study of these enabled scholars and naval architects to build the *Olympias*, a reconstruction of a Greek trireme.

The trireme's three banks of rowers, named "thalamites," "zygites," and "thranites," were carefully staggered at a slight diagonal to allow each man room to ply his oar. Fifty-four thalamites, 27 on each side, worked the lowest oars through ports lined with watertight leather sleeves. Fifty-four zygites sat above and slightly forward of them, and above these sat 62 thranites who rowed from an outrigger along the hull. In addition to these 170 rowers, a trireme's crew included a captain, helmsman, shipwright, a dozen deckhands and other sailing crew, and roughly a dozen soldiers, bringing the ship's complement to about 200.

Long and narrow, with a length six to seven times their width, triremes were built for short bursts of speed. Athenian triremes measured about 120.7 feet (26.8 meters) by 17.8 feet (5.45 meters). Their primary weapon was a bronze-sheathed ram bolted to the prow. Like other Greek ships, triremes were built shell first, using planks of oak and various lightweight woods, carefully aligned and bound with mortise and tenon joints. Ropes strung below deck from bow to stern further contributed to the trireme's remarkably strong, yet flexible hull.

The volunteer crews of the *Olympias* have achieved 50 strokes per minute, driving the ship to almost 9 knots. Experienced ancient crews likely did better, though speeds would have been half that for long voyages. On these, triremes employed rowers in shifts or relied on square sails hung from a mainmast and sometimes a foremast that projected ahead of the ship. Captains usually beached their ships each night to rest the oarsmen and procure drinking water. When triremes sailed into battle, they left sails and masts on shore.

Expensive to build and maintain, triremes also regularly had to be dried to prevent rot. An Athenian trireme cost about one talent to build, and almost as much to feed and pay its crew each month. Maintaining a 200-trireme fleet at sea for 6 months could cost more than the 1,200 talents required to build the Parthenon. Few Greek city-states boasted more than a dozen triremes.

Stephen K. Stein

Further Reading

Morrison, John S., and John F. Coates. 1996. *Greek and Roman Warships 399–30 B.C.* Oxford: Oxford University Press.

Morrison, John S., John F. Coates, and N. Boris Rankov. 2000. *The Athenian Trireme: The History and Construction of an Ancient Greek Warship,* 2nd ed. Cambridge: Cambridge University Press.

Wallinga, Herman T. 1993. *Ships and Sea-Power Before the Great Persian War: The Ancestry of the Ancient Trireme.* Leiden, Netherlands: Brill.

INDIA, 1000 BCE TO 300 CE

Geographically, the Indian Peninsula is bounded by the sea to east and west and by the Himalaya Mountain Range to the north. India's long sea coast encouraged many Indians to enjoy a close connection to the sea and maritime activities. As civilizations rose and fell on the subcontinent, Indians' connection with the sea persisted, and included fishing and pearling, as well as trade along the coast and to distant ports in the Middle East and Southeast Asia.

When Indians first took to the sea remains unknown, but coastal trade helped fuel urbanization and the emergence of the Harrapan civilization in the Indus River Valley before 3000 BCE. Harrapan traders traveled across the Indian Ocean and developed an extensive trade with Mesopotamia in the third millennium BCE. Although Harrapan civilization collapsed about 1700 BCE, maritime trade soon resumed. Indian traders reached the islands of Indonesia and rebuilt trade routes with the Persian Gulf. Greek traders from Egypt arrived in India in the second century BCE and Romans a century later. By the time of Augustus (63 BCE to 14 CE), 120 Roman ships sailed each year for India and emissaries from India visited Rome. As empires rose and fell in the ensuing centuries, India's important place in trade, both as a producer of goods and transshipment point for goods from other regions, continued thanks to its central position in the Indian Ocean, production of valuable goods ranging from gemstones to spices and textiles, and the activities of Indian traders who reached as far west as Arabia and east to Indonesia's spice islands and China.

Harrapan civilization, named after the large city of Harrapa, which archaeologists began excavating in the 1920s, flourished along the Indus River from roughly 3300 BCE to 1700 BCE. Contemporaneous with Old Kingdom Egypt and Sumeria, the Harrapans built sophisticated irrigation and drainage systems and became experts at metalworking, pottery, and other crafts. Archaeologists have discovered more than 1,000 Harrapan cities and towns, but have yet to decipher the Harrapan language, leaving much of this civilization's achievements uncertain. There is little doubt, though, that these people became expert seafarers and traveled widely. Harrapan port cities traded with one another, and Sumerian texts demonstrate the existence of substantial trade between Persian Gulf ports and the major Harrapan ports of Bharuch, Lothal, and Sopara. Lothal, located at the head of the Gulf of Khambhat in modern Gujarat, was a particularly active port. It had extensive warehouses, wharves, and other facilities built from brick, along with a dock, which—dating to 2400 BCE—is the world's oldest.

Harrapans sailed to the Maldive Islands where they collected cowrie shells, which were prized in Sumer. Indian teak, ebony, and other woods, along with pearls and other precious stones were traded for copper, gold, lead, tin, and other metals. Much of this trade flowed through Dilmun, the Persian Gulf's premier entrepôt. Sumerian artifacts are present in the ruins of Harappa, Mohenjo Daro, and other Harrapan cities and Harrapan artifacts have been found in Dilmun and throughout Arabia. Among these are many Harrapan seals, which depict reed boats and other watercraft. The Harrapans probably built their larger ships from teak, a particularly durable indigenous wood, though archaeologists have yet to find any remains.

Following the collapse of Harrapan civilization, new peoples entered the Indian subcontinent, inaugurating the Vedic Age (ca. 1500 to 500 BCE). This period was named after the Vedas, the oldest Hindu scriptures, which were composed in this era. Indian maritime technology advanced rapidly during the Vedic Age, and the Vedas reveal much about Indian maritime activity. In the *Rig Veda* (ca. 1500 to 1200 BCE), for example, hymns to the sea god Varuna, note the riches of the sea, describe important trade routes, navigational references, and ports commonly visited by traders, and beseech Varuna's help to protect one from the sea's many perils including storms and dangerous, rocky coasts. The *Ramayana* and the *Mahabharata*, epic poems dating from the fourth and fifth centuries BCE, describe voyages to Suvarna and Yavan Dvipa (Sumatra and Java) and Lohta Sayara (the Red Sea). Numerous later Sanskrit dramas, such as the *Ratnavali,* purportedly written by King Harsha (590–647 CE), describe great voyages of Hindu traders and their epic sea adventures. The *Manu Smriti,* India's earliest known law book, dating to sometime between the second century BCE and second century CE, includes discussions of maritime laws and disputes over commerce and seaborne trade.

Early Buddhist literature, such as the Milindapanha, written during the reign of King Menander (160–135 BCE) similarly recounts maritime activities, great ocean voyages, and traders who returned from these laden with wealth. The *Jatakamala* states that ship captains must know the seasons, locations, and movements of the stars—of which the *Jatakamala* noted 56 of importance to navigation—and a captain must be able to identify his location based on the color of the seawater, marine life, and soil samples of sea bottom.

Early Indian trade moved along the coast, but Indian navigators learned to navigate by the stars, particularly the Pole Star, and took to the open sea before the second century CE. They learned the pattern of the monsoons to facilitate long-distance trade, which later Greek sailors learned from them, and developed a sophisticated body of navigational knowledge later compiled and expanded by the astronomers Varahamihira (505–587 CE) and Aryabhatta (476–550 CE). Dugout canoes and reedboats remained in use throughout this period in coastal waters. Larger boats—those used for cargo—employed sewn-hull construction. This required dozens of miles of rope made from coconut fiber, but produced flexible hulls that resisted damage from storms and beaching on rocky coasts. The ropes stretched and wore out over time, needing replacement, but nonetheless supported the construction of large ships, which reached about 150 feet in length and could carry several hundred tons of cargo.

Indian mariners and merchants traveled throughout Southern Asia, west to the African coast, and as far east as Thailand and Vietnam. Traders circumnavigated the Indian peninsula and, by 500 BCE, Tamil ships sailed with the monsoons to Malaya, Java, and Sumatra, departing at the beginning of the year and returning with the opposite winds at its end. In Southeast Asia they entered local trade networks, visiting Java, Borneo, Cambodia, and Bali. Departing from Mahabalipuram, a port on India's east coast, Indian merchants traded in pepper, cinnamon, and

---

Monsoons

The prevailing winds change seasonally around the world, but nowhere is this change more apparent and dramatic than in the Indian Ocean and Southeast Asia. Derived from the Arabic word for season, "*mawsim*," the monsoons are two seasonal winds created by the difference in temperature between the Indian Ocean, which stays roughly the same temperature year round, and the Asian landmass, which warms and cools with the seasons. In the summer, between May and September, warm air rises over Asia and draws air from the Indian Ocean, creating the southwest monsoon. In winter, from November to March, warm air rises over the Indian Ocean, creating the northeast monsoon, which blows from China to Indonesia at one end of the Indian Ocean and from India to Africa at the other. Sailing against the monsoons is all but impossible, and at times their high winds even disrupt coastal sailing.

Greek sailors operating from Egypt were among the first to understand this annual pattern of reversing winds, and this understanding facilitated rapid, seasonal sailing across the Indian Ocean, linking, among others, the Roman Empire to Han China in the second century CE. Until the introduction of steamships in the 19th century, sailing schedules and the pattern of trade across the Indian Ocean followed the monsoons. Merchants sailed with their cargoes to India, blown by the southwest monsoon, traded in India, and then awaited the arrival of the northeast monsoon, which would take them home. The roundtrip voyage took about 12 months.

Stephen K. Stein

---

other spices and established trading posts in the major islands of Southeast Asia. Local traders, in turn, conveyed Indian goods as far as China. The island of Ceylon (modern Sri Lanka) became a key center of Indian Ocean trade, a transshipment point for goods moving east or west where merchants from the west met those from India, China, and other eastern lands.

In the second century BCE, Eudoxus of Cyzicus pioneered Greek trade with India, returning home with perfumes and precious stones. The *Periplus of the Ehrythraean Sea*—a first-century CE Greek guide to Indian Ocean trade—describes Greek merchants trading clothing, linens, topaz, coral, frankincense, glass vessels, wine, and gold and silver coins and plate for cotton cloth, indigo, silk, turquoise and other semiprecious stones, and spices, particularly pepper, which was grown in southern India. Berenice, a port on Egypt's west coast, flourished from the third century BCE through the sixth century CE thanks to Indian Ocean trade.

India's coastal population farmed fish in freshwater reservoirs by the fourth century BCE and farmed both fish and crustaceans along India's west coast and Bengal. First-century CE Tamil poems collected in the *Akananuru* note the importance of fishing, operations ashore to harvest salt, and pearling. The *Periplus of the Erythraean Sea* notes that pearls from the Tamil coast were far superior to those from Arabia. Another Tamil poem from this era, the *Pattinappalai,* notes that fishing families lived in the outer streets of towns and that ports bustled with activity and glowed with the lights of artisans and dockworkers who worked late into the night.

Alexander the Great (356–323 BCE) briefly conquered Northwest India. Moving down the Indus River, he established a port at Patala where he built the ships that brought part of his army home. Alexander's arrival precipitated a series of wars in India that culminated in the victory of Chandragupta Maurya (340–297 BCE) who established the Mauryan Empire, which endured for another century. Chandragupta was the first Indian ruler to establish a navy. His naval forces, directed by an admiral, helped him conquer and rule his empire, operating both on rivers and in coastal waters. Despite Chandragupta's efforts, piracy remained a problem in Indian waters.

A later Mauryan ruler, Ashoka (304–232 BCE), embraced Buddhism and worked to spread the religion, building temples, arranging gatherings of religious leaders, and encouraging missionaries to spread the faith overseas, among them his daughter who traveled to Sri Lanka. Others traveled to Afghanistan, Egypt, Greece, Nepal, Persia, Southeast Asia, and China. Along with Indian goods, Indian culture spread throughout the region, influencing art, literature, religion, and politics. Buddhism, in particular, found wide appeal in East and Southeast Asia. Buddhist writings and artifacts found a ready market in China and Southeast Asia and Buddhist pilgrims traveled to India to study and visit holy sites.

Roman and Greek traders faded from the Indian Ocean after the third century—displaced by Sassanian Persians and Arabs whose trade goods included horses that were praised in India. Arab traders, in particular, came to dominate trade in the western Indian Ocean and down the East-African coast. Indian mariners, though, remained active throughout the Indian Ocean and trade connections with China remained strong, as demonstrated by the fifth century travels of Buddhist monk Fa Xian from China to India and back.

Amitabh Vikram Dwivedi

Further Reading

Barnes, Ruth, and David Parkin. 2002. *Ships and the Development of Maritime Technology on the Indian Ocean*. London: Routledge.

Chakravarti, Ranabir. 2002. *Trade and Traders in Early Indian Society*. New Delhi: Manohar.

Chattopadhyaya, Brajadulal. 2014. *Essays in Ancient Indian Economic History*. Delhi: Indian History Congress in Association with Primus Books.

Chauduri, K. N. 1985. *Trade and Civilisation in the Indian Ocean*. Cambridge: Cambridge University Press.

Ray, Himanshu Prabha. 2003. *Archaeology of Seafaring: The Indian Ocean in the Ancient Period.* Cambridge: Cambridge University Press.

Sheriff, Abdul. 2010. *Dhow Cultures of the Indian Ocean: Cosmopolitanism, Commerce and Islam.* New York: Columbia University Press.

Sidebotham, Steven E. 2011. *Berenike and the Ancient Maritime Spice Route.* Berkeley: University of California Press.

PHOENICIA AND CARTHAGE, 1000 BCE TO 300 CE

The history of Phoenicia and Carthage is closely linked to the Mediterranean Sea and is centered on a handful of maritime city-states in the Levant, and on Carthage, the most successful colony they founded. The principal Phoenician cities, including Akhziv, Akko, Arvad, Berytos, Byblos, Sarepta, and Sidon, all were situated on the Levantine coast, and also were near sources of excellent timber, including the cedars, pines, and cypresses of Mount Lebanon. Their maritime position developed and encouraged maritime activities from fishing and trading to widespread exploration and travel. Described in ancient sources as excellent seafarers, the Phoenicians mastered navigational techniques and became skilled engineers and shipbuilders.

The Phoenicians, a Semitic people, shared the same cultural and linguistic base, but their cities remained independent of one another and they referred to themselves by city, such as Byblians, Sidonians, Tyrians, and Carthaginians, for example. The names by which we know them were those used by the Greeks (Phoenicians) and Romans (Punic). Canaan, the name used in the Hebrew Bible for the region, means "land of merchants," which is an apt description of the major Phoenician cities in the Levant. One of the threads that united them was their relation to the sea. Much of their history and culture, recorded on papyrus scrolls, has not survived, forcing scholars to rely on archaeological evidence and accounts of other people about them—particularly their repeated mention in the Hebrew Bible, records of them in Assyrian annals, and accounts by various Greek and Latin authors.

The economic and political disruptions that accompanied the end of the Bronze Age (ca. 1200 BCE) eroded the power of the great empires of the Middle East, allowing the indigenous societies along the Levantine coast to rise in importance and pursue their own interests. The Phoenician city-states—particularly Tyre, Sidon, Arvad, and Sarepta—developed substantial urban populations and grew wealthy through their mercantile interests and long-distance trade by sea. In the ninth and eighth century BCE, though, they fell under the sway of the Assyrian Empire, which expanded steadily and became the region's dominant power. Assyrian expansion increasingly depended on Phoenician sea power, and the favorable place of the

Alphabet

The Phoenician abjad (all-consonant writing system) is the longest-lived and most important contribution stemming from Mediterranean maritime trade. The script, developed around 1300 BCE, is believed to be a modification of proto-Sinatic, though it is possible that it was influenced by either Egyptian hieroglyphs or Mesopotamian cuneiform (both complicated pictographic/logographic writing systems, respectively). There is no evidence to support these hypotheses, however, and it is possible that the script developed independently. The Phoenician phonetic script, which consisted of 22 consonants, was simpler to learn than its contemporaries, as each letter was associated with one sound. The ease in learning and employing this alphabet facilitated writing and literacy throughout the Levant.

The alphabet spread through both trade and Phoenician colonies in North Africa and the Iberian Peninsula. In the Levant, societies in close proximity to the Phoenicians, such as the Israelites and Judeans, modified the abjad for their language (10th century BCE), which was later amended for Aramaic (eighth century BCE), Syriac (first century CE), and Arabic (fifth century CE). The Greeks adapted the Phoenician writing system (eighth century BCE), and added vowels. This version of the alphabet evolved into the Etruscan (sixth century BCE), Latin (eighth century BCE), and Coptic (from Egypt, fourth century CE) scripts. The Phoenician alphabet is also the ancestor of Ethiopic (Ge'ez) script (fifth and sixth centuries BCE), and the Sogdian alphabet (adapted from Syriac, second century CE), used in Mongolia. It is also possible that the Phoenician alphabet (and its adaptations) influenced Brahmi (third century BCE), an Indic script. Today, derivatives of the Phoenician alphabet are used in nearly every country that uses an alphabetic script.

Rachel J. Mittelman

Phoenician cities in the Assyrian Empire contributed to their economic development and fostered a greater confidence in maritime activity—which in these years reached the Strait of Gibraltar. The Phoenicians probably were the first to construct biremes (in the seventh century), which provided the backbone of the Assyrian fleet.

The Persians—who built an even larger empire on the wreckage of Assyria's—also relied on Phoenician maritime prowess. During the Persian period (539–332 BCE), Phoenicia, Cyprus, and Syria were part of the fifth satrapy of the Persian Empire. The Phoenician cities entered the category of autonomous states, preserving their political and economic system. It was the Persian practice to use existing institutions without interfering in the administration of the economy of provinces, and the Persians encouraged the economic development of Phoenician ports. The empire also did not prevent the Phoenician cities from negotiating with regions outside of the Persian Empire, including those who represented a political enemy, such as Athens. In the fifth century, Phoenician triremes supported the advance of the Persian Empire and its invasions of Greece, and they fought at Salamis and other naval battles.

Sailing westward from their homeland, Phoenicians traded with indigenous peoples and established colonies as far west as the Atlantic coasts of Spain and Morocco. They cemented their trade networks by establishing merchant enclaves in major ports, as well as in small coastal settlements, which they began establishing in the eleventh or 10th century BCE. Lixus in Morocco, Cadiz in Spain, and Utica in Tunisia were among the first colonies established by the Phoenicians according to Classical sources. Carthage, founded by the end of the ninth century, probably as a trading center, developed into an impressive city in the seventh and sixth centuries, thanks to its excellent natural harbor, fertile hinterland, and prime location on the east–west Mediterranean trade routes.

In the sixth century BCE, Carthage conquered Sardinia and expanded into Sicily, fighting regularly with Greek cities in eastern Sicily. At the Battle of Alalia (ca. 540–535 BCE), near Corsica, a Greek fleet narrowly defeated a combined Etruscan and Carthaginian fleet. Although Greek settlers established more colonies in the region, Carthage remained the region's strongest naval power well into the fourth century BCE, building large fleets of triremes and later quadriremes. The growing Roman Republic, however, proved a more serious threat than that of the Greek city-states of Sicily and Southern Italy. Rome, relying on a captured Carthaginian quadrireme as its model, constructed a navy in the First Punic War (264–241 BCE) and successfully challenged Carthage at sea, permanently weakening Carthaginian naval power. As a result, the Second Punic War (218–201 BCE), famous for Hannibal's invasion of Italy, featured hardly any naval battles at all. It ended when Carthage sued for peace following Rome's successful invasion of North Africa. The Third Punic War (149–146 BCE)—triggered by Roman fears that Carthage would regain its maritime power—ended in Rome's complete destruction of the city.

Until recently, Assyrian representations were the main source of knowledge on Phoenician ships. Underwater archaeologists, however, have discovered the wrecks of several Phoenician vessels which in recent years have dramatically advanced our understanding of Phoenician shipbuilding and trade. Two sunken Phoenician merchant ships, the *Tanit* and *Elissa*, were discovered in deep water near Ashkelon, Israel, and date from the eighth century BCE. Near Spain, divers discovered two off Mazzarón, and another near Bajo de la Campana. Two Carthaginian ships were discovered near Lilybaeum, Sicily (Marsala), once a major Carthaginian port, and another shipwreck recently was found near Malta. The Phoenicians built both cargo ships and warships, and both types are depicted on a relief in the palace of Sennacherib at Khorsabad (in modern Iraq), dating to the eighth or seventh century BCE. The warships, identified as biremes, have a less curvaceous hull with a metal-sheathed pointed ram at the bow and a stern, which, at the tip, curves back on itself. They appear to have a series of plain and cross-hatched panels between the upper oarsmen and the upper bulwarks. The cargo ships have a rounded hull in longitudinal profile, and are double-ended with near-vertical posts. Thus far, underwater archaeologists have only discovered Phoenician cargo ships. Their planks were fastened with mortise and tenon joints, which the Phoenicians might have pioneered in shipbuilding. Their superb joinery and wood-working techniques limited water seepage into the hull and allowed ships to flex with strain and helped establish the Phoenicians' reputation as master shipbuilders and seafarers.

For all that the Phoenicians contributed to navigation in the Mediterranean, relatively little is known about the lives and livelihoods of Phoenician sailors. They mastered both coastal and open sea navigation, developing an excellent knowledge of the shoreline (and best anchorages and stopping places), the sea routes, winds, sea currents, and astronomy. Early in their exploration of the Mediterranean, the Phoenicians established colonies at many of the sea's best natural harbors. Their ports were well cited and sturdily built and the Phoenicians mastered the construction of artificial harbors, using a double ashlar wall with a filling of fieldstones—known as the pier-and-rubble technique. This system has been noted at Sarepta, Lebanon, in a layer dated to the 11th century BCE. This technique possibly spread from the Levant to the western Punic colonies, Greece, and North Africa. The use

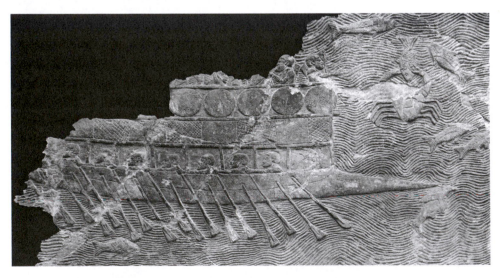

The Phoenicians were the greatest seafarers of their era and were responsible for innovations in warship design that produced the bireme. This bireme, portrayed in an Assyrian relief from the reign of Senacherib, clearly shows the ship's ram and two banks of oars. It was likely crewed by Phoenicians who played an important role in Assyrian—and later Persian—fleets. (Universal History Archive/UIG via Getty Images)

of ashlar techniques can be seen, for instance, in the Persian harbor of Akko (Israel); the Hellenistic harbor at Amathus in Cyprus; and the Roman quay at Sarepta, Dor, and Athlit (Israel). Iron Age Athlit is one of the best-studied Phoenician harbors. Others worthy of note include the harbors of Tabbat el-Hammam, Tyre, Sidon, Beirut, Akko, Kition, and Carthage. Carthage, according to the literary sources, possessed two harbors—one commercial and one military; the commercial harbor was rectangular and the military harbor circular, like an artificial lake or "*cothon*." The British excavations showed that they were built during the Punic wars, no earlier than the fourth century BCE.

The sea played an important role in the development of a maritime economy, providing the primary channel for trade and the basis for sea-centered industries. The Phoenicians obtained abundant material from the sea, particularly fish (which they salted for export), and murex (a sea snail used to make purple dye used in cloth), which became an important Phoenician export. They also evaporated seawater to produce salt, which they traded widely. The international trade with Egypt, the Aegean, and the Mediterranean developed largely between 1000 and 300 BCE. The Phoenicians also made exploratory trading voyages around the Mediterranean (Crete, Euboea, Chios, Malta, Sicily, Sardinia, North Africa, Spain) up to the Atlantic coast, in search of new sources of raw materials, mainly metals—gold, silver, copper, and tin. Progressively they acquired a good knowledge of the maritime routes, creating a Phoenician trade network and establishing trading enclaves around the Mediterranean. Literary sources and archaeological data show that they traded different types of commodities, including wood, wine, oil, salted fish, metals, slaves, pottery, textiles, metal vessels, glass beads, shells, and other luxury products. The *Odyssey* notes that the Phoenicians are the trading people, sailing all over the sea (the Mediterranean) and spending a whole year in selling their cargo; for example, the cargoes of wine destined for Egypt found in the two shipwrecks of *Tanit* and *Elissa*.

Known as the "rulers of the sea" (Ezekiel 26:16) the Phoenicians, and later the Carthaginians, played an important role in the history of the Mediterranean and the Near East, trading and exploring widely. Phoenician ports and warships proved important in the navies of Assyria, Persia, and other great empires, and Carthage became an important sea power in its own right, dominating the Western Mediterranean in the third and fourth centuries. Phoenician seafarers travelled widely, establishing trade routes that extended beyond the Mediterranean into the Atlantic and Indian Oceans and endured for centuries. Their exploits as explorers were among the most daring of the time and secured their reputation as the greatest seafarers of the period. The sea deeply shaped Phoenician culture, but also fostered the spread of Phoenician products, technology, and culture throughout the Mediterranean, such that this handful of coastal city-states has left a substantial legacy.

Iva Chirpanlieva

Further Reading

Aubet, M. E. 2001. *The Phoenicians and the West. Politics, Colonies, and Trade.* Cambridge: Cambridge University Press.

Ballard, R. et al. 2002. "Iron Age Shipwrecks in Deep Water off Ashkelon, Israel." *American Journal of Archaeology* 106: 151–68.

Baurain, Claude, and Corinne Bonnet. 1992. *Les Phéniciens. Marins des trois continents.* Paris: Armand Colin.

Doumet-Serhal, Claude (ed.). 2008. *Networking Patterns of the Bronze and Iron Age Levant. The Lebanon and its Mediterranean Connections. Symposium "Interconnections in the Eastern Mediterranean; The Lebanon in the Bronze and Iron Ages," 4–9 November 2008. Beirut.* Beirut: Printed ACPP.

Gras, M., P. Rouillard, and J. Teixidor. 1989. *L'Univers Phénicien.* Paris: Hachette, Collection Pluriel.

Lipinski, E. 2004. *Itineraria Phoenicia.* Studia Phoenicia, 18, Orientalia Lovaniensia analecta 127, Peeters Publishers and Department of Oriental Studies Bondgenotenlaan, Louvain.

Markoe, G. 2000. *The Phoenicians, People of the Past.* London: British Museum.

Sherratt, S., and A. Sherratt. 1993. "The Growth of the Mediterranean Economy in the Early First Millennium B.C." *World Archaeology* 24: 361–78.

Stager, L. E. 2003. "Phoenician Shipwrecks in the Deep Sea." In *Sea Routes: From Sidon to Huelva: Interconnections in the Mediterranean, 16th–6th c. BC.* Proceedings of the International Symposium held at Rethymnon, Crete, September 29–October 2, 2002, 233–48.

Hanno the Navigator, Fifth and Sixth Centuries BCE

Hanno, called "the Navigator" to distinguish him from others with the same name, lived during the fifth and sixth centuries BCE. A Carthaginian, he led a large expedition down the west coast of Africa around 500 BCE. His periplus (literally "a sailing around") describes ports and coastal landmarks, noting approximate distances between them. Hanno's original periplus, carved on a stone tablet, was hung in the temple of Ba'al Hammon in Carthage. It was lost when the Romans captured and razed Carthage in 146 BCE. An incomplete Greek translation, found in a medieval manuscript, is the only surviving account of his extraordinary voyage.

The periplus describes Hanno leading 60 pentekonters (ships with 50 oarsmen) and 30,000 men and women to establish colonies beyond the straits of Gibraltar. Because 60 pentekonters could not hold that many people, it is reasonable to assume one of the following hypotheses: the number was not translated correctly, the pentekonters escorted larger passenger ships, or the number was simply exaggerated. As the expedition traveled along the Moroccan coast, groups of settlers disembarked and founded eight colonies. Eventually, the fleet came to a small island at the mouth of a river. Scholars generally believe this was Herne Island at the mouth of the Rio de Oro, where the last of the colonists disembarked.

The expedition then continued south. The reasons are unclear, but it is likely that the Carthaginians sought trading opportunities. The expedition reached the mouth of a large river, possibly the Senegal. Following the waterway inland, they reached mountains inhabited by stone-throwing natives. Hanno describes finding elephants, hippopotamuses, and crocodiles. Returning to the coast, the expedition continued south for about two weeks and encountered the mouth of an immense river thought to be the Gambia estuary. Hanno describes a country burning with fires and strange perfumes, and streams of fire running into the sea. Three days after passing through this inhospitable region, they arrived at a large bay with an island full of hairy, savage people that their interpreters called "Gorillae" (from which the modern word "gorilla" is derived). Hanno reports capturing three females, but they proved so vicious that they were killed, flayed, and the skins brought back to Carthage.

Hanno's narrative ends abruptly at this point with the decision to return to Carthage due to dwindling supplies. The full purpose and effect of Hanno's voyage remains unclear. No mention of trade exists in the Greek translation, which only makes this theory more likely. Phoenicians were extremely competitive and secretive, so it is likely that existing documents are filled with misdirection and falsehoods to protect their trade network. The full purpose of Hanno's extraordinary voyage might never be known. Scholars continue to debate how far south Hanno traveled. He could have reached Mount Cameroon, roughly halfway to the southern tip of the African continent.

Jill M. Church

Further Reading

Hoyos, B. Dexter. 2010. *The Carthaginians*. New York: Routledge.

Metrology: The Forgotten Science. 2007. "The Voyage of Hanno." http://www.metrum .org/mapping/hanno/htm. Accessed November 11, 2014.

Roller, Duane W. 2006. *Through the Pillars of Herakles: Greco Roman Exploration of the Atlantic Ocean*. New York: Routledge.

ROME, 1000 BCE TO 300 CE

In Roman histories there are few references to state-sponsored naval ventures under the Roman kings (traditionally dated 753 to 509 BCE) or during the early Roman Republic (509 to 390 BCE). These eras largely are documented in sources written many centuries later; however, it is also clear that Rome's attention throughout the early centuries of its history was directed elsewhere. Rome regularly was engaged in territorial conflicts with the neighboring communities of Etruria, Latium, and the Italian interior. These annual conflicts were frequently brief and naval warfare was of little strategic value in this period.

Romans had regular contact and interaction with the coastal cities of Italy, including local maritime powers such as Antium (south of Rome) and the Greek colony of Neapolis in Campania. Farther south, sailors from the Sicilian cities—both Greek and Carthaginian (Punic)—had trade and military interests which reached up along Italy's Tyrrhenian coast. Rome engaged in a number of treaties with Carthage during its early history. The details and sequence of these treaties is debatable. They appear to have protected Carthaginian maritime affairs in Italy but did not make comparable provision for Rome, and even allowed for the potential that Carthage might acquire territories in Italy.

Rome's initial naval endeavors were modest. The Roman historian Livy claims that Rome sent a delegation in 454 to Athens to consult the laws of Solon in framing Rome's early legal system. An embassy sent to Delphi, Greece, in 394 was intercepted by pirates from the Lipari Islands. The solitary Roman vessel apparently was easy prey and suggests that Rome had little or no capacity to protect such ventures. The first indication of preparedness for naval warfare under the Republic is the appointment of "*duumviri navales*" in the fourth century. Even so, the naval powers of the Latin and Campanian coasts such as Antium and Neapolis appear to have been subjugated by land-based campaigns and not by sea-based campaigns. With Antium's surrender in 338, Rome captured the city's ships, some of which were taken to Rome while others were burned and their rams ("*rostra*") used to decorate the speaker's platform near the senate house. From this time forward, the *rostra* of enemy ships became emblematic of naval victory and images such as a ship's prow or naval spoils are depicted on early Roman coinage.

In 282, a duumviral fleet was intercepted and defeated off the southern coast of Italy by ships from Tarentum. Roman envoys seeking the return of hostages were insulted, leading to Pyrrhus (319–272 BCE), the king of Epirus (located between modern Greece and Albania), invading Italy with a large and experienced army on the behest of the Tarentines. Fighting largely occurred inland and naval fleets do not seem to have played a part in the eventual Roman victory over Pyrrhus and his army—even though Italy's geographic isolation thanks to the sea was an advantage to the Romans.

Roman armies in the Republic were mustered and placed under oath by the year's presiding magistrate annually in accordance with military needs. Similarly, Roman fleets were raised and disbanded as necessity dictated. The costs to the state of keeping a war fleet deployed were considerable; meaning that, in some instances (such as during the First Punic War), state-owned ships were leased out to be used as privateers or no fleet was put to sea at all. The maritime colonies possessed Roman citizenship, with the obligation to provide men for the fleets instead of the normal expectation to provide men to the legions. Rome also accorded select coastal cities in Italy with special status to supply sailors ("*socii navales*"). From 267 BCE, magistrates known as "*quaestores classici*" were appointed to coordinate these sailors. By the late second century BCE Rome primarily was engaged in conflicts away from Italy and some regular naval capacity can be inferred from references to the movement of men and resources overseas. Equally, emerging conditions could require additional ships for which a magistrate would be tasked with either overseeing the refit of existing vessels or the commissioning of new ships. In the absence of an available magistrate such as one of the praetors, a subordinate commander was tasked with the responsibility of commanding a fleet. In the second and first centuries BCE, fleets often were commanded by "*legati*" or "*praefecti*" operating under the supreme command of one of the consuls or promagistrates.

The Roman acquisition of large parts of Sicily during the First and Second Punic Wars opened up opportunities for the large-scale importation of produce by sea to Italy and, in particular, to the city of Rome. These trade networks expanded in parallel with the Republic, which by the mid-first century dominated large parts of the eastern Mediterranean. Imported grain purchased by the state was regularly distributed to the populace of Rome. An increasingly important social and political issue from the first century BCE onward was maintaining the security of the provision of basic foodstuffs to the populace of Rome by the state. Sicily, and then Sardinia and Corsica, and later Egypt and North Africa, were critical in producing adequate levels of grain surpluses to feed the population of Rome and Italy. The tonnages and distances involved meant that much of this grain was moved by sea by privately owned shipping operators, known as "*navicularii*." Remains of buildings at Ostia, the coastal port of Rome, demonstrate the diversity of trade by sea which flowed to the city, and the extent of the commercial operations which carried it out. When these supplies were interrupted, rioting and panic in Rome could rapidly follow. Thus, in the cases of Pompey in 57 BCE and Octavian in 22 BCE, short stoppages (possibly engineered for maximum political impact) led to a general panic and the voting of extraordinary powers granted to the ruler to deal with the food crisis. The management of the grain supply, the "*cura annonae*," became an important public position. Similarly, from the first century BCE on, Rome went to significant lengths to curtail piracy.

Roman combat at sea involved a combination of ramming enemy vessels, using projectiles and fire, and boarding enemy warships to engage in man-to-man combat. Warships typically were fitted with a metal reinforced prow for ramming (Latin: "*rostrum*"). These are depicted on numerous Roman coins, and a number of examples excavated from the sea floor have survived. Boarding enemy vessels was a combat tactic preferred by the Romans, as it allowed for the use of trained soldiers in combat at sea and made possible the capture of intact enemy vessels. As such, reports of naval battles in literary sources frequently reckon the number of ships sunk and captured. Use of a boarding bridge ("*corvus*"), which could be maneuvered and then dropped onto the enemy deck, is described in reference to the First Punic War, although ancient writers could have exaggerated its sophistication at this early period.

Fleets were important in the civil wars of the first century BCE for the range and speed of movement, which they afforded rival Roman generals. A series of civil conflicts was played out between generals who had ventured east against those remaining in Italy, demonstrated by the conflict between Sulla and the faction of Cinna and Carbo. So too, Cnaeus (Cn.) Pompeius Magnus and his supporters had sailed for the east and were followed by Caesar and defeated at Pharsalus in 48 BCE. The murderers of Caesar, having taken up commands in the east, raised a fleet of more than 100 warships with which to oppose Antonius and Octavian's crossing, the rival fleets seeking in turn to cut off one another's army's lines of supply, while the opposing armies met at Philippi. For Sextus Pompeius in Sicily, naval power was important for protecting the island from attempts by Octavian and Lepidus to dislodge him. At the battle of Naulochus in 36 BCE a fleet under the command of Octavian's chief lieutenant, M. Agrippa, defeated him. Agrippa's coordination of

Athlit Ram

The ram was the premier weapon of ancient Mediterranean warships. Bolted to the ship as a separate piece, rams could be dislodged in combat. Discovered in 1980 by Yehoshua Ramon in the Bay of Athlit off present-day Israel, the Athlit ram is the only ancient Mediterranean ram yet discovered. Made of bronze, the Athlit ram is 7 feet long, 30 inches wide, and 38 inches high. It weighs 1,025 pounds and was cast as a single piece, perfectly fitting the ramming timber to which it was attached. Three-pronged, it was designed to shatter an enemy ship's hull on impact.

There are four recognizable symbols on the ram: the trident of Poseidon, the wand of Hermes, the starred helmet of Dioscuri, and the head of an eagle (possibly a symbol of Zeus), all referring to Greek gods. Along with metallurgical analysis and carbon-14 dating, these symbols suggest the ram was cast in a port in Cyprus during the reign of Ptolemy V Epiphanes (209–181 BCE) or Ptolemy VI Philometer (185–145 BCE). The Athlit ram probably came from a trireme or perhaps a quadrireme. Its excellent condition has enabled scholars to determine the characteristics and likely sizes of ancient Mediterranean warships and their rams. The Athlit ram currently is on display in the National Maritime Museum in Haifa, Israel.

Matthew Blake Strickland

naval resources in the war against Antony gradually isolated Octavian's last serious rival and at Actium in September of 31 BCE Octavian soundly defeated Antony.

Roman military honors for naval victories appear to have been rare. Contributing factors likely were the rarity of outright victories at sea and the fact that from the early years of the Second Punic War subordinate commanders tended to be tasked with naval commands. C. Duilius was the first Roman general to celebrate a naval triumph ("*triumphus naualis*") in 260 BCE. This honor—distinct from the more ancient form of the Roman triumph (given for a victory on land)—was almost exclusively conferred upon generals in the period from Duilius's victory in 260 to the defeat of Macedon in 168. Subsequent great naval victories, such as Pompeius's defeat of Mediterranean piracy and the victories of Agrippa and Octavian at Naulochus in 36 BCE, were celebrated with public displays and honors which closely echoed earlier naval triumphs. Rostral columns ("*columna rostrate*"), a column bearing a statue and adorned with the captured rostra and other spoils from enemy ships were erected to commemorate a number of naval triumphs. A military award, the "*corona rostrata*," was a crown awarded to the first soldier to board an enemy vessel (on the model of the "*cornona muralis*"), a novel form was awarded to M. Agrippa as the commander of a naval victory. It is highly likely that, with monopolization of the triumph by the imperial family in the late first century BCE, Augustus's Actium triumph in which the rams of enemy ships were carried through the streets of Rome would prove the last major naval battle to receive the honors of a naval triumph.

In the Augustan era, Roman naval power became a standing force; a development which paralleled the increasing professionalization of the Roman military in general. Permanent naval bases were established in Italy; at Cape Misenum on the Tyrrhenian Sea and at Ravenna on the Adriatic. Praetorian prefects commanded these fleets. Roman control reached around the coasts of the Mediterranean, therefore these standing fleets were not required to engage in active military action often but rather served as an ongoing deterrent against uprisings, a check on piracy, a protection of the ever-important shipping networks, and—in the event of an unexpected crisis—as a manpower reserve for the empire. Thus, in 68 CE, in desperate circumstances, the legion I Adiutrix was raised from marines stationed with the fleet at Misenum. Over the course of the first century CE the standing naval power of the empire was expanded; such fleets included the Egyptian fleet ("*classis Alexandriana*"), those based on the Rhine (the "*classis Germanica*" based at Koln), and those on the upper and lower Danube ("*classis Moesiaca*"). Under Nero a fleet was established in the Black Sea ("*classis Pontica*"), and under the Flavian emperors a fleet was based on the Syrian coast (the "*classis Syriaca*" based at Seleuca Pieria on the mouth of the Orontes River, which linked the base to the city of Antioch). Roman military infrastructure became increasingly sophisticated under the emperors. Shipping was extensively employed upon the Rhine and Danube to connect and supply the important military bases of Rome's northern-most zone of control.

Throughout Roman history travel by sea remained a risky proposition for armies. Factors included the potential for losing ships and men in storms, the numbers of transports required to move the scale of Rome's military forces, and the difficulties of supplying a large army with basic necessities while shipboard. Under the empire, much of Rome's military forces were stationed in static forts in the provinces. In the event of a crisis, detachments drawn from these armies could be moved rapidly to reinforce another army. As such, even in the second and third centuries CE Roman armies often travelled by land.

Large-scale naval battles, such as those fought at Mylae (260 BCE), the Aegates Islands (241 BCE), Naulochus (36 BCE), and Actium (31 BCE) were rare. Although war fleets were especially critical to the conduct of the First and Second Punic Wars, later Roman fleets typically were used in transport, supply, and support roles. For instance, Julius Caesar's first incursions in Britain in 55 BCE had difficulty establishing a secure beachhead and also were hampered by storms. Caesar's subsequent invasion in 54 CE utilized a large fleet of both warships and transports. The successful invasion in 43 CE under Claudius utilized three coordinated fleets making separate landings. Germanicus commanded a campaign in Germany coordinated with a fleet which sailed into the North Sea. Agricola's campaign in northern Britain between 77 and 84 CE similarly utilized naval supply and support, with a fleet sailing along the northern Scottish coast. Campaigns in the east under Septimius Severus (145–211) utilized shipping along the Tigris and Euphrates in support of his army.

Christopher James Dart

Further Reading

Casson, L. 1995. *Ships and Seamanship in the Ancient World*. Baltimore: Johns Hopkins University Press.

Morrison, J. S., and J. F. Coates. 1996. *Greek and Roman Oared Warships*. Oxford: Oxford University Press.

Starr, C. G. 1960. *The Roman Imperial Navy: 31 B.C.–A.D. 324*. New York: Barnes & Noble.

Theil, T. H. 1954. *A History of Roman Sea-Power Before the Second Punic War*. Amsterdam: North-Holland.

Actium, Battle of, 31 BCE

The decisive naval battle of Actium was fought during the civil wars raging between Octavian (C. Julius Caesar *divi filius,* later known as Augustus) and Marc Antony (M. Antonius) that led to Octavian's victory in the war. The third century CE historian Cassius Dio preserves the most detailed ancient account of the battle in book 50 of his *Histories*.

Over the winter of 32–31 BCE, Antony moved to land in Italy. With his advance opposed by Octavian's ships, Antony entered the Gulf of Actium (modern Ambracian Gulf in western Greece) with a large fleet and anchored off the southern end of its two promontories for the remainder of the season. Octavian's chief lieutenant, Marcus Agrippa attacked strategic points along the Greek coast, and in early 31 BCE Octavian embarked at Brundisium (in southern Italy) and sailed with a fleet of more than 250 ships. He landed in Greece unopposed, took the strategic city of Corcyra, and then concentrated his forces on the northern promontory at Actium, overlooking the enemy positions to the south. Antony arrived in person and for several months the two opposing armies engaged in fortifying positions and conducting cautious maneuvers, attempting to draw one another into the field. Meanwhile Agrippa delivered a series of important victories in other parts of Greece, defeating fleets under the command of Antony's lieutenants and progressively cutting off Antony's lines of supply.

On the morning of September 2, Antony burned some of his ships, put to sea the largest vessels, and sailed out of the gulf. He formed up his warships in a line backed by 60 Egyptian vessels commanded by their queen, Cleopatra. Octavian's fleet—which consisted of smaller but more maneuverable vessels—formed up into lines to oppose them. The two fleets engaged fiercely for a time, but in the midst of the battle the Egyptian ships suddenly turned and fled, Antony following in his flagship. Ancient sources have variously sought to explain Antony's reasons, although modern debate has noted that he must have realized the consequences of abandoning his fleet; it would all but guarantee Octavian victory in both the battle and the civil wars. The battle continued into the afternoon. Octavian, who hoped to capture the enemy vessels and secure booty, eventually resorted to setting the ships ablaze before Antony's fleet surrendered. Although parts of Antony's army attempted to flee, Octavian's soldiers rapidly intercepted them and induced the men to surrender in the days that followed. Supposedly as few as 5,000 died in the battle although Octavian captured as many as 300 warships and transports.

In the following months, Antony and Cleopatra committed suicide, the Roman conquest of Egypt was achieved, and the foundations of the sole-rule of the future Augustus was firmly established. Actium was celebrated in Roman art (Cordoba relief) and literature (Virgil's *Aeneid* and Propertius's *Elegies*), primarily during the Augustan era, and was commemorated as one of Octavian/Augustus's greatest achievements—although much of the credit is due to his admiral Marcus Agrippa. Near the site of the battle, Octavian founded the city of Nicopolis, erected an altar to the victory, and set up a display of captured warships. At Octavian's triple triumph on August 15–17, 29 BCE, Actium was celebrated on the second day with the rams of enemy vessels ("*rostra*") carried in the pageant and used to decorate the speaker's platform in front of the Temple of the Divine Julius. The veterans of the battle were referred to as "*Actiaci*" in inscriptions.

Christopher James Dart

Fought in 31 BCE, the naval Battle of Actium secured the Roman Empire for Octavian who ruled as Augustus. In its aftermath, Romans could truly claim the Mediterranean as *Mare Nostrum*—Our Sea. (Jose Lucas/Alamy Stock Photo)

Further Reading

Carter, J. M. 1970. *The Battle of Actium: The Rise and Triumph of Augustus Caesar*. London: Hamilton.

Gurval, R. A. 1995. *Actium and Augustus: The Politics and Emotions of Civil War*. Ann Arbor: University of Michigan Press.

Lange, C. 2009. *Res Publica Constituta: Actium, Apollo and the Accomplishment of the Triumviral Assignment*. Leiden: Brill.

Piracy in the Mediterranean to 300 CE

Piracy was a common part of life for many ancient Mediterranean communities from the earliest documented times. There are frequent references in the works of Homer and other early Greek writers to the activities of pirates and seafaring bandits. Raids by marauders posed a major threat to Mediterranean coastal communities and, as a result, protection from piracy was an important factor in determining locations for settling cities. For many city-states in the Mediterranean, piratical ventures also were an accepted part of local economic activity. Pirates played an important part in the ancient slave trade and frequently kidnapped people to collect ransoms. The activities of pirates were not seen as wholly unacceptable even though many ancient writers tended to sympathize with the victims of such attacks, and the fear of seafaring marauders was commonplace. As such, the Greek hero Odysseus boasts without any shame in Homer's *Odyssey* of how he had frequently led raids by ship and carried off booty (Homer, *Odyssey* 14.229f).

In classical Greece, city-states developed powerful war fleets and pursued aspirations of asserting naval dominance over their rivals; however, pirates and plundering through seaborne raids remained common. The distinction between warfare, raiding, and piracy often was blurred, with Greek city-states supporting widespread marauders, both to harm enemy interests and to generate resources to fund further warfare. Many Greek city-states relied upon privately owned vessels to muster their war fleets, with ships readily available for raiding when not required by the state. The activities of pirates posed an ongoing threat to seaborne trade and travel, particularly for peoples with far-reaching trade interests. Conversely, in Illyricum, the late–third century ruler Demetrius of Pharus supported the numerous pirate communities of the Illyrian coast as a means of furthering his territorial ambitions.

The Romans viewed pirates with disdain, with victories over them deemed unworthy of the highest Roman military honor, the curule triumph. During the First Punic War (264–41 BCE), Rome at times leased ships to be used as privateers. The policy was the product of the depletion of resources needed to continue the war, and was rapidly abandoned in favor of fleets once again under the command of the annually elected magistrates. From the late third century BCE, Rome progressively became the dominant state in the Mediterranean and took repeated and increasingly ambitious actions to suppress piracy. Attempts were made to deal with pirates in notorious regions such as the Illyrian coast (late third century) and the Balearic Islands (122 BCE), and campaigns were directed eastward against pirates in Cilicia (102 BCE) and Crete (74 BCE). Piracy persisted, however, as is shown by the famous story of Julius Caesar being kidnapped and held by Cilician pirates in 75 BCE.

In 67 BCE, the Romans resolved to take decisive action against piracy in the Mediterranean. Pompeius Magnus (later known as Pompey the Great) (106–48 BCE) was appointed to an extraordinary command that empowered him to suppress piracy throughout the Mediterranean. With the commitment of vast military resources this task was accomplished in the space of months. The campaign involved the use of naval forces but also relied upon significantly curtailing the areas that pirates could use to base their operations. The magnitude of Pompeius's actions against piracy in the Mediterranean occasioned him to adopt many of the public honors associated with a naval triumph.

Under the Empire, Roman control of land and sea alike remained a check upon widespread piracy. Even so, piracy continued to be a threat to private shipping and to coastal communities, particularly in less-protected parts of the empire, such as Sardinia and Corsica. A resurgence of piracy occurred in the mid–third century, a period of numerous political and military crises for Rome. Gothic pirates are reported in the 250s and 260s CE operating in the Black Sea and the eastern Mediterranean. Similarly, Frankish and Saxon pirates attacked the British coast in the 280s.

Christopher James Dart

Further Reading

De Souza, P. 1999. *Piracy in the Graeco-Roman World*. Cambridge: Cambridge University Press.

Ormerod, H. A. 1996. *Piracy in the Ancient World*, 2nd ed. Baltimore: Johns Hopkins University Press.

Punic War, 264–146 BCE

The Punic Wars were a series of wars fought between Rome and Carthage over land and sea. Although previous relations had been peaceful, in the course of three major wars with two intervening periods of uneasy peace, the Carthaginian Empire—one of the era's great maritime powers—was dismantled, and Rome was established as ruler of the western Mediterranean. In the aftermath, Rome became the Mediterranean's dominant maritime power. The most important ancient accounts of the Punic Wars occur in the histories of Polybius and Livy.

The First Punic War erupted in 264 BCE when Rome intervened in the affairs of Messana (modern Messina, Sicily), then ruled by Italian mercenaries. For the first time, a Roman consular army crossed the sea and became engaged in hostilities with Sicily's two major powers: the Greek colony of Syracuse and the Carthaginians. Although Syracuse and its dependents in eastern Sicily concluded a treaty with Rome in 263 BCE, fighting with Carthage continued.

To combat Carthaginian maritime dominance, the Romans constructed a large war fleet during the winter of 261–260 BCE. At the Battle of Mylae in 260, consul Gaius Duilius won a decisive victory over a Carthaginian fleet and became the first Roman to receive the honor of a naval triumph. The victory broadened Roman ambitions and ineffectual campaigns against Carthaginian interests in Sardinia and Corsica followed in 259. Roman naval victories off Tyndaris in 257 BCE and Ecnomus (modern Licata) in 256 BCE permitted a large-scale invasion of North Africa commanded by Marcus Atilius Regulus. Despite initial success, the campaign ended in defeat in 255 BCE.

Roman fleets sustained heavy losses in storms in 255, 253, and 249, due to a fatal combination of incompetence and misfortune. Exploiting the substantial manpower resources of Italy, Rome built new fleets after each disaster and

Illustration of the Roman Siege of Syracuse during 213–212 BCE. The cranes protruding from the walls were used to drop grapples, known as "claws," into the Roman ships. The ships could then be lifted up and suddenly released, swamping and sinking them. (Photos .com)

frequently matched Carthaginian crews in battle, occasioning the celebration of several naval triumphs. The predominance of a pro-Roman perspective in the ancient sources, however, likely magnifies both Roman victories and Punic losses. The scale of naval warfare between the two powers was immense, both putting to sea in excess of 100 warships in many years. The war finally was brought to an end in 241 BCE when the Romans surprised and defeated a newly built Carthaginian fleet off the Aegates Islands (northwestern Sicily). Remains from the battle, including ships' rams, armor, and weapons, have been excavated from the sea floor in recent years.

After the war, Rome organized Sicily as a new province and later annexed Sardinia and Corsica. Carthage, having lost its footholds in these islands, expanded its influence on the east coast of the Iberian Peninsula.

The Second Punic War—sparked by Hannibal's siege and conquest of Saguntum, a city with ties to Rome—began in 218 BCE. Italy's geographic isolation and Rome's ability to put formidable war fleets to sea possibly encouraged the Romans to act slowly, assuming that the Carthaginians could be confronted away from the peninsula. The Carthaginian general Hannibal made a daring crossing of the Alps and caught the Roman consuls off guard—one in southern France and the other in Sicily.

Roman naval power established during the First Punic War proved valuable; the Roman commanders rapidly united their armies and were waiting for Hannibal as his army descended into Italy. Hannibal dealt the Romans a sequence of devastating defeats in the war's first years (Trebia and Ticinis in 218, Trasimene in 217, Cannae in 216), but was largely cut off from Carthaginian assistance as the Romans retained control of the western Mediterranean and the Italian coast. Capable Roman commanders progressively contained Hannibal in southern Italy and forced rebellious allies—such as Tarentum, Capua, and Syracuse, which had been emboldened by Hannibal's successes—to resubmit to Rome after long and bitter fighting.

In Spain, a protracted campaign waged by brothers Publius and Gnaeus Cornelius Scipio—and after their deaths in battle, the younger Publius Cornelius Scipio (later named Africanus)—expelled the Carthaginians. Roman fleets successfully supported armies in Spain, Sicily, the Adriatic coast, and Greece while deterring attacks on Italy. Indeed, Hasdrubal's attempt in 207 to open a second

Destroyed by the Romans following the Third Punic War, Carthage had been a great maritime city with an extensive harbor and large military and commercial ports. Its position was so advantageous that a new Roman city was soon founded near its ruins, pictured here in a modern photograph. (Itanart/Dreamstime.com)

front in Italy came not by sea but from the Alps. The Roman consuls—through a forced march—reached Hasdrubal's army, defeated it at the Metaurus in Umbria, and returned to the south to present Hannibal with his brother's head. In 204, Scipio (Africanus) mounted a coordinated invasion of North Africa. Hannibal, compelled to confront the Romans, successfully brought his army home by sea, but his defeat by Scipio at Zama in October 202 forced Carthage to end the war. Carthage agreed to abide by Roman treaties, surrender its war fleet, and pay 10,000 talents in war reparations over the next 50 years.

Roman distrust persisted, however, and the final payment of reparations only served to fuel Roman fears of a rearmed Carthage. In 149 BCE, Carthaginian military resistance to King Masinissa, a Roman ally in Africa, led to the Third Punic War. Ill-equipped to fight the emerging superpower, Carthage rapidly agreed to an unconditional surrender. The Romans answered by demanding that the entire city be relocated at least 10 Roman miles from the sea, something which proved intolerable to the once-great maritime power. A short period of fighting and a two-year siege ended in 146 BCE with the destruction of Carthage as an independent political entity and the death of many of the city's residents.

Christopher James Dart

Further Reading

Goldsworthy, Adrian. 2001. *The Punic Wars*. Cassell.

Hoyos, Dexter (ed.). 2010. *A Companion to the Punic Wars*. West Sussex: Wiley-Blackwell.

Livy; T. J. Luce (trans.). 1998. *The Rise of Rome*. Oxford: Oxford University Press.

Polybius; W. R. Paton (trans.). 2012. *Polybius: The Histories*. The Loeb Classical Library. Chicago: University of Chicago.

Rosenstein, Nathan. 2012. *Rome and the Mediterranean 290 to 146 BC*. Edinburgh: University of Edinburgh Press.

PRIMARY DOCUMENTS

The Voyage of Hanno, ca. 600–400 BCE

Heirs to the Phoenicians, the Carthaginians also were expert seafarers. They traded throughout the western Mediterranean and established new cities in North Africa and southern Spain. Like the Phoenicians, they also dispatched expeditions to explore new lands and to found new cities. Among the expeditions was that led by Hanno (described below). Generally called "Hanno the Navigator," he sailed in the sixth or fifth century BCE. As with the Phoenician expedition to circumnavigate Africa dispatched by Pharaoh Necho II, scholars continue to debate how far south Hanno's expedition sailed and seek to match his descriptions of the West African coastline with modern landmarks.

It was decreed by the Carthaginians, that Hanno should undertake a voyage beyond the Pillars of Hercules [the Strait of Gibraltar], and found cities. He sailed accordingly with sixty ships of fifty oars each, and a body of men and women to the number of thirty thousand, and provisions and other necessaries.

When we had passed the Pillars on our voyage, and had sailed beyond them for two days, we founded the first city, which we named Thymiaterium. Below it lay an extensive plain. Proceeding thence towards the west, we came to Soloeis, a promontory of Libya [possibly Cape Blanco, Morocco], a place thickly covered with trees, where we erected a temple to Neptune; and again proceeded for the space of half a day towards the east, until we arrived at a lake lying not far from the sea, and filled with abundance of large reeds. Here elephants, and a great number of other wild beasts, were feeding.

Having passed the lake about a day's sail, we founded cities near the sea. . . . On its banks the Lixitae, a shepherd tribe, were feeding flocks, amongst whom we continued some time on friendly terms. Beyond the Lixitae dwelt the inhospitable Ethiopians, who pasture a wild country intersected by large mountains, from which they say the river Lixus flows. In the neighborhood of the mountains lived the Troglodytae, men of various appearances, whom the Lixitae described as swifter in running than horses.

Having procured interpreters from them, we coasted along a desert country towards the south two days. Thence we proceeded towards the east the course of a day. Here we found in a recess of a certain bay a small island, containing a circle of five stadia, where we settled a colony, and called it Cerne. We judged from our voyage that this place lay in a direct line with Carthage; for the length of our voyage from Carthage to the Pillars, was equal to that from the Pillars to Cerne.

We then came to a lake, which we reached by sailing up a large river . . . we came to the extremity of the lake, that was overhung by large mountains, inhabited by savage men clothed in skins of wild beasts, who drove us away by throwing stones, and hindered us from landing. Sailing thence we came to another river, that was large and broad, and full of crocodiles, and river horses [hippopotamuses]; whence returning back we came again to Cerne. . . .

Thence we sailed towards the south twelve days, coasting the shore, the whole of which is inhabited by Ethiopians, who would not wait our approach, but fled from us. Their language was not intelligible even to the Lixitae who were with us. Towards the last day we approached some large mountains covered with trees, the wood of which was sweet-scented and variegated. Having sailed by these mountains for two days, we came to an immense opening of the sea; on each side of which, towards the continent, was a plain; from which we saw by night fire arising at intervals in all directions, either more or less.

Having taken in water there, we sailed forwards five days near the land, until we came to a large bay, which our interpreters informed us was called the Western Horn. . . . when we had landed, we could discover nothing in the daytime except trees; but in the night we saw many fires burning, and heard the sound of pipes, cymbals, drums, and confused shouts. We were then afraid, and our diviners ordered us to abandon the island.

Sailing quickly away thence we passed a country burning with fires and perfumes; and streams of fire supplied from it fell into the sea. The country was impassable on account of the heat. We sailed quickly thence, being much terrified; and passing on for four days, we discovered at night a country full of fire. In the middle was a lofty fire, larger than the rest, which seemed to touch the stars. When day came we discovered it to be a large hill, called the Chariot of the Gods. On the third day after our departure thence, having sailed by those streams of fire, we arrived at a bay called the Southern Horn; at the bottom of which lay an island like the former, having a lake, and in this lake another island, full of savage people, the greater part of whom were women, whose bodies were hairy, and whom our interpreters called Gorillae. Though we pursued the men we could not seize any of them; but all fled from us, escaping over the precipices, and defending themselves with stones. Three women were however taken; but they attacked their conductors with their teeth and hands, and could not be prevailed upon to accompany us. Having killed them, we flayed them, and brought their skins with us to Carthage. We did not sail farther on, our provisions failing us.

Source: A. H. L. Heeren (trans.). 1832. "The Voyage of Hanno, Commander of the Carthaginians, Round the Parts of Libya Beyond the Pillars of Hercules, Which He Deposited in the Temple of Saturn." In *Historical Researches into the Politics, Intercourse and Trade of the Carthaginians, Ethiopians, and Egyptians.* Oxford: D. A. Talboys, pp. 492–501.

Herodotus on Pharaoh Necho II, ca. 484–425 BCE

Herodotus (ca. 484–425 BCE) was one of the ancient world's greatest travelers. He gathered tales from throughout the Mediterranean world and incorporated them into his history of the Persian War. That book, titled simply Historia, *which meant "inquiry" in ancient Greek, made Herodotus the first historian. He was the first person to systematically collect data, question his sources, and weave the information he gathered into a coherent narrative of historical events. The passages below recount two stories that continue to inspire scholarly discussion today: Pharaoh*

Necho's efforts to build a canal connecting the Nile River and Red Sea and the Phoenician expedition he sent to circumnavigate Africa. Although most scholars doubt that the Phoenicians completed this circumnavigation, Herodotus provides the important detail that from the perspective of these Phoenician sailors, the position of the sun changed, which it would have once they crossed the equator.

2.157. Psammetichus [Psamtik I] ruled Egypt for fifty-three years; for twenty-nine of these he sat before Azotus, a great city in Syria, and besieged it till he took it. . . .

Psammetichus had a son Necos [Necho II], who became king of Egypt. It was he who began the making of the canal into the Red Sea, which was finished by Darius the Persian. This is four days' voyage in length, and it was dug wide enough for two triremes to move in it rowed abreast. It is fed by the Nile, and is carried from a little above Bubastis by the Arabian town of Patumus; it issues into the Red Sea. The beginning of the digging was in the part of the Egyptian plain which is nearest to Arabia; the mountains towards Memphis . . . come close to this plain; the canal is led along the lower slope of these mountains, where its longest reach is from west to east; passing then into a ravine it bears southward out of the hill country toward the Arabian Gulf. Now the shortest and most direct passage from the northern to the southern or Red Sea is from the Casian promontory, which is the boundary between Egypt and Syria, to the Arabian Gulf, and this is a distance of one thousand furlongs, neither more nor less; this is the most direct way, but the canal is much longer, inasmuch as it is more crooked. In Necos's reign, a hundred and twenty thousand Egyptians perished in the digging of it. Necos ceased from the work, being stayed by a prophetic utterance which bade him deal first with the barbarian. The Egyptians call all men of other languages barbarians.

Necos then ceased from making the canal and engaged rather in warlike preparation; some of his ships of war were built on the northern sea, and some in the Arabian Gulf, but the Red Sea coast: the landing-engines of these are still to be seen. He used these ships at need, and with his land army met and defeated the Syrians at Magdolus [Migdol], taking the great Syrian city of Cadytis [Gaza] after the battle. . . .

4.42. I wonder, then at those who have mapped out and divided the world into Libya, Asia, and Europe; for the difference between them is great, seeing that in length Europe stretches along both the others together, and it appears to me to be beyond all comparison broader. For Libya shows clearly that it is encompassed by the sea, save only where it borders on Asia; and this was proved first (as far as we know) by Necos [Necho II] king of Egypt. He, when he had made an end of digging the canal which leads from the Nile to the Arabian Gulf, sent Phoenicians in ships, charging them to sail on their return voyage past the Pillars of Heracles [Strait of Gibraltar] till they should come into the northern sea and so to Egypt. So the Phoenicians set out from the Red Sea and sailed the southern sea; whenever autumn came they would put in and sow the land, to whatever part of Libya they might come, and there await the harvest; then, having gathered in the crop, they sailed on, so that after two years had passed, it was in the third that they rounded the Pillars of Heracles and came to Egypt. There they said (what some may believe but I do not) that in sailing round Libya they had the sun on the right hand.

Source: Herodotus. A. D. Godley (ed. and trans.). 1921. 2.157–9 and 4.42. New York: G. P. Putnam's Sons. Volume 1, pp. 469–75 (1920); Volume 2, pp. 239–41.

Julius Caesar Battles the Veneti, ca. 100–44 BCE
Excerpt from *The Gallic War*, 56 BCE

Julius Caesar (100–44 BCE) fought a number of different peoples over several years to conquer Gaul (modern France). Although initially successful, his troops ran low on food. Caesar dispatched envoys to several tribes to procure food, among them the Veneti, the region's most accomplished seafarers. The Veneti seized the Roman envoys and organized an anti-Roman alliance, provoking one of the most interesting ancient naval battles, one that pitted oared Roman galleys against the sailing ships of the Veneti, which is described in the passage below.

Chapter 8

[T]he Veneti both have a very great number of ships, with which they have been accustomed to sail to Britain, and [thus] excel the rest in their knowledge and experience of nautical affairs; and as only a few ports lie scattered along that stormy and open sea, of which they are in possession, they hold as tributaries almost all those who are accustomed to traffic in that sea. With them arose the beginning [of the revolt]. . . .

Chapter 9

Caesar, being informed of these things . . . orders ships of war to be built in the mean time on the river Loire, which flows into the ocean; rowers to be raised from the province; sailors and pilots to be provided. . . . The Veneti, and the other states also, being informed of Caesar's arrival . . . resolve to prepare for a war . . . and especially to provide those things which appertain to the service of a navy, with the greater confidence, inasmuch as they greatly relied on the nature of their situation. . . .

Chapter 12

The sites of their towns were generally such that, being placed on extreme points [of land] and on promontories, they neither had an approach by land when the tide had rushed in from the main ocean, which always happens twice in the space of twelve hours; nor by ships, because, upon the tide ebbing again, the ships were likely to be dashed upon the shoals. . . .

Chapter 13

For their ships were built and equipped after this manner. The keels were somewhat flatter than those of our ships, whereby they could more easily encounter the shallows and the ebbing of the tide: the prows were raised very high, and, in like manner the sterns were adapted to the force of the waves and storms. . . . The ships were built wholly of oak, and designed to endure any force and violence whatever; the benches which were made of planks a foot in breadth, were fastened by iron spikes of the thickness of a man's thumb; the anchors were secured fast by iron chains instead of cables, and for sails they used skins and thin dressed leather. These [were used] either through their want of canvas and their ignorance of its application, or for this reason, which is more probable, that they thought that such storms of the ocean, and such violent gales of wind could not be resisted by sails, nor ships of such great burden be conveniently enough managed by them. The encounter of our fleet with these ships was of such a nature that our fleet excelled in speed alone, and the plying of the oars; other things, considering the nature of the place [and] the violence of the storms, were more suitable and better adapted on their side; for neither could our ships injure theirs with their beaks (so great was their strength), nor on account of their height was a weapon easily cast up to them; and for the same reason they were less readily locked in by rocks. To this was added, that whenever a storm began to rage and they ran before the wind, they both could weather the storm more easily and heave to securely in the shallows, and when left by the tide feared nothing from rocks and shelves: the risk of all which things was much to be dreaded by our ships.

Chapter 14

[A]bout 220 of their ships, fully equipped and appointed with every kind of [naval] implement, sailed forth from the harbor, and drew up opposite to ours; nor did it appear clear to Brutus, who commanded the fleet, or to the tribunes of the soldiers and the centurions, to whom the several ships were assigned, what to do, or what system of tactics to adopt; for they knew that damage could not be done by their beaks; and that, although turrets were built [on their decks], yet the height of the stems of the barbarian ships exceeded these; so that weapons could not be cast up from [our] lower position with sufficient effect, and those cast by the Gauls fell the more forcibly upon us. One thing provided by our men was of great service . . . sharp hooks inserted into and fastened upon poles, of a form not unlike the hooks used in attacking town walls. When the ropes which fastened the sail-yards to the masts were caught by them and pulled, and our vessel vigorously impelled with the oars, [the ropes] were severed; and when they were cut away, the yards necessarily fell down;

so that as all the hope of the Gallic vessels depended on their sails and rigging, upon these being cut away, the entire management of the ships was taken from them at the same time. . . .

Chapter 15

The sail yards [of the enemy], as we have said, being brought down, although two and [in some cases] three ships [of theirs] surrounded each one [of ours], the soldiers strove with the greatest energy to board the ships of the enemy; and, after the barbarians observed this taking place, as a great many of their ships were beaten, and as no relief for that evil could be discovered, they hastened to seek safety in flight. And, having now turned their vessels to that quarter in which the wind blew, so great a calm and lull suddenly arose, that they could not move out of their place, which circumstance, truly, was exceedingly opportune for finishing the business; for our men gave chase and took them one by one, so that very few out of all the number, [and those] by the intervention of night, arrived at the land, after the battle had lasted almost from the fourth hour till sunset.

Source: Julius Caesar. W. A. McDevitte and W. S. Bohn (trans). 1869. *The Gallic War.* Book III, 8–9, 12–15. New York: Harper & Brothers. Available at Internet Classics Archive http://classics.mit.edu/Caesar/gallic.html.

Excerpt from the *Pattinapalai*, ca. 100 BCE–100 CE

One of the Pattupattu, *the oldest collection of Tamil poems, the* Pattinapalai *was written at least 1,500 years ago, possibly as long ago as 2,000 years. Its author, Uruthirankannanar, was from Kadyalur—a seaport with an ancient history— located on India's southeast coast. The long poem tells the tale of a husband who must leave his wife to go to Kaveripattinam, a famous emporium and port and the capital of the Chola kingdom—the location of which is no longer known. It was a cosmopolitan city, home to people from many lands whom the sections below describe: fishers, foreign traders, local merchants, and many others.*

1 Though Venus, star of splendor bright,
Strays southward from its wonted course.
Cool showers fail to fall, and the lark
That feeds on rain in silence droops,
Yet sea-like Kaveri mountain fed
Its waters spread o'er golden sands.
The never failing fields extend
With green sweet cane and fragrant vats
That boil and make long water plants
Of neighboring fields grow pale and fade.
Here under stores of grain do sleep

Grown calves fed sleek with yellow rice.
Rich coconut and plantain trees
With bunches, fruitful areca palms.
Sweet mangoes, bunchy palmyras,
And rooty *sempu,* saffron sweet,
And tender ginger: these abound.

. . .

28 There gardens girt with loam are seen
Where pegs are driven to tie strong boats
That stand like steeds in stables tied,
Come fully laden with the grain
By barter bought of salt refined
Through Chola land extending wide
With many a hamlet closely set,
The groves are charming, rich in yield.
Beyond are gardens bright with flowers.
Long ponds are there with lofty banks
That look like the moon when girt with stars
In a cloudless sky. They shimmer bright
With a riot of gaudy tints that tinge
The fragrant flowers that edge the banks.
The ponds afford such joys as felt
In this our birth and in the next.

. . .

66 The fishers thrive on an evil trade.
They live close with their numerous kin
In wide, black, sandy mounds. There are
Seen wrestling grounds with ancient trees.
They eat sweet roasted shrimp, and feed
On turtles boiled. They wear the blooms
Of *Adampu* dry that creeps on land
And *ambal* that in water grows.

. . .

83 In the outskirts mud-walled wells are found,
Pigs with their young, and various fowls.
These rams with partridges do play.
Long fishing rods that lean against
The low-roofed huts resemble much
Memorial stones round which stand spears
And shields. In the center nets are spread

To dry on sandy yards that seem
Like gloom with moonlight patches mixed.
Here red-haired fishers garlands wear
Of blossoms, cool and white, and vines
Beneath the pines with hanging roots.
They plant the sword of the gravid shark
To seat their sea-god great, for whom
They wear the bloom of sheathed pine,
And toddy drawn from rugged palms
They drink. . . .

116 The ancient glories of the port,
So blessed with never-failing flowers,
Are rare, and match the pride of heaven.

In night's last watch, when eyes are tired,
The boatmen in their prow-bent crafts
Note well the lights that still burn bright
In stories high where artless dames
At night enjoyed their mates embrace,
Discarding silks for raiment white.
They wear the garlands of their wives,
And wine they shun for sweeter drinks.

. . .

141 As when the rainy season comes,
The copious waters drawn by clouds
Are shed on mountain tops and these
In turn flow down and fill the sea,
So goods flow in from sea to land,
And also flow from land to sea.
Unmeasured are the abundant wares
Here brought and piled. And watchmen strong
In depots guarded well do seal
These with the potent tiger mark
They pile in yards these bundled heaps
Of ware immense. . . .

. . .

211 The good and worthy gods protect
The city's limits. Here are brought
Swift, prancing steeds by sea in ships,
And bales of pepper black, by carts.
Himalayas sends gems and gold,

While Kudda hills, sweet sandalwood
And akhil; pearls from the south sea come,
Red coral from the eastern sea.
The Ganges and the Kaveri bring
Their yield; Ceylon provides its food,
And Burma, manufactures rare.
With other rare and rich imports
This wealth lies close and thickly piled,

Confused along the spacious streets,
Where merchants live the fish is safe
In the sea, and the cattle, in the land.
Quite free and happy are their lives
Amidst their multiplying kin
They know no foes; their fishes play
Near the fisher's quarters unafraid,
And cattle multiply untouched
In butcher's haunts. The merchants thus
Condemn the taking of these lives.
They tolerate not thieving vile.

. . .

Even so their hearts are poised and just.
They speak the truth and deem it shame
To lie. For others' goods they have
The same regard as for their own
In trade. Nor do they try to get
Too much in selling their own goods,
Nor give too little when they buy.
They set a fair price on all things.
Their ancient wealth was thus acquired.
It's here the merchants crowded live.

As those who are united close
By various cultures high, at times
Together come to ancient shrines,
So people speaking diverse tongues
That come from great and foreign homes
Mix free in friendly terms with those
Who occupy this glorious town.

Source: J. V. Chelliah. 1985. *Pattupattu, Ten Tamil Idylls: Tamil Verses with English Translation.* Thanjavur: Tamil University.

Strabo on Pytheas of Massalia, ca. 64 BCE–24 CE

Pytheas of Massalia, a fourth century BCE geographer, sailed to Britain and explored the North Atlantic, encountering fog and ice. Although many of his contemporaries doubted his reports, modern scholars give them more credence, but remain uncertain about how far north Pytheas sailed and the location of Thule, an island he visited that was north of Britain and near a frozen sea. Pytheas chronicled his travels in his book, On the Ocean, *but only small fragments of it have survived. In the passage below, Strabo (ca. 64 BCE to 24 CE), a preeminent Roman geographer, describes Pytheas's voyage, but then casts doubt on it.*

Polybius, in his account of the geography of Europe, says he passes over the ancient geographers but examines the men who criticize them, namely Dicaerchus, and Eratosthenes, who has written the most recent treatise on Geography; and Pythias, by whom many have been misled; for after asserting that he travelled over the whole of Britain that was accessible Pytheas reported that the coast-line of the island was more than forty thousand stadia, and added his story about Thule and about those regions in which there was no longer either land properly so-called, or sea, or air, but a kind of substance concreted from all these elements, resembling a sea-lung [an acaleph of the ctenophora]—a thing in which, he says, the earth, the sea, and all the elements are held in suspension; and this is a sort of bond to hold all together, which you can neither walk, nor sail upon. Now, as for this thing that resembles the sea-lungs, he says that he saw it himself, but that all the rest he tells from hearsay. That, then is the narrative of Pytheas, and to it he adds that on his return from those regions he had visited the whole coast-line of Europe from Gades to the Tanais.

Now Polybius says that, in the first place, it is incredible that a private individual— and a poor man too—could have traveled such distances by sea and by land; and that, though Eratosthenes was wholly at a loss whether he should believe theses stories, nevertheless he has believed Pytheas' account of Britain, and of the regions about Gades and of Iberia; but he says it is far better to believe Euhemerus, the Messenian, than Pytheas. Euhemerus, at all events, asserts that he sailed only to one country, Panchaea, whereas Pytheas asserts that he explored in person the whole northern region of Europe as far as the ends of the world—an assertion which no man would believe, not even if Hermes [the divine messenger and god of travel] made it.

Source: Horace Leonard Jones (trans.). 1917. *The Geography of Strabo* (Loeb Classical Library). Cambridge: Harvard University Press, 399–401 (lines 2.4.1– 2.4.2).

Periplus of the Erythraean Sea, ca. 60 CE

Compiled by an experienced seafarer, probably an Egyptian Greek living in the first century CE, The Periplus of the Erythraean Sea, *is a firsthand account of voyaging in the Persian Gulf and Indian Ocean. It describes two trade routes from Egyptian ports on the Red Sea—one east to Arabia and India, the other south along the East African coast. Greek seafarers produced many guides like this, but the Periplus of the Erythraean Sea is the only one that has come down to us through the years reasonably intact. About 20 pages long, it provided ancient seafarers a host of detailed information, including dangerous areas, ports and market places, safe anchorages, coastline features, and the bribes or gifts expected by local officials. It remains one of our best sources on ancient seafaring.*

Line 20. Directly below this place is the adjoining country of Arabia, in its length bordering a great distance on the Erythraean Sea . . . the country inland is peopled by rascally men speaking two languages, who live in villages and nomadic camps, by whom those sailing off the middle course are plundered, and those surviving shipwrecks are taken for slaves. . . . Navigation is dangerous along this whole coast of Arabia, which is without harbors, with bad anchorages, foul, inaccessible because of breakers and rocks, and terrible in every way. Therefore we hold our course down the middle of the gulf and pass on as fast as possible by the country of Arabia until we come to the Burnt Island; directly below which there are regions of peaceful people, nomadic, pasturers of cattle, sheep and camels.

21. Beyond these places, in a bay at the foot of the left side of this gulf, there is a place by the shore called Muza. . . .

24. The market-town of Muza is without a harbor, but has a good roadstead and anchorage because of the sandy bottom thereabouts, where the anchors hold safely. The merchandise imported there consists of purple cloths, both fine and coarse; clothing in the Arabian style, with sleeves; plain, ordinary, embroidered, or interwoven with gold; saffron, sweet rush, muslins, cloaks, blankets (not many), some plain and others made in the local fashion; sashes of different colors, fragrant ointments in moderate quantity, wine and wheat, not much. For the country produces grain in moderate amount, and a great deal of wine. And to the King and the Chief are given horses and pack mules, vessels of gold and silver, finely woven clothing and copper vessels. . . . The voyage to this place is made best about the month of September . . . but there is nothing to prevent it even earlier.

25. After sailing beyond this place about three hundred stadia [a Roman stade is about 600 feet], the coast of Arabia and the Berber country about the Avalitic Gulf now coming close together, there is a channel, not long in extent, which forces the sea together and shuts it into a narrow strait, the passage through which, sixty stadia in length, the island Diodorus divides. Therefore the course through it is beset with rushing currents and with strong winds blowing down from the adjacent ridge of mountains. Directly on this strait by the shore there is a village of Arabs. . . .

30. On this bay there is a very great promontory facing the east, called Syagrus; on which is a fort for the defense of the country, and a harbor and storehouse for the frankincense that is collected; and opposite this cape, well out at sea, there is an island, lying between it and the Cape of Spices opposite, but nearer Syagrus: it is called Dioscorida, and is very large but desert and marshy, having rivers in it and crocodiles and many snakes and great lizards [probably monitor lizards], of which the flesh is eaten and the fat melted and used instead of olive oil. The island yields no fruit, neither vine nor grain. The inhabitants are few. . . . They are foreigners, a mixture of Arabs and Indians and Greeks, who have emigrated to carry on trade there. The island produces the true sea-tortoise, and the land-tortoise, and the white tortoise which is very numerous and preferred for its large shells . . . those of value are cut apart and the shells made whole into caskets and small plates and cake-dishes and that sort of ware. There is also produced in this island cinnabar. . . .

[continuing north and east]

34. Sailing along the coast, which trends northward toward the entrance of the Persian Sea, there are many islands known as the Calxi, after about 2000 stadia, extending along the shore. The inhabitants are a treacherous lot, very little civilized [possibly pirates and smugglers].

35. At the upper end of these Calaei Islands is a range of mountains called Calon, and there follows not far beyond, the mouth of the Persian Gulf, where there is much diving for pearls. . . . To the left of the straits are great mountains called Asabon, and to the right there rises in full view another round and high mountain called Semiramis; between them the passage across the strait is about six hundred stadia; beyond which that very great and broad sea, the Persian Gulf, reaches far into the interior. . . .

Source: W. H. Schoff (trans. & ed.). 1912. *The Periplus of the Erythraean Sea: Travel and Trade in the Indian Ocean by a Merchant of the First Century.* London, Bombay & Calcutta, pp. 20–40.

■ CHAPTER 3

Exchange and Encounter, 300 CE to 1000 CE

INTRODUCTION

The period from 300 to 1000 CE was one of dramatic political and religious change—including the fall of the Roman and Persian empires, the emergence and rapid spread of Islam, and the rise of the Tang Dynasty in China—following centuries of war. At sea, the Polynesians sailed east across the Pacific, settling a succession of island chains, and the Vikings sailed west across the Atlantic. The Polynesians, in particular, developed a sophisticated system of navigation and land finding, and peoples around the world improved their navigational techniques and developed new instruments to aid navigation. Despite the political and religious disruptions of the era, long-distance trade continued, particularly in the Indian Ocean.

Well before the western half of the Roman Empire collapsed in the fifth century CE, Rome's ability to police the Mediterranean and suppress piracy faded away. Many of the peoples who invaded the empire moved along rivers and crossed seas. Angles, Jutes, and Saxons invaded Britain, and the Vandals moved across Spain and crossed the Mediterranean to North Africa where they overthrew Roman rule and established their own kingdom. Vandal fleets regularly crossed the Mediterranean raiding southern Europe, and in 455 sacked Rome itself.

Although of dramatic significance to the Mediterranean and Middle East, Rome's decline had little effect in the Indian Ocean where trading networks persisted and ships continued to sail the monsoon winds. Growing numbers of these ships originated in the Muslim World, which expanded rapidly after the seventh century, coming to include the Middle East, North Africa, Persia, and parts of the East African and Indian coasts. Arab and Persian scholars developed a sophisticated body of astronomical knowledge, which aided Muslim sea captains on their journeys. One of literature's greatest captains, Sinbad, sailed in these years, returning from India and other distant lands to his home port of Basra with cargoes of diamonds, spices, ivory, and other rarities. Leaving aside Sinbad's great adventures and encounters with strange creatures, the tales of his voyages capture the breadth and diversity of Indian Ocean trade in the last centuries of the first millennium CE.

Under the Tang Dynasty (618–907 CE), China expanded its trade west along the Silk Road and also exerted a more active maritime presence, particularly in the Yellow Sea, trading with Japan, Korea, and several Southeast Asian states. Chinese ports, particularly Guangzhou, bustled with activity and became home to communities of foreign merchants from more than a dozen different cultures. Chinese diplomats and traders sailed to Southeast Asia and India, some traveling as far as the Persian Gulf, Red Sea, and East Africa, and Chinese scholars regularly traveled to India to study at Buddhist monasteries.

European monks and pilgrims similarly took to the sea, traveling as pilgrims to Jerusalem and other holy sites, or as missionaries to spread Christianity. Among the latter were the Irish Peregrini, the sixth century Irish monks who sailed to the Orkney and Faroe Islands, as well as mainland Europe and Scandinavia, preaching their faith.

Two of history's greatest seafaring peoples reached their maritime peak in the last centuries of the first millennium. In Europe, the Norse (Vikings) sailed west, settling in Iceland (770 CE), Greenland (982 CE), and—for a time—North America (986 CE). Viking raiders struck throughout Europe and into the Mediterranean, which encouraged their targets—particularly England and France—to improve their maritime defenses and, in England's case, to develop a navy. In the Pacific, Polynesian navigators used their understanding of winds, currents, and wave patterns, in addition to stellar navigation, to guide voyaging canoes across vast distances. By 1000 CE, they had settled almost every habitable Pacific island—more than 500 in total—inside the triangle formed by New Zealand, Hawai'i, and Easter Island. The Vikings withdrew from their distant settlements over time, abandoning their North American settlement due to hostilities with local peoples and leaving Greenland due to climate change. Polynesian communities across the Pacific flourished, although some groups, such as the Hawaiians, abandoned long-distance seafaring.

Vikings learned to measure the angle of the Pole Star to stay on a straight east or west course, and several seafaring cultures used a polar stick to aid navigation. Holding the polar stick at arm's length, the user sighted the Pole Star and compared it to the latitudes of common destinations that were marked on the stick. Because a polar stick was held at arm's length, each stick was individual to its owner. During the day it could be used to determine the ship's rough position relative to the sun. Arab navigators developed a more sophisticated version of the polar stick called the "*kamal*." The kamal had a knotted string attached to the stick, and each knot represented the latitude of a particular destination. To reach their destinations, ships either hugged the coast and kept in sight of land, or relied on latitude sailing. Latitude sailing involved sailing north or south to the latitude of one's destination and then maintaining a straight course east or west at that latitude until reaching the destination. Devices like the kamal facilitated latitude sailing although it was not without risk, because pirates often congregated at the latitudes of heavily trafficked ports to await potential prey.

Viking ships are among the most interesting of the period. Built shell first with overlapping planks fastened by nails (clinker built), their hulls could withstand the rough seas of the Atlantic. A broad keel and shallow draft enabled Viking longships to navigate upriver substantial distances, facilitating their raids. For propulsion, they relied on a large, square sail at sea and oars in calm weather or when navigating coastal waters or rivers. In the Mediterranean, lateen sails largely displaced square, a transition that also took place in the Indian Ocean. Lateen sails can be cut larger and baggier than square sails, allowing them to catch more wind, and they can sail closer to the wind. The Byzantines, the only state to maintain a standing navy throughout this era, introduced frame-first construction which speeded shipbuilding, and equipped some of their warships with a devastating new

This Danish reproduction of a Viking longboat shows the overlapping clinker-built (lapstrake) construction and prominent prow of its hull. An onboard A-framed tent provides shelter for the ship's crew. (Jacob Jensen /iStockPhoto.com)

weapon: Greek fire. Byzantium's navy protected and saved the state in its greatest adversity in the seventh century and made possible a Byzantine resurgence in the 10th century.

People in this era traveled farther by sea than ever before and the maritime links between different cultures both deepened and broadened. The sea became a passage not only for trade but also for religious pilgrimage of Buddhists, Christians, and Muslims, and sea travel facilitated the spread of these faiths. The expanding Muslim world, in particular, was linked by the sea from East Africa through the Middle East and into India and later Southeast Asia. Muslim traders came to dominate the rich Indian Ocean trade in spices, silk, and other luxury goods, and the spread of Islam to new regions often enhanced trade. Ports along the Indian Ocean became points of connection for people of diverse cultures and home to communities of merchants and sailors from different lands. In microcosm, they displayed the connections between distant peoples made possible by sea travel.

Stephen K. Stein

Further Reading

Hourani, George. 1995. *Arab Seafaring in the Indian Ocean in Ancient and Early Medieval Times,* 2nd ed. Princeton: Princeton University Press.

Jones, Gwyn. 1984. *A History of the Vikings,* 2nd ed. Oxford: Oxford University Press.

Lewis, Archibald R., and Timothy J. Runyan. 1985. *European Naval and Maritime History, 300–1500.* Bloomington: Indiana University Press.

Lewis, David. 1994. *We, the Navigators: The Ancient Art of Landfinding in the Pacific,* 2nd ed. Honolulu: University of Hawai'i Press.

Pryor, John H., and Elizabeth M. Jeffreys. 2006. *The Age of the Dromon: The Byzantine Navy, c. 500–1204.* Leiden: Brill.

CHRONOLOGY

Chronology: Exchange and Encounter, 300 to 1000 CE

ca. 320 CE	Chandragupta founds Gupta Dynasty in India.
330 CE	Roman Emperor Constantine founds Constantinople as the empire's new capital.
ca. 350 CE	Emergence of Kingdom of Srivijaya in Sumatra, Indonesia.
380 CE	Christianity becomes the Roman Empire's official religion.
395 CE	Roman Empire divided into eastern and western halves.
399–414 CE	Chinese scholar Fa Xian travels to India to study Buddhism.

455 CE	Vandals sack Rome.
476 CE	Fall of the Western Roman Empire.
ca. 484–577 CE	Life of Saint Brendan.
527–565 CE	Reign of Byzantine Emperor Justinian.
541 CE	Outbreak of Black Death (Bubonic Plague) in Egypt, which quickly spreads, killing about a quarter of the population of the Byzantine and Persian empires.
579 CE	Irish monks establish a monastery in the Orkney Islands.
ca. 600 CE	China's Grand Canal is completed.
618 CE	Tang Dynasty founded in China.
632 CE	Death of Prophet Muhammad; Abu-Bakr becomes the first caliph.
641 CE	Arabs conquer Egypt.
655 CE	Muslims defeat Byzantine fleet in the Battle of the Masts.
661 CE	Founding of the Umayyad Caliphate.
670 CE	Irish monks reach the Faeroe Islands.
674–678 CE	First siege of Constantinople.
ca. 675–685 CE	Chinese monk Yiching travels to India and studies at Nalanda.
697 CE	Venice becomes an independent city-state.
711 CE	Muslim armies conquer most of Spain.
713 CE	Muslim merchants arrive in China.
717–718 CE	Second Arab siege of Constantinople.
731 CE	Indian ruler Yashovarman dispatches an embassy to China.
732 CE	Christian victory against Muslims at the Battle of Poitiers.
750 CE	Founding of the Abbasid Caliphate in Baghdad.
770 CE	Vikings settle in Iceland.
793 CE	In their first recorded raid, Vikings sack the monastery on Lindisfarne, a small island off the English coast.
800s CE	Tales of Sinbad the Sailor likely written.
800 CE	Charlemagne crowned the first emperor of the Holy Roman Empire.
814 CE	Death of Charlemagne.

820s CE	Spanish Muslims capture Sicily and Crete.
841 CE	Vikings settle in Dublin, Ireland.
844–845 CE	Viking fleets raid the Iberian coast.
ca. 850 CE	Founding of the Chola Dynasty in southern India.
854 CE	Vikings attack Paris, but fail to capture the city.
900s CE	Ibn Shahriyar compiles the tales that appear in *The Book of the Marvels of India*.
911 CE	Vikings allowed to settle in Normandy.
934 CE	Merchants from Oman establish a trading post at Mogadishu in East Africa.
936 CE	Tosa Diary, describing a Japanese sea voyage, is written.
958 CE	Byzantines recapture Cyprus from Arabs.
960 CE	Song Dynasty established in China.
961 CE	Byzantines recapture Crete from Arabs.
985 CE	Erik the Red begins Viking settlement of Greenland.
995 CE	Olaf Tryggvason becomes King of Norway.
999–1000 CE	Long Serpent constructed for King Olaf Tryggvason.
ca. 1000 CE	Vikings, led by Leif Eriksson, establish North American settlements.
ca. 1025 CE	*Serce Limani* ship sinks.
1190–1290 CE	Polynesians arrive in Hawai'i.
ca. 1200 CE	Peak of construction of monolithic heads on Easter Island (Rapa Nui).

CHINA AND EAST ASIA, 300 TO 1000 CE

People and goods traveled long distances between China and other regions via sea routes from the first century CE. Sun Quan (182–252 CE), who ruled the Kingdom of Wu, successfully unified mainland China in 229 CE, integrating the three kingdoms of Shu, Wei, and Wu. Afterward, he dispatched high officials on a diplomatic mission to Funan (68–550 CE), a Southeast Asian kingdom centered on the Mekong Delta in what are now southern Vietnam and Cambodia. The Chinese officials' journey is recorded in fragmentary historical accounts that originated from the lost Chinese manuscripts *Funan Yiwu Zhi* (*Record of Rarities of Funan*) and *Wu Shi*

Wai Guo Zhuan (Foreign Countries in the Period of the Kingdom of Wu). They described Southeast Asian seagoing ships constructed of tropical hardwoods, and which were more seaworthy than contemporary Chinese ships.

Funan was a tributary state to China, paying homage in the form of regular shipments of goods from tropical regions. These tributes included items such as pearls, coral, aromatic woods, and spices. Funan maintained an entrepôt port, which served as a hub of maritime trade between the West and the East, as evidenced by the Roman coins discovered by archaeologists in the ruins of Oc-Eo (a Mekong Delta city), and glassware from the Roman Empire and the Indian Ocean world which have been found in Japanese tombs dating to the fifth and third centuries. Interaction with other kingdoms lying along the sea routes benefited Chinese rulers, garnering them important knowledge about the world beyond China—such as the existence of the Roman Empire on the other side of the world—and enabling them to obtain precious exotic items which could be traded to other parts of East Asia. In addition to the tributary trade centered on the Imperial Court, diverse groups of people engaged in private trading.

Imperial Tribute in the Sui and Tang Eras

The tribute system was a form of diplomatic relationship between China's imperial court and neighboring countries, and it also functioned for authorized official trade. The emergence of a stable monarchy in both imperial and tributary contexts was essential for effective functioning of the tributary system. China's Jin Dynasty (265–420 CE)—which succeeded the Wu Dynasty in 280 CE—ushered in a period of political instability. The unification of political entities by the Sui Dynasty (589–618 CE) improved the situation. Although this dynasty did not last long, during their relatively short reign the Sui rulers ambitiously propelled territorial expansion into northern Vietnam and Korea. They also undertook massive construction projects, including the expansion of the Great Wall and the Grand Canal, which linked the Yangtze and Yellow Rivers. Socioeconomic conditions, culture, and Buddhism all advanced under Sui rule, which led to the development of the tributary system along with political centralization and the beginning of imperialism. For state rulers of countries near China, it was important to obtain diplomatic recognition from the Chinese emperor. The countries first had to send envoys to the Chinese imperial court with various tributes. In return, the Chinese emperor sent an envoy to the tributary state, in the belief that a China-centric order had to show influence over surrounding countries.

By the seventh century, Japan's political institutions were sufficiently mature to send envoys to China. According to accounts in the state chronicle *Nihon shoki (Chronicles of Japan)*, Japan sent envoys to the Sui court four or five times between 600 and 618 CE. Japanese ships departed from Osaka, crossed the Tsushima Strait, and then sailed along the west coast of Korea to land in northern China. The

Sui, in turn, sent missions to Japan with a number of imperial gifts. These exchanges enhanced diplomatic relations between China and Japan and established trade between them. The dispatch of envoys from Japan continued during the Tang Dynasty (618–907 CE). Envoys traveled to the Tang court at least 18 times between 630 and 894 CE. By then the envoys sailed in larger fleets, which carried people involved in a variety of missions beyond the official government trade and tribute, including merchants, translators, artisans, shipwrights, medical professionals, and Buddhist missionaries.

The voyages of these envoys were not without risk. The Japanese monk Ennin (794–864 CE) joined an envoy voyage in the 830s or 840s as a member of a pilgrim mission. In his record of his nine-year pilgrimage, *Nitto Guho Junrei Gyoki* (*Record of Pilgrimage to China in Search of the Law*), he describes a terrible storm his envoy ship encountered. The ship almost broke apart from the strain endured. The weakness of its structure combined with the crew's poor navigation skills made for an unsafe voyage. Moreover—in contrast to the previous era—the safe route along

Salt Production

Salt historically has been important for preserving food and hides, and is necessary in small quantities for human life. Based on archaeological evidence, it is likely that coastal inhabitants began producing salt as early as 15,000 years ago. As maritime-based production techniques were largely similar worldwide, a typical example of salt production practices can be found in Japan.

Evidence of a salt trade in Japan can be traced back as far as the Jōmon era (approximately 12,000–300 BCE), and salt is listed in 10th-century documents as required for certain ceremonies. It was a key product throughout the coastal areas of Japan. Salt was produced by commoners, shrine affiliates, and cultivators, and was accepted for rent payments by land owners in the capital at Kyoto. The basic method of seaside salt production entailed evaporating seawater until the salt remained. Early salt fields were called "*agehama*" ("lifting to the shore"), and required people to physically carry seawater to a sandy area, where the water would evaporate in the sun and leave the salt. By the 14th century, production shifted to "*irihama*" ("filling the shore") salt fields, where seawater was piped into a sandy area for natural evaporation. In both cases, the sand then was rinsed with seawater, further increasing the salinity, and then boiled to leave the salt behind. The *irihama* style decreased the amount of labor needed, allowing for increased production and opened up more land for use as salt fields. It continued to be a common style of salt production even into the 19th century. Sites of large-scale salt production also needed a sustainable lumber supply to fuel fires to boil water. The whole process thus required a significant area that included forestlands to facilitate the entire endeavor.

Michelle M. Damian

the Korean Peninsula no longer was an option because of political tensions between Japan and Korea. Instead, the envoy fleets embarked at islands in the Kyushu region of southern Japan and crossed the East China Sea directly to reach major ports on the middle coast of China (today's Zhejiang Province). Encountering new ideologies, technologies, and material culture, however, motivated these Japanese travelers to visit China despite the risks.

Buddhist Pilgrimage from China

The history of Buddhist travels from China to India and Indian-influenced regions demonstrates improvements in navigation and the development of a maritime network. Buddhism gradually became a prevalent faith in China during the Six Dynasties period (222–589 CE). First introduced by foreign monks, Chinese monks spread Buddhism widely during the Sui and Tang dynasties, helped by the patronage of China's rulers. Chinese monks translated and circulated Buddhist doctrines and important writings, and a number of Chinese monks made the long sea voyage to India to acquire Buddhist scriptures and relics. Several of them left records of their pilgrimages, which provide important information on the practice of and spread of Buddhism, and about the maritime routes to India and the societies these travelers encountered along their voyages and travels in India.

The earliest account of such a pilgrimage is *Fu Kuo Chi* (*Record of the Buddhist Kingdoms*) by Fa Xian (337–442 CE). He left Chang'an (modern Xi'an in China) for India in 399 CE, traveling by land through Dunhuang on the Silk Road. After six years' travel, he arrived in northern India—then ruled by the Gupta Empire—and proceeded south toward Ceylon (modern Sri Lanka). Fa Xian returned to China from Ceylon to China in 413 CE aboard a Southeast Asian ship. His account describes the voyage in detail, including rough weather and the tense relations among the ship's passengers, which included Buddhist monks and itinerant traders in addition to the crew. Damaged by storms, the ship barely reached the Nicobar Islands in the Bay of Bengal. Following repairs, it sailed eastward and arrived in an Indonesian chiefdom, where Fa Xian transferred to a different ship. His account of his voyage crossing the South China Sea was even more perilous and illustrates the sailors' rudimentary navigational techniques. The ship's captain aimed for Guangzhou, but navigational errors brought the ship to provinces much farther north.

Maritime travel improved and became safer in the Tang period. The monk Yiching (635–713 CE), who studied at Nalanda University in India for 13 years, became renowned for his Chinese translation of Sanskrit Buddhist scriptures. He also wrote two remarkable manuscripts about his voyage and stay in Indonesia, the Malay Peninsula, and India: the *Da Tang Xiyu Qiu Fa Gaoseng Zhuan* (*Buddhist Monk's Pilgrimage of Tang Dynasty*; 646 CE) and *Nanhai Jigui Neifa Zhuan*

(*Account of Buddhism Sent from the South Seas*; 712 CE). In 671 CE, Yiching embarked at Guangzhou—probably on a Persian ship—for the Kingdom of Srivijaya in Indonesia, which they reached in 20 days. Srivijaya appeared in the Tang court's accounts as a tributary country, probably based in modern Palembang in eastern Sumatra. Yiching described the heyday of Mahayana Buddhism and Chinese merchant settlements in Srivijaya. He stayed in Srivijaya for about six months to learn Sanskrit and then traveled by ship from Palembang to India—following the same route as Fa Xian's return voyage. Yiching returned to Palembang laden with the Sanskrit Buddhist scriptures he had gathered and remained there to translate them and write about his travels. He returned to Guangzhou in 695 CE, by which point the tributary relationship between the Chinese court and Srivijaya was fully developed. Ships plied regular trade routes between Guangzhou and Palembang, helped by knowledge of the monsoons, tides, and currents, which made the voyages safer and faster.

The Tang Dynasty Maritime Ceramic Route

Guangzhou during the Tang Dynasty period was a gateway linking China with the port cities of Southeast Asia and the Indian Ocean world. It was a terminal for what scholars have labeled the "Maritime Ceramic Route." Similar to the overland Silk Road, historical and archaeological resources provide evidence of merchant ships that made regular, seasonal voyages to Guangzhou. Tang chronicles, for instance, include the names of foreign merchant ships to record the contexts of maritime trade. Some of these ships represent specific ethnic groups operating the ships (e.g., Malay-Austronesian people) and their regional origins (e.g., India, Sri Lanka, Persia). Guangzhou became a flourishing and prosperous port city, through which most of China's maritime commerce passed, a status exemplified by the Tang court's founding, in this busiest international port, of the bureau Shi Bo Si (Sea Trade Department) to administer maritime trade.

The discovery of shipwrecks from the Tang period demonstrates the existence of the Maritime Ceramic Route. In 1998, an Indonesian sea-cucumber diver discovered the remnants of an Indian Ocean merchant ship. Known as the Belitung shipwreck, cargo salvaged from the wreck includes a number of Chinese ceramics made for export, such as bowls originating from the Changsha kilns in northern China. The kilns operated actively during the Tang Dynasty and the following Five Dynasties period (907–960 CE). A shipwreck found near Vietnam—dated to the eighth or ninth century—yielded many Changsha bowls and other ceramics with surface inscriptions in Chinese, Indic, and Arabic, indicating the different languages of the people who sailed the Maritime Ceramic Route. There was a huge demand for Changsha ware. This unique Chinese export commanded high prices in foreign markets and was traded as far away as East Africa. Bowls with a splash motif were rare and popular in the Islamic world, and local crafts people produced imitation splash ware. China's first large-scale enterprises emerged in the Tang period due to seaborne trade led by foreign merchants.

Seaborne Merchants of Silla, 668–935 CE

In the East Asian maritime world before the 10th century, Chinese itinerant traders and bureaucrats were not necessarily a majority among seafaring groups. Merchants and Southeast Asian seafarers played a key role in the Maritime Ceramic Route trade in the Indian Ocean, on the northern Chinese coast and in the Yellow Sea. For a time, the people of Unified Silla (668–935 CE), who unified the Korean Peninsula, dominated regional maritime trade. Adjacent to both Tang China and the Kingdom of Bohai (698–926 CE) in the north, the new Silla state occupied a geographically important position in East Asian maritime trade. In addition to authorized trading associated with tribute missions, a private trading system appeared whereby Silla merchants became involved in transit trade. Coincidentally, Silla communities arose along China's coast. Jang Bogo (787–841 CE), mainly known for his role as Silla's military governor late in his career, became a prominent figure among the Silla elite and engaged in merchant activities in Korea, China, and Japan. Jang Bogo increased trade with Japan, regularly dispatching ships to Dazaifu in Kyushu—at the time, the only Japanese port open to overseas traders. Yet, this Silla-Japan trade declined after Jang Bogo's death, and the network of Silla communities lost momentum. Moreover, in China the Song Dynasty (960–1279 CE) brought significant economic growth to China. The Song Dynasty devoted substantial efforts to shipbuilding, trade, and other maritime activities, stimulating a greater engagement of Chinese voyagers in overseas trade that stimulated maritime commerce throughout East Asia.

Jun Kimura

Further Reading

Kimura, Jun. 2016. *Archaeology of East Asian Shipbuilding*. Florida: University Press of Florida.

Needham, Joseph. 1971. *Science and Civilisation in China*. Vol. 4, "Physics and Physical Technology-Civil Engineering and Nautics." London: Cambridge University Press.

Reid, Anthony, Shiro Momoki, and Kayoko Fujita. 2013. *Offshore Asia: Maritime Interactions in Eastern Asia Before Steamships*. Singapore: ISEAS.

Reischauer, Edwin O. 1955. *Ennin's Travels in Tang China*. New York: Ronald Press Company.

Wade, Geoff (ed.). 2014. *Asian Expansions: The Historical Experiences of Polity Expansion in Asia*. New York: Routledge.

Wang, Gungwu. 1958. "The Nanhai Trade: A Study of the Early History of Chinese Trade in the South China Sea." *Journal of the Malayan Branch Royal Asiatic Society* 31(2): 1–135.

Yamamoto, Tatsuro. 1980. "Chinese Activities in the Indian Ocean Before the Coming of the Portuguese." *Diogenes III* 3: 19–34.

Yule, Colonel H. 1882. "Notes on the Oldest Records of the Sea-Route to China from Western Asia." *Proceedings of the Royal Geographical Society and Monthly Record of Geography* 4(11): 649–60.

Fa Xian, 337 to ca. 422 CE

Most of what is known about the Chinese Buddhist monk Fa Xian lies within the historical account of his travels around the Asian world (*A Record of Buddhist Kingdoms*) roughly from 399 to 414 CE. One of the greatest travelers of the era, Fa Xian set out on a quest to India, the "Holy Land" of Buddhism, to procure Buddhist texts to replace the dilapidated ones held within his temple. Setting out from Changan, present-day Xian, Fa Xian and his fellow travelers faced harrowing dangers as they took the overland Silk Road, through the Taklimakan Desert, to India.

After arriving in India, Fa Xian set about visiting sacred Buddhist sites, and studying Sanskrit texts with scholars. After remaining for a number of years collecting works in India, Fa Xian decided to return to China following the well-known maritime Silk Road route. Setting off from Sri Lanka aboard a merchant vessel, Fa Xian began his return journey across the expanse of the Indian Ocean; planning to sail through the Straits of Malacca, to eventually arrive in Guangzhou in southern China. Shortly after setting out, however, Fa Xian's vessel encountered a typhoon and started taking on water. After the storm subsided, the crew was able to repair the ship and reorient the ship to make landfall on the island of Java, approximately 120 days after setting out from Sri Lanka.

Fa Xian resided on the island for almost six months before embarking on the last leg of his return voyage. In late spring, he set off aboard a larger merchant vessel with provisions to last 50 days to make the trip to Guangzhou. However, after a month at sea Fa Xian's ship encountered another violent storm that caused the ship's navigators to lose their bearings. Around the 70th day, with almost no fresh water remaining, the navigators decided to change course and head northwest to try and find land. After 12 more days of apprehensive sailing, Fa Xian's vessel made landfall much farther north than intended on the Shandong Peninsula. After making his return to China, Fa Xian completed his 15-year quest, travelled south to Nanjing, and began translating the Buddhist works he had successfully transported. The two major historical contributions of Fa Xian consist of the record of his journey containing valuable information about early Indian Buddhism, and his role in expanding Chinese Buddhism. In addition to this, Fa Xian's descriptions also provide a looking glass to view historical land- and sea-based travel conditions as well as the historical transmission of information and ideas.

Zachary N. Reddick

Further Reading

Legge, James. 1965. *A Record of Buddhistic Kingdoms: Being an Account by the Chinese Monk Fa-Hien of His Travels in India and Ceylon in Search of the Buddhist Books of Discipline.* New York: Paragon Book Reprint Corp & Dover Publications Inc.

Waugh, Daniel. "The Journey of Faxian to India." 1999. https://depts.washington.edu/silk road/texts/faxian.html. Accessed February 15, 2015.

Grand Canal

Stretching 1,115 miles from Beijing in the north to Hangzhou in the south, China's Grand Canal (Da Yunhe) is the world's longest artificial river. For centuries, it has been the key artery between China's two great natural waterways, the Yellow River and the Yangzi River.

Although sections of the canal originated in the fifth century BCE, these disparate segments were not united until the Sui Dynasty (581–618 CE). Prior to the Industrial

The Grand Canal in China was constructed by the second Sui emperor, Yang Di, during the seventh century CE. (Yory Frenklakh/Shutterstock.com)

Revolution, the Grand Canal was unrivalled as the world's most extensive civil engineering project.

By the time of the Song Dynasty (960–1279 CE), the Grand Canal, along with China's major rivers and associated tributaries, served to integrate the world's most densely populous trading region—which spanned more than 30,000 miles and connected millions of peasants and urban dwellers. As an axis for grain, salt, and troop transportation, the Grand Canal allowed imperial officials to control the flows of commerce and military power and gave the state access to a vast array of ecological zones. Under the Ming (1368–1644 CE) and Qing (1644–1911 CE) dynasties, these diverse regions stretched from subarctic Manchuria to Hainan in the tropical south.

The Grand Canal's shifting fortunes had profound effects on China's maritime history. Completion of canal renovations in 1415 CE generated a more secure and efficient inland grain transportation network than those offered by sea routes, thereby leading to a decline in coastal trade within the empire. The Grand Canal also proved detrimental to weak states; during the waning months of the Ming Dynasty, the invading Manchu army made its southern advance along the canal.

Today, portions of the canal have fallen into disrepair from silting and disuse. However, the Chinese government is upgrading sections of this ancient waterway to serve as the eastern conduit for its South-North Water Transfer Project. In 2014, the United Nations Educational, Scientific and Cultural Organization (UNESCO) designated the Grand Canal as a World Heritage Site, in recognition of its historical importance to Chinese culture.

Edward D. Melillo

Further Reading

Dreyer, Edward L. 1982. *Early Ming China: A Political History, 1355–1435*. Stanford, CA: Stanford University Press.

Fairbank, John King, and Merle Goldman. 2006. *China: A New History*, 2nd ed. Cambridge, MA: Harvard University Press.

McNeill, J. R. 1998. "China's Environmental History in World Perspective," in Mark Elvin and Liu Ts'ui-jung (eds.), *Sediments of Time: Environment and Society in Chinese History*. New York: Cambridge University Press, 31–49.

INDIA, 300 TO 1000 CE

Between 200 and 550 CE, China's Han Dynasty, the Gupta Empire in Northern India, and the Western Roman Empire all collapsed. Yet, trade through the Indian Ocean continued and even grew over the succeeding centuries. From the west, Muslim Arab and Persian merchants increased their presence in the region and became the Indian Ocean's primary long-distance shippers. Traveling to India to study at its great temples and monasteries, Buddhist pilgrims from China strengthened ties between China, India, and Southeast Asia. The most valuable trade goods that moved through the Indian Ocean were black pepper, porcelain, sandalwood, and silk, which were exchanged for cotton textiles, horses, incense, ivory, and metal goods. In the years between 300 and 1000 CE, India's increasingly multiethnic and multicultural ports became centers not only for trade, but also as meeting places where people from a variety of cultures, met, mingled, and exchanged ideas.

Once Greek seafarers learned the direct, open-sea passage to India in the second century BCE, trade increased dramatically between India and the Mediterranean World. By the first century CE, the 120 ships sailed annually from Myus Hormus on Egypt's Red Sea coast to India where Greek and Roman merchants purchased spices and other goods. An extensive trade for silk developed between Rome and China, passing through India. Imports of these goods continued into the fifth century, despite the collapse of the Han Dynasty in China and the steady weakening of the Roman Empire. After the collapse of the Han Dynasty, kingdoms in southern China, no longer able to access the Silk Road, expanded maritime trade to Southeast Asia, exchanging silk and porcelain for spices and aromatic woods. Alaric the Goth (ca. 370–410 CE) provides evidence of this enduring trade. When his army besieged Rome in 408 CE, Alaric demanded 3,000 pounds of pepper and 4,000 silk tunics, and large quantities of gold and silver (Shaffer, 18).

Shipbuilding and Navigation

India has a long history of seafaring, and coins dating from 300 to 900 CE depict the classic, single-masted *dhows* that were the workhorses of Indian Ocean trade—sailing with the monsoon winds, whose patterns were by then well known to Indian captains. At least some Indian ships were larger, as accounts from Chinese travelers describe 1,000-ton ships with four masts that carried as many as 700 men. A three-masted ship with a steering oar is depicted in Aurangabad cave paintings. Some ships depicted in art from the fourth through sixth centuries show curved hulls and planking extending above the waterline. Most used sails but some were propelled by oars.

Numerous types of boats plied India's many rivers, which are generally large, easily navigable, and empty into estuaries near the sea. The Ganges-Brahmaputra river system extends from the Himalayas to the Bay of Bengal and links a variety of cultures and climates. It provides easy means to move people and goods from India's interior to the many ports that developed where rivers met the sea. Boats used in inland waters included *Sangara,* which were dug-out canoes yoked together, *shangadam,* which were log rafts, and *trappaga* and *kotymba,* which were probably oared vessels used as tug boats. Reed bundle rafts were also used in rivers and lakes, as well as for coastal voyages. Snake boats, made from a single log, hollowed out and shaped, employed as many as 20 paddlers, and were prized for speed by rulers who used them for messengers and ambassadors.

Indian navigators relied on landmarks, the characteristics of local waters and their changing, seasonal nature, and stellar navigation. The Gupta Empire inaugurated formal study of astronomy in which Indian astronomers and mathematicians made numerous significant advances. Aryabhata (476–550 CE), for example, who published his work in the book *Aryabhatiya,* noted that the earth was a sphere that rotated around its axis. He also accurately calculated a number of astronomical constants related to the periods of moon and planets and the timing of eclipses.

Buddhism Influence on Trade and Travel

Fa Xian (337 to ca. 422 CE), an elderly Chinese Buddhist monk, was among the first to travel to India, seeking Buddhist texts related to monastic rules and other religious topics. He wrote about his travels in *A Record of Buddhist Kingdoms,* which is the earliest firsthand account of the customs and practices of Buddhists in India and Southeast Asia written in Chinese. Fa Xian devoted his life to translating Indian Buddhist texts into Chinese, and his books encouraged a view of India as a pure land, a place of holiness and sophistication. This encouraged other Chinese Buddhists to follow in his footsteps and make a pilgrimage to India. Some of the works he translated exist today only in Chinese, making them an important work of preservation.

Northern India fragmented into numerous small polities following the collapse of the Gupta Empire in the sixth century. Harshavardhana (590–647 CE) united several of these in the Punjab and Bengal, earning the title of Maharaja in 606. He converted to Buddhism and attracted scholars, artists, and Buddhist monks to his court, among them Xuanzang (602–664 CE), a Chinese Buddhist monk who, inspired by Fa Xian, traveled to India over the Himalayas to visit sites of significance to the Buddha. Harshavardhana and Xuanzang came to admire one another and their relationship helped establish the first diplomatic relations between China and India. Growing numbers of Chinese monks followed in the footsteps of Fa Xian and Xuanzang and made pilgrimages to India, and their journeys expanded trade and travel between their nations. Growing numbers of Chinese diplomats and traders during the Tang (618–907 CE) and Song (960–1279 CE) dynasties sailed to Southeast Asia and India, eventually reaching as far as the Persian Gulf, the Red Sea, and East Africa.

The trade that emerged depended upon the seasonal winds. In the fall through the winter, Northern trade winds pushed Indian sailboats from ports along the east coast: Tamralipiti, Palur, Kalingapatnam, Dharanikota, Arkamedu, and Poompuhar to Sri Lanka, Sumatra, Java, and Bali as well as farther points in Southeast Asia. In

February the winds reversed, and a Southwest trade wind blew the merchants, monks, and pilgrims back to the east coast of India.

Pilgrimages were a robust part of the exchanges between the two civilizations and the many islands and mainland states of Southeast Asia. Hundreds of monks, artisans, pilgrims, and merchants made the voyage, some on large ships carrying more than 200 people. As Buddhism spread, local rulers, supported by traveling merchants and monks, funded monasteries along the pilgrimage routes through Southeast Asia and along India's east coast, and these provided medical care and hospitality to seafarers and travelers, as well as services to the local communities.

A host of goods flowed from India to China, including beads, gemstones, glass, pearls, pepper, pottery, punched metal coins, Roman gold coins, and worked ivory, and Buddhist relics, documents, and liturgical items. India, in turn, imported aromatic woods including cinnamon, cassia, and sandalwood from Sri Lanka and from Southeast Asia, tin, and Chinese silk. As trade increased, Indian merchants settled in Southeast Asia, accelerating the diffusion of Indian culture and religion into the region.

The Heart Sutra exemplifies the lively cultural interchange of this era. Scholars believe that Maka Hannya Haramitsu Prajna Paramita (*The Heart of Great Perfect Wisdom*) Sutra was written between the fourth and the seventh centuries. Today it is considered one of the most important Buddhist sutras worldwide, and the single most important for Zen Buddhism. It was written as part of the Mahayana Sutras, which were designed to popularize Buddhism among laypeople. Zen temples now recite this sutra in a language known as Sino-Sanskrit. Written originally in Sanskrit, visiting Chinese monks translated this sutra into Chinese. Later Chinese monks carried it to Japan where it was chanted using the Japanese pronunciation of the Chinese characters. As a result, it is difficult for modern Japanese to understand. Nonetheless, as Zen spread across the West in the 20th century, the Sino-Sanskrit language of the chant came with it, linking modern Zen Buddhists to Chinese monks who traveled to India more than 1,200 years ago.

Islamic Commercial Dominance

In addition to Southeast Asia, Indian trade extended into the Persian Gulf, Arabia, and up the Red Sea and through Egypt to the Mediterranean. From the first through the fifth centuries CE, much of this trade flowed to and from Rome. It declined as Rome weakened, but revived in the seventh century as the expansion of Islam brought new generations of Arab and Persian traders into the Indian Ocean. The first evidence of Muslim contact with the people of Gujarat was in 635 CE when Bahrain sent an expedition to the region. Arabs conquered the region of Sindh (part of Pakistan today) in 712 CE, and its port of Daybul—located on the Indus delta— became an important center of trade, linking maritime and land trade routes.

Following the conquest, growing members of the local population converted to Islam, particularly Buddhist artisans, merchants, traders, and sailors, because conversion allowed them to participate in mercantile activities on the same favorable terms as other Muslims. Those involved in agriculture, primarily Hindus, lacked the same commercial incentives to convert and therefore were less likely to do so. From Sindh, Islam spread to Gujarat and to ports across the Indian Ocean, as Muslim seafarers increasingly entered local trade, becoming the region's premier long-distance shippers and traders. Muslim merchants controlled the passages through the Red Sea and the Persian Gulf and the caravan routes that connected these sea routes; the flow of goods enriched Baghdad and other Muslim centers. In addition to silk and spices, Chinese porcelain became particularly popular among with Muslim elites in the Middle East, and the Chinese sought horses and also frankincense and other aromatic gums and resins from Arabia for use in incense and perfume.

Compared to later eras, when Indian Ocean trade passed through a succession of port emporia, direct voyages from Basra and other Arab or Persian ports to India, Sri Lanka, and even China were common enough that several guides to the route were published in the ninth century, such as the *Book of Roads and Provinces*, by Ibn Khurdadhbih (ca. 820–912 CE). Ships sailed from the Persian Gulf to Daybul, then around India to Ceylon, or sailed directly from Persian Gulf ports across the Indian Ocean to Ceylon. From there, ships crossed the Bay of Bengal, proceeded through the Strait of Malacca, and entered the South China Sea, following the coast along Vietnam to Guangzhou (Canton), China, trading textiles and metals for silk and porcelain. By the ninth century, buoys marked several major shipping lanes, especially in the Persian Gulf.

The Chola Empire

The Chola kingdom emerged among the Tamil people of southeastern India and flourished for several centuries before its dramatic expansion in the ninth. Moving north and south, Chola rulers absorbed neighboring kingdoms and soon controlled most of southern India. In 993 CE, the Cholas invaded Sri Lanka (Ceylon) and, after several years of fighting, gained control of its rich pearl beds. In 1007 CE, Chola Emperor Rajendra (r. 1014–1044 CE) dispatched a naval expedition against Srivijaya, a powerful Indonesian state that had controlled the Strait of Malacca since the fifth century. Continuing naval warfare between the Cholas and Srivijaya eroded Srivijaya's naval power. Massive Chola raids in 1024–1025 CE disrupted Srivijaya's control of the Strait of Malacca, but the Chola proved unable to expand into Indonesia. Srivijaya remained the region's preeminent naval power. Chola rulers dispatched several embassies to China and the Abbasid Caliphate and maintained good relations with both. Chola expeditions facilitated the spread of Hindu trading companies, which by the 10th century operated throughout southern India. Later, the Hindu companies entered Southeast Asian trade. Trade in India, in particular, increasingly came into the hands of trading guilds, which specialized in particular goods or regions, and operated in ports throughout the eastern Indian Ocean.

The years from 300 to 1000 CE evidenced growing trade and maritime activity in the Indian Ocean. Buddhist pilgrims from China and Southeast Asia strengthened relations between the Chinese court and India rulers, and increased the volume of trade between China and India and between China and Southeast Asia. Muslim Arab and Persian traders increased their presence in the Western Indian Ocean, and some intrepid Muslim captains sailed all the way to China. In part due to the influx of local converts, Muslims became the region's premier—though hardly exclusive—long-distance traders, and dominated trade in the western Indian Ocean between East Africa, the Middle East, and India. The Chola Empire formed in eastern and southern India in the ninth century and for the next several hundred years dominated the waters of Southern India and Sri Lanka. Yet, the diversity of trade and traders in the Indian Ocean continued. People from across the region sailed with the monsoons and traded goods, and the region's ports developed vibrant, multi-ethnic communities that persisted into the era of European colonialism.

Carolyn Stein
Stephen K. Stein

Further Reading

Alpers, Edward A. 2013. *The Indian Ocean in World History*. Oxford: Oxford University Press.

Chakravarti, Ranabir. 2002. *Trade and Traders in Early Indian Society*. New Delhi: Manohar.

Chaudhuri, K. N. 1985. *Trade and Civilization in the Indian Ocean: An Economic History from the Rise of Islam to 1750*. Cambridge: Cambridge University Press.

Hall, Kenneth R. 2011. *A History of Early Southeast Asia: Maritime Trade and Societal Development, 100–1500*. Lanham, MD: Rowman & Littlefield.

McGrail, Sean. 2004. *Boats of the World: From the Stone Age to Medieval Times*. Oxford: Oxford University Press.

McPherson, Kenneth. 1993. *The Indian Ocean: A History of People and the Sea*. Oxford: Oxford University Press.

Pearson, Michael. 2003. *The Indian Ocean*. New York: Routledge.

Sen, Tansen. 2016. *Buddhism, Diplomacy, and Trade: The Realignment of Sino-Indian Relations, 600–1400*. Lanham, MD: Rowman & Littlefield.

Shaffer, Marjorie. 2014. *Pepper: A History of the World's Most Influential Spice*. New York: St. Martin's.

Sheriff, Abdul. 2010. *Dhow Cultures of the Indian Ocean: Cosmopolitanism, Commerce and Islam*. New York: Columbia University Press.

Tripati, Sila. 2011. "Ancient Maritime Trade of the Eastern Indian Littoral." *Current Science* 100(7), 1076–87.

Pilgrimage, Buddhist

Siddhartha Guatama, the Buddha, encouraged pilgrimage and pilgrimage became important to Buddhists after his death sometime in the fifth century BCE. Buddhism spread from India by both land and sea after the third century BCE, gaining converts throughout Southeast Asia and China. In later years, monks and other pilgrims traveled to India to study and visit holy sites. Buddhism spread along established land and maritime trade routes and pilgrims, in turn, followed these routes in later years. By the seventh century, Chinese traded coral, pearls, glass, and silk for Buddhist texts and relics. Trade for religious texts and artifacts stimulated general trade among China, India, and Southeast Asia, which grew steadily over the years.

In the *Mahaparinibbana Sutta*, the Buddha advised his disciples to visit four places for their inspiration: Lumbini, Bodhgaya, Sarnath, and Kusinara. Each of these places is significant to Buddha's life. He was born in Lumbini, attained Enlightenment in Bodhgaya, preached his first sermon in Sarnath, and died and achieved Nirvana in Kusinara.

During the reign of King Ashoka (304–232 BCE), four more places became important Buddhist pilgrimage sites: Veshali, Rajagrah, Sankasia, and Savathi. All are closely associated with the Buddha's life and are scenes of his miracles. These eight sites are the most important places for pious disciples to visit and seek inspiration. The pilgrims look upon them with feelings of reverence, reflecting on the particular event associated with the life of Buddha. Lumbini is in Nepal; the other seven are in India.

Buddhism spread from India to other countries during and after the reign of King Ashoka. Buddhists from other countries, particularly China, traveled to India to learn more about Buddhism and seek enlightenment. Indian monks, in turn, traveled to China to share their knowledge. Buddhist monks traveled from China to India either over land, through mountainous Yunnan and Burma, or by sea around Southeast Asia. Over time, Buddhist temples sprang up along this route and temple complexes in Vietnam, Cambodia, Java, Sri Lanka, and Sumatra became important stops for pilgrims on the way to India, and even sites of pilgrimage in their own right. Hanoi alone boasted 20 temples by the third century CE.

The first well-documented account of a Chinese pilgrimage to India is the journey of Fa Xian (337–422 CE) who traveled to India by land and returned by sea.

Sixty years old when he embarked on the journey in 399 CE, he visited Kapilvastu, Lumbini, and Kusinara, and other holy sites and studied at several monasteries. His travelogue offers detailed descriptions of these temples, the legends associated with them, Buddhist practice and ritual, and his adventurous return home—which included encounters with pirates and visits to Buddhist temples in Sri Lanka and other locations.

Two other Chinese pilgrims, Xuanzang (ca. 602–664 CE) and Yijing (635–713 CE), also produced detailed accounts of their journeys in this era. Xuanzang made the difficult land journey to India. Setting out in 627 CE, he crossed the Gobi Desert and the Tian Shan mountain range to reach India, where he spent many years studying and learning from Buddhist masters. He returned home with 657 Sanskrit texts. Supported by Emperor Taizong (599–649 CE), Xuanzang established a major center of learning and translation.

Yijing departed the Chinese port of Guangzhou in 672 CE on a Persian ship bound for Srivijaya (today's Palembang, Indonesia), where he studied Sanskrit grammar and the Malay language before resuming his journey to India on a different ship. In India, he joined a group of merchants, traveling throughout the country and visiting 30 different principalities and numerous temples and religious sites. Yijing voyaged home by sea, again stopping at Srivijaya, where he spent two years translating Sanskrit texts before returning to China.

Fa Xian, Xuanzang, and Yijing are representative of what became a regular and growing pilgrimage of Buddhists from China and Southeast Asia to India. Although some traveled by land, the less arduous maritime route through Southeast Asia became preferred. Copies of sacred texts and Buddhist relics proved to be in high demand. One Chinese envoy, for example, paid 4,000 bolts of silk to purchase one of the Buddha's bones. Thus, trade mixed with pilgrimage, and triggered an exchange of religious texts and relics—as well as monks and scholars—between India, Southeast Asia, and China.

Amitabh Vikram Dwivedi

Further Reading

Forbes, Duncan. 1999. *The Buddhist Pilgrimage*. Delhi: Motilal Banarasidass Publishers.

Liu, Xinru. 1998. *Ancient India and Ancient China: Trade and Religious Exchanges AD 1–600*. Delhi: Oxford University Press.

Sen, Tansen. 2003. *Buddhism, Diplomacy and Trade: The Realignment of Sino-Indian Relations, 600–1400*. Honolulu: University of Hawai'i Press.

Sen, Tansen. 2009. "The Travel Records of Chinese Pilgrims Faxian, Xuanzang, and Yijing." *Education About Asia* 11(3), 24–33.

Weerawardane, Prasani. 2009. "Journey to the West: Dusty Roads, Stormy Seas and Transcendence." *Biblioasia* 5(2), 14–18.

ISLAMIC WORLD, 632 CE TO 1000 CE

The history of Muslim travel often focuses on its religious motivations—the pilgrimage to Mecca ("*hajj*") is required at least once in the lifetime of every financially and physically able Muslim. This requirement inspired the development of navigational instruments and technologies, because many Muslims lived far from the holy sites of Mecca and Medina and thus had to travel long distances over sea and land. At the same time, Muslim merchants, soldiers, and scholars moved regularly across the wider Muslim world. Conquest, commerce, and communication all fueled the development or dissemination of navigational, ship, and sail technologies—many of which were learned from the ancient Persians, Greeks, and Chinese. Medieval Muslim seafarers used instruments such as the astrolabe, quadrant, charts, and (later) the compass, although most ship captains preferred to navigate by sight, sticking close to the shorelines (coastal tramping). Arabic geographical treatises and traveler's accounts also were written to describe both seas (further subdivided into regional seas) and the lands that surrounded them, to aid pilgrim travel and spread scholarly knowledge of the world. Muslim merchants transmitted raw materials and commercial products, technologies, culture, and religion within and between the Indian Ocean and Mediterranean Sea regions. Sea travel also fostered the spread of Islam, as merchants established settlements beyond the political reach of Islamic rulers in the eastern Indian Ocean and coastal East Africa.

Although some Islamic legal experts prohibited sea travel because of the potential for danger or legal complications, medieval Islamic cultures were deeply involved in travel, trade, and communication over water, and developed a corpus of laws governing trade, transportation, and religious life that included shipwreck, piracy, and other maritime business matters. Of particular concern to jurists was how to dispose of commercial or personal property of a pilgrim or merchant who died at sea.

When the Prophet Muhammad died in 632 CE, the majority of the Arabian Peninsula was under the religious and political control of Islam—a region filled with desert nomads as well as cities along the long-distance trade networks connecting the Indian Ocean commercial sphere with that of the Mediterranean Sea. Within a century, Muslims controlled most of the regions bordering these seas—from central Asia to the far western edge of North Africa and the Iberian Peninsula, the southern and western shores of the Mediterranean Sea, and the western shores of the Indian Ocean. In addition to incorporating and adapting many of the administrative, cultural, and economic systems in place in conquered regions, Muslims took over many of the ships and sailing techniques of conquered peoples. Sea travel also fostered the spread of Islam itself, as merchants established Muslim settlements beyond the political reach of Islamic rulers, especially in the eastern Indian Ocean and coastal East Africa.

Serçe Limanı

In about 1025 CE, a Greek Christian merchant ship sailing toward Constantinople from Muslim Syria sank off the southwestern coast of Anatolia. Named the *Serçe Limanı* shipwreck for its location, or the "Glass Wreck" for its cargo, this mid-sized wooden-planked ship with a flat bottom and two lateen-rigged sails held three metric tons of broken glass intended for re-melting (cullet).

The glass came from Fatimid Syria, as did other commodities onboard, including intact glassware, ceramics, copper pots, gold jewelry, sumac (a spice), and raisins. Numerous "daily life" objects—grooming sets, small coins, well-worn ceramic dishes, weapons, tools, padlocks, scales, seals—teach us about the men who sailed the ship and the commerce, both large scale and small, in which they were engaged. Food evidence includes animal bones and jugs ("amphorae") of wine and olive oil—some with names to indicate their owners; "Michael" possessed most of the amphorae, suggesting that he was the captain. The sailors played games (backgammon, chess), fished, mended fishing nets, and had purchased small bundles of Islamic goods to resell back home. This shipwreck thus reveals both the patterns of Christian-Muslim trade in the 11th-century Mediterranean and aspects of life for sailors and merchants at sea.

Medieval sailing depended on weather and season, and shipwreck or poor weather was always feared. Most medieval ships sailed along the coasts, keeping shorelines in sight; poor weather could obstruct sightlines and allow ships to sail off course or, worse, could cause shipwreck. Other dangers lurking at sea included pirates, who were active in both the Mediterranean Sea and Indian Ocean.

The primary type of vessel in the Indian Ocean was a sewn-plank sailboat known today as the "*dhow*," which was long and thin with a triangular (lateen) sail. Mediterranean ships were larger, with nailed-plank hulls and flat bottoms. Merchant ships in the Mediterranean relied primarily on sails (both square and lateen), but warships also utilized oars and rowers for better handling in battle. Much remains unknown about medieval vessels and their details because there are few direct sources from these centuries that explain naval technologies, ships, and sails. Instead, the majority of sources include a combination of literary and graphic representations created by landlubbers rather than sailors, shipwrights, or shipowners. A major aid to present-day understanding of ships, their contents, and their routes comes from the growing field of maritime archaeology. The discovery of actual medieval ships—such as the Serçe Limanı wreck discovered off the coast of Turkey—and the study of their construction and cargos has contributed immensely to knowledge of pre-modern seafaring.

Dhow sailing boats on the Indian Ocean at sunset. Dhows have two distinctive characteristics: triangular, or lateen, sails and their stitched construction. (Steffen Foerster/Dreamstime.com)

Indian Ocean (Bahr al-Hind)

Before the advent of Islam, some Arabs and Jews from southern Arabia conducted seaborne trade in the western Indian Ocean and Red Sea, although—in the period immediately preceding Muhammad—the major sea powers in the region were the Sassanid Persian Empire and the various maritime states of India. Along with the overland Silk Road routes, the Indian Ocean was a conduit for trade goods from India and China, via the Persian Gulf (Bahr Faris) or the Red Sea (Bahr al-Qulzum), and from there into the eastern Mediterranean. By 1000 CE, Muslim merchants were the connection between these two commercial spheres.

The most valuable eastern goods were porcelain, spices (especially pepper, cinnamon, nutmeg, and medicinals), pearls, jewelry, precious stones, silks, and silkworms. Muslim traders also gained knowledge of many eastern agricultural products that spread to the Muslim lands and from there into Europe—including rice, sugarcane, citrus fruits, and cotton. The traders also learned and transferred several important technologies, including production of silk, porcelain pottery, and paper.

Within Muhammad's lifetime, Arabs from Aqaba to Yemen had sworn allegiance to Islam, opening Red Sea ports to Muslim control. Under the second caliph, Umar I (r. 634–644 CE), Muslim ships crossed the Persian Gulf, raided the Indian coast and established a Muslim presence in Indian Ocean trade. By 713 CE, Muslim merchants and ambassadors had reached China, and they dominated regional trade by 878 CE, when Chinese rebels massacred foreign merchants—many of them Muslims—in Canton (Guangzhou). Afterward, direct trade with China ceased in favor of trade at ports in India and nearby islands; it resumed about a century later. Beginning in the eighth century, Muslim merchants also sailed south along the African coast, reaching Sofala (modern Mozambique) and Madagascar. Commodities sought there included gold, ivory, iron, timber, and slaves—known in Arabic as "*Zanj*" ("black"), which gave their name to the southeast region of Africa.

Islam itself was also transmitted by merchants who established colonies and spread the religion along the coasts of eastern Africa and into the islands of the Indian Ocean. By the ninth century, Muslim colonies were established along Indian Ocean trade routes from the Persian Gulf to the Malabar Coast, Ceylon, the Maldives, through the Strait of Malacca and along the Malay coast, and from there into Indonesia and China. Islamic culture thus had the opportunity to interact with and influence the various Buddhist and Hindu cultures of China and India.

Under the Umayyad caliphs (661–750 CE), with their capital at Damascus, most seafaring took place via the Red Sea and the Mediterranean. After the change in dynasty in 750 CE and the establishment of the Abbasid capital at Baghdad, the bulk of trade shifted to the Persian Gulf route. Basra became the most important port, along with Sohar (Gulf of Oman) and Siraf (Persian Gulf). During early Abbasid rule, trade from the Persian Gulf into the Indian Ocean flourished, and a northern route developed via the Tigris and Euphrates Rivers to the Black and Caspian Seas and then to the Baltic Sea. The construction of a canal between the Tigris and Euphrates aided the development of this northern trade route. After the establishment of a rival Shiite caliphate—the Fatimids—in Egypt in 969 CE, significant trade shifted back to the Red Sea, from the ports of Jedda and Aden, and it became particularly important as a route for pilgrims to Mecca and Medina.

The seasonal monsoon winds were an important aspect of Indian Ocean seafaring, determining direction and timing of voyages: southwestward in the summer (June through September) and northeastward in the winter (October through January). The voyage from the Arabian Peninsula to the Far East took about six months, as did the return journey. Thus, roundtrip travel to China required about one and a half years, and midway trading centers in India arose to facilitate shorter or segmented trips. Merchants timed voyages to eastern Africa for the beginning or end of the monsoons, in April/May and August. June and July were too dangerous for sailing in the western Indian Ocean.

The Mediterranean Sea (Bahr al-Rum, or Bahr al-Sham)

Although most of the military conquests in the East resulted from land battles, much of the contest in the West was waged on the seas—particularly the battles over islands and port cities. Between the late 630s and the start of the eighth century, Muslim forces advanced across Byzantine North Africa. Alexandria, a major Byzantine port, fell to Muslim control in 641 CE, providing access to the ships and sailors docked there. Many of the seventh-century Muslim-owned ships were sailed by the Greeks and Copts who previously had sailed Byzantine galleys. Carthage fell in 698 CE, and nearby Tunis became the leading Muslim port in the western Mediterranean. By the mid- to late-seventh century, Muslim forces sailed regularly from North Africa into the Mediterranean on military raids (gathering goods and slaves) as well as diplomacy and commerce.

Muslim ships were victorious in early sea battles with the Byzantine navy—beginning with the Battle of the Masts in 655 CE. By this date the Muslim fleet numbered roughly 500–600 ships (Kennedy 2008, 327). From Tunis, the western Muslim fleet deployed for raids of conquest and commerce against islands such as Cyprus (649 CE) (raids continued until the Byzantines re-conquered the island in 958), Sardinia (from the early eighth century), the Balearic islands (from the early eighth century; incorporated into the Umayyad Caliphate of Cordoba from 902), Sicily (from the mid-seventh century; under Muslim rule from 827 CE), Malta (869 CE) and the Christian seacoasts of Italy, France, and Iberia (under Muslim dominion from 711 CE). Sicily, although not under Islamic control until the ninth century, experienced semi-regular attacks on its southern shores from the mid-seventh century.

Muslim forces attacked Constantinople, the capital of the Byzantine Empire, in 674–678 CE and again in 717–718 CE. These campaigns relied on a series of bases established along Anatolia to besiege the city, and both ended with the destruction of the Muslim fleets by "Greek fire." This did not mean the end of Muslim naval power, however, as their fleets recovered and thrived.

The port of Tunis housed the major western Mediterranean fleet, with other fleets based in eastern Mediterranean cities such as Acre, Alexandria, and Tarsus. Other ports and cities came under the control of Muslim sailors and of ships operating independently as pirates or privateers. Such independent Muslim settlements—called emirates but often referred to as "pirates' nests"—were established on the island of Crete (824–960/961 CE), in the French coastal town of Fraxinetum (ca. 889–973 CE), and in southern Italy at Bari (841–871 CE) and Taranto (840–880 CE)—all reconquered by Christian forces by the end of the 10th century. From these bases, Muslim ships conducted raids on both land and sea—on the towns and monasteries of southern Italy and France, and even Rome—and engaged in commercial trade with both Muslim and Christian towns.

Sea-borne trade between Muslims, Jews, and Christians continued despite and during periods of warfare throughout the medieval period. Trade in the medieval

Mediterranean brought products from the East—notably spices, silks, porcelain, pearls, coral, precious stones, and medicinals from the East in exchange for linens, wool, and cotton cloth, carpets, and metalwork. Commodities from the Near and Far East then traveled into Christian Europe and, by 1000 CE, Christian maritime cities in Italy were active in Mediterranean trade. The Umayyad Caliphate at Cordoba conducted a majority of its trade with the central Islamic lands via North Africa, although there is evidence of sea-based trade and travel, especially of Iberian pilgrims and scholars. After the breakup of the caliphate in 1031 CE, Muslim trade in the western Mediterranean was conducted by a number of the small "taifa" states of Iberia, such as Denia, which carried on extensive trade with Italian cities.

Many of the merchants active within the Muslim-controlled Mediterranean were Jews who lived and worked in Muslim lands, formed commercial partnerships with Muslims, sailed on Muslim-owned ships, and spoke Arabic. Jewish merchants from Egypt were the primary agents of a particularly active trade triangle between Egypt, Sicily, and Tunisia, in which eastern and Mediterranean goods were traded and then passed on to markets in the western Mediterranean and north into Christian Europe. Some of these Jewish merchants also traveled into the Indian Ocean and thus mediated trade between the two regions.

Mediterranean ships sailed eastward and westward from April to October, although most captains preferred to be off the seas during the winter months of November through March. Wind and current patterns in the Mediterranean follow a roughly counterclockwise direction, meaning that East-West travel depended on the ability to stop at ports along the northern shores (coastal tramping). Likewise, because the southern shores of the Mediterranean are rockier and more dangerous, the preferred route followed the northern shores and islands. Most of these islands were under Muslim control from the eighth or ninth century, giving them dominance over the sea-lanes. European Christians recaptured all of these locations by the end of the millennium, however, which assisted their later military campaigns.

Sarah Davis-Secord

Further Reading

Agius, Dionisius A. 2008. *Classic Ships of Islam: From Mesopotamia to the Indian Ocean*. Leiden: Brill.

Alpers, Edward A. 2014. *The Indian Ocean in World History*. Oxford: Oxford University Press.

Bass, George F., and Sheila Matthews, J. Richard Steffy, and Frederick H. van Doorninck Jr. 2004. *Serçe Limanı: An Eleventh-Century Shipwreck*. Vol. 1, "The Ship and Its Anchorage, Crew, and Passengers." College Station, TX: Texas A&M University Press.

Campbell, I. C. 1995. "The Lateen Sail in World History." *Journal of World History* 6: 1–23.

Chaudhuri, K. N. 1990. *Asia Before Europe: Economy and Civilisation of the Indian Ocean from the Rise of Islam to 1750*. Cambridge: Cambridge University Press.

Goitein, Shelomo Dov. 1967–1993. *A Mediterranean Society: The Jewish Communities of the Arab World As Portrayed in the Documents of the Cairo Geniza*, 6 vols. Berkeley: University of California Press.

Hourani, George. 1995. *Arab Seafaring in the Indian Ocean in Ancient and Early Medieval Times*. Princeton, NJ: Princeton University Press.

Kennedy, Hugh. 2008. *Great Arab Conquests: How the Spread of Islam Changed the World We Live In*. New York: Da Capo Press.

Khalilieh, Hassan Salih. 1998. *Islamic Maritime Law: An Introduction*. Leiden: Brill.

McCormick, Michael. 2001. *Origins of the European Economy: Communications and Commerce, A.D. 300–900*. Cambridge, UK: Cambridge University Press.

Power, Timothy. 2012. *The Red Sea from Byzantium to the Caliphate: AD 500–1000*. Cairo: American University in Cairo Press.

Pryor, John H. 1988. *Geography, Technology, and War: Studies in the Maritime History of the Mediterranean, 649–1571*. Cambridge: Cambridge University Press.

Christian Egyptians and the Umayyad Fleet

In the late seventh and early eighth centuries, the Byzantine navy threatened the Muslim holdings in the Mediterranean. Building a naval power became a compelling and urgent need for the nascent Islamic Empire. The Arab Muslims, who had little understanding of the sea or experience with naval warfare, sought to harness the maritime capabilities of Christian Egyptians who became a vital part of Muslim naval power.

For several millennia, the Nile and the Red Sea had been part of the nautical culture of Egypt. In conquering Christian Egypt in the seventh century, Muslim forces (including Arabs, Persians, and others), gained two major assets: the port of Alexandria, which included a naval base with excellent facilities; and a long-standing tradition of skilled maritime craftsmen, including carpenters, caulkers, navigators, sailors, and oarsmen. Christians played an important role in preparing and sailing the Muslim fleet that won the Battle of the Masts (655 CE) against Byzantium. In the aftermath of that battle, Egypt's Muslim rulers continued to draw on Christians with maritime skills.

The documentary and literary records from the Umayyad period (661–750 CE) in Greek, Coptic, and Arabic show that Christian Egyptian laborers (mostly Copts) were conscripted from the Egyptian provinces ("*pagarchies*") for the construction and refitting of ships. In addition to their poll tax ("*jizyah*"), some laborers paid for substitutes to take their place. Interesting topics such as fugitives and deserters, and obviously the punishments imposed by the Muslim rulers, are revealed in the papyri.

The first Muslim fleet was built in Egypt at the shipyards of Babylon (Old Cairo) and Alexandria. By the early eighth century, there were nearly 1,700 ships in the

Muslim fleet (Syriac Chronicle of Michael). The cities of Tyre (Lebanon) and Acre (Israel) served as the Muslim naval forward base.

Another base and fleet were created in Ifriqiya (Tunis) once again by the Christian Egyptians. Under the rule of 'Abd al-Malik ibn Marwan (685–705 CE), 1,000 Copts with their families were shipped to North Africa for the construction of the shipyard and the building of the fleet in Tunis (al-Tijani). Fearful of mass conversion to Islam of these Christian laborers, the Coptic Patriarch attempted to maintain ties by dispatching Coptic priests to both Cyrenaica (Libya) and Tunis. Yet there is scant evidence to suggest the ploy was successful.

Indeed during the Caliphate of Yazid ibn Mu'awiyah (680–683 CE) and Sulayman ibn 'Abdul Malik (715–717 CE), the Coptic Patriarchs were powerless to prevent their own monks, living in the remote areas of the desert, from being driven into servitude on both the labor camps (building and repairing the ships) and the fleets alongside the conscripts (*History of the Patriarchs of Alexandria*, 372–73). The enforced labor of the Copts was pivotal in the rise to naval supremacy of the Arab Muslims and facilitated Muslim raids on Cyprus, Malta, and Sicily, and the Islamic conquest of Western Europe.

Myriam Wissa

Further Reading

Allouche, A. 1991. "Coptic Contribution to the Umayyad Fleet." In Aziz S. Atiya (ed.), *The Coptic Encyclopedia* 7: 2286–87. New York: Macmillan.

Chabot, J. B. 1905, *Chronique de Michel le Syrien, Patriarche Jacobite d'Antioche (1166–1199). Éditée pour la première fois et traduite en français*, tome III. Paris.

Chiarelli, L. 1991. "Arsenal of Tunis." In Aziz S. Atiya (ed.), *The Coptic Encyclopedia* 1: 239. New York: Macmillan.

Evetts, B. T. A. 1910. *History of the Patriarchs of the Coptic Church of Alexandria*, and Part IV: *Mennas I to Joseph* (849) (*Patrologia Orientalis* X, fasc. 5). Paris.

Fahmy, A. M. 1948. *Muslim Naval Organisation in the Eastern Mediterranean from the Seventh to the Tenth Century A.D.* London: Lawrence Verry.

Greek Papyri in the British Museum. 1910. Catalogue, with Texts, Vol. 4. H. I. Bell (ed.), with Appendix of Coptic Papyri W. E. Crum (ed.)., London.

Dhow

The term "*dhow*" is a generic term used by westerners referring to a variety of large and small indigenous sailing vessels that dominated trade and navigation in the western Indian Ocean for centuries. Their sizes ranged from less than 50 tons up to 500 tons. There are many different types of dhows that, depending on size and place of origin, share enough common characteristic features to be considered a dhow.

The word dhow generally is considered to have been derived from the Farsi word "*dawh,*" which means "small ship" and predates the arrival of Islam. There is almost no pictorial evidence of early dhows. Much of what is known about the early construction of dhows comes from Greek and early Roman historians. Medieval writers observed dhows in the Red Sea, along the east African coast, along the Malabar and Coromandel coasts of India, and in the Maldives.

Dhow building was done close to the ports, estuaries, and inlets bordering the Indian Ocean, Persian Gulf, and the Red Sea. Early dhows were constructed from imported teak from Malabar in southwest India as teak does not crack, split, or shrink in saltwater.

Dhows had two distinctive characteristics: triangular or lateen sail and stitched construction. Hulls were assembled by laying wooden planks edge to edge. The planks were then held together by coir fiber stitching that passed through holes in the planks. The advantage of having a sewn hull was that it was able to endure the shock of driving ashore through the surf without suffering serious damage. The hull was made watertight by inserting resin between the planks. There were usually two pairs of triangular or lateen sails, one for daily use and the other for use at night or during storms. Early sails were woven from coconut palm leaves and eventually from cotton cloth. The masts for sails were made from either teak or coconut wood.

Dhows did not use keels but instead used either sandbags or cargo as ballast. It is interesting to note that dhows were built, and continue to be built, with no drawn plans. Carpenters typically carried out repairs onboard the dhow while major repairs were carried out at the dhow's first port of call.

Ballast

An anchor is a tool that uses weight to prevent a ship from drifting, and a ballast is a weight used to provide stability for a ship. This stability is achieved by having weighted material in the keel of a ship (or other vessel). This weighted material helps maintain balance to prevent capsizing. In modern times, the keels of boats and ships are built as heavy ballasts, but some ships use ballast tanks where water circulates in and out of the tank to maintain stability.

Throughout history, a multitude of items have been used to balance ships and boats. At times, crewmembers have acted as living ballasts. In many cases, the heavy cargo being transported was used to balance a ship. The oldest and perhaps most archaic way of balancing a ship was to use stones and sand. These items are obviously easily obtainable and provide a heavy counterweight to the winds and waves of the oceans and seas. Sand and stone have been used as naval ballasts since the prehistoric era, through antiquity, and up to modern times.

Matthew Blake Strickland

The arrival of the Portuguese in the Indian Ocean in the 15th century added new dimensions in hull design as well as the use of nails in construction. By the time the British East India Company arrived in the Indian Ocean, dhows were still a common site. Even today, dhows still ply the waters between the Persian Gulf and East Africa using sails as their sole means of propulsion.

Keith A. Leitich

Further Reading

Agius, Dionisius A. 2002. *In the Wake of the Dhow: The Arabian Gulf and Oman*. Ithaca: Garnet Publishing Ltd.

Hawkins, Clifford W. 1977. *The Dhow: An Illustrated History of the Dhow and Its World*. Lymington, Hampshire: Nautical Publishing Co. Ltd.

Prados, Edward. 1997. "Indian Ocean Littoral Maritime Evolution: The Case of the Yemeni *Huri* and *Sanbug*." *Mariner's Mirror* 83: 185–98.

Yajima, Hikoichi. 1976. *The Arab Dhow Trade in the Indian Ocean*. Tokyo: Institute for the Study of Languages and Cultures of Asia and Africa.

Masts, The Battle of the

The Battle of the Masts, also known as the Battle of Phoenix, was a naval engagement between the forces of Byzantine Emperor Constans II and a Muslim fleet commanded by Abdullah bin Sa'ad bin Abi'l Sarh. Fought sometime during 655 CE off the southern coast of Asia Minor near Cyprus, it marked the first major battle between Arab and Byzantine naval forces and the emergence of the Caliphate as a naval power in the Mediterranean. For the next 400 years, Arab fleets and ships posed a significant threat to Byzantium and sailed and raided across the Mediterranean. Trade patterns changed as well, and merchants residing in Muslim states came to dominate trade in the Eastern Mediterranean.

Islamic armies led by Caliph Uthman repeatedly bested Byzantine forces. They drove the Byzantines from Egypt in 642 CE and then advanced up the coast of Palestine. The Muslim advance, briefly checked by raids by the Byzantine navy, gathered strength following its successful siege of Caesarea (647 CE), a major Byzantine port on the Syrian coast. The conquest of Christian ports in Egypt, Palestine, and Syria allowed Arab leaders to expand their fleet, incorporating into it many Syrian and Coptic Christian sailors, whom Byzantium had persecuted. This growing fleet posed a serious threat to the Byzantine Empire and forced Emperor Constans II to take action. He gathered ships from throughout the empire and sailed with a fleet of approximately 500 ships.

The Byzantine fleet encountered and engaged bin Sa'ad's fleet of roughly 200 galleys off the coast of Anatolia, near Mount Phoenix. Crewed mostly by

Christians, the Muslim galleys carried numerous Arab soldiers. A variety of oral traditions attest to the religious implications of the battle. As the fleets neared one another, Christian crews reportedly nailed crosses to their masts and sang psalms. Muslim ships, in turn, affixed crescents to their masts and soldiers recited suras from the Quran. The Byzantine fleet rushed into battle in poor formation, expecting to overwhelm the outnumbered Muslim ships. Instead, the superior seamanship of the Muslim fleet's Christian sailors allowed them to slowly gain the upper hand in a daylong battle that resulted in heavy losses to both sides. Though a clear Muslim victory, the losses were such that the Muslim fleet retreated in its aftermath.

Islamic chroniclers interpreted these events as an affirmation of their faith. The battle might have swung the balance of power in the Eastern Mediterranean even more dramatically, but for the assassination of the Caliph Uthman the following year. His death precipitated a civil war, which gave the Byzantines a brief respite. Regardless of the internal conflicts within the Islamic camp, the battle proved a watershed event.

Kevin J. Delamer

Further Reading

Donner, Fred McGraw. 1981. *The Early Islamic Conquests*. Princeton, NJ: Princeton University Press.

Humphreys, R. Stephen. 2006. *Mu'awiya ibn Abi Sufyan: From Arabia to Empire*. Oxford, UK: Oneworld.

Kennedy, Hugh. 2007. *The Great Arab Conquests: How the Spread of Islam Changed the World We Live In*. Philadelphia: Da Capo Press.

Sinbad the Sailor

Sinbad the Sailor is a fictional character and hero of seven tales, each describing one of his voyages. Although often included in Scheherazade's *One Thousand and One Nights,* the stories of Sinbad originated separately, though they also likely date to the late eighth or ninth century CE. Sinbad, whose name might be of Persian origin, lived in Basra during the Abbasid Caliphate (750–1258 CE). A trader and sailor, he departed on a series of epic voyages, generally to the east and the south toward India. Reminiscent of Odysseus, Sinbad encounters a host of adventures and catastrophes. Often his ship is sunk or he is left stranded. He encounters numerous people in his adventures—some helpful, some not—in addition to giants, phantoms, half-men, and other monsters, most of whom seek to enslave or kill him. Sinbad always manages to cope with the dangerous situations he faces and outwit or outfight his foes, and each story resolves in a happy ending with Sinbad returning home wealthy. Retold over the centuries, the stories of Sinbad inspired and influenced a host of similar tales of nautical adventure. More recently, Sinbad has appeared in comic books and more than three dozen movies.

In the first voyage, Sinbad—having squandered the money his father left him—goes to sea to regain his fortune through trade. Sinbad's ships arrive at what appears to be a beautiful island, but it turns out to be a gigantic fish or whale. The fish dives into a deep sea and Sinbad saves himself by climbing onto a floating wooden box, which drifts ashore. Sinbad, left alone, finds shelter with the local ruler, saves his favorite horse from supernatural attack, and then works with local merchants and sailors until one day his ship arrives, he reclaims his goods, and Sinbad returns to home a rich man.

In his second voyage, Sinbad is accidently abandoned by his shipmates on a beautiful island. This island is home to giant birds and huge snakes that occupy a valley rich in diamonds. Sinbad tricks one of the birds, which eat the snakes, into carrying him back to its nest where he fills a sack with diamonds and then heads for home. In his third voyage, Sinbad and his crew encounter a giant. Much like Polyphemus in Homer's *Odyssey,* the giant begins consuming Sinbad's crew one by one. Like Odysseus, they escape by blinding the giant. Although additional members of his crew are killed by rocks hurled by the giant's wife, Sinbad again manages to return home rich.

In the fourth voyage, cannibals capture Sinbad and his crew and feed them a strange plant, which clouds their minds and makes them ravenous to fatten them up before the cannibals eat them. Sinbad, though, recognizes the danger, avoids the plant, and escapes. Again befriended in a nearby kingdom, he marries a beautiful woman presented to him by the king. Upon the death of his wife, however, Sinbad discovers that local custom is to bury the surviving spouse along with the dead one. Sinbad escapes this fate, returning home with gems from the tomb. His fifth voyage also goes badly at first. Sinbad is captured and enslaved by the "Old Man of the Sea" who makes Sinbad carry him on his back. Sinbad gets him drunk, escapes, and becomes wealthy by trading coconuts.

In the last two tales, Sinbad visits Serendip (Sri Lanka). In the sixth voyage, he is shipwrecked there, but again impresses the local king who rewards him. Returning there for his seventh voyage, Sinbad is attacked by pirates who capture him and sell him to a merchant as a slave. The merchant, in turn, promises Sinbad his freedom in exchange for 500 elephant tusks, which Sinbad manages to obtain by discovering an elephant graveyard.

Perhaps inspired by actual traders and sailors of the era, the tales of Sinbad provide insight into the societies and cultures along the Indian Ocean and Persian Gulf and the trading networks of the time. In addition to the coconuts, ivory, and precious stones mentioned above, Sinbad sought exotic woods and spices, particularly camphor, cinnamon, cloves, pepper, and sandalwood—goods that would attract merchants to India and Southeast Asia well into the modern era. In the modern era, several dozen movies have been made about Sinbad.

Amitabh Vikram Dwivedi

Further Reading

Haddawy, Hussain. 2008. *Sindbad: And Other Stories from the Arabian Nights*. New York: W. W. Norton & Company.

Hardy-Gould, J. 2005. *Sinbad*. Oxford: Oxford University Press.

Meisami, Julie Scott, and Paul Starkey. 1998. *Encyclopedia of Arabic Literature*. London: Routledge.

NORTHERN EUROPE, 300 TO 1000 CE

Europeans in the early Middle Ages, between 300 and 1000 CE, had diverse opportunities for seafaring (and overland) trade, pilgrimage, diplomacy, exploration, and adventure. Seafaring was an important part of life in the period, especially for elites who could, and did, travel widely.

Trade and Exchange

With the transformation of the Roman world in the Late Antique period (ca. 300–600 CE), northern Europe did experience a decline in volumes of trade and travel, but the narrative of catastrophic breakdown in economic and political function advanced by historian Edward Gibbon in the 18th century is no longer tenable, nor is the argument by Henri Pirenne in the early 20th century that it was the Arab attacks in the seventh and eighth centuries that ruptured the trade routes. Rather, current scholarship in textual and material culture emphasizes both continuity with the Roman world and dynamic change in Europe and the Mediterranean.

During the seventh century, a new exchange system was developed that connected the new rural elites of northwestern Europe with the old power centers in the Mediterranean basin. By 600 CE, secular and ecclesiastical elites (Franks and Gallo-Romans) had for the most part ceased organizing overland caravans south over the old Roman road network to ports such as Marseilles. Instead, the estuaries of great rivers became points of entry for travelers, diplomats, merchants, pilgrims, and missionaries across the North Sea, English Channel, and Irish Sea. Few Franks used these routes; it was mostly Anglo-Saxons, Norse, Danes, Frisians (modern Netherlands)—seagoing peoples who had the technology and the skill to exploit these waterways.

At these newly important places, trading towns were set up, called "*wics*" or "*emporia*," which were brand new trade sites in northern Europe. Important *wics* were founded in places such as Birka (Sweden) and Hedeby (Denmark) in Scandinavia; Dorestad (Netherlands) and Quentovic (France) on the Continent; and Jorvik (York, northern England) and Hamwic (Southampton, southern England) in the British Isles. Although scholars argue whether these were spontaneous creations, official royal foundations, or some combination thereof, it is certain that local kings and elites tried to take advantage of them by extracting customs duties from merchants and setting up mints for recasting foreign currency.

Many of these sites that have been fully excavated follow a similar pattern, each having a significant harbor, often slightly up a river to protect it, but within easy reach of the open sea. Beyond the harbor lay an industrial zone which has craftsmen and artisans. Outside of the urban settlement area was an agricultural and market gardening zone that served to supply food and necessities for travelers and locals alike. Passing through these *wics* were luxury goods from as far afield as Byzantium, the Islamic world, and East Asia, and included glass, pottery, textiles, and wine. Likewise, raw materials from the north flowed outwards, and included furs, skins, Baltic amber, and walrus tusk. These settlements were not occupied longer than 100 years in most cases, as they were natural targets for pirates and invaders, without protection of a navy or state.

Military and Naval Travel

Though it is commonly assumed that the Vikings represented a new sailing and naval tradition in northern Europe in the early medieval period, this story of early medieval Scandinavian naval supremacy lacks nuance and historical context. Indeed, the Anglo-Saxons of England and the Franks on the Continent did sail the coastal waters of the Channel, the North Sea, and the inland river systems successfully, though the earliest evidence of sailing (as opposed to oar-driven) ships in the region is in the sixth century, and sails were very certainly in widespread use by the late seventh century. It is still debated when the coastal piracy of the Angles, Saxons, and Jutes in Britain turned to full-scale settlement between the fifth and seventh centuries, but it is certain that both of these were accomplished using both oar- and sail-driven ships in the North Sea and the English Channel.

In the eighth century, the Frankish emperor Charlemagne had important naval endeavors, including an attempt to build a canal between tributaries of the Main and Danube rivers (although it failed because the route chosen passed over quicksand). Still, Charlemagne used ships logistically on rivers to move goods and people in his many wars against the Slavs, Saxons, and Avars. He and his successors also employed ships in tactical maneuvers against Vikings in the North Sea, as well as Muslim pirates in the Mediterranean. Indeed, the Franks, English, and others quickly adopted the Viking longship technology for themselves, leveling the playing field within 100 years or so. Most naval military activity by any group

William the Conqueror's fleet crossing the English Channel, detail from the Bayeux tapestry or the *Tapestry of Queen Matilda*. France, 11th century. (DeAgostini/Getty Images)

consisted of small raiding parties, the transport of armies, and various other logistical needs—naval warfare itself was quite rare in this period.

Although ship-to-ship battles were rare, they hold a large place in the literary textual sources, for the obvious reason that naval battles make for a good story. Even in the Scandinavian sagas they never took place on the open sea. When naval battles did occur, they would take place in confined waters such as estuaries or harbors, and ships might be lashed together to form a type of fighting platform for the opposing sides to engage one another upon. As the saga of the Norse king Olaf Tryggvason put it,

> This fight was very bitter and bloody. The men at the bows of [King Olaf Tryggvason of Norway's ships] threw anchors and grappling hooks into King Svein's [of Denmark] ships. They hurled weapons down on the men below them and cleared everyone off the ships they grappled. King Svein and the survivors of his army fled to other ships and got themselves out of weapon range as quickly as they could . . . they lost many men and some of their ships and, given the circumstances, they withdrew. (Ch. 106)

Although it is true that the Viking longship was an important technological innovation in seafaring in the early medieval period, it was not a wholly new idea from the Vikings, but rather was part of the evolution of seagoing technology in Europe before the year 1000 CE.

Mission and Pilgrimage

Trade and military advantage were not the only reasons that early medieval people traveled the sea, however. Religious travel—including pilgrimage, mission, and religious wandering—also was an important motivator for early medieval movement. Knowing about the importance of sea travel is key to understanding the religious and cultural transformations in early medieval Europe.

Travel is certainly an integral part of the Christianization process, as all missionaries are religious travelers. This is not necessarily their sole purpose, however, as they also could have diplomatic, economic, or political functions. The status of missionary travelers was important; they were representatives of powerful forces, from the temporal power of wealthy rulers such as Emperor Charlemagne and his successors, to the combination of temporal and divine power represented by the papacy, to the divine power of the Christian god himself. The reason that travel was such an important part of religious transformation and conversion was that missionary saints' knowledge of places of temporal and spiritual power—such as Charlemagne's capital at Aachen, or the Pope's Holy See in Rome—and their connections with these people of power, mirrored their connection with divine power; their holiness was dependent upon their connections to power through their stature as wanderers or travelers or missionaries. An important example of

---

On Christian Doctrine

One Christian pilgrim captured the apparent conflict of embarking on an arduous pilgrimage, but enjoying the journey.

Suppose we were travelers who could live happily only in our homeland, and because our pilgrimage made us unhappy, we wished to put an end to our misery and return there: we would need transport by land or sea which we could use to travel to our homeland, the object of our enjoyment. But if we were fascinated by the delights of the journey and the actual traveling, we would be perversely enjoying things that we should be using; and we would be reluctant to finish our journey quickly, being ensnared in the wrong kind of pleasure and estranged from the homeland whose pleasures can make us happy. So in this mortal life we are like travelers away from our Lord; if we wish to return to the homeland where we can be happy, we must use this world, not enjoy it.

Source: Saint Augustine. R. P. H. Green (trans.). 2008. *On Christian Teaching.*
Oxford: Oxford University Press, 1.4.4.

this traveling missionary saint is Boniface (ca. 672–754 CE), who was born in the kingdom of Wessex in southern England, crossed the sea to later become archbishop of Mainz in what is now northern Germany, and was killed in Frisia (modern-day Netherlands) while on a mission to convert pagans. Boniface also developed a close relationship with the papacy, having traveled to Rome three times in his life as a pilgrim and bishop, receiving permission to set up Christian dioceses beyond the old Roman imperial frontier of the Rhine and Danube rivers to Christianize both the elite and non-elite Germanic population. Boniface maintained close ties with both his native England and his ecclesiastical superiors in Rome from his mission fields on the continent, as his letter collection attests.

The Carolingian kings, centered in modern-day France, supported Boniface and other missionaries because the kings were engaged in long-term wars for territory and people with various Germanic tribes, such as Charlemagne's 30-year-long war against the Saxons. A major part of the non-military incorporation of the Saxons was forced conversion. Baptism was forced upon all conquered Saxons and pagan practices incurred the death sentence in conquered territories. Although these practices were at odds with the ideal of Christian conversion even in this period, it was a way of culturally decimating the population. Not every early medieval religious traveler was a missionary, and there is compelling evidence that many holy men wandered around seeking solitude on isolated islands in the north and the contemplative life in monastic foundations. These ascetics represented a different, apolitical Christian life than those of the missionaries, but they still demonstrated Christian life and Christian virtue to those they encountered.

More common were the pilgrims, both elite and non-elite, that traveled the early medieval world. These pilgrims—defined broadly as both local and long-distance travelers journeying for the purpose of religious devotion—utilized the same waterways and highways as missionaries, merchants, soldiers, and pirates. Indeed, at times the categories overlapped, as a man on a trading voyage might stop at a shrine to a saint, or a pilgrim might bring some items to trade during his trip and at his destination. Destinations for pilgrimage were many, from the holy places of Christ's life in Jerusalem, the tombs of the martyrs and saints in Rome, to innumerable shrines, reliquary churches, and local sites across Europe and the Mediterranean. Motivations for pilgrimage were just as diverse, from the expected piety, to a search for adventure, or the escape from troubles at home.

Early medieval people utilized the sea as a vector for many types of economic exchange, religious travel, and military movement. Though this primarily was the purview of the elites (and authors of the existing primary sources), the waterways of northwestern Europe in the early Middle Ages bustled with ships and people moving from place to place.

Courtney Luckhardt

Further Reading

Boniface. 2000. *The Letters of St. Boniface*. Ephraim Emerton (trans.). New York: Columbia University Press.

Haywood, John. 1991. *Dark Age Naval Power: A Reassessment of Frankish and Anglo-Saxon Seafaring Activity*, 2nd ed. New York: Routledge.

Hodges, Richard. 2012. *Dark Age Economics: A New Audit*. London: Bristol Classical Press.

McCormick, Michael. 2001. *Origins of the European Economy: Communication and Commerce, A.D. 300–900*. Cambridge: Cambridge University Press.

Sturluson, Snorri. 1964. "The Saga of Olaf Tryggvason." In *Heimskringla, the History of the Kings of Norway*. Lee M. Hollander (trans.). Austin: University of Texas Press, 144–243.

Wood, Ian. 2001. *The Missionary Life: Saints and the Evangelization of Europe, 400–1000*. Harlow: Longman.

Eriksson, Leif, ca. 970 to ca. 1020 CE

Leif Eriksson set sail circa 1000 CE from his home in the Eastern Settlement of Greenland towards an unknown western land, according to the sagas about his adventures, called the *Vinland Sagas*, written in Iceland in the early 13th century. These sagas contain the oldest written description of North America, filtered

This print depicts Leif Eriksson's sighting of Newfoundland circa 1000 CE. Eriksson and his Viking crew set sail from Greenland and landed on the northwest coast of Newfoundland where they established a settlement at L'Anse aux Meadows. (Library of Congress)

through at least 200 years of Icelandic oral tradition. They relate the story of Erik the Red, a chieftain exiled from Iceland to Greenland for his crimes and to prevent a blood-feud. The sagas also tell the story of his son Leif—nicknamed "the Lucky"—and his kin, who explored various lands, including Helluland (thought to be Baffin Island, Canada), Markland (Labrador), and most famously, Vinland, or "wine land" thought to be the land just south of the Gulf of St. Lawrence, Canada, the northernmost limit of wild grapes in eastern North America.

In contrast to the uninhabited north Atlantic islands the Vikings previously settled, such as Iceland and the Faroe Islands, Vinland and North America were filled with indigenous peoples, many of whom did not take kindly to Norse Greenlanders visiting or settling their lands. Eriksson and his companions called these local people "skraelings," which was a catch-all term for two different groups of indigenous populations of the eastern Arctic. The first group was the Dorset Paleo-Eskimos, descendants of the original inhabitants of the Arctic American continent who were living there when the Vikings first arrived in the late 10th century. The second group was the Thule Inuit people, ancestors of the present-day inhabitants of this area who immigrated to the area from Alaska in approximately the 11th through the 13th centuries. Although evidence from material culture of Norse interaction with local indigenous populations is still new and controversial, textual sources that speak of Leif the Lucky and his companions' interactions with "skraelings" are abundant. The *Vinland Sagas* tell of trade between the native inhabitants and the Vikings, including trading for furs—an important natural resource that Scandinavians were keen to exploit. The sagas also describe battles between them, including one that erupted after a Viking killed a native for trying to steal weapons. This killing provoked retaliation from the locals, and the sagas say that although the Vikings remained in Vinland the rest of that winter, by spring they all wanted to return home.

Although Leif Eriksson and his fellow Vikings did make it to North America around the year 1000 CE, they erected no permanent settlements, only winter camps such as L'Anse aux Meadows. Even the Norse settlements on Greenland did not survive; the last written record of Scandinavian presence there comes from the 15th century.

Courtney Luckhardt

Further Reading

Magnusson, Magnus, and Herman Pálson (trans.). 1965. *The Vinland Sagas, The Norse Discovery of America. Graelendinga Saga and Eirik's Saga*. New York: Penguin.

Seaver, Kirsten A. 1996. *The Frozen Echo: Greenland and the Exploration of North America, ca. AD 1000–1500*. Palo Alto, CA: Stanford University Press.

Sutherland, Patricia D., Peter H. Thompson, and Patricia A. Hunt. 2015. "Evidence of Early Metalworking in Arctic Canada." *Geoarchaeology* 30.1 (Jan/Feb): 74–78.

L'Anse aux Meadows

In 1961, archaeologists discovered the remains of an 11th-century Viking settlement at L'Anse aux Meadows, Newfoundland, Canada. This site represented the first evidence from material culture that the stories of Scandinavian travel to North America (found in Icelandic *Vinland Sagas*) were based on real travel.

Norse voyages in Vinland (so named because the land was far enough south for grape vines to grow) took them south following the St. Lawrence River. Situated at the tip of Newfoundland at the mouth of the Gulf of Saint Lawrence, L'Anse would have marked the jumping-off point between Vinland and the North Atlantic.

L'Anse aux Meadows itself was a place where ships could be hauled ashore and repaired for the voyage home to Scandinavia. The site was a base and winter camp for exploring regions farther away from Greenland, and for repairing ships for spring voyages back to the Vikings' native lands. The new land in North America was too far from home bases in Iceland and Scandinavia to make large-scale settlement an option, because Viking settlement colonies in the North Atlantic depended heavily on trade to sustain themselves. In addition to the distance, another reason was that the land was far from empty—it was occupied by indigenous peoples who resisted the establishment of permanent settlements in their territory.

The Norse site, fully excavated in the 1970s, included three complexes, each with dwellings and workshops. Although the major purpose of the buildings was to serve as winter living quarters for the whole group, each complex housed specialized craftsmen. The blacksmiths lived in the complex closest to the brook, smelting bog iron ore (impure iron found in bogs and swamps) in a furnace and smithing the resulting iron into finished objects in a forge. The furnace itself essentially was a pit lined with clay and topped by a frame of large stones. The quality of the production was not impressive: 80 percent of the iron stayed in the slag. This iron was sufficient for making the needed iron objects—mostly nails or rivets for ship repair.

The second building complex was home to carpenters, whose wood debris from smoothing and trimming logs and planks with metal tools was found in the bog below this area. There also were broken and discarded objects, including what was probably a floorboard from a small Norse boat. The third complex held the final major specialized activity: boat and ship repair. Here, excavators found many damaged rivets that had been removed from boats to be replaced with new ones forged in the smithy in the first complex.

Courtney Luckhardt

Further Reading

Ingstand, Helge. 2001. *The Viking Discovery of America: The Excavation of a Norse Settlement in L'Anse aux Meadows, Newfoundland.* St. John's, NF: Breakwater.

Kay, Janet E. 2012. *The Norse in Newfoundland: A Critical Examination of Archaeological Research at the Norse Site at L'Anse aux Meadows, Newfoundland.* Oxford: Archaeopress.

Magnusson, Magnus, and Herman Pálson (trans.). 1965. *The Vinland Sagas, The Norse Discovery of America. Graelendinga Saga and Eirik's Saga.* New York: Penguin.

Viking Longship

Scandinavians created a shipbuilding tradition independent from the rest of Europe by the eighth century. The ships they built were the most important means of maritime transport for the Vikings, as well as being embodiments of elite wealth and power. The Viking longship was an innovation in shipbuilding. Its ability to both cross the open ocean and sail up rivers made it ideal for staging raids. The longships earned their name because they could be built long relative to their widths—often at a five-to-one or six-to-one ratio.

The ships were "clinker built," meaning that they were constructed by laying the keel (the central spine of a ship) and then assembling a shell from slightly overlapping strakes (planks), riveting the strakes together to create a strong watertight hull. The ships had a single mast with a square sail, as well as oars and rowing benches for manual propulsion. The draught of the ships often was quite shallow, allowing the ships to sail up rivers far inland.

The Vikings built their ships with relatively simple tools. Trees were felled with long-handled axes and the trunks were split with wedges driven in with hammers and mallets. The planks were shaped using short-shafted T-shaped broad axes, and heat was used to bend the planks into shape to form the shell. Nothing is known of the measuring devices used, although scholars assume that marked strings or sticks were used. The clinker construction needed iron rivets, which require only simple smithing techniques, but the ships did have anchors as well, which were likely the largest and most advanced objects made by blacksmiths in the Viking Age.

Evidence about Viking longships has been considerably advanced in the past few decades with the development of the subdiscipline of maritime and underwater archaeology. The Skuldelev ships were the first Viking ships to be excavated underwater in Roskilde Fjord, Denmark, in the early 1960s (now the site of the Viking Ship Museum, which also houses the longest Viking ship yet discovered, the 37-meter *Roskilde* 6). Viking ships had been found buried on land, however; most famously the Gokstad ship, which was found in a burial mound in Norway in 1880. New technology has improved scholarly understanding of these ships immensely, including dendrochronological (tree-ring) dating, which precisely dated the Gokstad ship to 895–900 CE.

Viking longships and shipbuilding techniques spread rapidly in early medieval northern Europe, especially in the places most directly affected by Viking raiding

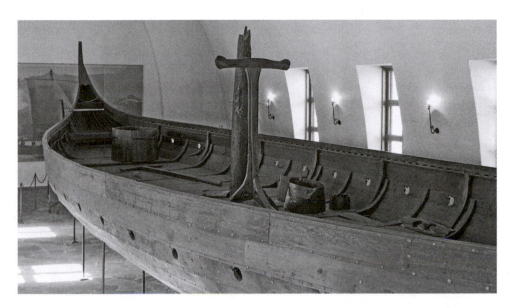

Gokstad longship on display at the Viking Ship Museum in Oslo, Norway. Discovered in 1880 at a burial site in Norway, scientists have dated the Gokstad ship to the ninth century CE. (Natalia Rumyantseva/Dreamstime.com)

and settlement, including the British Isles and the coasts of Normandy and Frisia on the continent.

Courtney Luckhardt

Further Reading

Bill, Jan. 2001. "Ships and Seamanship." In *The Oxford Illustrated History of the Vikings*. Peter Sawyer (ed.). Oxford: Oxford University Press, 182–201.

Crumlin-Pederson, Ole. 2010. *Archaeology and the Sea in Scandinavia and Britain: A Personal Account*. Roskilde, Denmark. Viking Ship Museum.

Vikings

Between the late 790s, when the first recorded Viking raid on Europe occurred, until about the end of the 11th century, medieval Scandinavians raided, traded, and settled in many parts of the European mainland, from Ireland to Constantinople. The term "Viking" generally was not used in the Middle Ages to describe Scandinavians—in Old Norse, "*víking*" is a verb, meaning "to travel abroad for adventure and profit." These Scandinavian seafarers were opportunists, raiding if a settlement appeared vulnerable, trading when it was well defended, and settling new lands when given (or taking) the chance.

The earliest recorded interactions of Vikings with Europeans were raids upon coastal and island monasteries and churches, starting with the raid at Lindisfarne ("Holy Island") off the coast of northeastern England in 793 CE. It was from accounts of these raids, written by churchmen who were their victims, that the Vikings gained their reputation as marauders and barbarians. The Vikings did attack towns and monasteries, though they also exploited fears of attacks to extort bribes to go away and "make peace," and captured hostages for ransom money or to sell as slaves. Scholars have proposed various theories as to why the raids began. Most, however, argue that a lack of arable land and the population pressures within Scandinavia, combined with the economic disparity between Western Europe and Scandinavia, and political instability on the Continent, all played a part. Most important though was the technological innovation of the development of the Viking longship that allowed Scandinavians to both cross the oceans and travel up rivers. Opportunists that they were, the Vikings used their technology to press their advantage throughout the ninth and tenth centuries, raiding coastal settlements in the west, including Britain, Ireland, Francia, the Netherlands, and Spain, as well as in the east, in the Baltic, Russia, Slavic lands, and the Black Sea. They even attacked Constantinople, but were unsuccessful. Scandinavians often lost pitched battles and the Franks and Anglo-Saxons built bridges and other defensive fortifications around towns as deterrents. Likewise, the Vikings could not maintain their technological advantage over the long term. By the 11th century, the Franks and others had adapted Scandinavian ship technology to their own ends.

Raids were not the Vikings' only methods for gaining the wealth of mainland Europe. The foundation of "*wics*" (trading centers) in the North Atlantic in the eighth century allowed for early contact, providing new markets for Scandinavian raw materials and whetting the Viking appetite for luxury finished goods from Europe and the Mediterranean. These early settlements also provided a model of centralized trade and urban development that the Scandinavians imported to their own lands, as the first towns in Scandinavia were founded as wics circa 800 CE, including Ribe in Denmark, Birka in Sweden, and the recently excavated Kaupang in Norway. The Vikings also exported these ideas about centralized trading settlements into lands they explored that did not have towns or cities. Dublin, Ireland, was founded by Vikings, as was the earliest town in Russia, Staraya Ladoga (near modern St. Petersburg), founded circa 753 CE. Scandinavians explored the rivers and waterways of Eastern Europe, founding Novgorod and Kiev, multi-ethnic cities of Scandinavians, Slavs, Bulgars, and Byzantine Greeks, which attracted traders from the Abbasid caliphate in Baghdad, as well.

Over time, the Vikings settled in the territories with which they raided and traded. In the west, this began in the early ninth century when Vikings set up winter camps at the mouths of key rivers from Thanet on the Thames River in Britain to Noirmoutier at the mouth of the Loire in France. Initially these bases were convenient spots from which to launch raids inland in early spring, but soon Scandinavians settled permanently in these territories, such as the Danelaw in eastern England, which came under direct Viking rule, and had its own law codes and coinage. Similarly, in 911 CE a group of Vikings led by Rollo settled in Normandy with the permission of the Frankish kings who hoped that these settlements would protect inland Frankish territories from raids. Scandinavians largely assimilated into the local cultures, intermarrying with native women, converting to Christianity, and speaking local languages. Scandinavians also settled the uninhabited islands of the North Atlantic, including the Faroe Islands and Iceland circa 870 CE. Although they kept their Scandinavian language in these new territories, it was not only Scandinavians who settled there. Recent DNA evidence from Iceland has shown that even though most of the male settlers were Scandinavian, most of the female settlers were from Celtic lands (Ireland, Scotland) and likely came as concubines and slaves.

The 11th century generally is considered the end of the "Viking Age." Although it is true that, following a succession of weak Anglo-Saxon kings, King Cnut the Great (ca. 985–1035 CE) conquered England, creating a North Sea Empire which in 1016 combined the lands of Denmark, Norway, and England under his leadership. King Cnut married Emma of Normandy, the widow of the previous king, thus preserving the alliance between those lands. Upon Cnut's death in 1035, the empire collapsed into its constituent parts. In 1066 CE, the tripartite struggle for rule over England came to a head. Harald Hardrada of Norway invaded Britain from the north, but was defeated by the Anglo-Saxon king, Harold Godwinson of Wessex, at the Battle of Stamford Bridge. Just three weeks later, Harold Godwinson himself was defeated at the Battle of Hastings in the south, as he attempted to repulse a second invasion, this one by William the Conqueror of Normandy, who thereafter completed the "Norman Conquest" of England. The Normans—French-speaking descendants of the 10th-century Viking settlers led by Rollo—settled England, adding to the melting pot of Germanic, Celtic, and Scandinavian peoples already living there. In the Scandinavian homelands, the local kings and their followers converted to Christianity, which brought them into closer social and cultural alignment with the rest of Europe. In the 11th and 12th centuries, the Scandinavians for the first time wrote down the sagas and myths associated with their raiding, trading, and settling days, creating important literary and historical traditions of their ancestors' seafaring past.

Courtney Luckhardt

Further Reading

Haywood, John. 1995. *Penguin Historical Atlas of the Vikings*. New York: Penguin.

Sawyer, Peter. 2001. *The Oxford Illustrated History of the Vikings*. Oxford: Oxford University Press.

Smiley, Jane, and Robert Kellogg et al. 2001. *The Sagas of the Icelanders*. New York: Penguin.

Somerville, Angus A., and R. Andrew McDonald (eds.). 2014. *The Viking Age: A Reader*, 2nd ed. Toronto: University of Toronto Press.

ROMANS AND BYZANTIUM

The men and women who lived in the Late Roman Empire called themselves "*Romanoi*" (Greek: "Romans"), though modern scholars call them "Byzantines" to distinguish them from the Romans of the classical, Latin-speaking ancient empire. Though the Byzantines spoke Greek in their capital of Constantinople (modern-day Istanbul, Turkey), they saw themselves as direct descendants of the Romans, and inheritors of the glory of Rome. The Byzantine Empire in the eastern Mediterranean Sea lasted for more than 1,500 years. Its capital at Constantinople stood in a strategically vital location—the intersection of Europe and Asia where the Mediterranean and the Black Seas meet, linked by the Bosporus Strait—and this location facilitated both Byzantine naval power and trade.

Trade and Exchange

Byzantine imperial trade dominated the maritime and land routes that surrounded Constantinople, maintaining control over lucrative markets and ports all over the Mediterranean and Black Seas, as well as the inland rivers that fed these bodies of water. Constantinople itself attracted foreign merchants from Europe, North Africa, and the Near East. The Byzantine government taxed merchants and their goods to control the export and import of valuable goods in and out of the empire, including silk. Although these customs duties did provide revenue, often a standard 10-percent duty, the most important source of governmental revenue was the land tax. Constantinople was by far the largest and most important Christian trading port throughout the early medieval period, with Syrian, Russian, Venetian and other merchants staying for months at a time. Each group was housed in its own section of the city with their own houses of worship—Arab traders stayed in lodging near local mosques, Jewish traders near their own synagogues, and European merchants stayed near Latin churches.

Evidence of Byzantines' maritime trading activity can be seen in the material culture as well. For example, the Yassi Ada wreck is a 70-foot-long cargo ship that sank just off the coast in the Aegean Sea—in what are now Turkish waters—with its goods aboard. The Yassi Ada ship sank in 626 CE, datable given the 16 gold coins and 50 copper coins recovered, all issued by Emperor Heraclius (575–641 CE), with the last coin dated to 625–26, which was at the tail end of a war between the Byzantine and Persian Empires. The ship sank with 900 amphorae, 700 globular jars, as well as cylindrical amphorae, that carried low-grade wine for soldiers. Based on the various Christian finds aboard, including a bronze censer (incense burner) topped with a cross and typically used in Byzantine Christian worship services, the ship itself was likely owned by the church. The connection between trade goods (such as wine), military troop supplies during war, and the church ownership indicates an interesting overlap between economic, political, military, and religious life in the eastern Mediterranean during the period.

Military and Naval Travel

This overlap also is seen in the way that Byzantine government officials regulated maritime trade for strategic military reasons. No products determined to be essential to the state were supposed to be exported. This included supplies of gold and salt, iron for making weapons or tools, wood for shipbuilding, as well as elements (likely naphtha) that made up the recipe for the unique Byzantine incendiary weapon, "Greek fire." An important part of Byzantine naval dominance involved advanced technology. The "dromon," a large galley ship, was the preeminent warship of the era. Propelled by both oars and sails, it was nimble, yet strong—a perfect offensive fighting vessel. The Byzantines also used Greek fire (a liquid petroleum-based incendiary weapon) shot from flamethrowers from the prows of dromons.

The role of the navy in defending the empire was especially important by the seventh century, during Byzantium's wars with both the Sasanian Persian Empire (602–628 CE) and the Arabs who conquered Syria, Egypt, and North Africa (634–698 CE). Although much of the fighting occurred on land, the Byzantine navy was the dominant force in the eastern Mediterranean, proving decisive in keeping the empire together (though vastly shrunken) during a century of external conflict. Constantinople itself, surrounded by water on three sides, depended on the navy for defense. During the Persian Wars (602–628 CE), the Persian army camped directly across the Bosphorus Strait from the old city at Chalcedon (now the neighborhood of Kadiköy, a suburb of modern Istanbul) to besiege the city in 626 CE. The Persians lacked a navy and depended on their Slavic allies to provide transport across the water. The Slavs' ships proved no match for the Byzantine navy, however, which destroyed them before they neared the Golden Horn.

The victory of Emperor Heraclius over the Persians proved to be pyrrhic, as it weakened both empires. Combined with a devastating plague that swept the empire, this allowed Arabs to conquer vast swathes of land, and conquer the Sasanian Persian Empire completely by 651 CE. The Byzantine Empire itself lost about two-thirds of its territory in the seventh century, including Jerusalem in the Holy

Land, and Alexandria in Egypt. Despite this loss of land, however, the sea still belonged to the Byzantines. Indeed, the tide of naval warfare did not begin to turn in favor of the Arabs until they captured Alexandria and other Byzantine ports and used these to build their own fleet. Arab forces then captured the eastern Mediterranean islands of Cyprus, Rhodes, and Kos, and defeated the Byzantine navy—commanded by Emperor Constans II himself—at the Battle of the Masts (655 CE), fought near Finike, a port on the southern Anatolian coast. This was not the end of Arab-Byzantine naval conflict, but rather the beginning, as the two empires battled for supremacy over the eastern Mediterranean trade routes through the 11th century, when the Crusades tilted the balance of power in favor of Europe.

After the seventh century, the Byzantine Empire turned its attention northwards, coming in contact with Scandinavian Viking raiders (the Rus) and traders for the first time in the ninth century in what is now Russia. The Rus were growing their trade routes along the Dnieper and Volga Rivers, coming into contact with Byzantines in the Black Sea, and Muslims on the Caspian. They founded a capital at Kiev (now modern-day Ukraine) in 882 CE, a multiethnic city with Scandinavians, Slavs, Finns, Balts, Khazars, and Bulgars. Kievan Rus war bands raided along the Black Sea, but the Byzantine navy easily protected Constantinople itself from attack. In 912 CE, the Byzantine emperor and the king of the Kievan Rus negotiated a treaty that laid out a series of trading rights, and by 950 CE there were huge flotillas between Kiev and Constantinople importing raw materials from the north, such as timber, amber, furs, and slaves, and exporting finished products from the south, from jewelry to fine glassware. In 961 CE, the strengthened Byzantine fleet recaptured Crete (lost to Muslim raiders from Spain in the 820s). The Byzantine navy again dominated the Aegean Sea and supported the empire's dramatic resurgence in the late 10th century.

Mission and Pilgrimage

Trade and military advantage were not the only reasons that Byzantine people traveled the sea. Religious travel, including pilgrimage and mission, were important motivators for travelers from the Byzantine Empire.

Pilgrims were motivated to travel by the power of a holy place, person, or relic, to venerate it, ask for divine aid, or discharge a religious obligation. Often these holy sites were accompanied by monastic religious communities made up of both locals and religious travelers who wished to remain at the holy places. By the fifth century in the Byzantine Empire, monasteries were both an urban and rural phenomenon, with many monasteries being founded in urban centers such as Constantinople and Jerusalem, but also in isolated places, for instance,

St. Catherine's in the Sinai Peninsula and St. Simeon Stylites outside Aleppo, Syria. Until the Arab conquests, these holy sites were under Byzantine control, and even afterwards Christian pilgrimage continued but in reduced numbers. After the seventh-century conquests, one of the most important sites of Byzantine religious travel and settlement was the monasteries of Mount Athos, or Holy Mountain, in the Aegean, in what is now northern Greece, accessible mainly via ship. In an imperial decree dated to 885 CE, the Holy Mountain is proclaimed a place of monks, and no laymen or farmers or cattle-breeders were allowed to settle there. In 958 CE, the monk Athanasios the Athonite (ca. 920–1003 CE) arrived. He later built the monastery of Great Lavra with the support of his patron, Emperor Nicephorus Phocas. It is still the largest and most prominent of the 20 monasteries existing on Mount Athos today. Great Lavra and the other holy sites enjoyed the protection of the emperors of the Byzantine Empire during the following centuries, becoming important centers of spiritual life and pilgrimage.

In addition to trading to maintain a positive relationship with the Kievan Rus, Byzantines thought that the best way to deal with them was not to fight them, but rather to convert them to Christianity and make them a part of Christendom, rather than attackers from outside of it. To this end, the Byzantines sent missionaries to the Scandinavians and Slavs, to convert them to Orthodox Christianity. Emperor Leo VI (886–912 CE) wrote an account of the missionizing efforts of his father, Emperor Basil I (867–86 CE). Basil persuaded the Slavs

> to change their old ways and, having Grecized [*graikosas*] them and subjected them to rulers on the Roman [Byzantine] pattern, and having honored them with baptism, he . . . schooled them in fighting against the peoples hostile to the Romans . . . on account of this he freed the Romans from care about the rebellions that had often been mounted by Slavs . . . (Leo VI, Tactica, XVIII.101)

This process of Slavic conversion was first taken on by two missionaries, Saint Cyril and Saint Methodius, who in 862 CE traveled to Moravia (now the Czech Republic) to evangelize the local population, primarily by creating a translation of the Bible into Old Church Slavonic, the first written Slavic language. To do so, Cyrul and Methodius created a new alphabet—Glagolitic—which is the precursor to Cyrillic, the alphabet of Russian and other modern Slavic languages. They also created a new Christian liturgy in Slavonic, based on the Greek liturgy in use in Constantinople. The Byzantine state attempted to bring other northern peoples and places into their political and religious sphere by sending missionaries to King Boris I of Bulgaria (852–889 CE) in 865 CE. The missionary travels of churchmen on the great rivers systems of Eastern Europe, from the Danube to the Dnieiper, allowed the Byzantine Empire to spread its religious, economic, military, and cultural reach in new areas.

With this new hegemony, the Byzantines turned their attention to the Aegean and Black Seas and their riverine hinterlands, a dramatic change over time in the geographical sphere of the Byzantine Empire's maritime activities between 300 and 1000 CE.

Courtney Luckhardt

Further Reading

Gregory, Timothy E. 2010. *A History of Byzantium,* 2nd ed. Oxford: Wiley-Blackwell.

Hattendorf, John B., and Richard W. Unger (eds.). 2003. *War at Sea in the Middle Ages and Renaissance*. Woodbridge, UK: Boydell Press.

Herrin, Judith. 2009. *Byzantium: The Surprising Life of a Medieval Empire*. Princeton: Princeton University Press.

Horden, Peregrine, and Nicholas Purcell. 2000. *The Corrupting Sea: A Study of Mediterranean History*. Oxford: Wiley-Blackwell.

Laiou, Angeliki. 2007. *The Economic History of Byzantium, from the Seventh Through the Fifteenth Century*. Washington DC: Dumbarton Oaks.

Pryor, John, and Elizabeth Jeffreys. 2006. *The Age of the Dromōn: The Byzantine Navy, ca. 500–1204*. Leiden: Brill.

Constantinople

Emperor Constantine I founded the city of Constantinople in 330 CE as a "New Rome," shifting the political and economic heart of the Roman Empire to the east. The city (now modern Istanbul, Turkey) is surrounded on three sides by the waters of the Bosporus Strait, which link the Mediterranean and Black Seas, and the continents of Europe and Asia. These features helped protect the city and also made it a center of trade by land and sea. Constantinople was built on an imperial scale, with a great hippodrome for horse and chariot racing, imperial palaces with statues and mosaics, Christian churches and basilicas, aqueducts and cisterns, great walls to protect the city from attack, and deep natural harbors and ports to berth the ships that connected Constantinople to Europe, North Africa, Central Asia, Anatolia, and Persia.

Constantinople's great wealth and power was built upon the city's connections to the sea and its key geographical place in the European and Asian trade and transportation routes. As the Byzantine historian Procopius put it circa 550 CE,

> Besides the city's other blessings the sea is set most beautifully all about it, forming curving bays, contracting into narrow straits, and spreading into a great open sea; and thus it makes the city exceptionally beautiful, and offers the quiet shelter of harbors to navigators, thereby abundantly providing the city with the necessities of life and making it rich in all useful things. (Procopius, 57)

Archaeologists recently excavated the city's major early medieval harbor, the Port of Theodosius, unearthing 37 ships dating from the fifth to eleventh centuries, including cargo boats, transport vessels, small lighters, fishing boats, and naval galleys, along with thousands of artifacts.

Between 330 and 602 CE, Constantinople accumulated wealth from trade and imperial taxation, funding harbors, ports, city fortifications, sea walls, as well as naval ships and technology. Constantinople's growth and its secure position both geographically and politically was a main factor in the survival of the Byzantine Empire after the military crises of the seventh century, including a devastating war with the Sasanian Persian Empire between 602 and 628 CE. Although the Byzantines won that protracted conflict, they were severely weakened and could not withstand the onslaught of the Muslim Arab armies, who conquered two-thirds of Byzantine territory between 644 and 698 CE. The landlocked Persian Empire fell completely to the Arabs in 651 CE, but the Byzantine Empire survived thanks to its naval power and impregnable capital at Constantinople. In a push to take over the Byzantine Empire completely, the Arab armies laid siege to the city by both land and sea between 717 and 718 CE. The Byzantines defeated the blockade of Constantinople with a superior navy, allowing the city to be supplied from the Black Sea region, while simultaneously cutting off supply sources for the Arab army encamped at the westward land walls. This marked the last major Arab assault on Constantinople. The city's superb maritime location, impressive fortifications and harbors, and strong navy allowed it to endure as the core of the Byzantine Empire for another 700 years.

Courtney Luckhardt

Further Reading

Haldon, J. F. 1990. *Byzantium in the Seventh Century: The Transformation of a Culture.* Cambridge: Cambridge University Press.

Harris, Jonathan. 2007. *Constantinople: Capital of Byzantium.* London: Hambledon Continuum.

Kocabaş, Ufuk. 2015. "The Yenikapı Byzantine-Era Shipwrecks, Istanbul, Turkey: A Preliminary Report and Inventory of the 27 Wrecks Studied by Istanbul University." *The International Journal of Nautical Archaeology* 44(1): 5–38.

Procopius, *On Buildings*, Loeb Classical Library, no. 343. H.B. Dewing (trans.). Cambridge, MA: Harvard University Press, 1940.

Dromon

The dromon was a large galley ship in active use in the Mediterranean by the Byzantine Empire during late antiquity and the early Middle Ages, ca. 500–1100 CE. These vessels were the preeminent naval warships of the era. Though they were valuable for carrying cargo, their principal use was for fighting. One of the key features of these warships was their propulsion by two banks of oars, one above the other, with men sitting on their own benches. In addition to the primary oars, the dromons also moved via lateen (triangular sail), which likely had been adopted from the Arab world. Another key feature of the dromon was its offensive fighting capability. Dromons were equipped with bow spurs to smash the oars of opposing vessels and tubes for carrying their primary weapon: Greek fire. Greek fire was a natural petroleum-based incendiary that ignited when pumped over flame and could not be extinguished by water. Although the formula was a closely held secret by Byzantine elites (and was lost during the Ottoman conquest of Constantinople), modern scholars think that it was similar to napalm.

Dromons were an integral part of the Byzantine dominance of the eastern Mediterranean Sea through the 12th century. As Byzantine politician Nikephoros Ouranos put it in his naval treatise, the *Peri Thalassomachias* ("*On Fighting Sea*"),

> It is appropriate that dromons should be built that are adequate for fighting the enemy at sea . . . let the dromon have suitable construction, so that it is not sluggish when sailing and is not broken up by waves in a gale and, when struck by the enemy, proves stronger than them. (Pryor and Jeffreys, 573)

Nautical archaeology has provided valuable information recently on the dromon and Byzantine galley warships. A military galley from the sixth century has been excavated off the coast of Cefalù, Sicily, and contained swords, iron tools, stone cannon balls, and an iron pipe set in a U-shaped cavity, which might have been a flamethrower for Greek fire. Even more recently the excavations at the ancient Port of Theodosius in modern Yenikapi, Istanbul, have yielded four galley warships that will certainly yield new information about the important warships of the Byzantine Empire.

Courtney Luckhardt

Further Reading

Haldon, John. 2006. " 'Greek Fire' Revisited: Recent and Current Research." In E. Jeffreys (ed.). *Byzantine Style, Religion, and Civilization: In Honour of Sir Steven Runciman*. Cambridge: Cambridge University Press, 290–325.

Kingsley, Sean. 2004. *Barbarian Seas: Late Rome to Islam*. London: Periplus.

Kocabaş, Ufuk. 2015. "The Yenikapı Byzantine-Era Shipwrecks, Istanbul, Turkey: A Preliminary Report and Inventory of the 27 Wrecks Studied by Istanbul University." *The International Journal of Nautical Archaeology* 44(1): 5–38.

Pryor, John and Elizabeth Jeffreys. 2006. *The Age of the Dromōn: the Byzantine Navy, ca. 500–1204*. Leiden.

Greek Fire

The most significant innovation of the Byzantine naval warfare in the early Middle Ages was Greek fire. Invented in the seventh century, Greek fire was a natural petroleum-based incendiary that ignited when pumped over flame and could not be extinguished by water. It was best fought by using sand or vinegar. The exact formula was a closely held secret of Byzantine elites and was lost during the Ottoman conquest of Constantinople. The major ingredients likely included naphtha, petroleum, sulfur, and pitch (perhaps in varying combinations).

Greek fire was used defensively, particularly in sieges, but is most famous for use aboard Byzantine dromons. Some dromons were equipped with a "*siphon*" (often translated as "flamethrower"), a complex apparatus that included a long tube of wood lined with bronze and attached to an air pump. As the Byzantine politician Nikephoros Ouranos said around 1000 CE,

> The dromon should have a *siphon* in the front of the prow, bound well in bronze as is the custom, so that processed fire can be thrown through it against the enemy. Above this *siphon* there should be planks, so that marines can stand on it to fight the enemy attacking them from the prow, or so that they can throw whatever weapons they want and can devise from there, not at the prow and stern of the enemy, but at the whole enemy ship. (Pryor and Jeffreys, 573)

> *Source:* Pryor, John H. and Elizabeth M. Jeffreys. 2006. *The Age of the Dromon: The Byzantine Navy, c. 500–1204*. Leiden: Brill.

Rhodian Sea Law

In the seventh and eighth centuries CE, the Byzantine Empire codified a collection of regulations governing maritime contracts and customs, called (in Latin) the *Lex Rhodia*, or (in English) the *Rhodian Sea Law*. Most of the laws dealt with compensation for damage or loss of goods at sea, ensuring that merchants received fixed amounts from the shipowners who had agreed to transport their wares. However, some of the laws did deal with broader issues of maritime commerce and life aboard ships in the Mediterranean and Black Seas.

The *Sea Law* emerged as the standard for resolving maritime disputes in the Mediterranean Sea. Byzantine merchants were involved in trade all over the region, including extensive commerce with Muslims in North Africa and the Levant, connecting to the trade routes of the Islamic, Central Asian, Indian, and East Asian worlds. Focused on maritime trade, the *Sea Law* helped regulate many aspects of these commercial relationships, including the rights of the owners of vessels, the rights of investors who might own shares of a particular voyage or ship, the obligations of the owner to his crew and vice versa, the duties of pilots who guided vessels into ports, the responsibilities of captains, owners, and crew in case of shipwreck or piracy, including the need to jettison cargo to save the ship in inclement weather.

The *Sea Law* itself was closely connected to other revisions of Roman law undertaken by the Byzantine emperors in the early medieval period, most notably the *Corpus Iuris Civilis* ("*Body of Civil Law*") that Emperor Justinian I (482–565 CE) revised in the sixth century. A section of the *Rhodian Sea Law*, preserved in Justinian's *Corpus*, states the mutual obligations involved in medieval maritime trade. "It is provided by the Rhodian Law that where merchandise is thrown overboard for the purpose of lightening a ship, what has been lost for the benefit of all must be made up by the contribution of all" (*Digest of Justinian*, Book XIV, Title 2).

The *Rhodian Sea Law* had a major influence on the maritime laws of Europe in later periods, especially the Italian city-states of Venice and Genoa, as well as other Mediterranean ports throughout the later medieval and early modern periods.

Courtney Luckhardt

Further Reading

Ashburner, Walter. 1909. *The Rhodian Sea-Law*. Oxford: Clarendon.

Maridaki-Karatza, Olga. 2002. "Legal Aspects of the Financing of Trade." In Angeliki Laiou, *Economic History of Byzantium*, vol. 3, 1097–1112. Washington, DC: Dumbarton Oaks.

Watson, Alan. 1998. *The Digest of Justinian*, vol. 1. Philadelphia: University of Pennsylvania Press.

Zimmermann, Reinhard. 1996. *The Law of Obligations, Roman Foundations of the Civilian Tradition*. Oxford: Clarendon.

T-O Maps

Early medieval maps were not intended to be practical cartographical tools for navigation, topography, or geography, but rather illustrations depicting cosmography, designed to detail the general features of earth and heaven (creation and the cosmos) in a Christian worldview.

The earliest known of these medieval maps are T-O maps, so called because they show the three continents known to medieval people (Asia, Europe, and Africa) in a circular schematic divided into three parts in a T shape. Unlike modern maps, medieval maps were oriented towards the east. So, within the circle the top half shows Asia (the east), the bottom-left quarter shows Europe (north), and the bottom-right quarter Africa (south). In the center of the map is Jerusalem, seen by many authors as the literal geographic center of the world, following Psalm 73 in the Vulgate Bible, which says that God "created salvation in the middle of the earth." Despite the fact that these two-dimensional representations show the earth as a disk, medieval people, like their counterparts in antiquity, knew that the world was spherical. The idea that medieval people thought the world was flat is a myth introduced in the Victorian Era. Medieval people believed that the other half of the sphere was an uninhabited ocean, and depicted it as a larger circle surrounding all the landmasses in the central circle.

These T-O maps are found in many manuscripts, including those accompanying the encyclopedic text, the *Etymologies* of Isidore of Seville from the sixth century, as well as the illuminated *Beatus* map, found in copies of the *Commentary on the Apocalypse* by eighth-century Spanish monk, Beatus of Liébana.

Courtney Luckhardt

Further Reading

Lozovsky, Natalia. 2000. *"The Earth Is Our Book": Geographical Knowledge in the Latin West ca. 400–1000*. Ann Arbor: University of Michigan Press.

Russell, Jeffery Burton. 1991. *Inventing the Flat Earth: Columbus and Modern Historians*. Westport, CT: Praeger.

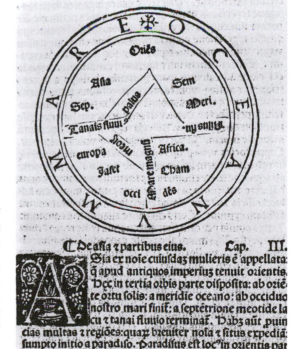

Mappa Mundi, Etymologiae, De Summo Bono, by Isidore of Seville (ca. 540–636), Peter Loslein edition, Venice, 1483. Within a circle, the top half shows Asia (the east), the bottom left quarter shows Europe (north), and the bottom right quarter Africa (south). (DeAgostini/Getty Images)

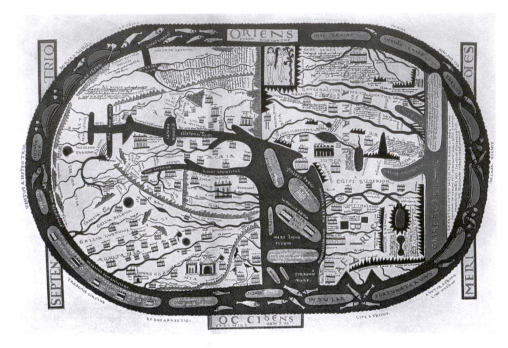

Beatus was a Spanish priest who died in 798 CE. He is credited as the originator of a world map whose style was copied from the 10th to the 13th centuries. This world map, modeled on the Beatus world map, is oriented with the East (Oriens) at the top and dates to around 1050 CE. It was drawn in the St. Sever Aquitanian monastery and is considered the most carefully executed and most detailed of all the Beatus maps. (Ivy Close Images/Alamy Stock Photo)

SOUTHEAST ASIA, POLYNESIA, AND THE PACIFIC

Covering approximately one-third of Earth's surface, the Pacific Ocean displays tremendous biological and human diversity. The nations and territories of the Pacific are home to nearly one-quarter of the world's languages, and the waters of this vast aquatic realm feature some of the planet's most species-rich ecosystems.

The 25,000 islands of the Pacific Basin experienced non-human and human colonization by air and water. For example, nearly 40 percent of Hawaiian plants reached the archipelago as seeds transported in the digestive tracts of birds. Other botanical arrivals, such as the coconut, dispersed across the Pacific through a combination of unassisted floatation and human carriage.

Humans entered the Western Pacific from Southeast Asia 40,000 to 50,000 years ago. The first group of these so-called "Austronesian" migrants arrived in Australia and New Guinea during a period of late Pleistocene glaciation when significant reductions in sea level exposed the "Sunda Shelf" and the "Sahul Shelf." The

Sunda Shelf encompassed the Malay Peninsula and the islands of Borneo, Java, and Sumatra, as well as smaller surrounding archipelagos. In places, only narrow oceanic straits—navigable by rudimentary rafts or dugout canoes—separated this peninsular extension of Asia from the Sahul Shelf, a mega-continent of dry land that included mainland Australia, Tasmania, New Guinea, Seram, Timor, and neighboring islands. New Guinea's mountainous terrain and Australia's immense terrestrial expanses help to explain the development of isolated hunter-gatherer societies, which exhibited striking linguistic and cultural variations after millennia of isolated existence. Throughout these regions, agrarian cultures also left durable legacies. In New Guinea, farmers domesticated one of the major species of sugar-cane (*Saccharum officinarum*) by 6000 BCE.

By approximately 30,000 years ago, Austronesians had reached Buka, the north-ernmost island in the Solomon chain. This migratory pulse represented the farthest eastward extent of early Pacific colonization in the region of Pleistocene human occupation known as Near Oceania.

The remainder of the Pacific Islands—often referred to as Remote Oceania—experienced much more recent settlement. For decades, archaeologists have known that human colonization of the South Pacific occurred relatively late in the chro-nology of global migrations. Even so, accumulating evidence supports a longer arc of Pacific Island colonization than previous theories had suggested. In 2011, re-searchers at Leeds University used mitochondrial DNA from current Polynesian populations to trace their ancestral lineages to travelers who began colonizing is-lands beyond New Guinea between 6,000 and 8,000 years ago. These findings undermined the prior hypothesis—known as the "Express Train Model"—that Pacific Islanders had arrived at the tail end of a migratory surge southeastward from Taiwan approximately 4,000 years ago.

This new evidence built upon earlier revelations about the eastward paths of several settlement stages in Pacific world history. During a 1952 excavation on the Foué peninsula of Grande Terre, New Caledonia's main island, archaeologists dis-covered distinctively decorated earthenware potsherds, which suggested the exis-tence of a previously unknown civilization. The highly mobile Lapita were an early Pacific Ocean people that flourished between 1600 BCE to 500 BCE. Their seafaring voyages represented the first eastward stage of human migration into Remote Oceania. In addition to fishing and hunting, and raising domesticated chickens, dogs, and pigs, the Lapita were intimately familiar with Melanesian tree crops, including coconut (*Cocos nucifera*), Tahitian Chestnut (*Inocarpus fa-giferus*), *Canarium* almond, and Vi apple (*Spondias dulcis*). Lapita reliance on flaked-obsidian tools, shell fishhooks, and ground-stone adzes left behind unique and durable traces of their material culture. From their emergence onwards, Lapita communities became increasingly integrated into a far-reaching trade network that eventually became the gateways to further exploration into the Central Pacific.

The settlement of East Polynesia—a geographical triangle consisting of Hawai'i at the northernmost tip, Rapa Nui (Easter Island) at the eastern point of its base, and Aotearoa (New Zealand) at the western point of its base—occurred relatively recently in world history. Colonization of the 15 archipelagos that comprise this region was swift and particularly significant, given that the voyagers had no metal tools or navigation instruments. Instead, they relied on wooden canoes fashioned with implements of bone, coral, and stone. European accounts made centuries later suggest the long-term accumulations of sophisticated engineering skills that were displayed in such seaworthy watercraft. After visiting the Society Islands in 1774, Spanish captain and explorer José Andía y Varela wrote, "These canoes are as fine forward as the edge of a knife, so that they travel faster than the swiftest of our vessels; and they are marvelous, not only in this respect, but for their smartness in shifting from one tack to the other" (Andía y Varela 1914, 2:283).

Travelling aboard double-hulled oceangoing canoes, settlers arrived in Samoa by around 800 BCE. Colonists settled the central Society Islands between 1025 and 1120 CE, and they reached Hawai'i, Rapa Nui (Easter Island), and other islands between 1190 and 1290 CE. As of 1000 CE, New Zealand had yet to be inhabited by Māori people, who did not arrive until between 1250 and 1300 CE. At this point, humans had colonized the region that would eventually become known as Polynesia.

"Polynesia" was not an indigenous term. Eighteenth-century French writer Charles de Brosses combined the Greek words *poly* ("many") and *nēsos* ("island") when introducing the concept of *Polynésie* to readers of his *Histoire des navigations aux terres australes* (*History of Navigations to the Southern Lands*, 1756). Initially, Europeans applied this expansive notion to all of the Pacific Islands. Following French expeditions to the Pacific in the late 1820s, however, explorer Jules Dumont d'Urville contrived a geographical division of the South Pacific into Melanesia, Micronesia (a term he borrowed from travel writer Grégoire Louis Domeny de Rienzi), Polynesia, and Malaysia.

The Pacific region's indigenous inhabitants have long contested outsiders' representations of their homelands. In his influential essay "Our Sea of Islands," Fijian-Tongan writer Epeli Hau'ofa contended,

> There is a gulf of difference between viewing the Pacific as "islands in a far sea" and as "a sea of islands." The first emphasizes dry surfaces in a vast ocean far from the centres of power. When you focus this way you stress the smallness and remoteness of the islands. The second is a more holistic perspective in which things are seen in the totality of their relationships. (Hau'ofa 1993, 7)

The historical routes of Pacific migratory surges have elicited similarly spirited debates. In 1947 CE, Norwegian adventurer and ethnographer Thor Heyerdahl questioned the orthodoxy of the East Asian origins of Polynesian settlement. In an attempt to prove that ancient navigators had followed prevailing trade winds and journeyed westward from the Americas, Heyerdahl and five crewmembers set sail in a handmade balsawood raft, *Kon-Tiki*. After 101 days at sea, they had travelled 4,300 miles from Peru to the Tuamotu Islands in the South Pacific. Heyerdahl claimed that the *Kon-Tiki*'s successful journey demonstrated the feasibility of the settlement of Polynesia by South American mariners. Most subsequent scholarship has rejected Heyerdahl's conclusions about the likelihood of such migratory trajectories. Linguistic, ethnographic, and ethnobotanical evidence, along with genetic and archaeological data refute Heyerdahl's theory.

Comparable to Heyerdahl in his iconoclastic bravado was New Zealand civil-servant-turned-historian Andrew Sharp. In his 1956 book, *Ancient Voyagers in Polynesia*, Sharp contended that the settlement of Polynesia had been both accidental and sporadic due to the primitive sailing and navigation technologies of Pacific Islanders. Sharp claimed that westerly storms had driven voyagers off course, leading to the discoveries of islands through inadvertent landfalls that led to settlement without further attempts to return home. This hypothesis amounted to a wholesale attack on the theory of deliberate migration in the remote Pacific.

Among the most significant challenges to Sharp's assertions came from experimental, real-life voyages. Field studies of traditional Polynesian navigation methods undertaken by anthropologist Ben Finney and adventurer David Henry Lewis in the 1960s were among the first such trials. During the following decade, Hawaiian writer and artist Herb Kawainui Kāne (1928–2011) built and sailed *Hokule'a*, a full-scale replica of a *wa'a kaulua*, a traditional double-hulled ocean canoe. Kane, who co-founded the Polynesian Voyaging Society with Finney, was part of the Second Hawaiian Renaissance, a movement that aimed to inspire renewed interest in the history of the Hawaiian peoples and their long-term seafaring prowess. In 1973, Kane wrote, "if a voyaging canoe were built and sailed today, it would function as a cultural catalyst and inspire the revival of almost-forgotten aspects of Hawaiian life" (Kāne 1973, 476). *Hokule'a*'s inaugural 1976 voyage from Hawai'i to Tahiti relied on the traditional knowledge of Micronesian navigator Mau Piailug (1932–2010 CE), a master mariner who taught non-instrument way-finding techniques to generations of Pacific Islanders.

A second set of experiments, using data-driven simulations, also called into question Sharp's assumptions. In 1973, computer scientist Michael Levison collaborated with geographers R. Gerard Ward and John W. Webb on an innovative computer model of Polynesian settlement. Their research effectively undermined the notion that Rapa Nui could have been reached by accidental drift from another Polynesian location.

Two decades later, in *The Prehistoric Exploration and Colonization of the Pacific* (1992), University of Auckland anthropologist Geoffrey Irwin augmented these earlier findings and drew upon his own extensive research when asserting, "The pioneering computer simulation by Levison, Ward and Webb (1973) proved that the remote Pacific was settled with intention. This study builds on their conclusion by approximating navigational method within the context of a continuing and rational tradition of ocean exploration and colonization" (Irwin 1992, 173).

Despite these conceptual advances to our understanding of Pacific World migrations, many topics await further exploration. Provocative new evidence indicates the possibility of extensive pre-Columbian exchanges in the Pacific World prior to Ferdinand Magellan's circumnavigation in the early 16th century and Captain James Cook's Pacific explorations in the late 18th century. In 1990, archaeologist Patrick Kirch found evidence of sweet potatoes in the Cook Islands dating back to 1000 CE. This confirmed the early introduction of these South American cultivars to central Polynesia long before European arrival. Likewise, recently published studies suggest that pre-Hispanic Mapuche peoples along South America's west coast experienced prolonged transpacific contact with Polynesian mariners. If it stands up to ongoing scientific scrutiny, chicken bone DNA taken from an archaeological site in southern Chile dated to the 14th century corroborates earlier "soft" evidence from linguistic cognates, similar material cultures, and analogous maritime technologies.

Edward D. Melillo

Further Reading

Andía y Varela, José [*Ship's Log*]. 1913–1916. In Bolton Glanvill Corney (ed.). *The Quest and Occupation of Tahiti by Emissaries of Spain During the Years 1772–76* (3 vols.). London: Hakluyt Society.

Carlquist, Sherwin. 1980. *Hawaiʻi: A Natural History*. Kauaʻi: Pacific Tropical Botanical Garden.

D'Arcy, Paul. 2006. *The People of the Sea: Environment, Identity, and History in Oceania*. Honolulu: University of Hawaiʻi Press.

Davis, Wade. 2009. *The Wayfinders: Why Ancient Wisdom Matters in the Modern World*. Toronto: House of Anasasi Press.

Gunn, Bee F., Luc Baudouin, and Kenneth M. Olsen. 2011. "Independent Origins of Cultivated Coconut (*Cocos nucifera* L.) in the Old World Tropics." *PLoS ONE* 6(6): e21143.

Hauʻofa, Epeli. 1993. "Our Sea of Islands." In *A New Oceania: Rediscovering Our Sea of Islands*. Vijay Naidu, Eric Waddell, and Epeli Hauʻofa (ed.). Suva: School of Social and Economic Development, The University of the South Pacific in association with Beake House, 2–16.

Heyerdahl, Thor. 1950. *The Kon-Tiki Expedition: By Raft Across the South Seas*. London: George Allen & Unwin.

Irwin, Geoffrey. 1992. *The Prehistoric Exploration and Colonization of the Pacific*. Cambridge, UK: Cambridge University Press.

Kāne, Herb Kawainui. 1976. "A Canoe Helps Hawai'i Recapture Her Past." *National Geographic Magazine* 149(4): 468–89.

Kirch, Patrick V. 1996. "Lapita and Its Aftermath: The Austronesian Settlement of Oceania." *Transactions of the American Philosophical Society* 86(5): 57–70.

Lewis, David. 1994. *We, the Navigators: The Ancient Art of Landfinding in the Pacific,* Revised ed. Honolulu: University of Hawai'i Press.

McNeill, John R. 1994. "Of Rats and Men: A Synoptic Environmental History of the Island Pacific." *Journal of World History* 5(2): 299–349.

Ramírez-Aliaga, José Miguel. 2011. "The Mapuche Connection." In *Polynesians in America: Pre-Columbian Contacts with the New World*. Terry L. Jones, Alice A. Storey, Elizabeth A. Matisoo-Smith, and José Miguel Ramírez-Aliaga (eds.). Lanham: AltaMira Press, 95–109.

Salesa, Damon Ieremia. 2012. "The World from Oceania." In *A Companion to World History*. Douglas Northrop (ed.). Chichester, UK: Wiley-Blackwell, 392–404.

Soares, Pedro et al. 2011. "Ancient Voyaging and Polynesian Origins." *American Journal of Human Genetics* 88(2): 239–47.

Wilmshurst, Janet M. et al. 2008. "Dating the Late Prehistoric Dispersal of Polynesians to New Zealand Using the Commensal Pacific Ra.," *Proceedings of the National Academy of Sciences of the United States* 105, no. 22: 7676–80.

Easter Island (Rapa Nui)

Rapa Nui—called "Easter Island" by Dutch navigator Jacob Roggeveen who encountered the remote island on Easter Sunday in 1722—holds a special place in the story of the Pacific. The tiny 64-square-mile island, some 2,300 miles off the coast of Chile, originally was discovered and settled sometime between 600–1200 CE by Polynesian explorers, probably from the Marquesas. As such, it represents a significant waypoint in traditional voyaging and human migration, lying upwind from the Marquesas in the prevailing trade wind circulation and presenting a very small landfall target in the large open ocean of the eastern Pacific.

Rapa Nui also is the eastern-most apex of the Polynesian Triangle, the farthest extent of ancient Pacific oceanic migration and colonization. This triangle stretches from Rapa Nui to Aoteroa (New Zealand) to Hawai'i, encompassing 16 million square miles and including the Marquesas, Samoa, French Polynesia, the Cook Islands, and Tonga. The Hawaiian voyaging canoe *Hokule'a* made a successful passage from the Marquesas via Pitcairn Island to Rapa Nui in 1999 using only traditional (non-instrument) navigation.

Most people are familiar with the monumental architecture of Rapa Nui, including ceremonial structures and platforms or *"ahu,"* and the hundreds of towering monolithic stone statues or "*moai*," stylized heads believed to portray the deified ancestors of the original inhabitants. This construction peaked around 1200 CE, when the population reached an estimated 12,000–15,000. This period of monumental architecture came to an end prior to western contact in 1722 and is attributed, in part, to deforestation and the environmental collapse of the island's ecosystem. The reasons for this collapse remain debated and include the overexploitation of resources, impacts of invasive species on the palm trees (Polynesian rats or *Rattus exulans*), slash-and-burn agricultural practices, warfare, and climate change. Today the island's archaeological legacy and unique cultural landscape is the focus of its national park and UNESCO World Heritage Site.

The isolated history of Rapa Nui reflects the nature of the sea, which can be both a barrier and a highway. Rapa Nui also highlights the achievements of ancient voyagers in the Pacific and raises interesting questions about navigation and maritime contacts.

Hans Konrad Van Tilburg

Further Reading

Hunt, Terry L., and Carl P. Lippo. 2009. "Revisiting Rapa Nui (Easter Island) Ecocide." *Pacific Science* 63(4): 601–16.

McCall, Grant. 1994. *Rapanui: Tradition and Survival on Easter Island*. Honolulu: University of Hawai'i Press.

Srivijaya

Srivijaya was the earliest maritime empire of Southeast Asia's classical period. It dominated seaborne trade throughout Southeast Asia's waters from the 7th to the 14th century CE. Srivijaya's ships carried spices and forest products—aromatic resins, animal parts, camphor, and sandalwood—to India and China on what can be called the Maritime Silk Road. Its ships brought back silk, cotton, porcelain, bronzes, and tea to the islands and coastal kingdoms within its network. Centered for most of its duration on what is now the city of Palembang on the island of Sumatra, the ethnically disparate states of this empire stretched from the southern reaches of present-day Thailand down the western coast of the Malay Peninsula and extended over all the trading ports of western Indonesia. It maintained a strict monopoly on maritime trade but allowed its member states to retain their political independence. Srivijaya employed powerful naval forces to thwart piracy and to crush any state that defied its rules for trade.

Despite its great wealth and power, Srivijaya exercised influence over only the trading ports and coastal towns of maritime Southeast Asia; its suzerainty did not extend far into the interior. Srivijaya had a strong cultural influence on the region.

Its rulers patronized Buddhism and promoted its ideals and imagery throughout its empire. This support contributed a strong Buddhist overlay to existing Brahmanist (Hindu) and indigenous belief systems. Srivijaya's method of maritime commercial domination was similar to that pursued later by European powers such as the Portuguese, the British, and the Dutch. None of the Western powers, however, knew of their indigenous pre-modern predecessor. Until the early 20th century, knowledge of Srivijaya was limited to brief descriptions in Chinese, Indian, and Arab accounts. More recently, archaeologists have discovered stone inscriptions near Palembang and in southern Thailand that have added greatly to knowledge about Srivijaya's rulers, systems, and parameters.

Srivijaya's reign came to an end because of military and commercial conflict with powerful rivals to its west and east. In the early 11th century, the Chola Empire that had dominated the states of southern India fought Srivijaya for control of trade coming from the Malacca Straits to South Asia. Although Srivijaya survived the Chola attack, the campaigns weakened the Southeast Asian empire. Shortly thereafter, powerful kingdoms centered on the island of Java emerged to challenge Srivijaya for exclusive control of its trading areas in the east. Srivijaya's decline was furthered in the 13th century when the rulers of Aceh and other kingdoms of western Sumatra embraced Islam and separated themselves from the Buddhist-oriented trading empire.

Richard A. Ruth

Further Reading

Cœdes, George. 1968. *The Indianized States of Southeast Asia*. Honolulu: The East West Center Press.

Hall, Kenneth R. 2011. *A History of Early Southeast Asia: Maritime Trade and Social Development*. Lanham, MD: Rowan & Littlefield.

Wolters, O.W. 1967. *Early Indonesian Commerce: A Study of the Origins of Srivijaya*. Ithaca, NY: Cornell University Press.

Wolters, O.W. 1970. *The Fall of Srivijaya in Malay History*. Ithaca, NY: Cornell University Press.

Tattooing

Tattooing involves marking the body with an indelible design by saturating skin punctures with pigments. The word "tattoo" emerged after the 18th-century appearance of the Polynesian term "*tatau*" in vernacular English.

Cultures throughout the South Pacific have practiced tattooing for millennia. In Samoa, "*tufuga ta tatau*" ("master tattooists") were creating traditional male tattoos ("*pe'a*") at least 2,000 years ago. These intricate designs cover the skin from the waist down to the knees and connote the rank or status of their bearer. Women also received tattoos, known as "*malu*." Prior to European contact, Tongan nobility frequently travelled to Samoa to undergo tattoo rituals. During the 1830s, English missionaries began arriving in Samoa and tried to ban tattooing. Despite these attempts to suppress this "heathen" practice, Samoan skin-adornment traditions persist to this day.

Similar varieties of skin inking have existed throughout the world. Prior to the late 1700s, French explorers and colonists used the term "*piquage*" to describe the bodily art that they observed on indigenous North Americans. Late medieval accounts in German depict the practice of "*stempeln*" ("pricking") and "*stupfen*" ("stamping") the skin to produce lasting designs. Likewise, in 1300, Marco Polo remarked upon travelers from northern India who journeyed to Kublai Khan's China to have their bodies "painted" with needles.

Maritime associations with tattooing expanded rapidly following European encounters with Pacific Islanders. In March 1770, as Captain James Cook's *Endeavor* was circumnavigating Aotearoa-New Zealand, naturalist Joseph Banks recorded his impressions of the inhabitants of the northern (*Te Ika-a-Maui*) and southern (*Te Waipounamu*) islands. Remarking on Māori bearers of *Ta Moko*—or traditional facial tattoos—Banks wrote, "their faces are the most remarkable, on them they by some art unknown to me dig furrows in their faces a line deep at least and as broad, the edges of which are often indented and most perfectly black" (Banks 1963, 2:13). Returning from its second voyage to the Pacific, the Cook expedition brought the tattooed Tahitian man Omai to London. For many European elites, the distinctive markings on Omai's hands and feet reinforced the exoticism of a distant ocean and its cultures.

By the early 1800s, 90 percent of the crewmembers aboard Euro-American vessels sported tattoos. This corporeal art offered one of the few forms of permanent identification for a mobile workforce afloat on the world's oceans. It could also indicate much about a mariner's boundary crossings; a turtle showed that its bearer had traversed the equator, an anchor implied extensive journeys across the Atlantic, and a dragon suggested service in the China trade.

For most of the 19th century, artists created tattoos by tying several needles in a bundle, dipping the needles into a colored amalgam of ink and gunpowder, stretching the skin tightly, and piercing it to the depth of the dermis. This technique fell out of favor after New York tattoo artist Samuel O'Reilly patented the first electric tattoo machine on December 8, 1891. His device featured a design based on the rotary technology of Thomas Edison's autographic printing pen.

During the 20th century, tattooing retained its powerful associations with the seafaring world. Norman Keith Collins (1911–1973), also known as "Sailor Jerry," achieved widespread recognition by tattooing young men on Hawaiian shore leave from the United States Navy. Considered the father of modern-day tattoo art,

Collins was based in Honolulu for most of his career. He developed new styles that fused maritime symbols, Pacific Island themes, and Japanese motifs. Collins achieved these groundbreaking designs with an innovative array of pigments, novel sterilization techniques, and more advanced needles that reduced skin trauma for his clients.

Tattooing has long been a part of the struggle over the politics of the body. In 2003, such debates were on vivid display after the U.S. Navy changed its uniform regulations, banning tattoos on the head, face, neck, or scalp and prohibiting tattoos that are visible through uniform clothing. Thirteen years later, in an attempt to retain and recruit sailors from a generation in which a third of young men and women have body art, the navy relaxed its tattoo policy.

Edward D. Melillo

Further Reading

Banks, Joseph. 1963. *The Endeavor Journal of Joseph Banks, 1768–1771*, Vol. 2. J. C. Beaglehole (ed.). Sydney: Public Library of New South Wales.

Caplan, Jane (ed.). 2000. *Written on the Body: The Tattoo in European and American History*. London: Reaktion Books.

Groebner, Valentin. 2007. *Who Are You? Identification, Deception, and Surveillance in Early Modern Europe*. New York: Zone Books.

Voyaging Canoes

Long before western navigators reached the Pacific, ancient navigators had contacted most, if not all, of its habitable islands in what is now recognized as the single greatest marine migration ever to take place. Over hundreds of years, double-hull voyaging canoes, guided by specialists trained in non-instrument navigation, sailed eastwards into the Pacific, bearing the people and supplies to support permanent remote settlement. Navigators relied on traditional wayfinding techniques, using observations of sea and sky to maintain their course, and cloud patterns, migratory birds, and other signs to find small islands and atolls.

That achievement also relied on the capabilities of double-hulled oceanic voyaging canoes. These were advanced pre–Iron Age vessels well-designed for their environments. Parallel wooden dugouts, their sides raised by hull planks or strakes lashed together with natural cordage, were joined by cross beams, which also supported the deck. Sails were often natural plaited fibers carried in curved "crab-claw" masts. A steering oar at the stern between the hulls provided control. There were many different canoe designs across the Pacific, but the largest types were double-hulled and decked sailing vessels for long oceanic passages.

Reference works by Haddon, Hornell, Kirch, Howe, and others provide excellent sources for understanding the cultural and environmental challenges and the technical evolution of Pacific voyaging canoes. The speed and carrying capacity of many types of canoes impressed 18th- and 19th-century western explorers such as James Cook. The modern catamaran design comes from the traditional double-hulled canoe. This voyaging canoe design was clearly the preeminent Pacific vessel of ancient exploration and migration, a marine platform of immense cultural importance.

Hans Konrad Van Tilburg

Further Reading

Haddon, A. C., and James Hornell. 1936. *Canoes of Oceania*. Honolulu: Bishop Museum Press.

Howe, K. R. 2006. *Vaka Moana, Voyages of the Ancestors: The Discovery and Settlement of the Pacific*. Honolulu: University of Hawai'i Press.

Kirch, Patrick V. 2000. *On the Road of the Winds: an Archaeological History of the Pacific Islands before European Contact*. Berkeley: University of California Press.

PRIMARY DOCUMENTS

The Travels of Fa Xian, 337 to ca. 422 CE

Fa Xian, or "Fa-hsien" as his name is rendered in the passage below, was a Chinese monk who travelled to India and back, visiting numerous Buddhist monasteries and temples along the way. His voyage from Java to Canton proved particularly difficult and is described here.

After having stayed in this country [Java] for five months or so, Fa-hsien again shipped on board another large merchant vessel which also carried over two hundred persons. They took with them provisions for fifty days and set sail on the 16th of the 4th moon, and Fa-hsien went into retreat aboard the vessel.

A northeast course was set in order to reach Canton; and over a month had elapsed when one night in the second watch [9–11 p.m.] they encountered a violent gale with tempestuous rain, at which the traveling merchants and traders who were going to their homes were much frightened. However, Fa-hsien once more invoked the Hearer of Prayers and was accorded the protection of their awful power until day broke. As soon as it was light, the Brahmans took counsel together and said, "Having this Shaman on board has been our undoing, causing us to get into this trouble. We ought to land the religious mendicant on some island; it is not right to endanger all our lives for one man." A "religious protector" of Fa-hsien's replied, saying, "If you put this religious mendicant ashore, you shall also land me with him; if not, you had better kill me, for supposing that you land him, when I reach China I will report you to the king who is a reverent believer in the Buddhist Faith and honors mendicants." At this the merchants wavered and did not dare to land him just then.

Meanwhile, the sky was constantly darkened and the captain lost his reckoning. So they went on for seventy days until the provisions and water were nearly exhausted, and they had to use sea water for cooking, dividing the fresh water so that each man got about two pints. When all was nearly consumed, the merchants consulted together and said, "The ordinary time for the voyage to Canton is exactly fifty days. We have now exceeded that limit by many days; must we not have gone out of course?"

Thereupon they proceeded in a northwesterly direction, seeking for land; and after twelve days and nights arrived south of the Lao mountain [on the Shantung promontory] at the boundary of the Prefecture of Ch'ang-kuang [modern Kiao-chou], where they obtained fresh water and vegetables.

And now, after having passed through much danger, difficulty, and sorrow, and fear, suddenly reaching this shore and seeing the old familiar vegetables, they knew it was their fatherland; but not seeing any inhabitants or traces of such, they did not know what part it was. Some said that they had not got as far as Canton; others declared that they had passed it. Being in a state of uncertainty, some of them got into a small and went up a creek in search of any one whom they might ask about the place. These fell in with two hunters and brought them back to the vessel, telling Fa-hsien to act as interpreter and interrogate them. Fa-hsien began by reassuring them, and then quietly asked them, "What men are you?" They replied, "We are followers of Buddha." "And what is it you go among the mountains to seek?" continued Fa-hsien. Then they began to lie, saying "Tomorrow is the 15th day of the 7th moon; we wished to get something for a sacrifice [a lie] to Buddha." Fa-hsien then said, "What country is this?" They answered this is the boundary of the Ch'ang-kuang prefecture; all these parts belong to the Liu family. When they heard this the merchants were very glad, and at once requested that their effects might be landed, sending men off with them to Ch'ang-kuang.

The prefect, Li I, was a devout believer in the Faith of Buddha; and when he heard that a Shaman had arrived who had brought Sacred Books and Images with him in a ship from beyond the sea, he immediately proceeded with his retinue to the sea-shore to receive these Books and Images and carry them to his official residence. The merchants then returned to Yang-chou (in Kiangsu), while Fa-hsien received an invitation to remain at Ch'ing-chou a winter and a summer. When his summer retreat was over, Fa-hsien, who had been far separated from his ecclesiastical authorities for many years, was desirous of reaching Chang'an; but because of the great importance of his undertaking he accordingly proceeded south to the capital [Nanking] and handed over to the ecclesiastics there the Sutras and the Disciplines he had collected.

Source: H. A. Giles. 1880. *The Travels of Fa-hsien, 399–414, or Record of the Buddhist Kingdoms.* London: Trubner & Company, pp. 111–16.

The Voyage of St. Brendan, ca. 484–577 CE

St. Brendan (ca. 484–577 CE), a sixth-century Irish monk, took 14 fellow Christian monks on a legendary search for a blessed island they believed to be the Garden of Eden. On their long voyage, they encounter sea monsters and other nautical dangers, including sea ice. They are protected from the worst of these by their faith and they also encounter people and creatures important to their faith, including Judas, and an island of birds that sing psalms. In the excerpts below, they encounter an island that turns out to be a whale, an event that appears in many maritime tales, and then—helped by a mysterious guide—they reach their destination, from which they return home with gems and other valuables.

When they drew nigh to the nearest island, the boat stopped ere they reached a landing place; and the saint ordered the brethren to get out into the sea, and make the vessel fast, stem and stern, until they came to some harbor; there was no grass on the island, very little wood, and no sand on the shore. While the brethren spent the night in prayer outside the vessel, the saint remained in it, for he knew well what manner of island was this; but he wished not to tell the brethren, lest they might be too much afraid. When morning dawned, he bade the priests to celebrate Mass, and after they had done so, and he himself had said Mass in the boat, the brethren took out some uncooked meat and fish they had brought from the other island, and put a cauldron on a fire to cook them. After they had placed more fuel on the fire, and the cauldron began to boil, the island moved about like a wave; whereupon they all rushed towards the boat, and implored the protection of their father, who, taking each one by the hand, drew them all into the vessel; then relinquishing what they had removed to the island, they cast their boat loose, to sail away, when the island at once sunk into the ocean.

Afterwards they could see the fire they had kindled still burning more than two miles off, and then Brendan explained the occurrence: "Brethren . . . [f]ear not . . . for God last night revealed to me the mystery of all this; it was not an island you were upon, but a fish, the largest of all that swim in the ocean, which is ever trying to make its head and tail meet, but cannot succeed, because of its great length."

. . . [T]hey saw towards the west another island [the Island of Birds] . . . and they bore away towards its landing-place.

[They spent several days there and found a guide, the Procurator, who helped them complete their journey.]

The brethren got the boat ready and set sail forth into the ocean, while all the birds sang in concert: "Hear us O God our Savior, the hope of all the ends of the earth, and in the sea afar off." After this St. Brendan and his brethren were tossed about to and fro on the billows of the ocean for the space of three months, during which they could see nothing but sea and sky, and they took refreshment only every second day. One day, however, an island came into view, not far off; but when they drew near the shore the wind drove them aside, and thus for forty days they sailed round about the island without finding a landing place. The brethren meanwhile besought the Lord with tears that He would vouchsafe to help them, for their strength was almost exhausted because of their great fatigue; and when they had thus persevered in frequent prayer for three days, and in fasting also . . . they found a narrow creek fit to receive one boat. . . .

[They later returned to] the Paradise of Birds, where . . . they sojourned until the Octave of Pentecost. When that solemn season had passed, their procurator, who was still with them, said to St. Brendan: "Embark now in your boat, and fill all the water-skins from the fountain. I will be the companion and the conductor of your journey henceforth, for without my guidance you could not find the land you seek, the Land of Promise of the Saints." Then, while they were embarking, all the birds of the island, as soon as they saw St. Brendan, sung together in concert: "May a happy voyage under his guidance bring you safely to the island of your procurator." They took with them provisions for forty days, as their course lay to the west for that space of time. . . .

At the end of forty days, towards evening, a dense cloud overshadowed them, so dark that they could scarce see one another. Then the procurator said to St. Brendan: "Do you know, father, what darkness is this?" And the saint replied that he knew not. "This darkness," said he, "surrounds the island you have sought for seven years; you will soon see that it is the entrance to it"; and after an hour had elapsed a great light shone around them, and the boat stood by the shore.

When they had disembarked, they saw a land, extensive and thickly set with trees, laden with fruits . . . a young man of resplendent features . . . came to them, and . . . said: "Peace be with you, brothers, and with all who practice the peace of Christ. Blessed are they who dwell in thy house, O Lord; they shall praise Thee for ever and ever."

He then said to St. Brendan: "This is the land you have sought after for so long a time; but you could not hitherto find it, because Christ our Lord wished, first to display to you His diverse mysteries in this immense ocean. Return now to the land of your birth, bearing with you as much of those fruits and of those precious stones, as your boat can carry; for the days of your earthly pilgrimage must draw to a close, when you may rest in peace among your saintly brethren. . . ." When St. Brendan inquired whether this land would be revealed unto men, the young man replied: "When the Most High Creator will have brought all nations under subjection, then will this land be made known to all His elect." Soon after, St. Brendan, having received the blessing of this man, prepared for his return to his own country. He gathered some of the fruits of the land, and various kinds of precious stones; and . . . embarked once more and sailed back through the darkness again.

When they had passed through this, they reached the "Island of Delights," where they remained for three days, as guests in the monastery; and then St. Brendan, with the abbot's parting blessing, set sail in a direct course, under God's guidance, and arrived at his own monastery, where all his monks gave glory to God for the safe return of their holy patron, and learned from him the wonderful works of God, which he had seen or heard during his voyage.

Source: Denis O'Donohue. 1893. *Brendaniana: St. Brendan the Voyager in Story and Legend.* Dublin: Browne & Nolan, pp. 126–28, 134–35, 173–75.

The Book of the Marvels of India, 900–953 CE

A 10th-century Persian merchant and seafarer, Ibn Shahriyar recounted a number of tales he gathered in his travels to India. One tale (14) recounts fish following ships for several days, hoping to feast on trash tossed overboard. Another (15) tells of an island populated only by women. Others note giant fish, sea monsters, exotic birds and animals, such as monkeys, and various mythical creatures, great storms, shipwrecked sailors, and skilled navigators and captains able to predict the arrival of storms before any visible sign of their approach. Tale 7, recounted below, is about a trading expedition to India that purchases slaves, only to have the slaves revolt and capture the ship, making it one of the oldest tales of the seaborne slave trade and shipboard revolt.

Tale 7

According to the story communicated to me by Abou-Mohammed el-Hassan, son of Amr, a ship's captain told him, that, being set out for Zabedj on a ship which belonged to him, the wind drove them towards the isles of Waqwaq [a general term for the Southwestern Indian Ocean], where they were obliged to put in not far from a village. Seeing them, the inhabitants fled into the country, carrying off such of their property as they were able . . . a sailor, who understood the Waqwaqian language, was put over the side, and ventured through the town, on his way towards open country. Lighting on a man hidden beneath a tree, he addressed him, offering him some dates, which he carried. Why had the natives all taken to their heels, he asked, promising that no harm would come to him, and that it would be worth his while if he told the truth.

The fellow replied that, seeing the ship, the inhabitants thought they would be attacked and, with their king, had run off into the open country and the forest. He agreed to follow the sailor back to the ship. Three companions were allotted him, charged with a fair message to the king, and also bearing a present, of . . . some dates and various trifles.

Reassured, the king came back with all his people. The sailors took up their lodging amongst them, and began bartering with the cargo of the ship.

But the twentieth day had not yet gone by, when up came another tribe to attack the first. "They are coming, you see" explained the townspeople's king, "to harry me and pillage my goods because they imagine that I have laid my fingers on the ship's cargo. So do you help me against them; help me by helping yourselves."

At dawn continued my narrator, the enemy was at the town gate, ready for battle. And the king and his men issued to meet them, supported by as many able-bodied men as the ship's company could muster and such of the merchants that were inclined to fight. Battle was joined, but, in the press, a sailor, a native of Iraq, drew from his girdle a sheet of paper on which was written a bill owing to him, and, unfolding it, held it up towards the sky, declaiming certain words at the top of his voice.

The attackers saw it, and straightaway paused. Some ran up to him, crying: "No more of that, for God's sake! We'll go quietly!" . . . And to one another they exclaimed: "Give over, give over fighting! Our enemies have put their quarrel in God's hands. We shall be beaten and cut to pieces." And they bowed down before the sailor, till he had tucked the paper away again, and presently withdrew, using the most humble language.

Thus rid of them . . . we returned to our usual business of buying and selling. The King was all ours. We never stopped swindling the natives, stole their children, bought them from their fellows . . . and so prospered that we have finally stocked our ship with a hundred head of slaves, big and little.

Four months passed, and now the time of departure drew in [the captain presumably waited for the monsoon to carry his ship home]. The slaves we had bought or stolen said to us: "Don't take us away! Leave us here! It is not right to carry us off into slavery and separate us from our families." But much we cared! On board, they were chained up, some manacled by the feet and others bound with cords. Five men of the crew stayed on board to guard them and tend the ship. One night, the prisoners hurled themselves on the guard, bound them, hauled up the anchor and set sail, stealing our ship under cover of darkness. Morning came, and it had gone. There we were stranded, reduced for sole property and provisions to what poor odds and ends we had left in the town. Nothing could be heard from the ship. Many months we had to stay there, till we had built a light skiff, which would bear us, and then embarked in the utmost destitution.

Source: Ibn Shahriyar. L. Marcel Devic (trans.). 1928. *The Book of the Marvels of India.* London: George Routledge & Sons, pp. 7–10.

The *Tosa Diary,* 936 CE

The record of a 55-day sea voyage, the Tosa Diary, *written in 936 CE, describes the return to Kyoto of the governor of Tosa Province, today's Kochi Prefecture on Shikoku Island. Published anonymously and ascribed to a woman, presumably a member of the governor's court, modern scholars believe it was probably written by the governor himself, the revered poet Ki no Tsurayuki (872–945 CE). The evocative diary, liberally sprinkled with poetry, illustrates the often-painstaking progress of ships sailing along the coast.*

28 January. One year on the twenty-first day of the month, a certain personage [the governor] left home. . . . He had just completed the usual four or five years as governor of a province . . . and now he was about to . . . travel by ship. . . .

29 January. He prayed for a calm voyage to Izumi Province. Fujiwara no Tokizane came to "turn his horse's head" [a farewell celebration]. . . . Upper, middle, and lower classes all drank too heavily, and, wonderful to relate, they were on the edge of the salt sea itself all useless and incompetent.

. . .

The steersman, who had been himself freely eating and drinking *saké* while all this was going on, now remorselessly said they must get away at once; for the tide was full, and he feared the wind might blow and they would have a rough tossing in the ship.

[The ship departed and sailed east to Urato and then along the Pacific coast of Shikoku to Ominato where it was delayed by poor weather. The next morning they sailed to Naha where well-wishers had gathered to see them off.]

14 February. They set out from Ominato the first thing in the morning and rowed on, intending to stop at Nawa . . . people all the way [a]long the route had come to see him off, and they all did it from kindness of heart. . . . After this, as they rowed gently forward, those who remained upon the shore grew further and further away, and they in their turn could no longer see those in the boat. . . . This being so, he [the governor] could only recite the following verse to himself:

Far across the sea
In my heart I fly to you
Bidding you farewell;
But no written work, alas!
From the ship to you may pass.

After this they passed the pine forest of Uta.

[A]dmiring the beautiful scene, they rowed gently forward; mountains and sea all became dim, and the night drew on. As he could no longer distinguish east from west, he left all thought about the weather to the steersman. Those of the men who were unused to the sea began to feel gloomy and pensive, while the women laid their heads upon the bottom of the boat and cried aloud. But the steersman and sailors thought nothing of it all and sang their boat song. . . .

16 February. [After stopping overnight at Nawa] the boat started at break of day and headed for Murotsu. There were all still half asleep, and accordingly took no notice of the condition of the sea. But the position of the moon indicated which was east and which was west, and so the day gradually became light.

[Bad weather twice delayed their departure from Murotsu.]

And while still travelling on, he who was "the passenger" [the governor] noticed the waves and remembered that the pirates had threatened to take revenge upon him, when once he had left the province; all his hair turned white, when the waves once more became rough. An age of seventy or eighty years is soon reached at sea!

> White as snow my hair,
> Waves roll in upon the shore
> Breaking into foam;
> "Which is whiter" Can'st thou say,
> Warder of the Isles, I pray
> Tell me, steersman

. . .

28 February. The sun shone forth from the clouds, and, as there was said to be danger of pirates, he prayed for protection to the Shinto and Buddhist Gods. . . .

3 March. Can this really be true? As they say the pirates are in chase, the boat is not to start before midnight, and offerings are to be made while rowing. The steersman accordingly offered prayer-papers, and, as these fluttered away to the east, he prayed, "Graciously allow our gallant ship to be rowed with all speed in the direction taken by these prayer-papers." On hearing this a child made the following verse:

> To the Deep Sea God,
> He who rules the ocean road,
> Make we now our prayer;
> For these flying *nusa* [prayer-papers] pray
> May the breeze not die away.

As the wind was fair at the moment, the steersman was proud and happy in hoisting sail on the boat. . . .

[The voyage continues, with many stops along the way.]

12 March. This day with difficulty they hastened on through the Sea of Izumi to the harbor of Ozu. . . . [S]uddenly the wind arose; and, though they rowed hard, they drifted quickly astern and nearly capsized. . . . The steersman said, "This holy Deity of Sumiyoshi is a well-known God, and he desires some gift." Someone suggested that *nusa* should be offered; so accordingly an offering of prayer-papers was made.

But . . . it began to blow harder than ever and the waves rose accordingly, so that they were in great danger. Then the steersman spoke again, and said, "As the august heart (of the God) has not been moved by the prayer-papers, the gallant ship does not proceed; something more valuable should be presented." . . . [H]e could only offer one mirror; so to his deep regret it was thrown into the sea. Well, immediately the sea became calm as the looking-glass itself and "a certain personage" composed this:

> In the raging sea,
> I have cast my looking-glass
> And the gift's result
> Shows the partiality
> Of the awful Deity

[They reached Naniwa (modern Osaka) the following day.]

Eleventh day: Gentle rain was falling, so they remained where they were for a little while. Then, on going forward, the Temple of Hachiman came into view. . . . There was no limit to their delight; and there, opposite the Soo Temple, the boat anchored.

Source: William N. Porter (trans.). 1912. *The Tosa Diary.* London: Henry Frowde, pp.13–121.

The *Long Serpent*, 1000 CE

The Long Serpent*, constructed near Nidaros/Trondheim, Norway, in the winter of 999–1000 for King Olaf Tryggvason of Norway (ca. 960–1000 CE) is one of the Viking Age's most famous warships—and at 130 feet in length, was one of the largest. The passages below discuss its construction and its boarding by enemy forces at the fiercely fought Battle of Svold (September 1000).*

The winter after, King Olaf came from Halogaland (A.D. 1000), he had a great vessel built at Hladhamrar, which was larger than any ship in the country, and of which the beam-knees are still to be seen. The length of keel that rested upon the grass was seventy-four ells. Thorberg Skafhog was the man's name who was the master-builder of the ship; but there were many others besides—some to fell wood, some to shape it, some to make nails, some to carry timber; and all that was used was of the best. The ship was both long and broad and high-sided, and strongly timbered.

While they were planking the ship, it happened that Thorberg had to go home to his farm upon some urgent business; and as he remained there a long time, the ship was planked up on both sides when he came back. In the evening the king went out, and Thorberg with him, to see how the vessel looked, and everybody said that never was seen so large and so beautiful a ship of war. Then the king returned to the town. Early next morning the king returns again to the ship, and Thorberg with him. The carpenters were there before them, but all were standing idle with their arms across.

The king asked, "[W]hat was the matter?" They said the ship was destroyed; for somebody had gone from, stem to stern, and cut one deep notch after the other down the one side of the planking. When the king came nearer he saw it was so, and said, with an oath, "The man shall die who has thus destroyed the vessel out of envy, if he can be discovered, and I shall bestow a great reward on whoever finds him out."

"I can tell you, king," said Thorberg, "who has done this piece of work."—

"I don't think," replies the king, "that any one is so likely to find it out as thou art."

Thorberg says, "I will tell you, king, who did it. I did it myself."

The king says, "Thou must restore it all to the same condition as before, or thy life shall pay for it."

Then Thorberg went and chipped the planks until the deep notches were all smoothed and made even with the rest; and the king and all present declared that the ship was much handsomer on the side of the hull which Thorberg, had chipped, and bade him shape the other side in the same way; and gave him great thanks for the improvement. Afterwards Thorberg was the master builder of the ship until she was entirely finished. The ship was a dragon, built after the one the king had captured in Halogaland; but this ship was far larger, and more carefully put together in all her parts. The king called this ship Serpent the Long, and the other Serpent the Short. The long Serpent had thirty-four benches for rowers. The head and the arched tail were both gilt, and the bulwarks were as high as in sea-going ships. This ship was the best and most costly ship ever made in Norway.

At the Battle of Svold, Olaf Tryggvason in the *Long Serpent* faced a coalition of Eirik Hakonarson (ca. 960s–1020s), King Olaf of Sweden (ca. 980–1022), and King Svein of Denmark (960–1014) who together amassed 71 ships against Tryggvason's 11. Caught by surprise and ambushed by the larger fleet, Tryggvason's outnumbered ships were boarded and captured one by one with the fiercest fighting on the *Long Serpent*, the last to be captured.

Desperate was the defence in the Serpent, and there was the heaviest destruction of men done by the forecastle crew, and those of the forehold, for in both places the men were chosen men, and the ship was highest, but in the middle of the ship the people were thinned. Now when Earl Eirik saw there were but few people remaining beside the ship's mast, he determined to board; and he entered the Serpent with four others. Then came Hyrning, the king's brother-in-law, and some others against him, and there was the most severe combat; and at last the earl was forced to leap back on board his own ship again, and some who had accompanied him were killed, and others wounded.

. . .

Now the fight became hot indeed, and many men fell on board the Serpent; and the men on board of her began to be thinned off, and the defence to be weaker. The earl resolved to board the Serpent again, and again he met with a warm reception. When the forecastle men of the Serpent saw what he was doing, they went aft and made a desperate fight; but so many men of the Serpent had fallen, that the ship's sides were in many places quite bare of defenders; and the earl's men poured in all around into the vessel, and all the men who were still able to defend the ship crowded aft to the king, and arrayed themselves for his defence. . . . But as many of the earl's men had now got into the Serpent as could find room, and his ships lay all round her, and few were the people left in the Serpent for defence against so great a force; and in a short time most of the Serpent's men fell, brave and stout though they were. King Olaf and Kolbjorn the marshal both sprang overboard, each on his own side of the ship; but the earl's men had laid out boats around the Serpent, and killed those who leaped overboard. Now when the king had sprung overboard, they tried to seize him with their hands, and bring him to Earl Eirik; but King Olaf threw his shield over his head, and sank beneath the waters.

. . .

[T]he report went immediately abroad and was told by many, that King Olaf had cast off his coat-of-mail underwater, and had swum, diving under the longships, until he came to the Vindland cutter, and that Astrid's men had conveyed him to Vindland: and many tales have been made since about the adventures of Olaf the king. . . . But however this may have been, King Olaf Trygvason never came back again to his kingdom of Norway.

Source: Snorri Sturluson. Samuel Laing (trans.) 1907. *Heimskringla: A History of the Norse Kings*. Norroena Society, London.Painting of the Battle of Lepanto (1571) by an unknown painter, in Saint Paul's Church, Antwerp, Belgium. (Jozef Sedmak/ Dreamstime.com)

■ CHAPTER 4
Global Interactions, 1000 CE to 1500 CE

INTRODUCTION

Between 1000 and 1500 CE, people introduced and spread more sophisticated navigational instruments—such as the compass—as well as new ship designs and construction techniques, which facilitated the construction of larger ships. The increasing sophistication and size of ships in these years fostered trade, which increased in volume, as well as fostering exploration and war. China, Portugal, and Spain reached farther out to sea than ever before, and used their growing naval power to expand their trading networks, explore and settle new lands, or exact tribute from distant states.

Developed in China, the compass spread across the world. Tenth-century wrecks recently discovered in Indonesia have compass bowls, and Arab seafarers used compasses by 1000 CE. Over the next century its use spread to Europe. People improved on the bowl compass and became more sophisticated compass users. By 1500 CE, they understood that compasses did not actually point true north, and the Portuguese developed navigation tables that listed the difference between true north and magnetic north at various locations. Other devices, such as mariner's astrolabe and the Arab kamal, aided stellar navigation. Mapmakers improved their techniques, resulting in the portolan chart, whose rhumb lines, based on compass directions, guided mariners to their destinations.

In Europe separate styles of shipbuilding solidified in this era. North Europeans adopted shipbuilding styles pioneered by the Vikings, building their ships from the outside in and up from the keel. Overlapping planks (clinker style), like shingles on a roof, were soaked or steamed, bent into shape, and fastened together by nails clinched on the inside. Builders then added internal bracing for additional strength. The cog, in use by 1250, typified their design with a deep, box-like hull and square sail.

Mediterranean builders adopted frame-first construction methods, building a keel and ribs to which planks were fastened edge to edge (carvel style) with nails and then caulked and waterproofed with grease or tar. This change required less skilled labor than older methods of shell-first construction in which planks were

A replica of a medieval astrolabe, which is a navigation instrument capable of 43 different astronomical calculations. (Brian Maudsley/iStockphoto.com)

fastened with mortise and tenon joints. Although not as robust as northern ships, they required considerably less wood. Mediterranean seafarers also favored lateen sails, which provided more maneuverability—a critical need in coastal navigation. The cog's square sail, though, propelled the ship faster in following winds and required fewer sailors to handle, resulting in significant cost savings.

The Chinese similarly transitioned to frame-first construction methods and pioneered several important technologies, including internal watertight bulkheads and the sternpost rudder. The Chinese favored fore/aft rigs for their sails, which had battens to allow easy and rapid adjustment. In the 12th century, China established a standing navy, and government shipyards began turning out warships of enormous size, some with as many as six masts. The sternpost rudder—developed around 1000 CE—replaced long steering oars and made sailing easier and safer, especially in bad weather. Like other Chinese developments, it slowly spread west, reaching Europe in the 12th century, around the same time as the compass. The Chinese also introduced paper currency (cash), which facilitated trade.

Sea power supported European crusaders and sustained Crusader states along the coast of today's Israel and Lebanon. Christian rulers steadily re-conquered the Iberian Peninsula, gaining control of its best ports: Lisbon (1147 CE), Cartagena (1245 CE), and Cadiz (1248 CE). Seaborne trade between northern and southern Europe increased in the 14th and 15th centuries, particularly after the Kingdom of Castile captured Gibraltar (1462), securing the strait for Christian shipping. One of the by-products of this trade was the gradual blending of ship design and construction techniques between northern Europe and the Mediterranean. The Portuguese, in particular, pioneered ships that employed both lateen and square sails, and these carracks and caravels—fast, maneuverable, and armed with cannon—facilitated Portuguese trade, exploration, and warfare.

Spices from Southeast Asia, including cinnamon, cloves, ginger, nutmeg, pepper, and sugar, became popular in China, the Muslim World, and later Europe, first for medical use, but soon for enhancing the flavors of food, making them the most valuable traded commodity in these years. India's Chola Empire (985–1297 CE) encouraged foreign trade, and a wide variety of other goods flowed through the Indian Ocean and Middle Eastern trading networks that linked Africa, Asia, and Europe, including ceramics, gemstones, metals (bronze, copper, iron, and tin—raw and worked), textiles (mostly cotton and silk), and of course, gold and silver. Indian merchants, often the middlemen in this trade, sailed to Arabia, Mesopotamia, Southeast Asia, Indonesia, and China, and many Indian ports boasted extensive communities of foreign traders, including Arabs, Chinese, Jews, and Persians. Jewish merchants, despite periodic persecution, operated in Christian Europe, the Islamic Middle East, and India. It was Jewish traders who first brought sugarcane from India and began planting it along the Nile, beginning the spread of what became the world's most profitable crop in the 17th and 18th centuries.

Cargos might pass through several hands before reaching their final destination. A North European cog, for example, might bring a cargo to Lisbon where it was loaded on a Portuguese ship that carried it to an Italian port, from which a Genoese or Venetian merchant would carry it to the Levant or Egypt. Arab traders then carried it overland to a Red Sea or Persian Gulf port from which it was shipped to India's west coast. Additional voyages might carry it through the Strait of Malacca and on to the Spice Islands or China. Several intrepid travelers, among them Marco Polo (1254–1324 CE) and Ibn Battuta (1304–1368 CE) travelled the length of this trade route, crossing the Mediterranean Sea and Indian Ocean to reach China.

Seaborne trade flourished when waterways were safe, as when policed by major maritime powers, or when merchant ships were able to protect themselves. Europe's lack of political unity required merchants to arm their ships to fight off attacks by pirates or rival states. North European builders added castles, located fore and aft, and these defensive platforms helped fight off boarding attempts. So, too, did the introduction of crossbows and gunpowder weapons. By the 14th century, North European merchants often sailed as part of convoys, which provided additional protection in dangerous waters.

From the earliest times, armies needed to cross water. Amphibious invasions, such as the first century CE Roman invasion of Britain, were rare. In the late Middle Ages, a number of states developed significant capabilities for amphibious warfare. Drawing on their seafaring heritage, the Normans successfully invaded England in 1066 CE. Venice developed impressive amphibious capabilities, which it demonstrated in successful assaults on Constantinople (1204 CE) and other fortified cities. The Mongols launched what were probably the largest amphibious invasions to date, against Japan (1274 and 1281 CE) and Java (1293). China's Song Dynasty (960–1279 CE) and the Ming Dynasty (1368–1644 CE) in its early years, maintained large fleets that exacted tribute from and ensured maritime access to states throughout Southeast Asia and across the Indian Ocean. Zheng He (1371–1435 CE), the greatest of the Ming admirals, commanded fleets of more than 200 ships carrying more than 25,000 sailors and soldiers, which swept pirates from the seas and established rulers favorable to the Ming throughout the region.

In 1291 CE, two Genoese brothers, Vandino and Ugolino Vivaldi, attempted to sail around Africa and were never heard from again. A century later, Musa Keita I (ca. 1280–1337 CE), who ruled Mali in West Africa, dispatched explorers into the Atlantic, but these, too, proved unsuccessful. The Sahara Desert extends to Africa's west coast, forcing ships to carry large quantities of water and supplies. Voyages of exploration were expensive, uncertain, and rarely attempted. The Portuguese succeeded, however, thanks to their perseverance, royal support, superior ships, and a methodical approach aided by science. Prince Henry the Navigator (1394–1460 CE), a veteran of Portugal's wars against Muslim states in Iberia and North Africa, funded maritime exploration as an extension of these wars, as well as to enrich Portugal and satisfy his own curiosity about the world. The Portuguese discovered winds that facilitated their exploration of the West African coast and led to the discovery of the Madeiras, Azores, and other uninhabited Atlantic islands. They settled these islands during the first half of the 15th century and began cultivating sugar there.

The European economy expanded rapidly in the 15th century and trade flourished, particularly in Italy, Portugal, and Spain. By the 15th century, Venetian ships annually carried more than three million pounds of spices from Alexandria across the Mediterranean to European ports. Although China withdrew from the sea following Zheng He's voyages, European ships—capable of ocean travel and armed with cannons—pushed farther and farther into the Atlantic Ocean. Maritime developments between 1000 and 1500 CE increasingly connected the peoples of Asia, Africa, and Europe, but also facilitated the spread of the Black Death (bubonic plague) across Asia, Europe, and North Africa in the 14th century. Successive waves of the plague devastated China, and weakened the Mongols' control of that

Black Death

Known as the "Black Death" due to its symptoms, which included black swellings (buboes), the Bubonic Plague devastated the major cities of Asia and Europe in the sixth century and again in the fourteenth. It is caused by the *Yersinia pestis bacillus*, which inhabits fleas whose bites spread the disease. Black rats, adept at climbing, hitched rides on Silk Road caravans and Indian Ocean trading ships and spread the disease when they bit humans.

The first documented outbreak occurred in Egypt in 541 CE. At that time, as part of the Byzantine Empire, Egypt was a nexus of trade between the Indian Ocean and the Eastern Mediterranean. Successive waves of plague struck over the next century, killing perhaps a quarter of the populations of the Byzantine and Persian Empires. As trading networks collapsed, the plague ebbed. Arab armies, recently converted to Islam, invaded the weakened empires.

The plague reappeared in the 14th century, spreading rapidly from China along recently reestablished trade routes. Mongol armies carried it to Kaffa, a Genoese trading outpost in the Crimea, which they besieged in 1347. Fleeing ships spread the plague to nearby ports and successive ships spread it further. It reached Alexandria and Sicily by the end of the year and Venice shortly afterward. From there it spread across the Mediterranean to the Atlantic. The plague killed a third of Europe's population over the next few years. The cities of Egypt and North Africa were particularly hard hit, losing up to half their populations. Among the dead was the mother of famed traveler Ibn Battuta.

Stephen K. Stein

nation. As much as half the populations of China and Europe died in the plague, which had the side effect of stimulating the development and adoption of labor-saving technologies and techniques in manufacturing and agriculture, among them frame-first shipbuilding techniques. The plague also could have contributed to China's retreat from the sea.

Stephen K. Stein

Further Reading

Flecker, Michael. 2004. "Treasure from the Java Sea: The Tenth Century Intan Shipwreck." *Asia Heritage Magazine* 2(2). Available at http://maritime-explorations.com/Intan.pdf. Accessed June 20, 2016.

Lane, Frederic C. 1934. *Venetian Ships and Shipbuilders of the Renaissance.* Baltimore: Johns Hopkins Press.

Lewis, Archibald R., and Timothy J. Runyan. 1985. *European Naval and Maritime History, 300–1500.* Bloomington: Indiana University Press.

Pryor, John H. 1988. *Geography, Technology, and War: Studies in the Maritime History of the Mediterranean, 649–1571.* Cambridge: Cambridge University Press.

Unger, Richard W. 1980. *The Ship in the Medieval Economy, 600–1600.* London: Croom Helm.

CHRONOLOGY

Chronology: Global Interactions, 1000 to 1500 CE

800s CE	Chinese develop the compass as a navigational device.
1000s CE	Chinese begin building ships with sternpost rudders. Thule Inuit spread across the Arctic of North America to Greenland.
1061–1091 CE	Normans conquer Sicily.
1066 CE	William the Conqueror invades Britain.
1070 CE	India's Chola Empire invades Srivijaya.
1071 CE	Seljuk Turks defeat Byzantines at the Battle of Manzikert.
1095 CE	Pope Urban II calls for a crusade to liberate the Holy Land.
1096–1099 CE	The First Crusade.
1104 CE	Venice Arsenal constructed.
1147 CE	Christian forces capture Lisbon, Portugal.
1160s CE	Benjamin of Tudela travels through the Middle East and Asia.
1161 CE	The Chinese navy repels Jurchen invasion.
1183–1185 CE	Ibn Jubayr's pilgrimage.
1187 CE	Saladin captures Jerusalem.
1191–1193 CE	England's Richard the Lionheart leads the Third Crusade against Saladin.
1200s CE	Cogs become the predominant North European cargo ship. Mariner's astrolabe introduced as a navigational aid. Portolan charts introduced in Europe. Development of mechanical clocks in Europe.
1204 CE	Fourth Crusade and the sack of Constantinople.
1215 CE	Magna Carta signed in England.
1217 CE	Ibn Jubayr's death.
1230s CE	Mongols conquer northern China.

1258 CE	Mongols sack Baghdad, ending the Abbasid Caliphate.
1265 CE	Hanseatic League requires all members to contribute to eradicating piracy.
1271 CE	Yuan (Mongol) Dynasty established in China by Kublai Khan.
1274 CE	First Mongol invasion of Japan.
1275 CE	Marco Polo arrives in China, along with members of his family.
1281 CE	Second Mongol invasion of Japan.
1291 CE	Fall of Acre, last Crusader city in the Holy Land.
1294 CE	Death of Kublai Khan.
1300s CE	Introduction of the dry compass in Europe. Portuguese develop the caravel, a nimble ship suited for trade and exploration.
1324 CE	Death of Marco Polo.
1325 CE	Ibn Battuta begins his journey across the Middle East and Asia
1337 CE	Beginning of the Hundred Years' War between England and France.
ca. 1340s CE	Aztecs establish their capital at Tenochtitlan.
1348 CE	The Black Death reaches Italy.
1354 CE	Ibn Battuta returns home.
1368 CE	Ming Dynasty founded in China.
ca. 1400 CE	Port of Malacca founded on the Malay Peninsula.
1402 CE	Kingdom of Castile begins occupying the Canary Islands.
1405 CE	Zheng He's first expedition departs China.
1415 CE	Portuguese capture port of Cueta in Morocco. England's Henry V defeats France in the Battle of Agincourt.
1420s CE	Henry the Navigator begins organizing and directing Portuguese expansion.
1431 CE	Portuguese discover the Azores.
1433 CE	Zheng He's fleet returns from its seventh and final voyage.
1440 CE	Portuguese sailors reach the Cape Verde Islands.
1444 CE	Portuguese ship African slaves to Portugal, beginning the transatlantic slave trade.

1453 CE	Ottoman Turks capture Constantinople. End of the Hundred Years' War between England and France.
1460 CE	Portugal's Prince Henry the Navigator dies.
1490 CE	Astronomer and navigator Ahmad ibn Majid completes *Kitab al-Fawa'id*, a detailed navigational guide to the Red Sea and Indian Ocean.
1492 CE	Spanish conquest of Granada, the last Muslim kingdom in Iberia. Jews expelled from Spain. Christopher Columbus's first voyage lands in the West Indies.

THE AMERICAS BEFORE 1500 CE

The Americas feature perhaps the richest range of prehistoric craft to have survived through history, with adapted versions of some aboriginal vessels remaining in use to this day, particularly off the coasts of Peru, Brazil, and Chile in South America. Because of the longevity of many American watercraft, the primary source of information on pre–Columbian seafaring, the corpus of drawings and descriptions provided by Europeans (primarily in the 18th and 19th centuries CE), is remarkably informative about prehistoric vessel types and their uses.

To take advantage of the opportunities and resources provided by the sea, prehistoric inhabitants of the American coasts developed and adopted different types of watercraft, and each type was specifically suited to its respective geographic region and purpose. Although it is difficult to gauge the antiquity of specific vessel types, the use of seagoing craft as early as 10,000 BCE is evidenced by the remains of water birds, marine mammals, and finfish that have been found on Pacific islands near southern California and northern Mexico. The use of oceangoing vessels in the Pacific Northwest by at least 3000 BCE is evidenced by deepwater fish and marine mammal remains from Vancouver Island. The appearance of sophisticated ceramics without local antecedent at the Ecuadorian coastal site of Valdivia, however, has led to the suggestion that oceanic voyages of communication also were taking place in northwestern South America by this time as well.

The design and construction of seagoing vessels varied widely according to the conditions and resources available in their region of use. Bark and hides were used to manufacture boats and canoes, although reed rafts and boats also were utilized, along with both boats and rafts made of logs. Reed-bundle boats, known as "*caballitos*," might be among the oldest of any watercraft. They are known from across the western Americas—from British Columbia to Chile—and also were used on

Caballitos de totora, straw boats still used by local fishermen in Peru. (Kseniya Ragozina/Dreamstime.com)

inland bodies of water, most notably Lake Titicaca in Peru. Composed of bundles of reeds lashed together, cut on one end and with a taper at the stern, the *caballito* was a single-person craft, and was ridden in the kneeling position or with legs extended in front of the rider. The prehistoric use of reed rafts might be reflected on the modern Andean coast, where they still are used to reach the fishing grounds of the Humboldt current several miles offshore. In some regions, particularly central and northern California, the single-person reed raft was further developed into the "*tule balsa*" (also called the "*sáka*"), a boat which consisted of a raft constructed of multiple bundles of reeds tied up with rope and joined together. Propelled with a paddle, these craft could carry a load of several hundred pounds, and were used on the open ocean as well as on rivers, lakes, and creeks.

Reed rafts and dugout canoes (from Spanish "*canoa*") seem to have had a mutually exclusive relationship, with the latter generally appearing in areas where agriculture was either present or emergent and supplanting the raft. The best known dugout canoes are from the Pacific Northwest, where vessels of significant length were carved from whole red cedar and spruce logs and used for ocean travel and subsistence. They were formed by splitting a log in two—creating "blanks" for two canoes—and then the logs were hollowed out, sometimes using smoldering charcoal to slowly burn away the interior wood. Dugouts were customized for specific tasks and sea conditions, including whale hunting, trade, and transportation. Not just limited to the Pacific Northwest, these craft were used throughout the Americas, and were crafted of pine, oak, and chestnut, as well as other wood types. By the time of European contact, the dugout canoe was the most important vessel used by the Maya, as well as by the peoples of the West Indies. A dugout made of pine and dating to 700 BCE was recovered from a lake in North Carolina and attests to the age of this design in eastern regions. In some areas, the dugout was developed into an extended form with strakes (continuous planking from stem to stern) added atop the dugout base, thus extending the craft's freeboard (the distance between the waterline and the top of the hull). Upon its arrival in the area of the Pacific coast from Colombia to Ecuador, the extended dugout supplanted most other indigenous watercraft in the region.

Bark canoes were used across the Americas, from the birchbark tradition of native North Americans to Tierra del Fuego in Chile, the southernmost tip of the South American mainland. In the south, bark canoes were sometimes mounted with a sealskin sail. These craft were capable of riverine navigation and sea travel, even in shallow waters, and could be carried over land (portaged) when necessary. The birchbark canoe reached the pinnacle of its development in North America, between Newfoundland and the Alaska coast, the swath of North America where paper birch (also known as "canoe birch") is indigenous. Outside this area, other types of birch were used for the canoe's skin, along with spruce, elm, hickory, and various other sources of bark; however, each of these had limitations not shared by the paper birch's bark. The majority of these craft were used for river and lake travel, although birchbark canoes used by the Beothuk tribe of Newfoundland were specifically designed for open-ocean voyages. This group and its ocean-going birchbark canoe might form the basis of a sea story about dark-skinned sailors wearing sealskins who were found floating in a canoe off the English coast in the early 16th century. In western South America, bark canoes could have evolved into the sewn plank boat, although both bark canoes and sewn boats coexisted in some locations, including islands off the coast of Chile, where the "*dalca*"—a long, narrow boat of sewn planks—was used alongside the canoe. In North America, only the Chumash of southern California seem to have used sewn plank boats prior to European contact. Called "*tomól*," these were built by connecting sanded planks together with tar or pitch and sewing them together with hemp or other plant fiber rope, which was strung through holes that had been drilled in adjacent planks.

Skin boats, constructed of a framework held together with animal skins, were used from the Arctic to the coast of Chile. These craft had shallow draft and easy rise on the waves, thus they generally were dry at sea, taking on little water despite wave conditions. Arctic waters are subject to violent storms, and skin boats had to

---

Balsa

The term *"balsa"* (Spanish for *"raft"*) encompasses a range of watercraft employed in modern Ecuador, Peru, and Chile from Pre-Columbian times to the present. Constructed of a variety of materials, including *totora* reeds, seal hides, and logs from the balsa tree (species *Ochroma*), *balsas* were employed on the navigable rivers of Ecuador's tropical forests and on the open sea for multiple purposes, including subsistence, exchange, and in some cases long-distance trade and exploration.

The largest seagoing *balsas* were composed of a flat deck of lashed balsa logs topped by a reed deckhouse. They were propelled by sails and steered with adjustable centerboards (*guaras*) placed vertically between deck logs. Seagoing *balsas* and their crews, called *"grandes marineros"* by the Spanish chronicler Agustín de Zárate, were capable of carrying significant loads and undertaking distant voyages even in the absence of favorable winds. A heavily laden *balsa* sailing close to the wind was encountered by Francisco Pizarro's pilot, Bartolomé Ruiz, in 1527, informing the first of many European accounts of these crafts. Computer models and experimental journeys of modern rafts like *Kon-Tiki*, *Illa-Tiki*, and *Manteño* have shown that *balsas* were capable of sailing from South America to Mexico and Polynesia. Andean legend held that Inca ruler Túpac Inca Yupanqui (r. 1471–1493 CE) led a fleet of *balsas* and 20,000 men on a voyage of Pacific exploration, returning nine months later with a rich cargo of gold, brass, "dark-skinned" prisoners, and other plunder.

Jeffrey P. Emanuel

---

be designed to survive these conditions. The main types of skin craft were the umiak, kayak, and rafts made of skin floats fitted into a framework. Both umiaks and kayaks essentially were seagoing craft. Umiaks primarily were used by the Inuit, who constructed them from the inside out, sewing skins around a framework and allowing them to shrink until they became smooth and tight. Kayaks were remarkably seaworthy, and were designed for particular environmental requirements. Thus, there was significant variation in kayak form and size over the wide geographic range of their use, which extended from the Bering Sea to the north Atlantic, as well as on inland lakes and rivers. The appearance of skin floats was limited to latitudes between 40° North and South, though they primarily were used on the coasts of South America—including in Peru and Chile—where they could be fastened side by side with cane decking.

The log raft, or balsa, occupies an important and controversial place in American maritime prehistory, particularly Ecuador and northern Peru. The decks of these stable craft were constructed of lashed or pinned-together logs from the balsa tree, a "featherweight wood" buoyant enough to allow rafts to ride high on the waves. Larger craft could have multiple decks, with a hut sometimes placed upon the topmost level, and were evidently capable of carrying up to 70 tons of cargo. Rafts typically were paddled or rowed, but those balsas that were outfitted with a sail for propulsion also featured adjustable centerboards ("*guaras*"), which were placed vertically between deck logs and lifted or lowered in concert with sail adjustments to provide steering control. Although log rafts were used for transport, fishing, and other local maritime activities, sailing craft also could have been instrumental in the development and maintenance of expansive trading networks, transporting goods and culture along the Pacific coast from Peru to Panama, and possibly as far north as Mexico. Each of these voyages would have been a minimum of 600 nautical miles (1,100 kilometers), with the southward trek from Ecuador to Peru being particularly difficult, as both wind and current would have been against the craft, requiring significant sailing and navigational acumen. Log rafts have been associated with trans–Pacific voyages, including to the Galapagos Islands and to Oceania, although there is no conclusive proof that such voyages ever were purposely carried out. This vessel type is associated with several legends, including the founding myth of the Lambayeque civilization on the north coast of Peru. According to this legend, the dynastic founder Naymlap arrived from the south on a fleet of balsas in the mid–eighth century CE, carrying with him a royal retinue of wives, concubines, a servant who scattered the dust of the *mullu* shell on the ground wherever he walked, and other courtiers, along with an idol of green stone (iconographic representations of Naymlap also depict him riding alone on a *caballito*, although these might be more symbolic in nature than reflective of his court's arrival at Lambayeque). Much later legend held that Túpac Inca Yupanqui, who ruled from 1471–1493 CE, led a fleet of balsas and 20,000 men on a voyage of Pacific exploration, returning nine months later with a rich cargo of gold, brass, "dark-skinned" prisoners, the jaw of a zebra, and other fantastic plunder. This voyage has been associated with another legend, from Mangareva in French Polynesia (more than 2,000 nautical miles, or 6,400 kilometers, from Peru), of a visitor named "Topa" (or "Tupa") who arrived from the east on a fleet of rafts and stayed a short time, making significant contributions to indigenous civilization, before sailing back across the ocean to his land of powerful kings.

A similar craft, called the "*jangada*," was used in similar latitude on the eastern coast of South America. Built of various wood types that are collectively referred to as "*pau de jangada*" ("raft-woods"), the decks of these rafts were bound or pinned together and fitted with a triangular sail and single centerboard. Although the chronology of the sail's addition to the *jangada* is unclear, a 19th-century account of these craft described them as having the same form and use as before European contact, suggesting that they could have been sailed prior to 1500 CE. Like many other pre-Columbian watercraft of the Americas, *jangadas* remain in use to the present day, primarily in the easternmost regions of Brazil.

Jeffrey P. Emanuel

Further Reading

Ames, Kenneth M., and Herbert D. G. Maschner. 1999. *Peoples of the Northwest Coast: Their Archaeology and Prehistory*. London: Thames & Hudson.

Anderson, Atholl, Helene Martinsson–Wallin, and Karen Stothert. 2007. "Ecuadorian Sailing Rafts and Oceanic Landfalls." In Atholl Anderson, Kaye Green, and Foss Leach (eds.). *Vastly Ingenious: The Archaeology of Pacific Material Culture, in Honour of Janet M. Davidson*. Dunedin: Otago University Press, 117–33.

Dewan, Leslie and Dorothy Hosler. 2008. "Ancient Maritime Trade on Balsa Rafts: An Engineering Analysis." *Journal of Anthropological Research* 64: 19–40.

Edwards, Clinton R. 1965. "Sailing Rafts of Sechura." *Southwestern Journal of Anthropology* 16: 368–91.

Erlandson, Jon M. et al. 2011. "Paleoindian Seafaring, Maritime Technologies, and Coastal Foraging on California's Channel Islands." *Science* 331: 1181–85.

Estrada, Emilio. 1955. "Balsa and Dugout Navigation in Ecuador." *The American Neptune* 15: 142–49.

Heyerdahl, Thor. 1952. *American Indians in the Pacific: The Theory Behind the Kon–Tiki Expedition*. London: Allen & Unwin.

Johnstone, Paul. 1988. *The Sea–Craft of Prehistory*, 2nd ed. Sean McGrail (ed.). London: Routledge.

McGrail, Sean. 2015. *Early Ships and Seafaring: Water Transport Beyond Europe*. Havertown: Pen and Sword.

Thule Inuit

The Thule people, also called "proto-Inuit," were the ancestors of all modern Inuit. Thule culture evolved along the coast of northern Alaska about 1000 CE and spread eastward across Canada, reaching Greenland by 1200 CE. They flourished until 1600, when the severe climate change associated with the "Little Ice Age" caused them to leave the High Arctic. The Thule culture is characterized by a strong maritime focus, demonstrating innovations and adaptations in sea-hunting, transportation, and tools that enabled them to thrive in the Arctic for several centuries.

The first people to migrate to the high latitudes, called "Paleoeskimos"— "*Paleo*" meaning "of ancient times," and "*Eskimo*" meaning "eaters of whale meat"—crossed the Bering Strait from Siberia about 4,000 years ago, during a period of global warming and retreating glaciers. By about 500 BCE, the Dorset culture evolved from these earliest inhabitants. Their settlements were more permanent than those of earlier peoples, and the artistic Dorset people decorated everyday implements, and traded over a wide geographic area.

An even more sophisticated culture displaced the Dorset about 1,000 years ago. The Thule period coincided with an era known as the "Medieval Warm Period," which lasted from about 950 to 1250 CE. The climate was warmer in the Northern Hemisphere, allowing bowhead whales access to Arctic waters. It is entirely possible that the Thule simply were following this valuable resource as they traversed the far north. The Thule developed a remarkable technology to flourish in the Arctic. They invented umiaks—large, multi-person boats framed with walrus ribs covered with walrus hide. They also developed toggling harpoons attached to seal-skin floats. Umiaks and the larger harpoons enabled hunters to go far out to sea to hunt bowhead whales, assisted by individuals in smaller kayaks. Whales could be harpooned in their feeding grounds, and the floats would keep them from diving to escape the hunters. These whales provided enormous amounts of food to support a village through the long winters. Seal hunters also perfected methods for taking seals at breathing holes, after ice clogged waterways in winter and whales were out of reach.

Thule women served a critical survival role. Hunters had to stay warm and dry. Any body part that got wet could develop frostbite, resulting in possible gangrene and death. The sewing skills of Thule women were vital to the community. The women sewed incredibly tiny, tight stitches using caribou sinew for thread. Caribou skin leggings, parkas, and other clothing was well-tailored, lightweight, and incredibly warm. Caribou hairs are hollow and filled with air, an excellent insulator. The Thule used waterproof sealskin for boots.

Thule transportation was well adapted to arctic life. Dogs were used to pull strong, light sleds crafted from driftwood with whalebone runners. Water poured on the runners would freeze instantly, making sleds that would glide easily over snow and ice. Umiaks could transport groups of hunters, dogs, and sleds over a great distance in search of food. Cooperation was crucial in surviving such a harsh environment. Small family groups would travel together in spring and summer, gathering in large permanent camps in winter for seal hunting. The Inuit reached the Atlantic coast at about the same time as the earliest Norse explorers, but little is known about the contact between them. As the climate grew colder during the Little Ice Age, the Thule abandoned their northernmost sites and concentrated their subsistence efforts on smaller marine mammals, notably ringed seals. As contact with Europeans increased, the Thule population decreased. The Thule are the immediate antecedents of contemporary Inuit.

Jill M. Church

Further Reading

McCannon, John. 2012. *A History of the Arctic: Nature, Exploration, and Exploitation.* London: Reaktion Books, Ltd.

McGhee, Robert. 1997. *Ancient People of the Arctic.* Vancouver: UBC Press.

Stern, Pamela R. 2010. *Daily Life of the Inuit.* Santa Barbara, CA: Greenwood.

CHINA AND EAST ASIA, 1000 TO 1500 CE

The years 1000 to 1500 CE, during which the Song (960–1279) and Yuan (1271–1368) dynasties flourished and fell, and the emperors of the Ming Dynasty (1368–1644) dispatched vast treasure fleets, were a remarkable time, though intermittent, of Chinese maritime activity and innovation. Innovative designs made seafaring more predictable and safe, increased trade, and made exotic goods from previously unimaginable foreign lands accessible to the Chinese court. Following their conquest of the Song and establishment of the Yuan Dynasty, the Mongols launched an ambitious invasion of Japan with a huge, newly constructed fleet. Pirates operating from outlying Japanese islands remained a problem, ravaging coastal communities and preying on merchant ships, prompting the Korean, Japanese, and Chinese governments to act against them.

The Song Dynasty inaugurated a period of unprecedented Chinese maritime activity. Jurchen nomads swept in from the north in 1127 CE, forcing the Song court to relocate from the landlocked capital city of Kaifeng to the coastal city of Hangzhou. Previously, taxes on land provided most of the state's revenues, and their loss encouraged emperors to seek new revenues from maritime trade. Traditional Chinese thought discouraged foreign trade for two reasons: encouraging the elite to pursue civil-service careers, and maintaining China's isolation from a world they thought had little to offer. Both dominant strains in Chinese philosophy—Confucianism and Legalism—thought poorly of mercantile pursuits. Confucianism encouraged the pursuit of scholarship and civil service as a means to fulfill filial piety to the emperor. Legalists—who ranked the social order—placed merchants last, following scholars, peasants, and craftsmen. Yet, the flight of the imperial court to coastal Hangzhou encouraged a reconsideration of merchants and trade, and the Song court increasingly relied on maritime activity for its survival. As profits from foreign trade rose, so too did the status of merchants.

Chinese overseas exports in the 11th century included iron, steel, crafts, and textiles, particularly silk. Chinese ships carried these goods throughout Southeast Asia, trading for tropical commodities, particularly spices. During the 12th century, the Song court encouraged innovation and oversaw the development of the junk, a new ship design that came to typify Chinese nautical architecture. These innovative ships were the most highly developed seafaring vessels of their time, equipped with magnetic compasses, interior compartments separated by bulkheads, and sails that could be raised and lowered with ropes and pulleys from the deck rather than requiring sailors to climb the masts. Junks also were larger than older ships, generally at least 100 feet long, with later models perhaps reaching more than 300 feet, thus they carried more cargo. Merchant junks traveled in fleets in search of trade to the east with Japan, Korea, Southeast Asia, and Indonesia; and to the west, crossing the Southeast Pacific and the Indian Ocean, reaching as far as

Compass

Thanks to a magnetized needle, a compass constantly points north (or south, depending on one's perspective). During the Han dynasty (206 BCE–220 CE) the property of a loadstone to consistently point south or north was used for divination and geomancy. Later, magnetic properties were transferred by induction to small pieces of iron. During the Qin dynasty (221–206 BCE) philosopher Han Fei refers to a "south-pointer" used to determine position.

The secretive nature of divination and geomancy, the agrarian character of China's civilization, and the passage of most trade by river and canal, limited the compass's diffusion to seafaring. It likely entered seafaring use during the Tang dynasty (618–907 CE) and was definitely in use after 850 CE. In *Mengxi Bitan* ("*Dream Pool Essays*") of 1088, cartographer, Shen Kuo (1031–1095 CE) described for the first time the magnetic compass and its maritime use. The *Pingzhou ketan* (1119 CE) of Zhu Yung reports that at night captains determined a ship's position by looking at the stars, but in bad weather they used the south-pointing needle. Floating compasses spread from China to the Islamic World and Europe, where they were refined into the dry compass, a pivoting needle over a wind rose in a glass-topped box, by 1300 CE. Floating compasses remained in use in China, though, into the 16th century when the Dutch introduced the dry-pivoted needle.

Claudia Zanardi

the East African coast. Hangzhou developed into a booming port city with resident foreign merchants offering the Chinese exotic curiosities, as well as medicines and spices from faraway lands.

In 1132, the Song court established a permanent navy, constructing warships to patrol the coast, as well as rivers and canals—particularly the Yangzi River to the north, where strong naval forces provided protection from the nomadic Jurchens who controlled large parts of China north of the river where they established the Jin Empire. In 1161, in the Battle of Caishi, Chinese warships repulsed a major Jurchen effort to cross the Yangzi River, and successfully defended Hangzhou from naval attack. Among the innovative warships deployed by the Song were 24 ships driven by human-powered paddle wheels. Chinese warships, armed with catapults and trebuchets, launched a variety of projectiles at enemy ships including clay pots filled with metal fragments, lime, and gunpowder, which exploded and ignited fires on enemy ships. The Song navy continued to grow; by 1237 CE it numbered 52,000 personnel who staffed a host of shore establishments and sailed more than 100 river- or seagoing warships, which patrolled China's many waterways and projected Chinese strength into the East China Sea, and the Korean and Japanese coasts.

The Jin Empire of the Jurchens, though, fell to Genghis Khan (1162–1227 CE) and his Mongol warriors, who captured Zhongdu (modern-day Beijing) in 1215 CE. Genghis Khan's grandson, Kublai Khan (1215–1294 CE), completed the conquest in 1233 CE, capturing Kaifeng. The growing Mongol Empire posed a much greater threat to the Song. Kublai, determined to conquer the rest of China, built his own navy with the help of former Song merchants and naval officers. In 1274 CE, Mongol ships raided Japan, landing troops on several islands. Despite several victories, increasing Japanese resistance and a typhoon which sank many Mongol ships forced the Mongols to withdraw.

The Mongols again turned their attention to the Song, capturing towns along the Han and Yangzi rivers and enlarging their navy with captured ships, as well as new construction facilitated by its conquest of river towns. Mongol ships dominated the Yangzi River by the end of 1275 CE, and Song merchants—sensing this shift of power—traded with the Mongols, even supplying them with ships and crews. The enlarged Mongol fleet captured the Song capitol of Hangzhou the following year, and members of the Song court took to the sea in junks. In 1279 CE, a Mongol fleet trapped the remnants of the Song navy off the coast of Guangzhou, and the Song emperor leapt from his vessel to his death, opening the way for Kublai Khan to claim the throne and establish the next Chinese dynasty, the Yuan. Emboldened by his success, Kublai Khan again focused on Japan, launching an even larger effort to capture the islands in 1281 CE. This campaign, too, failed, due to another typhoon—an enormous storm that wrecked hundreds of Mongol ships and inspired the Japanese to claim divine protection of the "*kamikaze*" winds.

The Yuan Dynasty, like the Song, embarked on expansive maritime ventures. Yuan-era fleets traveled to Annam (modern-day Vietnam), Java, Sumatra, Ceylon, and India. According to Marco Polo (1254–1324 CE), they even reached Madagascar. Missions ranged in purpose from diplomacy and trade to military reprisal and conquest, including repeated efforts to conquer Vietnam. Marco Polo reported seeing vessels of the Yuan court at the port city of Quanzhou, describing the junks as four-masted with crews numbering more than 150 people. The Yuan capital, Khanbalik (modern-day Beijing), was supported by products from across China, such as grain, via internal waterways and from across the world via its extensive trade-route networks. In addition to trade and its military and political endeavors, Yuan maritime activities fostered a great exchange of thought between China, India, and lands farther west. Buddhist texts and relics continued to find a ready market in China.

Despite the naval power of the Song and Yuan dynasties, formidable bands of pirates established themselves throughout East Asia in these years, attacking ships and ravaging coastal communities in Korea, Japan, and China. These pirates earned the name "*wokou*" in Chinese, meaning "Japanese bandits," based not on their ethnicity, as their number included Chinese and Koreans, but rather because many of the bands operated from Japan. In the 11th century, Korean builders designed warships armed with rams to combat the *wokou*, which proved successful against both pirates and Yuan warships during an aborted 13th-century invasion. Pirates, though, remained a problem, and were particularly active in the 12th and 14th centuries, in the eras of Song, and later Yuan, decline.

Less than 100 years after coming to power, the Yuan rule weakened. Famines, droughts, and floods plagued the land and quarrelling government leaders lost popular support. Ethnic Chinese, treated harshly by Kublai's successors, provided ready support for rebels, two of which—the Han and the Ming—met in battle in 1363 CE at Lake Poyang. The victorious Ming displaced the remnants of Mongol (and Han) power, and established a dynasty that would rule until 1644 CE.

The highlight of Ming maritime activity was the construction and voyages of the great treasure fleets commanded by Zheng He (1371–1435 CE). A Ming court eunuch with a military background, the emperor appointed Zheng He to lead seven overseas expeditions between 1405 CE and 1433 CE. The primary mission of these voyages was not trade. Rather, these were diplomatic missions that established and enhanced Chinese presence overseas. Destinations included Southeast Asia, India, the Middle East, and East Africa. Although varying in size among the expeditions, Zheng He's fleets numbered more than 60 ships and 25,000 crew members, and the ships themselves were of previously unprecedented size—several times the size of contemporary European ships. Zheng He's flagship measured about 450 feet long and 180 feet wide. The treasure fleets departed with silk, porcelain, gold, and silver, which they offered to faraway rulers as gifts, receiving in exchange curiosities and tribute ranging from ivory, precious stones, spices, and exotic animals—including lions, ostriches, and giraffes, which found particular favor in the imperial court. Heavily armed and loaded with troops, Zheng He's ships also spread Chinese influence by force of arms, destroying pirates, and settling local disputes by placing pro-Chinese rulers on several thrones.

The seventh treasure fleet returned in 1433 CE, and China never dispatched another. Within the court, Confucian scholars regained their traditional ascendance and their resurgence coincided with declining profit from foreign ventures, a situation exacerbated by the immense cost of Zheng He's treasure fleets. Once again, the imperial court emphasized agricultural production and discouraged foreign ventures and overseas trade. As isolationist thought returned, naval funding declined and the great Ming navy withered. Confucian scholars disparaged merchants for acting in self-interest rather than the interests of the state. Increasingly, Ming rulers restricted foreign trade, and eventually placed all overseas trade under government control. Soon, foreign trade only could occur within the confines of the tribute system. Merchants who traded outside these strictures were considered pirates, which further encouraged the resurgence of piracy along China's coast as the Ming navy declined in strength. For a time the Ming court hired Shaolin monks to fight the pirates, but these efforts met with limited success. A great era in Chinese maritime activity, which included substantial innovation in naval technology, the construction of large numbers of ships of enormous size and sophistication, and a sporadic but steady increase in both the scale and the scope of Chinese activity at sea, came to an end. As the Ming court turned inward, European explorers and traders entered the Indian Ocean and became increasingly important to regional trade and eventually trade with China.

Amanda Yeargin

Further Reading

Curtin, Philip D. 1984. *Cross Cultural Trade in World History*. London: Cambridge University Press.

Delgado, James. 2010. *Khubilai Khan's Lost Fleet: In Search of a Legendary Armada*. Oakland, CA: University of California Press.

Dreyer, Edward L. 2006. *Zheng He: China and the Oceans in the Early Ming Dynasty, 1405–1433*. New York: Longman.

Levanthes, Louise. 1994. *When China Ruled the Seas*. Oxford: Oxford University Press.

Lo, Jung-Pang. 1957. *China As a Sea Power*. Seattle: NUS Press.

Reddick, Zachary. 2014. "The Zheng He Voyages Reconsidered: A Means of Imperial Power Projection." *Quarterly Journal of Chinese Studies* 3.1.

So, Billy K. L. 2000. *Prosperity, Region, and Institutions in Maritime China: The South Fukien Pattern, 946–1368*. Cambridge: Harvard University Asia Center.

So, Kwan-wai. 1975. *Japanese Piracy in Ming China During the Sixteenth Century*. Lansing: Michigan State University Press.

Junk

The junk is the typical sailing ship found on rivers, canals, lakes, and at sea in South and East Asia. The term "junk" comes from the Portuguese word "*junco*" or the Dutch word "*jonk*," which in turn likely derived from the word for ship in Malay ("*Jong*"), Javanese ("*djong*"), or most likely, Chinese ("*rongke*"). Built of wood, its flat or slightly rounded bottom hull was made of multiple transverse bulkheads (compartments), which could be made watertight. The planking of the hull did not close in towards the stern as in it did in other vessels. Rather, a transom of straight planks closes it. Fewer bulkheads were required than frames or ribs to give the same degree of strength and rigidity than vessels built with different designs. Junks had square and full battened sails, and long strips of wood were inserted in the sails. Well before their adoption in the West, junks had stern-mounted rudders. Rudders with holes (fenestrated rudders)—which made steering the rudder easier—were introduced in the 13th century.

A term applied to a wide variety of Chinese sailing ships, junks were traditionally made of teak and employed sails with battens as shown in this illustration. In the 15th century, Zheng He's fleet included very large junks, perhaps as long as 500 feet. (Corel)

The lost naval section of the *Yüeh Chüeh Shu* (circa first century CE), provided the military strategist Zixu's description of the navy of the Wu Kingdom during the Western Zhou Dynasty (1046–771 BCE) and the Spring and Autumn period (771–476 BCE). It listed the great wing ("*da yi*"); little wing ("*xiao yi*"); stomach striker ("*tu wei*"); tower, deck, or castle ship ("*lou chuan*"), and bridge boats ("*qiao chuan*"). It also explained that the navy applied land techniques to fighting at sea. Hence, "the great wings are used as the heavy chariots of the land forces, the little wings are used as the light chariots of the land forces. The deck ships are like the infantry . . . and the bridge boats are like the light cavalry" (Lo 2012, 28).

Different types of ships characterized different geographical regions. In the north, on canals and rivers, sable ships ("*shachuan*"), large flat-bottom sailing junks with no keel (the lowest longitudinal timber of a vessel on which framework the ship is built) prevailed. Ocean-going junks were diffused along the southern coasts of the empire (Guangdong, Fujian). In the 10th century, maritime trade soared and under the Song Dynasty (960–1279 CE) some ocean-going junks called "giant ships" ("*jujian*") reached 300 feet in length and 1,250 tons. Smaller versions ("*gezhou*") were diffused south along the coasts of Zhejiang and Fujian, and were used to transport people, mainly on rivers. The large ships used to transport tributes such as the ships of Zheng He's expeditions (1405–1433 CE) were called treasure ships ("*baochauan*").

Claudia Zanardi

Further Reading

Levathes, L. 1996. *When China Ruled the Seas: The Treasure Fleet of the Dragon Throne, 1405–1433*. New York: Oxford University Press.

Lo, J.-P. 2012. *China As a Sea Power, 1137–1368. A Preliminary Survey of the Maritime Expansion and Naval Exploits of the Chinese People during the Southern Song and Yuan Periods*. B. A. Elleman (ed.). Hong Kong: Hong Kong University Press.

Needham, J. 1970. *Science and Technology in China*. Vol. 4, Pt. 3, sec. 29, "Nautical Technology," 379–699.

Worchester, G. R. G. 1971. *The Junks of the World*. Annapolis: Naval Institute Press.

Mongol Invasions of Japan

The Mongol invasions of Japan are among the largest naval invasions in history. While on his way to conquer the Southern Song Dynasty of China, the Mongol Emperor Kublai Khan (1215–1294 CE) dispatched 900 ships from Korea to invade Japan in 1274 CE. The fleet landed in Hakata—a flourishing center of international trade in western Japan—set fire to the city and advanced farther inland. Nevertheless, it is recorded that the invading troops suddenly retreated to their ships and returned to Korea. The reasons for the retreat remain vague. Scholars have suggested that a strong storm is to blame for the failed invasion. This is debatable, however, because returning to ships in a storm—instead of staying on land—is an illogical and hazardous decision. Some Chinese accounts indicate that Japanese Samurai offered strong resistance to the invasion, and this might have instigated the withdrawal. Whatever the case, the first invasion of Japan ended in failure.

Kublai's attention returned to Japan after he defeated the Southern Song Dynasty and cemented his rule over all of China. This time, he amassed a massive fleet of more than 4,000 vessels from both China and Korea, which sailed in 1281 CE. The 900 ships from Korea arrived first, however, and the departure of the remaining ships from China was delayed for more than a month. The fleet from Korea failed to secure a land base in Japan, perhaps prevented by defensive stone walls constructed between the two invasions. When the two fleets finally met, they landed on Takashima Island in Imari Bay north of Nagasaki. Historical records indicate that strong wind and waves crushed the invading fleet, destroying 9 out of 10 ships and killing an equal portion of the troops. The Japanese believed that the storm was brought by the gods, thus the belief in "*Kamikaze*" ("divine wind") was born.

Until recently, the only way to study the Mongol invasions of Japan was through historical sources. Underwater archaeological excavation conducted at Takashima Island, however, has begun to shed new light on the details of the second invasion of Japan. Artifacts—including swords, helmets, arrows, ceramic storage jars, ship timbers, and anchors—were found underwater and some naval aspects of the invasion have been revealed. Four anchors were found intact in the seabed in a single line, which suggests that a strong wind was blowing at the time of the ships' sinking. Perhaps the most important artifact, if not the most interesting, is "*Tetsuhau*"—a type of grenade made of ceramic. This ordnance packed with scrap metal was most likely thrown using a catapult. The study of artifacts from underwater archaeological sites is time-consuming because conservation of artifacts requires years, and sometime even decades. So far, it appears that there were several types of vessels present at Takashima, such as large cargo ships and miscellaneous medium-sized vessels, as well as smaller landing-craft. Surprisingly, the majority of the finds (including hull timbers) were from southern China. There is some evidence of possible repairs on the hull timbers, but no clear conclusion can be drawn. A 2015 survey project at Takashima has led to the discovery of a well-preserved vessel for the first time. The naval organization of the invasion might soon be deciphered thanks to this discovery. This Chinese vessel, approximately 39 feet in length, was a fast-moving vessel that perhaps carried troops to shore.

Randall Sasaki

Further Reading

Conlan, Thomas. 2001. *In Little Need of Divine Intervention.* Ithaca: Cornell University Press.

Delgado, James. 2008. *Khubilai Khan's Lost Fleet: In Search of a Legendary Armada.* Berkeley: University of California Press.

Ota, Koki. 1997. *Mōko Shūrai: Sono Gunjishiteki Kenkyū* (*Mongol Invasion: The Study of Its Military History*). Tokyo: Kinseisha.

Sasaki, Randall. 2015. *The Origins of the Lost Fleet of the Mongol Empire.* College Station: Texas A&M University Press.

Zheng He, 1371–1435 CE

Zheng He was a Ming Dynasty military leader who achieved legendary status for his command of fleets that conducted seven unprecedented voyages across the Indian Ocean. Born with the name "Ma He" near Kunming, the provincial capital

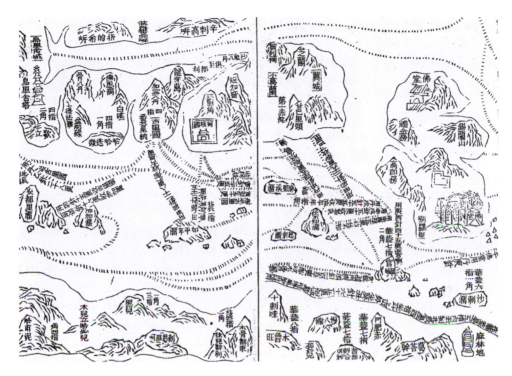

Zheng He (1371–1435) led a succession of Chinese fleets that sailed throughout Southeast Asia and the Indian Ocean. His sailing charts were published in 1628 in *Wubei Zhi* (*Treatise on Armament Technology*). This chart shows India (top left), Ceylon (far right) and Africa (bottom). (Cartography/Universal History Archive/UIG/Bridgeman Images)

of China's Yunnan Province, he was the scion of an influential Muslim family originating from Bukhara in present-day Uzbekistan. Ma He's father was killed during the1381 Ming invasion of Yunnan and in 1382 CE Ma He was taken prisoner, castrated, and put to work as a eunuch official in the household of the future Ming Dynasty Yongle Emperor (1360–1424 CE). Although born a Muslim, as an adult Zheng He practiced Buddhism and paid tribute to Chinese gods.

Zheng He excelled in his official duties, serving, among other functions, as a military commander in the civil war that put Yongle on the throne. When Yongle formed his court in 1402, Zheng He was assigned the rank of grand director, the highest rank a eunuch could achieve. As director of palace servants, his responsibilities included the construction and maintenance of the palace buildings. In 1403 CE, Yongle ordered construction of a fleet to project Chinese power across the South China Sea and into the Indian Ocean, and appointed Zheng He its commander. In 1404 CE, Yongle changed Ma He's name to "Zheng He," in recognition of his distinguished leadership during the defense of the Zheng Village Dike and its associated reservoir during the civil war.

When Zheng He's first expedition sailed from Nanjing, China, in 1405 CE, the 255-ship fleet contained a variety of vessels, including 62 described as enormous "treasure ships." Although the specific design and the structural characteristics of these ships are lost, the vessels were certainly of unprecedented scale. Usually estimated to have been between 385 and 440 feet long with breadths between 150 and 180 feet, some writers argue that they might have been as long as 600 feet. These treasure ships were most likely enlargements of the compartmented and relatively flat-bottomed Chinese river barges common in the early Ming Dynasty. They are believed to have incorporated an off-center and off-vertical arrangement of nine masts arrayed in three banks. The six subsequent expeditions were of roughly the same size and composition.

These expeditions are better understood as assertions of imperial power among tributary states than voyages of exploration or trade. The roughly 28,000 members of each fleet were predominantly soldiers, but also included sailors, navigators and other ship's officers, craftsmen, and other specialists. The destinations to which the fleets sailed were relatively well known and many already boasted sizeable Chinese communities. Zheng He bestowed gifts of paper money and imperial recognition upon the regional rulers he encountered and carried those rulers' tributes and ambassadors to China.

The first expedition visited the Hindu kingdom of Champa, a Chinese ally against Annan, the Vietnamese state on China's southern border. It continued to Java and then through the Malacca Strait calling at several entrepôts. After resupplying in the Andaman Islands, Zheng He's fleet visited Sri Lanka and proceeded to the Indian cities of Quilon and Cochin prior to reaching its farthest destination, Calicut, the port that dominated Indian Ocean trade. The return journey retraced the outward route, detouring slightly to visit Palembang where Zheng He's forces captured a troublesome Chinese pirate and installed a Chinese merchant as the port's administrator.

The second and third journeys departed in 1407 and 1409 CE, and generally followed the route of the first. When visiting Java, the second expedition settled a Chinese dispute with the declining Majapahit Empire and thereby underpinned the succeeding Singosari Dynasty. The strength of Zheng He's forces usually intimidated rulers, allowing him to achieve his goals without resorting to violence—but, when necessary, he employed force. During the third expedition, for example, Chinese troops battled local forces to settle a leadership dispute on Ceylon. Probably during this visit, although possibly during the return transit from the second voyage, Zheng He erected the surviving Galle Stone praising Buddha, Vishnu, and Allah in Chinese, Tamil, and Persian.

Zheng He's fourth, fifth, and sixth expeditions (departing in 1412, 1417, and 1421 CE) took the same route to India, but then continued westward. The fourth expedition visited the Maldives and Hormuz, the most important trade hub in the western Indian Ocean. The fifth and sixth expeditions likely again visited Hormuz and then sailed to Aden, Mogadishu, and Malindi. Their stopovers in East Africa are remembered for the giraffes they carried home among the tribute cargo. On arriving in China, these animals were greeted as mythical "*kirin*," heavenly creatures that only appear when the Middle Kingdom has entered into alignment with the heavens and thus powerful symbols of imperial virtue.

In 1421 CE, likely shortly after the departure of the sixth voyage, Yongle suspended support for future voyages. Later that year, his son ascended to the throne as the Hongxi Emperor (1378–1425 CE) and made the suspension permanent. Hongxi charged Zheng He with supervising construction of the Great Baoen Temple in Nanjin. After the temple was completed, the next emperor, Yongle's grandson Xuande (1399–1435) ordered a seventh expedition which departed in 1430 and traveled as far as Hormuz.

Over the past six centuries, Zheng He's voyages have been interpreted by oral tradition, plays, novels, films, and other media. Luo Maodeng's 1597 novel *Sanbao Taijin Xia Xiyang Ji Tongsu Yanyi* ("*The Grand Director of the Three Treasures Goes to the Western Ocean*") was particularly important in moving the legend Zheng He away from its historical basis. Gavin Menzies's 2002 work of nonfiction, *1421*, became a global bestseller despite dubious reception from scholars who rejected Menzies's argument that Zheng He visited Australia, the Americas, and even Greenland. In recent years, the Chinese government has promoted Zheng He's image as a peaceful and inclusive forbearer of China's current economic rise and expanding naval power. Beijing has financed conferences, publications, monuments, study centers, and commemorative societies dedicated to Zheng He's legacy.

John F. Bradford

Further Reading

Dreyer, Edward L. 2006. *Zheng He: China and the Oceans in the Early Ming Dynasty, 1405–1433*. New York: Pearson.

Levathes, Louise. 1994. *When China Ruled the Seas*. New York: Simon and Schuster.

Suryadinata, Leo. 2005. *Admiral Zheng He and Southeast Asia*. Singapore: Institute of Southeast Asian Studies.

EUROPE, 1000 TO 1500 CE

The seas surrounding the European continent played an important role in shaping European politics and society between 1000 and 1500 CE and continued afterward. Europe is bordered to the north by the North Sea and Baltic Sea, to the west by the Atlantic Ocean, and to the south by the Mediterranean Sea; Europeans thus had ready access to water routes in every direction. Although much foreign influence flowed into Europe via these seas, the intense European exploration of and expansion across these seas also connected Europe to—and allowed it to influence—the rest of the world.

These seas teemed with all types of activity by the end of the first millennium. Piracy became a threat to northern Europeans by the late eighth century, when the Vikings began conducting raids along the coasts and up the river systems of England, Ireland, and Continental Europe, as far south as Italy, and as far east as Russia and Byzantium. Slavic pirates preyed so relentlessly on North and Baltic Sea trade routes by the 12th century that merchants of German port cities banded together to form an association—the Hanseatic League—to protect and regulate maritime trade.

The Mediterranean's well-developed trade networks combined with plentiful, readymade hiding places such as islets, bays, and coves made it an attractive workplace for pirates. Piracy flourished in the medieval Mediterranean, as the Slavic pagan Narentines raided extensively from their Dalmatian coastal base into eastern and southern Italy. The Narentines were such a formidable force in the ninth-century Adriatic that they defeated the powerful Venetians in naval battle. North African Muslim pirates wreaked havoc from Iberia to Crete early in this period, preying on the fledgling trade networks of western Mediterranean port cities. In fact, the expansion of cities such as Genoa into the wider Mediterranean world began as an effort to protect their nascent trade networks from Muslim pirates, who had sacked the city in 934–35 CE. The Genoese took to the seas in the following decades and, in the process of combating these raiders, mastered galley warfare and emerged as a maritime power in the western Mediterranean. The Italian city of Pisa similarly emerged as a regional power, and by 1016 CE it had allied with Genoa to repulse Mujahid al-Siqlabi (n.d.), the Muslim ruler of Denia in eastern Spain, from Sardinia. The attraction of Sardinia to the Genoese and Pisans was its abundant supply of sheep, slaves, salt, and grain, the last of which both were needed due to scarce agricultural lands at home; the two rivals knew that securing such precious resources meant their cities' survival, but also expanded trade opportunities.

The years before the turn of the millennium had seen the westward movement of Europeans across the North Atlantic. As the Vikings continued to raid and colonize northern Europe, livestock farmers by the ninth century had begun to colonize Iceland. Overpopulation and famine fueled their westward expansion, leading to Erik the Red's (ca. 950–1003) discovery of Greenland in the late 10th century, where the Vikings established numerous farmsteads and engaged in trade. The Vikings used Greenland as a springboard for their advance to North America, either by accident or intent, where Erik the Red's son, Leif Eriksson (ca. 970–1020 CE) established a temporary settlement in modern-day Newfoundland. Named

"Vinland," it flourished briefly, but hostile relationships with locals eventually led to its abandonment. The Vikings were thus the first Europeans to connect their continent to North America via the sea, but were unable to establish a permanent presence there.

Economic stagnation plagued Europe following the Roman Empire's demise, but the "Agricultural Revolution" near the turn of the millennium increased crop yields, which spurred population growth and increased seaborne trade. Agricultural innovations included a more durable plow, improved horse collar and horseshoes, and more productive crop-rotation patterns, which further boosted yields. The resultant growth in agricultural productivity and labor-saving effects of these developments freed many Europeans—who previously had been tied to the fields—to move to nearby towns and pursue occupations beyond farming. Urban life grew and thrived, producing what scholars have labeled the "Commercial Revolution," as cities became the centers of local, then regional, then long-distance trade across Europe and the Mediterranean. The Crusades, beginning in the late 11th century, proved an important catalyst for this growing commerce. Defending the Crusader States' important port cities was mostly the responsibility of western merchants/colonists from Genoa, Venice, Pisa, Marseille, and other port cities. Crusade leaders granted them financial and legal privileges—and even control of their own respective city neighborhoods—in return for naval support. Numerous Italian merchant colonies sprang up along the Levantine Coast in Acre, Tyre, Beirut, Tripoli, and other cities, and trade flowed from west to east through them, sustaining the Crusader States. Of equal importance was the flow of eastern luxury items such as Chinese silk and Asian/Indian spices to the West, which increased trade flowing through European cities.

The lucrative nature of this eastern trade spurred innovations in maritime technology that facilitated the movement of goods westward in high volume. The Vikings had long used a small cargo vessel, the "*knarr*," for trading ventures along Scandinavian, Irish, and Greenlandic coasts, but it proved to be incapable of hauling the larger cargoes of long-distance trade. The popular oared galley, although useful for lessening the problem of erratic Mediterranean winds, was expensive to operate and less suitable for long-distance trade than was the *knarr*. Shipbuilders responded by developing the two workhorses of high-medieval seaborne transportation: the cog, followed by the hulk. Both ships were designed for transporting bulkier loads over longer distances. They had wide, flat bottoms and steep sides—which maximized cargo capacity and facilitated loading and unloading in port—one mast and sail, as well as a stern-mounted rudder for improved maneuverability. This rudder, which first appeared on late-12th-century cogs in the North Sea and Baltic Sea and then quickly spread to the Mediterranean, was the first to be mounted permanently on a ship's hull. The design of cogs and hulks was excellent for long-distance shipping, but sacrificed speed. Late-medieval shipbuilders addressed this deficiency by introducing two new ship designs that were large enough to maintain stability in rough waters and carry provisions for long voyages. The Portuguese developed the caravel for long-distance exploration, rigging it with triangular lateen sails, which gave it speed and the ability to sail into the wind. Later appearing in southern Europe was the carrack, which was larger than the caravel, and thus had room for up to four masts to the caravel's two or three. It was in fact these types of ships that carried Christopher Columbus and his crew to the New World on his famous 1492 voyage; the *Santa Maria* was a carrack, and the *Niña* and the *Pinta* were both caravels.

Beyond improvements in ship design, the 12th and following centuries were a time of innovations in maritime navigation that were instrumental in both increasing long-distance seaborne trade across Europe and initiating an age of European exploration of and expansion into the Indian and Atlantic Oceans. The adoption and late-12th-century improvement of the magnetic compass by northern Europeans began a navigational revolution and spread throughout the continent. The earliest compasses were simply a magnetized pointer floating in water. By 1300 CE,

---

Portolan Chart

Portolan charts were a major innovation in early European cartography. Originating in Italy and Spain in the 13th century, and based on compass directions and distances estimated from seafarers' observations, they preserved, in cartographic form, the experiences and wisdom of mariners who had navigated the Mediterranean Sea for generations. The charts recorded landmarks, ports, and trade routes (indeed, the derivation of "portolan" is the Italian word "*portolano*," meaning a book of sailing directions and port locations).

These maps reveal the importance medieval cartographers and mariners placed on having a thorough knowledge of Mediterranean wind patterns. A characteristic feature of a portolan is its network of "wind rose lines" emanating from compass roses placed strategically across the map; the wind rose lines' purpose is to display typical wind directions and compass points for the map reader. Portolan charts were not merely maps, however, but also works of art, often including intricately drawn cityscapes, geographic features/flora/fauna/peoples characteristic of a particular region, and even ships and sea monsters on the high seas. Over time, these maps became prized for their accuracy throughout Europe, which most likely explains why mapmakers eventually adopted the practice of including on them a cartouche for the purpose of advertising their names and the charts' creation dates. Their importance was such that competing maritime nations during the Age of Discovery often classified them as state secrets.

Brian N. Becker

Europeans had produced the dry compass, which consisted of a magnetized needle attached to a compass rose and covered by glass or contained within a wooden box. Mariners later added a gimbal to the compass to preserve its horizontal position relative to the ocean's surface, minimizing its jostling in rough seas. The introduction and development of the compass came at roughly the same time that seafarers developed more accurate ways to calculate their ship's position through dead reckoning, using the ship's former position in combination with its speed and direction over time.

Additionally, the development of portolan charts by Italian and Spanish mapmakers in the early 14th century greatly aided mariners' navigation of the Mediterranean. These charts contain representations of trade routes, harbors, and important geographical features, a thorough knowledge of which was crucial to successfully navigate dangerous seas. Portolans almost always display wind roses, compasses, and rhumb lines (which indicate wind direction). They primarily are a functional tool, but also are works of art—usually displaying detailed images of Mediterranean port cities and elaborately drawn animals, people, and even sea monsters.

In combination, these innovations fundamentally altered mariners' relationship with the Mediterranean both by allowing for more precise maritime navigation and lengthening the sailing season to include most of the winter, a season previously viewed as too dangerous for long-distance seafaring. Mediterranean maritime trade experienced sustained expansion in these centuries, which eventually went beyond southern Europe to include the entire continent. The earliest surviving evidence of direct maritime trade between the Mediterranean and the English Channel comes from the end of the 13th century.

By the 14th century, piracy replaced Viking raids as the most serious threat to northern seas trade. The Hanseatic League had grown to include nearly 200 port cities from England to Russia and succeeded in curbing piracy and dominating trade in northern Europe until the 16th century. The emergence and uniting of powerful northern European nation-states, however, served to diminish the access of member cities to many important domestic markets in the northern seas. Another problem for the league was the development of new maritime connections, between both the Baltic and Mediterranean, and Europe and the Americas, which redirected trade westward to ports facing the Atlantic Ocean. In the late-medieval Mediterranean, the citizens of Barcelona, Marseille, Genoa, Venice, and other Mediterranean maritime cities continued to engage in widespread piracy, both private and state sponsored.

The Byzantine Empire's decaying naval power had, by the 14th century, created an opening for the Ottoman Empire to assert itself in eastern Mediterranean waters. A strong Ottoman naval presence in the eastern Mediterranean, including the pirates in its employ who preyed on east-west shipping, soon forced western merchants to abandon the traditional trade routes linking East and West through the Levant and search for new ones. The kingdoms of the Iberian Peninsula took the lead in this search, as first the Portuguese and then the Spanish embarked on sustained, long-distance maritime exploration, inaugurating what later scholars labeled the "Age of Discovery." Portugal's Prince Henry the Navigator (1394–1460 CE) was a key figure in this age's initiation, recruiting some of his day's best cartographers, geographers, and pilots to his kingdom with promises of financial backing for maritime expeditions to the west and south. The Portuguese discovered and settled Madeira (1418 CE) and the Azores (1431 CE), and sailed south along the African coast, discovering some gold and entering the slave trade.

Expeditions rounded Africa's southern tip in 1487, and reached India in 1498, establishing direct European-Indian Ocean trade. Portugal's successes motivated Spain to fund similar voyages, among them Columbus's 1492 voyage that claimed the Americas and Caribbean for Spain. This, however, only was the beginning of European expansion across the seas. By the mid-16th century, the Portuguese controlled the Indian Ocean spice trade and established trading networks that reached Japan, and Spanish expeditions had discovered the Pacific Ocean, circumnavigated the globe, claimed the Philippines, and explored the interior of the Americas.

Brian N. Becker

Further Reading

Adams, Jonathan. 2013. *A Maritime Archaeology of Ships: Innovation and Social Change in Late Medieval and Early Modern Europe*. Oxford: Oxbow Books.

Brummett, Palmira. 1994. *Ottoman Seapower and Levantine Diplomacy in the Age of Discovery*. Albany: State University of New York Press.

Dollinger, Philippe. 1970. *The German Hansa*. D. S. Ault and S. H. Steinberg (trans.). Stanford: Stanford University Press.

Dor-Ner, Zvi, and William Scheller. 1991. *Columbus and the Age of Discovery*. New York: William Morrow and Company, Inc.

Eddison, Jill. 2013. *Medieval Pirates: Pirates, Raiders and Privateers 1204–1453*. Stroud, Gloucestershire: The History Press.

Graham-Campbell, James. 1980. *The Viking World*. London: Frances Lincoln.

Konstam, Angus. 2008. *Piracy: The Complete History*. Oxford: Osprey Publishing.

Meier, Dirk. 2006. *Seafarers, Merchants and Pirates in the Middle Ages*. Angus McGeoch (trans.). Woodbridge, England and Rochester, NY: Boydell and Brewer.

Rose, Susan. 2012. *Medieval Naval Warfare 1000–1500*. London and New York: Routledge.

Rose, Susan. 2012. *The Medieval Sea*. London and New York: Hambledon Continuum.

Scammell, Geoffrey V. 1981. *The World Encompassed: The First European Maritime Empires c. 800–1650*. Berkeley: University of California Press.

Stockwell, Foster. 2003. *Westerners in China: A History of Exploration and Trade, Ancient Times Through the Present*. Jefferson, NC and London: McFarland & Company.

Stuckey, Jace (ed.). 2014. *The Eastern Mediterranean Frontier of Latin Christendom*. Aldershot: Ashgate Variorum.

Benjamin of Tudela

Benjamin of Tudela was one of the most famous travelers of the Middle Ages. He traveled extensively throughout Europe, Asia, and Africa from the early 1160s to 1173 CE, recording his experiences in detailed notes over the course of his journeys. These notes, written in the simple Hebrew of a merchant or trader, later were compiled by an acquaintance to form the "Itinerary of Benjamin of Tudela," which scholars justly regard one of the most valuable sources for the history of Jewish communities in the medieval Mediterranean world.

Benjamin wrote virtually nothing about himself; he instead recorded the distance and interesting geographical features located between the Jewish communities he visited, the leaders and sizes of these communities, and the presence of Talmudic schools. It is clear from his itinerary that Benjamin viewed these communities as component parts of a more-broadly conceived community of "Mediterranean" Jews who were bound together by the sea. There is no scholarly consensus on what motivated Benjamin's travels. Nothing suggests that he was commissioned by a secular ruler, or that a Jewish community sent him, but his consistent inclusion of local holy sites, traditions, and miracles make it probable that the journey was, at least in part, a pilgrimage. The probability of this is strengthened by both the reverence and grief with which Benjamin describes the Holy Land's sacred sites and their post-crusade Christian appropriation, respectively. Benjamin's profession also provided an impetus for his long journey, as it was not uncommon during the 12th century for Jewish merchants to undertake commercial expeditions measuring thousands of miles.

Readers of the itinerary gain good information on various aspects of the Mediterranean economy and the numerous merchants who plied their trade across the sea. Benjamin describes such goods as the high-quality sugar produced at Tyre; Chios' mastic trees; the snow-white pepper, calamus, and ginger of Khulam; and the silk produced at Thessalonica. He further notes the presence of foreign merchants in numerous locales, including Byzantines and Egyptians in Barcelona and Montpellier; Genoese throughout Greece; Moroccans in Montpellier and Alexandria; and Babylonians, Persians, Medians, Egyptians, Canaanites, Russians, Hungarians, Patzinakians, Khazarians, Lombards, and Spanish in Constantinople. Benjamin's writings are made even more valuable by his observations concerning the physical appearance and layout of the cities he visited. He remarks that a wall surrounds the city of Genoa, and that each house has a tower from the top of which they fight each other in times of strife. Benjamin even compliments the architect of Alexandria—Alexander the Great—for building a city with great understanding, "for its streets are wide and straight, so that a man can look along them for a mile from gate to gate, from the gate of Reshid to the gate by the sea" (Adler 2007, 104). Benjamin of Tudela could have been a typical Jewish merchant-traveler for his day but, because of the survival of his travel account, he has ultimately made an invaluable contribution to our knowledge of trade, travel, and Jewish life in the medieval Mediterranean world.

Brian N. Becker

Further Reading

American-Israeli Cooperative Enterprise. 2015. "Benjamin of Tudela." http://www.jewish virtuallibrary.org/jsource/biography/BenjaminTudelo.html. Accessed January 15, 2015.

Benjamin, Sandra. 1995. *The World of Benjamin of Tudela: A Medieval Mediterranean Travelogue.* Teaneck, NJ: Fairleigh Dickinson University Press.

Benjamin of Tudela. Marcus Nathan Adler (trans.). 2007. *The Itinerary of Benjamin of Tudela.* Gloucester, United Kingdom: Dodo Press.

Jacoby, David. 2008. "Benjamin of Tudela and His 'Book of Travels'." Klaus Herbers and Felicitas Schmieder (eds.). In *Venezia incrocio di culture.* Rome: Edizioni di storia e letteratura, 135–64.

Shatzmiller, Joseph. 1998. "Jews, Pilgrimage, and the Christian Cult of Saints: Benjamin of Tudela and His Contemporaries." In *After Rome's Fall: Narrators and Sources of Early Medieval History. Essays Presented to Walter A. Goffart.* Alexander C. Murray (ed.). Toronto: University of Toronto Press, 337–47.

Cog

The cog was one of the main types of medieval ship used in maritime trade and military roles on northwestern European seas from about the 11th to the 15th century. Some elements of the structural form of the cog have been traced to vessels as early as the fourth century BCE, though recent researchers place greater emphasis on Romano-Celtic shipbuilding techniques in the development of the cog.

The first known use of the term "cog" to refer to a ship appears in the ninth century. Images that could represent cogs appear on coins recovered at Hedeby, a medieval trading center on the Jutland Peninsula near modern Schleswig. Other documents from the same period mention the cog as "the ship of the Frisians," traders who lived on the European coast between the Rhine and Elbe Rivers (Hutchinson 1994, 15). In the 12th to 15th centuries, the cog was the mainstay of the Hanseatic trading cities that dominated North Sea and Baltic Sea trade.

The cog had a flat-bottomed, double-ended hull. Bottom planks were flush-laid (i.e., positioned side by side without overlapping), and the bottom transitioned abruptly upward where it joined the straight stem- and sternposts that extended from the keel at an angle to form the ends of the ship. Thick overlapping planks running from end to end ("staves") were nailed together to complete the high-sided hulls. Cogs bore a single square sail for propulsion and, after the mid-12th century, were steered by a centerline rudder hung from their sternpost using a hinge-like arrangement of iron pins ("pintles") and hollow cylindrical sockets ("gudgeons"). The result was a sturdy ship with ample cargo space.

Their strong roomy structure also fitted cogs well to military roles, and by the late 10th century they were being used to transport soldiers. Their high sides provided a height advantage over the oar-driven galley in ship-to-ship combat. To overcome this disadvantage, raised structures in the form of bow and stern fighting castles were built, leading to a cycle of building as each builder sought the advantage. One document (a grant of rights to a Danish monastery at Næstved) might indicate the outfitting of cogs as warships by 1249 CE. The Hanseatic cities had armed their ships with cannon by the late 14th century. Soon afterward, sailing ships replaced oar-driven ships in the English fleet. The utility of the vessel eventually led to its widespread use as far away as the Mediterranean Sea.

Larry A. Grant

Further Reading

Hattendorf, John B., and Richard W. Unger (eds.). 2003. *War at Sea in the Middle Ages and the Renaissance*. Rochester, NY: Boydell Press.

Hutchinson, Gillian. 1994. *Medieval Ships and Shipping*. London: Leicester University Press.

McCarthy, Michael. 2005. *Ships' Fastenings: From Sewn Boat to Steamship*. College Station, TX: Texas A&M University Press.

McGrail, Seán. 2014. *Ancient Boats in North-West Europe: The Archaeology of Water Transport to AD 1500*. New York: Routledge.

McGrail, Seán. 2004. *Boats of the World: From the Stone Age to Medieval Times*. Oxford: Oxford University Press.

Cresques, Abraham, 1325–1387 CE

Scholars consider Cresques—a master mapmaker and builder of nautical navigational instruments from Palma, Majorca—to be one of the leading cartographers of the Majorcan cartographic school. Modern literature commonly refers to him as Abraham Cresques, but this is incorrect. His parents, Abraham and Astrugona, named him "Cresques," which, according to Catalan Jewish custom, would have made his name "Cresques (son of) Abraham"; it is for this same reason that we know his son (also a respected cartographer) as "Judah (son of) Cresques."

The Majorcan cartographic school holds an important place in mapmaking history as an early innovator in combining the functionality and accurate coastal details of a mariner's (portolan) chart with a medieval world map's ("*mappa-mundi*") elaborate decoration and informative inscriptions. The cartographers of this school also centered their maps on the Mediterranean, unlike earlier *map-paemundi* which often centered on Jerusalem. Cresques's skills in painting and illuminating these maps earned him both the reputation of being the premier cartographer of his day and the patronage of both King Peter IV and his son Prince John of Aragon, who bestowed upon him the title "*magister mapamundo-rum et buxolarum*" ("master of world maps and compasses"). It was at the behest of Prince John that Cresques—possibly in collaboration with his son Judah—produced the famous Catalan Atlas, which is the only extant map that scholars confidently attribute to him. John commissioned from him a world map as a gift for his cousin, Prince Charles VI of France, in 1375 CE or shortly thereafter, although Charles would only receive John's gift upon becoming king in 1381 CE.

The Catalan Atlas, which currently resides in the Bibliothèque Nationale in Paris, is celebrated as one of the finest surviving examples of late-medieval cartography. It is ambitious when compared to the geographic scope of contemporary portolan charts, covering lands from the Atlantic to China and from Scandinavia to Africa. Yet, it was also clearly meant to be of practical use for mariners, because it denotes the political and religious allegiances of cities, as well as provides information useful for daytime and nighttime navigation.

Brian N. Becker

Further Reading

Abraham, Cresques. 1978. *Mapamundi, the Catalan Atlas of the Year 1375*. With commentary by Georges Grosjean (ed.). Dietikon-Zurich: Urs Graf Verlag.

Bibliothèque Nationale de France. 2015. "Atlas de cartes marines, dit [Atlas catalan]." http://gallica.bnf.fr/ark:/12148/btv1b55002481n/f1.image. Accessed February 16, 2015.

Ceva, Juan. 2015. "The Cresques Project." http://www.cresquesproject.net/home. Accessed February 16, 2015.

Crusades

The Crusades were a series of military campaigns undertaken predominantly by western European Christians with the pope's approval and an offer of some form of spiritual reward such as the forgiveness of the participant's sins. Beginning in the late 11th century, the initial purposes of these campaigns included the recovery of the Holy Land from and defense of it against Muslims, but the movement

Crusaders embarking, 15th-century manuscript. Although this 15th-century painting portrays the voyage in a cheerful way, the actual conditions must have been squalid and uncomfortable; knights traveled with retinues of servants and squires, and the ships were often too crowded to afford sleeping quarters for all of them. (The British Library)

expanded over the following centuries to include new targets and geographical foci such as Muslims in Iberia, heretical Christian groups in southern France, pagans in Eastern Europe, and Orthodox Christians in Byzantium. Historians traditionally considered only those campaigns against Muslims in the Holy Land to be "official" crusades. More recently, however, the argument that many campaigns against non-Christians outside of the Holy Land also deserve this designation has gained popularity. Historians supporting this argument contend that the crusading movement continued into the 16th century, well beyond the traditionally accepted end date of the late 13th century.

Historians consider the First Crusade (1096–1099 CE) to be the most successful of all campaigns to the Holy Land, because it alone accomplished its primary goal:

Jerusalem's recovery from the occupying Muslim Seljuk Turks. This crusade had furthermore conquered a sizeable amount of Seljuk territory in parts of modern-day Turkey, Syria, Lebanon, Jordan, and Israel, which its leaders eventually divided into four Crusader States: the County of Edessa (1098 CE), the Principality of Antioch (1098), the Kingdom of Jerusalem (1099 CE), and the County of Tripoli (1109 CE). The primary goal of all subsequent Holy Land crusades was to defend these states, but varying combinations of poor organization, lack of focus, strengthened Muslim resistance, and diminished European interest made these campaigns significantly less effective than the First Crusade, if effective at all. In fact, most historians consider these later campaigns failures.

In the early 12th century, the lack of adequate land forces led crusading knights to form "military religious orders" such as the Templars and Hospitallers, whose sworn duty was to protect Christian holdings in, and increased pilgrimage traffic to, the Holy Land. Conversely, defending the Crusader states' important port cities was mostly the responsibility of western merchants and colonists. An important result of this was the establishment of numerous Italian merchant colonies along the Levantine Coast in towns such as Acre, Tyre, Beirut, Tripoli, etc., through which flowed from west to east items crucial to the Crusader States, including manpower and other supplies. One cannot know exactly how much wealth Europe sent to the East through these Levantine ports, but it was certainly a great deal. A significant number of Italian settlers migrated to the East both to work in the Levantine cities' industries and to man Crusader fortifications, although they never constituted anything approaching a majority population in any of the Crusader states.

Maritime warfare did not play a significant role in the various northern crusades against pagans in Eastern Europe and the Baltic or the *Reconquista* against Iberian Muslims, although a crusader fleet's capture of Muslim Lisbon in 1147 was one of the Second Crusade's few successes. Conditions were different for the Crusader states, however, whose very survival depended upon Italian naval forces for supplies and coastal protection. The preservation of their merchant quarters and privileged status in the Crusader East indeed motivated the Italian cities to provide these services from the time of its foundation, but an equally important motivation was the need to consolidate maritime routes from Europe to the Holy Land for trade and for troop and pilgrim transportation. Egypt initially posed the greatest Muslim threat to the eastern portion of these routes; later Levantine crusades indeed had its conquest as their initial goal, but factional strife combined with the 1191 CE conquest of Cyprus by Richard I of England, prevented Egypt from ever truly challenging Italian naval supremacy in the region.

It is also important to note that a thriving trade existed between the Islamic world and the Far East, which helps to explain the lack of Muslim resistance to European dominance of eastern Mediterranean waters; a flourishing trade with the

Far East lessened the urgency to establish commercial ties with a hostile West. Once consolidated, the relative security and speed of these routes led later crusade organizers to opt for seaborne troop transportation eastward rather than overland marching. Also, Italian merchant ships dominated these routes, across which flowed to Europe a lucrative trade in eastern goods such as textiles, spices, and other regional products that would continue well after Acre, the last remnant of the Crusader states, fell in 1291 CE.

The Crusades did not initiate European exposure to Islamic culture, but the movement certainly intensified that exposure. This exposure was made possible mostly by the Mediterranean Sea. Its well-established contact points linked Europe and the Islamic world, such as Iberia and Sicily, and served as conduits through which Islamic medicine, science, geographical knowledge, architecture, and philosophy passed from East to West during this period. The sea thus played a significant role in Europe's introduction to this body of knowledge, which led to Western innovation in many fields. The very idea of crusading also proved influential in Europe, as popes and secular rulers—oftentimes for personal advantage—expanded the movement by couching campaigns against non-Muslims outside of the Holy Land as crusades. Pope Innocent III, for example, proclaimed a crusade against Christian heretics in southern France, the Albigensians, as a show of papal power against lay challengers. Christian kings in both Iberia and Eastern Europe used crusading ideology to expand their territory at the expense of Muslims and Pagans, respectively. The sea thus was not much of a factor in later European crusades, but it was vitally important to the movement's early success, subsequent plans for future success, and Europe's intellectual maturation.

Brian N. Becker

Further Reading

Chazan, Robert. 1987. *European Jewry and the First Crusade.* Berkeley: University of California Press.

Christiansen, Eric. 1980. *The Northern Crusades: The Baltic and the Catholic Frontier, 1100–1525.* London; New York: Macmillan.

Courbage, Yousef, and Phillipe Fargues. 1998. *Christians and Jews Under Islam.* London: I. B Tauris.

Harris, Jonathan. 2003. *Byzantium and the Crusades.* London: Hambledon Continuum.

Hillenbrand, Carole. 1999. *The Crusades: Islamic Perspectives.* Edinburgh: Edinburgh University Press.

Housley, Norman. 1992. *The Later Crusades, 1274–1580. From Lyons to Alcazar.* Oxford: Oxford University Press.

Maalouf, Amin. 1984. *The Crusades Through Arab Eyes.* Jon Rothschild (trans.). London: Al Saqi Books: Distributed by Zed Books.

Maier, C. T. (ed.). 2000. *Crusade Propaganda and Ideology. Model Sermons for the Preaching of the Cross*. Cambridge: Cambridge University Press.

O'Callaghan, J. F. 2003. *Reconquest and Crusade in Medieval Spain*. Philadelphia: University of Pennsylvania Press.

Riley-Smith, Jonathan. 1987. *The Crusades: A Short History*. New Haven: Yale University Press.

Hanseatic League

The Hanseatic League was a Northern European trading confederation. At its greatest extent, it encompassed more than 200 cities and towns, many of them ports, and was active from the mid-12th through the mid-17th centuries.

The Hanseatic League had its origin in 12th-century "*hanses*" ("associations") of German merchants trading overseas. During an age of weak nation-states and endemic piracy, entering into such groups enabled merchants to provide for their mutual protection and well-being. The league came into existence when *hanses* based in the ports of Lübeck in northern Germany and Visby on the Baltic island of Gotland joined forces with other *hanses* in the region. Within a short time this larger group had extended its activities throughout the lands bordering the Baltic and North seas, establishing trading centers in participating settlements. As the league's operations grew, it became a confederation of cities and towns rather than merchants.

Inevitably the league's widening activities led to increased shipbuilding in the region, which in turn encouraged the adoption of new methods and designs. The earliest Hanseatic ships were cogs—flat-bottomed, single-masted ships carrying one square sail. These were supplanted over the course of the 14th and 15th centuries by hulks, which were larger, more advanced ships with rudimentary keels and more elaborate superstructures. Hulks could carry more than twice the cargo of cogs, but their rounded hulls allowed them to land easily on flat shores. In the latter half of the 15th century Hanseatic shipbuilders began to turn out even larger, faster ships called caravels.

The cost of shipbuilding in league ports generally was borne by a number of individuals, as was the cost of cargoes in later years. Such practices allowed for sharing of profit as well as risk, and became particularly important as ships' capacities and the value of their cargoes increased. They also ensured that more and more members of the community were invested in the success of the league's seaborne enterprises.

Typical Hanseatic cargoes included ore, timber, furs, honey, grain, dried fish, and textiles. It is estimated that by the 15th century the league's merchants were trading with a fleet of about 1,000 ships, ranging from large seagoing vessels to smaller coasting craft, with a total tonnage of about 60,000 tons.

Although it preferred to expand in the wake of German conquest and settlement, the Hanseatic League occasionally participated in conflicts. One of the most significant was a naval war with Denmark that, under the terms of the Treaty of Stralsund of 1370, resulted in uncontested Hanseatic supremacy in the Baltic region. Over the course of the following century, however, the league's power was eclipsed by increasingly powerful nation-states and by the expanding sea power of the Dutch merchant marine.

Grove Koger

Further Reading

Halliday, Stephen. 2009. "The First Common Market?" *History Today* 59.7: 31–37.

Schildhauer, Johannes. 1985. *The Hansa: History and Culture.* Leipzig: Edition Leipzig.

Schulte Beerbühl, Margrit. 2011. "Networks of the Hanseatic League." *European History Online.* http://www.ieg-ego.eu/schultebeerbuehlm-2011-en. Accessed Dec. 7, 2014.

Normans

The Normans are best known for their seafaring raids and colonization of wide areas of Europe and the Mediterranean. Norman territories stretched across the northern and western coasts of France, the British Isles, Sicily, and Northern Africa to the Levant. The name "Norman" came from groups of Viking invaders, and meant, "the men of the sea." "Norman" is used either for the Scandinavian people as a group (which plundered and pillaged foreign countries from the 8th to the 11th century and founded settlements across Europe), or—as described here—for the Danes and Norwegians (whose territory reached into western and southern Europe), particularly those who in the 10th century settled in northern France and founded the duchy of Normandy.

In Christian sources, "Normans" soon became a collective name for raiders from the north. When the 11th-century historian William of Jumièges tried to define for his contemporary readers what is meant by "Normans," he wrote that "they, however, are called Northmen, for in their language 'Boreas' is called 'North', and 'homo' 'man'; thence the men from the north are called 'Northmen'" (Van Houts 1992, 17).

Originally pagan pirates from Scandinavia, the Normans started to make predatory raids on European coastal regions from the eighth century on. In the ninth century, Normans devastated Britain, Ireland, and the Frankish Empire. The raiders sailed along the rivers inside the country with their swift and versatile longships and pillaged even important cities like Canterbury, York, Paris, Chartres, and Hamburg. Seasonal raids grew in scale and frequency and the Normans began to stay in fortified places through the winter—where they could trade—instead of returning home each year. After 900 CE, the Normans showed a tendency to settle in the northwest of the Frankish Empire. Probably in 911 the Frankish King Charles III the Simple (879–922 CE) granted the region around Rouen to the Viking leader Rollo (846 to ca. 928 CE) and the settlement he established developed into the principality of Normandy. The Norman settlers converted to Christianity and intermarried with the indigenous population. Within a generation the Vikings—or Normans, as they came to be known—established themselves as a dominant force.

The prerequisite for the rapid Norman expansion was their maritime technology and seafaring abilities. Economically, the process of integration of Northern Europe into the Latin-Christian world and Mediterranean trade networks began with the Norman raids. The naval capabilities of European states declined following the collapse of the Roman Empire, and the Vikings and Normans benefited from this decline. Norman longships, shown in the Bayeaux Tapestry preparing for the 1066 CE invasion of England, were similar to earlier Viking longships. Eminently seaworthy, they carried a large number of troops for their size. Of shallow draft, they handled well in coastal waters and rivers, and were easily beached, facilitating raids and invasions.

From their settlements in Normandy, the Normans embarked on several major campaigns of conquest, which they secured with impressive castles and fortifications. The most important of these were the capture of Southern Italy, including Sicily and parts of North Africa (around 1015–1112 CE) by the Hauteville and Drengot families, and the conquest of England (1066 CE) by William the Conqueror. Norman warriors appeared in Southern Italy prior to the conquest of Sicily as pilgrims and later established the Principality of Antioch under Bohemond I in the wake of the First Crusade (1096–1099 CE). Throughout the Middles Ages, the Norman Kingdoms of Sicily and England created innovative military and political structures that aided their conquests. The Norman Kingdom of Italy, for example, blended Arab, Byzantine, and West European political structures in which a multi-ethnic and multi-religious meritocratic bureaucracy served their Norman rulers.

From the perspective of Christian Europe, the Normans began as pagan destroyers but ascended to the first rank of Latin-Christian politics. By the 12th and 13th centuries, though, the Normans had largely blended into the indigenous population of their conquests. Their political and military adaptability along with their prowess as seafarers and warriors enabled them to conquer lands throughout Europe and the Mediterranean and to play a leading role in the Crusades.

Stephan Köhler

Further Reading

Bates, David. 2013. *The Normans and Empire*. Oxford: Oxford University Press.

Chibnall, Marjorie. 2006. *The Normans*. Oxford: Blackwell.

Davis, Ralph H. C. 1976. *The Normans and Their Myth.* London: Thames and Hudson.

Van Houts, Elisabeth M. C. 1992. *The Gesta Normannorum Ducum of William of Jumièges, Orderic Vitalis, and Robert of Torigni.* Oxford: Clarendon Press.

Van Houts, Elisabeth M. C. 2000. *The Normans in Europe.* Manchester: Manchester University Press.

Pilgrimage, Christian

Christian pilgrimage to biblical sites—particularly those associated with the life and death of Jesus Christ and the ministry of the apostles—began in Late Antiquity and has continued into the modern era. Pilgrimage to the Levant took off after the Roman co-emperors, Constantine I and Licinius, issued the Edict of Milan in 313 CE. This edict ended persecutions of Christians, allowing open practice of their religion and facilitation of pilgrimage. Constantine (280s to 337 CE) ultimately became a great patron of the church, granting privileges to members of the clergy and sponsoring the construction of Christian basilicas. In ruins after its destruction under Titus in 70 CE, Jerusalem underwent a restoration at Constantine's direction. Christian pilgrims from other parts of the Empire flocked to the region to visit biblical sites.

Beginning in Late Antiquity and continuing throughout the Middle Ages, devout Christians sought spiritual guidance or healing at holy sites where they sometimes encountered saints' relics, which included bones and objects associated with the saint through which Christians believed God acted due to the saint's close connection to the divine. One of the earliest relics, they believed, was discovered by none other than Constantine's mother Helena. During her pilgrimage to Jerusalem, she reportedly found a fragment of the True Cross on which Jesus had been crucified. Early locations of pilgrimage in the Levant included a variety of sites, such as the Church of the Holy Sepulchre, built in the 300s CE atop the believed location of Christ's rock-cut tomb.

Itineraries and travel accounts of several Christian pilgrims from the late Antique and Medieval periods survive, illuminating the human, cultural, religious, and physical landscapes of the Levant and Mediterranean world. Some of these extant or partially extant accounts that involve pilgrimage to Levantine sacred sites include the "*Itinerarium Burdigalense*" ("*Bordeaux Itinerary*"), an anonymous account composed ca. 333 CE; the pilgrim Egeria's account written in the late 300s CE; a sixth-century itinerary ascribed to Antoninus of Piacenza; and *De Locis Sanctis* ("Of Sacred Places"), authored ca. 670–80 CE and based on recollections of Arculf, a bishop of Gaul.

The Romans called the Mediterranean Sea, "*mare nostrum*" ("our sea"), and Rome facilitated pilgrimage between East and West through the creation of a space with relatively limited piracy and brigandry. Rome also maintained a complex network of highways with staging posts of which pilgrims made use. The fourth-century pilgrim, Egeria, made her way, mostly by sea, from the western province of Spain to the Levant where she spent three years (381–384 CE), traveling also to Egypt and visiting a multitude of sites including those that Christians associated with both Old and New Testament accounts. Egeria's account of her experiences survives in fragmentary form, yet it provides an important narrative description of the region as well as evidence for the diversity of early Christian religious practices and the development of a Christian liturgy and liturgical calendar.

The account of her excursion to the Sinai includes a brief description of Clymsa (modern Suez), which was situated between the Red Sea and the Mediterranean Sea. Egeria notes that the harbor was populated by numerous ships and functioned as a port of trade for goods coming from "India" (likely Ethiopia and Arabia) to the Roman world. She also mentions that Rome sent an ambassador to "India" every year, indicating their deep overseas networks of trade and diplomacy. The text also includes an informed description of the Red Sea itself, which Egeria compares favorably to both the Atlantic Ocean and the Mediterranean Sea. She notes that the title "red" is not reflective of the water's hue but rather of the red and purple stones quarried in the area. She mentions ruts along the shoreline that probably were evidence of the spot where vessels were pulled onto land for cleaning or repair. Egeria believed they were chariot tracks marking the spot where the Israelites had been pursued by the Egyptian pharaoh during the Exodus.

One of St. Jerome's (ca. 342–420 CE) fifth-century epistles provides insight into the modes of transport used by pilgrims to the Levant. In this letter Jerome praises the ascetic Roman noblewoman, Paula, who left her family and wealth behind in Rome to join him in Bethlehem where they established monastic houses for men and women. Jerome describes Paula boarding a cargo ship propelled by its sails and by oarsmen from Rome through the Tyrrhenian Sea. It made numerous stops in the ports of the eastern Mediterranean, including Melea, Rhodes, Cyprus, and several Phoenician cities. Over the course of her sojourn, Paula, like Egeria and others, encountered a number of sacred sites.

By the late 600s CE the Levant was part of the Umayyad Caliphate, and Christian pilgrimage to biblical sites continued in now Muslim-ruled lands. Approximately 300 years after Egeria wrote her account, Bishop Arculf of Gaul recalled (ca. 670–80 CE) both the biblical sites that pilgrims wished to explore and the impressive number and diversity of people who regularly gathered in Jerusalem. Presumably these individuals included western and eastern Christians, Jews, and Muslims.

Christian pilgrimage to these sacred sites continued well into the Middle Ages, creating opportunities for interaction between east and west. Venetian ships, in particular, carried many pilgrims across the Mediterranean. In 1095 CE, Pope Urban II (d. 1099 CE) gave a speech at the Council of Clermont in which he called for a

"Great Pilgrimage," more commonly known as the First Crusade—a Christian holy war. Crusaders set off as pilgrims to Jerusalem where Urban suggested that Muslim Seljuk Turks, then advancing into Christian Byzantine lands, had disrupted pilgrimages to holy sites, including the Church of the Holy Sepulchre. Urban sought the "restoration" of the Holy Land to Christian hands and the liberation of eastern Christians from Muslim rule.

Indeed, the First Crusade resulted in the creation of four Christian-ruled Crusader states, which relied on the sea for their survival and benefitted from regular arrivals of pilgrims at Acre and other ports. These kingdoms also served as loci for significant interaction between Christians and Muslims, as the Islamic pilgrim Ibn Jubyar (1145–1217 CE) recounts in his 12th-century *Travels*. These connections had a significant impact on the development of late-medieval and early Renaissance intellectual culture.

Holle Canatella

Further Reading

Egeria. 1999. *Egeria's Travels*, 3rd ed. John Wilkerson (trans.). Warminster, England: Aris and Phillips, Ltd.

Elsner, Jás. 2000. "The *Itinerarius Burdigalense*: Politics and Salvation in the Geography of Constantine's Empire." *The Journal of Roman Studies* 90: 181–95.

Hunt, E. D. 1982. *Holy Land Pilgrimage in the Later Roman Empire, AD 312–460*. Oxford: Clarendon Press.

Polo, Marco, ca. 1254–1324 CE

Marco Polo, traveler and author of a famous travelogue, hailed from a Venetian merchant family whose extensive eastern trading—especially by his father, Niccolò, and uncle, Maffeo—earned it wealth and prestige. After returning to Venice in 1270 CE, the brothers embarked on another eastward journey in 1271 CE, this time accompanied by 17-year-old Marco. His experiences on this trip form the basis for *The Travels of Marco Polo*, which he completed after returning to Italy in the late 1290s CE. Widely read, its descriptions of China's wealth and sophisticated culture excited European interest in the East.

After being captured in war and imprisoned by Venice's archrival, Genoa, in 1296, Marco met Rustichello of Pisa, a romance author to whom he dictated his tales of the East. The original title of this work in Franco-Italian, *Description of the World*, is actually more appropriate for their collaboration, because it is not firmly an autobiography, recollection, or itinerary, but rather medieval didactic literature, which informs and entertains readers simultaneously. Marco relates that the Polos traveled to Acre, and then braved miles of dangerous deserts in what are now southeastern Turkey, Iraq, and Iran to arrive at Hormuz on the Persian Gulf.

Judging a sea journey to India too risky, they turned inland. By 1275 CE, the Polos had traveled northeast through modern-day eastern Iran, Afghanistan, and found the Silk Road, which they followed into China, eventually arriving at Mongol Great Khan Kublai's summer residence of Shangdu. Kublai was delighted to see the elder Polos again, and meet young Marco, whose eagerness to learn Mongol customs and local languages (Mongol, Turkish [Cuman], Uighur, Persian, and Chinese) impressed him greatly.

The Polos spent nearly two decades traveling throughout Kublai's empire, though the embellishments and digressions of *The Travels* make it difficult to track their activities accurately. Marco claims dubiously that the Polos acted as Mongol military advisors, even designing siege weapons to help them take Xiangyang, and that he governed Yangzhou for three years. More credible are Marco's claims to have been a Mongol customs inspector and personal explorer for the Great Khan, who delighted in hearing stories of the Polos' encounters with strange lands and peoples and sent Marco on information-gathering missions to the far reaches of his lands, including China and possibly Myanmar. *The Travels* records much about the people and places of Kublai's empire, and digresses to discuss topics such as the

One of history's greatest travelers, Marco Polo, shown here entering the port of Hormuz on the Persian Gulf, traveled from Italy to China. The chronicle of his journeys excited European interest in China. (*The Travels of Marco Polo* by Marco Polo, 1958 reprint of the 13th-century original)

Caliphate of Baghdad; the Old Man of the Mountain and his Assassins; the origins, customs, and old capital of the Mongols (Karakorum); and the splendor of Kublai's new capital of Khanbalik (now Beijing), but Polo's observations often are detached and lack specific travel details such as arrival and departure times and the distance between locations.

The Polos returned to Venice predominantly by sea through the Pacific and Indian oceans, making *The Travels* valuable for the study of medieval maritime history. *The Travels* describes Japanese ships; Kublai's unsuccessful Japanese naval expedition; the seas surrounding Java, Sumatra, and Sri Lanka; the coastlines and people of India; and the existence of Ethiopia and Madagascar. Although most scholars agree that Polo (and Rustichello) sensationalized his account by meshing what he had seen with tales that he had heard, the intention was to inform and entertain, not to deceive, their readers. Undisputable is the enormous popularity of Polo's travelogue, as numerous, widespread surviving manuscripts of it in multiple languages attest. Also undisputed is that Polo's geographic descriptions helped inspire later European explorers. Indeed, Christopher Columbus owned a well-annotated copy of *The Travels*, and, hoped to reach the fabulously wealthy China that Polo described.

Brian N. Becker

Further Reading

Bergreen, Laurence. 2007. *Marco Polo: From Venice to Xanadu.* New York: Alfred A. Knopf.

de Rachewiltz, Igor. 1997. "Marco Polo Went to China." *Zentralasiatische Studien* 27: 34–92.

Haw, Stephen G. 2006. *Marco Polo's China: A Venetian in the Realm of Khubilai Khan.* London; New York: Routledge.

Larner, John. 1999. *Marco Polo and the Discovery of the World.* New Haven: Yale University Press.

Olschki, Leonardo. 1960. *Marco Polo's Asia: An Introduction to His "Description of the World" Called "Il Milione."* Berkeley: University of California Press.

Wood, Francis. 1996. *Did Marco Polo Go to China?* Boulder: Westview Press.

Piracy in Europe, 1000–1500 CE

The Mediterranean's combination of well-developed trade networks and plentiful hiding places such as islets, bays, and coves, led to piracy flourishing there in ancient Phoenician and Greek times. It was still flourishing in the medieval Mediterranean, as the Slavic pagan Narentines raided extensively from their Dalmatian coastal base into eastern and southern Italy. The Narentines had become such a formidable force in the ninth-century Adriatic that they defeated the powerful Venetians in naval battle, an event still celebrated in Croatia today. North African Muslim pirates also wreaked havoc from Iberia to Crete early in this period, and citizens of Barcelona, Marseille, Genoa, and Venice engaged in widespread piracy, both private and state-sponsored. Further, the withering of Byzantine naval power by the 14th century led to a strong Ottoman presence in the eastern Mediterranean, including those pirates they employed to prey on east-west shipping.

Pirates threatened northern European sea travel from at least the fifth century CE. St. Patrick (ca. 390–460 CE) wrote in his *Confession* that Irish pirates captured and enslaved him when he was 16. So, piracy was an established threat to northern Europeans by the late eighth century, when the Vikings began their raiding. Slavic pirates preyed so relentlessly on North and Baltic Sea trade routes by the 12th century that merchants of German port cities banded together to form the Hanseatic League, an association to protect and regulate maritime trade. The League eventually grew to include nearly 200 port cities from England to Russia, and successfully curbed piracy and dominated trade in northern Europe until the 16th century.

Piracy threatened seaborne commerce in this era, but states also used piracy to harass their political rivals. This helps to explain why many western maritime law codes treat piracy ambiguously. A state often deemed its own piracy permissible, but that of rival states and their citizens illegal. The high cost of containing piracy also influenced authorities' attitudes towards it, namely, that its suppression was a responsibility shared by government and citizen. In 1265 CE, the Hanseatic League required all member cities to combat piracy, and the Court of Admiralty in 14th-century England expected its ports to defend themselves against piracy. Authorities recognized that containing piracy was crucial to preserving good foreign relations. The Commune of Genoa established an Office of Piracy around 1300 CE to compensate victims of piracy.

Brian N. Becker

Further Reading

Appleby, John C., and Paul Dalton. 2009. *Outlaws in Medieval and Early Modern England: Crime, Government and Society, c. 1066–c. 1600*. Farnham: Ashgate.

Eddison, Jill. 2013. *Medieval Pirates: Pirates, Raiders and Privateers 1204–1453*. Stroud, Gloucestershire: The History Press.

Khalilieh, Hassan S. 2014. "Perception of Piracy in Islamic Sharīa." In *Jews, Christians and Muslims in Medieval and Early Modern Times: A Festschrift in Honor of Mark R. Cohen*. Arnold E. Franklin, Roxani Eleni Margariti, Marina Rustow, and Uriel Simonsohn (eds.), 226–47. Leiden: Brill.

Meier, Dirk. 2006. *Seafarers, Merchants and Pirates in the Middle Ages*. Angus McGeoch (trans.). Woodbridge, England and Rochester, NY: Boydell and Brewer.

Tai, Emily Sohmer. 2012. "The Legal Status of Piracy in Medieval Europe." *History Compass* 10: 838–51.

Venice Arsenal

A large state-owned shipyard containing shipbuilding facilities, basins, and docks as well as adjoining rope, sail, and munitions factories, the Venice Arsenal helped assure Venice's position as the strongest mercantile and naval power in the eastern Mediterranean Sea during the late Middle Ages.

Venice's Old Arsenal dates from 1104 CE, but a considerably larger New Arsenal was built east of the city in the early 14th century, and an addition known as the Newest Arsenal was constructed in the late 15th century. By the 16th century, the Arsenal had become the largest industrial complex in the world, covering about 60 acres and surrounded by two and a half miles of walls and moats.

The Arsenal also was one of the earliest examples of assembly-line production. Workers, known as "*arsenalotti*," applied their skills to particular aspects of the shipbuilding process. Usually members of guilds, the *arsenalotti* numbered in the thousands and formed their own community. They drew their wood supply from Arsenal-owned forests on the mainland, and although they were responsible for most aspects of the shipbuilding process, the Venetian government imposed certain standards on their ships. Merchant vessels, for instance, were built in such a way that they could be adapted for warfare if necessary. Thanks to its efficient organization, the Arsenal was capable of completing a ship in a single day, and its fame attracted travelers from all over Europe.

Although the Arsenal never enjoyed a monopoly on Venetian shipbuilding, it accounted for a large percentage of the city's merchant ships and warships, which in the early 15th century included 45 galleys and 300 "round ships"—two- and three-masted vessels with forecastles, stern castles, "fighting tops" (crow's nests), and triangular lateen sails. In later years the Arsenal turned out galleons as well.

The importance of the Arsenal declined in the 16th century as the Venetian mercantile fleet shrank. Napoleon Bonaparte (1769–1821 CE) burned its docks when he conquered the city in 1797, but the complex was reconstructed under later Austrian occupation. Its docks were finally dismantled by the Italian government in 1917.

Grove Koger

Further Reading

Crowley, Roger. 2011. "Arsenal of Venice." *Military History* 27.6: 62–70.

Davis, Robert C. 1991. *Shipbuilders of the Venetian Arsenal: Workers and Workplace in the Preindustrial City.* Baltimore: Johns Hopkins University Press.

Lane, Frederic Chapin. 1934. *Venetian Ships and Shipbuilders of the Renaissance.* Baltimore: Johns Hopkins Press.

INDIA AND SOUTHEAST ASIA, 1000 TO 1500 CE

The peoples of the Indian Ocean boast a rich body of nautical knowledge, and diverse peoples—including Arabs, Chinese, Indians, and Malays—sailed its waters. In the last decades of the first millennium CE, two powerful dynasties arose, the Cholas (985 CE) in India and the Song (960 CE) in China. Both looked to the sea and worked to stimulate Indian Ocean trade. The nations of Southeast Asia played a crucial role in this trade and developed diplomatic relations with both China and India. Increasing trade spread Indian culture and religion (Buddhism and Hinduism) across Southeast Asia. This peaceful interaction changed in the second millennium CE when the Chola invaded Srivijaya (present-day Palembang).

King Rajaraja (947–1014 CE) established the Chola Empire and continued to expand his borders, as did his son and successor Rajendra Chola (r. 1014–1042 CE). Rajaraja systematically subdued the kingdoms of southern India. Expanding along the coast, the Cholas captured the flourishing ports of the Coromandel and Malabar coasts, which provided bases to successfully invade Sri Lanka and the Maldive Islands, both important trading centers. Rajendra Chola launched two expeditions into Bengal, which cemented control over India's eastern coastline and facilitated trade farther east. An inscription at the temple in Tanjavour, located in the modern-day south Indian state of Tamil Nadu, records that king Rajendra Chola in 1025 CE "dispatched many ships in the midst of the rolling sea and having caught Sangrama-vijayottunga-varman, the king of Kadaram (on the Malay Peninsula), together with the elephants and his glorious army took large heaps of treasure" (Sastri 1995, 211). Chola forces struck 12 other ports in the Malay Peninsula and Sumatra, as well as Nicobar Island. In 1070, King Kulottunga I (1070–1118 CE) led a naval expedition against Kadaram, the capital of Srivijaya, a powerful mercantile kingdom that controlled the Straits of Malacca, the gateway to the Chinese market. Previously, the Cholas maintained friendly relations with Srivijaya, which had sent several friendly missions to India, but the Chola Empire increasingly clashed with Srivijaya over control of key trade routes in Indonesia and to China.

Although there are numerous references to trade and the Chola's military expeditions in temple inscriptions and other sources, less is known about Chola warships and naval organization. The navy maintained extensive facilities, including specialized shipyards, along the Indian coast, as well as two naval bases in Sri Lanka. Warships periodically escorted trade fleets and also patrolled to suppress piracy. Many warships were converted merchant ships (strengthened sides and boarding impedimenta), but at least some were purpose-built warships. The designs of these remains uncertain, but the largest of them carried about 400 troops in addition to sailing crew.

The commercial activities in the Indian Ocean trading network during the early 11th century became complex as China emerged as one of the lucrative places for international commerce, due to increasing demand for silk and porcelain across Asia. Strategically located, Srivijayans began to dominate commercial exchanges through the Straits of Malacca, and Cholas increasingly started expanding its commercial and political sphere in the Indian Ocean region. The triangular relation between Chola, Srivijaya, and China played a crucial role in interlinking the commercial and diplomatic exchanges in the region. The confrontation between the Cholas and Srivijayans resulted from competition to access markets in Song China, the profit from which enriched and strengthened the Chola state.

The two important maritime centers of India's trade with Southeast Asia were Gangaikondacholapuram and Nagapattinum. Founded by Rajendra Chola in 1020 CE, Gangaikondacholapuram was the imperial capital of the Cholas until the 13th century. Increasing trade led to the growth of prosperous towns and markets. There were organized guilds known as "*nagaram*" located in each port city. Recent archaeological remains excavated from the site reveal important antiquities, decorative items, and ceramics traded in the region from China. Nagapattinum, a seaside port town located along the east coast of South India, was an important center for

Astrolabe

An astrolabe is an astronomical instrument designed for measuring the altitude of celestial bodies and for determining the time. Its use enabled mariners to determine their latitude while at sea.

Astrolabes were invented in Greece in the second or third century BCE and were later used throughout Europe and the Islamic world. During the Renaissance they were used to teach astronomy, although their primary use was for casting horoscopes. The planispheric astrolabe is the oldest type. It consisted of a brass disk marked with degrees, with several thin plates stacked on top. The back of the astrolabe was marked with scales and fitted with a rotating arm, or "alidade," that was used to measure the altitude of the sun or moon.

Mariners' astrolabes, in use since the early 13th century, were simpler than planispheric models and consisted of a single ring inscribed with degrees and fitted with an alidade. Sailors measured the noon altitude of the sun and consulted an almanac to find the sun's declination for that date. Using mathematical calculations they were able to fix their latitude. At night readings could be taken from stars. Astrolabes were displaced by more sophisticated instruments in the 17th century.

Karen S. Garvin

commercial and religious exchange between India and Southeast Asia. Numerous inscriptions in the Kayarohanaswamin temple in Nagapattinum record trade and gift exchanges between the Cholas and Srivijaya, which included jewels and religious artifacts for the temple, donated by Srivijaya's ruler. Another inscription from the same period refers to diplomatic donations made by officials of the king of Kidara (modern-day Kedah in Malaysia) to install a specific deity—*Ardhanariswara*—in the temple (Kulke et al. 2009, 122, 124).

The merchant guilds of South India played a significant role in establishing the Chola Empire and often were the driving force behind its naval expeditions. The largest of these operated on the Kerala and Tamil coasts and dominated local maritime trade. They employed soldiers to protect their merchant fleets and were capable of launching substantial armed overseas expeditions. Several of the guilds, particularly the Manigramam and Ainurruvar, included foreign merchants from West Asia, Arabia, and Persia, including Jews, Christians, and Muslims among their members. To encourage trade, many local rulers offered tax exemptions and other privileges to attract foreign traders, among them the Anjuvannam, a guild of Jewish merchants at Cochin. Abraham Ben Yiju, a successful Jewish trader from Tunisia, relocated to India. Ship owners ("*nauvittakas*") generally remained at home, trusting their ships and goods to captains ("*nakhudas*") and sailors ("*navikakarmakaras*") who spent much of their lives on long voyages.

Temple inscriptions from the port of Belur on India's west coast note 62 traded commodities. Those most mentioned are pepper, areca nuts, betel, leaf, paddy, rice, sandalwood, cotton thread, and cloth (Kulke et al. 2009, 140). India's weaving and dyeing industries improved their techniques and expanded in these years. By the 11th century, painted and block-printed textiles became popular export commodities. The introduction of the spinning wheel in the 13th century further increased production. Indian block-printed textiles—which used mordant to bind the dye to fabric and preserve its color—featured intricate patterns and were exported throughout Southeast Asia in exchange for spices from as far as away as the Banda Islands, which Indian merchants re-exported throughout the Indian Ocean. Indian textiles, in turn, found markets throughout the region and into China. Marco Polo, a 13th-century Italian traveler, described the arrival of large ships loaded with Indian textiles that sailed from India's Coromandel Coast to Southeast Asia and China. Nobles on Java and Sumatra, in particular, sought Indian patterned cloth.

Along with Indian goods came Indian culture. Earlier Indian traders already had introduced Buddhism to Southeast Asia. Tamil traders introduced brahmanical court culture and Hindu deities to Southeast Asia, and later Cambodian and Javanese rulers came to trace their descent from two of these: Vishnu and Shiva. Thailand's kings, in turn, presented themselves as incarnations of Indra. Throughout Southeast Asia, people incorporated Indian artistic styles as well as religious ideas, and this process of amalgamation and acculturation was accelerated by the Cholas' increasing activity in Southeast Asia, both peaceful and military. Cham sculptures in Vietnam exemplified the Indian Brahmin pantheon interpretation. Celestial deities from Hindu mythology found favor in the Thai court, as did depictions of Indian deities rising from lotus flowers with folded hands. Chola temples, in turn, were influenced by Southeast Asian styles, particularly the grand style of Angkor, the capital of the Khmer Empire centered in modern Cambodia.

India's trade with Southeast Asia remained strong even as the Chola Empire declined in the late 12th and 13th centuries. Arguably, its decline might have facilitated increased trade as local kingdoms, particularly in the Bay of Bengal, sought new, distant markets. In the 14th century, the Delhi Sultanate increasingly expanded into central and southern India, bringing with it Islam. Muslim trading communities spread to more and more Indian ports, and Muslim sailors and ships became more prevalent in the Indian Ocean. In the early 15th century, the Chinese, too, became more active in the Indian Ocean and dispatched a series of expeditions under the legendary admiral Zheng He (1371–1435 CE), which expanded Chinese influence beyond the Strait of Malacca and exchanged goods with peoples across the Indian Ocean as far as East Africa. Following the last of Zheng He's expeditions (1433 CE), though, the traditional trading patterns of small merchants and merchant guilds resumed.

Adwita Rai

Further Reading

Abraham, Meera. 1988. *Two Medieval Merchant Guilds of South India*. New Delhi: Manohar Publications.

Barker, Graeme, Craig Benjamin, Jerry H. Bentley, David Christian, Candice Goucher, Benjamin Z. Kedar, J. R. Mcneill et al. 2015. *The Cambridge World History. Expanding Webs of Exchange and Conflict, 500 CE – 1500 CE 5 5*. Cambridge: Cambridge University Press.

Chakravarti, Ranabir. 2010. *Exploring Early India, up to c. AD 1300*. Delhi: Macmillan Publishers India.

Champakalakshmi, R. 1996. *Trade, Ideology, and Urbanization: South India 300 BC to AD 1300*. Delhi: Oxford University Press.

Kwa, Chong Guan. 2013. *Early Southeast Asia Viewed from India: An Anthology of Articles from the Journal of the Greater India Society*. New Delhi: Manohar.

Kulke, Hermann, K. Kesavapany, and Vijay Sakhuja. 2009. *Nagapattinam to Suvarnadwipa: Reflections on the Chola Naval Expeditions to Southeast Asia*. Singapore: Institute of Southeast Asian Studies.

Malekandathil, Pius. 2010. *Maritime India: Trade, Religion and Polity in the Indian Ocean*. Delhi: Primus Books.

Ray, Himanshu Prabha, and Edward A. Alpers. 2007. *Cross Currents and Community Networks: The History of the Indian Ocean World.* New Delhi: Oxford University Press.

Ray, Himanshu Prabha, and Jean-Francois Salles. 1996. *Tradition and Archaeology: Early Maritime Contacts in the Indian Ocean: Proceedings of the International Seminar, Techno-Archaeological Perspectives of Seafaring in the Indian Ocean, 4th cent. B.C.–15th cent. A.D.* New Delhi: Manohar Publishers and Distributors.

Sastri, K. A. N. 1995. *The Cholas Vol. I.* University of Madras.

Sen, Tansen. 2015. *Buddhism, Diplomacy, and Trade: the Realignment of India-China Relations, 600–1400.* Lanham: Rowman & Littlefield.

Wade, Geoff. 2009. "An Early Age of Commerce in Southeast Asia, 900–133 CE." *Journal of Southeast Asian Studies* 40(2): 221–65.

Banda Islands

Roughly 1,200 miles east of Java, the Banda Islands are 10 small volcanic islands. Until the 19th century, they were the only source of nutmeg and mace, valuable spices produced from the seeds of the nutmeg tree that were used in both food and medicines. The largest of the islands, Banda Neira, became their commercial center and a major spice port.

The poor soil of the Banda Islands encouraged farmers to specialize in spices, and the Bandanese came to depend on imported rice. Chinese traders visited the islands in the late 14th century, and traders based in Java and Malacca sailed annually to Banda, trading cargoes of cotton cloth, silk, rice, ivory, and ceramics in exchange for nutmeg, mace, and other spices. The Bandanese, in turn, re-exported some of these goods to Maluku, a two-week voyage farther east, where they traded for cloves. Foreign traders generally avoided the voyage to Maluku because of the strict timetable dictated by the monsoons; they had to return west while the winds were favorable.

Less hierarchal and more communal than neighboring societies, most Bandanese lived in hinterland villages. They preferred to avoid foreigners, and over time delegated commercial matters to the residents of Banda Neira's port. These residents, in turn, intermarried with the Javanese settlers and emerged as a wealthy, elite group which monopolized local trade and were called "*orang kaya*," roughly translated as "rich men."

The location of the Banda Islands at the periphery of Southeast Asian trade routes made invasion difficult, and local powers preferred peaceful trade with the *orang kaya*. The arrival of the Europeans, however, ignited conflict. The Bandanese successfully resisted a Portuguese invasion in 1529 CE, after which peaceful trade resumed. The Dutch East India Company, however, steadily displaced the Portuguese in the later 16th century and established a base on Banda Neira in 1602 CE. Escalating trade disputes with the Dutch—who soon claimed a monopoly on trade with the islands—led to war. In 1621 CE, the Dutch conquered the islands, killing or expelling much of the population. Afterward, they brought in indentured servants and slaves to help cultivate the nutmeg plantations alongside the remaining Bandanese.

The Dutch repeatedly clashed with the British over the islands. In 1810 CE, the British conquered and briefly ruled them before returning them to the Dutch. When the British departed, they took nutmeg trees and transplanted them in Ceylon. This ended the Dutch monopoly and the importance of the Banda Islands to the spice trade.

Stephen K. Stein

Further Reading

Andaya, Leonard Y. 1993. *The World of Moluku: Eastern Indonesia in the Early Modern Period.* Honolulu: University of Hawai'i Press.

Hanna, Willard A. 1991. *Indonesian Banda: Colonialism and Its Aftermath in the Nutmeg Islands.* Bandanaira: Yayasan Warisan dan Budaya Banda Naira.

Milton, Giles. 1999. *Nathaniel's Nutmeg: Or the True and Incredible Adventures of the Spice Trader Who Changed the Course of History.* New York: Farrar, Straus, and Giroux.

Villiers, John. 1981. "Trade and Society in the Banda Islands in the Sixteenth Century." *Modern Asian Studies* 15(4): 723–50.

Ben Yiju, Abraham, ca. 1120 to 1156 CE

Abraham Ben Yiju was a Jewish merchant from Tunisia active in the trade networks of the 12th-century Indian Ocean. About 80 documents from the Cairo Geniza concern Ben Yiju and his extended family, providing an excellent window onto the lives of Jewish traders active in the Mediterranean and Indian Ocean.

Ben Yiju travelled to Egypt and Yemen before settling on the Malabar Coast of India where he imported and exported goods such as pepper and iron, and owned a bronzeware factory. Ben Yiju's letters demonstrate the existence of a number of merchant networks connecting Mediterranean markets with the Red Sea, Yemen, and the coasts of India. Personal ties, reputation, and trust bound the members of these networks that were meticulously maintained through constant correspondence. Merchants bought and sold goods as agents for each other in a system of mutual aid and support. Ben Yiju's letters also highlight the many risks run by those who traded across the Indian Ocean. The letters mention pirate attacks on ports and ships, deaths of colleagues, and the loss of entire shipments and considerable investments in shipwrecks. The inherent risks in this system encouraged merchants to diversify their activities and partnerships.

Ben Yiju's activities as a factory owner point to the sophisticated nature of trade in the Islamic and Indian Ocean worlds. Merchants in Aden ordered bronzeware such as candlesticks, basins, and lamps from Ben Yiju's Indian factory. The merchants provided the materials—especially the copper—and specified in detail the styles, dimensions, and decorations they desired. These merchants were thus ordering goods for their local Yemeni market, or perhaps for export elsewhere, benefitting from the craftsmanship of workers in India. This illustrates the interconnected hemispheric system of trade.

Letters concerning Ben Yiju also portray the sometimes difficult life of a Jew living in a foreign land—maintaining ties to his home, religion, and culture, but also interacting with the local population. Ben Yiju bought, liberated, and then married an Indian slave girl shortly after his arrival in India, and faced criticism in his efforts to reconcile this relationship with the legal and religious strictures of the Jewish community. He employed an Indian slave as his agent, a common merchant practice, entrusting him with much responsibility for his affairs. After 17 years away, Ben Yiju returned to the Mediterranean to reunite with his family shortly before his death in 1156 CE.

Travis Bruce

Further Reading

Goitein, S. D., and M. A. Friedman. 2008. *India Traders of the Middle Ages. Documents from the Cairo Geniza ("India Book")*. Leiden: Brill.

Gordon, Stewart. 2008. *When Asia Was the World*. Cambridge: Da Capo Press.

Simonsohn, Shlomo. 1997. *The Jews in Sicily (383–1300)*. Leiden: Brill.

ISLAMIC WORLD, 1000 TO 1500 CE

As in the early Middle Ages, later medieval Muslims traveled by sea for trade, pilgrimage, scholarship, and conquest. Muslim merchants transmitted raw materials and commercial products, technologies, and culture both within and between the Indian Ocean and Mediterranean Sea. Arabic geographical treatises and traveler's accounts were written to describe both seas (further subdivided into regional seas) and the lands that surrounded them, to aid both travel and scholarly knowledge of the world. Maritime commerce also fostered the spread of Islam itself, as the religion spread along trade routes—especially on the coasts of the western Indian Ocean and eastern Africa, where Islam was well established by the late 11th century. The religion spread to Southeast Asia more slowly, but by 1500 CE Islamic principalities ruled in Malaya, Java, Sumatra, and the Philippines. Not only traders and rulers, but networks of Islamic scholars were scattered around both seas, and intellectuals ("*ulama*") traveled by land and sea to learn, study, and earn patronage. The 14th-century Muslim traveler Ibn Battuta witnessed mosques, Quranic schools, scholars, and Muslim communities all around the Indian Ocean and eastern Africa.

To navigate, Muslim seafarers used instruments such as the astrolabe, quadrant, charts, and later the compass. Most ship captains preferred to navigate by sight, however, sailing close to shore ("coastal tramping"). The great navigator and author Ahmad ibn Majid (ca. 1432 to ca. 1500 CE) wrote numerous treatises describing Indian Ocean ports, monsoons, navigational techniques, and new ship technologies (such as the axial rudder) and tools (such as the magnetic compass). Even with such technological advances medieval seafaring was dangerous—shipwreck and poor weather always were feared. Most captains sailed along the coast, keeping shorelines in sight; however, poor weather could obstruct sightlines and allow ships to sail off course or, worse, could cause shipwreck. Other dangers lurking at sea included pirates, who were active in both the Mediterranean Sea and Indian Ocean. Ships often sailed in convoys for safety. Islamic maritime law was developed to adjudicate disputes and deal with the risks associated with sea travel.

As in the early medieval period, winds and weather patterns dictated sailing seasons. Mediterranean ships sailed eastward and westward from April through October, with most seafaring halted in the winter months of November through March. Wind and current patterns in the Mediterranean follow a roughly counterclockwise direction. In the Indian Ocean, seasonal monsoon winds determined the direction and timing of voyages. These predictable wind and current patterns allowed for southwestward sailing in the summer (June through September) and northeastward in the winter (October through January). The voyage from the Arabian Peninsula to the Far East took about six months, as did the return journey. Mercantile roundtrips to China required about 18 months, and midway trading centers in India arose to facilitate shorter segmented trips. The voyage to eastern Africa was timed for the beginning or the end of the monsoons in April, May, and August; the weather in June and July was too dangerous for sailing in the western Indian Ocean.

The primary category of Indian Ocean vessels is called the "*dhow*," which refers to various sizes of boats that were made of sewn and sealed wooden planks and had long, thin double-ended hulls and stern-post rudders. Although it has long been believed that iron never was used in medieval Indian Ocean vessels, the recently excavated Thaikkal-Kadakkarappally wreck (provisionally dated to between the 11th century and the 15th century) is an early example of an iron-nailed ship built in India. The late medieval period saw significant development in Mediterranean galleys, but virtually none of these were owned or captained by Muslims.

Indian Ocean

Between the 7th and 11th centuries CE, Muslim mariners established a unified Indian Ocean (Bahr al-Hind) commercial sphere that, along with the overland "Silk Road" routes, was a conduit for trade goods from India and China via the Persian Gulf (Bahr Faris) or the Red Sea (Bahr al-Qulzum), and from there into the Mediterranean. By 1000 CE, Muslim merchants had established routes all the way to China, along with a series of intermediary ports and methods of intercultural interaction that had been developed to facilitate trade and community in the multi-cultural and multi-religious ports. In the later Middle Ages this trade flourished, with Arabic as the common language of traders and Islamic law as the prevailing legal framework in the western Indian Ocean. By 1500 CE, this trade was so lucrative that western Christian merchants sought a direct route to the Indian Ocean to bypass the Mongols, Mamluks, and Ottomans who served as middlemen. Vasco da Gama, a Portuguese explorer, was the first European to successfully make this journey (1497–1499 CE), opening a new era of seaborne trade that fundamentally altered the preexisting patterns of seafaring and commerce.

The most valuable goods imported from the East were porcelain, spices (especially pepper, cinnamon, nutmeg, and medicinals), pearls, jewelry, precious stones, silks, and silkworms. Trade in foodstuffs, coins, timber, and cloths also was significant. Muslim traders gained knowledge of many eastern agricultural products, which then spread to Muslim lands and from there into Europe—including rice, sugar cane, citrus fruits, and cotton. Muslim traders also adopted and transferred several important technologies, including production of silk, porcelain pottery, and paper. The East African ports—notably Mogadishu, Mombasa, Kilwa, and Sofala—were important exporters of gold, ivory, timber, and slaves. This lucrative trade promoted both the economic and political power of the Muslim African rulers of the Swahili coast.

Between 1000 and 1500 CE, the Indian Ocean was much more significant to the economic and political power of the Muslim world than was the Mediterranean Sea. Both the Sunni Abbasid Caliphate based in Baghdad (750–1258 CE) and the Shi'ite Fatimid Caliphate based in Cairo (909–1171 CE) focused on military expansion toward the East and the import of eastern luxury goods. The Abbasids and their regional governors promoted the Persian Gulf ports, particularly Basra, Hormuz, and Sohar, replacing Siraf. The establishment of the Fatimid capital in Cairo redirected much of the Indian Ocean shipping toward the Red Sea ports, especially Aden, and helped promote the spread of Shi'ite Islam along the East African coast (where it was predominant until the 14th century).

Not long after Saladin dismantled the Fatimid Caliphate in 1171 CE, Aden—and, along with it, control of trade with the East—was transferred to the rulers of Yemen. Aden remained the primary entrepôt for this long-distance trade, and its rulers collected tolls on all its traffic. By the 15th century, however, Jeddah (the main port for pilgrimage to Mecca) had surpassed Aden thanks to official support from the Mamluk Sultanate (1250–1517 CE) based in Cairo. It was not until 1517 that the Ottomans conquered Mamluk Egypt, and attempted to capitalize on their new Red Sea ports to regain Muslim ascendancy in the Indian Ocean. This led to a series of conflicts in the 16th century between the Ottomans and the Portuguese, vying for control over Indian Ocean commerce.

Mediterranean Sea

At the approach of the first millennium CE, Muslim powers dominated the Mediterranean (Bahr al-Rum, or Bahr al-Sham) but, soon after the year 1000, the balance of power in and around the sea began to tip in favor of Christian forces. The Crusades, the Spanish "*reconquista*," and aggressive Italian seaborne traders all participated in a large-scale advance of Christians onto the southern and eastern shores of the Mediterranean, which eroded Muslim sea power in the region. In the later Middle Ages, Christian forces conquered Islamic territories in the Mediterranean.

In the 960s CE, the Byzantines already had recovered the eastern Mediterranean islands of Crete and Cyprus, and Christian forces in Italy and Iberia soon became dominant in the central and western Mediterranean. Also in the 960s CE, the Shi'ite Fatimid Caliphate established its capital at Cairo, which led to an increased significance of Red Sea trade and heightened attention to land and sea territories to the East. The Fatimids continued to control northern Africa and Sicily until the middle of the 11th century, but their direct influence in those regions was negatively impacted by conflict with their governors in Ifriqiya (Tunisia), where famine, warfare, and Berber invasions led to a sharp decline in both economic and political power and, thus, the ability to mount effective naval defense of the territories.

Indeed, in the mid-11th century the Ifriqiyans sent ships to defend Muslim Sicily from the invading Christian Normans, but were unable to prevent the island from falling under Christian control between 1061 and 1091 CE. The Norman realm established there (a kingdom from 1130 CE) further diminished Muslim naval power in the central Mediterranean and, by the mid-12th century, Norman kings had conquered cities and islands along the North African coast, though they held them only briefly. Christian Normans and northern Italian merchants, who had long been active throughout the Mediterranean, gained control of seaborne trade between North Africa and Sicily. Over the course of the later Middle Ages, these Italian maritime city-states—most notably Venice, Genoa, and Pisa—became the dominant economic and political players in regions of the Mediterranean formerly controlled by Islamic or Byzantine rulers.

Venice and Genoa, in fact, came to control much of the seaborne trade in the Mediterranean Sea by the 12th century, establishing mercantile hostelries and warehouses ("*fondacos*" or "*funduqs*") in port cities across the southern Mediterranean. Both city-states also profited from the establishment of trading outposts in crusader cities on the Levantine coast (especially Tyre, Sidon, and Beirut, but also Acre, Jaffa, and others) and participated in battles that further advanced their commercial interests, such as the joint attack on the Tunisian port of Mahdia by Genoa and Pisa in 1087 CE.

As transporters and suppliers for the crusades, Italian mercantile city-states gained concessions and control over eastern Mediterranean ports that allowed them to dominate regional trade and begin to establish economic empires. Most of the first crusaders traveled over land, but in later crusades travel and supply by sea were routine, and the Italian merchant-sailors became integral players in the crusading enterprise. The Levantine ports were the last crusader cities recaptured by Muslim forces (the last being Acre in 1291 CE)—but they were conquered on land, not at sea. No major crusading battles took place at sea.

In the western Mediterranean, Christian Iberian forces gradually eroded Muslim power in al-Andalus, beginning in earnest with the conquest of Toledo in 1085 CE, and later becoming integrated with the crusading movement. During the Second Crusade, fleets from England and Flanders participated in the *reconquista* by sailing along the Atlantic coast and assisting the 1147 CE siege of Almoravid Lisbon before entering the Mediterranean and proceeding to the Levant. Such voyages began to link the North Sea and the Mediterranean and, by 1500, both entrance and exit through the Straits of Gibraltar were common. By 1250 CE, the only Muslim state left in Iberia was Granada (conquered in 1492 CE). In this region, the primary form of Muslim seafaring was privateering—what would come to be known as the Barbary pirates—much of it state sponsored (especially by the Ottomans). Even though Muslim sea trade and naval power had declined, Muslims continued to travel by sea across the Mediterranean for pilgrimage, trade, and study. They simply sailed on Christian ships, took overland routes, or combined these modes of travel, as did Ibn Jubayr and Ibn Battuta.

The eastern Mediterranean from the late 11th century was embroiled in the Crusades and the decline of Byzantine power in the face of new Turkish powers (Seljuks and later Ottomans). The Fatimids and their Sunni successors the Ayyubids and the Mamluk Sultanate concentrated on land power and the Indian Ocean trade, further diminishing Muslim sea power in the Mediterranean Sea. Mediterranean seafaring began to revive starting in the 14th century under the Ottoman Empire, with the creation of a navy intended to wrest control of vital ports and trade routes from the Italians. Several Venetian-Ottoman wars in the 15th century eroded the territory and commercial power of the Italians. Under the admiralty of Kemal Reis (d. 1511 CE), the uncle of cartographer Piri Reis, the Ottoman navy defeated the Venetians at the Battle of Zonchio in 1499 CE, in which ship-mounted cannons were decisive and which returned much of the Aegean and Adriatic to Muslim

Painting of the Battle of Lepanto (1571) in Saint Paul's Church, Antwerp, Belgium. (Jozef Sedmak/Dreamstime.com)

control. Such artillery would be a hallmark of sea battles of the 16th century, particularly in the Battle of Lepanto (1571), in which a Christian coalition defeated a large Ottoman fleet.

Sarah Davis-Secord

Further Reading

Abulafia, David. 2011. *The Great Sea: A Human History of the Mediterranean*. New York: Oxford University Press.

Agius, Dionisius A. 2008. *Classic Ships of Islam: From Mesopotamia to the Indian Ocean*. Leiden: Brill.

Alpers, Edward A. 2014. *The Indian Ocean in World History*. Oxford: Oxford University Press.

Chaudhuri, K. N. 1990. *Asia Before Europe: Economy and Civilisation of the Indian Ocean from the Rise of Islam to 1750*. Cambridge: Cambridge University Press.

Constable, Olivia Remie. 2003. *Housing the Stranger in the Mediterranean World: Lodging, Trade, and Travel in Late Antiquity and the Middle Ages*. Cambridge: Cambridge University Press.

Dotson, John E. 2001. "Foundations of Venetian Naval Strategy from Pietro II Orseolo to the Battle of Zonchio, 1000–1500." *Viator* 32: 113–26.

Gertwagen, Ruth, and Elizabeth Jeffreys. 2012. *Shipping, Trade and Crusade in the Medieval Mediterranean.* Farnham, Surrey; Burlington, VT: Ashgate.

Khalilieh, Hassan Salih. 2006. *Admiralty and Maritime Laws in the Mediterranean Sea (ca. 800–1050): The Kitāb Akriyat al-Sufun vis-a-vis the Nomos Rhodion Nautikos.* Leiden; Boston: Brill.

Pearson, M. N. 2003. *The Indian Ocean.* London: Routledge.

Pryor, John H. 1988. *Geography, Technology, and War: Studies in the Maritime History of the Mediterranean, 649–1571.* Cambridge: Cambridge University Press.

Tomalin, Victoria, V. Selvakumar, P. K. Gopi, and M. V. Nair. 2004. "The Thaikkal-Kadakkarappally Boat: An Archaeological Example of Medieval Shipbuilding in the Western Indian Ocean." *The International Journal of Nautical Archaeology* 33.2: 253–63.

IBN BATTUTA, 1304 TO 1368 OR 1369 CE

Ibn Battuta was an Islamic jurist and traveler whose journeys across Eurasia are recorded in the *Rihla*. The *Rihla* was commissioned by the Marinid Sultan of Morocco and was composed—with the assistance of a scholar who recorded and edited Ibn Battuta's dictations—upon the completion of Ibn Battuta's three decades of travels. Although the *Rihla* (an Arabic term for "book of travels") primarily is concerned with politics and religion, it contains Ibn Battuta's descriptions of his voyages across bodies of water stretching from the Indian Ocean to the South China Sea, including his accounts of surviving shipwrecks and pirate attacks.

Born in 1304 CE in the Moroccan city of Tangier on the Strait of Gibraltar, Ibn Battuta belonged to the Sufi sect of Islam and followed his family's tradition by studying to become an Islamic jurist—a profession that would prove profitable during his journeys. In 1325 CE, Ibn Battuta began the initial leg of his globetrotting adventures, making a hajj pilgrimage to the holy Islamic city of Mecca. After completing his pilgrimage in 1328 CE, he traveled to Jeddah and boarded a *jalba* (a two-masted ship commonly used in the Red Sea) bound for Yemen. Violent weather forced Ibn Battuta's vessel to land in Africa before spending another six days at sea to reach its destination. Following a respite in Aden, Ibn Battuta traveled across the Indian Ocean to Mogadishu and Kilwa on the East African coast. At Mogadishu he observed the tradition of local men greeting newly arrived merchants with platters of food—which actually was part of a scheme that obliged the foreign merchants to accept the services of local trade brokers.

In 1332 CE, Ibn Battuta traveled to Anatolia where he boarded a Crimean-bound vessel on the southern shores of the Black Sea. Rather than sail along the safety of the coast, the ship's captain attempted to cross the treacherous open sea and finally reached Crimea after several failed attempts and near disaster. In Crimea, Ibn Battuta visited Kaffa, an important port and transit point for goods traveling along the Silk Road between China, Persia, and Europe. Ibn Battuta then turned east and travelled through Central Asia and on to India, where in 1334 CE he enlisted as an Islamic jurist in the services of the Sultan of Delhi. His stay in India was long and profitable. In 1341 CE, the Sultan appointed Ibn Battuta ambassador to the Mongol rulers of China. Unfortunately the diplomatic mission was aborted soon after it began, after most of the members of the mission—including hundreds of horses and slaves—perished at sea during a storm off Calicut. Ibn Battuta fled the disaster and relocated to the Maldives archipelago, where he was appointed chief Islamic judge. Ibn Battuta observed and experienced firsthand that, in the Maldives, sailors and local women entered temporary marriages that ended in divorce once the ships departed. Ibn Battuta's stay in Maldives ended with a falling out with the local rulers and he departed the Maldives in 1344 CE. Shortly after, he nearly drowned in a shipwreck off the coast of Sri Lanka, which was followed by a humiliating sea heist committed by a dozen pirate ships off the coast of India.

While in South Asia Ibn Battuta encountered Chinese junks and marveled at their roomy facilities that could house hundreds of passengers and crew members. The one criticism Ibn Battuta had about the junk was that—unlike the common vessels of the Indian Ocean that were held together by rope—the planking of the junk was nailed together and it easily broke apart when the junk ran aground.

Ibn Battuta then visited the Sultan of Samudra on the island of Sumatra in modern-day Indonesia before heading to China. Much of Ibn Battuta's commentary about China is unreliable—if not fictitious—although his description of the Muslim trading community in Quanzhou in southern China is considered accurate. During his travels back west, he survived the carnage wrought by the onslaught of the bubonic plague. In 1351 CE, Ibn Battuta made his final journey to the West African kingdom of Mali before retiring to Morocco, where he died in either 1368 or 1369 CE.

David Straub

Further Reading

Dunn, Ross E. 1986. *The Adventures of Ibn Battuta*. Berkeley: University of California Press.

Husain, Mahdi. 1976. *The Rehla of Ibn Battuta* (*India, Maldive Islands and Ceylon*). *Translation and Commentary*. Baroda: Oriental Institute.

Waines, David. 2010. *The Odyssey of Ibn Battuta*: *Uncommon Tales of a Medieval Adventurer*. London: I. B. Tauris.

IBN JUBAYR, D. 1217

Ibn Jubayr, a Muslim pilgrim from Granada, Spain, sailed across the Mediterranean Sea and back, and across the Red Sea, between 1183 and 1185 CE. His trip highlights the transformations of Mediterranean seafaring by the 12th century: Muslims traveled by sea, but now they traveled on Christian ships, particularly those from Italian mercantile city-states such as Genoa—the origin of all three Mediterranean ships on which Ibn Jubayr traveled. Many former Muslim territories had come under Christian control, and Ibn Jubayr visited several of them. His voyages also demonstrated the methods and perils of sea-travel: Coastal tramping and island-hopping often were hindered by storms that pushed ships into open waters and obscured the sightlines needed for navigation. Multiple ships often sailed together for protection against pirates and to aid in navigation. Shipwreck was a constant fear.

Each of Ibn Jubayr's voyages on the Mediterranean and Red Seas experienced storms, high winds, and navigational difficulties. He first sailed 30 days from Granada to Alexandria, Egypt, passing Sardinia and Sicily (both of which he saw) and Crete (which he could not see), and experiencing frightful storms. From Alexandria he traveled overland to the Red Sea, where he boarded a *jalba*—a small vessel sewn together with coconut fibers—which made him fear for his life, both because of the *jalba*'s construction and because it was overfilled with passengers. Shallow reefs and strong winds made navigation treacherous, but after a week Ibn Jubayr landed and traveled overland to Mecca and Medina. After performing the pilgrimage rituals and seeing the sights, he traveled north via Baghdad and Syria. To get on a westbound ship, he traveled through Crusader territory to Acre and took passage alongside hundreds of Christian pilgrims.

Ibn Jubayr's trip home entailed two voyages, the first of which was his most terrifying. Too late in the year for safe sailing, the normally two-week trip from Acre to Sicily took 40 days. Tempests drove the ship off course and destroyed part of the mast, which the sailors rebuilt in the midst of the storm. The Genoese captain's skillful maneuvering kept the ship afloat, but he lost sight of land and passengers ran short of provisions. Finally, Sicily's shores appeared, but they still were not safe. Violent storms, during which they again had to repair the masts and sails, caused the Christians to despair, but Ibn Jubayr said the Muslims calmly submitted to God's will. Near Messina, the ship broke apart. Rowboats dispatched from there rescued the passengers.

After wintering in Sicily, Ibn Jubayr departed on another Genoese ship, which sailed in convoy with three other Christian ships. Slowed at first by contrary winds, they gathered speed after passing Sardinia and soon spied the coast of Spain, along which they sailed until landing at Granada. During his two-year trip, Ibn Jubayr experienced storms and shipwreck, heard tales of pirates capturing slaves, saw dead passengers thrown overboard, and nearly starved. He also experienced the multicultural Mediterranean, fulfilled his religious duty, and left an invaluable account of his experiences.

Sarah Davis-Secord

Further Reading

Broadhurst, R. J. C. (trans.). 1952. *The Travels of Ibn Jubayr*. London: Jonathan Cape.

Kahanov, Yaacov, and Iskandar Jabour. 2010. "The Westbound Passage of Ibn Jubayr from Acre to Cartagena in 1184–1185." *Al-Masaq* 22: 79–101.

Netton, Ian Richard. 1996. "Ibn Jubayr: Penitent Pilgrim and Observant Traveler," 95–101. In Ian Richard Netton, *Seek Knowledge: Thought and Travel in the House of Islam*. Wiltshire, UK: Curzon Press.

IBN MAJID, AHMAD, CA. 1432 TO CA. 1500 CE

The son and grandson of prominent navigators, Ahmad Ibn Majid (full name: Shihab al-Din Ahmad ibn Majid al-Najid) was born in Julfar (modern-day Ras al-Khaimah) around 1432 CE. The greatest Arab navigator of his age and a prolific writer and poet, Ibn Majid authored more than 40 works on navigation. In addition to detailed navigational and technical data, his works often include poetry, evocative descriptions of places and peoples, and his often pithy observations on these topics. Many of his works have survived to the present, including *Kitab al-Fawa'id f i usul al-bahr wa'l-qawa'id* (*The Book of Profitable Things Concerning the First Principles and Rules of Navigation*), Ibn Majid's most important work.

Completed in 1490, *Kitab al-Fawa'id* was the most detailed guide to navigating the Red Sea and Indian Ocean of its time, and remained in common use for more than a century. It included a detailed discussion of major ports, navigational hazards, trade routes, the monsoons, winds, and currents, and the customs of local peoples, as well as a history of Arab seafaring. Ibn Majid describes the use of rhumb lines (and the stars associated with each of them), the compass, and other navigational instruments, and details how to compute one's latitude by measuring the height of the polestar with a "*kamal*," a knotted string attached to card with each knot representing the latitude of a major port. A voracious compiler of information, Ibn Majid's other works detail the east coast of Africa, almost as far south as the Cape of Good Hope, as well as China, Taiwan, and other parts of East Asia.

Ibn Majid's works are full of advice and warnings for sailors, ranging from the importance of staying alert at sea to treating other seafarers with respect. Much of this advice is provided in poetry, as in the selection below on when to sail to India.

> Whenever Gurab shines in the dawn, the heavier ships
> In Yemen are prevented from crossing to India.
> And for some time after the winds are full of rain.
> But it is possible for them to reach Shir with much trouble.

(Tibbetts 1971, 240)

After his death, several Arab writers suggested that Ibn Majid was the Muslim navigator who joined Vasco da Gama's expedition in East Africa, shared navigational information with him, and assisted in his voyage to India. There is no evidence to support these claims, and modern scholars discount the accusation. Ibn Majid penned his last work in 1500 CE, and likely died shortly afterward.

Stephen K. Stein

Further Reading

Clark, Alfred. 1993. "Medieval Arab Navigation on the Indian Ocean: Latitude Determination." *Journal of the American Oriental Society* 113: 360–74.

Tibbetts, G. R. 1971. *Arab Navigation in the Indian Ocean Before the Coming of the Portuguese, Being a Translation of Kitab al-Fawa'id f i usul al-bahr wa'l-qawa'id of Ahmad b. Majid al-Najdi.* London: The Royal Asiatic Society of Great Britain and Ireland.

PILGRIMAGE, MUSLIM (*HAJJ*)

The *hajj*, the spiritual journey to Mecca in present-day Saudi Arabia, is one of the five pillars of Islam. Every Muslim is required to make the trip to Mecca once during their lifetime if they possibly can. Mecca was the city where the Prophet Muhammad was born and where he is said to have received revelations from God. The journey is to take place during the last three months of the Islamic calendar. Because the Islamic calendar is based on lunar cycles, the *hajj* can take place on various dates on the Western calendar. Before his death Muhammad returned to Mecca and his pilgrimage set the example for the *hajj*. The dramatic expansion of the Muslim community across the world meant that, from its earliest days, sea travel was important for many of those traveling to Mecca.

Either sailing across the Mediterranean to Egypt and from there across the Red Sea, or across the Indian Ocean and around the coast of Arabia, ships brought *hajj* pilgrims to Jedda, Arabia's primary Red Sea port, known as the gateway to Mecca. From there, pilgrims traveled 60 miles overland to Mecca. The growing Muslim populations of South Asia and Southeast Asia meant that, for some Muslims, *hajj* journeys could be several thousand miles long. Often, pilgrims booked passage on cargo ships, and carrying these passengers became an important part of their cargo ships' business during the *hajj* season. Some of these ships were large enough to transport the camels of wealthy pilgrims who brought their own rather than hiring camels after arriving in Arabia.

Although land routes had their dangers—which ranged from attacks by bandits to dying of thirst, hunger, or heat—sea pilgrimages had their own disadvantages. Storms were always a danger. The winds of the Red Sea, often powerful and

The Kaaba in al-Masjid al-Haramat, Mecca, Saudi Arabia. The Kaaba is a shrine that houses the Black Stone of Mecca, the focal point for Muslim prayer and final destination for pilgrims to Mecca. (Sufi70/Dreamstime.com)

contrary, made it difficult for ships to navigate its treacherous, rock-strewn coastline. Larger ships often needed to transfer their passengers to smaller boats to complete the voyage to Jeddah, Arabia's primary Red Sea port from which pilgrims proceeded inland to Mecca.

Pirates often threatened pilgrim ships. In the 12th century, Crusader Raynald of Châtillon (ca. 1125–1187 CE) commanded five ships in the Red Sea that attacked ships carrying *hajj* travelers. After their arrival in the Indian Ocean at the end of the 15th century, Portuguese warships repeatedly attacked ships carrying pilgrims to the *hajj* and raided ports important to their travel. During parts of the 16th century, sea travel became so dangerous that some Muslim leaders declared that the *hajj* would not be mandatory for those who faced serious dangers.

Colonial powers later sought to gain control of the *hajj* travel business. Great Britain gave exclusive privileges to the Peninsular and Oriental Steamship Company (P&O) to convey pilgrims from India to Arabia. The Dutch colonial rulers in what is now Indonesia sought not only to control the travel routes, but to control what happened en route to Mecca. In the later years of Dutch control, fearing that pilgrims would be exposed to anti-colonial influences, authorities sought to isolate larger groups of pilgrims from those holding extremist views.

Beginning in the 19th century, cholera became widespread in the holy cities of Arabia. Efforts were made on both sides of the *hajj* trip to lessen the spread of this and other diseases. In areas around Arabia quarantine stations were set up. Ships carrying pilgrims often were forced to dislodge their passengers for a stay in these stations. Inspections also were made to determine whether disease was noticed among passengers.

Changing transportation technology altered traditional *hajj* routes. Railroads eased the journey, as did steamships. The opening of the Suez Canal allowed North African Muslims to book passage directly to Jeddah, omitting the previous journey up the Nile and across Egypt. Sailing ships might take weeks to cross the Red Sea, but steamships sailed from Suez to Jeddah in only three days. After World War II (1939–1945 CE), growing numbers of pilgrims traveled by air, and airlines displaced steamships as the primary transporter of pilgrims on *hajj*. In recent years, however, some cruise lines have begun serving *hajj* travelers.

Kenneth B. Taylor

Further Reading

Agius, Dionisius A. 2013. "Ships that Sailed the Red Sea in Medieval and Early Modern Islam: Perception and Reception." In Venetia Porter and Liana Saif (eds.). *The Hajj: Collected Essays*, 84–95. London: British Museum Press.

Alexanderson, Kris. 2014. "A Dark State of Affairs: Hajj Networks, Pan-Islamism, and Dutch Colonial Surveillance during the Interwar Period." *Journal of Social History* 47(4) (Summer): 1021–41.

Ladjal, Tarek. 2013. "Asian Hajj Routes: The Reflection of History and Geography." *Middle-East Journal of Scientific Research* 14(12): 1691–99.

Peters, F. E. 1994. *The Hajj: The Muslim Pilgrimage to Mecca and the Holy Places*. Princeton, NJ: Princeton University Press.

Tagliacozzo, Eric. 2013. *The Longest Journey: Southeast Asians and the Pilgrimage to Mecca*. Oxford University Press.

Slave Trade, 1000–1500 CE

One of the outcomes of the earliest global interaction, other than the exchange of goods and ideas that shaped world history, was the slave trade. Slavery is one of the oldest institutions in history—a social practice that has existed in every human society at different times and places. The period from 1000 to 1500 CE played a significant role in formalizing and institutionalizing the slave trade. Slaves—often war captives or people held in lieu of debt—were considered property and were bound to serve their owners. During the early Middle Ages, however, slavery acquired a new form as the establishment of large slave markets led to the commercialization of slaves who could be bought and sold like commodities. The slave trade became international and multi-directional. Many nations and peoples participated in the trade, which took place by land and increasingly by sea.

The Vikings (793–1100 CE), famous for their sea raids, played a crucial role in expanding the slave trade. They captured and enslaved a great number of Irish and Scandinavian natives in their raids and sold them as slaves to the Byzantine Empire and Muslim states. "The Annals of Ulster," for example, records the Viking raid of Dublin in 821 during which many women were carried away. The business became so lucrative that during the 11th century Irish kings entered the trade, selling war captives to the slave markets. Slaves were used as tribute and as payment for military service. Dublin, York, Chester, and Bristol became important ports for exporting slaves. Like the Vikings, Arab seafarers regularly raided Europe for slaves. In 1189, the Almohad caliph led a fleet that raided Lisbon, captured 3,000 women and children, and sold them as slaves.

The Turks (900–1200 CE) captured or purchased European slaves and trained them as soldiers for their armies. The most famous of these were the Janissaries of the Ottoman Empire, but many other Islamic states also formed corps of slave soldiers. In a few cases, these slave soldiers ("mamlukes") rose to become kings, establishing the Delhi Sultanate in India (1206–1290 CE) and the Mamluke Sultanate in Egypt (1250–1517 CE). Constantinople, long a center of the slave trade, declined following the Fourth Crusade (1202–1204 CE).

Italian merchants, who increasingly dominated Mediterranean seaborne commerce, established new trade routes that reached into the Black Sea. They sold Armenian and Georgian slaves to the Turks, and imported thousands of others to Italy, particularly after 1380 due to labor shortages following the Black Death.

Modern readers most closely associate Africa with the slave trade. Initially, Africans were captured by other Africans and used as slaves. The states of Ghana, Mali, and Songhai developed and maintained their ties with European and Near East culture through trade of gold, ivory, and slaves. The leaders of the Abbasid Caliphate brought large numbers of East African slaves, called "*Zanj*," from the Swahili coast and shipped them north to farm Iraq's marshes. Conditions were so poor that the slaves revolted at end of the ninth century. It was largely this trade between East Africa and the Islamic World that formalized and institutionalized the slave trade—a trade that Europeans later entered and enlarged. In 1440, Portuguese sailors reached the Cape Verde Islands and soon traded for African slaves to farm the previously uninhabited islands. In 1452, Pope Nicholas V issued a bill authorizing Portuguese enslavement of prisoners of wars, including women and children. The 1453 CE Ottoman conquest of Constantinople disrupted the eastern routes of the slave trade, but European colonization of America in the following century dramatically increased the slave trade in the West.

Slaves in this era often performed more varied work than those of later centuries, and were employed in homes, the military, and on farms and plantations. Many of them were women, and slavery in this era lacked the racial distinction of white slave owner and black male slave worker that typified the later transatlantic slave trade.

Adwita Rai

Further Reading

Alpers, E. A. 2014. *The Indian Ocean in World History*. Oxford: Oxford University Press.

Campbell, G. 2006. *The Structure of Slavery in Indian Ocean Africa and Asia*. London: Frank Cass.

Eltis, D., and S. L. Engerman. 2011. *The Cambridge World History of Slavery: Vol. 3*. Cambridge: Cambridge University Press.

Rodriguez, J. P. 1997. *The Historical Encyclopedia of World Slavery*. Santa Barbara, CA: ABC-CLIO.

PRIMARY DOCUMENTS

Letter from a Medieval Jewish Trader, ca. 950–1250 CE

Letters and documents found in Cairo's Ben Ezra synagogue in 1896 demonstrate the extensive travels and business dealings of a number of Jewish merchants. More than 300,000 in all, the documents span 1,000 years of history (870 to 1880 CE) and describe long-distance business relationships, patterns of trade, and even a few lawsuits. Trading partnerships transcended political, cultural, and religious boundaries and spanned North Africa, the Arabian coast, Persian Gulf, and India. Between 950 and 1250, Jewish traders were particularly active in Aden, a center of trade in the Indian Ocean and between the Indian Ocean, Egypt, and the Mediterranean. The letter provided below, written by an Italian living near Amalfi who went to sea against his parents' wishes, describes the dangers he faced at sea and his hopes to establish a new life in the Holy Land.

I faced death and unbearable dangers from the day I parted from my parents, whom I disobeyed. Likewise, when I visited Amalfi, there were difficulties when I was preparing to leave the city. Disturbances surrounded [it?] and I wondered why all that should happen. M. Hananel and M. Menahem—may they be remembered with a thousand blessings—were very good to me. [They introduced me] to the merchants, and all my dealings were carried out according to their instructions; also all other matters, such as the customs to be paid to the city. . . . They also tried to persuade us not to continue on our way. But we did not listen, for thus it was destined by God.

We arrived in Palermo . . . and paid our customs for everything in addition to the duties [a tip] for . . . the sailors of the ship. We were [there] a week and waited. Finally we found a large ship there, which sailed to Alexandria, Egypt. We paid the fare and embarked before the New Year Holiday. But on the fifth of Tishri, on Monday at noontime, a storm broke loose . . . storming upon us for three days. On the third day the ship began to leak and water penetrated into it from all sides. [We worked hard] to reduce its load and to bale the water out, for there was a big crowd on the ship, about four hundred persons. . . . The sea became even wilder and the ship was tossed about with its entire load. All the people lay down, for no strength was left to anyone [and cried to] God. Then they approached the captain and pleaded with him, saying, "Save us! Turn the ship toward the land as long [as there is daylight], before the sun sets, when everything will be lost." And all cried with a loud voice. The ship was steered toward the coast and all embraced one another, trembling. I am unable to describe how we cried. For when I saw those who knew how to swim had given up hope for life, what should I do who cannot stand water as high up as the ankles?

Finally, the ship touched ground and cracked asunder, as [an egg] would crack when a man presses it with his two hands. Passengers began to drown here and [there and pieces from] the ship floated above them. We three stood on a cabin on the uppermost part of the ship and did not know how to escape. People from below called us saying: "Come down quickly, each of you, catch a piece of wood and ride upon it, perhaps God will grant you rescue." [We cried to God with a bitter voice, but when I saw that everyone was riding on a piece of wood I said to Elijah [one of his companions]: "Why should we sit here, let us do as they do." I emitted a loud cry [and moved. We went down] together, one helping the other, [praying] to Him who hears Israel [. . .] and he got upon a piece of wood.

They survived and settled in Tyre, Lebanon, though much of the letter's end is missing. The writer concludes:

Money is nothing. . . . I shall replace.

Source: Shelomo Dov Goitein. 1973. *Letters of Medieval Jewish Traders* (Princeton: Princeton University Press), 40–41. Used by permission of Princeton University Press through Copyright Clearance Center, Inc.

"A Viking Raid"; Excerpt from *Gesta Normannorum Ducum*, 1060 CE, by William Jumièges

William of Jumièges, an 11th-century monk, wrote the Gesta Normannorum Ducum *(Deeds of the Norman Dukes) around 1060 CE. William the Conqueror (1028–1087 CE) later ordered the monk to expand that work to cover William's conquest of England, and 12th-century writers extended the work further. Written to glorify Norman deeds, it remains one of our best sources on the Normans. The passage below recounts the devastating Viking raids of 851 and 852 CE in which Vikings sailed up the Seine River, and raided throughout France, leaving Rouen and many other cities in ruins.*

Thereafter the Danish population grew so rapidly that soon the islands were overrun by people and many men were forced by royal edict to migrate from their homes. . . . For after his sons had grown up a father had to evict all of them except one, who was heir to his right.

. . .

Prompted by the laws of his ancestors, Lothbroc drove into exile his son Björn Ironside, together with a large group of young men compelled by a similar lot, and his tutor Hasting . . . in order that he might explore foreign countries and win by force new lands to settle. . . . Hasting as an exile, banished from his country with his pupil sent out messengers inviting soldiers of nearby provinces, who were impulsive and eager to fight, to join the expedition, and so gathered an army of innumerable warlike recruits. What more is there to say? They built ships, restored shields, repaired cuirasses, polished hauberks and helmets, sharpened swords and lances, and carefully strengthened their army with all manner of weapons. On the appointed day the ships were pushed into the sea and soldiers hastened to go aboard. They raised the standards, spread the sails before the winds, and like agile wolves set out to rend the Lord's sheep, pouring out human blood to their god Thor.

All alike partook of this blood sacrifice; a favorable wind blew them and they came [to] a harbor in Vermandois, in the year of our Lord 851. They sprang from their boats and immediately set fire to the county. In raging madness they burnt down the monastery of Saint-Quentin. . . . Emmo, bishop of Noyon, together with his deacons perished by their swords, and the common people, deprived of their pastor, were cut to pieces. They went from there to the mouth of the Seine, drew up their ships there and set up their siege camp near Jumiéges. . . . When the monks and other inhabitants of Jumiéges heard about the arrival of the heathens, they fled, burying some of their possessions in the earth and taking others with them, thus with God's help saving themselves [but] all the buildings were razed to the ground. . . .

From there they sailed up the River Seine and arrived at Rouen, which they destroyed by fire, and where they committed violent crimes against the Christians. Penetrating deeper into the interior of France, they invaded, with the fury that characterizes the Vikings, almost the whole of Neustria, which stretches from the city of Orléans all the way to Paris. During their raids they marched on foot, lacking the skills of horsemanship, but later on they rode on horseback as our fellow countrymen do, laying waste everything they found in their way. Then they harbored their ships near an island south of the monastery of Saint-Florent, which served as a place of refuge in case of danger. They put up huts and so created a sort of fortress, where they kept their prisoners in chains, and where they themselves seized the opportunity to refresh themselves after their exertions in order to set out straight[a]way on new expeditions. From this island they organized unexpected raids by ship or on horseback and ravaged the surrounding region. Then they traversed Anjou, where they burnt down Angers. Towns and villages all over the country, from the sea to the city of Poitiers, fell prey to massacre. Thereafter they sailed to Tours, filling it in their usual way with slaughter; they set fire to the town and destroyed the surrounding country. Not long afterwards, navigating their ships along the River Loire, they reached Orléans, which they captured and robbed of all its gold. . . .

Hasting and his accomplices, ambitious that their lord should occupy a high position, began seriously to consider the imperial crown. Finally, after taking counsel, they sailed their ships across the sea, determined to seize Rome by a secret raid. But a terrible storm arose and the wind forced them to land near the city of Luni. . . .

After the destruction of the city the heathens . . . took counsel and decided to return. On his way back to his native country, Björn, standard-bearer of the destruction and king of the armies, suffered shipwreck and barely reached the coast of England, while a number of his ships were lost.

Source: Elisabeth M. C. Van Houts (ed. and trans.). 1995. *The Gesta Normannorum Ducum of William of Jumièges, Orderic Vitalis, and Robert of Torigni.* Volume 1. Oxford: Clarendon Press, pp. 17–25. Used by permission of Oxford University Press.

Kingdoms and Marvels of the East, 1299 CE, by Marco Polo

A merchant from Venice, Marco Polo (1254–1324 CE) traveled with his father and uncle to China where they spent time in the court of Kublai Khan (1215–1294 CE). On his return, he chronicled his travels, and for more than a century his book was Europeans' premier guide to the Far East. In the passages below, he discusses Java, a central market in the spice trade, some navigational reference points, and kingdoms west of Java near which pirates lurk.

When you sail from Chamba, 1500 miles in a course between south and southeast, you come to a great Island called Java. And the experienced mariners of those islands who know the matter well, say that it is the greatest Island in the world, and has a compass of more than 3000 miles. It is subject to a great King and tributary to no one else in the world. The people are Idolaters. The Island is of surpassing wealth, producing black pepper, nutmegs, spikenard, galingale, cubebs, cloves, and all other kinds of spices.

This Island is also frequented by a vast amount of shipping, and by merchants who buy and sell costly goods from which they reap great profit. Indeed the treasure of this Island is so great as to be past telling. And I can assure you the Great Kaan never could get possession of this Island, on account of its great distance, and the great expense of an expedition thither.

. . .

Melibar is a great kingdom lying towards the west. The people are idolaters; they have a language of their own, and a king of their own, and pay tribute to nobody.

In this country you see more of the North Star, for it shows two cubits above the water. And you must know that from this kingdom of Melibar, and from another near it called Gozurat, there go forth every year more than a hundred corsair vessels on cruize. These pirates take with them their wives and children, and stay out the whole summer. Their method is to join in fleets of 20 or 30 of these pirate vessels together, and then they form what they call a sea cordon, that is, they drop off till there is an interval of 5 or 6 miles between ship and ship, so that they cover something like an hundred miles of sea, and no merchant ship can escape them. For when anyone corsair sights a vessel a signal is made by fire or smoke, and then the whole of them make for this, and seize the merchants and plunder them. After they have plundered them they let them go, saying: "Go along with you and get more gain, and that mayhap will fall to us also!"

But now the merchants are aware of this, and go so well manned and armed, and with such great ships, that they don't fear the corsairs. Still mishaps do befall them at times.

There is in this kingdom a great quantity of pepper, and ginger, and cinnamon, and turbit, and of nuts of India. They also manufacture very delicate and beautiful buckrams. The ships that come from the east bring copper in ballast. They also bring hither cloths of silk and gold, and sendals; also gold and silver, cloves and spikenard, and other fine spices for which there is a demand here, and exchange them for the products of these countries.

Ships come hither from many quarters, but especially from the great province of Manzi. Coarse spices are exported hence both to Manzi and to the west, and that which is carried by the merchants to Aden goes on to Alexandria, but the ships that go in the latter direction are not one to ten of those that go to the eastward; a very notable fact that I have mentioned before.

. . .

Gozurat is a great kingdom. Their people are Idolaters and have a peculiar language, and a king of their own, and are tributary to no one. It lies towards the west, and the North Star is here still more conspicuous, showing itself at an altitude of about 6 cubits.

The people are the most desperate pirates in existence, and one of their atrocious practices is this. When they have taken a merchant-vessel they force the merchants to swallow a stuff called *Tamarindi* mixed in seawater, which produces a violent purging. This is done in case the merchants, on seeing their danger, should have swallowed their most valuable stones and pearls. And in this way the pirates secure the whole.

In this province of Gozurat there grows much pepper, and ginger, and indigo. They have also a great deal of cotton. Their cotton trees are of very great size, growing full six paces high, and attaining to an age of 20 years. It is to be observed however that, when the trees are so old as that, the cotton is not good to spin, but only to quilt or stuff beds withal. Up to the age of 12 years indeed the trees give good spinning cotton, but from that age to 20 years the produce is inferior.

Source: Henry Yule (trans. and ed.). 1903. *The Book of Ser Marco Polo the Venetian Concerning the Kingdoms and Marvels of the East.* 2 vols. London: John Murray, 217, 324–35, 328.

Ibn Battuta's *Journey*, 1354 CE

Over the course of about 30 years, Ibn Battuta (1304–1369 CE), a 14th-century Muslim scholar, travelled across the Muslim world from Spain, through North Africa, the Middle East, the Horn of Africa, and then to India and Southeast Asia. From there, he sailed north to China. Ibn Battuta spent time in numerous countries and wrote about them on his return in a book he titled simply Journey. *The passages below describe some of the places he visited, including the lighthouse of Alexandria and the busy port of Aden, as well as pearl divers and other people he met.*

I left Tangier, my birthplace, on Thursday, 2nd Rajab 725 [June 14, 1325], being at that time twenty-two years of age, with the intention of making the Pilgrimage to the Holy House [at Mecca] and the Tomb of the Prophet [at Medina]. I set out alone, finding no companion . . . and no party of travelers with whom to associate myself. Swayed by an overmastering impulse within me, and a long-cherished desire to visit those glorious sanctuaries, I resolved to quit all my friends and tear myself away from my home. As my parents were still alive, it weighed grievously upon me to part from them, and both they and I were afflicted with sorrow.

[Crossing the Mediterranean, he arrived at Alexandria where he visited its famous lighthouse.] It is a very high square building, and its door is above the level of the earth. Opposite the door, and of the same height, is a building from which there is a plank bridge to the door; if this is removed there is no means of entrance. . . . It is situated on a high mound and lies three miles from the city on a long tongue of land which juts out into the sea from close by the city wall, so that the lighthouse cannot be reached by land except from the city. On my return to the West in the year 750 [1349] I visited the lighthouse again, and found that it had fallen into so ruinous a condition that it was not possible to enter it or climb up to the door.

[Ibn Battuta traveled overland through Syria to Mecca, spending some time in the area before departing Arabia from the port of Jedda and sailed south.]

We took ship at Sawakin [in modern Sudan] for Yemen. No sailing is done on this sea at night because of the number of rocks in it. At nightfall they land and embark again at sunrise. The captain of the ship stands constantly at the prow to warn the steersman of rocks. Six days after leaving Sawakin we reached the town of Hali, a large and populous town inhabited by two Arab tribes. The sultan is a man of excellent character, a man of letters and a poet. I had accompanied him from Mecca to Jedda, and when I reached his city he treated me generously and made me his guest for several days. I embarked in a ship of his and reached the township of Sarja, which is inhabited by Yemenite merchants.

. . .

I travelled thence to Aden, the port of Yemen, on the coast of the ocean. It is surrounded by mountains and can be approached from one side only; it has no crops, trees, or water, but has reservoirs in which rainwater is collected. The Arabs often cut off the inhabitants from their supply of drinking water until they buy them off with money and pieces of cloth. It is an exceedingly hot place. It is the port of the Indians, and to it come large vessels from Kinbayat [Cambay], Kawlam [Quilon], Calicut and many other Malabar ports [on the south-west coast of India]. There are Indian merchants living there, as well as Egyptian merchants. Its inhabitants are all either merchants, porters, or fishermen. Some of the merchants are immensely rich, so rich that sometimes a single merchant is sole owner of a large ship with all it contains, and this is a subject of ostentation and rivalry amongst them. In spite of that they are pious, humble, upright, and generous in character, treat strangers well, give liberally to devotees, and pay in full the tithes due to God.

. . .

From there we journeyed to the town of Qays, which is also called Siraf. The people of Siraf are Persians of noble stock, and amongst them there is a tribe of Arabs, who dive for pearls. The pearl fisheries are situated between Siraf and Bahrayn in a calm bay like a wide river. During the months of April and May a large number of boats come to this place with divers and merchants from Firs, Bahrayn and Qathif. Before diving the diver puts on his face a sort of tortoiseshell mask and a tortoiseshell clip on his nose, then he ties a rope round his waist and dives. . . . When he reaches the bottom of the sea he finds the shells there stuck in the sand between small stones, and pulls them out by hand or cuts them loose with a knife which he has for the purpose, and puts them in a leather bag slung round his neck. When his breath becomes restricted he pulls the rope, and the man holding the rope on the shore feels the movement and pulls him up into the boat. The bag is taken from him and the shells are opened [to find] pearls. These are then collected large and small together; the sultan takes his fifth and the remainder are bought by the merchants. . . Most of them are the creditors of the divers.

. . .

On leaving Zayla [in modern Somalia] we sailed for fifteen days and came to Maqdashaw [Mogadishu], which is an enormous town. Its inhabitants are merchants and have many camels, of which they slaughter hundreds every day [for food]. When a vessel reaches the port, it is met by sumbuqs, which are small boats, in each of which are a number of young men, each carrying a covered dish containing food. He presents this to one of the merchants on the ship saying "This is my guest," and all the others do the same. Each merchant on disembarking goes only to the house of the young man who is his host, except those who have made frequent journeys to the town and know its people well; these live where they please. The host then sells his goods for him and buys for him, and if anyone buys anything from him at too low a price, or sells to him in the absence of his host, the sale is regarded by them as invalid. This practice is of great advantage to them.

Source: Gibbs, H. A. R. (trans. and ed.). 1929. *Ibn Battuta Travels in Asia and Africa, 1325–1354*. London: Routledge, pp. 43, 46, 87, 107–11, 121.

Zheng He's Voyages, 1405–1411 CE

The Ming Dynasty's greatest admiral, Zheng He (1371–1435 CE), commanded large Chinese fleets on six voyages through Southeast Asia and the Indian Ocean. In modern parlance, Zheng He was "showing the flag," demonstrating the might of China and its ability to intervene in affairs far from home. On the voyages, Zheng He gave and received gifts that affirmed tributary relationships with China, suppressed pirates, and installed local rulers favored by China. The passages below from the "Ming Shi-lu," a collection of Ming government documents, describe the emperor's orders to Zheng He and his triumphant return from his third voyage.

July 11, 1405 [First Voyage]

The eunuch Zheng He and others were sent to take Imperial orders of instruction to the various countries in the Western Ocean, and to confer upon the kings of those countries patterned fine silks and variegated thin silks interwoven with gold thread, as appropriate.

October 2, 1407 [Second Voyage]

The Eunuch Director Zheng He who had been sent to the various countries of the Western Ocean, returned, bringing the pirate Chen Zu-yi and others in fetters. Previously, when he had arrived at Old Port, he came across Zu-yi and so on and sent people to bring them to negotiated pacification. Zu-yi and the others feigned surrender but secretly plotted to attack the Imperial army. [Zheng] He and the others found out about this and, marshaling the troops, prepared defences. When the forces led by Zu-yi attacked, He sent his troops out to do battle. Zu-yi suffered a great defeat. Over 5,000 (Alt: 50) of the bandit gang were killed, while ten of the bandit ships were burnt and seven captured. Further, two false bronze seals were seized and three prisoners, including Zu-yi, were taken alive. When they arrived at the capital, it was ordered that all the prisoners be beheaded.

October 17, 1408 [Third Voyage]

The Eunuch Director Zheng He and others were sent with Imperial orders to proceed as envoys to the countries of Calicut, Melaka, Samudera, Aru, Jia-yi-le, Java, Siam, Champa, Cochin, A-bo-ba-dan, Xiao Ke-lan, Nan-wu-li, and Gan-ba-li. They were also to confer brocades, fine silks and silk gauzes upon the kings of these countries.

July 6, 1411 [Return from Third Voyage]

The eunuch Zheng He and others, who had been sent as envoys to the various countries in the Western Ocean, returned and presented Ya-lie Ku-nai-er, the captured king of the country of Sri Lanka, and his family members. Previously, [Zheng] He and the others had been sent as envoys to the various *fan* countries. However, when they reached Sri Lanka, Ya-lie Ku-nai-er was insulting and disrespectful. He wished to harm [Zheng] He, but He came to know of this and left. Ya-lie Ku-nai-er also acted in an unfriendly way to neighbouring countries and repeatedly intercepted and robbed their envoys. All the *fan* countries suffered from his actions. When He returned, he again passed Sri Lanka and the king enticed him to the country. The king then had his son Na-yan demand gold, silver and precious objects, but He would not give these to him. The king then secretly despatched over 50,000 *fan* troops to rob He's ships. They also felled trees to create obstructions and impede He's route of return, so that he could not render assistance. He and the others found out about this and they gathered their force and set off back to their ships. However, the route had already been blocked. He thus spoke to his subordinates, saying: "The majority of the troops have already been despatched. The middle of the country will be empty." He also said: "Our merchants and troops are isolated and nervous and will be unable to act. If they are attacked by surprise, the attackers will achieve their purpose." Thus, he secretly ordered persons to go to the ships by another route with orders that the government troops were to fight to the death in opposing the attackers. He then personally led 2,000 of his troops through a by-path and attacked the royal city by surprise. They took the city and captured alive Ya-lie Ku-nai-er, his family members and chieftains. The *fan* army returned and surrounded the city and several battles were fought, but He greatly defeated them. [Zheng] He and the others subsequently returned to the Court. The assembled ministers requested that the king be executed. The Emperor pitied the king for his stupidity and ignorance and leniently ordered that he and the others be released and given food and clothing. The Ministry of Rites was ordered to deliberate on and select a worthy member of the family to be established as the country's king in order to handle the country's sacrifices.

Source: Geoff Wade (trans.). *Southeast Asia in the Ming Shi-lu: An Open Access Resource*, Singapore: Asia Research Institute and the Singapore E-Press, National University of Singapore. Entries 533, 605, 1048, 1778. http://epress.nus.edu.sg/msl/. Accessed June 29, 2016. Used by permission of National University of Singapore Press.

■ CHAPTER 5
The First Global Age, 1450 CE to 1770 CE

INTRODUCTION

Vasco da Gama (ca. 1469–1524 CE) opened a new European route to the riches of Asia, and Christopher Columbus (1451–1506 CE), seeking a route to those same riches, instead bumped into the Americas—a whole new world from the perspective of Europeans. Their voyages, only six years apart, together marked a dramatic moment in world history. Before then, the world's societies lived in relative isolation. Cultures knew their immediate neighbors and trading partners—for example, as Italians and Arabs knew one another—but possessed only fragmentary information on more distant civilizations, such as China. The voyages of Columbus, da Gama, and later European explorers and adventurers connected the peoples of the world as never before. The scale of their achievements was such that it required almost a century for Spain's rulers to understand the size of the Americas and for European cartographers to produce reasonably accurate maps of Asia and the Americas.

The voyages of those who followed in Columbus's wake, such as that of John Cabot (ca. 1450–ca. 1500 CE) who sailed north and of Pedro Alvares Cabral (ca. 1467–1520 CE) who sailed south, quickly demonstrated that Columbus had not located new islands off Japan, but rather had found a whole new continent. Ferdinand Magellan (1480–1521 CE) discovered the long-sought strait to reach the Pacific, and demonstrated that the world's oceans were all interconnected and that Asia's Spice Islands were not a short sail west of Panama—rather, several thousand miles of the Pacific Ocean separated them. The wealth of Asia was such that explorers dispatched to the Americas continued to devote much of their attention to finding a route to China and India through a northwest passage, or to simply attacking Spanish shipping. Russian explorers similarly sought a passage north over Russia to Asia.

These voyages were made possible by improvements in shipbuilding and navigation, which spread quickly around Europe thanks to Johannes Gutenberg (ca. 1398–1468 CE), who revolutionized printing with movable type. The first printed Bible appeared in 1455 CE, and over the next 50 years Europeans printed about 20 million books. This unprecedented outpouring spread knowledge across Europe and accelerated developments in a host of fields including astronomy and navigation.

By the 15th century, portolan charts detailed coastlines and ports and provided compass directions for sailing between them. Once beyond sight of land, navigators relied on stellar objects to determine their position north or south. In the northern hemisphere, they relied on the polestar and used a quadrant—a quarter circle marked with a scale to read the star's altitude. The Portuguese compiled existing navigational knowledge, disseminated it to their sailors, and systematically improved their navigational expertise and instruments. By 1480 CE, sailing south of the equator, they determined their north/south position by the sun's declination and later the Southern Cross constellation, the polestar's southern equivalent.

The Portuguese caravel, a product of blending northern and southern European building styles, was a three-masted, full-rigged ship equipped with square and lateen sails that allowed it to sail in almost any conditions. Armed with cannon and guided by officers with new navigational knowledge and instruments (including astrolabes, quadrants, and cross staffs), it was the first ship capable of sailing anywhere in the world. Copied by other European builders, caravels and similar ships carried Europeans across the world's oceans.

Portugal's leaders were quick to understand the Indian Ocean's maritime geography. They lacked the population to support significant conquest, but in a carefully planned campaign they sought to gain control of its commerce, systematically expanding their maritime empire in Asia. The tremendous advantage of Portuguese ships in quality and quantity of cannon enabled them to destroy local naval opposition, establish bases throughout the region, seize control of the Straits of Malacca (1511 CE) and Hormuz (1515 CE), and disrupt Arab shipping through the Red Sea, which allowed Portugal to become Europe's primary supplier of Asian spices, bringing in about 30 tons of cloves and 10 tons of nutmeg annually between 1513 and 1530 CE (Reid 1993, 14).

Although profitable, Portugal's empire also was vulnerable and steadily lost ground to European rivals who imitated the Portuguese by establishing fortified trading outposts of their own and disputing Portuguese control. After establishing their base at Batavia (modern Jakarta) in 1619 CE, the Dutch steadily displaced the Portuguese from the spice trade. The English, in turn, fought three wars with the Dutch in the 17th century over trade. It was not until the arrival of the Dutch and English that Europeans gained almost complete control of the spice trade, squeezing out local shippers. European ships, often heavily armed, sailed for the East Indies in spring and summer, stayed to trade over the winter, and returned the following year. The length of voyages and their inherent dangers fueled the development of maritime lending and insurance to finance them and joint stock companies to spread the risk.

Well into the 17th century, Europeans had little of interest to trade in the Indian Ocean, and so they paid with gold, silver, or goods purchased elsewhere in Asia, such as Chinese silk. In the 1640s CE, Southeast Asia annually exported about 6,500 tons of pepper—the most sought after spice—in exchange for 25 tons of sliver. By the mid-17th century, Dutch merchants estimated that Europeans consumed between a third and a half of Southeast Asia's entire spice production. In the 15th century, they had consumed less than 10 percent (Reid 1993, 19, 24).

Spain's burgeoning American empire owed much to chance and the independent actions of conquistadors. Perceived by Europeans as sparsely inhabited after epidemic diseases devastated local populations, the Americas attracted growing numbers of Europeans. More than 200,000 Spaniards immigrated to the New World in the century following Columbus's return, and immigration increased in the 17th and 18th centuries as other European states established New World colonies, shipping African slaves to them, as well as European settlers. Crops and animals also moved between the old and new worlds, changing agriculture and diet around the world. The potato, previously found only in Peru, became a staple for people from Ireland to Russia. Many spices, previously grown on distinct Southeast Asian islands, were transplanted and grown throughout the tropics, as were bananas and other fruits. Spanish sailors adopted the hammock, used by Caribbean islanders, for shipboard use, and other navies followed suit, making it a staple of shipboard life.

Despite its settlement of the Americas and extraction of wealth from them, the Spanish, too, focused on Asian trade, which was epitomized by Spain's Manila galleons. Sailing annually, these traded New World silver for Chinese porcelain and silk. They relied on European navigational knowledge and two great wind systems for their 20,000-mile round trip. The first, which aided Columbus, blows from east to west in the tropical latitudes and sped them from America to China. The second, first sailed by Magellan's expedition, blows from west to east in the temperate latitudes (particularly those between 40 and 50 degrees in both northern and southern hemispheres), and these "Roaring Forties," returned them home. Spain's coinage of New World silver, immortalized in pirate lore as pieces-of-eight (an eight-real coin or Spanish dollar), helped produce a global currency.

Increasingly, it was the Dutch who dominated international trade. Their merchant fleet expanded from about 2,500 ships in the 1630s CE to more than 12,000 in the 1660s CE, and these accounted for about two-thirds of total European shipping. The Dutch pioneered economical, purpose-built ships, epitomized by the "*fluyt*," a boxy cargo ship with a capacious hull, and the herring bus, an unusually large fishing vessel designed to stay at sea for up to two months and process and pack herring as it was caught. Both relied on simplified rigging and a host of pulleys and other labor-saving devices to handle the sails and cargo, which kept their crews small. England became the primary competitor and grew its own fleet, in part, by capturing Dutch cargo ships in war—more than a thousand in the First Anglo Dutch War (1652—1654 CE) alone (Hugill 1993, 22; Misa 2011, 38).

Europeans continued to improve their navigational expertise. Flemish cartographer Gerardus Mercator (1512–1594 CE) developed a more accurate system to display the curved surface of the earth on flat maps, which stimulated an outpouring of mapmaking. In 1584, Dutch cartographer Lucas Janszoon Waghenaer (1533–1606) published *Mariner's Mirror*, the first bound collection of nautical charts and sailing directions. Later editions, translated into several languages, extended the scope of this indispensable guide from Western Europe covering all waters from the Baltic Sea to the Canary Islands.

Calculating a ship's East/West position (longitude) remained a problem. Estimates depended on calculations of a ship's speed and the time, measured with an hourglass. Combining speed, direction, and time—called "dead reckoning"— allowed one to estimate a ship's position, and Columbus and other transatlantic explorers relied on this system to approximate their locations. In 1714, the British government established the Board of Longitude and offered a £20,000 reward to

Mercator, Gerardus (1512–1594 CE)

Gerardus Mercator—born Gerard De Cremer on March 5, 1512, in what is now Belgium—was a Flemish cartographer who studied mathematics and astronomy and is best known for creating the Mercator projection. Mercator attended the Catholic University of Leuven and later worked with Gemma Frisius to create some of the most advanced maps, globes, and astronomical instruments. Although Mercator questioned his faith at times, he tended to favor Christian belief over philosophy. In 1544 CE, he was accused of Protestant sympathies and imprisoned for seven months, but resumed his cartographic work upon release.

In the 1560s, Mercator developed a technique that allowed ships to sail a straight line course over the Earth's curved surface. This Mercator projection facilitated sea travel because the latitudinal and longitudinal lines were straight; this allowed for a direct path to be followed to a certain point on the map rather than the curved lines of previous maps. The longitudinal lines were spaced farther and farther apart as they moved away from the equator to account for the spherical shape of the earth.

In the 1580s, Mercator began compiling an atlas, a term possibly first used by Mercator to describe a compilation of maps. Mercator's son, Rumold, completed the *Atlas*, which included ancient maps and contemporary maps created by Mercator, in 1595 CE, a year after his father's death.

Matthew Blake Strickland

whoever solved the problem of calculating longitude, a prize not collected until 1761 CE when John Harrison (1693–1776 CE) received it for his chronometer, which kept exact time, allowing the precise calculation of longitude.

Ships continued to increase in size, growing from a few hundred tons to more than a thousand tons by the end of the 16th century. Purpose-built warships displaced the improvised warships of the Middle Ages, and these galleons—so called because they came to resemble galleys in their increasingly sleek lines as builders eliminated the large fore and aft castles of the past—mounted more (and larger) cannon on two or even three decks, thanks to watertight gun ports. By the mid-17th century, English and French warships carried up to 70 guns and displaced as much as 2,000 tons. A century later, they approached 3,000 tons, straining the practical limits of wooden shipbuilding. In contrast, Asian ships became smaller as Europeans dominated the most important trade routes. Starved of business, Asian shippers focused on local markets, carrying rice, grain, and other common goods in ships that rarely reached 200 tons.

Europeans benefitted disproportionately from the international market they created, importing a host of goods—once seen as luxuries—that became increasingly commonplace in the 18th century: coffee, pepper, sugar, tea, tobacco, and manufactured goods ranging from Chinese porcelain and silk to calico and muslin fabrics from India. Apart from the Arctic and Antarctic, only the Southern Pacific had escaped European influence, and a new generation of explorers, most notably James Cook (1728–1779 CE) pushed into the region in the mid-18th century, bringing with them scientists who made observations, studied local flora and fauna, and gathered samples. By 1770 CE, Europeans dominated the maritime world—a world they had largely shaped.

Stephen K. Stein

Further Reading

Boxer, Charles R. 1969. *The Portuguese Seaborne Empire, 1415–1825.* New York: Alfred A. Knopf.

Hugill, Peter J. 1993. *World Trade Since 1431: Geography, Technology, and Capitalism.* Baltimore: Johns Hopkins University Press.

Love, Ronald. 2006. *Maritime Exploration in the Age of Discovery, 1415–1800.* Westport, CT: Greenwood.

Misa, Thomas J. 2011. *Leonardo to the Internet: Technology and Culture from the Renaissance to the Present.* Baltimore: Johns Hopkins University Press.

Philips, William D., and Carla R. Philips. 1993. *The Worlds of Christopher Columbus.* Cambridge: Cambridge University Press.

Reid, Anthony. 1993. *Southeast Asia in the Age of Commerce, 1450–1680, Volume 2: Expansion and Crisis.* New Haven: Yale University Press.

CHRONOLOGY

Chronology: The First Global Age, 1450 to 1770 CE

1450s CE	The printing press is introduced in Europe.
1484 CE	King John II of Portugal establishes maritime advisory committee.
1488 CE	Bartolomeu Dias reaches the Cape of Good Hope, laying a foundation for Portuguese voyages into the Indian Ocean.
1492 CE	Christopher Columbus crosses the Atlantic and explores several Caribbean islands.
1494 CE	Portugal and Spain sign the Treaty of Tordesillas.
1497 CE	On his first voyage of exploration, John Cabot arrives in Newfoundland.
1498 CE	Vasco da Gama arrives at Calicut, India.
1500 CE	Pedro Alvares Cabral lands in Northeastern Brazil.
1501 CE	First African slaves arrive in Spain's Caribbean colonies.
1506 CE	Death of Christopher Columbus. Portugal establishes the Estado da Índia to oversee its Indian Ocean empire.
1510 CE	Afonso de Albuquerque leads Portuguese conquest of Goa.
1517 CE	Martin Luther launches the Protestant Reformation. Ottoman Empire conquers Egypt.
1518 CE	First outbreak of smallpox in America.
1520 CE	Suleiman the Magnificent becomes Sultan of the Ottoman Empire. Ferdinand Magellan discovers the Strait of Magellan in South America and sails into the Pacific.
1521 CE	Hernan Cortes conquers the Aztec Empire in Mexico. Ferdinand Magellan is killed in the Philippines. Magellan's fleet finishes its circumnavigation of the globe.
1524 CE	Giovanni de Verrazano explores North American coast for France.
1534 CE	Jacques Cartier claims Canada for France and begins exploring the St. Lawrence River.
1535 CE	Viceroyalty of New Spain founded.
1537 CE	Pedro Nuñes appointed Cosmographer of the Kingdom of Portugal.

1538 CE	Hayreddin (Barbarossa) defeats Christian fleet at the Battle of Prevesa.
1545 CE	English warship *Mary Rose* sinks.
1555 CE	Muscovy Company founded in England to trade with Russia and the Baltic.
1560s CE	Gerardus Mercator improves the navigational accuracy of maps.
1565 CE	Spain's first Manila Galleon sails across the Pacific.
1571 CE	Portuguese establish trading post at Nagasaki, Japan. A Genoese, Spanish, and Venetian fleet defeats the Ottomans at the Battle of Lepanto.
1577–1580 CE	England's Sir Francis Drake circumnavigates the globe after raiding Spanish settlements and shipping in the Americas.
1582 CE	Richard Hakluyt publishes *Divers Voyages Touching the Discoverie of America* to promote English colonization of the Americas.
1584 CE	Dutch cartographer Lucas Janszoon Waghenaer publishes *Mariner's Mirror*, the first bound collection of nautical charts and sailing directions.
1587 CE	Sir Walter Raleigh establishes an English colony on Roanoke Island. Its inhabitants mysteriously disappear within a few years.
1588 CE	Voyage and defeat of the Spanish Armada.
1591 CE	Dutch introduce the "*fluyt*," an economical cargo ship.
1592–1598 CE	The Imjin War between Korea and Japan.
1600 CE	English East India Company founded.
1602 CE	Dutch East India Company (VOC) founded.
1603 CE	Tokugawa Shogunate established in Japan. Death of Queen Elizabeth I of England.
1605 CE	Samuel de Champlain establishes French colony in Nova Scotia.
1607 CE	English settlers establish colony at Jamestown, Virginia.
1609 CE	Dutch jurist Hugo Grotius publishes *Mare Liberum* on the free use of the sea for trade.
1619 CE	First African slaves arrive in Virginia. Dutch East India Company captures Jakarta; renamed "Batavia," it becomes the company's center of operations in Southeast Asia.

1620 CE	The *Mayflower* lands pilgrims in New England.
1621 CE	Dutch capture Banda Islands.
1633–1653 CE	Construction of the Taj Mahal in India.
1634 CE	Japan's government restricts foreign merchants to Dejima, a small island off Nagasaki.
1641 CE	Dutch defeat the Portuguese and take control of Malacca.
1644 CE	Qing Dynasty established in China.
1648 CE	End of the Thirty Years' War in Europe. The Dutch Republic secures its independence from Spain.
1651 CE	England passes the first Navigation Acts.
1652 CE	Dutch settlers establish Cape Town near the Cape of Good Hope.
1652–1654 CE	The First Anglo Dutch War.
1655 CE	England captures Jamaica.
1661 CE	The first yacht race pits English King Charles II against his brother James. Portugal cedes Tangier, its last holding in Morocco, to England in exchange for English support against Spain.
1662 CE	English East India Company captures Bombay, India.
1665–1667 CE	Second Anglo Dutch War.
1671 CE	Sir Henry Morgan leads English buccaneers on their largest raid, sacking Panama City.
1672–1674 CE	The Third Anglo-Dutch War.
1674 CE	French establish base at Pondicherry, India.
1687 CE	Isaac Newton publishes the *Prinicipia Mathematica*.
1688 CE	The Glorious Revolution in England. Lloyd's of London begins insuring ships and expeditions.
1690s CE	Vladimir Atlasov explores and charts Kamchatka.
1700 CE	The Great Northern War between Russia and Sweden begins.
1703 CE	The Great Storm of 1703 sinks ships across England.
1715 CE	Tsar Peter the Great founds Russian Naval Academy in St. Petersburg.

1718 CE	The pirate Blackbeard (Edward Teach) dies in battle.
1719 CE	Daniel Defoe's *Robinson Crusoe* published.
1721 CE	End of the Great Northern War.
1733–1743 CE	Vitus Bering's Second Kamchatka Expedition maps the Siberian coastline and explores the Bering Strait, Aleutian Islands, and Alaskan coast.
1740–1748 CE	War of Austrian Succession.
1756–1763 CE	The Seven Years' War, also known as the French and Indian War.
1757–1759 CE	Invention of the sextant.
1761 CE	John Harrison wins prize for his chronometer, which enabled the accurate calculation of longitude.

AFRICA, 1450 TO 1770 CE

Sub-Saharan Africa is bordered by thousands of miles of coastline, bisected by rivers, and pockmarked by lakes. The Niger River's sweeping arch frames its northeastern limit, and the Congo River plunges through its southern reaches. Many rivers are several miles wide and deep enough to allow tallships to sail upwards of 100 miles inland. Most people lived near water and societies were not dichotomized into discrete terrestrial and maritime worlds. Many early modern Africans were fishing farmers and farming fishermen who wove terrestrial and aquatic experiences into *amphibious* lives, incorporating economies, social structures, and political institutions—their very way of life—around relationships with water.

Africans developed robust maritime traditions centuries before the Europeans' arrival, permitting them to master and exploit their waterways. Accounts indicate that most Africans were strong swimmers and underwater divers, using these abilities to fish, salvage goods from sunken vessels, and relax. Dugout canoes, the most ubiquitous watercraft, were used for commerce, warfare, and fishing. Together, swimming and canoeing enabled African societies to gain intimate understandings of their world and to exploit natural resources. Trade always involved the exchange of cultural practices and ideas and short- and long-distance canoe-born commerce wove waterside societies into a community of communities. Prior to the 15th century, trade flowed inland towards trans-Saharan markets. The arrival of Europeans along the coast, beginning in 1444 CE, and access to faster seaborne commercial routes and overseas markets reoriented trade towards the Atlantic. Canoes facilitated the fast shipment of goods to coastal African markets. Through the 18th century, African maritime skills promoted friendly reciprocal commercial relationships with Europeans.

African societies valued swimming as a life-saving skill and source of pleasure and profit and this was inculcated into children at a young age. "Once the children begin to walk by themselves, they soon go to the water in order to learn how to swim," observed Dutch merchant Pieter de Marees (de Marees 1987, 26). Parents promoted expertise through play. Youth used coastal, river, and lacustrine beaches as playgrounds. At Elmina (in modern Ghana), Jean Barbot watched "several hundred . . . boys and girls sporting together before the beach, and in many places among the rolling and breaking waves, learning to swim," concluding Africans' dexterities "proceed from their being brought up, both men and women from their infancy, to swim like fishes" (Hair 1992, II, 532). Similar scenes unfolded in the interior. Near Timbuktu, Mali Réné Caillié "amused" himself "observing groups of young negroes of both sexes, who were bathing, dancing and gamboling about it the water" (Caillié 1830, II, 5–6).

Swimming was regularly employed to generate incomes. Atlantic Africa possesses few natural harbors and most "ports" were actually "surf-ports," or landings situated on surf-battered beaches. They offered little protection from the sea and possessed no wharves, compelling shipmasters to anchor a couple miles offshore. Captains then hired African surf-canoemen to transport goods and people between ship and shore because slower and more cumbersome boats typically capsized in the surf. As heavily laden canoes were launched, canoemen often swam alongside to help keep bows pointed seaward, preventing capsizing. European slave traders employed African lifeguards to protect their investments. French slave trader Theophilus Canneau hired a "swimming party" to "swim off whenever a canoe should capsize" in high surf and rescue captives whose shackles inhibited swimming (Canneau 1976, 256).

Divers played a central role in some states' political and economic development by earning hard currency and trade goods. Men and women harvested oysters for their meat and burned their shells to produce lime for construction. The Mbamba province in the Kongo Kingdom controlled Luanda Island and its surrounding areas, where "*nzimbu*" ("cowry") shells were harvested for circulation. Others collected gold. Barbot reported that the "Kingdom of Sakoo produces much gold, which the blacks fish for, diving under the rocks and into the waterfalls" (Hair 1992, II, 338).

The diving skills of Africans impressed white travelers and European shipowners hired them to scrape barnacles from ships' hulls. *Kru* watermen repeatedly cleaned the *John H. Jones* in Monrovia, Liberia, impressing Charles Stewart who wrote, "their power of remaining underwater" was "truly remarkable" (Stewart 1936, 12–13). Diving served as a spectacle for white travelers who watched

Africans retrieve trinkets tossed overboard, as Bosman noted while on the Ivory and Grain Coasts.

> Whenever they were on Board, and I threw a string of Coral, or any thing else into the Sea, one of them would immediately dive after it, and tho' almost got to the bottom fetch it up again. This they seldom missed of, and were sure of what they brought up as their Reward. (Bosman 1705, 491)

Although Europeans wanted to conquer African polities, ecological advantages favored Africans who also possessed iron weapons, forcing Europeans to treat them as equals. Into the 18th century, Africans largely controlled the terms of commerce, using swimming and canoeing to undercut European exploitation.

Waterways were inherent to Africans' geopolitical spaces. When ships sank or ran ashore they became contested places with Africans and Europeans claiming ownership of them. Europeans wanted Africans to adopt Western salvage traditions dictating that shipowners maintained possession of stricken vessels, permitting salvagers to collect compensation for recovering goods. African rulers exercised traditional discretionary powers permitting them to claim a portion of game animals killed within their boundaries to appropriate grounded ships, their cargos, and, sometimes, crewmembers, whom they ransomed. They typically dispatched male and female divers to salvage shipwrecks. In 1615 CE, Father Manuel Álvares complained that the Bijago averred "what arrives on the beaches belongs to the first who seizes it." If a vessel "wrecked on any of their islands, they consider it fair gain; and . . . retain the unfortunate individuals whom they may have taken with it in captivity, until ransomed by friends" (Álvares 1990, 3).

Because the Atlantic slave trade could deplete populations and create political instability, some oligarchs worked to repel European slavers. The Faloup of Guinea-Bissua opposed the slave-trading of their Cassanga neighbors and discouraged Portuguese slavers by attacking their vessels and selling shipwrecked mariners into slavery.

Rulers did not always appropriate distressed vessels. To facilitate future trade, some commanded citizens to recover goods and refloat vessels belonging to African, North African, and Western merchants. Still, when Europeans retained possession of grounded vessels, they employed African divers to recover their goods.

Aquatics also undercut European attempts to project power across African waters. William Smith of the (English) Royal African Company reported how a Sierra Leonean ruler swam to safety when Smith tried to kidnap and force him to accept his commercial terms. Others swam off with stolen merchandise. While on the Grain Coast (now Liberia) in 1600 CE, Johann von Lübelfing reported that a man with a "pewter tankard of beer in his hand and a soldier's helmet on his head, jumped into the water with them and swam thus a great distance underwater; then he re-emerged and jumped into his little boat." He knew Europeans could not swim well enough to capture him. Indeed, they remained transfixed by his ability to "swim like a fish" despite being impeded by ill-gotten gains (Jones 1963, 12).

Enslaved Africans frequently took to the water during attempts to re-secure freedom. Many leapt from canoes while heading towards the coast. Men and women similarly jumped from slave ships lying off offshore and sometimes managed to escape.

Dugout canoes were central to Atlantic Africa's social, cultural, political, and economic development, providing three primary functions: trade, fishing, and warfare. Without canoes, travel in tropical Africa would have been exceedingly difficult as tsetse flies spread "*nagana*" disease to draft animals, which usually proved fatal in weeks. Consequently, human porters and canoemen were the primary modes of transport, with canoes being far more efficient. Dugouts were versatile vessels, fast and responsive, and with a shallow draft they could navigate waters only a few inches deep. The largest of them could carry several tons of cargo or more than 150 people.

Canoemen wove Africa into a community of communities bound together by commercial and cultural exchanges. Transporting commodities across coastal waters and along rivers, merchants circulated ideas, traditions, and spiritual beliefs as diverse peoples interacted and intermarried. Pidgin languages developed, and some languages—including Wolof, Bobangi, Fulani, KiKongo, Lingala, Hausa, Arabic, and European languages—became languages of trade.

To consolidate wealth and protect commerce, many merchants organized themselves into what scholars call "canoe houses." These were trading and fighting companies that maintained fleets of war canoes to protect and project their commercial interests. Rapidly evolving, they met the commercial demands of intensifying transatlantic trade. Traditionally consolidated along bloodlines and led by the oldest male family member, these firms developed into corporations of related and unrelated merchants, paddlers, warriors, and slaves, bound together by fictive kinship and market capitalism. As overseas trade expanded, leadership shifted to the wealthiest member, reflected in the titles the Efik of the Nigeria Delta bestowed upon the heads of their trading houses: "*Ete Ufok*," meaning "father of the house," was replaced by "*Etubom*," meaning "father of the canoe" (Sparks 2009, 40).

By the 1490s, fishermen in the eastern Niger Delta conducted brisk business with the Portuguese and transformed their fishing communities into commercial states. In 1699 CE, Jean Barbot observed the region's expanding slave-trading role, writing "long and large canoes, some sixty foot long and seven broad" carried "European goods and fish to the upland Blacks; and bring down to their respective towns, in exchange, a vast number of slaves, of all ages and sexes, and some large elephant teeth [tusks]" (Hair 1992, II, 675).

Crass at it sounds; humans were bulky, perishable commodities, requiring fast shipment to slave markets. They required food and water, with food costs and mortality rates increasing the longer they were en route. Hence, it was more profitable to ship slaves to the coast than march them overland. It could take months to walk to the coast and mortality rates were high. Water voyages were faster and less strenuous, reducing deaths and enabling merchants to sell healthier humans at higher prices than those trekked overland.

The currents of Atlantic commerce generated tremendous revenues for Africans, Europeans, and Americans. From the 15th through the early 20th century, virtually all the goods flowing out of Africa—including the roughly 12 million human beings bound for the New World bondage—were trans-shipped from shore to ship in surf-canoes. For example, surf-canoemen transported some "40,000 tons of goods" into and out of "colonial Dahomey at the end of the nineteenth century" (Manning 1985, 62). Surf-canoemen leveraged their expertise to inflate wages.

Most polities situated along navigable waterways possessed navies, which protected commerce and territorial waters. During conflicts, polities also pressed trade and fishing dugouts and crewmembers into service. Those built for warfare could exceed 80 feet in length and carry upwards of 200 people. Their length and relative narrowness made them unstable in rough waters, confining them to lagoons, lakes, and sluggish rivers. Those employed on coastal waters ranged from 20 to 40 feet in length.

Warriors were expected to both navigate and fight. Missiles included javelins, spears, and arrows, often dipped in poison, which precipitated slow painful deaths and terrified Europeans. At a given signal, warriors lay down their paddles to loose volleys of arrows or javelins. Shields, swords, knives, stabbing spears, and short axes were then used during hand-to-hand combat as canoes came alongside each other and during amphibious assaults. Most battles between ships and canoes ended in a stalemate and negotiation, as Africans had difficulty boarding high-sided ships.

Navies could defend territorial waters against European encroachment, capturing numerous ships in the process. The Bijago, who lived on the Bijago Archipelago, preyed upon European merchants operating on the Guinea-Bissua mainland from the 15th through early 19th century. They captured ships and sacked coastal and riverside European trade forts, prompting Portuguese priest Manuel Álvares to lambaste

those not aboard the Bijago's fleet cannot escape their claws. . . . If they encounter two or three canoes from other points on the coast they do not avoid them, even if they are war-canoes, unless they are stronger. Hence they say that all the other nations on the sea are their chickens. (Álvares 1990, 2)

War canoes built for calm waters were large enough to be fitted with fixed and swivel European-purchased guns. Some polities began adopting cannons during the late 17th century. This was especially true on the lagoon system paralleling the Bights of Benin and Biafra. Larger caliber guns were fixed to prows allowing canoes and surrounding waters to absorb their recoil. Canoes' maneuverability made it easy to align bow-guns with targets. Side-mounted swivel guns had to be smaller, because the recoil of larger guns could precipitate capsizing.

Naval guns were used against ships and canoes, to bombard land forces, and to support and defend against amphibious assaults. In July 1737 CE, a Little Popo and Hueda naval force commanded by Ashangmo, ruler of Little Popo, used muskets and cannons to destroy an invading army of 13,000 Dahomian soldiers, which he lured onto a narrow island. After his navy destroyed their canoes, trapping them ashore, the Popoes fired "at them at their leisure, from their canoes" and wiped them out (Norris 1789, 55–56).

Swimming and canoeing were widely held skills used to exploit natural resources, permitting Africans to efficiently weave rivers, lakes, and coastal waters into vast cultural and commercial networks. Canoemen moved copious quantities of European imports inland and carried African products seaward. War canoes protected trade and commerce, and divers recovered goods from capsized canoes and sunken ships. The arrival of Europeans provided opportunities to expand canoe-born commerce and generate incomes through swimming. From 1444 CE through roughly 1700 CE, cooperation and collegial maritime trade typified African and European relationships. This steadily gave way as European powers sought to control African markets and the production of raw materials. The European colonization began in earnest during the second half of the 19th century.

Kevin Dawson

Further Reading

Álvares, Manuel. 1990. *Ethiopia Minor and a Geographical Account of the Province of Sierra Leone (c. 1615)*. P. E. H. Hair (trans. and ed.). Liverpool.

Bosman, William. 1705. *A New and Accurate Description of the Coast of Guinea, Divided into the Gold, the Slave, and the Ivory Coasts*. New York.

Brooks E. George, Jr. (ed.). 1968. "A.A. Adee's Journal of a Visit to Liberia in 1827." *Liberian Studies Journal* Vol. II.

Caillié, Réné. 1830. *Travels Through Central Africa to Timbuctoo; and Across the Great Desert, to Morocco; Performed in the Years 1824–1828*. 2 vols. London: H. Colburn and R. Bentley.

Canneau, Theophilus. 1976. A *Slaver's Log Book, or 20 Years' Residence in Africa*. Englewood Cliffs, NJ: Prentice-Hall.

de Marees, Pieter. 1987. *Description and Historical Account of the Gold Kingdom of Guinea.* Albert Van Dantzig and Adam Jones (trans.) (1602, first ed.). New York: British Academy.

Hair, P. E. H. 1992. *Barbot on Guinea: The Writings of Jean Barbot on West Africa, 1678–1712.* 2 vols. London: Hakluyt Society.

Jones, Adam. 1983. *German Sources for West African History, 1599–1669.* Wiesbaden: Steiner, Franz.

Jones, G. I. 1963. *The Trading States of the Oil Rivers: A Study of Political Development in Eastern Nigeria.* London: Oxford University Press.

Manning, Patrick. 1985. "Merchants, Porters, and Canoemen in the Bight of Benin: Links in the West African Trade Networks." Catherine Conqury-Vidrovitch and Paul Lovejoy (ed.). *The Workers of the African Trade.* London: Sage.

Norris, Robert. 1789. *Memoirs of the Reign of Bossa Ahadee of Dahomey, King of Dahomy an Inland Country of Guineay.* London: W. Lowndes.

Sparks, Randy J. 2009. *The Two Princes of Calabar: An Eighteenth-Century Atlantic Odyssey.* Cambridge: Harvard University Press.

Stewart, Charles Jones. 1936. *"Home at Last!": A Voyage of Emigration to Liberia, West Africa in 1861–1862.* Cold Spring Harbor: Whaling Museum Society.

Thomas, Chas. W. 1860. *Adventures and Observations on the West Coast of Africa, and its Islands.* New York: Derby & Jackson.

Mozambique Island

Mozambique Island (Ilha de Moçambique) is an island situated in the northern part of the Mozambique Channel, the passage between the African mainland and island of Madagascar in the western Indian Ocean. A strategic location, it became an important trading post and part of Portugal's overseas empire. The Portuguese named it "Ilha de Moçambique," probably after local sheikh Ali Musa Mbiki.

Only 1.86 miles long with a maximum width of 0.31 miles, the island lacks fresh water. Nonetheless, by 900 CE, it was an important Arab and Swahili trade post. Vasco da Gama arrived at the island in early March 1498. Recognizing its strategic importance, as well as the fine protected harbor in Mossuril Bay, the Portuguese conquered the island and integrated it into their State of India (Estado da Índia). First construction of a stone-built and fortified trade post, a church invoked to Saint Gabriel (São Gabriel), a cemetery, and a hospital for the sick seafarers began during the reign of King Manuel I (1495–1521 CE), followed by the construction of the chapel invoked to Our Lady of the Bulwark (Nossa Senhora de Baluarte) and the Saint Sebastian fortress (Fortaleza São Sebastião) at the northernmost end of the island protecting the entrance channel to the inner harbor.

Mozambique Island became one of the most important waystations along the Portuguese India route known as the Carreira da Índia, and after 1558 CE was the capital of the eastern provinces of Portugal's Estado da Índia. It served as a trade post and a center for Christian missionary expeditions and a port for slave trade in the Atlantic as well as the Indian Ocean regions. Withstanding the Dutch sieges in 1604, 1607, and 1608 CE, the island remained as the capital of the eastern provinces of the State of India until 1752 CE, when it received its administrative independence. Mozambique Island lost its importance for navigation following the opening of the Suez Canal and the capital was removed to Lourenço Marques (today's Maputo, the capital of the Republic of Mozambique) in 1898 CE.

Due to its historical importance and well-preserved 16th- and 17th-century European stone buildings and fortifications, UNESCO classified Mozambique Island a World Heritage Site in 1991 CE.

Torsten dos Santos Arnold

Further Reading

Baxter, T. W., and A. da Silva Rego. 1962–1989. *Documentos sobre os Portugueses em Moçambique e na África Central* (*Documents on the Portuguese in Mozambique and Central Africa*), *1497–1840*. Lisbon: Centro de Estudos Históricos Ultramarinos. 11 vols.

Boxer, Charles R. 1961. "Moçambique Island and the 'Carreira da Índia.'" *STVDIA* 8: 95–132.

Henricksen, Thomas H. 1978. *Mozambique: A History*. London: Rex Collings.

Newitt, Malyn. 1995. *A History of Mozambique*. Bloomington: Indiana University Press.

Newitt, Malyn. 2005. *A History of Portuguese Overseas Expansion, 1400–1668*. London, New York: Routledge.

Slave Trade, 1450–1770 CE

The transatlantic slave trade was the largest forced migration in human history and one that intimately linked the economies of Africa, Europe, and the Americas. The trade ebbed and flowed in volume throughout its duration, revolving around innovations in crop production, evolving market necessities, and labor demands. Portuguese sailors initiated the trade in the 1440s CE by capitalizing on advancements in maritime technology, navigational expertise, innovations in mapmaking, and a more sophisticated comprehension of West Africa's wind currents. Such innovations made oceanic contact a more expedient venture for European traders and helped maintain contact with various West African communities. The Portuguese occasionally raided local villages for slaves, but found that negotiating trading partnerships with local communities was more sustainable to their interests. As colonial ambitions surged in the western hemisphere the trade expanded to include various European nations, ushering in new economic systems that molded imposing maritime empires.

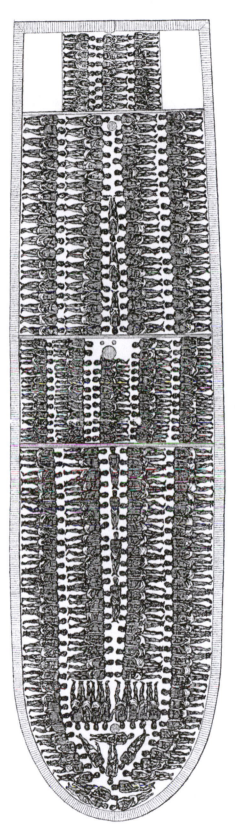

This 1788 diagram popularized by the anti-slavery movement shows the crowded conditions in which slaves were transported, in this case aboard the ship *Brookes*. (Pictorial Press Ltd/Alamy Stock Photo)

Gold was the initial item that Europeans most craved. Deeming one section of West Africa the "Gold Coast," Europeans offered favorable terms to local kingdoms for access to this mineral. Initially, the Portuguese imported slaves from other areas of western Africa into the Gold Coast to labor in the mines. West African gold bolstered the global presence of Portuguese mariners, even financing Vasco Da Gama's voyage around Southern Africa's Cape of Good Hope in the late-15th century. The Atlantic trade, however, heightened the demand for human commodities as European voyagers shifted their focus toward the Atlantic.

By the late-15th century, Iberian colonists occupied several Atlantic islands south of Europe and just west of Africa's coastline. The islands of Madeira, São Tomé, and the Canaries were crucial in developing the plantation complexes that would eventually dominate the slave societies of the Americas. Motivated by the cultivation of sugar—a crop largely unknown to most Europeans in the early 16th century—Iberian colonists exploited African, European, and Indigenous laborers in the deadly occupation of sugar production. As colonial ambitions expanded westward toward the Atlantic Ocean, slave trafficking obtained normalcy in the relations between West Africans and Western Europeans.

Plantation owners initially opted for a combination of African servitude, European indentured labor, and the enslavement of indigenous Americans, but the latter two proved unsuccessful in the long term. The contracts of indentured servants eventually expired and American Indian slaves either fled too frequently or died from the foreign diseases of the colonists. In consequence, Europeans tapped their existing African markets to expand trade in human chattel. Coupled with an escalating anti-black racism throughout Western Europe, the transatlantic slave trade ripped millions of people from the African continent. The early centuries of this trade were particularly devastating for those taken aboard the slave ships. Historians calculate that in the 16th and early 17th centuries nearly 20 percent of all African slaves perished on the "Middle Passage," the name given to the voyage from Africa to the Americas (Lindsay 2008, 95).

Although Europeans extracted millions of people from western Africa, historians generally agree that local communities controlled the flow of slaves that entered the Middle Passage. African rulers engaged in the trade through their own volition, and when Europeans attempted to force local communities to comply they were often met with resistance through physical and economic means. West Africans not only resisted European encroachments militarily, but they cleverly pitted slave traders against one another. In one example, African trader John Corrantee was courted by the French and English as they both sought to acquire a foothold in the slave trade at the Gold Coast. Records indicate that Corrantee often manipulated both empires if he was dissatisfied with the conditions of the trade, often outwitting his European counterparts and increasing his own wealth. Additionally, the mixed-race progeny of European sailors and African women largely controlled the volume of slaves that passed through the port cities, and some operated extensive trading networks that spanned Europe, Africa, and the Americas. As slavery was an indigenous institution throughout western Africa, most societies held few quarrels about selling slaves into the Atlantic network.

The individuals taken during the early Portuguese raids of the 15th century were largely reserved for European elites who employed them as domestic servants to enhance their status. Upon successful cultivation of sugarcane in the Atlantic islands and the voyage of Christopher Columbus in 1492, however, monocrop agriculture spread to the Caribbean islands and parts of the American mainland. Sugar was best cultivated in tropical environments and the labor conditions required that the workforce be constantly replenished. Due to disease, abuse, and physical exhaustion the birth rates in sugar-producing regions stayed low but the labor requirements remained high. As sugar fetched a high price in the booming European markets, Caribbean planters increased their demands for human chattel. Consequently, the forced transportation of human commodities intensified throughout the sugar colonies during the 17th, 18th, and 19th centuries.

Rice, coffee, indigo, cocoa, tobacco, and cotton also facilitated the expansion of black labor in the Americas. Each staple crop fed the market demands for products not indigenously grown in Europe. This combination of land conquest and crop production ultimately led to inter-colonial rivalries and the rise of European empires built upon African labor. Racist theories of natural subservience provided the impetus for this reliance upon chattel bondage, as black slaves were considered the absolute property of white slave owners. Anti-black philosophies existed in Western Europe for centuries prior to the Atlantic trade, but white supremacy codified this doctrine into the laws and social conditions of the Americas and rendered few liberties to the enslaved population. Pro-slavery apologists often argued that Africans became civilized under their European master's tutelage, entirely ignoring how slaves were forced to endure mental, physical, and sexual violence. The idea that slaves were defined by their production decisively minimized the value of black lives and enabled the trade to grow.

Although the Iberians led the colonization of the Americas and expanded African slavery in multiple areas, England, France, Sweden, the Netherlands, Denmark, and sections of Germany also invested in human commodities. By the 18th century, the British Empire asserted itself most forcefully among the naval powers of Western Europe and became one of the most prolific slave-trading empires in the Americas. Much of Great Britain's economy was tied to the slave trade and stimulated the expansion of British capitalism by introducing consumers to products such as sugar, tobacco, cotton, and coffee.

Tyler D. Parry

Further Reading

Eltis, David. 2000. *The Rise of Slavery in the Americas*. Cambridge: Cambridge University Press.

Lindsay, Lisa A. 2008. *Captives As Commodities: The Transatlantic Slave Trade*. New Jersey: Pearson Education, Inc.

Lovejoy, Paul E. 2011. *Transformations in Slavery: A History of Slavery in Africa*, 3rd ed. Cambridge: Cambridge University Press.

Northup, David. 2013. *Africa's Discovery of Europe*, 3rd ed. Oxford: Oxford University Press.

Rediker, Marcus. 2007. *The Slave Ship: A Human History*. New York: Penguin Books.

Schwartz, Stuart B. (ed.). 2004. *Tropical Babylons: Sugar and the Making of the Atlantic World, 1450–1680*. Chapel Hill: University of North Carolina Press.

Sparks, Randy J. 2014. *Where the Negroes Are Masters: An African Port in the Era of the Slave Trade*. Cambridge, MA: Harvard University Press.

Thornton, John K. 2012. *A Cultural History of the Atlantic World, 1250–1820*. Cambridge: Cambridge University Press.

THE AMERICAS, 1450 TO 1770 CE

Flanked by the Atlantic and the Pacific Oceans and smaller maritime realms such as the Caribbean Sea, the massive coastline of the Americas naturally influenced its history. Although standard narratives of American maritime history emphasize the absence of a high-seas maritime tradition in pre-Columbian times, wherever newly arrived Europeans encountered coastal communities they actually marveled at the natives' fishing and navigating skills. Spanish, French, and English accounts described in detail indigenous light boats, including canoes carved from single tree trunks and more elaborate birch bark canoes. Christopher Columbus compared the vessels he saw in the Caribbean with rowing galleys and remarked at their strikingly different construction from European plank-on-frame technology. The native population used them mainly for voyages in protected coastal water, for fishing and transporting warriors. In South America, people used balsa rafts to establish trade routes that reached across its entire west coast. Indigenous American craft, though, were suited mostly to river and coastal navigation, or inter-island travel in the Caribbean. The arrival of Europeans significantly shaped the Americas' maritime development by introducing high-sea navigation and connecting these native peoples to the rest of the world.

Spanish America

Apart from legendary Viking explorers who had explored North American waters and coastlines from their settlements in Iceland and Greenland, the first recorded

European seafarer to cross the Atlantic and reach America was Christopher Columbus (1451–1506 CE), sailing for the soon-to-be-unified Spanish crown. In his first of four voyages, in 1492, the Genoese navigator led three vessels (*Niña*, *Pinta*, and *Santa Maria*) from Palos de la Frontera via the Canary Islands to the Bahamas, Cuba, and Hispaniola. What later was recognized as the European discovery of the Caribbean was believed at the time to be the discovery of a West passage to Asia. Columbus returned to Spain with gold, curiosities, and prospects for successful colonization and proselytization of the new territories. Spain's rulers responded quickly and attempted to monopolize trade with the Indies and using American riches to increase their power on the Iberian Peninsula and Western Europe.

By the end of the 16th century, two viceroyalities (one in Mexico City and another in Lima) along with 10 *Audiencias* (Guadalajara, Mexico, Guatemala, Santo Domingo, Panama, Santa Fé de Bogotá, Quito, Lima, Charcas, and Chile) were in charge of the colonial administration. The House of Trade in Seville—enjoying a monopoly over the American trade—and the overseas colonies introduced a long list of regulations. A major factor was the discovery of enormous silver deposits in Potosí in the Viceroyalty of New Castile and the introduction of mercury amalgamation, which facilitated the extraction of silver from even low-grade ore, in the 1560s. The rich mines of Potosí might have accounted for 80 percent of global silver production between 1493 CE and 1800 CE. This bullion funded Spanish military operations in Europe, and facilitated trade across the world to China and Southeast Asia. Following the discovery of a transpacific route, Spain's Manila galleons or *Nao de la China*, sailed regularly between Acapulco and Manila, paying for Chinese and other Asian goods with silver. Their success depended not only on the effort of many individual groups such as sailors, miners, and mule drivers who operated between the main American ports of Vera Cruz in Mexico and Portobelo in Panama, but also on the weather. Spanish treasure fleets became targets for Dutch and English privateers and pirates operating in the Atlantic during the 16th and 17th centuries (until the Treaty of Madrid between Spain and England outlawed piracy in 1670 CE), forcing them to travel in convoys escorted by warships.

Vera Cruz became the main port for trans-shipment in the Viceroyalty of New Spain. Both Acapulco and Vera Cruz, being only of seasonal importance, however, lacked the splendor of other port cities. Prior to the 17th century when the Atlantic economy connected mines, haciendas, fisheries, plantations, and trading posts, cross-Atlantic encounters triggered lasting environmental consequences known as Columbian exchange: Although the export of staple crops such as potatoes, corn, tomatoes, and beans led to a population explosion in Africa, Asia, and Europe, wheat, grapevine, and sugarcane—but most dramatically germs and diseases brought by the Europeans in return—had dramatic agricultural and demographic consequences for the New World. A smallpox epidemic, for example, killed 90 percent of the population of the Aztec capital Tenochtitlan and facilitated its capture by Spain in 1521 CE. Over the following centuries, both free and forced migration across the Atlantic transformed and increased the American population.

Portuguese Brazil

In 1500 CE, Pedro Álvares Cabral (1467–1520 CE) landed in Northeastern Brazil and claimed it for Portugal. Unlike Spain's territorial colonization, the Portuguese mainly settled in coastal enclaves, where they initially focused on the export of brazil wood used for dye in Europe. Because Portuguese explorers initially found no silver or gold, they concentrated on the production of cash crops. Brazil's colonizers exported tobacco and cotton, but sugarcane—introduced from Europe—remained the most important and profitable product on transatlantic ships until the early 18th century.

Yet, early Portuguese colonizers struggled with a constant labor shortage, which settlers and indigenous people proved insufficient to meet. The need for labor on Portuguese sugar plantations helped produce the transatlantic slave trade. In the so-called Atlantic system based on triangular trade, Africa supplied labor, the Americas land and minerals, and Europe technology and military power. The first slaves arrived at Portugal's Brazilian sugar plantations in the 1530s. Sugar production boomed, and by the end of the 16th century, more than 100 ships sailed annually between Recife, Brazil, and Lisbon, Portugal. Like Spain, Portugal sought a monopoly on trade with its colonies, which was embodied in the 1494 Treaty of Tordesillas it negotiated with Spain. Both Dutch and French expeditions sought to penetrate Brazil and displace the Portuguese, but without long-term success. Increasing competition from sugar producers in the Caribbean, however, reduced the profitability of Brazilian sugar plantations by the end of the 17th century.

The English in North America and the Caribbean

The first documented, English-funded crossing of the Northern Atlantic was by the Genoese John Cabot (ca.1450–ca.1500 CE), who left Bristol in 1497 CE and returned with reports of rich fishing grounds, but no trade goods. Only after several decades, though, did the English crown actively participate in transatlantic activities, first by issuing letters of marque to privateers. In 1579 CE, Queen Elizabeth secretly supported Sir Francis Drake (ca. 1540–1596 CE), who captured the richly laden Spanish vessel *Nuestra Señora de la Concepción* off Columbia before sailing up the west coast of America and raiding Spanish settlements and then crossing the Pacific. Over the following decades various institutions sent colonists to the east coast of the present-day United States.

Before the establishment of coastal trade between the Dutch trading post in New Amsterdam (1624–1664 CE) and Boston (founded as a Puritan settlement 1629 CE), English settlers struggled to survive disease and famine, which reduced their numbers. Many of those Calvinists who failed as farmers took to the sea as fishermen and traders, and connected the growing number of English settlements scattered along the east coast of North America, which included "semitropical plantations, raucous fishing camps and pious communities of religious zealots" (Roland 2007, 10). Over time, these developed into a vibrant maritime community. In the 1630s, 138 ships crossed the Atlantic to New England, without a single ship lost on voyages that averaged 10 and one-half weeks. Inter-colonial trade with the Caribbean began during the English Civil War (1642–1646 CE), when ships from Massachusetts delivered timber to Caribbean sugar plantations and stayed to fish in these rich waters.

By the 17th century, North American shipwrights from ports between New Amsterdam and Maine built increasingly larger ships, including small warships for Britain's Royal Navy. In fact, shipbuilding became the colonies' most profitable export manufacture. Small bluff-bowed sailing vessels carrying news, goods, and passengers between England's 13 disparate mainland colonies played a role in the colonies' political integration and eventual independence. Although aimed primarily at their Dutch competitors, England's Navigation Acts (1651, 1660, and 1663 CE) also restricted the shipbuilding and trade of its American colonies. England's rulers, however, focused more attention on Caribbean trade, which was closely linked to plantation production of sugar, coffee, and tobacco. Together with other colonial latecomers, England's economic success in the Caribbean relied on plantations worked by slaves. English merchants entered the slave trade, annually transporting thousands of slaves across the Atlantic in inhumane conditions.

The French

King Francis I (1494–1547 CE) sponsored Jacques Cartier's (1491–1557 CE) expeditions to North America in the 1530s/40s. Rivalry with English adventurers encouraged the French explorers to move westward from Newfoundland to Nova Scotia and the Gulf of Maine, and they soon recognized the area's potential for fur trade. The French colony in Nova Scotia, established by Samuel de Champlain in 1605 CE, as well as future French colonization projects relied more on cooperation with indigenous peoples than on their conquest, particularly around Quebec, where the first French colonists traded with indigenous people for beaver and other furs. French fur traders moved west and then south down the Mississippi River, establishing settlements around the Great Lakes and eventually Louisiana in 1682 CE.

The Dutch

In 1609 CE, English explorer Henry Hudson (d. 1611 CE), claimed parts of North America for the Dutch while seeking a Northwest Passage to Asia. The Dutch established their first North American settlement and trading post, Fort Nassau, in 1615 CE near modern New York. The Dutch expanded their operations in the region following the 1621 CE founding of the Dutch West India Company (WIC). In 1626 CE, company director Peter Minuit (ca. 1580–1638 CE) purchased the island of Manhattan from its Lenape natives, and over the next generation established settlements along the Connecticut and Delaware Rivers. Dutch seafarers successfully undermined Spanish and Portuguese claims in the Americas, capturing ships and raiding—and sometimes capturing—poorly defended coastal settlements. The WIC established settlements in Venezuela, Guiana, the Caribbean, and northeastern Brazil, whose major port of Recife, captured from Portugal, became the WIC's hosting American headquarters. West India Company vessels became major carriers of sugar from Brazil and salt and tobacco from Venezuela to Europe, but in 1661 CE the resurgent Portuguese successfully drove the Dutch out of Brazil. The Caribbean, however, remained an important center of WIC operations, which established its first colonies there at Tobago (1628 CE), Curaçao (1634 CE), and Aruba (1637 CE).

Piracy and warfare were regular features in American waters in these years and rich colonies might change hands several times. During the Anglo-Dutch Wars (1652–1674 CE), for example, the Dutch colony of Suriname, north of Brazil, repeatedly changed hands before 1667 when England exchanged it to secure its claim to New Amsterdam (modern New York). Throughout these years, maritime activity increased steadily and many European colonies developed their own shipping shipbuilding facilities, which helped facilitate their movement to independence in the late 17th and 18th centuries.

Birgit Tremml-Werner

Further Reading

Crosby, Alfred. 1972. *The Columbian Exchange. Biological and Cultural Consequences of 1492.* New Haven: Yale University Press.

Elliott, John H. 2006. *Empires of the Atlantic World. Britain and Spain in America, 1492–1839.* New Haven: Yale University Press.

Parry, J. H. 1990. *The Spanish Seaborne Empire.* Berkeley: University of California Press.

Rediker, Markus. 2007. *The Slave Ship. A Human History.* New York: Viking/Penguin.

Rediker, Markus. 2014. *Outlaws of the Atlantic.* Boston: Beacon Press.

Roland, Alex. 2007. *The Way of the Ship. America's Maritime History Reenvisioned, 1600–2000.* Malden: Wiley.

Smith, Joshua M. (ed.). 2009. *Voyages. The Age of Sail, Documents in American Maritime History, 1492–1865,* vol. 1. Gainesville: University Press of Florida.

Hakluyt, Richard, 1552–1616 CE

A veritable jack-of-all-trades, Richard Hakluyt is best remembered as a geographer, translator, writer, and editor. Despite never travelling across the Atlantic, the legacy of Hakluyt is found in his two most important works: *Divers Voyages Touching the Discoverie of America* (1582 CE) and *The Principall Navigations, Voiages, Traffiques and Discoveries of the English Nation* (1589 CE). In *Divers Voyages*, Hakluyt promoted English colonization of North America. Hakluyt's cousin, Sir Humphrey Gilbert, had been granted the rights of this exploration by Queen Elizabeth, and five years after Hakluyt's publication, the Roanoke Island colony in Virginia was settled by Gilbert's half-brother, Sir Walter Raleigh.

At an early age Hakluyt lost his father and became a ward of his cousin who shared the same name; his cousin is normally referred to as Richard Hakluyt the lawyer while the subject of this entry is sometimes known as Richard Hakluyt the younger. A Queen's Scholar at Westminster School, Hakluyt later received a BA and MA from Oxford. By 1580 CE, he was ordained as an Anglican priest. Furthermore, he also served with the English ambassador to France; his journey to Paris was Hakluyt's only journey abroad.

After the colony at Roanoke failed (now recognized as the "Lost Colony") Hakluyt continued to support English settlement of North America. His name appears in the petition to King James I for a colonial charter in Virginia; it was from these efforts that Jamestown was chartered and settled in 1607.

Principall Navigations is Hakluyt's most famous work. Keeping in mind that Hakluyt did not participate in any English voyages personally, compiling the numerous voyages spanning the time period of almost a thousand years was no easy task; it was in this work that Hakluyt showed his skills in translating, editing, and writing. Hakluyt successfully recounted English voyages while also including letters and journals written by those who participated. This multivolume work was popular enough to be printed in subsequent editions. Hakluyt used his *Principall Navigations* as a means of extolling the past and contemporary successes of the English. It was through this praise that Hakluyt promoted future successful voyages and truly believed the English could advance their colonization of North America and extend their dominion throughout the Atlantic.

Despite the importance of the two works mentioned in detail, more than 20 other writings are attributed to Hakluyt. These include other discourses of travel, trade, and even a presentation to Queen Elizabeth detailing the means by which the English could profit from colonization in the New World. The Spanish and Portuguese used conquest for the purposes of gold and silver mining but Hakluyt believed the English could use the wealth of farming and shipping to grow their economy and develop a maritime empire; he was absolutely correct in his analysis.

Matthew Blake Strickland

Further Reading

Hakluyt, Richard. Reissue 1972. *Voyages and Discoveries: Principal Navigations, Voyages, Traffiques and Discoveries of the English Nation.* Jack Beeching (ed.). New York: Penguin Books.

Mancall, Peter C. 2007. *Hakluyt's Promise: An Elizabethan's Obsession for an English America.* New Haven: Yale University Press.

Parks, George Bruner. 1928. *Richard Hakluyt and the English Voyages.* New York: American Geographical Society.

Manila Galleons

The "Manila Galleon" or "Nao de China" was a heavily armed, multi-decked Spanish merchant ship with three to four masts, a lateen-rigged mizzen and a distinguishing square gallery at the stern. Between 1565 CE and 1815 CE an average of two Spanish galleons crossed the Pacific nearly annually from Manila, Philippines, to Acapulco, Mexico, and vice versa, making it the longest uninterrupted sea journey of its time. The Manila Galleons triggered socioeconomic processes through the exchange of New World silver and Chinese manufactured goods including silk and porcelains together with specific inter-imperial migration flows. Mexican merchants and colonial and church authorities from the Iberian Peninsula traveled from New Spain to the Philippines, while on the return route, passengers included Hispanic returnees, Filipino-Malay sailors, Chinese craftsmen, and even East Asian slaves. Transpacific exchange rested upon the coinciding discovery of silver mines in Potosí (Peru) and Ming China's currency crisis; together they encouraged a shift in maritime trade in the China Seas and stimulated demand for luxury goods and spices from Western Europe to Japan.

Five Pacific expeditions after Ferdinand Magellan's (1480–1521 CE) arrival on the Philippine archipelago (1521), Augustinian friar Andrés de Urdaneta (1498–1568 CE) used his knowledge about yearly monsoon and typhoon conditions and the Black Current ("*Kuroshio*") for establishing a navigable return route ("*tornaviaje*") to New Spain in 1565. Both east- and westbound routes averaged 9,000 nautical miles, despite a difference of 20 degrees in latitude, and required several months of sailing. Although westbound galleons could reach Manila in less than two months, journeys from Asia to Acapulco could take up to one year. Next to tempestuous weather and shortage of provision, passengers also were exposed to potential attacks by Spain's enemies or by individual pirates attracted by the galleon's valuable cargo. The costly galleons were mostly constructed in Cavite, Manila's international port, which benefitted from nearby good timber and a ready work force. Being a crown monopoly, all galleon-related matters—from the participating ports of call to the purchase of construction materials—followed royal decrees. In 1593 CE, King Philip II (1527–1598 CE) defined the maximum carrying capacity at 300 tons per galleon and limited the annual amount of silver sent to one million pesos (about 28 tons of silver). Because Spaniards on both sides of the Pacific soon found ways to circumvent these restrictions, the amount shipped was actually much greater.

Birgit Tremml-Werner

Further Reading

Buschmann, Rainer F. et al. 2014. *Navigating the Spanish Lake: The Pacific in the Iberian World, 1521–1898.* Honolulu: University of Hawai'i Press.

Schurz, William Lytle. 1959. *The Manila Galleon.* Boston: D. P. Dutton.

Suárez, Thomas. 2004. *Early Mapping of the Pacific. The Epic Story of Seafarers, Adventurers and Cartographers Who Mapped the World's Greatest Ocean.* Singapore: Periplus.

Mayflower

The *Mayflower* has a well-known place in the history of the United States as the ship that famously transported the Pilgrims to the New World where they established the Plymouth Colony. This event has been the subject of great historical analysis for its importance in British colonization and has also been mythologized with the Thanksgiving holiday.

The precise origin of the famous ship that carried the Pilgrims to present-day Massachusetts is unknown. It is believed that Christopher Jones and other businessmen purchased the ship around 1607 CE for trade purposes. However, the first documented voyage found in historical records occurred in 1609 CE. After what appears to be that maiden voyage, the *Mayflower* transported goods around the Atlantic coast of Europe. In September 1620 CE, the *Mayflower* made its first journey across the Atlantic to North America—this is the voyage that made it famous. The *Mayflower* was only in service for a few years after its first transatlantic voyage. The ship was declared unseaworthy in 1624 CE and is believed to have been broken apart.

The *Mayflower* is representative of what was occurring in the 17th century. Ships transporting large groups of people and diverse commodities sailed throughout the Atlantic Ocean basin between Europe, Africa, and the New World. Many other ships like the *Mayflower* provided the means by which Europeans could begin to settle in areas not previously colonized by European nations; the *Mayflower* found in the history of North American colonization happens to be one of the more famous.

Matthew Blake Strickland

The *Mayflower*, which carried Pilgrims to Plymouth Rock to start a new colony in 1620. (Library of Congress)

Further Reading

Caffrey, Kate. 1974. *The Mayflower*. New York: Stein and Day Publishers.

Dillon, Francis. 1973. *The Pilgrims*. New York: Doubleday & Company.

Hilton, Christopher. 2005. *Mayflower: The Voyage That Changed the World*. Phoenix Mill, UK: Sutton Publishing.

Philbrick, Nathaniel. 2006. *Mayflower: A Story of Courage, Community, and War*. New York: Viking.

Piracy in the Americas, 1450–1770 CE

Piracy in the Americas began shortly after Spain established its first colonial settlement in 1493 CE and increased rapidly after Hernando Cortés (1485–1547 CE) defeated the Aztec Empire in 1521 CE, and Francisco Pizarro (ca. 1471–1541 CE) looted the Incan Empire in the 1530s. As Spanish ships carried Aztec and Incan treasure across the Atlantic, other European powers looked on greedily. French corsairs presented Spain's first significant challenge in the Caribbean, attacking ships and settlements in the 1520s and 30s. These attacks forced the Spanish to create an expensive convoy system called the *Carrera de Indias* ("the Indies run"), which lasted into the 18th century. Spain's establishment of the rich Zacatecas (Mexico) and Potosí (Bolivia) silver mines in the late 1540s amplified the need for naval protection and coastal fortifications.

By the 1560s, the wealth flowing to Spain from its colonies in the Americas lured English seamen to the region. At first, the English smuggled African slaves into Spanish America, but after the Battle of San Juan de Ulúa in 1568 CE, during which the Spanish sank an English smuggler, the 700-ton *Jesus of Lubeck*, English seafarers turned to piracy. Sir Francis Drake (ca. 1540–1596 CE), the most famous of these enterprising pirates, formed alliances with French corsairs and runaway indigenous and African slaves, called "*cimarrones*," to menace Spanish shipping and colonies in both the Atlantic and Pacific Oceans. His successes outraged King Phillip II of Spain (1527–1598 CE) and contributed to Phillip's 1588 CE attempt to overthrow Queen Elizabeth I (1533–1603 CE).

During the 16th and 17th centuries, piracy was intricately linked to national interests and competing European empires. Typically, English, French, and Dutch pirates—or "buccaneers" as they were called in the 17th century—colluded and attacked, and pillaged Spain's American Empire. Pirates received toothless public reprimands from their monarchs, but private encouragement to weaken Spain's Empire. Spanish loot, meanwhile, either augmented monarchs' coffers or helped develop nascent colonies in the Caribbean and North America. English leaders considered early colonization efforts as potential bases for pirate and privateering attacks against the Spanish. Indeed, England's 1655 CE conquest of Jamaica from Spain ushered in the great buccaneer era of Sir Henry Morgan (1635–1688 CE) who sacked Puerto Principe, Porto Bello, and Panama City. More than 2,000 buccaneers soon called Port Royal, Jamaica, home and Jamaican merchants invested their plunder in slaves and sugar plantations. England valued these men as national assets rather than judging them to be criminals.

As English, Dutch, and French American colonies developed in the late-17th century, pirates lost their usefulness to established powers and colonial elites. The benefits of Atlantic commerce in sugar, tobacco, and other commodities came to outweigh pirated loot. After 1689 CE, escalating hostilities between England and France strained the maritime labor market in the Americas, leading to large-scale naval impressments in West Indies and North American ports. Consequently, many ex-buccaneers abandoned the West Indies for the Indian Ocean where they amassed riches plundering the Mughal Empire's weakly defended ships. Much of this fortune made its way to English-American ports where pirates had important political and mercantile connections. The Indian Ocean pirates, however, soured relations with England's mercantile community. Parliament recalled colonial governors that consorted with pirates, passed *An Act for the More Effectual Suppressing of Piracy* in 1700 CE, publically tried and executed Indian Ocean pirate William Kidd, and dispatched a naval squadron that eradicated the pirate base on St. Mary's Island near Madagascar. Along with Queen Anne's War (1702–1713 CE), these actions halted most pirate activity.

In 1716 CE, piracy resurfaced with a vengeance and produced some of history's most colorful and powerful pirates, including Edward Teach (Blackbeard), Stede Bonnet, Charles Vane, Calico Jack Rackham, Edward England, Bartholomew Roberts, Edward (Ned) Low, and William Fly. Roughly 4,000 men sailed under the black flag, plundering at least 2,400 vessels in this era. Unlike their predecessors, they attacked the shipping of all nations and had no national support. Of the pirates listed above, only Edward England escaped death in combat or by hanging. By the mid-1720s, the Royal Navy and colonial officials drove the pirates into marginal places such as Newfoundland and the Bay of Honduras where they scraped by

Blackbeard

The notorious pirate Blackbeard is known for terrorizing the Atlantic Ocean and Caribbean Sea from 1716–1718 CE. His early years are a mystery; however, historians believe he was born Edward "Teach" or "Thatch" between 1680 and 1690 CE in Bristol, United Kingdom. Archival evidence reveals a record from early December 1716 that lists Blackbeard as a lieutenant on Benjamin Hornigold's (ca. 1680–1719 CE) privateer vessel during the War of the Spanish Succession (1701–1714 CE). After a few years plundering French and Spanish vessels, Blackbeard joined a band of Caribbean pirates, stole a pirate sloop, and became captain. In the fall of 1717 CE, Blackbeard and his crew captured the French slave ship *La Concorde* off the coast of Martinique in the Caribbean. He renamed the vessel, "*Queen Anne's Revenge*," and it became his flagship. Along with three smaller pirate sloops, Blackbeard attacked and captured ships along the North American coast, terrifying shippers.

In May 1718 CE, the pirates returned to their base in the Carolinas and blockaded Charleston, South Carolina, for nearly a week—capturing ships and holding passengers and crew as hostages, ransoming them for expensive medicines for shipboard diseases. The pirates sailed upon receiving the ransom, but their ships ran aground on sandbars at Old Topsail Inlet in North Carolina. Blackbeard abandoned the *Queen Anne's Revenge* and another sloop, marooning some crewmembers on a nearby island, and sailed for Ocracoke Island, North Carolina. At this inescapable hideaway in November 1718 CE, Lieutenant Robert Maynard (ca. 1684–1751 CE), commanding the HMS *Pearl*, attacked and captured Blackbeard's remaining sloop in a fierce battle. Maynard shot and beheaded Blackbeard, then hung the pirate's head from the *Pearl*'s bow and threw Blackbeard's body into Pamlico Sound. The location of his rumored buried treasure died with him.

Samantha J. Haines

looting food, liquor, and supplies from fishing and logwood vessels. After 1726 CE, pirates reemerged in only sporadic and isolated cases or under the guise of state-sanctioned privateers. Nevertheless, this generation of pirates left a lasting legacy on global commerce and in the realm of public opinion both past and present.

Steven Pitt

Further Reading

Baer, Joel. 2007. *Pirates*. Great Britain: Tempus.

Earle, Peter. 2003. *The Pirate Wars*. New York: Thomas Dunne Books.

Lane, Kris. 1998. *Pillaging the Empire: Piracy in the Americas 1500–1750*. Armonk and London: M.E. Sharpe.

Rediker, Marcus. 2004. *Villains of All Nations: Atlantic Pirates in the Golden Age*. Boston: Beacon Press.

Ritchie, Robert C. 1986. *Captain Kidd and the War Against the Pirates*. Cambridge: Harvard University Press.

Salem, Massachusetts

Salem, Massachusetts became one of the principal ports of colonial America and the early United States.

Long before Europeans arrived in the 1620s, the Naumkeag people, an Algonkian-speaking band of the Pawtucket Tribe, which occupied a large swath of coastal New England, settled the area that became Salem. They farmed corn, beans, and squash, and fished with dugout canoes, nets, and weirs.

During the winter of 1623–1624 CE, England's Dorchester Company established an outpost on the rocky headlands of Cape Ann, 30 miles northeast of Boston's future location. After three years, former Plymouth colonist Roger Conant led a contingent of settlers to the mouth of the Naumkeag River. The residents subsequently renamed the settlement Salem for "*Shalom*," the Hebrew word for peace.

In the popular imagination, Salem's cultural identity reflects its role as the site of the 1692 CE witch trials, which later featured prominently in Arthur Miller's *The Crucible* (1953). However, it was Salem's connections to the world's oceans through which the city's fortunes ebbed and flowed. As maritime historian Samuel Eliot Morison remarked, "Salem, with a little under eight thousand inhabitants, was the sixth city in the United States in 1790. Her appearance was more antique than even that of Boston, and her reek of the salt water, that almost surrounded her, yet more pronounced" (Morrison 1922, 79).

The Revolutionary War (1775–1783 CE) and the War of 1812 (1812–1815 CE) bookended Salem's heyday as a leading North American port city. Exports of Atlantic codfish and imports of West Indian molasses proved lucrative trade ventures for seafarers like Richard Derby (1712–1783 CE) and George Crowninshield (1733–1815 CE). Other Salem captains travelled farther, making their fortunes in the so-called "East India and China Trades." In fact, Salem ships were so commonly at anchor in major Asian entrepôts that many traders there concluded that Salem was a sovereign nation. The depth of such international connections is apparent from Salem's city seal, which features the motto, "*Divitis Indiae usque ad ultimum sinum*," which is Latin for "To the rich East Indies until the last lap."

Extant bills of lading indicate the stunningly diverse cargos carried by Salem ships. Silver, sandalwood, tobacco, and opium proved to be the most desirable commodities on outgoing voyages. Sumatran pepper, tree resins from Zanzibar, and Chinese tea, silk, and porcelain ranked among the most coveted goods on return trips to New England.

The decline of Salem's seafaring fortunes began with the Embargo Act of 1807 and the War of 1812, both of which hindered the city's commercial connections to the world. Additionally, Salem's harbor was unable to compete with wider, deeper ports such as those of Boston and New York.

Even so, Salem's ship traffic did not come to a complete halt. Novelist Nathaniel Hawthorne was the port's overseer between 1846 CE until 1849 CE, working in the Customs House near Pickering Wharf—which served as the setting for the opening of *The Scarlet Letter* (1850 CE).

By the late 19th century, Salem's economy had turned to industry. Tragedy struck on June 25, 1914, when a fire spread from the Korn Leather Factory, destroying more than 1,376 buildings and leaving 20,000 Salem residents homeless. The concentration of federal architecture on Chestnut Street was spared and remains a favorite site for tourists looking to witness durable displays of the city's past maritime wealth.

Edward D. Melillo

Further Reading

Morison, Samuel Eliot. 1922. *The Maritime History of Massachusetts, 1783–1860*. Boston: Houghton Mifflin.

Morrison, Dane Anthony, and Nancy Lusignan Schultz (eds.). 2004. *Salem: Place, Myth, and Memory*. Boston: Northeastern University Press.

United States Department of the Interior, National Park Service. 1987. *Salem: Maritime Salem in the Age of Sail*. Washington, DC: Government Printing Office.

Smuggling

Rampant smuggling defined commerce in the Americas during the colonial era. Some historians have estimated that smuggled goods constituted up to 50 percent of all goods traded but accurate figures for this shadow trade are difficult to determine. Large-scale smuggling arose out of the restrictive mercantilist economic policies of major European powers such as England, Spain, France, and Portugal. The strict prohibitions on American commerce and production of manufactured goods ensured that colonial merchants actively smuggled to increase their profit margins and obtain desired goods cheaper. Only the Dutch eschewed most of these policies, maintaining free ports in Curaçao, St. Eustatius, and Suriname, and allowing their goods to be carried on foreign vessels.

During the 16th century, most smuggling entailed Northern European ships and sailors infiltrating the wealthy Spanish American Empire to sell African slaves and depart with silver, cochineal, chocolate, and other rare New World commodities. As English, French, and Dutch colonies matured during the 17th century, smuggling became more complex and encompassed a wider array of commodities. In 1651 CE, the English Parliament, desperate to challenge Dutch supremacy in trade, passed the Navigation Acts, limiting English commerce to English ships and ports. The renewed acts of 1660 CE decreed that enumerated goods such as tobacco, sugar, indigo, logwood, rice, and eventually most other colonial commodities—with the exception of fish—had to be exported to England, Wales, Ireland, other English colonies, and, after 1707 CE, Scotland.

The increased limitations under the Navigation Acts opened up new realms for smuggling among all nations. British colonial merchants ignored the laws by shipping enumerated goods directly to European ports, especially Amsterdam, Leghorn (Livorno), Hamburg, and Lisbon, and returning with smuggled manufactured goods, wines, and brandy. Although widely accepted by colonial elites, smuggling still had to be carried out in secrecy. Merchants regularly wrote clandestine letters to their ship captains with orders to avoid popular trade routes and talking with other vessels. The captain should also maintain crew morale with higher wages and good food and drink and ensure that crewmembers did not write to their wives, mingle with townsfolk, or sneak off to taverns prior to safely delivering smuggled goods. To accomplish this, smugglers generally offloaded illicit goods away from the prying eyes of customs officials in the larger towns. Favorite locations included Noodles Island near Boston, Tarpaulin Cove near Newport, Sandy Hook near New York, and Lewes and Newcastle in Delaware near Philadelphia.

As the 18th century progressed, legislation against smuggling became harsher, especially following complaints against colonial merchants for smuggling goods with enemy nations during wartime. The perceived disloyalty of many British colonial merchants led to new customs laws after the French and Indian War (1754–1763 CE), attacking the pervasive practice of smuggling. Parliament eventually deemed smuggling a capital offense. In 1773 CE, Parliament passed the Tea Act to undercut American smuggling with the Dutch, further disrupting colonial merchants' illicit trade. The Boston Tea Party therefore had its roots in Parliament's crusade against smuggling. Indeed, embittered smugglers became some of the most ardent and active Patriots when the United States declared independence in 1776 CE.

Steven Pitt

Further Reading

Carp, Benjamin L. 2012. "Did Dutch Smugglers Provoke the Boston Tea Party?" *Early American Studies: An Interdisciplinary Journal* 10: 2, 335–59.

Chet, Guy. 2014. *The Ocean is a Wilderness: Atlantic Piracy and the Limits of State Authority, 1688–1856*. Amherst and Boston: University of Massachusetts Press.

Tyler, John W. 1986. *Smugglers & Patriots: Boston Merchants and the Advent of the American Revolution*. Boston: Northeastern University Press.

Teixeira, Pedro de, d. 1641 CE

A Portuguese military officer and explorer, Pedro de Teixeira's voyages along the Amazon River valley and through South America influenced European exploration and the expansion of the Portuguese Empire in the New World. Teixeira is most known for his role in the 1637–1639 CE Amazon expedition, during which he became the first European to travel the length of the Amazon River, eventually exploring from what is now Belem, Brazil, to Quinto, Ecuador. His career in South America spanned more than three decades, during which time he helped establish Portuguese rule in Brazil, outmaneuver Spanish competitors, and advance Portugal's territorial claims beyond those granted by the Treaty of Tordesillas (1494 CE).

Born sometime between 1575 and 1587 CE in Cantanhede, Portugal, little is known about de Teixeira's early life other than that he embarked on a military career. In many ways his career was defined by the rising European colonial competition of the period, increasing Portuguese concerns regarding Spanish trading gains, Spanish Imperial land acquisitions in the New World, and growing demands for Portuguese Independence. In 1607 CE, Captain de Teixeira traveled to Brazil and subsequently repulsed French attempts to control and settle São Luís do Maranhão. He helped establish Fort Presépio on the northern coast of Brazil. The Fort developed into the city of Belém, led military patrols along both the Xingu and Amazon Rivers, and protected Portugal's monopoly on local trade from British, Dutch, and French merchants who occasionally arrived.

In 1637 CE, de Teixeira's skills were challenged when two Spanish Franciscan friars arrived in Fort Presépio, having abandoned their mission due to hostile indigenous people. Concerned about this Spanish activity in the region, the governor of Maranhão, Jacome Raimundo de Noronha, commissioned de Teixeira to lead an expedition up the Amazon River. His orders were to escort the Spanish friars to Quito in Spanish Peru, ascertain the extent of the Spanish expansion in the Amazon valley, and identify sites for future Portuguese forts and settlements.

De Teixeira prepared his expedition thoroughly and set out in four-dozen canoes loaded with weapons, food, and trade goods and crewed by a combination of native Brazilians and Portuguese soldiers. The expedition—roughly 1,000-strong—explored parts of the Rio Negro and Madeira Rivers, identified Spanish settlements, systematically mapped the Amazon River valley, and successfully arrived in Quito after an eight-month journey where its members were well received by the Spanish, who were themselves concerned about the progress of Portuguese expansion.

A Spanish Jesuit priest, Cistobal de Acuna, accompanied de Teixeira on his return voyage in 1638–1639 CE, and reported to his superiors on Portuguese expansion. Spanish officials proved slow to act on these reports and de Teixeira's expedition cemented Portugal's claim to the Amazon River valley, which reached beyond the limits agreed to in the Treaty of Tordesillas. Promoted and made governor of Pará (northern Brazil) for this success, de Teixeira, already in poor health, died on June 4, 1641, in Sao Luis do Marahao, Brazil.

Sean Morton

Further Reading

Goodman, Edward J. 1972. *The Explorers of South America*. New York: Macmillan.

Smith, Anthony. 1994. *Explorers of the Amazon*. Chicago: University of Chicago Press.

CHINA AND EAST ASIA, 1450 TO 1770 CE

By the 15th century, China had 1.5-millennia-long relationships with East Asia by overland contact (beginning with the Western Han) and half a millennium–long links to the rest of East Asia by sea (beginning with the Northern Song). This long seafaring tradition was capped by the epic voyages of the Ming Era Eunuch–turned admiral Zheng He (1371–1435 CE) who led an armada through the Western Pacific and Northern Indian Oceans for 28 years from 1405 to 1433 CE. Both the scale and scope of this Ming naval operation were unprecedented in East Asia—and probably in the world—at that time. After 1433 CE, however, state-led naval operation in China came to a sudden stop. There are several reasons, both political as well as personal, for the voluntary withdrawal of Chinese sea power in East Asia, but among the most important was the heavy financial burden of the Ming naval expeditions.

Even so, benefits remained from the Ming voyages. The most obvious one was a China-centered "tributary trade," a self-contradictory term, for the exchange relationship between China and some other Asian countries between 1450 and 1770

CE. It was trade, although in a disguised form. A foreign trade delegate usually paid symbolic tribute to the Imperial Court of China. Such tribute was generously awarded with money and goods of several times this tribute's value. After the protocol and ritual, the foreign trade delegate was free to sell its cargo inside China without government interference. The fact that all the goods, including the "tribute," brought in by foreign delegates were compensated by the state or the market in China indicates that tributary trade was dictated by market exchanges between China and the outside world. During its heyday, the "tributary trade" network had more than 30 member countries along the Pacific-Indian Ocean sea routes that dispatched trade missions to China once every 2 to 3 years. To safeguard this China-centered trading system the Imperial government issued permits to tributary countries without which foreign vessels and delegates' entry to China was denied. This was probably the first recorded centrally controlled customs system in East Asia.

The majority of "tributary traders" were based on what some have called the "Asian Mediterranean," the South China Sea. Sailing was largely dictated by the predictable Asian monsoon pattern in which the prevailing wind blows from the north to the south in autumn and from the south to the north in spring.

The main items for tributary trade were pharmaceutical materials, such as minerals, plants, and animal parts, and luxuries such as spices, perfumes, rare feathers and shells, and tropical hardwoods, for which the Chinese exchanged manufactured goods, including paper, fans and umbrellas, ceramics, lacquer wares, porcelain and crystal beads, gold and silver products (bullion, beads, and sheets), copper products (coins, balls, pots, plates, and blocks), lead and lead weights for fishing nets, iron products (cooking pots, wires, blocks, and needles), mercury, sulfur, cotton (dyed and printed), tung oil, and others. In addition, large quantities of Chinese bronze coins were exported to the Asian Mediterranean as international currency—despite the perpetual official Chinese ban on the export of precious metals.

A subtle change took place after 1500 CE, with the rise of the mining and refining of silver in the Spanish New World. As the appetite for Chinese goods increased in the West, Spanish traders found a seemingly unlimited demand for silver in China. This led to the Manila Galleon Trade, which lasted 250 years—1565 CE to 1815 CE. The Spanish shipped large quantities of silver—thousands of tons per year—to the Chinese market in exchange for Chinese manufactures, mainly silk. In the 1630s, for example, a Spanish cargo ship sailing from Manila to Mexico would have 300 to 500 boxes of silk products with a net total weight of 69,000 to 115,000 pounds. Neighboring Japan joined this silver trade, shipping several thousand tons of silver to China between 1530 CE and 1700 CE in exchange for Chinese manufactured products, such as textiles, paper, stationeries, and books. Foreign silver served in China as a means to store value (hoarding) in an economy where a base-metal currency made of bronze coins was the only legal tender until the

1890s. The silver trade was a natural extension of China's tributary trade. In most cases, the imported foreign silver pieces remained in China in their original sizes, shapes, and styles and were treated as ingots instead of currencies. About 7 percent of China's total silver intake, though, was smelted and refined into ingots with 98-percent silver content. The ingots were called "*sycee*" which was "fiscal silver" used to pay taxes and to fulfill government spending.

The tributary trade network and the consequent China-centered trade pattern (meaning other countries coming to China for trade) had an unintended consequence for China's economy. It made sailing by Chinese commercial ships largely redundant. This was particularly true of European traders whose goods had global appeal and whose ships were heavily armed, able to sail in dangerous waters. This planted the seed for the gradual deterioration of China's maritime capacity over the next two centuries. China's naval weakness was first exposed between 1522 CE and 1566 CE when Japanese pirates ("*wokou*") infested the waters of China's East Coast. These pirates soon controlled local sea routes and even attacked China's coastal cities. Yet, Ming officials identified more than 70 percent of the alleged Japanese pirates as Chinese outlaws. China's declining sea power was finally and fully exposed in the First Opium War (1839–1842 CE) with the British East India Company, in which it suffered defeat at the hands of modern British warships.

At the same time, China's private sector boomed. Investors funded the construction of large ships which traded throughout China's old tributary system. This was most evident in Japan. From 1642 to 1684 CE, private Chinese traders were responsible for 66 percent of the silk imported into Japan (more than five million pounds) and 70 percent of all copper exported from Japan (more than 80 million pounds). The activities of these Chinese maritime traders peaked in 1688 CE when 193 Chinese ships and 9,128 merchants docked at Nagasaki. So great was the scale of this trade that the Tokugawa government worried about its effect on Japanese resources and society. That same year, the Japanese government imposed a restriction on Chinese traders. Only 70 Chinese ships were allowed to visit Nagasaki each year with a ceiling on the value of goods set at 100,000 taels of silver (equal to about four tons). Evidence indicates that Chinese private traders played a similar role in the Spanish Philippines and Dutch East Indies. By the 18th century, Chinese communities (diasporas) in Southeast Asia became so powerful that European colonizers massacred them to eliminate their Chinese competitors. In 1740–41 CE, Dutch forces slaughtered 100,000 Chinese in Batavia. Earlier, in 1603 CE, Spanish forces massacred 24,000 Chinese in Manila. Despite these, the Chinese maritime and trading population in Southeast Asia recovered quickly, suggesting that the private sector was not deterred by these atrocities.

Historians have long debated the results of the maritime bans issued by China's Imperial authorities. It is true that the bans on maritime trade were officially announced, such as Emperor Zhu Yuanzhang's 30-year ban (1368–1398 CE) during the Ming Era, and another 30 years (1664–84 CE, 1717–27 CE) ordered by Emperor Kangxi (1661–1722 CE) of the Qing. The effectiveness of these bans, however, is questionable. Smuggling was common. During the Qing ban, Shen Shangda, an army general, was able to make 4,000 to 5,000 taels of silver (328 to 410 pounds) from each trip. He was not stopped until 1681 CE by which time he amassed a total of 975,936 taels of assets (40 tons). The most famous case was Zheng Chenggong's (known as "Koxinga" in the West) maritime empire, stretching from coastal China to Japan and the rest of Southeast Asia. Zheng's trade operation is believed to have been seven to eleven times greater than that of his Dutch competitors in Japan. The Qing ban of the 17th century had no effect on Zheng's businesses, which earned enough from their maritime operations to maintain 170,000 troops and a fleet of 8,000 ships for some 40 years. In 1662 CE, Zheng's fleet launched a major attack from the Penghu Islands and captured Taiwan from the Dutch.

On the mainland, China's links to East Asia experienced dramatic changes. In 1644 CE, the Manchus were invited through the Shanghai Pass (*"shanhai guan"*) along the Great Wall defense line and entered China as mercenaries, helping put down a major rebellion led by Li Zicheng (1606–45 CE) whose followers captured the capital, Beijing, and established the new, but short-lived, Dashun regime. The last Ming emperor, the Chongzhen Emperor (r. 1627–44 CE), committed suicide. The Manchus fulfilled their mercenary duty, toppling Li Zicheng, but refused to return home. Instead, they seized power in China and established a new dynasty, the Qing, which ruled from 1644 to 1911 CE. This fundamentally altered the geopolitical equilibrium in East Asia in several ways.

- It made China's permanent defense line, the Great Wall, redundant. Troops and artisans were no longer needed to garrison and maintain the wall.
- China's territory expanded in the north and west to double its size under the Ming Dynasty.
- Farming resettlement schemes in China's newly captured regions enlarged China's agricultural economy and reduced its rate of urbanization.
- The Qing state in 1715 CE, unilaterally froze its total tax revenue, which remained unchanged regardless of China's future expansion in territory, economy, and population, the last of which quadrupled after 1700 CE.

Through the long peace of the 18th century, the Qing state withered, steadily withdrawing from governance. By 1850 CE, China's population reached 400 million, but there were fewer than 30,000 mandarins on the Qing government payroll. This produced huge gaps between not only population and officials but also between the gentry class (Imperial degree holders) and the paid officials. In the absence of government authority, self-governance at the grassroots level not only became common but soon was expected by the Qing state.

Although individual Chinese merchants and traders thrived in these years, the Qing government's power gradually withered, and along with it the naval power needed to protect Chinese trade in the future. Although little noticed for much of the 18th century, it resulted in disastrous consequences in the 18th century when China suffered from a succession of internal rebellions, including the White Lotus Rebellion (1794–1804 CE), Taiping Rebellion (1850–1864 CE), Nian Rebellion (1851–1868 CE), Miao Rebellion (1854–1873 CE), and Muslim Rebellion (1862–1877 CE), and lost wars with several foreign powers, most notably the Opium Wars (1839–1842 and 1856–1860 CE), the Sino-French War (1884–1885 CE) and the Sino-Japanese War (1894–1895 CE).

Kent G. Deng

Further Reading

Deng, Gang. 1997. *Chinese Maritime Activities and Socio-Economic Consequences, c. 2100 b.c.–1900 a.d.* New York, London and West Port: Greenwood Publishing Group.

Deng, Gang. 1999. *The Premodern Chinese Economy—Structural Equilibrium and Capitalist Sterility*. London and New York: Routledge.

Deng, Gang. 1999. *Maritime Sector, Institutions and Sea Power of Premodern China*. New York, London and West Port: Greenwood Publishing Group.

Frank, A. G. 1998. *ReOrient: Global Economy in the Asian Age*. Berkeley: University of California.

Gipouloux, Francois. 2011. *The Asian Mediterranean, Port Cities and Trading Networks in China, Japan and Southeast Asia, 13th–21st Century*, London: Edward Elgar.

Hobson, J. M. 2004. *The Eastern Origins of Western Civilisation*. Cambridge: Cambridge University Press.

Jones, E. L. 1988. *Growth Recurring: Economic Change in World History*, Oxford: Clarendon Press.

Mokyr, Joel. 1990. *The Lever of Riches*. Oxford: Oxford University Press.

Vries, Peer. 2015. *State, Economy and the Great Divergence*, London and New York: Bloomsbury Press.

PIRACY IN EAST ASIA, 1450 TO 1770 CE

Piracy increased following the decline of the Yuan Dynasty (1271–1368 CE) and was a recurrent problem during the Ming Dynasty (1368–1644 CE). Called Japanese bandits ("*Wukou*") by the Chinese, even though many of them were from China or other parts of Southeast Asia, pirates operated from a host of Japanese and Chinese offshore islands, attacking shipping and raiding coastal settlements, particularly along China's southern coast. Raids peaked in the mid-16th century and declined in the 17th century following the establishment of strong centralized governments in China, the Qing Dynasty (1644–1912 CE), and Japan, the Tokugawa Shogunate (1603–1867 CE).

The first Ming emperor, Hongwu (1368–1398 CE), unable to convince a divided Japanese government to suppress piracy, constructed forts along the coast. After the Ashikaga unified Japan, Emperor Yongle (1402–1424 CE) reestablished Japan's tributary relationship with China, which helped reduce piracy. China also built a powerful navy in these years, which culminated in the great voyages of Zheng He (1405–1433 CE), whose demonstration of China's military might and attacks on their bases, substantially reduced piracy.

As China withdrew from the sea in succeeding years—eventually prohibiting maritime trade—piracy and smuggling returned to Chinese waters. The Ming court frequently requested the Japanese government act to suppress Wokou operating from Japanese islands, but with limited results. Wokou raids reached their peak in the 1550s. Pirates established strong bases on offshore islands and isolated coastal enclaves and raided deeply inland, once even threating Nanjing.

China's scattered antipiracy efforts often failed. In 1557 CE, however, a Chinese force defeated a substantial pirate fleet. In 1563 CE, General Yu Tayu garrisoned the Penghu islands near Taiwan, where pirates often set up bases. The forces patrolled the area, defeating numerous pirates. His force, though, was withdrawn following this success, and pirates soon returned. In general, China's antipiracy efforts were most successful when government and military officials worked together closely and sustained their efforts over many years, as occurred in Hainan. The inconsistent and disunited effort in Taiwan helped make it a haven for pirates.

In the 17th century, Zheng (1604–1661 CE), a successful merchant, turned to piracy. The Dutch believed that piratical attacks on Chinese shipping would help them gain control of Chinese trade, and with their support Zheng amassed a fleet of several hundred ships and defeated Chinese fleets sent against him. Faced by invading Manchus, the Chinese government appointed Zheng an admiral in 1628 CE, hoping that his large fleet could turn the tide, but in 1646 CE he defected to the Manchus. Zheng's son, Zheng Chenggong (1624–1662 CE), led the remnant of Ming loyalists. Forced to retreat to Taiwan, he defeated a Dutch garrison and established his rule there until being overwhelmed by the Manchus (by then the Qing Dynasty) in 1683 CE. Afterward, piracy dwindled in the face of Qing armies and well-armed European ships, which increasingly dominated local trade.

Claudia Zanardi

Further Reading

Amirell, Stefan, E., and Leon Mueller. 2014. *Persistent Piracy: Maritime Policies & State Formation in Global Historical Perspective*. New York: Palgrave.

Dabringhaus, S., and Ptak, Robert (eds.). 1997. *China & Her Neighbours. Borders, Visions of the Other, Foreign Policy 10th to 19th Century*. Wiesbaden: Harrassowitz Verlag.

Shapinsky, Peter. 2014. *Lords of the Sea: Pirates, Violence, and Commerce in Late Medieval Japan.* Ann Arbor: University of Michigan Press.

So, Kwan-wai. 1975. *Japanese Piracy in Ming China During the 16th Century.* Michigan State University Press.

Willis, John E., Jr. 2007. "The Seventeenth-Century Transformation: Taiwan under the Dutch & the Cheng Regime." Murray A. Rubinstein (ed.). *Taiwan. A New History.* New York: M. E. Sharpe, 84–106.

ENGLAND, 1450 TO 1770 CE

Between the 15th and 18th centuries, England transformed from a relatively minor state to the world's dominant naval power and most important maritime state. In a succession of wars and lesser conflicts, England's Royal Navy defeated the Spanish, Dutch, and French fleets, enabling English merchants—often supported by the government—to enter markets around the world. English colonies in the Caribbean, North America, and India played an important role in spreading English influence and trade, and a growing share of the world's goods moved in English ships.

On March 5, 1496, Italian navigator Giovanni Caboto (John Cabot, 1450 to ca. 1500 CE) and his three sons received letters patent from the English monarch, Henry VII (1457–1509 CE) entitling them to sail westward to China in the name of Albion. Cabot sailed the following year in one ship with 20 men. They reached North America, claimed it for England, and returned—too few in number to accomplish much else. Cabot's two subsequent expeditions explored North America in more detail, though it would be another century before England's rulers sought to establish New World colonies. Cabot's expeditions were a response to Portuguese and Spanish Atlantic expeditions, and Cabot built on preexisting English knowledge of the North Atlantic Ocean. English fishermen, especially from Bristol, had long fished these waters, sailing to Iceland in the early 15th century and later reaching as far as Greenland, Labrador, and perhaps Newfoundland. English merchants sailed to the Baltic and Mediterranean and traded with the newly discovered Atlantic islands such as Madeira and the Canaries.

Several expeditions followed in Cabot's wake. William Weston, a Bristol merchant who might have sailed in Cabot's first expedition, crossed the Atlantic in 1499 CE, and landed in North America, probably in Canada. The Tudor monarchs continued to support exploratory voyages, dispatching Hugh Elliot and Robert Thorne to the New World in 1502, and several others over the next half century. Their goal, though, was to discover a route to Asia, a Northwest Passage through the Americas, which they failed to find. A 1517 CE expedition failed to reach America, but a 1527 CE expedition led by John Rut (d. 1528 CE) reached Newfoundland and also visited Santo Domingo, a Spanish colony. That of Richard Hore (d. 1540 CE), dispatched in

1536 CE by Henry VIII (1491–1547 CE), also landed in Newfoundland, but his reports did little to excite interest in the New World.

Although English rulers proved slow to pursue wealth in the New World, they rejected Portuguese and Spanish claims to this territory, and codified it in the Treaty of Tordesillas (1494).

Queen Elizabeth I (1533–1603 CE) insisted that the sea belonged to everyone, a position later argued by Dutch jurist Hugo Grotius (1583–1645 CE) in *Mare Liberum* (1609 CE). Increasingly, in the second half of the 16th century, English sailors, drawn by profit, interacted with Portugal's and Spain's colonial empires, first as traders and smugglers, and soon thereafter as privateers or pirates.

In 1530 CE, Plymouth merchant William Hawkins (1495–1555 CE) extended his trade activities to the Atlantic and over the next decade was probably the first Englishman to complete the trade triangle between Europe, West Africa, and Brazil. In 1542 CE, England intervened to support Emperor Charles V (1500–1558 CE) in the Italian War of 1542–1546 CE against France and the Ottoman Empire. Hawkins, with friends James Horswell and John Elyot, turned to privateering—outfitting ships that successfully attacked French commerce. After the war, English merchants increasingly entered the slave trade. Thomas Wyndham made a successful slave trading trip to West Africa in 1553 CE and followed it with two others, each noted for its brutality and aggressiveness. Although opposed by both Portugal and Spain, English traders successfully entered the slave trade. Most of the expeditions were either private ventures or supported by joint stock companies. Only a few received financing from the monarchy.

Henry V (1387–1422 CE) developed a small navy to support his operations in the Hundred Years' War (1337–1453 CE), but it was not until the threat of Spain's force increased in the 16th century that England substantially enlarged its navy. Even then, England's most talented commanders spent much of their time privateering. John Hawkins (1532–1595 CE), son of William Hawkins, led three privateers in 1562–63 CE, which captured a Portuguese slaver and sold its cargo of 301 slaves in Santo Domingo. In response, Spain banned English ships from its Caribbean colonies. Hawkins sailed again in 1564–65 CE and 1567–68 CE, accompanied by his second cousin Francis Drake (1540–1596 CE). Their venture was successful, as they captured several ships, secured a cargo of slaves in Africa, and in Venezuela sold the 400 who survived the voyage. The 1567–68 CE voyage ended in disaster. After again securing slaves in Africa, a cargo they augmented by capturing a Portuguese slaver, they sailed for America, landing at San Juan de Ulua where they encountered a Spanish squadron, which attacked and captured three of Hawkins's five ships.

Hawkins's near escape did not diminish English activity. Rather, English piracy and privateering increased. Hawkins, Drake, Thomas Cavendish, Martin Frobisher, Richard Grenville, Humphrey Gilbert, and Walter Raleigh sailed as explorers, privateers, smugglers, or traders, as the need required. Often financed by the crown, they operated with a great deal of independence and in the second half of the 16th century, substantially increased England's presence at sea. Drake and Cavendish were the first to follow in Magellan's footsteps, completing round-the-world voyages in 1577–80 CE and 1586–88 CE, respectively. Both attacked Spain's Pacific settlements and shipping, plundering widely. Only in the aftermath of Cavendish's expedition, did Spain seek to secure the passage through the Strait of Magellan and its Pacific colonies.

Escalating raids and England's support for Dutch rebels fighting for independence from Spain, led Philip II (1527–1598 CE) to mount a massive expedition against England. In 1587, Drake led an English fleet against Spain's port of Cadiz, which destroyed 37 ships and delayed the departure of the Spanish Armada until the following year. The Armada—one of the largest fleets ever assembled—found itself outmatched by more maneuverable English warships in several battles, which led to its commander's ill-fated decision to sail around England where storms wrecked many of his ships. Hostilities continued afterward and English privateers continued to prey on Spanish shipping until Queen Elizabeth's death in 1603 CE, after which peace was concluded.

In addition to privateering, Martin Frobisher (1535–1594 CE) led three expeditions to North America and mapped parts of its northeastern shore while searching for a Northwest Passage. Early reports that he discovered gold proved false after he returned to England with 1350 tons of iron pyrite (fool's gold). Henry Hudson (d. 1611 CE), working for the Muscovy Company, unsuccessfully sought a passage north of Russia in 1608 and twice explored the northern latitudes of North America near the Arctic Circle (1607 and 1609 CE). In his third, most ambitious expedition, he reached and mapped what is now Hudson Bay. After being stranded in the ice over the winter, though, members of Hudson's crew mutinied and sailed home, stranding Hudson and seven others whose fate remains unknown. These expeditions all reported rich fishing off Newfoundland, the Grand Banks, which Bristol fishers began to exploit. Some fishermen spent the winter in Newfoundland to process and salt their catch, and some of these sites developed into permanent settlements. A 1614 CE expedition led by John Smith (1580–1631 CE) found rich fishing off the coast of Maine, which quickly attracted cod fishers and whalers to the area.

Walter Raleigh (ca. 1554–1618 CE), supported by a 1584 CE charter issued by Queen Elizabeth, launched and helped finance the first substantial English efforts to establish settlements in North America. His 1587 CE expedition established a colony on Roanoke Island, off the Carolina coast. War with Spain, though, delayed the sailing of a planned follow-up expedition with additional supplies and settlers. When a second expedition finally arrived in 1590 CE, they found no trace of the Roanoke Colony, and its fate remains unknown.

The first monarchs of England's Stuart dynasty intensified colonization efforts and for a time improved relations with Spain. James I (1566–1625 CE) signed a peace treaty with Madrid, which forced English privateers to pursue other maritime enterprises, alternatively trading and smuggling with the growing number of New World colonies. England established its first permanent American colonies in Virginia in 1607 CE and Massachusetts in 1620 CE, the former by a joint stock company, the latter by religious dissidents. After struggling in their early years, settlements in both areas thrived, and tobacco exports from Virginia plantations became an important part of England's growing transatlantic trade. England also established colonies on several Caribbean islands, including St. Kitts (1624 CE), Barbados (1627 CE), and Nevis (1628 CE), and trading posts along the West African shore in Guinea and Benin. In 1670 CE, Charles II chartered the Hudson's Bay Company, which monopolized the fur trade in that region. Over time, patterns of trade developed between England, the Caribbean colonies, and the North American colonies, which involved African slaves, Caribbean sugar, and tobacco, rum, timber, furs, and other goods from the North American colonies.

It was to protect and encourage this growing trade that, in 1651 CE, England issued the first of what became a succession of Navigation Acts. These aimed to restrict English goods and trade to English ships and unseat the dominant position in maritime trade held by the Dutch. At the time, about two-thirds of world shipping was Dutch, and increasing English efforts to restrict Dutch trade led to three wars between England and the Netherlands (1652–1654 CE, 1665–1667 CE, and 1672–1674 CE). The English proved successful in these wars, capturing more than a thousand Dutch merchant ships in the first, the Dutch colony of New Amsterdam (New York) in the second, and substantially reducing Dutch naval power in the third. In 1692 CE at the battles of La Hague and Barfleur, fought roughly a week apart, English fleets, this time allied with the Dutch, defeated French fleets and established England as the region's dominant naval power.

England's Royal Navy emerged substantially stronger from these wars, and the English government increasingly took control of the private colonial endeavors in the Atlantic and integrated them into a growing empire. In Asia and the Pacific, though, the East India Company operated with substantial independence and remained the dominant English trading company in the region well into the 18th century. Although Queen Elizabeth I chartered the East India Company in 1600 CE, English merchants did not enter the Pacific and the Indian Oceans in significant numbers until late in the 17th century. Over time, though, English interests in the region grew, as did their possessions, which grew from the ports of Surat (1615 CE), Bombay (1662 CE), and Calcutta (1690 CE) to encompass most of the Indian subcontinent following the 1757 CE defeat of Bengal and its French allies at the Battle of Plassey by the soldiers of the East India Company.

Grog

"Grog" became a generic term for a variety of weak alcoholic beverages served to sailors in 18th-century navies. In Britain's Royal Navy, it was a mixture of rum and water, with a little lemon or lime added for flavor and as a preservative. Later, people recognized that lime also helped prevent scurvy. Grog's development generally is credited to Vice-Admiral Edward Vernon (1684–1757 CE), nicknamed "Old Grog" for the grogram ("grosgrain") cloth cloak he favored.

The mandated ratio of water to rum and addition of other ingredients varied depending upon the ships' captains; however, it was standardized by the Royal Navy in the 18th century as a mixture of one-quarter rum and three-quarters water, issued twice per day. Although rum—a cheap byproduct of Caribbean sugar production—was favored, other sources of cheap alcohol could be substituted. Unlike beer and water, distilled liquor did not spoil during the months-long voyages of ships. By mixing water and rum, the sailors received the ration of alcohol they desired, which also helped them cope with the cold, hard labor aboard ship, and grog made the shipboard water—which became stale sitting in barrels for prolonged periods—more palatable.

Matthew Blake Strickland

The Atlantic Ocean also became an arena of British-French conflict. In 1714 CE, Britain (Britain since the 1707 Act of Union that united England and Scotland) gained from Spain, the right (Asiento) to import slaves and other commodities to Spanish colonies. British trade with Spain's colonies flourished for the next 30 years, but European politics increasingly involved Britain in wars against France and Spain. To finance these wars, the British government founded the Bank of England, and Britain's superior financial system, along with its growing navy and commercial shipping, helped win the War of the Spanish Succession (1701–1714 CE), which ended Spanish ambitions to dominate Europe, and in which Britain conquered Gibraltar, a strategic position at Spain's southern tip that allowed Britain to police shipping in and out of the Mediterranean Sea.

British relations with France and Spain remained poor and exploded into war in two related conflicts: The War of Jenkins' Ear (1739–1748 CE), which centered in the Caribbean, and the War of Austrian Succession (1740–1748 CE), which focused on European matters. The War of Jenkins' Ear, named for British merchant captain Robert Jenkins, whose ear was cut off by Spanish officers after they caught him smuggling, was fought over British rights to trade with Spain's colonies. British fleets raided Spanish colonies throughout the Caribbean, which steadily ground until 1744 CE when France entered the war in support of Spain. This shifted the focus on hostilities to Europe where England, Austria, and the Netherlands fought France, Prussia, and Spain. A British expedition in the Caribbean failed to capture Cuba, but in European waters British ships regularly raided the French coast and British fleet twice decisively defeated French fleets off Cape Finisterre capturing several ships of the line. The Treaty of Aix-la-Chapelle ended the war in 1748 CE. Apart from territorial changes in Europe, the treaty affirmed British rights to trade with Spain's colonies. In 1756 CE, however, Britain and France went to war again in the Seven Years' War (1756–1763 CE). Britain's Royal Navy dominated the fighting at sea from start to finish, defeating or containing French fleets and supported British expeditions that expanded British possessions in India and conquered Canada.

In 1763 CE, Britain emerged from war as the world's dominant naval power and in possession of lucrative colonies that straddled the globe from the Caribbean to North America to Asia. Although these wars left the British government deeply in debt, this seemed of little concern at the time, as British warships controlled the high seas and its merchants traded at will throughout the world, controlling roughly half of world trade.

Jakub Basista

Further Reading

Andrews, Kenneth R. 1984. *Trade, Plunder and Settlement: Maritime Enterprise and the Genesis of the British Empire, 1480–1630*. Cambridge: Cambridge University Press.

Armitage, David and Michael J. Braddick. 2002. *The British Atlantic World, 1500–1800*. New York: Palgrave.

Benjamin, Thomas. 2009. *The Atlantic World*. Cambridge: Cambridge University Press.

Elliott, John H. 2007. *Empires of the Atlantic World: Britain and Spain in America 1492–1830*. New Haven: Yale University Press.

Friel, Ian. 2003. *Maritime History of Britain and Ireland*. London: British Museum Press.

O'Hara, Glenn. 2010. *Britain and the Sea: Since 1600*. New York: Palgrave Macmillan.

Raudzens, George. 1999. *Empires: Europe and Globalization, 1492–1788*. Phoenix Mill: Sutton Publishing.

Rodger, N. A. M. 1996. *The Wooden World: An Anatomy of the Georgian Navy*. New York: Norton.

Rodger, N. A. M. 2005. *The Command of the Ocean: A Naval History of Britain, 1649–1815*. New York: Norton.

Cabot, John, ca. 1450–1500 CE

John Cabot (*Giovanni Caboto* in Italian) was a sailor, navigator, and explorer, best known for exploring North America; the first European to do so since the Vikings.

Probably born in Genoa, Italy, Cabot's family later moved to Venice and he received Venetian citizenship in 1476 CE. Much of his life before 1496 CE remains uncertain. He traded throughout the Mediterranean and relocated to Valencia, Spain after 1488 CE, perhaps to escape his creditors, and then to Seville. Like several other Italian seafarers, he sought royal sponsorship for voyages of exploration, but without success until he relocated to England, probably in 1495 CE.

Perhaps supported by Italian bankers in London, Cabot and his three sons received letters patent from Henry VII on March 5, 1496, entitling them to broadly explore the seas. Cabot outfitted his expedition in Bristol, at the time England's second largest port. Cabot's first expedition sailed in 1496 CE, but soon returned without success. His second, aboard the 50-ton *Matthew*, sailed on May 20, 1497, and reached North America on June 24. Cabot's expedition explored North America for four weeks, remaining close to the coast. They found evidence of human habitation, but encountered no locals. Where they landed remains uncertain, with Newfoundland, Nova Scotia, Maine, and Labrador all considered likely.

They returned to Bristol on August 6 and a few days later Cabot had an audience with Henry VIII, who rewarded him and later gave him a pension of 20 pounds per year. In February 1498 CE, Cabot received a royal patent to organize another expedition, which several English merchants also helped fund. In May 1498 CE, Cabot departed with five ships loaded with textiles and other trade goods. Damaged by storm, one of the expedition's ships soon returned, but the fate of the other four remains a mystery. They could have been lost at sea; some historians believe that they returned successfully, but that records of the expedition were lost. The historians of the Cabot Project, founded in 2009 and located at the University of Bristol, currently search for clues to the fate of John Cabot and his last expedition.

Jakub Basista

Further Reading

Jones, Evan T. 2010. "Henry VII and the Bristol Expeditions to North America: The Condon Documents." *Historical Research* 83 (August).

Jones, Evan T. and Alwyn Ruddock. 2008. "John Cabot and the Discovery of America." *Historical Research* 81 (May): 224–54.

Quinn, D. B., A. M. Quinn, and S. Hillier (eds.). 1979. *New American World: A Documentary History of North America to 1612*, 1.

Ruddock, A. A. 1966. "John Day of Bristol and the English Voyages Across the Atlantic Before 1497." GJ 132: 225–33.

Williamson, J. A. 1962. *The Cabot Voyages and Bristol Discovery under Henry VII*. Hakluyt Society, 2nd ser. 120.

Defoe, Daniel, ca. 1660–1731 CE

Famous for writing *Robinson Crusoe*, Daniel Defoe was a man of many talents and interests. He was a spy, merchant, prolific author (more than 300 books), and journalist, who created the syndicated column and helped shape the modern English novel. Although Defoe never crossed the ocean, he wrote movingly about the sea in both his fictional and nonfiction works.

Published in 1719 CE, *Robinson Crusoe* quickly became popular. Using elements of travel books that were fashionable at the time, Defoe based his character loosely on the factual account of stranded sailor Andrew Selkirk, whose adventures as a marooned sailor in the South Pacific were published in 1712 CE. Soon translated into many languages, *Robinson Crusoe* continues to resonate with people around the world due to its exploration of universal human values as well as European colonialism. The story and its main themes repeatedly show up in various guises, including movies entitled *Robinson Crusoe* in 1954 and 1997, the hit Tom Hanks movie, *Cast Away* (2000), and modern "reality" TV shows such as *Survivor* (2000–) and *Naked and Afraid* (2013–). Defoe wrote a sequel to his book, as well as several other exciting sea-faring adventures. His book *The Storm* (1704), which provided vivid descriptions of the Great Storm of 1703 CE that meshed first-person accounts and scientific analysis, stands as a landmark in journalism.

Defoe's greatest fascination, however, was with trade and commerce. He was involved in brick making, and the wine and tobacco trade, and he had an astonishing knowledge of many branches of English commerce. Although he often lost money in risky investments, his infatuation with commerce led him to propose new plans for colonization and trade to English King William III (r. 1689–1702 CE). One idea was for British merchant ships to steer east, anchor off of Manila, Philippines, where they would meet a ship flying a French flag and trade secretly for silks, china, nutmeg, and cloves. The British ship then would sail to South America and engage in similar secret trading. He also proposed a plan for two new English settlements in South America near modern Valdivia, Chile, and on the southeast coast between the Plate River and the Straits of Magellan.

Defoe also turned his attention to the Royal Navy, suggesting that it build a naval yard in Scotland, which would provide jobs and protect the English and Scottish coasts. He also suggested that the navy find ways other than impressment to attract sailors.

He hoped to make London the center of world trade. In *The Complete English Tradesman* (1726 CE), Defoe argued that British merchants were superior to those of other nations and that Britain should attain a dominant position in the world through trade rather than military might. This feat was achieved through a combination of commerce and military power, less than 100 years after Defoe's death on April 24, 1731 CE.

Joyce Sampson

Great Storm of 1703 CE

The Great Storm of 1703 CE, a massive hurricane, devastated coastal England on November 26, 1703 (December 7, of the modern calendar). Although wind speeds and trajectories are uncertain, given the state of meteorological measurements at the time, contemporary accounts indicate that this storm was among the worst natural disasters of the era. People received no advance warning before the storm appeared on the horizon. Winds uprooted thousands of trees and heavy rains flooded fields, drowning people and cattle. In London, thousands of brick chimneys were toppled and many homes were destroyed.

Losses were particularly heavy among sailors and shipping. Several dozen ships were lost at sea, along with most of their crews; other ships were blown hundreds of miles off course. Hundreds of ships anchored in the Thames River were torn from their moorings and blown upriver, suffering heavy damage. The Royal Navy lost 10 ships of the line, including the 90-gun *Vanguard*, and several smaller warships. The exact death toll is uncertain, but exceeded 10,000 people—many of them sailors who went down with their ships. Sailors on board had little chance of survival because of the condition of the seas they found themselves in.

Matthew Blake Strickland

Further Reading

Backscheder, Paula R. 1989. *Daniel Defoe: His Life*. Baltimore and London: John Hopkins University Press.

Healey, George Harris. 1955. *The Letters of Daniel Defoe*. Oxford, Clarendon Press.

Richette, John. 2008. *The Cambridge Companion to Daniel Defoe*. Cambridge University Press.

Drake, Sir Francis, ca. 1540–1596 CE

Sir Francis Drake was an English explorer and privateer who became famous for his successful raids against Spanish ports and shipping. He attacked the port of Cadiz in 1587 CE and fought against the Spanish Armada in 1588 CE.

Born in Crowndale, Devon, Drake was the first child of Edmond Drake, and a cousin of John Hawkins (1532–1595 CE), a famous admiral who introduced him to life at sea. Francis Drake sailed with Hawkins on several raiding and slaving expeditions in the 1560s, and by 1568 CE he commanded his own ship. Between 1569 and 1575 CE, Drake attacked Spanish settlements, ships, and caravans in Central America—often cooperating with other English or French privateers, as well as *cimarrons* (escaped black slaves). He acquired a small fortune in the process, which he used to purchase land for his family and a ship for himself.

In 1577 CE, Drake developed a plan with Sir Francis Walshingham for a privateering voyage around the world. Walshingham, John Hawkins, and Queen Elizabeth I (1533–1603 CE) helped finance the voyage. The five-ship expedition, led by Drake in the *Golden Hind*, departed in the fall and set sail for the African coast, planning to continue to South America and then circumnavigate the continent and attack Spain's possessions on its Pacific coast. Drake's subordinate captains proved unruly and two of them were later convicted of mutiny and beheaded, but the fleet successfully captured Spanish and Portuguese merchant ships off the coast of Morocco. Three of his captains turned back for England rather than navigate the Straits of Magellan, and thus Drake entered the Pacific with only two ships. Sailing north along the coast Drake attacked ships and settlements, spreading fear and acquiring more loot than his ships could carry. Off Lima, Peru, he captured a Spanish treasure ship loaded with gold. Reaching roughly as far north as modern San Francisco, they turned west and crossed the Pacific, arriving home at Plymouth on September 26, 1580 CE. Having amply rewarded his investors and completed the first round-the-world voyage since Magellan's expedition, Queen Elizabeth knighted him the following year. Afterward, he was briefly mayor of Plymouth and served in Parliament.

Battle between Sir Francis Drake's ship, the *Golden Hind,* and the Spanish ship, *Nuestra Señora de la Concepción,* in March 1579. Sir Francis Drake was an English explorer and privateer who became famous for his successful raids against Spanish ports and shipping. (Library of Congress)

In 1585–86 CE, Drake commanded 21 ships and 1,800 men. He led them to the Caribbean where they raided Spanish shipping and settlements, holding some settlements for ransom—which failed to yield the wealth Drake expected. On the return voyage, they evacuated the settlement established at Roanoke by Walter Raleigh (1552–1618 CE).

In 1587 CE, Drake sailed again, this time against Spain itself. His fleet attacked the port of Cadiz where he captured four ships and destroyed more than two dozen others. This disrupted Spain's most important port and delayed the military preparations of Spain's King Philip II (1527–1598 CE). Afterwards, Drake's fleet cruised off Spain and intercepted several Spanish convoys, further delaying Philip's planned expedition against England.

The following year, the Spanish Armada sailed against England, expecting to escort troop transports across the English Channel. Drake—a vice admiral in the English fleet—helped repulse the Armada. Drake led an English squadron in the initial engagement and captured a Spanish ship. Afterward, Drake organized a fire ship attack on the anchored Spanish fleet, and then led his squadron at the Battle of Gravelines—the climactic battle of the campaign, which repulsed the Armada.

The following year, Drake, together with Sir John Norris, set out in command of 100 ships and approximately 19,000 soldiers to invade Portugal, aiming to liberate Portugal from Spanish rule and capture the Azores. The task proved beyond his force's means. Although it did provide some support to rebels fighting Spain, the expedition lost 20 ships and more than 10,000 men to combat and to disease. Despite this failure, Drake remained an active commander, sailing in August 1595 CE with John Hawkins and a large fleet to again raid Spain's Caribbean possessions. After some early successes, the expedition's attack on Puerto Rico failed. Drake landed in December at the Isthmus of Panama, but the fleet was driven back by Spanish soldiers. At sea, a deadly fever spread through the fleet, killing many people—including Drake, who died on January 27, 1596 CE. He was buried at sea in a lead coffin.

Jakub Basista

Further Reading

Bawlf, Samuel. 2003. *The Secret Voyage of Sir Francis Drake, 1577–1580.* Walker & Company.

Hakluyt R. 1589 [1965 ed.]. *The Principall Navigations, Voiages and Discoveries of the English Nation.* Cambridge: Published for the Hakluyt Society and the Peabody Museum of Salem at the University Press.

Hughes-Hallett, Lucy. 2004. *Heroes: A History of Hero Worship.* New York: Alfred A. Knopf.

Kelsey, Harry. 1998. *Sir Francis Drake, the Queen's Pirate.* New Haven, CT: Yale University Press.

East India Company, 1600–1874 CE

The English East India Company (EIC) (1600–1874 CE) was one of the world's first companies, and it played a key role in the creation of the British Empire and the integration of global commercial markets. It is also perhaps the most important business for understanding the evolution of the modern world. In general world or European history text books, the EIC, along with the Dutch East India Company (founded in 1602 CE) (DIC) and the French East India Company (founded in1664 CE) (FIC), are discussed under the term "mercantilism," an aspect of the Commercial Revolution whereby governments chartered (licensed) companies to operate and endowed them with special rights. The alliance was mutually beneficial because overseas trade required large amounts of capital, and special privileges with—and protection from—native rulers in distant lands. Essentially, company merchants received two main benefits from this relationship: a monopoly on trade in the region where it was chartered to operate and limited liability. It is debatable whether the EIC was the world's first limited liability company (LLC), as some popular business magazine articles claim. In return for government backing, the company was expected to find new markets for national trade and bring home gold and silver. The EIC primarily used gold to pay for goods in the East Indies, including pepper, cinnamon, cardamom, nutmeg, cotton, dyes, textiles, spices, saltpeter, silk, and indigo. It also established permanent agents in ports and founded new cities, including Singapore City and Hong Kong, to foster trade with those areas in Asia.

When chartered by Queen Elizabeth I on December 31, 1600, the company's name was "The Governor and Company of Merchants of London Trading into the East Indies." Unlike its Dutch and French counterparts, however, the EIC focused strictly on trade and did not initially engage in military conquest. The EIC's initial governing board consisted of 24 shareholders who were elected to manage the company's affairs from London. Regional administrative sub-units called "presidencies" were established in Bombay, Madras, and Calcutta to direct day-to-day operations. Initially, EIC merchants arranged, invested in, and received payment for, individual voyages. Early excursions thus followed no pattern, and they were as much explorations as economic ventures.

The company's royal charter ended when King Charles I was executed (1649 CE), but Lord Protector Oliver Cromwell (r. 1653–1658 CE) renewed it in October 1657 CE. The new charter made the EIC a joint stock company, which paid dividends to investors based on the company's overall operations, rather than on a per-voyage basis. This change gave the EIC attributes of modern companies, which have an overarching direction and strategy. The EIC's charter was in limbo between Cromwell's death (1658 CE) and Charles II's ascension to the throne (1660 CE). King Charles II issued a new royal charter that gave the company extraordinary powers—similar to those of a nation—including the authority to wage war, administer justice, engage in foreign diplomacy, acquire territories, raise and command armies, and plunder ships that violated its monopoly. Over time, the EIC came to maintain a standing army of more than 200,000 men and possessed its own navy. At its height, it was responsible for half of global trade. The company ceased to operate as an active entity by the terms of the India Act of 1858, but the process was not complete until its last charter expired in 1874 CE.

Within 100 years of its founding, the EIC's operations made an extensive impact on English society, economy, and domestic policy. By 1699–1701 CE, East Indies trade goods constituted 13 percent of England's overseas imports. The EIC also loaned money to the English government out of the company's funds from the sale of stocks to shareholders. This made the EIC one of two organizations (the other was the Bank of England, founded in 1694 CE) that held most of the debt Great Britain accumulated in wars between 1689 CE and 1713 CE. Coffee houses sprung up throughout the country and the affordable cotton textiles imported from India created a demand that spurred the English textile industry which, in turn, was an important basis of the Industrial Revolution that occurred in England in the 18th and 19th centuries.

The need to pay dividends to shareholders from its overall profit led to one of the EIC's greatest contributions to world travel and trade—the development of a formal body of knowledge about the oceans and seas. Whereas popular history portrays John Harrison's invention of the chronometer (1714 CE) as the final piece of the world navigational puzzle, the reality is that, without accurate knowledge of the oceans' currents and circulation patterns and the outlines of coasts, the chronometer is simply another navigation aid. Such information was needed if EIC captains were to maintain a steady pattern of voyages where ships visited the same ports at predictable times. This type of maritime information was critical, because the most dangerous part of a voyage is approaching coastlines—it's the most likely time for a profit-losing shipwreck to occur. Although the EIC never established a hydrography office (as the DIC and FIC had), it employed a number of professional hydrographers, such as Alexander Dalrymple (1737–1808 CE) and James Horsburg (1762–1836 CE), who compiled and researched the information necessary for navigating the world's seas that began to appear in printed books and depicted on sea charts. As the EIC's monopoly on trade in the eastern part of the world deteriorated in the 18th century, and with the end of its shipping monopoly to China in 1834 CE, the hydrographers' work became a service industry to the world's commercial shipping.

Cumulatively, the changes to the EIC's charters and organization from the mid-17th to the early 18th century made it one of the most powerful companies in the world. During that period, the company became as much an agent of British colonization as commercial adventurists. As the Mughal Empire crumbled, local Indian rulers sought help from the European trading agents there to aid them in rebellion. The company acquired its first territorial acquisitions when Sir Robert Clive

(1725–1774 CE) gained control of Bengal and its 30 million inhabitants as a result of his victory in the Battle of Plassey (June 23, 1750).

The EIC also has a strong association with piracy. The company's lucrative maritime trade made the Indian Ocean and South China seas attractive areas for pirates to prey on shipping. The EIC therefore maintained its own navy and hired private ships and captains to fend off pirates. Not all such attempts to hire privateers benefitted the EIC, however. The renowned pirate, Captain William Kidd (1645–1701 CE), for instance, originally was hired to protect the company's trade. This association of piracy together with being an agent of the British Empire continues in the modern popular imagination. The company is part of the generic backdrop for numerous swashbuckling stories and films. For instance, Kidd is most likely the inspiration for Johnny Depp's character, Captain Jack Sparrow in the hit film series, *Pirates of the Caribbean*. In that series, the EIC and the British government are the antagonists against Sparrow and his merry band of pirates, who represent the struggle for freedom. In 2010 CE, a London-based luxury goods

---

Shipboard Life in the Age of Sail

Despite their often-romantic depictions, conditions aboard ships in the Age of Sail were harsh. Sailors endured poor pay without contact with home or the outside world for months or even years. Although specific hazards depended upon the voyage (a Navy midshipman might fall in battle; a Yankee harpooner might lose his life fighting a sperm whale in the South Sea), many dangers shadowed all ships at sea, including storms, running aground, a fall from the rigging, and disease (especially the scourge of the age, scurvy).

In such conditions, maintaining order aboard a ship was the captain's highest priority, and punishments for any infraction were swift and brutal (often a flogging with the cat-o-nine-tails). In the absence of such peril, however, life at sea also could be numbingly tedious. Sailors kept boredom at bay and buoyed morale with games, storytelling, singing, and crafts including tattooing and intricate scrimshaw. Officers could expect better food and berthing, but average seamen (many just boys) lived and worked in cramped, often unhygienic conditions without privacy, tapping the insects out of their biscuits before a meal (which might also include cured meats and other provisions which did not require refrigeration).

These conditions led Frederick William Wallace to title his famous 1924 book about the end of the Age of Sail, *Wooden Ships and Iron Men*, which (although it ignores the surprising number of women who also toiled in maritime trades) has since become common nomenclature for these sailors and their vessels. One of the benefits of sailing for the East India Company was that even average sailors received a small cargo allotment that enabled them to trade goods on their own.

Kelly P. Bushnell

trading company gained the rights to use the EIC's name and trademarks, and now operates as the East India Company, linking its heritage to the historic company.

Joyce Sampson

Further Reading

Bowen, H. V., Margarette Lincoln, and Nigel Rigby. 2015. *The Worlds of the East India Company*. Boydell Press.

Brown, Stephen R. 2009. *Merchant Kings: When Companies Ruled the World, 1600–1900*. St. Martin's Press.

"The East India Company: The Company That Ruled the Waves." *Economist*, December 17 2011. http://www.economist.com/node/21541753. Accessed December 1, 2016.

Erickson, Emily. 2014. *Between Monopoly and Free Trade: The English East India Company, 1600–1757*. Princeton University Press.

Farren, John, and Sarah Jobling (producers). 2014. *The Birth of Empire: The East India Company*. Presented by Dan Snow. Documentary TV mini-series.

Wild, Antony. 1999. *The East India Company: Trade and Conquest from 1600*. Harper Collins.

Halley, Edmond, 1656–1742 CE

Astronomer Edmond Halley—best known for the comet that bears his name—made significant contributions to sea navigation by improving a number of navigational instruments, charting stars, and surveyed magnetic variation in the Atlantic.

Born in Shoreditch, a suburb of London, Halley matriculated at Queen's College, Oxford in 1673 CE and before graduation wrote three scientific papers on astronomy which were published in the *Philosophical Transactions* of the Royal Society. Two were coauthored with John Flamsteed (1646–1719 CE), the first Astronomer Royal, who was particularly consumed with the problem of how to accurately determine longitude at sea. Flamsteed believed that the best way to calculate longitude was to create an accurate chart of navigational stars and the motion of the moon. It then could be used to determine longitudinal distance from a fixed reference point, such as a homeport. To assist Flamsteed in creating a global chart, Halley traveled in 1676 CE, along with several telescopes and other self-modified astronomical and navigational tools, to the island of St. Helena in the South Atlantic, then the southernmost British territory. During his two years there, Halley helped improve a variety of navigational instruments, invented a new type of ship's log to determine a vessel's speed through water, and accurately charted the position of more than 340 stars in the Southern hemisphere, publishing them shortly after his return to England. His nautical contributions aided in his election as a Fellow of the Royal Society before his 23rd birthday. That fellowship placed

Halley in close contact with Isaac Newton, and it was ultimately Halley who persuaded Newton to publish his magnum opus, the *Principia Mathematica*, fully subsidizing the cost of the first edition himself.

Making vast contributions to meteorology, physics, mathematics, classical scholarship, and natural history, Halley remained interested in the longitude problem. For years he collected observations on variations of the compass from mariners, hoping to find a way to determine longitude through an understanding of magnetic variation and accurate determination of latitude. Backed by the English Board of Admiralty, he carried out several voyages surveying magnetic variation in the South Atlantic during 1698–1700 CE. The result of these trips was the production of two oceanic charts featuring Isogonic—or Halley—lines, which join points of equal magnetic variation. Following the charts' publication, Halley went on to map the tides, depths, currents, and winds in the English Channel, producing yet another valuable maritime compendium. Never one to focus his attention on a singular problem, he also improved underwater diving bells, noting how pressure changed air volume and innovating ways to maintain a fresh air supply, later continuing along this interest by inventing a diving helmet for marine salvaging. In 1703 CE, Halley took up the post of Savilian Professor of Mathematics at Oxford, which he would occupy for the rest of his life, adding to his title that of Astronomer Royal after Flamsteed's death.

Timothy Daniels

Further Reading

Cook, Alan. 1998. *Edmond Halley: Charting the Heavens and the Seas*. Oxford: Clarendon Press.

Thrower, Norman (ed.). 1981. *The Three Voyages of Edmond Halley in the* Paramore, *1698–1701*. Burlington, VT: Ashgate.

Wakefield, Julie. 2005. *Halley's Quest*. Washington, DC: Joseph Henry Press.

Harrison, John, 1693–1776 CE

John Harrison was an English carpenter from Yorkshire who is best known for inventing the marine chronometer—basically a spring-driven clock—in an attempt to accurately determine the longitude of a ship at sea.

In the 17th century, ships determined their position by "dead reckoning": calculating their location using a previously determined position and advancing it based on estimated speeds over elapsed time and course. This process was subject to many errors, largely because tides and currents vary constantly, and those errors proved costly for merchant and naval vessels. Notably, in 1707 CE, because of navigational errors British Admiral Cloudesley Shovell's fleet struck several rocks near the Scilly Islands. Four men-of-war sunk, and nearly 2,000 sailors drowned. In response to the disaster, as well as the constant predation on merchant ships that travelled across predictable shipping lanes, in 1714 Parliament established a Board of Longitude to explore solutions to determine longitude at sea. The board offered prizes of up to £20,000 for individuals who could demonstrate a working device or method to determine longitude accurately at sea within one-half to one degree of longitude (or between 30 and 60 nautical miles).

Several different proposals were advanced over the following century, but the two most promising methods relied on being able to accurately measure time when on board a ship, because a difference in longitude between two specific locations corresponds to a difference in time. By knowing the difference in time at a reference point (such as Greenwich) and that on board ship (most easily calculated at noon), a navigator could reckon his longitude relative to the point of reference. Harrison recognized that the more popular approach—determining time via celestial navigation—required clear skies, access to good charts, and expensive navigational tools operated by competent navigators. After consulting with astronomer royal Edmund Halley (1656–1742 CE) and several accomplished clockmakers, Harrison used the skills he honed as a carpenter to craft a clock that would not succumb to the vicissitudes of sea travel. He tested his "H1," as it came to be called, in 1736 CE, and was awarded £500 to further improve it. He crafted two more substantial timepieces before finally producing his masterpiece, the three-pound, 5.2-inch-diameter "H4" in 1760 CE. On its sea trial, it lost only 5 seconds over 81 days. The Longitude Board, headed by astronomers who held their profession in much higher regard than that of manual craftsmen, blocked Harrison from receiving the prize. He spent nearly the rest of his life wrangling with the board over compensation, finally receiving a settlement just three years before his death. James Cook (1728–1779 CE) used a copy of the H4 to chart his voyages of discovery. Harrison's chronometers can be seen today at the National Maritime Museum in Greenwich.

Timothy Daniels

Further Reading

Hobden, Heather, and Mervyn Hobden. 1988. *John Harrison and the Problem of Longitude*. Lincoln, England: Cosmic Elk.

Quill, Humphrey. 1966. *John Harrison: The Man Who Found Longitude*. New York: Humanities Press.

Sobel, Dava. 1995. *Longitude*. New York: Walker & Company.

Mary Rose

Built in 1510 CE, the 500-ton *Mary Rose* was enlarged in 1536 CE to 700 tons and armed with new, heavy guns fired through gunports, a recent invention. One of

England's largest and most modern ships, the *Mary Rose* sank on July 19, 1545, during the Battle of Solent. The redesigned ship proved unstable. As the *Mary Rose* maneuvered, a wind gust heeled the ship. Water flooded in through the open gunports, sinking the ship in about 35 feet of water off the Isle of Wight. Anti-boarding netting prevented all but two- or three-dozen of the 415 sailors and marines from escaping.

Salvaging this prized ship precipitated a court case that questioned English ideas of race and status. In July 1546 CE, the Admiralty appointed Venetian Petri Paulo Corsi, adept in the latest techniques, to direct the salvage. In July 1547 CE, Italian merchants hired Corsi to salvage the *Sancta Maria* and *Sanctus Edwardus* off nearby Southampton. Corsi employed Jacques Francis and seven other African divers who secured lines to items to hoist them to surface.

Salvaging proceeded until the Italian merchants accused Corsi of stealing goods from the *Sancta Maria* and sued him. The merchants, who previously applauded Francis's expertise, attempted to deny Francis's legal personhood based on his purported inferiority, calling him a "slave," "Blacke more," and "morisco born where they are not christened" (Anthonius de Nicholao Rimero Deposition). Perhaps the best diver in England, Francis testified that he "dyd handell and see under water" the allegedly stolen items were "saved" and would have been restored, but for Corsi's arrest. The merchants, he said, inhibiting recovering the king's property (the *Mary* Rose) by arresting Corsi in May, "the beste tyme" for diving, when seas were calm (Jacques Francis Deposition). Even as some claimed African inferiority, Francis demonstrated African expertise. His testimony and professionalism during two years upon the wrecks challenged ideas of race, slavery, and status. England had not yet legalized slavery and the court accepted Francis's expertise.

The trial halted salvage operations and the *Mary Rose*'s location slipped from memory. A layer of mud entombed and preserved the lower half of the hull. In the summer of 1836 CE, fishermen snared their nets on some of her timbers and the wreck was superficially worked in 1836 CE and 1840 CE. Rediscovered in 1971 CE, the Mary Rose Trust salvaged the mud-encased portion of the ship in 1982 CE in one of the most complex underwater excavations to date. The remains of the ship are preserved in the Mary Rose Museum in Portsmouth, England.

Salvage of the ship provided a wealth of artifacts including sailing equipment, naval stores, weapons, food, and personal and specialized equipment ranging from musical instruments, surgical instruments, and navigational devices to clothing, rosaries, and other religious items, and even a backgammon set. These provided an unparalleled portrait of 16th-century shipboard life.

Kevin Dawson

Further Reading

Childs, David. 2014. *The Warship Mary Rose: The Life and Times of King Henry VII's Flagship*. London: Chatham.

Dawson, Kevin. 2006. "Enslaved Swimmers and Divers in the Atlantic World." *The Journal of American History* 92(4) (March): 1327–55.

de Nicholao Rimero, Anthonius. 1548. Deposition made on May 28, 1548, PRO, HCA 13/93, ff. 275–6, and Interrogation of and Deposition made by Jacques Francis on Tuesday, February 8, 1548 (O.S.), 18 February 1548 (N.S.), PRO, HCA 13/93/202v-203r. http://www.nationalarchives.gov.uk/pathways/blackhistory/early_times/settlers.htm. The *Mary Rose* website. http://www.maryrose.org. Accessed December 15, 2015.

McElvogue, Douglas. 2015. *Tudor Warship Mary Rose*. Annapolis: Naval Institute Press.

Navigation Acts

Mercantilism, the dominant economic theory of the 17th and 18th centuries, encouraged nations to develop positive trade balances by developing colonies and limiting trade with rival nations. This would keep wealth within the particular empire. The Navigation Acts, also known as the Acts of Trade and Navigation, passed by England epitomized its adoption of mercantilism. The acts restricted English colonies from trading with other states, such as Spain, Portugal, France, and the Netherlands, and their colonies, and restricted all British colonies to trading solely with British merchants. Britain's European rivals passed similar acts.

The first Navigation Act was enacted in 1651 CE during Oliver Cromwell's rule. The Dutch were rapidly becoming Europe's leading traders and increasingly dominated Atlantic trade. The act aimed to hinder Dutch trade and encourage the development of British trade and naval power. It forbade any non-English ship from trading with the British Isles.

When the English monarchy was restored in 1660 CE under Charles II, the government passed a new act that expanded the 1651 CE act to include newly obtained Caribbean colonies. The 1660 act also required that the colonies trade only with England, and that their goods be carried in English ships with English captains, the majority of whose crews were also English. The Navigation Act of 1663 restricted trade between English colonies by requiring that their products, with a few exceptions like slaves and Madeira wine, first be shipped to England and then dispersed to other colonies to be sold. This, of course, further enriched English merchants at the expense of the colonies. Additional acts continued to add restrictions and close loopholes, and the various Navigation Acts were consolidated in the 1696 Navigation Act. Minor revisions continued until Parliament repealed the Acts of Trade and Navigation in 1849 CE.

Merchants from England's American colonies were among those most hindered by the Navigation Acts, which helped lead to the American Revolution. The 1764 Sugar Act—designed to force the colonists to buy higher-priced sugar produced in British colonies rather than cheaper sugar from the French West Indies—triggered colonial protests, as did the later Stamp Act (1765 CE), Tea Act (1767 CE), and

Townsend Acts (1767 CE). The protests against these taxes and restrictions eventually helped produce the American Revolution in 1775 CE. After the passage of the first Navigation Act, though, growing numbers of merchants evaded these restrictions, becoming smugglers. Throughout the New World, American smugglers traded illegally with French, Dutch, Portuguese, and Spanish colonial merchants, and smugglers from those nations and their colonies similarly evaded trade restrictions, seeking the lowest prices for goods regardless of trade restrictions and tariffs.

Matthew Blake Strickland

Further Reading

Armitage, David and Michael J. Braddick (eds.). 2009. *The British Atlantic World, 1500–1800*, 2nd ed. New York: Palgrave Macmillan.

Dickerson, Oliver Morton. 1951. *The Navigation Acts and the American Revolution*. Philadelphia: University of Pennsylvania Press.

Harper, Lawrence A. 1939. *The English Navigation Laws: A Seventeenth Century Experiment in Social Engineering*. New York: Columbia University Press.

Raleigh, Sir Walter, 1554–1618 CE

Sir Walter Raleigh, a courtier of Queen Elizabeth I, used his influence at court to encourage English exploration and colonization. He received a royal patent to explore part of the American coast, which he named Virginia in honor of the queen, and sponsored several voyages of exploration. In addition to searching for El Dorado, a mythical city of gold rumored to be somewhere in South America, Raleigh established an English settlement on Roanoke Island, in what is today Virginia, and popularized tobacco smoking in the English court. He never himself, though, set foot in North America.

Raleigh began planning North American colonization as early as 1583 CE. He applied for a colonizing patent and commissioned Richard Hakluyt to write a pamphlet in 1584 CE that supported a colony in North America. After securing funds from prominent London merchants, Raleigh sent out an expedition of around 600 men in 1585 CE. They settled on Roanoke Island. Within a year, however, the colony faced starvation and was abandoned; its colonists were carried home by Francis Drake, who was returning from raids on Spanish shipping. Raleigh dispatched a second expedition in 1587 CE, which reestablished the colony. A planned supply convoy, though, was delayed by war with Spain. Following the defeat of the Spanish Armada (1588 CE), the leaders of the supply convoy instead sailed to Cuba, hoping to raid Spanish shipping. A supply ship did not reach Roanoke Island until 1590 CE, and found the colony abandoned. Discussion of the fate of the "lost colony of Roanoke" continues to this day.

In 1594 CE, Raleigh led an expedition to Guiana on the northwest coast of South America, where he heard and became enthralled by Spanish stories of El Dorado, a city of gold. He published an account of the voyage, *The Discovery of Guiana* (1596 CE), which exaggerated his finds and further fueled the growing legend of El Dorado. Raleigh participated in several battles against the Spanish, including a 1596 CE raid on Cadiz, and briefly served in Parliament. He lost influence following Elizabeth's death in 1603 CE, and was tried, convicted, and imprisoned in the Tower of London for plotting against King James. Released in 1616 CE to lead a second expedition to South America, he again searched for El Dorado. Not finding it, his men attacked and sacked the Spanish settlement of San Thomé in Guiana, violating the tenuous peace between Spain and England and outraging the Spanish who insisted that Raleigh be punished. On his return, Raleigh wrote an *Apology for the Voyage to Guiana* in which he justified his actions, but to no avail. He was beheaded on October 29, 1618 at Westminster.

Matthew Blake Strickland

Further Reading

Armitage, Christopher M. 1987. *Sir Walter Raleigh: An Annotated Bibliography*. Chapel Hill: University of North Carolina Press.

May, Steven W. 1989. *Sir Walter Raleigh*. Boston: Twayne Publishers.

Popper, Nicholas. 2012. *Walter Raleigh's "History of the World" and the Historical Culture of the Late Renaissance*. Chicago: University of Chicago Press.

FRANCE, 1450 TO 1770 CE

People lived along the seacoasts of France from prehistory, but what we today know as France first met the sea in the 15th century. From 1450 to 1770 CE, France opened up transoceanic trade routes, founded overseas colonies, created a navy, and clashed with rival maritime states, particularly Great Britain. Coastal communities flourished and increased their role in the French economy and society. By the 18th century's end, France was among the world's leading maritime states and the French public had adopted a positive—even romantic—view of the sea.

The medieval kingdom of France took its first steps to becoming a maritime state in the middle 15th century by gaining access to two separate coasts: the Atlantic Ocean and the Mediterranean Sea. From the 12th century English-held possessions on the continent (the Angevin Empire) blocked the French state's access to the Atlantic coast. In the last years of the Hundred Years' War (1337–1453 CE), French armies displaced the English, conquering Dieppe in Normandy in 1443 CE, Rouen on the Seine River a few years later, and then Harfleur at the mouth of the Seine. A patchwork of independent feudal states blocked France's access to the Mediterranean Sea, but the largest of these, Provence, became French in 1486 CE.

King Francis I (r. 1515–1557 CE) further extended the boundaries of maritime France. He opened a new port at Le Havre in 1572 CE, which became the principal oceanic port of Paris, France's capital. Francis I completed an official union between the crown of peninsular Brittany and France in 1532 CE, joining a vast stretch of rocky Atlantic seacoast with the interior. That same year, an agreement with Ottoman emperor Suleiman the Magnificent (1694–1566 CE) permitted the establishment of French trading posts at Constantinople, Smyrna, Aleppo, Alexandria, Tunis, and Algiers. Through these Turkish-controlled ports and then across the Mediterranean, France imported cottons, muslins, silks, precious stones, and spices. French merchants in Marseilles prospered from the "Levant" or eastern trade, and the royal family, French nobles, and elite bankers enjoyed this new abundance of eastern luxuries.

The discovery of the New World in 1492 CE inaugurated a new era of opportunity for France overseas. Seeking a western trade route to China, the source of Levant trade luxuries, in 1523 Francis I dispatched Italian navigator Giovanni de Verrazano (1485–1528 CE) to explore the coast between Florida and Newfoundland. Beginning in 1534 CE, Jacques Cartier (1491–1557 CE) made three further voyages to these coasts. During that same period, intrepid fishermen from the Basque region of France braved the icy seas of the northern Atlantic. They fished for cod off the Grand Banks of Newfoundland and hunted whales and seals off the frozen coast of Norway. The codfish harvest nourished French people during the meatless holy days of the year as dictated by the religious calendar of predominately Catholic France. Voyages of discovery and returning fishing fleets from distant places excited the imagination of the French court, but they faced competition from European rivals.

Spain and Portugal insisted on their rights under the Treaty of Tordesillas (1494 CE) dividing the New World and excluding all others from trade and settlement. French traders ignored their pretensions and penetrated Spain's American markets. Contraband leather, sugar, and tobacco from Spain's colonies arrived in increasing quantities at Le Havre and other French Atlantic ports in the 16th century. French corsairs—privateer ship captains who were licensed by the crown to conduct a maritime war—attacked the Spanish town of Cartagena de Indies in Colombia in 1554 CE and burned Havana, Cuba, in 1555 CE. Soon afterward, France sought to establish its own colonies in Brazil (1562 CE) and Florida (1567 CE), but these efforts failed due to resistance from neighboring Portuguese and Spanish colonies.

France proved more successful in the 17th century. In 1603 CE, Samuel de Champlain (1574–1635 CE) founded Port Royal on the island of Acadia (Nova Scotia). Three years later, Quebec City on the banks of the St. Lawrence River was founded. Maritime Normandy supplied the majority of settlers to these colonies in present-day Canada.

In the Caribbean, the American Islands Company (*Compagnie des Îles de l'Amérique*) established plantations throughout the Lesser Antilles or Windward islands: St. Christophe, 1626 CE (modern-day St. Kitts and Nevis); Dominica, 1635 CE; Guadeloupe, 1635 CE; Martinique, 1637 CE; St. Barths, 1648 CE; St. Martin, 1648 CE; St. Croix, 1650 CE; and Saint Lucia, 1650 CE. The Breton town of Nantes prospered from an exclusive monopoly on Caribbean trade that was granted by the crown. French Tortuga off the coast of present-day Haiti was officially established in 1659 CE. Before that, it had served as a haven for French, English, and Dutch buccaneers who called themselves the "Brethren of the Coast." From Tortuga it was only a small step for France to establish in 1697 CE the colony of Saint-Domingue (today's Haiti) on the western third of the Spanish island of Hispaniola. Life in the French Caribbean colonies soon centered on vast plantations—almost entirely devoted to growing sugar, and worked by thousands of African slaves. A network of transatlantic trade routes, Mediterranean trade routes, cod fisheries, transatlantic colonies, and West African stations for the slave trade connected France to the wider world. The increasing volume of overseas trade meant that France could no longer afford a collection of ad hoc warships (mostly converted merchant vessels) but required a permanent navy.

King Louis XIV (r. 1661–1715 CE) supported the creation of a navy to support France's overseas interests. Jean-Baptiste Colbert (1619–1683 CE), the king's minister of finance, colonies, and navy, ordered an inventory of every vessel—large and small—capable of war or trade, including the names of ship owners and the number of sailors employed. Based on information gathered on harbors and port facilities, Colbert developed Toulon to support a French naval squadron in the Mediterranean, and stationed another squadron at Brest in Brittany from which it could sail into the English Channel or out into the Atlantic. A naval school at Saint-Malo would educate the navy's officers. Between 1661 CE and 1671 CE, France constructed 106 warships, which quadrupled the navy's size.

The construction of a royal navy under Louis XIV profoundly affected France's economy and ecology. Oak forests were exploited for the production of timber for masts, decks, and hulls. Forges produced artillery and anchors but also exhausted supplies of accessible French coal. Near the coasts, rope-sheds and sail-making sheds further depleted France's ancient forests. The arsenals in Toulon and Brest, the nexuses of this activity, became the largest concentrations of workers in preindustrial France.

The seamen of the new navy were drawn from fishermen and other mariners. In the past this had meant the employment of the press gang. Typically, the gates of a coastal town were barred and maritime workers ruthlessly rounded up. In place of this haphazard approach, Colbert instituted a system of maritime conscription for the nation's roughly 50,000 maritime workers (of a total population of nearly 20 million). Conscription proved unpopular and protests and resistance ensued, which forced the navy to maintain press gangs to supplement conscription.

A mercantilist like most of his contemporaries, Colbert believed there was a limited quantity of precious metals (gold and silver) in the world. In such a zero-sum view of wealth, only a favorable balance of foreign trade would bring riches to the state. Colbert's policies emphasized tariffs on imports of overseas goods, subsidies for French industries involved in overseas trade, and the establishment of overseas colonies for the benefit of the mother country. Colbert created in 1664 CE the French Company of the Indies as part of this program. As a result, French colonies and trading posts were extended to the Indian Ocean on the Île de Bourbon (Réunion) and the Île de France (Mauritius) and in India at Chandernagore and Pondichéry. Lorient in Brittany, where the company was headquartered, boomed thanks to the India trade.

In the Atlantic world, a triangular trade developed between the Caribbean, Africa, and France. In 1669 CE, Louis XIV authorized the export of slaves to the Antilles to support Caribbean sugar production. Following the arrival of wealthy Irish Catholic refugees between 1685 and 1688 CE, Nantes in Brittany took a leading role in the slave trade. Typically, captains sailed from Nantes to Senegal in West Africa, purchasing men and women in exchange for manufactured goods; they next sailed to the Antilles and sold the slaves to plantation owners. The vessels then returned to Nantes with Caribbean spices and sugar.

The creation of a Royal French Navy and Colbert's mercantilist polices that encouraged overseas trades and colonization led to a series of ruinous wars with Great Britain and the Dutch Republic. Although initially victorious in the Dutch War (1672–1678 CE) when France and England combined against the Dutch Republic, the naval balance subsequently turned against France in the Nine Years' War (1688–1697 CE), when France fought alone against the English, Dutch, and their Spanish allies. At the battle of Beachy Head (1690 CE) the French navy defeated the combined Dutch and English fleets, but in 1692 CE the French fleet was decisively defeated at the battle of La Hogue. In the subsequent, exhausting, War of Spanish Succession (1702–1713 CE), France's naval effort declined and launches of new vessels were suspended. In the Treaty of Utrecht (1713 CE) ending the war, France surrendered its fishing settlement on Newfoundland and evacuated Port Royal on Acadia (Nova Scotia).

Despite these setbacks, Louis XIV did not end France's overseas adventures. On the contrary, French overseas trade increased in the 1720s, particularly transatlantic trade, which by 1740 CE represented half of French overseas trade. Nantes and Bordeaux prospered more than ever. In Asia, the French Company of the Indies equaled the English East India Company in volume of trade, and reached two-thirds that of the Dutch East Indies Company. In French India, new trading posts were established along the Malabar Coast under the able leadership of Joseph-François Dupleix (1697–1763 CE). In the Atlantic, Louisbourg was built on Isle Royale (modern-day Cape Breton Island) to defend the entrance to New France.

France's renewed overseas success predictably led to further hostilities with Great Britain. When war began in 1744 CE (part of the War of Austrian Succession, 1740–1748 CE), the minister of the navy, Jean Frédéric Phélypeaux (Count of Maurepas) (1701–1781 CE), adopted a defensive strategy that emphasized escorting merchant convoys, and transporting troops to secure the overseas colonies. Maurepas sought to avoid a major fleet engagement with Britain's numerically superior Royal Navy. In the treaty of Aix-la-Chapelle (1748 CE), which ended the conflict, Britain returned Louisbourg to France in exchange for the port of Madras in India. It was an even swap, but the risk of conflict remained. In 1754–1755 CE, an anti-French fever gripped Parliament and brought William Pitt the Elder (1708–1788 CE) to power. Pitt was determined to break France's overseas empire, which he largely did in the Seven Years' War (1756–1763 CE) also known as The French and Indian War. France lost several Caribbean colonies and all of Canada.

Yet, these losses were offset by the continuation of a profitable overseas trade. By the 1780s, France boasted the largest overseas trading economy in Europe— surpassing even Great Britain (Daudin 2004, 144). The French artist Claude Joseph Vernet (1714–1789 CE) portrayed the bustle of France's ports in a panoramic series of oil paintings. At the end of the 18th century, Bordeaux overtook Nantes as the busiest of the French Atlantic ports. Marseilles became the third largest city in France with a population exceeding 120,000.

Despite wartime losses, public attitudes toward the sea changed for the better during the 18th century. From being a harsh and unforgiving place associated in popular culture with meatless holy days and tragedy and death, the sea was re-imagined as a place of beauty and mystery. From the mid-18th century, wealthy financiers constructed summer homes along the coasts of France. Accounts of voyages of scientific exploration and discovery and prints of distant islands and unusual sea life became popular. In 1707 CE, explorer Michel Dubocage (1676–1727 CE) ventured into the Pacific Ocean on board the *Découverte* and reached Clipperton Island. Located about 1,500 miles west of Costa Rica, Clipperton remains a French possession. Other expeditions visited Peru (1733 CE) and Lapland (1736 CE) to measure the meridian arc and determine the earth's shape. Among the most impressive expeditions was that of Louis Antoine de Bougainville (1729–1811 CE) who, accompanied by geographers and naturalists, explored the Pacific between 1766 and 1769 CE and laid the foundations of French Polynesia. France's connections with sea grew steadily in the 18th century.

George Satterfield

Further Reading

Ames, Glenn J. 1996. *Colbert, Mercantilism and the French Quest for the Asian Trade*. De Kalb, IL: Northern Illinois Press.

Bamford, Paul. 1956. *Forests and French Sea Power*. Toronto: University of Toronto Press.

Curry, Anne. 2002. *The Hundred Years' War, 1337–1453. Essential Histories*. Oxford: Osprey Publishing.

Daudin, Guillaume. 2004. "Profitability and Long-Distance Trading in Context: The Case of Eighteenth Century France." *The Journal of Economic History* 64: 144–71.

Dull, Jonathan. 2005. *The French Navy and the Seven Years' War*. Lincoln, NE: University of Nebraska Press.

Eccles, W. J. 2010. *The French in North America, 1500–1783*. Ontario: Fitzhenry & White-side.

Rognzinski, Jan. 2000. *A Brief History of the Caribbean: From the Arawak and Carib to the Present*. New York: Penguin Books.

Vergé-Franceschi, Michel. 1996. *La marine française au xviiiᵉ siècle: guerres, administration, exploration*. Paris: SEDES.

Cartier, Jacques, 1491–1557 CE

A French navigator and explorer, Jacques Cartier claimed Canada for France in 1534 CE and explored and mapped the St. Lawrence River in a succession of expeditions that established French control of the region.

Little is known about Cartier's early life. Born in Saint Mallo, France, on the Brittany coast in 1491, Cartier married Mary Catherine des Granches, who belonged to the local elite, in 1520 CE. Little is known of his early career, but he presumably participated in early voyages of exploration, perhaps that of Giovanni de Verrazano. In 1534 CE, King Francis I appointed him to command an expedition to explore North America to locate a northwest passage to Asia. The two-ship expedition sailed on April 20, 1534, and reached Newfoundland 20 days later. Over the next few weeks Cartier then explored the Island of the Birds (where his crew killed more than 1,000 birds), Prince Edward Island, Anticosti Island, and the Gulf of St. Lawrence. They encountered natives and captured two, whom they took to Europe. On the shore of Gaspé Bay, Cartier planted a 30-foot cross and claimed the land for France before returning home after the 137-day expedition.

Cartier set out again the following year with three ships, 110 men, and the two Indians he had brought home the previous year. They sailed up the St. Lawrence River as far as the Iroquois Indian capital of Hochelaga (today's Montreal). Welcomed there, they traded successfully and then returned upriver, spending the winter near modern Quebec, where they established a fort near several local Indian villages. The severe winter and accompanying illness, possibly scurvy, claimed the

La Grande Hermine, the galleon sailed by French explorer Jacques Cartier during one of his expeditions to North America, ca. 1535. (Library of Congress)

lives of 25 men along with 50 Indians. They sailed for home in May 1536 CE, again taking Indian captives with them. In France, Cartier reported his discovery of a wealthy kingdom and suggested that the St. Lawrence could provide passage to Asia.

European politics delayed King Francis I from dispatching Cartier on another expedition for five years. Cartier sailed to Canada for the third time in 1541 CE, as the principal navigator of a colonizing expedition commanded by Jean-François de La Rocque, sieur de Roberval. Cartier sailed first, with five ships and about 1,500 men, and Roberval was delayed for almost a year waiting for supplies. Cartier arrived in Quebec on August 23, 1541. Fearing Indian attack, he established a fortified settlement for the colonists who accompanied him farther up the river, at today's Cap Rouge, which he named Charlesbourg-Royal. From there, he continued exploring the St. Lawrence, but never journeyed beyond Montreal. The Iroquois attacked that winter, killing several of the settlers, and in the spring Cartier decided to return to France, bringing with him samples of "gold" and "diamonds" discovered by his men.

Cartier sailed for France in the spring, ignoring Roberval, recently arrived, who requested that he remain. Without Cartier, Roberval led his expedition to Charlesbourg-Royal, but continuing poor relations with the Iroquois, along with disease and poor weather, forced its abandonment the following year. Cartier's gold and diamonds, however, proved to be worthless quartz crystals and iron pyrite. Cartier retired to his Saint Mallo estate and continued to write about the potential wealth of Canada, dying on September 1, 1557. France would not establish permanent settlements in Canada until 1605 CE.

Jakub Basista

Further Reading

Blashfield, Jean, F. 2001. *Jacques Cartier in Search of the Northwest Passage*. Compass Point Books.

Cook, Ramsey (ed.). 2015. *The Voyages of Jacques Cartier*. Toronto: University of Toronto Press.

Hoffman, Bernard G. 1961. *Cabot to Cartier*. Toronto: University of Toronto Press.

Champlain, Samuel de, 1574–1635 CE

Samuel de Champlain was a noted French explorer, cartographer, the founder of Quebec City, and a colonial leader. Often called the "Father of New France," he encouraged settlement, oversaw development of the region, improved relations with indigenous peoples, and promoted trade. Champlain explored the Ottawa River, the St. Lawrence Seaway, parts of the eastern Great Lakes and New England, discovered Lake Champlain, and wrote extensively about his explorations and Native American society.

Born in 1574 CE in Brouage, France, little is known of Champlain's early life. He participated in several expeditions to the West Indies and Central America, winning renown as a navigator. He served as cartographer for King Henry IV (1553–1610 CE) from 1601–1603 CE, and then joined an expedition led by François Gravé Du Pont that explored Canada. In 1604 CE, Champlain was the cartographer for Pierre Du Gua de Monts' expedition to Canada where he helped establish the settlement of Port Royal, now Annapolis, on the coast of the Bay of Fundy. From 1605–1607 CE, Champlain explored the Bay of Fundy, the St. John and St. Croix River systems, and mapped the Atlantic coastline of southeast Canada and what became New England.

Champlain subsequently participated in an expedition up the St. Lawrence River and founded a trading fort on July 3, 1608, which became Quebec City. While there, Champlain improved French ties with the Huron and Algonquin peoples and helped them defeat the Iroquois in 1609–1610 CE. Named commandant of New

France by King Louis XIII (1601–1643 CE) in 1613 CE, Champlain continued exploring the region. In 1615 CE, he voyaged to Lake Huron where he again fought with France's Huron allies against the Iroquois. Injured in the fighting, Champlain spent the winter with the Huron and wrote a comprehensive account of their life and culture before returning to France later in 1616 CE.

Champlain continued to write and publish, winning recognition as an ethnographer. He returned to Canada in 1620 CE and worked to improve its administration. He established or enlarged several French forts and trading posts and in 1627 CE Cardinal de Richelieu placed him in charge of the Company of the Hundred Associates, which controlled the lucrative fur trade from French Canada. Champlain's administration was troubled by continuing hostilities with both England and the Iroquois. English privateer David Kirke besieged Quebec City and Champlain, who lacked the forces to defend the colony, surrendered the city on July 19, 1629. France regained its colony when the Treaty of Saint-Germain-en-Laye ended hostilities in 1632 CE, and Champlain, who had spent the interim writing books on leadership and navigation, returned to Quebec to begin its reconstruction. Unfortunately, his declining health led him to retire by the end of 1633 CE. He died on December 25, 1635 CE in Quebec City.

Sean Morton

Further Reading

Champlain, Samuel de. 1922–1936. *The Works of Samuel de Champlain.* H. P. Biggar (ed.). 6 vols. Toronto: Champlain Society.

Dionne, N. E. 1963. *The Makers of Canada: Champlain.* Toronto: Morang & Co. Ltd.

Morison, S. E. 1972. *Samuel de Champlain: Father of New France.* Boston: Little Brown Press.

French East India Company

The French East India Company is an umbrella term for French trading companies active in the Indian Ocean, the most important of which were the *Compagnie française pour le commerce des Indes orientales* and the *Compagnie des Indes* (French East India Company). They were created to compete with the British and Dutch East India companies, which had operated profitably since the early 17th century.

The first French attempts to establish sea trade with the Orient failed for several reasons, including poor financing and the active enmity of the Dutch. The *Compagnie des Moluques*, chartered by Marie de Médicis in 1615 CE, was somewhat more successful, as it established a short-lived trading post at Pondicherry on the southeast coast of India.

Subsequent French trading companies included the *Compagnie d'Orient*, the *Compagnie de Madagascar*, and the *Compagnie de Chine*. Under the guidance of

Jean-Baptiste Colbert, minister to King Louis XIV, these three merged in 1664 CE as the *Compagnie française pour le commerce des Indes orientales*. A joint stock venture chartered by the king, it enjoyed a monopoly on French trade throughout the Indian and Pacific oceans, carrying back cargoes of spices, textiles, coffee, and tea to the mother country. Shipbuilders in the French ports of Le Havre, La Rochelle, and Saint Malo turned out vessels for the company's fleet, as a new port—destined to become the site of the country's most important naval yards—was built at Lorient in 1666–1667 CE.

Although the French East India Company failed to colonize the large Indian Ocean island of Madagascar, the company succeeded on the smaller islands of Réunion and Mauritius, both of which would prove to be ideal provisioning stations and locations for growing spices. Its agents also set up several trading posts in India, including Surat in the northwest in 1668 CE and Chandannagar in the northeast in 1673 CE, and reopened the post at Pondicherry in 1674 CE. By 1719 CE, however, the company's finances were failing and it merged with several other companies to become the *Compagnie des Indes*, with a monopoly on French trade in both the Old and New Worlds.

Joseph François Dupleix, governor general of French settlements in India, strove to expand his country's territory on the subcontinent, but was checked during the Carnatic Wars (1746–1763 CE) by British East India Company forces commanded by Robert Clive (1725–1774 CE). Dupleix's defeat marked the end of French political and commercial aspirations in India. The *Compagnie des Indes* was dissolved in 1769 CE, reestablished in 1785 CE, and dissolved once again during the French Revolution of 1789–1799 CE. Pondicherry and a few other coastal enclaves remained French until their transfer to the newly independent nation of India in the mid-20th century.

Grove Koger

Further Reading

Das, Sudipta. 1992. *Myths and Realities of French Imperialism in India, 1763–1783*. New York: P. Lang.

Ray, Indrani. 1999. *The French East India Company and the Trade of the Indian Ocean: A Collection of Essays*. New Delhi: Munshiram Manoharlal.

Wellington, Donald C. 2006. *French East India Companies: A Historical Account and Record of Trade*. Lanham, MD: Hamilton.

Verrazano, Giovanni de, 1485–1528 CE

Often overshadowed by other explorers, Giovanni de Verrazano was the first European to survey the North American coast between the Carolinas and

Newfoundland, and discovered the fine natural harbor that later became New York.

Like many contemporary explorers, Verrazano hailed from Italy. Born into a noble Florentine family, he received an excellent education and sailed both Mediterranean and north European waters, often operating from the French port of Dieppe. In 1522, he captured two Spanish ships. Perhaps inspired by the return of the survivors of Magellan's round-the-world voyage, Verrazano attracted the support of King Francis I of France (1519–1559 CE) who supplied him with four ships. They sailed in the autumn of 1523 CE, ostensibly to explore the New World and seek a route to India, but also to raid Spanish shipping. Two of Verrazano's ships were damaged by storms and the third, *La Normandie*, returned to France with several merchant ships captured off Spain's coast. So, in early 1524 CE, Verrazano sailed from the Madeira Islands alone in *La Dauphine*, a royal ship with a crew of 50 and provisions for eight months.

Verrazano sailed a northerly course avoiding the Caribbean, and arrived at the barrier islands of the Carolinas. From there he sailed north, explored New York Bay, Long Island, the Hudson River, and Narragansett Bay, where he landed and traded with the indigenous population. Continuing north, they sailed about 900 more miles along the coast, regularly landing, meeting, and sometimes trading with indigenous peoples. They were particularly impressed by local furs, about which Verrazano reported at length. Continuing along the east coast of Newfoundland, they reached almost 50-degrees N latitude when, running low on supplies, they sailed for home. Crossing the Atlantic in only two weeks, they arrived in Dieppe on July 8, 1524.

Verrazano, who correctly reported that a passage through North America to Asia was unlikely, proved unable to convince King Francis I to fund further exploration. Instead, Verrazano turned to financiers in Dieppe who funded two more expeditions. In 1527 CE, Verrazano sailed to Brazil and returned with a cargo of exotic woods used to dye cloth. He sailed again in 1528 CE. Still seeking a route to India, he explored several Caribbean islands including Guadeloupe, where Carib warriors killed him. King Francis I—engaged in a bitter war in Italy—never capitalized on Verrazano's discoveries.

Stephen K. Stein

Further Reading

Murphy, Henry Cruse. 1875. *The Voyage of Verrazano: A Chapter in the Early History of Maritime Discovery in America.* New York: Press of J. Munsell.

Thrower, Norman. 1979. "New Light on the 1524 Voyage of Verrazzano." *Terrae Incognitae* 11:1, 59–65.

Wroth, Lawrence. 1970. *The Voyages of Giovanni da Verrazzano, 1524–1528.* New Haven: Yale University Press.

INDIA AND SOUTHEAST ASIA, 1450 TO 1770 CE

The collapse of the Chola state in the 13th century ended a great era of Indian seafaring during which a succession of Chola kings waged naval campaigns in Burma and Indonesia, and Indian merchants operated throughout the Indian Ocean and established trading posts throughout Southeast Asia, East Africa, and Egypt. Indian merchants remained active afterward, but Arab and Persian traders increasingly dominated trade between the Middle East and India. Merchants from throughout Southeast Asia sailed the eastern Indian Ocean, as did Chinese traders. When Vasco da Gama (ca. 1460–1524 CE) arrived off Calicut, India, in 1498 CE, his expedition encountered wealthy local kingdoms, successful merchants, and trading networks that crisscrossed the region. Da Gama began a process of European conquest in the Indian Ocean that required more than 250 years to complete, as Spanish, Dutch, English, and French merchants and fleets arrived in the region and fought both one another and local kingdoms. Local maritime traditions and seafaring persisted as European conquest transformed the region and Europeans gained increasing control of Indian Ocean trade. Following a succession of wars, Britain emerged as the region's dominant power in the late-18th century.

In the mid-15th century, India remained at the center of trade across the Indian Ocean. Indian merchants operated from a variety of Indian and foreign ports. Although India itself was politically divided, trade flourished across the Indian Ocean, carried by ships from diverse ports. The most common ships, collectively called "dhows," generally employed a single mast, triangular lateen sail, sternpost rudder, and a hull made from planks sewn together with coconut-fiber rope (several hundred miles of which were needed for a 100-foot ship). Indian builders produced ships of varying sizes, generally between 50 and 500 tons. They carried a variety of cargos, ranging from spices, metals, and textiles to pearls, rare gems, and even elephants (for which there was a small export market). The ships of Gujarat, built of teak, were prized for their longevity and Gujarati merchants continued to trade with the Persian Gulf, sailing along the coast, into the 20th century. Much of the region's trade focused on spices, pound-for-pound the most valuable trade good: cinnamon from Ceylon (Sri Lanka), pepper from India's Malabar coast and Sumatra in Indonesia, mace and nutmeg from the Banda Islands in eastern Indonesia, cloves from the Molucca Islands, and sandalwood and other aromatic woods and resins from numerous Southeast Asian ports.

China's government officially discouraged foreign trade after the 1430s, but private junks continued to travel to Indonesia and the Philippines to trade copper, iron, musk, porcelain, pottery, satin, silk, and other products for local goods. China, in fact, was the primary customer for Southeast Asia spices in the 16th century, consuming about three-quarters of the output, particularly pepper. Most of the remaining spices were exported to India, and—along with pepper and other Indian spices—exported west to the Islamic World through the Persian Gulf or Red Sea. Some of the spices were re-exported from there to Europe—a trade dominated by Venetian merchants. Apart from spices, the major products traded in the Indian Ocean were silk and porcelain from China; cotton textiles and precious stones from India; and glass, jewelry, and pottery produced in a number of locations. Several regions, particularly Bengal, exported rice to the Middle East, and Bengal also produced and exported a number of manufactured goods. Long voyages that spanned the length of the Indian Ocean, which were common in the past were rare in this era. Rather, goods passed through a succession of traders who carried them on short voyages. These traders included Arabs, Armenians, Burmese, Chinese, Indian, Javanese, Jews, Malay, Persians, and many other ethnicities.

Many traders were members of multi-ethnic trading communities or guilds, and these, particularly in Indonesia, proved a check on the power of local rulers, who often exercised little authority beyond port centers. Tension between ports, enriched by growing trade, and increasingly multi-ethnic and multi-cultural, and the agricultural interior of most Indonesian islands was endemic. Ferdinand Magellan (ca. 1480–1521 CE) was drawn into one of these disputes after arriving in the Philippines and died as a result. No polity dominated Southeast Asian trade as Srivijaya had at its peak 500 years earlier, although Malacca's excellent port and location dominating the Strait of Malacca made it a nexus of trade between China, India, and Indonesia, as well as an importer of cloth, porcelain, and other goods thanks to its growing wealth.

Vasco da Gama's 1498 CE arrival at Calicut, the largest port on India's Malabar Coast, sparked little immediate interest among local rulers, and the trade goods he offered generated even less. Although Europeans had become sophisticated seafarers whose ships outclassed those common to the Indian Ocean, they had little to offer local merchants other than precious metals. Portuguese captains quickly learned about local trade, in part by hiring local navigators, and also were quick to recognize the opportunities presented by the region's maritime geography. Trade passed through several chokepoints, and Portuguese leaders focused their attention on capturing these, along with strategically located and defensible ports. They hoped to achieve something unprecedented in the region's history, a complete monopoly on trade through the Indian Ocean.

The tremendous firepower and strong hulls of European warships often enabled them to overwhelm local defenses and seize ports—especially among the islands of Indonesia—but India's many coastal principalities, as well as the powerful Mughal Empire, which conquered Gujarat in 1572 CE, successfully resisted most European assaults. Successive Portuguese fleets defeated Calicut's navy and its Muslim ruler appealed to Fatimid Egypt for help, and Egypt dispatched a large naval expedition that reinforced Calicut's navy. Defeated off Diu in 1509 CE, the Egyptians withdrew. Periodically supported by the Ottoman Empire, which conquered Egypt in 1517 CE, Calicut intermittently ambushed isolated Portuguese ships and squadrons, but proved unable to project power far from home or dislodge the Portuguese from the island bases they steadily acquired.

Led by Alfonso de Albuquerque (1453–1515 CE), the Portuguese conquered the island of Goa in 1510 CE after learning that its majority Hindu population disliked the Muslim ruler. The following year, the Portuguese conquered Malacca. Efforts to conquer Aden at the mouth of the Red Sea failed, but the nearby island of Hormuz fell to them in 1515 CE. Along with Mozambique in East Africa and Cochin (Kochi) on India's west coast, captured respectively in 1507 CE and 1508 CE, they became the foundation of Portugal's Indian Ocean empire, the Estado da Índia. The Portuguese grew wealthy by dominating these chokepoints of trade, raiding local shipping, selling safe conduct passes to local shippers, and shipping home spices on the six-month voyage around Africa to Europe. Ottoman efforts to dislodge the Portuguese failed repeatedly, including major offensives from the Red Sea against Diu in 1538–1539 CE and Hormuz in 1554 CE. Similarly, the Sultanate of Aceh on Sumatra proved unable to dislodge the Portuguese from Malacca, despite a well-equipped navy equipped with Ottoman cannon. Nonetheless, Portuguese resources were strained. Ships regularly evaded Portuguese blockades. Over time, the Portuguese came to favor cooperative participation in local trade and licensing local merchants to operate in areas it dominated, to its earlier efforts to violently seize complete control of the spice trade.

Other Europeans eventually followed the Portuguese to the Indian Ocean. The Spanish, operating from the Americas, colonized the Philippines in the 1560s and established trade with China via their Manila Galleons. Dutch companies began arriving in 1595 CE and united to form the Dutch East India Company (VOC) in 1601 CE. Three years later, the Dutch concluded a treaty with Calicut's ruler, who still was at war with Portugal. The Dutch established their base at Batavia (Jakarta) in Java in 1619 CE, conquered the Banda Islands in 1622 CE, gained a monopoly on nutmeg and mace, and captured Malacca from Portugal in 1642 CE. The Dutch then steadily displaced the Portuguese from Ceylon. They captured the port of Colombo in 1654 CE and completed their conquest in 1665 CE, which gave them a monopoly on cinnamon. Portugal also lost Oman, which with Ottoman support successfully expelled the Portuguese in 1650 CE. Oman maintained a tenuous independence for more than a century, defeating a Persian invasion in 1741 CE, and actively traded with East Africa where its merchants established trading posts as Portuguese influence in the region declined.

England's East India Company arrived in 1601 CE, only a few years after the Dutch, but the English company proceeded more slowly, establishing bases at Madras (Chennai, 1640 CE), Bombay (Mumbai, 1661 CE), and Calcutta (Kolkata, 1690 CE). English merchants periodically encroached on Dutch trade and the two nations fought three wars between 1652 and 1674 CE, but the two companies often avoided direct hostilities and both prospered. By the 1640s, almost all the pepper and other spices arrived in Europe on ships of the VOC or EIC, a feat Portugal never managed. Into the early 19th century, Europeans paid for most Asian goods with gold and silver, which entered the region from Europe and the Americas via Spain's Manila Galleons. There also was a small demand in Asian markets for dyes, wool cloth, copper, iron, and other metals.

Europeans also entered local trade. The Dutch traded copper from Japan and cloth from India for spices in Indonesia, often coercing local rulers to trade only with them. Many Asian merchants came to prefer sending goods via European ships, which were often faster and whose armament made them difficult prey for the region's pirates, some of whom were also European. So, European shippers profited both by shipping spices and other goods back to Europe via the Cape of Good Hope and by trading among Asian ports.

By mid-18th century, the English East India Company had a lucrative business bringing Chinese tea to Europe, and the Dutch brought coffee from Java. Coffee was one of a number of products transplanted to new locations by Europeans. Before the 15th century, coffee was grown and drunk only in Yemen. Coffee-drinking spread to Egypt in the 16th century. Exported from Yemen's port of Mocha, coffee became increasingly popular in the Islamic World and reached northern Europe in the following century. To meet growing demand, the Dutch brought coffee cultivation to Java. Europeans also introduced potatoes and other New World crops into the Indian Ocean region, and these became staples of the Indian diet.

Formed in 1664 CE, the French East India Company posed a challenge to the English for the next century. It established bases off the African coast at Réunion and Mauritius and later in India at Pondichery and Chandernagore, which remained French possessions into the 20th century. Periodically supported by powerful fleets dispatched from France, the French East India Company cemented alliances with several Indian states and regularly maneuvered against its English competitor. Conflict raged in the 1740s and 1750s, culminating in the Battle of Plassey (1757 CE) at which British forces—many of them Indians—defeated the Nawab of Bengal, a key French ally.

Afterward, Britain steadily expanded its rule over all India, defeating individual rulers and states one by one over the next 50 years, and defeating a French fleet led by the redoubtable Admiral Pierre André de Suffren (1729–1788 CE) in the early 1780s. Contemporaneously, English traders steadily displaced the Dutch, especially after the Fourth Anglo-Dutch War (1781–84 CE) and the French occupation of the Netherlands during the French Revolution and Napoleonic Wars (1795–1810 CE). The India Act, passed by Britain's parliament in 1784 CE, established a

Board of Control that oversaw the EIC's operations in India and the process of establishing formal British rule over the parts of India it occupied.

After 1500 CE, a succession of European powers and merchant companies attempted to monopolize Indian Ocean trade and eliminate indigenous competition. Although they managed to gain control of long-distance trade, they never completely displaced indigenous traders and seafarers. Indians, Javanese, Malays, and others continued to sail widely and dominated coastal trade. Polities in Burma, Java, Sumatra, Vietnam, and elsewhere managed to maintain their independence and control most local trade. Nonetheless, Europeans gained control of the most profitable parts of Indian Ocean trade. As Europeans settled in the region, they entered more fully into local trade and also introduced European techniques into local shipbuilding, particularly the smaller ships used in coastal trade, which were purchased by both European and Indian merchants. European control of local trade did not become overwhelming until the introduction of steamships and the 1869 CE opening of the Suez Canal.

Stephen K. Stein

Further Reading

Alpers, Edward A. 2013. *The Indian Ocean in World History.* Oxford: Oxford University Press.

Bose, Sugata. 2009. *A Hundred Horizons: The Indian Ocean in the Age of Global Empire.* Cambridge: Harvard University Press.

Chaudhuri, K. N. 1985. *Trade and Civilization in the Indian Ocean: An Economic History from the Rise of Islam to 1750.* Cambridge: Cambridge University Press.

Furber, Holden. 1976. *Rival Empires of Trade in the Orient, 1600–1800.* Minneapolis: University of Minnesota Press.

Hall, Kenneth R. 2011. *A History of Early Southeast Asia: Maritime Trade and Societal Development, 100–1500.* Lanham, MD: Rowman & Littlefield.

Mathew, K. S. 1997. *Shipbuilding and Navigation in the Indian Ocean Region AD 1400–1800.* New Delhi: Munshiram Manoharlal.

McPherson, Kenneth. 1993. *The Indian Ocean: A History of People and the Sea.* Oxford: Oxford University Press.

Pearson, Michael. 2003. *The Indian Ocean.* New York: Routledge.

Goa

An Indian state on the western coast of the subcontinent, Goa once was a Portuguese colony. Ruled successively by Hindu and Muslim kingdoms, it was seized by Portugal in 1510 CE and became one of the most important possessions in Portugal's far-flung maritime empire in Asia.

Ruled by the Muslim dynasty of Adil Shahi since 1496 CE, Goa fell easily to General Afonso de Albuquerque's Portuguese troops in February 1510 CE. Muslim forces retook the city in May, but Albuquerque recaptured it in November with a fleet of 34 ships and the help of Hindu rebels.

Drained by several rivers (including the Mandovi and the Zuari) and possessing fine harbors, Goa was one of the busiest entrepôts on the western coast of India and had long been an important shipbuilding center. Under Portuguese rule, its dock-yards and arsenal grew to be among the most productive naval facilities in the Estado da Índia Portuguesa (the Portuguese territories in Asia). Spurred by Albuquerque's establishment of a mint in the territory, the city also flourished as a center of the spice trade—a highly lucrative activity in which the Portuguese had begun to supplant the Arabs and Venetians. The Portuguese monarchy financed Catholic missionary activity in the colony, and it served as a base for subsequent Catholic activity in Asia.

Goa became capital of the Estado in 1530 CE, replacing the port of Cochin on the southwestern coast of India. Famed for the splendor of its architecture (much of it ecclesiastical) and the elegance of its daily life, the city was known as "Golden Goa." Toward the end of the 16th century, however, its fortunes began to decline. Ships of the increasingly active Dutch navy blockaded its harbors in 1603 CE, an epidemic swept the city in 1635 CE, and another Dutch blockade followed in 1639 CE.

In the wake of aggressive British expansion during the 18th and 19th centuries, Portuguese territories in India were reduced to Goa and the small coastal enclaves of Damão and Diu. All three were forcibly annexed by the nation of India in late 1961 CE.

Grove Koger

Further Reading

Jayasuriya, Shihan de S. 2008. *The Portuguese in the East: A Cultural History of a Maritime Trading Empire.* London; New York: Tauris Academic Studies.

Pearson, M. N. 1987. *The Portuguese in India.* Cambridge; New York: Cambridge University Press.

Rao, R. P. 1963. *Portuguese Rule in Goa, 1510–1961.* Bombay; New York: Asia Publishing House.

Malacca (Melaka)

The name Malacca (also spelled "Melaka") can historically refer to one or a combination of several things: a port city; an historic sultanate or empire of the 15th and early 16th centuries; a Portuguese, Dutch, and later British colony; a province of present-day Malaysia; a synonym for the Malay Peninsula as a whole; and the Straits that separate the Malay Peninsula from the island of Sumatra.

The port of Malacca was founded around the year 1400 CE, and reached its apex a half-century later. According to legend, Malacca's rise took place against the backdrop of ancient Singapura-Temasek's decline and became the commercial, political center of the Melaka Sultanate. At its peak, this empire straddled the Malay Peninsula as well as the central-eastern parts of Sumatra and the Riau Archipelago. In the 15th century, Melaka was the foremost center of Malay culture and its ruler was also known as the "Emperor of the Malay Kings." Its thriving trade attracted the attention of a succession of European powers.

Alfonso de Albuquerque conquered the port and some surrounding lands in 1511 CE after which Malacca remained a Portuguese colony until 1640 CE when it was lost to the Dutch East India Company (VOC). Although the port and city had been taken by the Portuguese, the loyalties among the Melaka Sultan's subjects remained largely intact. The Sultanate did not end in 1511 CE, but rather in 1528 CE when the two sons of the last Sultan founded new polities: Perak and the Johor-Riau Empire. Dutch rule continued from 1641 to 1795 CE when, during the French Revolutionary Wars, the VOC colony was taken over by the British East India Company. Resulting from the Anglo-Dutch Treaty of 1824, Malacca remained a British possession, initially under East India Company rule, and together with Penang and Singapore as one of the Straits Settlements. Malacca and its surrounding territories became a state of Malaysia in 1963 CE.

Peter Borschberg

Further Reading

Borschberg, P. 2010. *The Singapore and Melaka Straits: Violence, Security and Diplomacy in the 17th Century.* Leiden and Singapore: KITLV Press and NUS Press.

Hashim, Yusoff Muhammad. 1992. *The Malay Sultanate of Malacca. A Study of Various Aspects of Malacca in the 15th and 16th Centuries in Malaysian History.* Kuala Lumpur: Dewan Bahasa dan Pustaka/Ministry of Education.

Singh Sandhu, K., and P. Wheatley. 1983. *Melaka: The Transformation of a Malay Capital, c. 1400–1980*, 2 vols. Kuala Lumpur: Oxford University Press.

Wheatley, P. 1961. *The Golden Khersonese: Studies in the Historical Geography of the Malay Peninsula before A.D. 1500.* Kuala Lumpur: University of Malaya Press.

Orang Laut

Malay for "Sea People," the term "orang laut" can refer generically to any of the nomadic maritime peoples of archipelagic Southeast Asia including the Moken of the Myanmar and Thailand Andaman coast, and the Sama-Bajau of the waters around Borneo, the Sulu archipelago, Sulawesi, and the Maluku islands. The term is used more specifically, however, to identify the proto-Malay maritime nomads that inhabit the littoral areas around the Strait of Malacca, the Indonesian Riau-Lingga archipelago, and the southern South China Sea. Orang laut primarily lived in family-sized groups aboard boats called "*sampan panjang*" ("longboats"), but sometimes employed larger craft. Their economic activities centered on fishing and gathering of foodstuff and trade products such as pearls and turtle shells from littoral zones. They were also regularly involved in piracy and provided naval and maritime constabulary forces for shore-based Malay states.

The orang laut were of particular importance to the success of Malacca Strait polities until the 19th century. Coastal states that built alliances with orang laut leaders could rely on their naval strength to protect friendly shipping and to act as privateers against rivals, thereby influencing trade patterns to create mutual profit. Under these arrangements, orang laut also provided valuable services such a harbor piloting, military scouting, slave raiding, transportation of messages and passengers, boatbuilding, and collecting rare woods. Such an alliance was a central element in the rise of Malacca as the predominant regional entrepôt during the early 15th century and is believed to have had a similar role in the enabling Svirijaya as the regional hegemon in the 7th to 10th centuries. Alliances between orang laut and Malay states ashore where similarly critical to the less-efficacious and more temporary rises of maritime polities such as Johor, Palembang, and Jambi in the 16th to 18th centuries.

The arrival of steamships and Anglo-Dutch commitment to eradicate regional piracy in the 19th century broke the political and military strength of the orang laut. By the early 20th century, many had elected to move from their boats to permanent settlements, often built on stilts. In the latter half of the 20th century, policy efforts by the modern regional states settled almost all of the families remaining afloat. The orang laut, however, remain an identifiable ethnic community with a unique Malay dialect that relies heavily upon the harvesting of maritime resources for its economic livelihood. Settlement has progressed in parallel to a general conversation from animism to Islam.

John F. Bradford

Further Reading

Andaya, Leonard. 2008. *Leaves of the Same Tree: Trade and Ethnicity in the Straits of Melaka*. Honolulu: University of Hawai'i Press.

Chou, Cynthia. 2003. *Indonesian Sea Nomads: Money, Magic and Fear of the Orang Laut*. New York: Routledge Curzon.

Sopher, David. 1977. *The Sea Nomads: A Study of the Maritime Boat People of Southeast Asia*. Singapore: National Museum.

JAPAN, 1450 TO 1770 CE

This three-century period spans a major rupture in the Japanese political structure: from the late medieval period, to the transition of power in the warring period, to the beginning of the Tokugawa (Edo) period, best known for the unbroken shogunal reign of more than 250 years (1603–1867 CE). That political restructuring had significant ramifications for maritime concerns. The earlier period saw an increase in domestic trade as central control weakened. As contact with European powers was established, foreign trade blossomed briefly, but the transitional era was also characterized by attempts at developing a centralized navy to prepare for an assault on the Korean peninsula. During the Edo period foreign contact was highly restricted, and domestic maritime-based trade again began to flourish.

Late Medieval, 1450–1550 CE

The traditional estate-based economy of the medieval period involved the tiered payment of rents and dues to proprietors, usually located in or near the central capital at Kyoto. Ships' captains were tasked with transporting those rents and dues to the overseers. In the late medieval period, however, central control over the peripheries was weakening, and local authorities were able to exert power in their immediate vicinities. As the estate system broke down, local autonomy increased. As such, marketplaces began to spring up well away from the central capital at Kyoto, and the thriving economy resulted in a growing maritime-based trade network.

Maritime Trade and Shipping

In the late medieval period, trade with China was conducted under the auspices of the central government ("*bakufu*"). Periodic delegations were sent to and from the mainland. Trade with Korea was more frequent and often bypassed official channels, as local Japanese families conducted direct exchanges with the peninsula. Major exports from Japan included sapanwood, sulfur, swords, and copper ore, and were exchanged mostly for coins, silver, silk, and brocades from China, and rice, beans, ginseng, and textiles from Korea.

Domestic maritime-based trade routes became important conduits for goods and people as local port-based marketplaces developed. Technological improvements, surplus commodity production, and the increasing use of coin as payment for those commodities all contributed to a growing need to send larger quantities of goods via ship. The thriving nature of this trade is exemplified in a record from 1445 CE, which denotes nearly 2,000 domestic vessels passing through a checkpoint at Hyōgo (modern-day Kobe). Ships as large as 150 tons transported more than 50 different types of cargo, ranging from marine goods to pottery to grains.

Piracy was an issue both domestically and abroad, and ships often paid a "protection fee" to local sea lords to ensure their safe passage through treacherous waters.

Maritime Governance

During this period there was no centralized navy or attempt to control domestic maritime infrastructure. Local rulers asserted their influence by taking control of maritime checkpoints, usually located at geographically or economically strategic chokepoints, or by commanding the right to be exempt from tolls at those checkpoints. Administrative oversight of port facilities also contributed to the local authority's coffers, as they had the right to authorize the creation of port infrastructure that would allow larger vessels into the harbor and increase the potential to bring in more trade goods.

In certain cases prominent families attempted to challenge central control over foreign trade. The Ouchi family, headquartered in Suo province (modern Yamaguchi prefecture), had been operating in conjunction with the shogunate since as early as 1398 CE. The shogun Ashikaga Yoshimitsu had requested that the Ouchi forward a request to the Choson court for a copy of the Korean Tripitaka, a set of Buddhist sutras. Despite a series of ups and downs in the meantime, the Ouchi pressed their advantage in 1468 CE. Officially accompanying a shogunal trade mission, the Ouchi family not only seized part of the shogun's cargo on its return, but also commandeered the tallies—official trade permits presented by the Chinese court to the shogunate—for future trade missions. This crippled immediate shogunal attempts to continue direct trade with China, though they soon used Korean intermediaries to explain the situation to the Chinese court and reasserted their control over foreign trade.

Warring Period and Early Unification, 1550–1600 CE

The first Europeans to arrive in Japan were the Portuguese in 1543 CE, followed soon after by the English and Dutch. Although initially trade flourished, in the late 16th and early 17th centuries Toyotomi Hideyoshi and his Tokugawa successors gradually constrained official interactions with the western nations. They enacted edicts expelling the Portuguese Jesuit missionaries and executing both foreign and Japanese Christians alike. Dutch traders stationed at the island of Dejima off the coast of Nagasaki, with less of an investment in religious conversion, were allowed to remain throughout the fluctuating fortunes of the Portuguese.

In 1592 CE, Hideyoshi invaded Korea as a first step toward his intended conquest of China, marking a rare centralized attempt at organizing a naval-based attack on the peninsula. The Japanese naval vessels were likely to have been repurposed fishing and cargo boats, and not constructed specifically for warfare. The invasion was ultimately unsuccessful, and Japan would not develop a large, centralized navy again until the late 19th century.

As terrestrial-based local lords ("*daimyo*") jockeyed for power during this period, many of the pirate families based in the Seto Inland Sea region also made efforts to legitimize their position as "sea lords." Hideyoshi, further consolidating his power over the archipelago, issued an edict in 1588 outlawing piracy in part to neutralize potential threats to his power. In effect he provided the pirate families with the legitimacy they sought, rendering them his retainers and using those former pirates to combat other pirates.

Early Tokugawa Period, 1600–1770 CE

After the Tokugawa shogunate came into power and relative peace descended on the archipelago, external sea-based threats were largely absent and once again internal maritime trade networks began to grow.

Maritime Trade and Shipping

Merchants relied heavily on immense vessels to ship their goods throughout Japan. Coastal cargo boats generally ranged from about 200 to 400 *koku* (one *koku* was thought to be roughly equivalent to about 330 pounds) in capacity in the early Edo period, and increased to up to 1000 *koku* after the restrictions on trade vessel construction were eased. As trade among different far-flung locales within Japan increased, coastal circuit routes developed that centered on Osaka as a start- or end-point. Eventually, the shogunate commissioned nautical charts and lighthouses along the coast to facilitate the sea circuit routes. Many local "*daimyo*" abolished port taxes, allowing for free trade in their domains and encouraging local growth, and emphasizing the importance of unencumbered maritime movements in stimulating the economy.

The high volume of domestic maritime trade and its effects upon the Edo's marketplaces is exemplified in the development of a ticketing system. Established to ensure higher product standards as well as equalize the chance to share in the profits, the system stipulated that at an agreed-upon date, each Osaka-based merchant company would launch a set number of ships in the first fleet of the season to Edo. Large ships waited in the harbor while a smaller, faster boat from each merchant's fleet registered at the warehouse, receiving a time-stamped ticket. The ships would then race to Edo, vying with the other merchant companies' fleets to be the first to arrive at the port of Uraga. The winning company not only would have the advantage of being first to sell their goods in Edo that season, but the captain of the winning ship also would receive a bonus and the honor of being known as the fastest boat captain along that trade route.

Maritime Governance

To enforce the isolation acts put into place by the shogunate, outside influences were prohibited not only by relegating all European trade to Dejima, but also by enacting laws forbidding Japanese ships from traveling beyond sight of the coastline. One law mandated that coastal and fishing vessels be constructed with a weak stern and a hung rudder, which resulted in a craft unsuitable for rough seas. The rudder was removable, and when in use was hung over the transom into the water. Planks extended out beyond the transom to enclose the rudder, providing some protection, but in stormy seas the rudder often was quick to break or unship. In the event that a Japanese ship was blown off course in a storm or shipwrecked and rescued by a foreign vessel, the crew often was not permitted to return directly to Japan. Although foreign visitors interpreted this legislation as strengthening isolationist policies, other evidence shows that such centrally enacted laws could have been directed at limiting naval power development in the outlying provinces. Limitations on the size of trade vessels were relaxed as early as 1638 CE, indicating that the construction limits were likely to prevent "*daimyo*" from building large military vessels.

The shifting power structure of late medieval and early modern Japan thus had dramatic ramifications on maritime practices within the archipelago. Prominent local families exerted their power as the medieval estate system weakened, allowing them to vie for control over domestic and foreign trade. Late-16th-century events ranged from first contact with European missionaries and traders to an expulsion of nearly all Western foreigners as central control over Japan was consolidated in the hands of the Tokugawa. These restrictions caused seafarers to focus again on domestic concerns, refining coastal trade and local defense networks.

Michelle Damian

Further Reading

Batten, Bruce L. 2003. *To the Ends of Japan: Premodern Frontiers, Boundaries, and Interactions*. Honolulu: University of Hawai'i Press.

Berry, Mary Elizabeth. 1989. *Hideyoshi*. Cambridge: Harvard University Press.

Damian, Michelle M. 2010. "Archaeology through Art: Japanese Vernacular Craft in Late Edo-Period Woodblock Prints." MA Thesis: East Carolina University.

Shapinsky, Peter D. 2014. *Lords of the Sea: Pirates, Violence, and Commerce in Late Medieval Japan*. Ann Arbor: University of Michigan.

Verschuer, Charlotte von. 2006. *Across the Perilous Sea: Japanese Trade with China and Korea from the Seventh to the Sixteenth Centuries*. Cornell East Asia Series. Ithaca, NY: Cornell University Press.

Wilson, Noell. 2015. *Defensive Positions: The Politics of Maritime Security in Tokugawa Japan*, 1st ed. Cambridge: Harvard University Press.

Imjin War, 1592–1598 CE

The Japanese invasion of Korea in 1592 CE marked the beginning of the seven-year Imjin War. Named after the Korean *"Imjin waeran"* or "bandit invasion," of the year *imjin* ("water dragon"), it featured several naval battles that relied on innovative warships and tactics.

Toyotomi Hideyoshi (1536–1598 CE) having recently emerged victorious from a series of civil wars, securing his rule as Shogun of Japan, dispatched an army of 150,000 to conquer Korea. His precise goals remain uncertain. He simply could have sought to keep his warriors occupied elsewhere as he consolidated his rule. Within three months, Japan's large army captured most of Korea's major cities and began preparations to invade China. Korean resistance continued, however, and Korea's naval forces attacked Japanese troop transports and supply ships, destroying many of them and disrupting the planned invasion.

Stimulated by Japanese pirate attacks, Korean Admiral Yi Sun-Shin (1545–1598 CE) developed a small but effective navy prior to the war. Like many of their contemporaries, Japanese warships carried large number of heavily armored troops to board enemy ships. Yi countered Japanese tactics by relying on maneuver and developing ships that proved difficult to board, particularly the *"geobukseon"* or "turtle ship," which relied on an armored deck to protect its oarsmen and rows of sharp spikes to deter boarders. In several battles, Yi deployed his ships in a U-shaped formation, dubbed the crane wing, enveloped the Japanese fleet, and then relied on superior maneuverability and cannons—Korean weapons being larger and having longer range—to smash the enemy fleet.

Unable to win control of the sea or secure their conquests on land, Hideyoshi agreed to a truce in 1596 CE before invading again the following year. This invasion, too, met with initial success, and Japan won its only naval victory of the war, catching most of Korea's fleet poorly deployed at the Battle of Chilchonryang and destroying most of it. The disaster forced the reinstatement of Admiral Yi, who had been dismissed for political reasons. Yi lured an overconfident Japanese force of about 133 warships and 200 supply ships into the narrow waters of the Myeongnyang Strait. The narrow waters and strong currents disrupted the Japanese fleet, and Yi, commanding only 13 warships, won a great victory, sinking or seriously damaging more than 24 Japanese warships and killing the Japanese admiral. Yi, too, died in the battle, and Hideyoshi's death shortly afterward brought the war to its end. Korean sea power had saved the nation.

Harry Barber

Further Reading

Hawley, Samuel. 2005. *The Imjin War: Japan's Sixteenth-Century Invasion of Korea and Attempt to Conquer China*. Seoul: The Royal Asiatic Society Korea Branch.

Turtle Ships

"Turtle ships" ("*Geobukseon*") were a class of early modern Korean warships. Often referred to as the world's first ironclad vessels, turtle ships employed enclosed decks and wooden roofs, covered in metal plates and spikes to protect personnel from musket and archery attacks and boarding. Some historians have disputed these assertions, however, arguing that the ship's "shell" was not actually clad in metal and comparing them to contemporary Japanese warships such as the *Atakebune*, which also likely had iron plating on the superstructures. The turtle ship, however, had a unique flat-bottom hull design that enabled its adept use in the shallow waters of the Korean littoral and its many small islands.

Turtle ships are closely associated with Admiral Yi Sun-Shin (1545–1598 CE), who scored naval victories against larger Japanese forces during the Imjin War (1592–1598 CE). Records suggest the first-ever "turtle-like" warship design dates to 1411 CE, during the reign of King Sejong (1397–1450 CE), who prioritized fielding gunpowder weapons in response to the pillaging Jurchens along Korea's northern border and the Japanese pirate raids along its coast. The turtle ships reemerged under Yi's leadership; the size was noticeably increased and the design was optimized to more effectively employ naval gunnery.

Turtle ships were used alongside the Joseon capital ships, "*Panokseon*," which had wide decks to accommodate cannons and archers, higher freeboard to increase range of fire, and protected decks for rowers. Although turtle ships have been popularized as having been keys to naval victory during the Imjin War, it is unlikely that more than four were in service at any time during the conflict.

John F. Bradford
Mingi Hyun

Holz, Heidi. 2009. "Complementary Keys to Naval Victory." *Naval History Magazine* 23(4).

Lee, Min-Woong. 2004. *Naval History of the Imjin Waeran*. Seoul: Chungaram Media.

Lim, Won-Bin. 2005. *Discussing Yi Sun-Shin's Strategy and Tactics*. Seoul: Shinseowon.

Swope, Kenneth M. 2005. "Crouching Tigers, Secret Weapons: Military Technology Employed During the Sino-Japanese-Korean War, 1592–1598." *The Journal of Military History* 69(1): 11–41.

Turnbull, Stephen. 2002. *Samurai Invasion: Japan's Korean War, 1592–1598*. London: Cassel and Co.

Nagasaki

Beginning in 1571 CE and continuing for nearly three centuries, Nagasaki was Japan's premier transpacific trading port. The only place the Shogun's government allowed Western ships to land and the hub of a thriving inter-Asian maritime trade, Nagasaki was the door through which goods, people, and ideas from around the world entered Japan.

Nagasaki is located on the western edge of Kyushu Island. In the 16th century that put it right at the crossroads of an emerging transpacific trade network linking China, Southeast Asia, and Western Europe. Eager to capitalize on this, the warlord Omura Sumitada (1532–1587 CE) shepherded Portuguese ships to a fishing village in his domain in 1571 CE. The experiment worked. Nagasaki quickly became a thriving mercantile center, with Portuguese and Spanish ships trading goods from Goa, Macau, Manila, and Lisbon in return mostly for Japanese silver. Concerned, however, that Portuguese missionaries and traders saw Nagasaki as their foothold for larger conquest, the Shogun Toyotomi Hideyoshi (1536–1598 CE) and his successors clamped down. They expelled missionaries in 1587 CE, outlawed Christianity in 1614 CE, and finally banished the Portuguese entirely in 1639 CE.

Nagasaki adapted. To appease the Shogun's suspicions, in 1634 CE merchants built a small island called Dejima to contain the Portuguese. When the Portuguese were ousted, Dejima hosted the Dutch East India Company in return for a trade monopoly: no other Western nation could land ships in Japan. Crammed onto Dejima's three-square acres, where—forbidden to cross the narrow, gated bridge between their island and the city—Dutch traders jostled for space with barnyard animals, a vegetable garden, servants, and warehouses. To compound their isolation and boredom, the Shogun permitted only two Dutch ships to land each year. Their goods, however, were welcomed. From cane sugar to scientific instruments, novelties flowed into Dejima that spread throughout Japan, making Nagasaki one of the more exotic places in the Shogun's realm. Those eager to learn more about the West flocked to Nagasaki where they could learn Dutch and read and translate Western books on mathematics, astronomy, medicine, and natural sciences. From 1641 CE until American ships arrived in 1853 CE and upended the Dutch monopoly, Nagasaki was Japan's only Western portal.

Despite its fame as a Dutch trading port, however, Nagasaki depended far more on the China trade. Although the Shogun allowed the Dutch only two vessels a year, in the late 1600s CE as many as 200 Chinese ships sailed into Nagasaki annually. Fearing Japanese silver mines would be emptied to pay for these goods, the Shogun restricted the number of Chinese ships, but captains and merchants simply offloaded sugar, ginseng, silk, medicine, and ivory at nearby smuggler's coves instead. Profits overwhelmed caution. Also, although laws restricted the Nagasaki Chinese to a residential quarter, their influence was still great. Only a handful of Japanese could read Dutch, but many could read the Chinese books flooding the city, which kept Japan updated about world events and new ideas. Chinese traders, moreover, transshipped goods from across Southeast Asia, providing Japan a link to its Pacific neighbors.

Gavin James Campbell

Further Reading

Clulow, Adam. 2013. *The Company and the Shogun: The Dutch Encounter with Tokugawa Japan*. New York: Columbia University Press.

Hellyer, Robert I. 2009. *Defining Engagement: Japan and Global Contexts, 1640–1868*. Cambridge: Harvard University Press.

Jansen, Marius. 1991. *China in the Tokugawa World*. Cambridge: Harvard University Press.

THE NETHERLANDS, 1450 TO 1770 CE

The "Republic of the Seven United Netherlands"—familiarly known as the "Dutch Republic" or the "United Provinces"—emerged as a consequence of political and religious rebellion against Philip II of Spain (1527–1598 CE). Following 80 years of war, the Calvinist Dutch Republic secured independence in 1648 CE. During the war's course, the Republic became one of Europe's most powerful states, due in large part to its domination of maritime trade. The combination of maritime technology, financial innovation, trade networks, and public investment made the Dutch Republic Europe's most vibrant and efficient state, able to transform its growing wealth into economic and military power. The founding of the east and west India trading companies, established the Republic as a global power, with Amsterdam its financial center and trade entrepôt. Yet, Dutch dominance of world trade led to a series of wars that eroded its position. After 1715 CE, the Netherlands entered a period of decline due to exhausting warfare, changing market conditions, and structural weaknesses. Although it remained a financial power through the end of the century, by 1750 CE Britain had replaced the Dutch Republic as Europe's leading maritime power.

Origins and Revolt, 1516–1572 CE

The Dutch Republic's history is closely tied to its geography. Low-lying territories in the Rhine and Meuse River delta, the Netherlands or "Low Countries" developed through the reclamation of land from the sea in the 12th century, fostering agricultural innovation. With access to the English Channel, the North Sea, and the Rhine, these towns used their wealth—developed through maritime activities, manufacturing, and agriculture—to gain significant political autonomy. Unified in the 15th century by the Dukes of Burgundy, the "Burgundian Netherlands," later termed the "Seventeen Provinces," were among Emperor Charles V's (1500–1558 CE) wealthiest domains.

Among the Seventeen Provinces, Flanders and Brabant became Europe's most populous and economically advanced territories. Antwerp, their preeminent city, developed into northern Europe's economic and financial hub boasting a population of more than 40,000 inhabitants and several luxury manufactures including the Flemish cloth industry. At the same time, Holland and Zeeland became the Seventeen Provinces' most important shipbuilders and cargo haulers. The development of the full-rigged herring buss in the early 15th century—a ship that enabled a small crew to catch and process their herring at sea—led to Holland's and Zeeland's virtual monopoly of the North Sea herring grounds for centuries. By mid-century, the northern provinces boasted 500 herring busses (Van Houtte 1977, 152–53; Israel 1989, 24). Holland displaced the Hanseatic League in Baltic shipping in the 15th century and by 1550 CE dominated Baltic trade. Its 1,800 merchant ships accounted for 70 percent of Seventeen Provinces' shipping. Toll registers reveal Dutch ships transported 66 percent of the salt, 74 percent of the Rhine wine, and 76 percent of the herring entering the Baltic, and 70 percent of the outward bound wheat and 81 percent of the rye were carried in Dutch hulls (Israel 1989, 24; Van Houtte 1977, 184–85).

The Seventeen Provinces' tradition of independence ultimately led to conflict with Spain. Philip II's (1556–1598 CE) succession to the Habsburg throne in 1556 CE brought greater Spanish influence to the Seventeen Provinces through which Calvinism spread. Attacks on Catholic Church iconography in 1566 CE led Philip to dispatch the Duke of Alba (1507–1582 CE) with an army to suppress the rebellion. Alba's brutal repression, which included the execution of several high-ranking nobles, led to open war with Netherlandish nobility in 1568 CE. Some nobles left for the Holy Roman Empire to raise armies; others took to the sea—the so-called "Sea Beggars"—to raid Spanish shipping as privateers. Prince William I of Orange (1533–1584 CE), a member of the States General and leading Netherlandish noble, became the rebellion's leader. Defeated by Alba's army, he retreated to Germany leaving the Low Countries under Alba's control.

Establishing the Dutch Republic, 1572–1609 CE

Alba's unpopular rule provoked new rebellions. The Sea Beggars' seizure of Brielle (Brill) on April 1, 1572, followed by the defection of several nobles to the rebels, led William to reassert his position as *Stadholder* of Holland and Zeeland— the *de facto* chief executive of those provinces—and renew rebellion in the north. Alba responded with calculated brutality, murdering the inhabitants of several captured towns. This strengthened Dutch resistance and William, supported by the Sea Beggars' ships, recaptured most of the northern towns. For much of the 1580s, the Dutch struggled both to establish a government and survive the Spanish onslaught. The 1585 CE fall of Antwerp marked a low point, as thousands of Calvinists fled north ending that city's preeminence and inadvertently contributing to Holland's economic expansion. Alliance with England, the Spanish Armada's defeat (1588 CE), and civil war in France all diverted Spain's attention and energies, which enabled the fledgling Dutch state to forge a government capable of sustaining the war.

The Union of Utrecht—and the Act of Abjuration (1581 CE) that officially separated the northern provinces from Spain—defined the emerging Dutch state's confederate structure. Disagreement amongst the provinces over government structure left the States General as their central federal institution. Although in theory the States General required unanimity to act, in reality Holland and the Stadholders—drawn from the noble houses of Orange and Nassau—exercised tremendous influence. Maurice of Nassau's (1567–1625 CE) appointment to Holland's stadholderate, following William of Orange's 1584 assassination, and the 1586 elevation of Johan Oldenbarnevelt (1547–1619 CE) to Land's Advocate—the Republic's most important political positions—exemplify Holland's sway.

The organization of the navy mirrored the Republic's confederate nature. From the revolt's inception, the provinces' maritime interests were a central concern. The character of the early rebellion resulted in northern cities and towns developing their own fleets, harbor facilities, and naval administrations. Although the States General desired a unified navy, provincial rivalry prevented it. In 1597 CE, the Republic established five separate admiralties—three in Holland (Amsterdam, the *Maze* [Maas], and *Noorderkwartier*), and one each in Zeeland (Middelburg) and Friesland (Dokkum/Harlingen). The admiralties were responsible for their own incomes, collecting a variety of tolls, taxes, and duties—established by the States General—to pay for escort ships for the merchant fleets. Additionally, the admiralties organized convoys and employed privateers to raid enemy shipping. Special subsidies from the States General provided additional funds as needed, especially for warship construction.

Spain's 1598 CE embargo of Dutch trade fostered a change in Dutch strategy that transformed the war and the nature of the Dutch state. Instead of a naval war aimed at controlling the sea lanes, Dutch maritime strategy targeted Spain's trade and economy and simultaneously expanded its own. In 1599 CE, Dutch ships attacked Portuguese settlements in Africa and Brazil for the first time, and armed merchantmen entered the Indian Ocean and Caribbean Sea with the goal of disrupting and displacing Iberian trade. The establishment of the Dutch East India Company in 1602 CE—better known by its Dutch acronym "VOC"—epitomized this strategy, bringing the promise of private investment and profit to the conflict. Governed by a board of directors working closely with the States General, investors and shareholders financed the VOC's military operations and reaped profits from the ships' cargoes. In 1605 CE, the VOC seized the Spice Islands from Portugal giving the Dutch a monopoly in the world's supply of nutmeg, mace, and cloves. Two years later, Dutch forces defeated a Spanish fleet off Gibraltar, demonstrating the Dutch navy's growing effectiveness.

From Golden Age to Disaster, 1609–1674 CE

The Twelve Years' Truce (1609–1621 CE) with Spain brought the Dutch Republic official recognition, improving its diplomatic status throughout Europe, but it did not bring peace. Domestic quarrels, culminating in Oldenbarneveld's clash with Maurice (and the former's defeat and execution for treason), exposed rifts in the Dutch polity between a "States" party—championed by Holland—and an "Orangist" faction supported by the stadholder's followers. Maurice's victory, coupled with the eruption of the Thirty Years' War (1618–1648 CE), and the Republic's eagerness to expand its overseas trade and possessions led to the resumption of hostilities in 1621 CE.

The Republic resumed its earlier maritime and economic strategy. Armies maneuvered across the fortress-dotted Low Countries, and the Republic expanded its overseas attacks and established the Dutch West India Company (WIC). A joint-stock company like the VOC, the WIC targeted Portuguese colonies and shipping in Africa and the Americas, especially the slave and sugar trades. During the company's first decades, the WIC seized Portuguese colonies on the Gold Coast and Slave Coast of Africa, and attacked Brazil's lucrative sugar trade. By 1640 CE, it had established colonies and installations in West Africa, South America, the Caribbean, and in North America (present-day New York). In 1628 CE, it attacked and captured a Spanish treasure fleet.

In Asia, the VOC expanded its trade network in the Indian Ocean and the South China Sea, becoming the region's dominant maritime power. From its headquarters in Batavia (present-day Jakarta) in Indonesia, VOC soldiers and ships—more than a thousand of all types—used force to eliminate competitors and increase market share. By 1640 CE, it had broken the Portuguese cinnamon monopoly, capturing Galle on Ceylon and established trading posts and factories in India, Malacca, Taiwan, and Japan.

In European waters, victory over Spain's fleet at the Downs in 1639 CE cemented the Republic's reputation as Europe's most powerful naval power, and Dutch merchants expanded their share of Europe's trade, in large part due to the development of the "*fluyt*," a cheap, purpose-built merchant ship designed to haul large cargoes with minimal crews. The Republic's dominance first of the Baltic trade and then the Iberian, Mediterranean, and Asian trades made Amsterdam Europe's premier trade entrepôt. By the mid-17th century, the Dutch owned close to 15,000 merchant ships, three-quarters of Europe's total (De Vries 1976, 118).

The Peace of Munster (1648 CE) ended the Eighty Years' War, but also brought the Republic new challenges. Renewed war with Portugal in the 1650s ejected the

WIC from Brazil, the first of many blows to the company. More significantly, resentment of the Republic's trade primacy led to a series of naval wars with England, followed by more dangerous wars with France. The First Anglo-Dutch War (1652–54 CE) found the Dutch navy outclassed by England's new purpose-designed warships and line-ahead tactics, but Johan de Witt's (1625–1672 CE) shipbuilding program redressed the balance and the Republic won the Second Anglo-Dutch War (1665–67 CE). France's King Louis XIV, however, united France and England in common cause during the Third Anglo-Dutch War (1672–74 CE), part of the larger Franco-Dutch War (1672–78 CE). As the French invasion exposed the Dutch army's lack of preparedness, Dutch fleets, led by Michiel de Ruyter (1607–1676 CE) dominated the sea, finally driving England from the war in 1674 CE. The French land invasion was more dangerous, causing panic that led to the elevation of 21-year-old Prince William III of Orange as Stadholder following de Witt's murder.

War and Decline, 1674–1795 CE

The Anglo-Dutch Wars did little permanent damage to Dutch trade, despite the loss of several thousand merchant ships. More significant were the continuing threat Louis XIV posed, and the Republic's temporary loss of its spice trade monopoly—an indication of weaknesses in the VOC's trade model. War with France not only deprived the Republic of significant markets, but directly threatened the state itself, requiring increasing defense expenditures. The Nine Years' War (1688–97 CE) and War of the Spanish Succession (1701–14 CE) marked the high point in the Republic's military power. With a population of slightly less than 2 million inhabitants, the Dutch Republic fielded 120,000 troops and 113 ships, financed mostly through borrowing (Glete 2002, 155–71). The Republic's public debt increased from 38 million guilders in 1678 CE to 128 million in 1714 CE, at the very time the Dutch economy was under the most distress (Israel 1995, 985–86). Wars with France not only deprived Amsterdam merchants of their French markets, but of their Mediterranean ones as well. The Anglo-Dutch alliance, established by William III's "Glorious Revolution" (1688 CE), opened Dutch-dominated markets to English merchants, especially the Baltic trade. Concurrently, Dutch financiers found new investment opportunities in the Bank of England, the East India Company, and the English National Debt which buoyed Britain's economy and hurt the Republic's. By the conclusion of the War of the Spanish Succession, the structure of world trade had shifted in Britain's favor. The lost primacy in the Mediterranean to France; Britain gained access to Spain's colonial trade; and the Dutch lost their virtual monopoly over the Baltic trade.

In the years following the Peace of Utrecht (1714 CE), the Republic's economic decline continued. Although still a considerable trading power, growing protectionism in European markets hurt Dutch manufacturers, undermining one of the last pillars of the Dutch economy. Changes in the structure of Dutch society and the nature of capital markets led Dutch capital to flow to safer investments and enabled fiscally conservative oligarchs to dominate politics. Even in Asia, where the VOC continued to prosper through the 18th century, its infrastructure costs—ships, fortresses, soldiers, and warehouses—increasingly cut into profits, as European competitors employed leaner, more cost-effective business models. The War of the Austrian Succession marked the Republic's definitive exit from the ranks of Europe's great powers. Its abysmal performance in that conflict followed by political revolution marked the beginning of the end. A final conflict with Britain—the catastrophic Fourth Anglo-Dutch War (1780–84 CE)—confirmed the Republic's fall as a maritime power.

John M. Stapleton

Further Reading

Bruijn, Jaap R. 1990. *The Dutch Navy of the Seventeenth and Eighteenth Centuries.* Columbia, SC: University of South Carolina Press.

De Vries, Jan. 1976. *The Economy of Europe in an Age of Crisis, 1600–1750.* London: Cambridge University Press.

Gastraa, Femme S. 2003. *The Dutch East India Company: Expansion and Decline.* Zutphen: Walberg Pers.

Glete, Jan. 2000. *Warfare at Sea, 1500–1650: Maritime Conflicts and the Transformation of Europe.* London: Routledge.

Glete, Jan. 2002. *War and the State in Early Modern Europe: Spain, the Dutch Republic and Sweden as Fiscal-Military States, 1500–1660.* London: Routledge.

Harding, Richard. 1999. *Seapower and Naval Warfare, 1650–1830.* London: UCL Press.

Israel, Jonathan I. 1989. *Dutch Primacy in World Trade, 1585–1740.* Oxford, UK: Clarendon Press.

Israel, Jonathan I. 1995. *The Dutch Republic: Its Rise, Greatness, and Fall, 1477–1806.* Oxford, UK: Clarendon Press.

Parthesius, Robert. 2010. *Dutch Ships in Tropical Waters: The Development of the Dutch East India Company (VOC) Shipping Network in Asia, 1595–1660.* Amsterdam: Amsterdam University Press.

Van Houtte, J. A. 1977. *An Economic History of the Low Countries 800–1800.* New York: St. Martin's Press.

Anglo-Dutch Wars, 1652–1674 CE

The Anglo-Dutch Wars were a series of maritime conflicts fought in the second half of the 17th century between England and the United Provinces of the

Netherlands. Although traditionally portrayed as economic affairs fought for trade and colonies, nationalism, domestic politics, and religion influenced all three conflicts. Fought largely at sea, by the conclusion of the Third Anglo-Dutch War in 1674 CE it was clear that the Dutch Republic had retained its primacy in European trade, though English maritime trade and power continued to grow, surpassing the Dutch by the mid-18th century. The two would fight a fourth war—an offshoot of the American War for Independence—but by then England had become Europe's dominant maritime power and the war confirmed this status.

The first war's origins can be traced to English jealousy created by the disparity between Dutch and English maritime trade, coupled with the political unrest created by the English Civil War (1642–1651 CE). By the 17th century, the Dutch Republic dominated Europe's carrying trade and also rapidly was becoming Europe's dominant naval power. Cheaper to build and operate, Dutch *fluyt* ships carried more than half of Europe's cargoes, enabling the Republic to ship goods far cheaper than any of its competitors. England's Parliament passed the Navigation Acts (1651 CE) to redress the Anglo-Dutch trade balance, but this had little real impact except to demonstrate England's growing frustration with Dutch trade supremacy. The execution of King Charles I of England (1649 CE)—linked to the Dutch House of Orange through marriage—further antagonized Dutch officials, and Dutch refusals of English proposals for an Anglo-Dutch political union further increased tensions. England's seizure of Dutch merchant ships and their insistence on receiving salutes from Dutch warships in the English Channel led to hostilities in May 1652. The First Anglo-Dutch War (1652–54 CE) proved brief but eventful. The English Royal Navy—with its more modern ships and line-ahead tactics—held the upper-hand for much of the war. Nevertheless, the Dutch victory at Scheveningen (August 1653 CE) broke the English blockade. Peace was concluded in April 1654 CE, but it did little to resolve the war's issues. The Dutch remained Europe's dominant trading power and immediately embarked upon a shipbuilding program to modernize the fleet.

The Second and Third Anglo-Dutch Wars were more politically driven than the first. Although trade and maritime rivalry remained central, domestic politics in England and the Dutch Republic also were important factors. Initially, England's King Charles II (1630–1685 CE) had little desire for war, having spent his exile in the Dutch Republic, but concern over the political future of his nephew—Prince William III of Orange—in the Dutch Republic, coupled with the colonial ambitions of his brother James (1633–1701 CE), convinced him to go to war. A series of unprovoked English assaults on Dutch colonies and shipping led to formal hostilities on March 4, 1665. A more evenly matched contest than the first, the Second Anglo-Dutch War (1665–67 CE) soon devolved into an attritional struggle as both sides won costly but inconclusive battles. Although England captured the Dutch colony of New Netherlands (modern New York), King Charles's inability to finance the war produced one of the most humiliating defeats in Royal Navy history. The Dutch raided the Medway (June 1667 CE) where many English ships were laid up, capturing two and burning more than a dozen others. Charles agreed to peace two months later.

Humiliated by his defeat, Charles II seized the opportunity to support France in the Franco-Dutch War (1672–78 CE), a conflict initiated by Louis XIV (1638–1715 CE) with the aim of cowing the Dutch Republic. Charles II believed victory in a third war would strengthen his domestic political position, but few in Parliament supported a renewed war and a French alliance proved politically (and religiously) problematic. He justified his decision for war as a strategic opportunity that he could not pass up. The French invasion of the Netherlands in May 1672 CE almost made Charles's war plans moot, as French armies tore through the Dutch defenses. By the end of June, Utrecht had fallen and Amsterdam itself was threatened. Only by flooding the countryside was Holland saved. In contrast, the Third Anglo-Dutch War (1672–74 CE) went poorly for Charles. Led by Admiral Michiel de Ruyter (1607–1676 CE)—the age's greatest naval commander—the outnumbered Dutch stymied the Anglo-French fleet at every turn, defeating it at Solebay (June 1672 CE). Charles's nephew William III (1650–1702 CE), elevated to stadholder, rebuffed his peace offers and the Anglo-French alliance fractured as Louis XIV's ambitions to conquer the Spanish Netherlands became obvious. Support for Charles II evaporated. After de Ruyter defeated another Anglo-French fleet at Texel (1673 CE), Charles agreed to peace. The Treaty of Westminster (1674 CE) largely reaffirmed the provisions of the 1667 CE treaty.

Although the Dutch remained preeminent at sea for the time being, the domestic struggle between England's Parliament and king continued, leading to the Glorious Revolution (1688 CE) in which William III and Mary II succeeded to the throne. Ultimately, it was political revolution, Anglo-Dutch cooperation, and two exhausting wars with Louis XIV's France, rather than Anglo-Dutch conflict, that allowed England to surpass the Dutch Republic as Europe's dominant maritime power in the mid-18th century.

John M. Stapleton

Further Reading

Hainsworth, Roger, and Christine Churches. 1998. *The Anglo-Dutch Naval Wars, 1652–1674*. Thrupp.

Jones, J. R. 1996. *The Anglo-Dutch Naval Wars*. New York.

Rodger, N. A. M. 2004. *The Command of the Ocean, A Naval History of Britain, 1649–1815*. New York: W.W. Norton.

Rommelse, Gijs. 2007. *The Second Anglo-Dutch War (1666–1667): International Raison d'Etat, Mercantilism, and Maritime Strife*. Hilversum.

Dutch East India Company

The *Vereenigde Nederlandse Geoctroyeerde Oostindische Compagnie* or "United Netherlands Chartered East India Company"—better known by its Dutch acronym VOC—was a powerful company that dominated the Asia trade in the 17th and 18th centuries. Established in 1602 CE, the VOC was among the earliest joint-stock companies and is considered the world's first multi-national corporation. With the power to wage war, negotiate treaties, mint coins, and establish colonies, the VOC was almost a state unto itself. It employed more than one million Europeans during the company's lifetime and shipped more than 2.5 million tons of Asian goods to Europe and the world. After a century of spectacular growth, however, the VOC gradually declined in the 18th century, a consequence of the growing influence of other European trading companies in the region and the VOC's own structural weaknesses. Nevertheless, the VOC remained an important trading concern until its demise in 1795 CE, paying an annual dividend of 18 percent for much of its 200-year history.

Origins and Organization

The VOC had its origins in Dutch merchants' desire to develop contacts in the Portuguese-dominated Asian spice trade. Increasing demand for Asian spices in northern Europe—when changing Portuguese trade practices limited its availability—created an opportunity for ambitious Dutch merchants anxious to develop their own

An illustration of the flag of the Dutch East India Company, headquartered in Batavia (now Jakarta) in Java. (Library of Congress)

Asian trade. Having gained firsthand knowledge of Portugal's "secret" trade routes and practices, Dutchmen who had worked for the Portuguese in Asia provided the information needed to make the journey. Cornelis de Houtman's successful 1595 CE voyage convinced Dutch merchants and investors of their financial potential. Between 1595 CE and 1601 CE, they sent 15 separate fleets to Asia, but their successes unintentionally increased the price of pepper in Asia and caused it to plummet in Europe, endangering the Dutch economy. This situation led the Dutch States General—the Republic's governing body—to intervene. In 1602, the States General and the companies forged a compromise: the "United Netherlands Chartered East India Company," commonly referred to as the VOC.

The VOC's organization mirrored the decentralized Dutch Republic itself. Its six *Kamers*—or "Chambers"—had their own boards of directors, warehouses, and facilities headquartered in cities representing the founding companies. A 17-member board of directors, called the "*Heren XVII*" or "Gentlemen Seventeen" managed the chambers. The VOC was closely tied to the Dutch state. The States General required senior VOC officials to swear oaths of loyalty and submit regular situation reports. It also encouraged VOC fleets to attack Portuguese and Spanish ships—states with which the Republic was at war. After 1609 CE, the VOC appointed a governor-general. The company's highest authority in Asia, the post also presided over the Council of the Indies formed to oversee company interests in the region.

Early expeditions to Asia required significant capital outlays that, during the first decade, exceeded their profits. Like modern limited liability companies, investors were only liable for the amount of their investment, though they also had considerably less control over the VOC's management. In 1610 CE, shareholders began receiving dividends on their investments, and the VOC remained highly profitable through the end of the century.

Expansion and Growth, 1602–1672 CE

The VOC's original charter granted a 21-year monopoly on Dutch trade east of Cape Good Hope, which its directors were willing to wage war to protect. Jan Pieterzoon Coen, Governor-General from 1617 CE to 1623 CE, established the aggressive strategy that characterized the company's operations during the early 17th century. Coen believed force would be central to the VOC's future success stating, "Trade without war, and war without trade cannot be maintained" (Parthesius 2010, 38). Fighting local magnates and European trading companies alike, the VOC "literally conquered their supremacy in the spice trade" (Parthesius 2010, 38). Central to Coen's strategy was establishing a permanent base to serve as headquarters, rendezvous for European-bound return voyages, and entrepôt for trade-goods and supplies. When the VOC captured Jakarta in 1619 CE—renamed

Batavia—it became that headquarters. With its powerful fleet, army, and logistical infrastructure, the VOC used trade and war to cow the English and supplant the Portuguese as the dominant European power in Asia. By 1660 CE, Dutch fortresses and factories dotted the Indian Ocean and South China Sea, from South Africa and the Malabar Coast in the west, to Taiwan and the Moluccas in the east.

Stagnation and Decline, 1672–1799 CE

The model that made the VOC the most powerful European power in Asia in the 17th century was one of the principal reasons for its decline in the 18th. The infrastructure that enabled the VOC to defend its monopolies through trade and war was ill-suited to changed markets in the 18th century. During the Third Anglo-Dutch War (1672–1674 CE), England broke the Dutch pepper monopoly, the first of many events that exposed the structural weaknesses of the VOC. The Republic's costly wars with Louis XIV's France further undermined the Dutch economy as Britain eclipsed the Republic as Europe's most dynamic economic power. The emergence of rival English, French, and Danish India companies, combined with the changing political situation on the subcontinent further weakened the VOC's position. Although the VOC still commanded a significant share of the Asia trade, it was not enough to offset the cost of its infrastructure. The Fourth Anglo-Dutch War (1780–1784 CE) delivered the VOC its deathblow; destroying one-half of the VOC's shipping at the very time when it could least afford it. Although Holland and Zeeland tried to nationalize the company, its charter was allowed to expire in 1799 CE, marking the end of the once great company.

John M. Stapleton

Further Reading

Boxer, Charles R. 1965. *The Dutch Seaborne Empire, 1600–1800.* London: Hutchinson.

Gaastra, Femme S. 2003. *The Dutch East India Company: Expansion and Decline.* Zutphen: Walburg Pers.

Israel, Jonathan I. 1989. *Dutch Primacy in World Trade, 1585–1740.* Oxford: Oxford University Press.

Parthesius, Robert. 2010. *Dutch Ships in Tropical Waters: The Development of the Dutch East India Company (VOC) Shipping Network in Asia, 1595–1660.* Amsterdam: Amsterdam University Press.

Fluyt

The "*fluyt*" (also called *fluitschip*, *flyte*, or *flute*) was a 17th-century Dutch merchant ship. Efficiently designed as an all-purpose cargo vessel, the oceangoing *fluyt* maximized cargo space and required only a small crew. In the early 17th century they became the ship of choice for Dutch traders.

The first *fluyt* was designed and built in 1595 CE by Pieter Jansz Vael (also called Pieter Jansz Liorne) (1561–1620 CE). It was the first ship built specifically for commerce. Earlier ships were intended for both warfare and cargo; they were big and heavy to support cannon and accommodate a large crew.

A typical *fluyt* measured about 80 to 100 feet in length with a tall, narrow stern. The hull was rounded with a bulge near the waterline and narrowed toward the top, a feature known as tumblehome architecture. This design placed the weight of the cargo near the waterline, which lowered the ship's center of gravity, increasing its stability. It also reduced the tolls *fluyts* paid, because they generally were calculated based on a ship's deck surface. The economical *fluyt* could carry twice the cargo of a similarly sized vessel.

Usually the *fluyt* was fitted with three masts. The fore and main masts carried square sails and the mizzen mast had a lateen (triangular) sail, all of which employed a simplified rigging system that improved handling against the wind and requiring fewer sailors—sometimes as few as a dozen men, though three dozen was more common.

At first, *fluyts* primarily were used in the Baltic trade routes and the coastal routes of Northern and Western Europe, which were relatively safe from pirates, thus enabling them to carry minimal armament. The Dutch East India Company (VOC), which favored the box-shaped *fluyts* for transporting its precious cargoes of spices and coffee, armed its Asian-bound vessels with cannon.

Inexpensive to build and operate, *fluyts* gave Dutch traders a tremendous advantage in the 17th century, and were instrumental in building the Netherlands' trading empire. Their efficient design inspired later Dutch, British, French, and Swedish merchant ships, particularly East Indiamen.

Karen S. Garvin

Further Reading

Boxer, C. R. 1990. *The Dutch Seaborne Empire: 1600–1800*. London: Penguin.

Hoving, A. J. 2012. *Nicolaes Witsen and Shipbuilding in the Dutch Golden Age*. College Station, TX: Texas A&M University Press.

Konstam, Angus. 2003. *The Pirate Ship 1660–1730*. Botley, UK: Osprey Publishing.

Lavery, Brian. 2004. *Ship: The Epic Story of Maritime Adventure*. New York: Dorling Kindersley Limited.

Parthesius, Robert. 2010. *Dutch Ships in Tropical Waters: The Development of the Dutch East India Company (VOC) Shipping Network in Asia 1595–1660*. Amsterdam: Amsterdam University Press.

Grotius, Hugo, 1583–1645 CE

Huig de Groot—better known by his Latinized name, Hugo Grotius—was a Dutch jurist and diplomat. He is remembered today for his contributions toward the development of modern international law and maritime law.

Grotius was born into a patrician family in the Dutch city of Delft on April 10, 1583. An exceptionally gifted child, King Henri IV of France dubbed him "the Miracle of Holland." Hugo matriculated at the age of 11 at the States College (now University) of Leiden, and obtained a *doctorate utriusque juris* from the University of Orléans in France in 1598 CE. This marked the beginning of a steep career in politics in the Dutch Republic. He became a right hand of the Republic's senior statesman Johan van Oldenbarnevelt, whose patronage helped him rise quickly through the government. He served as Historiographer of Holland, Advocaat Fiscaal (a type of public prosecutor), Pensionary of Rotterdam (secretary to the city government), and as a delegate to the provincial and federal estates. Concurrently, Grotius acted as a lobbyist for the Dutch East India Company (VOC).

After 1610 CE, he became increasingly involved in the religious disputes within Dutch Calvinism. These disputes erupted into a constitutional crisis which ended when Stadholder Maurice of Nassau, the Prince of Orange, staged a coup in August 1618 CE. Grotius was arrested with a number of other leading figures in politics and the judiciary. Oldenbarnevelt was executed, and Grotius was sentenced to life imprisonment.

Grotius used his time in prison to write. He escaped in 1622 CE and fled to Paris, where he entered into the employ of Louis XIII of France. There, he penned what is arguably his most famous book today: *Three Books on the Law of War and Peace* (*De Jure Belli ac Pacis Libri Tres*) published in 1625 CE, and subsequently revised until the author's death. Prevented from returning to the Dutch Republic, he later entered the service of Queen Christina of Sweden and her powerful chancellor, Axel Oxenstierna. He became a Swedish subject and served as Sweden's ambassador to France during the final phase of the Thirty Years' War. Financially stretched by the war effort, Grotius was recalled from Paris, and traveled via Hamburg and Lübeck to Stockholm where he received a handsome pension. After turning down a position as councilor in the Swedish government, he departed for an unknown destination. Grotius's ship was caught in a terrible storm and wrecked off the coast of Poland. Exhausted and ill, Grotius headed overland to Rostock where he died in an inn located just off the main market square on August 28, 1645.

A prodigious author, his works range from poetry, history, and biblical criticism to commentaries on natural law and international law. Maritime historians remember Grotius for a pamphlet which he originally published anonymously in 1609 titled, "The Free Sea." In this he sets out the legal argument for the Dutch to defy Portuguese acts of obstruction, sail the high seas at will, and call at ports and emporia in the East Indies that were not controlled by the Portuguese or Spanish. In doing so, he laid a foundation for later maritime law. Later, as a VOC lobbyist and delegate to Anglo-Dutch colonial conferences of 1613 CE in London and 1615 CE in the Hague, he fiercely defended Dutch efforts to exclude competitors from the spice trade and so played a role in the genesis of the Dutch spice monopoly in Asia. Throughout, Grotius grounded his arguments in law and history and thus contributed to the law of nations.

Peter Borschberg

Further Reading

Borschberg, P. 2011. *Hugo Grotius, the Portuguese and Free Trade in the East Indies*. Singapore and Leiden: NUS Press.

Clark, G. N., and W. J. M. van Eysinga. 1940 and 1951. *The Colonial Conferences between England and the Netherlands* in 1613 and 1615, 2 vols. Leiden, Netherlands: Brill.

Grotius, H. 2004. *The Free Sea*, ed. and intr. D. Armitage, tr. R. Hakluyt. Indianapolis: Liberty Fund.

Ittersum, M. J. van. 2006. *Profit and Principle: Hugo Grotius, Natural Rights Theories and the Rise of Dutch Power in the East Indies, 1595–1615*. Leiden: Brill.

Nellen, H. J. M. 2014. *Hugo Grotius, A Lifelong Struggle for Peace in Church and State, 1583–1645*. Leiden: Brill.

Tasman, Abel Janszoon, 1603–1659 CE

Abel Janszoon Tasman was a Dutch explorer, merchant and navigator who for most of his career sailed for the Dutch East India Company (VOC). He explored and charted much of the Indian and South Pacific Oceans, discovered the Van Diemen Land Islands (present-day Tasmania), circumnavigated Australia, and mapped the New Zealand coastline and several other Pacific Islands including Tonga and Fiji. He was the first European to visit many of these islands.

Born in 1603 CE in Lutjegast, Netherlands, Tasman later lived in Batavia in the Dutch East Indies. He joined the Dutch East India Company in 1633 CE. Well regarded, he sailed as second-in-command of an expedition that explored the North Pacific between 1639 CE and 1642 CE, visiting the Philippines, Taiwan, and Japan. Afterward, company leaders dispatched Tasman in command of one of the great exploratory projects of the period, a two-ship expedition to investigate the South Pacific and what some geographers at the time labeled "Terra Australis," a southern continent whose size and location remained unclear. Between 1642 CE and 1644 CE, Tasman's expedition discovered Tasmania, and visited Mauritius, New Zealand, and other islands. Most importantly, it circumnavigated Australia, proving that it was not connected to Antarctica to the south and that sea passage existed between the two. Returning home, Tasman discovered Tonga. In a subsequent voyage in 1644 CE, he mapped the north coast of Australia. Yet, Tasman assessed Australia as a poor prospect for the Dutch East India Company, unlikely to produce a profit. Europeans therefore largely ignored Australia and surrounding islands until the 18th century.

Tasman later led a trade mission to Thailand (1647 CE) and commanded a fleet that sailed to intercept a Spanish treasure fleet near the Philippines (1648–1649 CE), but failed to catch its quarry. Convicted in 1649 CE for hanging one of his sailors without trial, he was fined and suspended. He soon sailed again for the Dutch East India Company, but retired in 1653 CE to Batavia and became a successful cargo merchant and one of the region's largest landowners. He died on October 10, 1659.

Sean Morton

Further Reading

Anderson, Grahame. 2001. *The Merchant of the Zeehaen: Isaac Gilsemans and the Voyages of Abel Tasman.* Wellington: Te Papa Press.

Sharp, A. 1968. *The Voyages of Abel Janszoon Tasman.* Oxford: Oxford University Press.

Slot, B. 1992. *Abel Tasman and the Discovery of New Zealand,* Amsterdam: O. Cramwinckel.

Velde, Willem van de, the Elder, 1611–1693 CE

A renowned Dutch draughtsman and painter of naval and maritime themes, Willem van de Velde, known as "the Elder" to differentiate him from his son who also painted maritime themes, was born in 1611 CE in Leiden, Holland. His work holds exceptional historic value as he documented key maritime actions during the height of the 17th-century Dutch Golden Age of naval expansion and maritime trade. His paintings and drawings feature exceptional attention to detail, allowing for intricate analysis of 17th-century naval architecture. He often accompanied Dutch fleets to sea and observed battles from small boats, risking his life to capture the heat of action and produce remarkably authentic portrayals of the Battle of Scheveningen (1653 CE) and other actions in the Anglo-Dutch Wars.

Van de Velde's celebration of Dutch naval accomplishments and dedication to documenting naval battle brought him to the attention of Britain's King Charles II (1630–1685 CE), who, following his restoration to the throne in 1660 CE, expanded the Royal Navy and worked to make Britain a global naval power. In 1672 CE, during the Third Anglo-Dutch War (1672–1674 CE), van de Velde made the bold decision to accept a commission from Charles II, which required him to relocate to England and paint for his country's enemy. Van de Velde moved to the Greenwich neighborhood of London, which has historically held strong ties with maritime

The Battle of Sole Bay, June 7, 1672, from the northwest. (Rijksmuseum Amsterdam)

ventures, being the former residence of the Old Royal Naval College and the current location of The National Maritime Museum. Van de Velde set up his painting studio in Queen's House, which was the royal residence designed by Inigo Jones in 1616 CE for Queen Anne of Denmark, grandmother of Charles II. As van de Velde had created a national Dutch narrative through painting, he now did the same for Britain, creating a grand, larger-than-life depiction of the Royal Navy and its conquest of the high seas in the last decades of the 17th century.

Van de Velde had a stormy relationship with Judith Adriaensdochter van Leeuwen, whom he married in 1631 CE. They divorced in 1662 CE, but later reconciled. They had three children: Magdalena (1632–? CE), Adriaen (1636–1672 CE), a landscape painter, and Willem the Younger (1633–1707 CE), who often worked with his father and became well-known for his own paintings, many of which, like his father's, were commissioned by the British government. With the accession of William and Mary to the throne in 1689 CE, Van de Velde lost his royal commission and moved away from Greenwich to near Piccadilly Circus, London. He died on December 13, 1693, in London and was buried at St. James's Church, Westminster, in London.

Jennifer Daley

Further Reading

Cordingly, David. 1982. *The Art of the van de Veldes*. "Introductory Chapter." London: National Maritime Museum.

Robinson, M. S. 1953 and 1978. *Van de Velde Drawings: A Catalogue of Drawings in the National Maritime Museum Made by the Elder and the Younger Willem van de Velde*, 2 vols. Cambridge: Cambridge University Press.

Robinson, M. S. 1990. *The Paintings of the Willem Van de Veldes*. Greenwich: National Maritime Museum.

OTTOMAN EMPIRE, 1450 TO 1770 CE

Tracing the history of Ottoman naval power frequently highlights Ottoman leaders adapting to changing geopolitical conditions when Ottoman expansion necessitated investment in creating and maintaining a navy. At the beginning of the rise of the Ottoman polity, ca. 1300 CE, a navy was unnecessary as the "*beylik*" (territory ruled by an independent Turkish lord) of Osman (r. 1299–1326 CE) was landlocked. Rival Turkish lords in western Anatolia with seacoasts on the Aegean and Mediterranean Seas, however, formed effective navies in the early 14th century when the Ottomans solely depended on land forces. Umur Bey (1334–1348 CE) the ruler of the Aydın beylik on the Aegean coast, was known by the title "Gazi" ("raider" or "warrior for the faith"), because of his naval attacks from Izmir on the Aegean islands, the Balkans, and the Black Sea coasts. The precedent of naval warfare with the claim of religious justification set by these sea gazis would be adopted by seamen associated with the Ottoman Empire in the late 15th and 16th centuries.

Once the Ottomans acquired a coastline the necessity of developing maritime power arose, if only for defense. When naval power was neglected the fortunes of the empire suffered. The Ottomans gained seacoasts by conquering their neighbors, simultaneously acquiring territories and experienced seamen. These seamen usually were drawn from the inhabitants of the coastal regions, which by the 14th century were mixed ethnically and religiously. Ottoman seamen were thus drawn from many different ethnic backgrounds, but those who were successful had the common characteristic of personal seafaring experience.

During the 15th century, the Ottoman navy was integrated with the deployment of land forces to facilitate conquests for the sultans. At the beginning of his reign, Mehmed II (r. 1451–1481 CE) was determined to conquer Constantinople due both to its strategic and symbolic significance. This conquest required coordination between land and sea forces. Mehmed II first gained control of the Bosphorus by building a fort, Rumeli Hisar, on the European shore, opposite Anadolu Hisar, the castle built by Bayezid I (r. 1389–1402 CE), on the Asian shore. Next, Ottoman forces occupied seaports along the Sea of Marmara, after which an Ottoman fleet constructed in Gallipoli sailed through the Dardanelles into the Sea of Marmara where it coordinated with the Ottoman army besieging Constantinople. The Byzantines had stretched a chain across the inlet known as the Golden Horn to keep the Ottoman fleet from opening another position on the walls of the city. During one night in April, the Ottoman forces dragged galleys over the Galata hill to the Golden Horn to bombard the sea walls. On May 29, 1453, the fleet broke the chain, entered the Golden Horn, and assisted the land forces in the conquest of the city.

The Ottoman navy played an increasingly important role in continued Ottoman expansion as Mehmed's son Bayezid II (r. 1481–1512 CE), began to include corsairs (privateers) in official Ottoman naval forces. The foundations of Ottoman sea power in the 16th century were laid in the later 15th century. Two of the most famous seamen of the 16th century—Piri Reis (d. 1553 CE), known for his cartographic work and Hayreddin Pasha (d. 1546 CE) renowned for his victories as the admiral of the Ottoman fleet—owed their naval expertise to their training as corsairs. Although both men came from the core lands of the Ottoman Empire, they achieved success independently from the Ottoman state before later serving it in an official capacity.

Naval power was crucial to Ottoman power during the reign of Süleyman the Magnificent (r. 1520–66 CE). After Selim I (r. 1512–20 CE) defeated the Mamluks in 1517 CE, the Ottomans ruled Egypt, Syria, and Arabia. To defend these territories and to benefit from their trade and resources, an effective navy was essential. In the 1530s, Süleyman recognized the necessity of finding men with naval expertise to lead Ottoman naval forces. Under the leadership of Hayreddin Pasha, Ottoman naval forces exerted control over the entire Mediterranean Sea especially after his victory at Preveza in 1538 CE. The Ottomans also influenced the balance of power in Europe as the Ottomans formed a military alliance with France. An essential component of this alliance was supporting French initiatives with the Ottoman fleet in the western Mediterranean in the 1540s and 1550s. In 1543 CE, the Ottoman fleet combined with French forces to besiege Nice and then wintered in France before returning to Istanbul in 1544 CE. Ottoman naval power continued to impact events in the 1560s, with the defeat of Habsburg forces at Djerba in 1560 CE. In 1571 CE, the Ottomans suffered a major naval defeat at Lepanto; nevertheless their naval forces facilitated the conquest of Cyprus. In 1574 CE, Ottoman land and sea forces together conquered Tunis, which ensured their control of most of the North African coast except for Morocco. The neglect of the navy after these conquests, however, which continued into the early decades of the 17th century, left Ottoman possessions vulnerable to naval attacks, especially by the Knights of Malta and other Christian corsairs.

The conquest of Egypt in 1517 CE also impacted maritime trade in the Ottoman Empire. Alexandria had been a center of trade under previous dynasties and this continued under Ottoman rule. Although many European vessels continued to trade there, in addition Ottoman maritime trade between Egypt and Istanbul become essential to the well-being of the empire. Egypt became a source for grain and treasure for Istanbul. Major naval battles between the Ottomans and the Habsburgs ceased after the Battle of Lepanto (1571 CE), but attacks on each other's merchant shipping increased in the later 16th century and in the first half of the seventeenth century. Usually the vital maritime trade between Egypt and Istanbul was protected by the Ottoman navy, but if this protection was unavailable then Ottoman shipping losses could be substantial. Controlling Egypt also led to Ottoman trade in the Indian Ocean where they encountered the Portuguese. Although the Ottoman Empire devoted most of its resources to protecting trade in the Mediterranean and Black Seas, it clashed with the Portuguese in the Indian Ocean, and prevented the Portuguese from monopolizing shipping in the region and gaining complete control of the Indian Ocean. In addition to maritime trade, Ottoman subjects traveled by sea from Istanbul to Egypt to perform the *hajj*. In the 17th century, the Ottoman-Venetian war over Crete was ignited by an attack on an Ottoman ship carrying high-ranking individuals to Egypt for the pilgrimage.

Ottoman naval success diminished as the empire's expansion came to a halt in the latter half of the 17th century. In 1644 CE, the Ottomans decided to conquer Crete, a possession of Venice. This was the empire's last major territorial acquisition. The expedition against Crete began in the spring of 1645 CE and although most of the island was quickly conquered, the fortress city of Candia (Heraklion) did not submit until 1669 CE. The delay in the conquest of this city for 24 years resulted from the inability of the Ottoman fleet to mount an effective naval blockade of the island. Even more revealing of diminished Ottoman sea power was the frequent ability of the Venetian fleet to obstruct Ottoman sailing through the Dardanelles between 1647 CE and 1656 CE. In 1656 CE in the straits the Venetians inflicted the worst defeat on an Ottoman fleet since Lepanto. The weakness of the Ottoman navy can be explained by the lack of effective naval leaders because the Ottomans had failed to adequately utilize their naval forces during the 75 years of corsair warfare. Often this has been explained as a reluctance to modernize their ships, and to employ galleons rather than galleys.

Realizing the vulnerability of many of its territories—including the capital—due to naval weakness, the Ottoman navy formed a squadron of sailing warships in 1682 CE, commanded by an officer with the title "*kapudane*." These officers frequently were competent seamen. The overall commander of naval forces continued to be the commander of the galley fleet, however, who often was recruited from the traditional administrative elite with little or no naval experience. Because the admiral outranked the commander of the sailing ships, the *kapudane*'s expert advice could be ignored—sometimes with disastrous results. During the 18th century the principal enemy of the Ottoman Empire was the Russian Empire. During Catherine the Great's reign (1763–1794 CE) a Russian fleet sailed from the Baltic through the Straits of Gibraltar, across the Mediterranean and into the Aegean Sea. The original aim of this expedition was to assist the Greeks in the Peloponnesus in an uprising against the Ottomans. When this became untenable, the Russian fleet's goal changed to controlling maritime traffic through the Dardanelles. The expedition caught the Ottoman fleet off guard despite being warned that this fleet was en route to the Mediterranean. In July 1770 CE, the Russians employed fire-ships to destroy the Ottoman fleet, which had taken refuge in the harbor of Çeşme. This defeat resulted in Russian dominance in the Black Sea as outlined in the Treaty of Küçük Kaynarca (1774 CE) and an increased impetus to revamp the training of the Ottoman navy and to professionalize it.

War with Russia—usually linked to its support of Balkan nationalism—continued into the 19th century. During the Greek War of Independence (1821–1832 CE), a combined Russian, British and French fleet defeated the combined Ottoman and Egyptian fleet at the Battle of Navarino in 1827 CE. To replace the warships lost in this battle, Mahmud II (r. 1808–39 CE) recruited skilled foreigners for Istanbul's shipyards. The first Ottoman steamship was launched in 1837 CE, and others were constructed in the 1840s, though they relied on British boilers and guns. Not only was there a delay in learning to construct the warships demanded by advances in naval technology, but also a shortage of trained Ottoman naval officers and sailors to sail these new ships. The Ottomans brought in foreign advisers to train the navy, with mixed results. This was because training Ottoman naval officers—a high priority for the Ottoman government—was not always a priority for these foreign appointees. Because naval officers frequently lacked navigational training and sea experience, additional disasters occurred, such as Russia's destruction of the unprepared Ottoman fleet at Sinop in 1853 during the Crimean War (1853–1856 CE).

In 1869 CE, the Ottoman Empire purchased new armored ships from Britain and France to use against the rebels in Crete. An 1897 CE war with Greece, again over Crete, revealed the full extent of Ottoman naval weakness. The Ottoman fleet's failure forced Abdul Hamid II (r. 1876–1909 CE) to modernize the navy. He established a commission to assess the state of the navy, which recommended modernizing the existing armored warships and purchasing six foreign-built warships. In his reign's final years, Abdul Hamid II used the possibility of purchasing ships to improve relations with Europe's Great Powers.

Government leaders made the final attempts to reform the Ottoman navy just before World War I (1914–1918 CE), however poor finances and political infighting prevented much progress. There had been a British naval mission at Istanbul for more than 100 years, in 1908 CE the new head, Sir Douglas Gamble, attempted to introduce significant changes in the Ottoman navy. Several factors limited the success of this program, including that—due to the often ceremonial nature of naval command—many officers were paid although they never sailed in their ships. During the intense internal political turmoil brought on by the Young Turk Revolution, the minister of the navy was changed nine times between 1908 and 1911 CE. The major obstacle to reforming the navy, however, revolved around the necessity of purchasing new ships. The Ottoman Empire, deeply in debt, lacked the means to purchase expensive modern warships. The most intense negotiations involved buying warships from Britain and Germany. Despite many financial obstacles, in early 1914 CE British firms were building two battleships for the Ottoman Navy paid for, in part, by a public subscription program. In August 1914, as World War I loomed, the British government exercised its right to seize these ships despite the fact that Ottoman crews had already arrived in Britain to take possession of the *Sultan Osman I* and the *Reshadiye*. Shortly after this, two German cruisers—the *Goeben* and the *Breslau*—fleeing a British fleet in the Mediterranean, took refuge in the Dardanelles and were "purchased" by the Ottomans, although the German crews remained on board and they remained under the command of German Admiral Wilhelm Souchon (1864–1946 CE). Although the Ottoman decision to enter World War I alongside the Central Powers was much more complex than Britain's seizure of two battleships and the arrival of two German warships, the events did influence public opinion in favor of supporting Germany.

For centuries, Ottoman naval power was an essential but often neglected aspect of the empire's military forces. The empire's geopolitical situation made neglecting the navy dangerous, but the empire's large size and diversity of threats also made maintaining powerful naval forces difficult. As the empire's finances were strained, it was often the navy that suffered, and along with it Ottoman shipping in general.

Christine Isom-Verhaaren

Further Reading

Çelebi, Katip. 2012. *The History of the Maritime Wars of the Turks*. Princeton: Markus Wiener.

Guilmartin, John. 1974. *Gunpowder and Galleys*. Cambridge: Cambridge University Press.

Imber, Colin. 1980. "The Navy of Süleyman the Magnificent." *Archivum Ottomanicum* 6: 211–81.

Isom-Verhaaren, Christine. 2011. *Allies with the Infidel: The Ottoman and French Alliance in the Sixteenth Century*. London: IB Tauris.

Soucek, Svat. 2008. *Studies in Ottoman Naval History and Maritime Geography*. Istanbul: Isis Press.

Soucek, Svat. 2013. *Ottoman Maritime Wars, 1700–1914*. Istanbul: Isis Press.

Soucek, Svat. 2015. *Ottoman Maritime Wars, 1416–1700*. Istanbul: Isis Press.

Zorlu, Tuncay. 2011. *Innovation and Empire in Turkey: Sultan Selim III and the Modernisation of the Ottoman Navy*. London: IB Tauris.

Galley

Galleys remained the primary Mediterranean warships throughout the Middle Ages. The galley used by the Byzantine Empire, the *dromon*, evolved during the early medieval period in four main areas: variation in the number of banks of oars, lateen sails replaced square sails, the galley became fully decked, and the underwater ram was replaced by an above-water spur, which could destroy the oars of an enemy ship and cripple it. Rowing systems changed over time, shifting from each oarsman pulling an individual oar to several oarsmen seated together pulling the same oar.

Later Italian and Muslim galleys in the Mediterranean derived from Byzantine galleys. Italian maritime cities employed galleys throughout the medieval period and their vessels evolved to accommodate new conditions. Muslim polities also built war fleets of galleys and various names described different sizes of ships. In the 1290s, the Venetians began employing great galleys to transport high-value goods such as silk, spices, and gems. The great galleys had the lines of a galley and the usual number of oarsmen, but were larger and carried more cargo and more sail, because they had three masts. These great galleys also transported pilgrims from Europe to the Holy Land. In the 14th century, these galleys were the preferred way to travel because they stopped frequently, allowing pilgrims to visit many lands on their journey.

The great galleys ceased being used for trade in the 16th century but they were adapted into the "*galleass*," which the Venetians employed as battleships. These ships had a gun deck and their firepower made them superior to regular galleys although they were slower. Ultimately, these larger vessels—which required larger numbers of oarsmen—became too expensive to maintain. The greatest expenses of galley fleets remained food and other supplies for the oarsmen, which increased as galleys grew in size. Gathering these supplies required regular landings ashore and protected bases for fleets.

Galleys did not depend on the wind, therefore they were superior to sailing ships for some missions and the Ottomans and Venetians maintained galley fleets into the 17th century. Ultimately, their tactical advantages were undermined by their strategic limitations. Improvements in sailing ships led to their eventually replacing galleys even in the Mediterranean.

Christine Isom-Verhaaren

Further Reading

Gardiner, Robert. 1995. *The Age of the Galley: Mediterranean Oared Vessels Since Pre-Classical Times*. London: Conway Maritime Press.

Guilmartin, John. 1974. *Gunpowder and Galleys*. Cambridge: Cambridge University Press.

Lepanto, Battle of

The Battle of Lepanto, October 7, 1571, in which the fleet of the Holy League, a hastily concluded alliance of Christian states, defeated an Ottoman fleet in a closely fought action, was the last major sea battle between galley fleets in the Mediterranean.

Müezzinzade Ali commanded the Ottoman fleet of 251 galleys. The Holy League—commanded by Don Juan of Austria and composed of ships from Spain, Venice, Genoa, the Papacy, and a few lesser powers—totaled 206 galleys and 6 *"galleasses"* ("great galleys"), which boasted substantially more cannon than the average galley. Roughly 80,000 Ottoman sailors and soldiers faced about 70,000 in the Holy League's fleet, though the latter's ships carried more cannon, outnumbering the Ottomans' 750 guns more than two to one. The members of the Holy League, organized on May 25, 1571, hoped to prevent the Ottoman conquest of Cyprus, a Venetian possession.

According to the 17th-century Ottoman naval historian, Katib Çelebi, Uluj Ali (later Kilij Ali)—an experienced fighter and governor of Algiers who commanded part of the Ottoman fleet—advised against seeking battle. It was near the end of the campaign season and Ottoman manpower was low. Uluj Ali also advised against allowing any ships to be positioned too close to land, as the temptation to beach and flee in the event of defeat would be too strong, which proved the case for some ships deployed on the right flank near the shore. Nonetheless, Müezzinzade Ali, confident that his force outnumbered the enemy, sought battle.

As the fleets approached one another, the six galleasses, deployed ahead of the Christian fleet, inflicted substantial damage on the center of the advancing Ottomans. Nonetheless, Ottoman forces maneuvered to overlap and turn the Christians' flanks. Genoese admiral Giovanni Andrea Doria, commanding the Christian right, successfully blocked Uluj Ali, commanding the Ottoman left, but in doing so opened a gap between his forces and the Christian center, which Uluj Ali exploited, breaking through and capturing several ships. Christian forces in the center and left, though, overwhelmed their Ottoman opponents in heavy fighting. As the battle turned against the Ottomans, Uluj Ali abandoned most of his prizes and led his squadron to safety. Most of the rest of the Ottoman fleet, roughly 200 ships, were sunk or captured.

Often viewed as a turning point in history, the battle's immediate impact was minimal. The Ottomans conquered Cyprus and lost no territory to Christian forces. Yet, the loss of trained manpower, conservatively estimated at 30,000, proved difficult to replace. These included not only sailors, but also elite Janissary soldiers and skilled archers who usually served as cavalrymen in land battles. Still, the Ottomans launched a new fleet the following campaign season and, despite its inexperienced crews, it proved adequate. Disagreements among members of the Holy League, particularly between longtime rivals Genoa and Venice, soon led to its dissolution, and irregular actions by privateers again became the primary form of naval warfare in the Mediterranean.

Christine Isom-Verhaaren

Further Reading

Capponi, Niccolo. 2007. *Victory of the West*. Cambridge, MA: Da Capo Press.

Guilmartin, John. 1974. *Gunpowder and Galleys*. Cambridge: Cambridge University Press.

Imber, Colin. 1996. "The Reconstruction of the Ottoman Fleet After the Battle of Lepanto." Imber, *Studies in Ottoman History and Law*. Istanbul: Isis, 85–101.

Mahri, Sulaiman al, 1480–ca. 1554 CE

Sulaiman al Mahri was one of the most important Arab navigators of the 16th century. His works on maritime navigation of the Indian Ocean and the islands of Southeast Asia helped establish and promote trade and shipping routes throughout the region.

Sulaiman was born in 1480 CE in Shihr, a coastal town in modern-day Yemen. His name indicates that he was a member of the Arabic tribe of Mahara. Little is known of his personal life, but as a young man he became a pupil of Ahmad ibn Majid (1421–ca. 1500 CE), a famous Arab navigator and cartographer. Together, ibn Majid and Sulaiman al Mahri composed the *Book of Useful Information on Principles of Navigation*, one of the most important works of Arabic navigation of the period. In general, ibn Majid tended to focus on the theory of navigation and al Mahri provided details useful to the average mariner, making their collaboration useful to a broad range of seafarers. For example, ibn Majid highlighted 70 stars as useful for navigators and referenced them in his works. Al Mahri reduced this number to 15 essential stars, which aided greatly in learning to navigate the Indian Ocean and the islands of the Southeast Asia, a region through which he travelled extensively and on which he focused most of his attention.

Al Mahri worked to combine the empirical knowledge of experienced seafarers with his own scientific investigations. He composed five books and several shorter works on sailing and navigation. Mostly published between 1511 and 1513 CE, they melded practical and theoretical knowledge, detailing nautical astronomy; currents; coastal and open-sea navigation; meteorology and the timing of the monsoons; the major sea routes through the Indian Ocean, Persian Gulf, Red Sea, and the South China Sea; and the locations of harbors and other important landmarks. They also introduced readers to the magnetic compass. Together, al Mahri's works aided navigation in the Indian Ocean and promoted trade by identifying important markets and trading centers including Malacca, Singapore, and several of the Spice Islands. Translated into Turkish, his works proved important for the Ottoman expansion into Arabia and participation in Indian Ocean trade.

Edward Salo

Further Reading

Newton, Lynne S. 2009. *A Landscape of Pilgrimage and Trade in Wadi Masila, Yemen: Al-Qisha and Qabr Hud in the Islamic Period.* Oxford: Archaeopress.

Sezgin, Fuat. 2000. *Mathematical Geography and Cartography in Islam and Their Continuation in the Occident.* Frankfurt am Main: Institute for the History of Arabic-Islamic Science.

Pasha, Hayreddin (Barbarossa), ca. 1466–1546 CE

Born about 1466 CE on the island of Lesbos, Hayreddin Pasha, known to Europeans as "Barbarossa," became the most renowned Ottoman seaman of the 16th century. Hayreddin's father, Yakub, the son of a cavalryman from the Balkans, participated in the conquest of Lesbos in 1462 CE. Yakub remained on the island and married a local Christian woman. They had four sons, two of whom—Oruç and Hızır (later known as Hayreddin)—became famous seafarers. Oruç was authorized to engage in privateering against the Knights of Rhodes by Sultan Bayezid II's (1481–1512 CE) son Korkud. But Korkud lost the succession battle to Selim I (1512–1520 CE), and in 1513 CE Oruç and Hızır had to flee Ottoman territories, choosing to relocate in the vicinity of Tunis where they established a base. Oruç was killed in 1518 CE and thereafter Hızır worked alone to establish himself at Algiers. Hayreddin's control of Algiers was tenuous and in 1519 CE he sent an embassy to Selim requesting assistance. After the sultan provided 2,000 Janissaries along with artillery in September 1520, Hayreddin was able to rule Algiers as an Ottoman governor. During the next decade, Hayreddin's fortunes in Algiers fluctuated but he had achieved firm control of the region by 1530 CE.

In 1533 CE, Sultan Süleyman (1520–1566 CE) summoned Hayreddin to Istanbul and appointed him admiral in command of the Ottoman navy, which had lost several battles to Andrea Doria, the Genoese admiral commanding the navy of Habsburg Emperor Charles V. Hayreddin acted as an intermediary between Francis I of France and Süleyman even before his official appointment began. He received an ambassador from Francis I shortly before he sailed to Istanbul. As grand admiral, Hayreddin was promoted from the governor of a remote Ottoman outpost engaged in privateering to the head of Ottoman naval forces, with responsibilities that included all aspects of naval leadership.

For the next 12 years, until his death in 1546 CE, Hayreddin led Ottoman naval forces to victory after victory. In 1534 CE, he briefly gained control of Tunis, although in 1535 CE Charles V conquered the city and installed a puppet ruler. Hayreddin returned to Istanbul, but the following year he attacked the coast of Calabria. In 1537 CE, Hayreddin prepared a fleet to support the French in an attack on Habsburg possessions in Italy, in accordance with the wishes of Francis I. In

1536 CE, Francis's ambassador had negotiated a military alliance between the Ottomans and the French, with Grand Vizier Ibrahim. The proposed joint expedition of 1537 CE failed due to logistical problems and difficulties coordinating the French and Ottoman fleets. When the French fleet failed to arrive in Avlona as arranged, Hayreddin led the Ottoman fleet in a failed effort to besiege Corfu, and the successful conquest of several Aegean islands belonging to Venice. Hayreddin won his greatest victory in 1538 CE at the battle of Prevesa. There he defeated a combined fleet of forces of Venice, the pope, and Charles V, led by Andrea Doria. His judgment and daring turned a potential defeat into a resounding victory. In 1539 CE, he reconquered Castelnuovo, which had been captured by Doria following Prevesa.

Hayreddin's last major expedition was to support Francis I against Charles V in 1543 CE, another expedition arranged after negotiations with a French ambassador. Hayreddin sailed with the Ottoman fleet to southern France, directed the siege of Nice, and protected the fleet during its wintering in the port of Toulon. In the spring, after receiving permission from Süleyman to return home, he led the fleet in raids against the Italian coast, then under Habsburg rule.

Süleyman included Hayreddin among his favorites and depended on his knowledge of the western Mediterranean. This is demonstrated by their correspondence during 1543–44 CE. Hayreddin died in 1546 CE in the midst of preparing the fleet for another expedition. Although he was succeeded by a succession of court favorites who had little naval experience, these admirals relied on the advice of Turgud Pasha (d. 1565 CE), who had fought with and been mentored by Hayreddin.

Christine Isom-Verhaaren

Further Reading

Bradford, Ernle. 1968. *The Sultan's Admiral: The Life of Barbarossa.* London: Hodder & Stoughton.

Isom-Verhaaren, Christine. 2011. *Allies with the Infidel: The Ottoman and French Alliance in the Sixteenth Century.* London: IB Tauris.

Reis, Piri, ca. 1465–1554 CE

Piri Reis, a famous Ottoman cartographer, was born between 1465 and 1470 CE, probably at Gallipoli. He went to sea with his uncle, Kemal Reis (1451–1511 CE), in about 1481 CE, and for 14 years Piri and Kemal were privateers, sea *"ghazis"* ("religious warriors") who attacked Christian merchant shipping. Piri learned navigation from Kemal as they sailed throughout the Mediterranean from the Aegean as far as the Algerian coast. In 1495 CE, Ottoman Sultan Bayezid II (1447–1512 CE) recruited both Kemal and Piri into his service.

Kemal Reis's significant contribution to establishing Ottoman naval power included battling the Venetians in the Mediterranean and challenging Spain and Portugal's maritime expansion. As an advisor and successful naval commander, Kemal won the sultan's favor—thereby arousing the jealousy of educated palace Ottoman officials. It is thought that perhaps Admiral Iskender caused Kemal's death by sending him to sail in an unsound ship, which sank in a storm in 1511 CE. Thus Piri lost his uncle, his mentor, and his influence at court.

After 1511 CE, Piri's activities on shore at Gallipoli were at least as important as those at sea. In 1513 CE, Piri produced a map that included the Americas. Piri combined information from approximately 30 maps including one made by Christopher Columbus, which he obtained from a Spanish slave who accompanied Columbus on the American voyages. Piri presented his map to Sultan Selim I (1465–1520 CE) at Cairo in the summer of 1517 CE after the Ottoman conquest of Egypt. Piri continued to sail the length and breadth of the Mediterranean, participated in the most important naval conflicts of the period, and also studied and created maps.

Due to his skill as a navigator, in 1524 CE Piri was selected to act as pilot when Sultan Süleyman (1494–1566 CE) sent Grand Vizier Ibrahim Pasha (1493–1536 CE) to Egypt to organize its administration. Ibrahim encouraged Piri to revise a rough version of *Kitab-ı Bahriye* ("*Book of the Sea*"), a description with charts of the entire Mediterranean, and he produced an elegant version for the sultan in 1526 CE. Piri's final surviving cartographic achievement is a world map that was completed in 1528 CE.

Piri Reis then disappeared from Ottoman records until he was appointed "*Mısır Kapudanı*" (admiral of the fleet at Suez) that sailed the Indian Ocean in 1547 CE. Piri's first assignment was to re-conquer Aden, which he accomplished in 1549 CE. In 1552 CE, Piri sailed from Suez with a small fleet of 30 ships to attack Hormuz, another strategic port held by the Portuguese. The attack failed and Piri sailed for Basra in the summer of 1553 CE and then returned to Suez, leaving most of the fleet at Basra. From Suez he proceeded to Cairo, where in 1554 CE he was executed, probably for his failure at Hormuz. Piri's fame dates from the 20th century, when his maps were recognized as cartographic masterpieces.

Christine Isom-Verhaaren

Further Reading

Isom-Verhaaren, Christine. 2014. "Was There Room in Rum for Ottoman Corsairs: Who Was an Ottoman in the Naval Forces of the Ottoman Empire in the 15th and 16th Centuries?" *The Journal of Ottoman Studies* XLIV: 235–64.

Soucek, Svat. 1996. *Piri Reis and Turkish Mapmaking after Columbus*. London: Oxford University Press.

PORTUGAL, 1450 TO 1770 CE

The kingdom of Portugal as a state and entity emerged from the small earldom ("*condado*") of Portucalense that was established around 1095 CE in the northwest part of the Iberian Peninsula. Its territory encompassed the lands between the Douro and Mondego rivers and bordered Castile and Galicia. Following the battle of Mamede (1128 CE), Afonso Henriques proclaimed himself King of Portugal and expanded his territory to the south in a series of campaigns that included the successful siege and capture of Lisbon (1147 CE). His successors continued these campaigns, completing the conquest of the kingdom of the Algarve in 1249 CE, which established Portugal's modern boundaries. Its position on the route from the northern European markets of England, France, and Central Europe to the Mediterranean Sea, made Portugal an important hub of trade and the nation experienced steady economic growth. The Portuguese exported mostly agricultural produce, such as rock salt, fruits, wine, and cork. Additionally, its growing population demanded a constant import of cereals, mainly originating from the Baltic Sea and shipped from Danzig and Riga. Hanseatic cogs departing these Baltic port-towns also transported wood and timber for ship masts for the growing Portuguese shipbuilding industry, as native Portuguese tree species were not tall enough or strong enough to serve as masts. In the late 14th century, the Portuguese also established trading relationships with Italian merchants.

Generally speaking, the Portuguese maritime discoveries and expansion can be divided into the following four chronological eras: the time of discovery and expansion onto the Atlantic islands (1415–1497 CE); the time of great voyages of discovery and the establishment of a maritime empire spanning South America, Africa, and the Indian Ocean (1497–1580 CE); the Union of the Two Iberian Crowns and the emergence of European competitors such as the Dutch and English India Companies (1580–1640 CE); and the restoration of Portuguese rule and the reorganization of the empire by Marquês de Pombal (1640–1755 CE).

Portugal's maritime discoveries and exploration began with the conquest of Ceuta in 1415 CE during the reign of King John I (1358–1433 CE). Situated at the northern tip of the African continent and separated from the Iberian Peninsula by the Straits of Gibraltar, the conquest of this particular port-town was initiated by a conjunction of political, religious, and economic factors and signified the possibility of expanding Portuguese rule outside the Iberian Peninsula. The Catholic Church authorized crusades against the Muslims—both in the Iberian Peninsula, where Christian states fought with Muslim Granada, and in North Africa, where the Portuguese captured Ceuta, an important marketplace for African commodities brought by caravan through the Sahara, as well as locally grown cereals.

During the first decades of the 15th century, the Portuguese explored the Atlantic Ocean, discovering and establishing plantations on the archipelagoes of Madeira and the Azores, and voyaging south along the African coast. Directed by Prince Henry the Navigator (1394–1460 CE), they reached the Gulf of Guinea and the Cape Verde Islands, and explored up the Senegal River. Later voyages explored the Gold Coast (roughly modern Ghana), and established trading relations with local peoples, trading grain and cloth for gold (and later for slaves). Bartolomeu Dias (1451–1500 CE) completed the exploration of Africa's Atlantic coast in 1488 CE, circumnavigated the southern tip of Africa in the same year, and entered the Indian Ocean reaching as far as what is today known as Agulhas Bay in South Africa.

To maintain and expand their political and economic activities in these new lands, the Portuguese constructed fortified trading posts ("*feitorias*") as well as fortresses at strategic places, including Arguin (Western Mauritania) and São Jorge da Mina (Gulf of Guinea), from which they could project their power and maintain their ships. The Portuguese crown granted monopoly rights to explore and commercialize the Cape Verde islands to Fernando Gomes, a Venetian merchant, during the 1460s. By the end of the 15th century, the Portuguese government centralized Atlantic economic activities under the Lisbon-based House of Guinea and Mina ("*Casa de Guiné e da Mina*"). Founded in 1482 CE during the reign of King John II (1455–1495 CE), it was here that the crown planned and executed the voyages to Portugal's overseas trading posts, including São Jorge da Mina, Arguin, and the Cape Verde islands, which in these years became an important entrepôt of the slave trade supplying the sugar plantations on the Madeira archipelago and the Canary Islands. In exchange, Central European metalware such as copper and brass bracelets, kettles, and knives were exported to African markets.

The second phase of Portuguese expansion followed the voyages of Vasco da Gama to the Indian Ocean (1497–1499 CE) and Pedro Álvares Cabral to Brazil (1500 CE) and created the first European maritime empire. The Treaty of Tordesillas—signed several years earlier in 1494 CE by Portuguese King John II and Spanish rulers Isabel I of Castile and Ferdinand II of Aragon—secured Portuguese claims to these newly discovered territories, having divided the world, and territories in the Atlantic and Indian Oceans yet to be discovered by Europeans, between the Iberian powers. Following da Gama's and Cabral's successful voyages, Portuguese exploration and expansion accelerated, following different patterns in the Indian Ocean and the Atlantic. Portugal's rulers, however, controlled trade and prohibited direct sailing between the various regions of its growing empire, requiring that trade among its constituent parts—the Indian Ocean, Western Africa, and Brazil—passed through Lisbon, Portugal's capital and major port.

The eastern part of the Portuguese empire, the *Estado da Índia*, officially established in 1506 CE and governed by a viceroy, stretched from the Cape of Good Hope in Africa as far as Malacca, East Timor, and Macau. Trade was organized by the Lisbon-based India House ("*Casa da Índia*"), a central royal organization with its roots in the *Casa de Guiné e da Mina*, established by Henry the Navigator to

---

Careening

Careening is a technique employed for cleaning and repair to reach portions of a ship's hull that normally are underwater.

Ships' hulls—particularly wooden hulls immersed in tropical waters—are susceptible to attack and even destruction by marine life such as shipworms (*Teredo navalis*). Other marine organisms including barnacles and seaweed also accumulate on underwater surfaces and interfere with the smooth flow of water along the hull, reducing speed and increasing operating costs. Cleaning restores the efficiency of the hull and protects it from the destructive effects of marine growth.

Prior to careening, crewmen lighten the ship by offloading as much of the cargo, stores, and other portable material as possible. Careening is accomplished by running the ship into shallow water and allowing it to settle onto the ground as the tide ebbs. To expose more of the lower hull, lines and pulleys can be rigged to tilt the ship further. Crewmen remove weed and other growths from the exposed hull before repairing and resealing the hull planking. The ship is then heeled in the opposite direction to expose the other side. After cleaning and repairs are complete, the ship is refloated on the flood tide.

Larry A. Grant

---

oversee his monopoly on trade with Africa. This royal Portuguese institution regulated the majority of the nation's maritime activities including the design and building of ships. It annually outfitted and organized the trading fleets that sailed to its overseas possessions and trading outposts, and controlled the selling of overseas products. Long-distance trade between Europe and Asia—which the Portuguese hoped to monopolize—focused on importing large quantities of Asian spices, particularly pepper, via the Lisbon and Antwerp markets and exporting European metalware and copper ingots.

Indo-Portuguese navigation and commercial activities relied on a system of annual fleets of *Naus* (high-board Portuguese armed merchant ships) and galleons, known as the *Carreira da Índia*, that linked the capital of the empire, Lisbon, with Goa, the capital of the *Estado da Índia*. As navigation in the Indian Ocean during the Age of Sail was governed by the monsoons, these fleets followed a regular calendar of outward and homeward voyages. They left Lisbon between March and May, reached India in late August or September, and began the return voyage in late December or January, arriving back in Europe in August or September. In total, the round-trip voyage required almost one-and-a-half years. Goods from throughout the *Estado da Índia*—mainly spices and porcelain—were shipped to Goa, and from there went to Lisbon. European goods, in turn, flowed to Goa and then to the rest of Asia from there.

Exploration and settlement of Portugal's western empire, particularly Brazil, followed a different pattern. During its first decades, the king granted monopoly privileges to several private merchants—among them Fernão de Noronha (ca. 1470–1540 CE)—which gave them the right to export Brazilian commodities, such as Brazil-wood, for a period of several years. In exchange, the king required these merchants to establish fortified trade posts and explore the surrounding area of these *feitorias* at their own expense. These proprietary holdings created the basis of permanent settlements and towns, such as Pernambuco and Bahia, which flourished around them. Because the Atlantic Ocean lacked the rigid pattern set by the monsoons, trading fleets conducted several voyages per year.

As profits from the Asian spice trade declined during the 1570s, successful sugarcane plantations in Brazil offered a new source of royal revenues. This initiated a shift of emphasis from the eastern parts of the Empire to the transatlantic trade that continued for the next two centuries.

By the end of the 16th century, the Portuguese faced increasing competition from the Dutch and English East India Companies, and Portugal itself fell under the rule of Spanish kings between 1580 and 1640 CE. Commercial competition led to naval warfare in both the Atlantic and the Indian Ocean, extending to Southeast Asia. Internal political conflict and corruption within Portuguese India further compounded Portugal's problems, as did the decline in pepper prices, which resulted from this competition and the increasing shipments to Europe. A combined English-Persian force defeated the Portuguese and expelled them from Hormuz in 1622 CE. The Dutch, increasingly active in Southeast Asia, defeated the Portuguese in 1641 CE and seized Malacca from them. The Portuguese position in Asia continued to decline over the next century.

The Dutch also attacked Portuguese holdings in the West, occupying parts of northeastern Brazil and its rich sugar plantations, from 1624 CE, when the Dutch seized, until 1654 CE, when the Portuguese expelled the Dutch from Recife. The Brazilian sugar plantations continued to flourish and grow, and Portugal's participation in the transatlantic slave trade provided labor both for them and for Spain's silver mines in Peru. The export of sugarcane remained the major source of revenue for the Portuguese crown, later joined by tobacco and cattle, which also flourished in Brazil. The discovery of gold in Brazil ignited a gold rush in the 1700s and further added to Portugal's revenues as miners rushed the region of Minas Gerais, north of Rio de Janeiro.

The export of Brazilian tobacco to the Indian Ocean revitalized the *Estado da Índia*, as did participation in the slave trade off East Africa during the late 17th century. Portuguese trade with China continued through Macau, and increased after Portugal's government allowed direct shipping between Brazil and Portuguese territories in the East, particularly Goa and Macau. Trade throughout Portugal's empire increased as a result. Ships stopped at Brazil, loaded tobacco and gold, and sailed for India, where they offloaded their cargoes and then sailed for Lisbon with new cargo. Other ships would stop at Mozambican ports to pick up slaves for Brazil and then sail to Lisbon with tobacco, sugar, and gold, destined for European markets.

In the mid-18th century, particularly after the devastating 1755 CE Lisbon earthquake, Portugal implemented profound structural reforms in its empire, many at the behest of Sebastião José de Carvalho e Melo (1699–1782 CE), Portugal's Secretary of State at that time. In general, these further opened the empire to trade. Mozambique, previously governed as part of the *Estado da Índia*, gained administrative independence in 1752 CE, as did other parts of Portugal's eastern empire over time. Concurrently, more and more plantations were established in Brazil, growing cotton, cocoa, and coffee, in addition to sugar and tobacco, increasing the flow of African slaves to Brazil and increasing Portugal's participation in the slave trade.

Torsten dos Santos Arnold

Further Reading

Borschberg, Peter. 2010. *The Singapore and Melaka Straits: Violence, Security and Diplomacy in the 17th Century.* Singapore. NUS Press.

Boxer, Charles R. 1991. *The Portuguese Seaborne Empire, 1415–1825.* Manchester: Carcanet.

Boxer, Charles R. 2001. *The Church Militant and Iberian Expansion, 1440–1770.* Baltimore: Johns Hopkins University Press.

Boyajian, James C. 1993. *Portuguese Trade in Asia under the Habsburgs 1580–1640.* Baltimore: Johns Hopkins University Press.

Disney, Antony R. 2009. *A History of Portugal and the Portuguese Empire.* Cambridge: Cambridge University Press. 2 vols.

Fonseca, Luís Adão da. 1999. *The Discoveries and the Formation of the Atlantic Ocean: 14th Century to 16th Century.* Lisbon. Comissão Nacional para as Comemorações dos Descobrimentos Portugueses.

Newitt, Malyn. 2005. *A History of Portuguese Overseas Expansion, 1400–1668.* London, New York: Routledge.

Newitt, Malyn. 2010. *Portugal in European and World History.* London: Reaktion Books.

Russel-Wood, A. J. R. 1998. *The Portuguese Empire, 1415–1808—A World on the Move.* Baltimore: Johns Hopkins University Press.

Souza, George Bryan. 2004. *The Survival of Empire: Portuguese Trade and Society in China and South China Sea, 1630–1754.* Cambridge: Cambridge University Press.

Subrahmanyam, Sanjay. 1993. *The Portuguese Empire in Asia 1500–1700: A Political and Economic History.* London, New York: Longman.

Albuquerque, Alfonso de, 1453–1515 CE

The second governor of Portuguese India, Alfonso de Albuquerque was one of the architects of Portugal's empire. A successful diplomat and general, he helped Portugal gain a monopoly on the Asian spice trade, which it maintained for much of the 16th century.

The second son of Gonçalo de Albuquerque, Lord of Vila Verde dos Francos, and Dona Leonor de Menezes, nobles with friends in the royal court, Albuquerque participated in several campaigns in North Africa under Portuguese kings Alfonso V, John II, and Manuel I. Following Vasco da Gama's successful return from his first voyage to India, Manuel I dispatched a succession of expeditions to India. Albuquerque commanded the fifth of them, which departed on April 6, 1503 CE and arrived in Cochin on September 2. There, Albuquerque toppled the local ruler, the "*Zamorin*," and replaced him with one friendly to Portugal. He built and garrisoned a fortress at Cochin to ensure Portuguese control, and also established a trading post at Quilon before returning home with a rich cargo of spices.

After prolonged discussions of Portugal's policy in Asia with the royal court, Albuquerque sailed for India on April 6, 1506 with its eighth expedition to the subcontinent, commanded by Tristão da Cunha, a favorite of the king. En route, Albuquerque opened sealed orders from the king appointing him governor of Portuguese India in place of Francisco de Almeida, Portugal's first viceroy of India. Albuquerque and da Cunha defeated an Arab fleet and established a stronghold at Socotra in East Africa to control the passage between the Red Sea and the Indian Ocean. Afterward, Albuquerque parted with da Cuhna, and led seven ships to capture Hormuz at the mouth of the Persian Gulf in August 1507 CE. Forced to abandon this possession due to lack of resources, and dissension among his officers, Albuquerque departed for India, raiding the Arabian and Persian coasts along the way. In India, he confronted Almeida, who refused to relinquish his post until he avenged his son's death. Almeida, who won a decisive victory at Diu in February 1509 against an Ottoman-led coalition fleet, retained his post until November when a large Portuguese fleet arrived and forced Albuquerque's installation as governor.

Albuquerque hoped to seize control of trade routes across the Indian Ocean by gaining control of and garrisoning the region's major ports. His first assault on Cochin failed, but in November 1510 CE, after a protracted struggle, he captured Goa—which he made the capital of Portugal's Indian Ocean empire. In July 1511, he captured the rich port of Malacca whose strategic location enabled Portugal to dominate trade with the Spice Islands to the east. Albuquerque, however, spent as much time defending Portugal's empire as he did enlarging it—and his meager forces made continued expansion difficult. Vigorous campaigning in 1513 CE in the Red Sea resulted in no new conquests, but in February 1515 CE, his forces drove the Persians from Hormuz and made its ruler a Portuguese vassal. Albuquerque became ill during this campaign and died en route to Goa where he had expected to face off against political rivals eager to displace him as he had Almeida.

Jakub Basista

Further Reading

Bouchon, Geneviève. 1992. *Albuquerque. Le lion des mers d'Asie.* Paris: Editions Desjonquéres.

Disney, A. R. 2009. *A History of Portugal and the Portuguese Empire.* Cambridge: Cambridge University Press.

Prestage, Edgar. 1929. *Afonso de Albuquerque, Governor of India: His Life, Conquests and Administration.* Watford, England: Voss & Michael.

Cabral, Pedro Álvares, ca. 1467–1520 CE

Pedro Álvares Cabral was a Portuguese sailor and navigator and is generally credited as the first European to explore the coast of Brazil. One of 12 children, Cabral was the son of poor nobles Fernão Cabral and Isabel de Gouveia. He served at the royal court of Manuel I (1469–1521 CE) and received a position in the King's Council and the Military Order of Christ. Very little is known about Cabral's early life and career. He must have earned royal trust, because in February 1500 CE he was appointed command of the second Portuguese armada bound for India.

Cabral left Lisbon on March 9 in command of 13 ships and 1,500 men. The fleet followed a well-known route along the west coast of Africa passing the Canary Islands. As they sailed southwest, they spotted land on April 22, which they explored for 10 days. Originally assumed to be an island, they soon realized they had discovered a large land mass—which was later named Brazil after a species of local timber. They traded with locals, held a mass, and claimed the land in accordance with the Treaty of Tordesillas. One ship returned to Portugal to report the find and the others continued south, encountering a serious storm on May 23 or 24 in which several ships were lost.

The surviving ships rendezvoused off the African coast near the Cape of Good Hope where they conducted repairs before continuing the voyage to India. Sailing along the east coast of Africa, Cabral met with local rulers in Malindi and then crossed the Indian Ocean, arriving at Calicut on September 13. There, Cabral successfully established relations with the local ruler, the "*Zamorin*," and gained permission to set up a trading post. On December 17, however, local Arab merchants along with some Indians attacked the post, killing most of its staff. After the *Zamorin* refused Cabral's demands to punish the attackers and provide restitution, he bombarded the city and attacked local shipping, capturing 10 Arab ships whose crews he executed.

The expedition then sailed southeast to Cochin, a rival to Calicut whose rulers welcomed Cabral warmly. After trading successfully, they sailed home in 1501 CE, shortly after the New Year. Cabral sent his fastest caravel ahead to report news of his successes. Cabral, himself, arrived with his remaining ships in Portugal on July 21, 1501, having reunited with one of the ships lost in the previous year's storm. All told, seven of his ships returned to Portugal, five of them loaded with trade goods, which allowed the expedition to return an almost tenfold profit despite its high losses in ships and crew.

King Manuel I was pleased with the expedition's results, and initially assigned Cabral to lead another expedition to India, having already dispatched several ships to explore Brazil before Cabral returned. For reasons that remain unclear, Cabral lost the king's favor and was relieved of command while supervising the preparation of this fleet. Cabral retired to his estate at Beira Baixa and died in 1520 CE, never having sailed again.

Jakub Basista

Further Reading

Greenlee, William Brookes (ed.). 1938. *The Voyage of Pedro Alvares Cabral to Brazil and India from Contemporary Documents and Narratives.* London: Hakluyt Society, 2nd series, no. 81.

MacClymont, James Roxburgh, William Brooks Greenlee, Pero Vaz de Caminha et al. 2009. *Pedro Cabral.* Middlesex: Viartis.

Caravel

Although the caravel was employed in a variety of seagoing roles including as warships, its most significant historical role was its use by Portuguese explorers to overcome the navigational hazards of the African coast. Portuguese and Spanish explorers continued to use caravels, including Christopher Columbus's *Niña* and *Pinta*, as the principal ship for many voyages of discovery in the 14th, 15th, and 16th centuries.

The use of "caravel" to describe all of these ships does not mean that they were built according to a standard design. Individual caravels often differed according to the requirements of the individual shipbuilder and explorer, and the basic characteristics of the type varied significantly over the period of its use. Most descriptions of the ship rely on fragmentary references and conjecture, thus only general characteristics are known.

The caravels of the European explorers were about 60 feet in length, with lengths of 40 to 75 feet not uncommon. Viewed in profile, the line of the main deck followed a smooth and continuous curve (the sheer line) over the vessel's length, rising to its highest points above the waterline at the bow and stern. Although the bow was free of any raised superstructure, the ship carried a raised poop deck over an enclosed cabin at its stern. Several features of the caravel including the use of triangular (lateen) sails and the general shape of the hull might have originated with Arab *dhows*. Whatever its origin, caravels were in use in the Mediterranean by the mid-12th century and the Atlantic by the mid-13th century.

Early caravels used the all-lateen rig of triangular sails, which allowed them to "beat to windward" ("sail into the wind") more efficiently than when using square sails alone. After about 1400 CE, many caravels employed a composite rig that combined lateen with square sails for greater flexibility on both up- and downwind courses. Normally fitted with two masts, some caravels carried three or even four masts.

The hull of the caravel was built up from a straight keel using planks laid edge-to-edge (without overlapping) over an internal frame in a method called "carvel" construction. This produced a strong, smooth hull that could carry more sails and pass more efficiently through the water. The flat bottom and the overall strength of the hull also made the caravel suitable for use in shallow water. Initially rounded at the stern, by the end of the 15th century, caravels had adopted a flat transom stern with a rudder fixed on the centerline. As European trade with the rich entrepôts of the East, ships with larger cargo holds displaced caravels.

Larry A. Grant

Further Reading

Parry, John Horace. 1974. *The Discovery of the Sea*. New York: Dial Press.

Unger. Richard W. 1980. *The Ship in the Medieval Economy, 600–1600*. London: Croom Helm.

Villain-Gandossi, Christiane, Salvino Busuttil, and Paul Adam (eds.). 1989. *Medieval Ships and the Birth of Technological Societies: The Mediterranean Area and European Integration*. Valetta, Malta: European Coordination Centre for Research and Documentation in Social Sciences.

Dias, Bartolomeu, ca. 1450–1500 CE

A Portuguese explorer and navigator, Bartolomeu Dias was the first European explorer to sail around the southern tip of Africa and into the Indian Ocean. During that voyage, he discovered that by sailing south from the Cape Verde Islands and away from Africa, a ship could avoid the contrary winds that halted previous circumnavigation attempts. Once far enough south, westerly winds carried a ship around the cape and into the Indian Ocean. This discovery facilitated future Portuguese expeditions into the Indian Ocean, particularly that of Vasco da Gama (1469–1524 CE).

Little is known about Dias's early life or where he gained his maritime experience before King João II of Portugal (1455–1495 CE) appointed him to lead an

Statue of Bartolomeu Dias (1450–1500), a nobleman of the Portuguese royal household. He sailed around the southernmost tip of Africa in 1488, reaching the Indian Ocean from the Atlantic, the first European known to have done so. (Saphire Ovadia/Dreamstime.com)

expedition to circumnavigate Africa. In August 1487 CE, Dias departed Lisbon, Portugal, with three ships, made his way around Africa's southernmost point while well out to sea, and entered the Indian Ocean.

A storm blew the ships off course from the coast, but on February 3, 1488, Dias reached Mossel Bay, 160 miles east of the southernmost point of Africa. They continued their journey to Algoa Bay and then to the mouth of Bushman's River, where on March 12, 1488, Dias placed a padrão—a large limestone marker that the Portuguese used to stake claims and serve as guideposts. It was on the return voyage that Dias's expedition first saw the southern tip of Africa where the Atlantic and Indian Oceans meet. Dias named the point Cabo Tormentosa, or Cape of Storms. In December 1488, King João II renamed it Cabo da Boa Esperanca, the Cape of Good Hope, to reflect the opportunities offered by entering Indian Ocean trade. According to some accounts, Christopher Columbus (1451–1506 CE) was present when Dias recounted his journey to the king following his return, and Dias's report could have influenced Columbus's decision to explore west.

Several years later, at the request King João's successor, Manuel I (ca.1469–1524 CE), Dias accompanied Vasco da Gama (ca. 1469–1524 CE) for the first leg of his expedition to the Indian Ocean. Dias departed at the Cape Verde Islands to pursue trade opportunities in Ghana and what Europeans soon labeled the slave coast of Africa. In 1500 CE, Dias commanded four ships of the large expedition led by Pedro Álvares Cabral (ca. 1467–1520 CE), which by sailing a westerly route, became the first Europeans to sight Brazil. Cabral's fleet encountered a major storm on May 24 in which several ships were lost, including those commanded by Dias.

Samantha J. Haines

Further Reading

Bartolomeu Dias Museum Complex. 2015. "Historical Background." http://diasmuseum .co.za/index.php/about-the-dias-museum/historical-background. Accessed June 15, 2016.

Ravenstein, Ernst Georg, William Brooks Greenlee, and Pero Vaz de Caminha. 2010. *Bartolomeu Dias*. London, England: Viartis.

Estado da Índia

The Estado da India (Portuguese India State) is a term used to describe the several characteristics of the Portuguese presence in the Indian Ocean and Asia. The Estado da Índia was created as a kingdom governed by a viceroy to implement and defend Portuguese political and economic interests in the region, and to gain supremacy over Indian Ocean maritime trade, particularly the Euro-Asian spice trade. It consisted of a chain of fortified coastal settlements, "*feitorias*" ("trade posts") that served administrative, diplomatic, and economic interests.

Although the Portuguese presence rarely extended into the hinterlands, it was accompanied by missionary expeditions of religious orders, such as the Dominicans, Franciscans, and Jesuits, that had formed the Society of Jesus ("*Copanhia de Jesus*") in 1540 CE. Famous fathers such as Francis Xavier and António Vieira conducted missions to spread Roman-Catholic Christianity, known by the term "*Padroado da Índia*" ("patronage of India").

When D. Francisco de Almeida, its first viceroy, established the Estado da Índia in 1506 CE, Portugal did not possess any territory east of Africa's Cape of Good Hope. It expanded rapidly under Afonso de Albuquerque, governor from 1509–1515 CE, who conquered several key outposts including Malacca and Goa, to which he relocated the Estado's capital. At its peak, the Estado da Índia included all Portuguese territory between the Cape of Good Hope, and its eastern outposts at Macao, East Timor, and Nagasaki—where Portugal received permission to establish a trading post in 1571 CE.

Fleets of naus, known as the "*Carreira da Índia*," were the principal means of communication as well as the means to execute political, economic, and military strategies abroad. In addition to directing Portuguese expansion in the region, the Estado also oversaw Indo-Portuguese trade. Trade was based on a centralized system of intra-Asian ports of call, such as Malacca and the Moluccas, both from and to the Estado's capital, and annual direct voyages from the Estado's capital to Portugal's capital of Lisbon. Portugal's Dutch, English, and French competitors later adopted some of the Estado's trade practices, particularly local routes that linked to central hubs from which direct voyages to European ports took place.

Starting in the 17th century, the Portuguese presence in the Indian Ocean and Asian waters slowly declined due to European competitors and indigenous opposition. Hormuz fell to England in 1622 CE and Malacca to the Dutch in 1641 CE. Mozambique became separately administered in 1752 CE, as did Macau and Timor in 1844 CE. The final dissolution of the Estado da Índia came in 1961 CE, when India took control of Goa and the remaining Portuguese possessions along the Indian Subcontinent.

Torsten dos Santos Arnold

Further Reading

Boxer, Charles R. 1991. *The Portuguese Seaborne Empire, 1415–1825.* Manchester: Carcanet.

Disney, Antony R. 2009. *A History of Portugal and the Portuguese Empire.* Cambridge: Cambridge University Press.

Newitt, Malyn. 2005. *A History of Portuguese Overseas Expansion, 1400–1668.* London: Routledge.

Subrahmanyam, Sanjay. 1993. *The Portuguese Empire in Asia 1500–1700: A Political and Economic History.* New York: Longman.

Gama, Vasco da, ca. 1469–1524 CE

Dom Vasco da Gama, Count of Vidigueira was the first European to reach India by sailing from the Atlantic Ocean into the Indian Ocean. Over the course of his three voyages to India, da Gama helped establish a sustained European presence in and trade with East Africa, India, and the Indian Ocean. His violent attacks on local peoples also created tense relationships between Europeans and many peoples living in Africa and the Indian subcontinent.

Little is known of da Gama's life prior to his first voyage. He was likely born to a family of the minor nobility in the Portuguese province of Alentejo. He joined the military Order of Santiago in 1481 CE. His name first appears in contemporary records only in 1492 CE when King John II (1455–1495 CE) gave da Gama the command over a particular naval mission. This command suggests that the king knew and respected da Gama and his maritime skills as early as 1492 CE.

John II's successor, Manuel I (1469–1521 CE), selected da Gama to lead the 1497 CE fleet to India as its captain-major. This fleet built on decades of Portuguese land expeditions to India as well as previous sea voyages that had attempted to reach it and failed. Da Gama was given the specific task of reaching the Malabar Coast of India, known for its pepper. He also was told to establish friendly relationships with any Christians he might meet along the way.

Da Gama and his fleet, including four ships and about 170 crew members, set out from Portugal in early July 1497 CE. Rather than sailing down the west African coast—which often involved fighting contrary winds and currents—da Gama and his fleet swung out wide into the Atlantic Ocean to take advantage of favorable winds and currents to blow them around the southern tip of Africa. Making landfalls throughout south and east Africa, da Gama's interactions with the peoples and city-states he encountered set up a pattern typical for him on all three of his voyages. He tended to be personally suspicious, and assaults and all-out war between da Gama's crews and the peoples they encountered were frequent. He was also able to exploit tensions among local rulers to his own advantage. One such friendly ruler, the sultan of Malindi, provided a pilot knowledgeable about the India Ocean, who led da Gama's fleet to the Malabar Coast. It anchored outside the wealthy and powerful state of Calicut on May 20, 1498. Though da Gama hoped to cultivate an official trading agreement with the Zamorin (from "*Samudri raja*," meaning "sea lord") of Calicut, their relationship eventually soured. The Portuguese were able to do some trading during these negotiations, but they ended in multiple violent confrontations with the fleet having to leave the Malabar region quickly. The journey back to Portugal proved long and difficult. Roughly half of the expedition's members died of scurvy, forcing da Gama to abandon one of his ships. He arrived in Lisbon in late August or early September of 1499.

King Manuel reward him with the title, "Dom," the privilege of attending the royal council, an annual stipend, trading privileges in India, and the title "Admiral of the Sea of India." Manuel continued to sponsor yearly fleets to the Malabar Coast in an attempt to set up a successful spice trade with the region. Da Gama was given the command of the fourth such fleet leaving for India in 1502 CE. Engaging

---

Scurvy

People living in northern climates might have experienced scurvy during winter, when fruits and vegetables were scarce, but symptoms would likely have been mild. Scurvy was not recognized as a disease until the long voyages of Europe's age of exploration began, and first was noted in Vasco da Gama's return voyage from India. Sailors—at sea for months—experienced symptoms including extreme fatigue; spongy, bleeding gums; bleeding sores, and later internal bleeding; delusions; fever; heart problems; and eventually, death.

Ignoring local advice and sailing against the monsoons, Vasco da Gama's return voyage across the Indian Ocean required four months and cost the lives of almost half of his 170 sailors. Seriously weakened, crewmembers continued to die on the voyage home, among them da Gama's brother, Palo.

Caused by a Vitamin C deficiency, scurvy was the most common nutritional deficiency to afflict sailors in the sailing era. At sea for months, living on hard biscuits and salted meats, nutritional deficiencies were common. Many captains, such as James Cook, experimented with cures of their own devising, but with inconsistent results. By the mid-18th century, people recognized that fresh food prevented scurvy, but only later—following detailed experiments—did doctors identify the best foods for treating scurvy. In 1795 CE, convinced by growing medical evidence, the British Admiralty mandated that lemon juice be included for the fleet.

Stephen K. Stein

---

in piracy of Muslim ships in retaliation for Portuguese killed in Calicut as well as negotiating an official trading relationship with Cochin, a rival of Calicut, he returned to Portugal in 1503 CE, carrying between 30,000 and 35,000 quintals of spices.

The next two decades of da Gama's life included tension with King Manuel. In 1518 CE, he threatened to leave Portugal and sell his navigational skills elsewhere until Manuel made him Count of Vidigueira in 1519 CE. After Manuel died in 1521 CE, his son, John III (1502–1557 CE), decided to send da Gama on another voyage to India in the hopes of cleaning up corruption within the Portuguese administration there and to cultivate friendlier relationships with local peoples. Da Gama was made Viceroy of India, and he set out for the region on April 9, 1524. Though he reached Cochin in October 1524 CE and began his tasks, his health quickly deteriorated, and he died in India in late December 1524 CE.

When da Gama died, he had witnessed and taken part in unprecedented changes. His voyage of 1497 CE established a sea route to India that would continue in use for hundreds of years, allowing for the development of sustained trading relationships among Europeans, east Africans, Indians, and other merchants of the Indian Ocean. This route helped turn Portugal into a major imperial power of the 16th and

17th centuries. His attitude toward local populations and his ability to capitalize on tensions also helped ensure that this Portuguese empire would be based on violence and conquest.

Lindsay J. Starkey

Further Reading

Aimes, Glenn. 2005. *Vasco da Gama: Renaissance Crusader*. New York: Pearson Education, Inc.

Disney, Anthony, and Emily Booth (eds.). 2000. *Vasco da Gama and the Linking of Europe and Asia*. Oxford: Oxford University Press.

Subrahmanyam, Sanjay. 1997. *The Career and Legend of Vasco da Gama*. Cambridge: Cambridge University Press.

Watkins, Ronald. 2003. *Unknown Seas: How Vasco da Gama Opened the East*. London: John Murray.

Henry the Navigator, 1394–1460 CE

Infante Dom Henrique de Avis, Duke of Viseu, more commonly known as "Henry the Navigator," was a Portuguese prince, who played a significant role in 15th-century Portuguese politics as well as encouraged the expansion of European

Padrao dos Descobrimentos (Monument to the Discoveries), Lisbon, Portugal. The main statue is Prince Henry the Navigator, who expanded European knowledge of the African and Atlantic oceans. (Coplandj /Dreamstime.com)

power and trade into North Africa, the Atlantic Islands, and on the coast of Western Africa. Prince Henry was the third surviving son of King John I of Portugal (1358–1433 CE). Through his personal interest in crusading against Muslims in Africa and through patronage, Henry aided the development of Portuguese exploration and maritime trade.

As a third son, Henry was unlikely to inherit his father's throne. Instead, his livelihood depended on land grants, offices, privileges over trade, and military campaigns. In the early 1410s, Henry along with his brothers convinced his father to send a military expedition to Northern Africa. Setting out in 1415 CE, this expedition captured the major Moroccan trading port of Ceuta. John I made Henry the Duke of Viseu, the Lord of Covilhã and king's lieutenant for the affairs of Ceuta when Henry returned to Portugal. He was also made governor of the military Order of Christ in 1420 CE. This successful military campaign provided Henry with one of the main focuses of the rest of his life—the continued expansion of Portuguese power and influence throughout Northern Africa, helping lead attacks on Tangier in 1437 CE and on Alcazar in 1458 CE.

The resources and the powers Henry gained from his new role in Ceuta and as governor of the Order of Christ propelled his interest in Portuguese maritime activities. Moroccan forces continually attacked the Portuguese troops stationed in Ceuta's fortress. Henry's role as king's lieutenant in Ceuta meant that it was his job to oversee the provisioning of this garrison by Portuguese ships. There is no evidence that Henry sailed on these ships; however, there is evidence that Henry owned ships by the early 1420s and that he gave command of these ships to members of his household. These ships supplied food for the Portuguese in Ceuta and also raided the African coast for slaves and other goods they sold in Europe.

Throughout the 1420s and into the early 1430s, the corsairs that Henry supplied and oversaw began to encounter islands off the coast of Western Africa. Though unsuccessful in claiming the Canary Islands from Castile, Henry and his men were able to establish Portuguese control over Madeira, the Azores, and eventually the Cape Verde Islands. Henry petitioned and was granted jurisdiction over Madeira in 1433 CE, over the Azores in 1439 CE, and over the Cape Verde Islands shortly before his death. This jurisdiction allowed Henry to appoint the men who would oversee the settlement and development of these islands and provide Henry with a percentage of their profits.

Using both Ceuta and these islands as a base, corsairs on his payroll also raided down the west coast of Africa, capturing people to sell as slaves. This lucrative raiding and Africans' reactions to these raids increased both Henry's and wider European interest in traveling farther south down the coast and eventually encouraged the establishment of trading relationships between European merchants and various West African peoples. Once Europeans had raided a particular

African settlement, the people tended to move inland, forcing European sailors to travel farther south to find easier targets for their slave raids. By the later 1440s, these ships had sailed beyond Cape Bojador and reached territory in what is today Sierra Leone. The African peoples they encountered south of the Sahara Desert put up much stronger resistance. This opposition encouraged the Portuguese to set up factories and cultivate trade relationships with African groups. In exchange for slaves and gold, Europeans offered wheat, horses, salt, and cloth. Henry was extremely interested in this trade. He petitioned for control over it and was granted a monopoly in 1443 CE, meaning that any ships trading in West Africa required a license from him. In 1444 CE, he also set up a consortium at Lagos to send ships to West Africa, and he established a trading post on the island of Argium off the coast of modern Mauritania after 1445 CE. Throughout the 1450s, he worked to consolidate his personal gains and provide further support for them by petitioning popes for recognition of Portuguese claims over territories in Africa and in the Atlantic.

Though Henry did not personally undertake many voyages to Africa, his role in Ceuta, his jurisdiction over Atlantic Island settlements, and his monopoly on trade in West Africa meant that he provided encouragement as well as ships and supplies to those Europeans who were exploring these territories and creating and developing settlements, trade, and new contacts with Western African peoples.

Lindsay J. Starkey

Further Reading

Diffie, Baily W., and George D. Winius. 1977. *Foundations of the Portuguese Empire 1415–1580*. Minneapolis: University of Minnesota Press.

Newitt, Malyn. 1986. "Prince Henry and the Origins of Portuguese Expansion." Malyn Newitt (ed.). *The First Portuguese Colonial Empire*. Exeter: University of Exeter Press, 9–35.

Russell, Peter. 2000. *Prince Henry "The Navigator:" A Life*. New Haven: Yale University Press.

Zurara, Gomes Eannes de. 1896. *The Chronicle of the Discovery and Conquest of Guinea*. Charles Raymond Beazley and Edgar Prestage (ed. and trans.). London: Hakluyt Society.

Nau

Naus were high-board Portuguese armed merchant ships mainly used for the Cape route trade between Lisbon and India, the Carreira da Índia. From the early days of Portuguese navigation in the Indian Ocean by Bartolomeu Dias's circumnavigation of the Cape of Good Hope (1488 CE) and Vasco da Gama's (1497–1499 CE) voyage of discovery, the long-distance voyages of the maritime trade route to India required a new and more resistant ship type able to navigate in open seas and having a greater cargo capacity than the caravels used during the voyages of discoveries in the Atlantic.

Mostly built in the Lisbon shipyards (Ribeira das Naus) but also in Oporto and Goa (India), naus were based on a carvel-built hull structure characterized by the skeleton-first planking method commonly used in southern European countries. The naus were of a general length to width proportion of 3/1. Designed with three or four decks, a forecastle and aftcastle, these three-masted ships were rigged with square sails at the foremast and the mainmast and a lateen sail at the mizzenmast. An additional foremast also was rigged with a square sail. The capacity of naus was measured by tonéis of which 1 tonel was equivalent to 1.368 m^3 or 334 U.S. gallons. During the course of the 16th towards the early 17th century, the maximum capacity of the naus was increased from about 450 tonéis to approximately 800 to 900 tonéis. Famous Portuguese naus are the *Flor de la Mar*, the flagship of Afonso de Albuquerque in the battle off Malaka (1510 CE), and the *Nossa Senhora dos Mártires* (1606 CE) commonly known as the Pepper Wreck. The use of this particular ship type in the service of the Portuguese India shipping is documented until the early 19th century.

Torsten dos Santos Arnold

Further Reading

Fernandez, Manoel. 1995. *Livro de Traças de Carpintaria—Book of Draughts of Shipwrights*. Lisbon: Academia de Marinha.

Gardner, Robert (ed.). 1994. *Cogs, Caravels, and Galleons: The Sailing Ship, 1000—1650*. London: Conway Maritime Press.

Newitt, Malyn. 2004. *A History of Portuguese Overseas Expansion 1400–1668*. New York: Routledge.

Oliveira, Fernando. 1991. *O Livro da Fábrica das Naus—The Book of Shipbuilding*, Lisbon: Academia de Marinha.

Nuñes, Pedro, 1502–1578 CE

Pedro Nuñes was one of the most prestigious scientists of the Renaissance. During the Age of Discovery, this Portuguese mathematician and cartographer wrote extensively on cosmography, navigation, algebra, spherical geometry, and astronomy. He is best known for his contributions to the nautical sciences, which he was the first to approach via mathematics. He invented several measuring devices to aid in ship navigation.

Born in 1502 CE in Alcácer do Sal, Portugal, he studied at the University of Salamanca and the University of Lisbon. Graduating in 1523 CE he married a Spanish woman, Giomar de Arias, and they had six children together. Nuñes served as tutor to Prince Luis, the brother of King John III of Portugal (1502–1557 CE), and taught navigation and mathematics to Martim Afonso de Sousa (ca.1500–1564 CE), who led the first colonizing expedition to Brazil in 1530 CE, João de Castro (1500–1548 CE), a scientist, explorer, and writer who served as Portugal's fourth Viceroy in India, and other prominent individuals.

From 1532 CE to 1544 CE, Nuñes taught courses in mathematics, philosophy, and other fields at the University of Lisbon, and supervised numerous doctoral students while writing several books. He began writing *Libro de Algebra* in 1534 CE, but did not publish the completed work until 34 years later. He published *Tratado da Sphera* in 1537 CE, followed by two works on navigation, which at the time marked the pinnacle of nautical science. King João recognized Nuñes for his expertise by appointing him Cosmographer of the Kingdom of Portugal in 1537 CE. Nuñes continued to teach and write about navigation and mathematics, including *De Crepusculis* (*About the Twilight*, 1542 CE), which addressed the day with the shortest twilight, a problem posed by one of his students, and the *Book of Algebra in Arithmetic and Geometry* (1567 CE). His writings contributed to the development of new scientific methods and the construction of new navigational instruments.

Previously, it had been impossible to precisely measure small portions of an arc using an astrolabe. Nuñes conceived the idea of a nonius—an instrument that could be attached to an astrolabe for measuring fractions of a degree. It used 44 concentric auxiliary circles to allow precise readings of the height of stars on a quadrant. His other important discovery was the loxodromic curve on a globe—also called rhumb lines—a spiral that converges at the poles. The loxodromic curve is a line that maintains a fixed angle with the meridians. A ship following a fixed compass direction that is not exactly north-south or east-west follows a loxodromic curve. Nuñes discovered these lines and advocated drawing maps in which loxodromic spirals appear as straight lines. This eventually led to the Mercator projection, which is still in use today.

Jill M. Church

Further Reading

Martyn, John R. C. (ed. and trans.). 1996. *Pedro Nuñes (1502–1578): His Lost Algebra and Other Discoveries*. New York: Peter Lang Publishing, Inc.

O'Connor, J. J., and Robertson, E. F. 2010. "Pedro Nuñes Salaciense." http://www-history.mcs.st-andrews.ac.uk/Biographies/Nunes.html. Accessed January 25, 2016.

Randles, W. G. L. 1997. "Pedro Nuñes' Discovery of the Loxodromic Curve (1537)." *Journal of Navigation* 50/1: 85–96.

RUSSIA, 1450 TO 1770 CE

Russia's maritime tradition is most commonly associated with Peter the Great (1672–1725 CE; r. 1682–1725 CE), who secured for Russia a Baltic Sea port and founded the imperial Russian Navy. Peter famously proclaimed, "any potentate with an army has one hand, but he who also has a fleet has two hands." The idiom was inscribed into the opening pages of his Naval Statute ("*Morskoi Ustav*") of 1720 CE, the official regulation for activity at sea. Linking Russian seafaring to Peter I is accurate, but one-sided; it emphasizes the founding of the state navy, but ignores the vast experience and the rich maritime traditions of various subjects of the Russian empire pursued without the direct oversight of the state. Peter extended his vision beyond the strategic and commercial benefits of the navy. His vision of transforming Russia into a European state included building St. Petersburg, the northern capital he founded in 1703 CE, as a city of rivers and canals like Venice and Amsterdam. The city was located across several islands and riverbanks, with boats being the primary mode of travel. Peter also initiated the construction of a system of canals to facilitate transportation of goods to the capital, which he sought to make Russia's most important port. Russia's "window to Europe" has retained the nautical motif associated with its founder to this day.

Sixteenth Century: Muscovy Looks Outward

Before Peter I, early Russian polities had their own rich traditions of fishing, river navigation, and even overseas travel. There is some evidence to suggest that subjects of the first Russian state, Kievan Rus' (founded ninth century CE), expertly navigated and traded on the Black Sea. Muscovy, the reconstituted Russian entity after the Mongols were repelled in the middle of the 15th century, drew on these maritime traditions and established trade routes along river systems between the Baltic, Black, and Caspian Seas.

Ivan IV's (1530–1584 CE) acquisition of several strategic ports opened new possibilities for Russian trade with the civilizations around them. The conquest of Narva (1558 CE) in the course of the Livonian War (1558–1583 CE) gave Russia a highly desired Baltic Port, but it was returned to Sweden in 1581 CE at the end of the war. The tsar's conquests of Kazan (1552 CE) and Astrakhan (1556 CE) on the Volga River opened up the river valley and the Caspian Sea to Russian trade. Russian merchants regularly navigated the Caspian Sea from Astrakhan, which was positioned where the Volga flowed into the sea. They traded with the Khanates, Khiva, and Bukhara, and with the coastal cities Baku and Derbent. The Muscovy Company merchant Anthony Jenkinson reported the presence of Russian flotillas and boats on the Caspian Sea as early as 1561 CE.

The port of Astrakhan became the main focus of Russian-Asian trade in the 17th century. Expansion into Central Asia was highly desirable for access to the eastern luxuries but, with the exception of Peter the Great's short-lived campaign which allowed Russians to occupy the western shores of the Caspian Sea from 1722 to 1735 CE, it remained out of Russian reach until the 19th century.

In 1583–1584 CE, Tsar Ivan IV ordered the construction of the port of Arkhangel'sk (known as "Archangel" in English-language sources) on the White Sea. Situated at the mouth of the North Dvina River, Arkhangel'sk was better suited to dock deep-sea going vessels than the less-favorably situated Kholmogory and Severodvinsk (sometimes referred to as St. Nicholas) also along the North Dvina. Its construction allowed English and Dutch merchants to conduct business directly with Russian merchants, cutting out the Swedish middlemen who monopolized the Baltic trade. Referred to by Muscovites as Russia's "gate to the seas," Arkhangel'sk became and remained Russia's busiest port until the 18th century. The Muscovite state depended on indirect taxes and customs revenues associated with foreign trade passing through there for more than 40 percent of its revenues. The main exports passing through Arkhangel'sk were furs, "*iufti*" (a specially treated leather product), potash, tallow, and grain. With all the characteristics of a frontier town, Arkhangel'sk also was notorious for its foul smell, owing to the local industry of blubber distilleries, tallow and salt works, and ship construction. Even Peter the Great declined to stay in the town on each of his three visits to learn the art of seafaring.

Seventeenth Century: Drive and Consolidation

The Russian North's fishing industry operated nearly year-round to harvest freshwater fish, marine fish, and marine-mammal products. The Pomors ("*pomory*") ("people of the sea") as well as indigenous ethnic groups, lived, fished, and hunted in the circumpolar region around the White Sea and in nearby rivers and lakes. For the *pomory*, freshwater fish such as pike, whitefish, perch, herring, and smelt provided cheap, everyday food for consumption, and migratory salmon was a valuable catch. Herring, cod, and halibut were important commodities acquired from the marine environment off the coast of the Kola Peninsula. The hunters also sought out walruses for their valuable blubber and tusks, and some even went as far away as Spitsbergen to hunt whales.

The Murmansk coast of the Kola Peninsula was an important point of encounter with fishermen and hunters from the Danish-Norwegian kingdom, occasionally resulting in disputes over fishing rights in the area. The daily catch was preserved with salt and distributed to distant parts of the Russian empire.

In the far north, monks and local monasteries played an important spiritual and practical role in the fishing industry. In the dangerous marine environment the locals developed an array of rituals that combined pagan superstitions with tenets of the Orthodox Christian faith. The communities sought divine protection and drew on the support of the Orthodox churches. Fishermen and hunters often donated a portion of their profits to a local church upon their return home. Monasteries also provided a range of skilled experts in carpentry and blacksmithing for construction of river- and seagoing vessels, and facilitated trade in fish and marine mammal products.

Much like European expansion in the Americas, Russia's expansion eastwards into the heart of Siberia and to the Pacific Ocean was a story of conquest, displacement, violence, exploitation, and conversion. In the late 15th century, Muscovite raids into Siberia pushed Russia's presence north and east. Muscovy annexed the independent city of Novgorod, Russia's historic outlet to the Hanseatic trade on the Baltic Sea, and launched military expeditions beyond the Urals where encounters with Siberian indigenous tribes yielded tribute and furs. In the 16th century, state-sanctioned groups of Cossacks or other military persons travelled east to collect "*iasak*" ("tribute") adding to Muscovy's knowledge and control of the region. Russian exploration to the east made use of the riverine network, with the Ob', Enisei, Lena, Iana, Indigirka, and Kolyma forming successive frontiers for Russian expansion. The mythical Cossack Ermak Timofeev, credited with conquering the Khanate of Sibir' (1581–1585 CE), brought the Russians to the Irtysh river. Ivan Moskvitin reached the Pacific coast in 1639 CE. Vasilii Poiarkov was the first European to reach the Amur River, and his travels along the Amur brought the region into the Russian fold (1649–1652 CE). Through their explorations, some Cossack leaders traveled along the highly sought-after Northeast Passage. In the middle of the 17th century, Semen Dezhnev sailed from the Kolyma River, along the Arctic coast, and into the Pacific Ocean. In the 1690s, Vladimir Atlasov's exploratory party charted the Kamchatka peninsula and the Okhotsk seacoast. Russian expansion into the region was also propelled by countless unnamed "*promyshlenniki*"—entrepreneurial fur-trappers, traders, and prospectors who moved into Siberia in search of "soft gold." When the Siberian furs had been exhausted, they moved on to the marine environment of the North Pacific. On the Commander, Aleutian, and Bering Islands stretching all the way to Alaska, they hunted sea otters, fur seals, and blue foxes almost to the point of extinction.

Eighteenth Century: The Russian Empire Flourishes

Because of these earlier traditions, it would be far more accurate to say that the maritime tradition that Peter the Great established was to bring Russian seafaring under the eye of the state. Under Peter I, this tradition came to include his naval campaigns at Azov (1695–1696 CE), on the Caspian Sea (1722–1723 CE), and in the Great Northern War (1700–1721 CE). The Treaty of Nystadt (1721 CE), ending the

Great Northern War between Russia and Sweden, ceded the territories of Estonia and Livonia to the Russian Empire, giving Russia permanent access to Baltic ports. Peter built naval infrastructure such as wharves and sea fortresses, including Kronstadt near St. Petersburg to house the Baltic Sea Fleet. Peter also founded the School of Mathematical and Navigation Sciences in Moscow (1701 CE) and a Naval Academy in St. Petersburg (1715 CE) to provide technical education to sailors and naval engineers.

Exploration of the Russian north and the Pacific coast also took a decidedly more scientific turn under Peter, part of the state's increasing "territoriality"—greater attention paid to the space and resources of the empire used to inform practices of governance (Sunderland 2007, 34). The First Kamchatka Expedition (1725–1730 CE), led by the Danish captain Vitus Bering, established the presence of a strait between the continents of Asia and America. The Second Kamchatka Expedition (1733–1743 CE), also under Bering's command, included a significant academic component and yielded the first natural historical descriptions of the Kamchatka peninsula and the North Pacific marine environment. The Russian Academy of Sciences, founded in 1724 CE, had begun to play a larger role in directing and utilizing knowledge gained from these expeditions. Better understanding of geography and natural resources of the region were also put to use by *promyshlenniki*, who continued trapping furs and exploiting the environment.

The reign of Catherine II (1729–1796 CE; r. 1762–1796 CE) proved to be a boon for Russian seafaring. The Empress reorganized the administrative structure of the Admiralty, allocated immense resources to the construction of the Black Sea fleet, and reinvigorated scientific exploration of the North Pacific region. Some projects of commerce and exploration were waylaid by several wars with the Ottoman Empire (1768–1774 CE; 1787–1791 CE) and Sweden (1788–1790 CE), but others, such as the Billings Expedition to the North Pacific (1789–1795 CE) pressed on. Known for her legislative projects, Catherine the Great sought to secure an optimal international maritime legal regime for Russian trade through the League of Armed Neutrality (1780 CE).

One of Catherine's grand undertakings was the First Archipelago Expedition (1769–1774 CE). After the breakout of the 1768 Russian-Ottoman War, Catherine dispatched five squadrons from the Baltic Sea fleet to circumnavigate the European continent and enter the Aegean Sea. The squadrons arrived to support a Greek rebellion against the Ottoman Empire. The uprising in the Morea failed, but after the Russian naval victory in the Battle of Çeşme on July 5–7, 1770, the naval leadership undertook Russia's first overseas imperial project in the Aegean Archipelago. Representatives of nearly 30 islands from the Greek archipelago took an oath for their islands to come under Russian suzerainty, and the naval command proceeded to implement imperial rule in an effort to teach the Greeks to eventually govern themselves. The Expedition provided the Russians with an opportunity to create naval maps and charts of the region, as well as to bring artifacts of classical civilization back to Russia. The Russians gave up the so-called Archipelago Principality in the 1774 peace treaty with the Ottoman Empire in return for other concessions, thereby ending Russia's first attempt at overseas rule.

Throughout the 18th century, the Russian Empire had endeavored to wrest from the Ottoman Empire the rights to navigate on the Black Sea and secure passage through the Bosporus and Dardanelles Straits. The 1774 Treaty of Kuçuk-Kainarca was the first step in realizing these ambitions. The treaty concessions given by the Ottoman Empire continued to be challenged through the 19th century, and the Bosporus and Dardanelles Straits became subject of much geopolitical contention.

Although few Russians lived near the sea, the idea of the sea played a significant role in the popular imagination. In Russian folklore, they had always been a maritime power, shown by the plentiful allusions to the "ocean-sea" (as large bodies of water appeared on 18th-century maps). The romantic poetry of Vasilii Zhukovsky and Alexander Pushkin features images of the sea, and many characters in Pushkin's fairy tales lived along seashores. The Russian state's explorations and discoveries of marine environments on the outskirts of the empire were kept secret from the international public, adding to the perceived image of Russia as a land-based empire. Within the empire, however, ceremonies, arts, and literature told a different story of the Russian self-image as a seafaring empire.

Julia Leikin

Further Reading

Bonhomme, Brian. 2012. *Russian Exploration, from Siberia to Space: A History*. London: McFarland & Co.

Jones, Ryan Tucker. 2014. *Empire of Extinction: Russians and the North Pacific's Strange Beasts of the Sea, 1741–1867*. New York: Oxford University Press.

King, Charles. 2004. *The Black Sea: A History*. Oxford: Oxford University Press.

Kivelson, Valerie A. 2006. *Cartographies of Tsardom: The Land and Its Meanings in Seventeenth-Century Russia*. Ithaca, NY: Cornell University Press.

Kotilaine, Jarmo. 2004. *Russia's Foreign Trade and Economic Expansion in the Seventeenth Century*. Leiden: Brill.

Kraikovski, Alexei. 2015. "'The Sea on One Side, Trouble on the Other': Russian Marine Resource Use before Peter the Great." *Slavonic and East European Review* 93(1) (January 2015): 39–65.

Sunderland, Willard. 2007. "Territorial Thought and Practice in the Eighteenth Century." In *Russian Empire: Space, People, Power, 1700–1930*. Jane Burbank and Mark Von Hagen (eds.), 33–66. Bloomington: Indiana University Press.

Bering, Vitus, 1681–1741 CE

Vitus Bering was a Danish-born sea captain who explored the North Pacific for the Russian Empire in the 18th century. He crossed the Bering Sea—which is named after him—and landed in Alaska, opening Alaska to Russian traders, trappers, and whalers.

Born to Jonas Svendsen and his wife Anna Bering in Horsens, Denmark, Vitus Bering, named after a maternal great-uncle, spent his childhood in Jutland. After receiving basic naval training in Amsterdam, he moved to St. Petersburg where he advanced rapidly in the Russian Navy, recently founded by Tsar Peter the Great. Russia was a latecomer to maritime explorations, and the tsar commissioned foreigners not only as officers in his fleet, but also to lead expeditions searching for a route through the Arctic Ocean to China and Japan. Among the former was Cornelius Cruys, born of Norwegian and Dutch parents, he entered the Russian Navy, rose to the rank of admiral, and attracted other foreigners to Russian service, among them Vitus Bering. Scandinavian navigators such as Cruys and Bering strongly influenced the growing Russian Navy.

Bering led two expeditions to Kamchatka. These were combined sea-land enterprises with three important outcomes: rendering Siberia's geographical scope more precisely, charting the North Pacific between the East Siberian coast and Alaska, and providing the basis for the future colonization of Alaska by Russia. The contribution of Bering and his crew enlarged Imperial Russia's knowledge of her seas and demonstrated that the Russia Empire could compete with other European sea powers.

The purpose of the first Kamchatka expedition, which departed in August 1724 CE, was to determine whether Asia and North America were connected by land. Sailing north from Kamchatka, Bering and his crew charted the strait between Eastern Siberia and Alaska—which was named after Bering. A previous Russian seafarer, Semyon Dezhnev, also had discovered the strait, but records of his expedition were lost. The reason why Bering gained more credit than Dezhnev was that in the 17th century Russia's exploration of the Arctic Ocean was made by individuals, but in the 18th century it became a state-endeavored enterprise with expeditions directed by scientifically trained officers. In 1731 CE, Bering led a second expedition which further explored the strait and, most importantly, sighted and landed on the Alaskan coast. German naturalist Georg Wilhelm Steller, who accompanied both expeditions, recorded their results, which included noting the large populations of sea otter, fur seals, and sea lions that soon attracted hunters. The prolonged expedition took a heavy toll on Bering's crew, many of whom succumbed to scurvy, including Bering himself who died on December 8, 1741. His second-in-command—Sven Waxell—led the survivors home the following year.

Eva-Maria Stolberg

Further Reading

Frost, Orcutt. 2003. *Bering. The Russian Discovery of America.* New Haven: Yale University Press.

Lauridsen, Peter. 2012 (first ed. 1889). *Vitus Bering. The Discovery of the Bering Strait.* Cambridge: Cambridge University Press.

Oliver, James. A. 2006. *The Bering Strait Crossing. A 21st Century Frontier Between East and West.* Exmouth: Company of Writers.

Steller, Georg Wilhelm. 1988. *Journal of a Voyage with Bering, 1741–1742.* With an Introduction by O.W. Frost (ed.). Margritt A. Engel and O. W. Frost (trans.). Stanford: Stanford University Press.

Dezhnev, Semyon Ivanov, 1605–ca. 1673 CE

Semyon Dezhnev was the first Russian explorer to pass through the Bering Strait. In 1648 CE, he sailed from the mouth of the Kolyma river in Eastern Siberia eastbound along the Arctic shores to the mouth of the Anadyr River on the peninsula Chukotka. At that time, sea expeditions were not recorded in the Tsarist Empire and thus Dezhnev's discovery fell into oblivion. The strait between Chukotka and Alaska instead was named after Captain Vitus Bering who sailed the strait 100 years later.

Born and raised on the White Sea, the western part of the Russian Arctic Ocean, Dezhnev developed a lifelong passion for the Arctic Ocean. Before his expedition in 1648 CE, he had sailed along various Siberian rivers including the Irtysh and Yenisei. These rivers flowing into the Arctic Ocean were the path to the far North. After serving as a government agent in Western Siberia, Dezhnev went to Yakutia in the 1640s where he worked to expand the fur trade. This required the exploration of the rivers and seaway to the east. Blocked by local tribes that fought with both the Russians and each other, Dezhnev successfully mediated among them.

Dezhnev then led several expeditions to the East. The first expedition, financed by a Moscow merchant and launched in 1647 CE, failed due to thick ice. The following year they tried again and proved successful, although some ships were wrecked by storms. This expedition, which lasted a year, reached the strait between Chukotka and Alaska and passed along shores inhabited by the warlike Chukchee tribe. The colonial administration of Siberia, however, saw no practical use for the passage Dezhnev discovered because thick ice made it impassable most of the year. Thus, the passage through the waters between the East Siberian coast and Alaska was forgotten, only to be rediscovered in the 18th century. Modern Russian historiography credits Semyon Dezhnev as a great explorer of the Arctic Ocean. One cape and an icebreaker are named after him. In 1983, the film "Semen

Dezhnev," directed by Nikolai Gusarov, premiered in Soviet cinema and promoted Russia's importance in Arctic exploration.

Eva-Maria Stolberg

Further Reading

Black, Lydia. 2004. *Russians in Alaska, 1732–1867*. Fairbanks, Alaska: University of Alaska Press.

Fisher, Raymond F. 1981. *The Voyage of Semen Dezhnev in 1648. Bering's Precursor with Selected Documents.* London: The Hakluyt Society.

Myarikyanova, Elvira. 2005. "Dezhnev, Semyon." Mark Nuttal (ed.). *Encyclopedia of The Arctic. Volumes 1, 2, and 3. A–Z.* New York: Routledge.

Muscovy Company

The Muscovy Company, also known as the Russia Company, was an English joint stock company that held a monopoly on that country's trade with the Kingdom of Muscovy (present-day Russia) from 1555 to 1649 CE. The company received its charter on February 26, 1555, and in October received permission from Russian Tsar Ivan IV to trade in Russia. At first, the company operated a trade route on the White Sea to the Russian city of Severodvinsk (known to the English as "St. Nicholas"); however, within a decade the Muscovy Company's activities expanded to the Baltic port of Narva—conquered by Russia in 1558 CE—and through the Tsar's lands to Persia.

The Company's imports from Russia were commodities and raw materials, and its exports to Russia were manufactured goods. Cordage—cables and ropes used for rigging a ship—was the most important commodity imported by the Muscovy Company into England. The expansion of English shipping in the first decades of the 17th century increased the demand for cordage, and the largest consumers were the English navy and the East India Company. Tallow—animal fat essential to manufacture of candles, soap, cloth, and leather—was a second essential commodity, virtually all of which was imported into London from Russia. Other items included *"iuft"* (high-quality Russian leather), caviar, and potash (used in manufacture of cloth, soap, and glass). For Russia, the two main imports were luxury cloths such as Italian silk desired by the Russian nobility and non-precious metals such as lead, tin, and copper for production of armaments and munitions.

The Muscovy Company's successes owed much to the special privileges it received from the Russian government, including the right to trade in Russia's interior and an exemption from paying customs duties, tolls, and other taxes. These privileges put the English merchants well ahead of the Dutch and Swedish merchants also trading in Russia. Moreover, even the top corporation of

Russian merchants was not exempt from paying customs duties. Tsar Ivan IV's favorable treatment was provided in the hope of a political and military alliance with England against neighboring powers. When the English refused, the Russian government began curtailing some of the privileges the English merchants received; however, the English managed to hold on to their full duty exemption until 1646 CE.

By the beginning of the 17th century the Muscovy Company's position was precarious. Although the company's trade remained lucrative, the political situation in Russia at the turn of the century—the Time of Troubles—jeopardized its business. The company lost much of its property and many of its debtors. It refinanced and reorganized in 1620 CE; political turmoil in England hindered its operations for the rest of the century. In June 1649 CE, Tsar Aleksei Romanov revoked the company's charter to trade in Russia. Although he cited the execution of King Charles I as a factor, it is likely that Russian merchants' petitions to curtail West European merchants influenced the decision. Successive English missions sought to reinstate the company's privileges, but only a handful of merchants received permission to trade in the Russian interior. By the end of the 17th century, the Muscovy Company's membership fell to about a dozen merchants. A 1699 act of Parliament to enlarge trade with Russia ended its monopoly and removed restrictions on membership, and the company reconstituted itself as the Russia Company.

Julia Leikin

Further Reading

Arel, Maria Salomon. 1999. "Masters in Their Own House: The Russian Merchant Élite and Complaints Against the English in the First Half of the Seventeenth Century." *The Slavonic and East European Review* 77(3) (July): 401–47.

Baron, Samuel H. 1991. *Explorations in Muscovite History*. Hampshire: Variorum.

Willan, Thomas S. 1956. *The Early History of the Russia Company 1553–1603*. Manchester: Manchester University Press.

Peter the Great, 1672–1725 CE

Peter the Great ruled Russia jointly with his older brother, Ivan V, from 1682 to 1696 CE. Following his brother's death, Peter was the sole ruler until his own death in 1725 CE. Among his many accomplishments was the founding of St. Petersburg as Russia's new capital on the Baltic Sea in 1703 CE, and encouraging a maritime vision for Russia.

Born June 9, 1672, Peter developed an interest in the sea and at age 16 learned to sail under the supervision of the Dutch Franz Timmermann. As Tsar he instituted a host of political and military reforms, expanded the Russian army and navy, and fought successful wars against both Sweden and the Ottoman Empire. Eager to modernize Russia, in 1697–1698 CE he traveled through Western Europe, observing and learning. He learned carpentry and shipbuilding in Zaandam, near Amsterdam, and visited the English docks at Deptford. Peter admired the British as a seafaring people and an English acquaintance, John Perry, reported Peter once remarking that it would be "a much happier life to be an admiral in England, than Czar in Russia."

The English 18th century biographer of Peter the Great, Alexander Gordon, reported that the Tsar inspected towns which were suitable for shipbuilding and located on rivers. Following his return, Peter founded several ports and enlarged others, including Riga, Reval, and Viborg. He increased funding for the Russian navy, and hired shipbuilders from England, the Netherlands, and Scandinavia to build a modern fleet of sea-going and river-going vessels. Showcased in parades of ships and other maritime displays, Peter's new fleet proved successful in wars against both the Swedes and the Ottomans.

Peter's motives for expanding the navy were threefold: commercial, military, and scientific. Under Peter, the Baltic, White, and Caspian Seas, the Sea of Azov, and the North Pacific were increasingly connected with Russia's interior waterways, fueling commerce, which included grain, timber, hemp, iron, potash, and Russia's famous caviar destined for Western markets.

Continuing the professionalization and modernization of Russian seafaring, Peter founded the Moscow School of Mathematics and Navigation in 1700 CE. A decade later the navigation school transferred to St. Petersburg. The goal was to provide academic training in geodesic measurement, sea surveying, and ship engineering. Modeled after English patterns, a first textbook on navigation in Slavonic dialect was published. Peter also ordered the Kamchatka expedition, led by Vitus Bering, to explore the North Pacific. He died on February 8, 1725, shortly after the expedition set out.

Eva-Maria Stolberg

Further Reading

Bushkovitch, Paul. 2001. *Peter the Great.* Lanham: Rowman & Littlefield Publishers.

Cross, Anthony. 1997. *By the Banks of the Neva. Chapters from the Lives and Careers of the British in Eighteenth-Century Russia.* Cambridge: Cambridge University Press.

Gordon, Alexander. 1755. *The History of Peter the Great, Emperor of Russia.* Aberdeen: F. Douglass & W. Murray.

Hughes, Lindsey. 2002. *Peter the Great. A Biography.* New Haven: Yale University Press.

Philipps, Edward J. 1995. *The Founding of Russia's Navy. Peter the Great and the Azov Fleet, 1688–1714.* Westport, CT: Greenwood Publishers.

SPAIN, 1450 TO 1770 CE

The maritime history of the realms that would become unified Spain extend over a number of different maritime stages in the Mediterranean, the Atlantic, and the Pacific Ocean. Because the territories on the Atlantic coast and those on the Mediterranean historically were not under the same rule, they underwent different socioeconomic developments. The dynastic marriage between Isabella I of Castile (1451–1504 CE) and the Aragonese king Ferdinand II (1452–1516 CE) in 1469 CE, laid the foundation for far-reaching unification and hispanization. As Catholic Monarchs ("*Reyes Católicos*," a title given by Pope Alexander VI in recognition of their defense of Catholicism in 1494 CE) they completed the Reconquista on the Iberian Peninsula in 1492 CE, following their victory over the Nasrid-Emirate of Granada, the last Muslim kingdom in Spain. In addition to territorial consolidation and forced conversion, Jews were likewise expelled from the composite monarchy.

Although Castile historically was intertwined with Portugal, the composite monarchy of the Crown of Aragon turned into a Mediterranean empire during the 14th and 15th centuries, controlling the Balearic Islands (Mallorca 1344 CE), Sicily (1381 CE), Sardinia (1297 CE), and the kingdom of Naples (1442 CE). The western Mediterranean kingdom was famous for the predominately Jewish cartographers of Majorca (School of Cartographers). Mercantile self-administration known as "Llotja" (also known as "Consulate of the Sea") with juridical functions for maritime and commercial law, helped well-organized merchant communities in port cities such as Barcelona, Palma, and Valencia prosper during the golden age of the 15th century. Catalans moreover participated in explorations of the Canaries, Azores, and the West African coastline from the 13th century onwards together with Portugal and Genoa.

Castilian Atlantic expansionism started in the Canary Islands, an archipelago about 60 miles west of the southern coast of Morocco and more than 600 miles from the Spanish coast. Castile had laid claim to the archipelago since the expeditions led by Jean de Béthencourt (1362–1425 CE) to Lanzarote and Fuerteventura in 1405 CE, before gradually establishing colonial rule and single-crop cultivation on Gran Canaria and Tenerife in 1480 CE and 1495 CE, respectively. In 1462 CE, the first Duke of Medina Sidonia, Juan Alonso de Guzmán (1405–1468 CE), captured Gibraltar and in 1497 CE Melilla on the Moroccan coast. The Treaty of Alcáçovas of 1479 CE, which ended the Portuguese-Castilian war of succession, excluded Castile from any activities south of Cape Bojador on the West African coast. This restriction influenced Isabella's decision to sponsor Christopher Columbus's (ca. 1451–1506 CE) expedition to seek a western route to East Asia. On his first of a total of four journeys, Columbus unknowingly discovered a "new" continent when landing with his modest three-ship fleet in what is now the Bahamas. The following year Columbus set out with 17 ships and 1,500 men (including soldiers and settlers) to explore and colonize the Antilles.

In their maritime projects, the crowns of Aragon and Castile benefited from far-reaching trading networks open to foreign investments (from Genoese financiers and Portuguese "*conversos")* as well as from Arab-Muslim-Jewish nautical heritage. Reliable oceangoing ships, knowledge of currents and winds, and the use of naval instruments and advanced map-making were the pillars of Iberian maritime expansion and facilitated the first recorded crossings of both the Atlantic and Pacific Oceans. Experienced foreign seafarers and scholars would also help to design ships for the transport and defense of large tonnage over far distances. In the early stage of Atlantic expansion, the most common ship was the *nao* (also "*carrack*"), a three-masted Mediterranean merchant ship, usually constructed and outfitted in the shipyards of northern Spain. It often served as flagship, as was the case of the *Santa Maria* in Columbus's first voyage and the *Victoria*, the only ship that returned from Ferdinand Magellan's (1480–1521 CE) circumnavigating project. Yet, the most famous oceangoing vessels employed in Spain's long-distance trade were galleons. Developing alongside coastal trade with Flanders and France, the multi-decked galleon with three to four masts and a cargo space of up to 2,000 tons became the preferred sailing ship for Atlantic and Pacific commercial voyages.

Diving Bell

A diving bell is an enclosed metal compartment hooked to a rope or chain and tethered to a ship. Air becomes trapped within the bell due to water pressure, enabling divers to descend in the bell and explore the sea and the seabed. Limited by the ship to which they are tethered, the divers themselves cannot move the bell. First described by Aristotle (384–322 BCE), diverse peoples have used diving bells since antiquity—long before the invention of submarines in the modern era. Aristotle and Alexander the Great (356–323 BCE), for example, used a diving bell to explore the Mediterranean seabed.

Reinvented at various times, diving bells have proven particularly useful in salvage operations. The Spanish Crown, for example, used bronze diving bells to salvage treasure from the *Nuestra Señora de Atocha*, a treasure ship sunk by a hurricane off the Florida Keys in 1622 CE. Over the next few years, they recovered roughly half of the ship's cargo, though many of the Native American slaves employed in the operation died from the effects of rapid decompression when rapidly hauled to the surface from a depth of 60 feet. Eighteenth-century diving bells used bellows to pump fresh air into the bell allowing prolonged operation. By the 20th century, diving bells could operate in depths of several hundred feet and divers were brought to the surface slowly to protect them from the effects of decompression.

Matthew Blake Strickland

A few months after the first Spanish ships arrived in the Caribbean, the famous papal bulls *inter caetera* and *dudum siquidem*, or Bulls of Donation of 1493 CE, recognized Spanish claims to all new territories that lay west of an imaginary line of demarcation 100 leagues west of the Azores and Cape Verde Islands. Practically all Spanish overseas possessions enjoyed legitimization by the pope. The Portuguese, fearing Spanish intrusion in the South Atlantic, called for modifications to these bulls. The famous Treaty of Tordesillas of 1494 thereafter divided the world theoretically 370 leagues (1,770 km) west of the Cape Verde Islands between Portugal and Castile. It was an attempt to create two separate spheres of influence, assuring the Portuguese Crown the exclusive use of the route to India via the Cape of Good Hope as well as active participation in America by way of Brazil. The terms of the treaty encouraged the Castilians to expand via the Antilles to the American mainland. Once the Spaniards had crossed the Pacific following Vasco Nuñez Balboa's (ca. 1475–1519 CE) "discovery" (with Indian help) of the Isthmus of Panama in 1513 CE and Ferdinand Magellan's attempted circumnavigation of 1519–20 CE with landfalls in the Moluccas and the Philippines, the terms for Portuguese-Spanish division of influence were extended to Asia and defined in the 1529 Treaty of Zaragoza.

New overseas territories and growing aspirations of transatlantic trade required extensive royal administrative institutions. Queen Isabel founded the *Casa de Contratacíon* ("House of Trade") in 1503 CE in Seville to direct exploration, conquest, and trade with the new territories (similar to Portugal's *Casa da Índia*, established as *Casa de Ceuta* in 1434 CE in Lisbon). It levied the "*quinto real*" (a 20 percent tax) on all precious metals entering Spain, licensed pilots, and was in charge of protecting and regulating trade fleets such as the transatlantic *Carrera de India* or New Spain fleet (travelling in May and September), and the transpacific Manila Galleon (*Nao de la China*). It produced the "*Padrón Real*," a master map template for maps used on all Spanish ships after 1508 CE, offered naval training, and recorded information about new discoveries. The lawyers of the Council of the Indies (*Consejo de Indias*) implemented by Charles V (1500–1558 CE) in 1524 CE made all the laws and decisions for the Americas and the Philippines. Seville, which came under Christian rule in 1248 CE, was situated beside one arm of the Guadalquivir River 50 miles from the Atlantic Ocean. The city became the center of Atlantic trade and its prosperity was characteristic of Spain's golden age when the Atlantic system supported brisk economic growth during the 16th century. The *Carrera de India* linked Seville with Cartagena in Colombia and Veracruz in Mexico and from Acapulco to Manila. Spain's involvement in triangular trade meant that ships to the Americas carried slaves, liquor, textiles, grain, weapons, royal orders, settlers, missionaries, and colonial personnel, and returned with bullion, dyes, exotic timber, and tropical commodities. At the same time, it contributed to both negative biological and ecological consequences of the *Columbian Exchange* on both sides of the Atlantic.

With the Union of Crown between Spain and Portugal from 1580–81 to 1640 CE, Philip II of Spain (1527–1598 CE) became a truly global ruler and the country was on the peak of political and economic power. Yet, this was also the period of increasing tensions with Protestant rulers in northwestern Europe, including the Seven Provinces of the Low Countries, which successfully revolted against Philip II. During the second half of the 16th century, France and England joined the Dutch in challenging Spain at sea and its monopoly on Atlantic trade. When attacks on Spanish treasure fleets and raids of both Atlantic and Pacific ports by English privateers increased, Spain dispatched the 130-vessel-strong "Spanish Armada" in 1588 CE in a failed attempt to invade England and end English interference in the Netherlands.

At the same time, Spain's maritime frontier in the Mediterranean became a stage for hegemonic struggles with Christian rulers as well as Spain's battle against Islam. In 1510 CE, King Ferdinand built a Spanish garrison in Tripoli. A few decades later, Ottoman westward expansion alarmed Christian rulers—including the pope—and resulted in the forming of various holy leagues with Spanish participation. The Ottoman victory in the Battle of Preveza (1538 CE) marked the beginning of a new Ottoman order in the Mediterranean. Charles I of Spain, grandson of the Catholic Monarchs, continued his crusade against Islam, including the sultanates of Barbary Coast of North Africa and their corsairs which regularly attacked Spanish ports. He led an expedition against Algiers in 1541 CE but—similar to the 1560 Battle of Djerba under his successor Philip II—it ended with crippling losses to the Spanish fleet. With regard to Spanish conflicts over influence in Italy, Charles's imperial admiral Andrea Doria successfully extended Spanish Habsburg dominion over Italy. By the Battle of Lepanto (1571 CE), Spanish naval power had increasingly become dependent on Italian resources. Yet, the combined Christian fleet of the Holy League (Republic of Venice, Spain, Papal States, Republic of Genoa) initiated by Pope Pius V and led by Don Juan de Austria (1547–1578 CE) against the Ottoman naval forces under admiral Ali Pasha (supported by the corsairs Mehmed Sioco of Alexandria and Uluç Ali) prevented the Ottoman Empire from expanding farther West. The project was largely financed by the Spanish Habsburgs and was of great symbolic value for Catholic Europe.

The economic and political crisis in 17th-century Spain affected maritime matters in various ways. After 1609 CE, when the crown ordered the expulsion of up to 300,000 Moriscos—former Muslims who had converted to Catholicism—many of them settled in North Africa and joined anti-Spanish corsairs in attacking their original homeland. In addition, the Moriscos' expulsion and the loss of their knowledge and skilled labor reduced sugar production. After the decadent reigns of the last Habsburg kings and the childless death of Charles II (1661–1700 CE), Spain was drawn into a war of succession (1700–1713 CE) that involved Europe's major powers. It ended with Philip of Anjou (1683–1746 CE) ascending to the Spanish throne as Philip V, but also had consequences for Spanish overseas possessions such as Gibraltar, which became an English outpost.

In 1717 CE, Cadiz replaced Seville as seat of the House of Trade. The new Bourbon kings instituted economic and political reforms that aimed to regain control over transatlantic trade and establish tighter control over the empire. In the 1760s, King Charles III (1716–1788 CE) established A Coruña on the Galician Atlantic as a post port (*Correo Ultramarino*) from where frigates carried mail to Havana and Montevideo every three months, dramatically improving communications within Spain's empire. That empire, though, soon was disrupted by a succession of wars including the American War of Independence and the Wars of the French Revolution and Napoleon, which weakened Spain's hold on its colonies, many of which won their independence in the first decades of the 19th century.

Birgit Tremml-Werner

Further Reading

Abulafia, David. 1994. *A Mediterranean Emporium. The Catalan Kingdom of Majorca* Cambridge: Cambridge University Press.

Elliott, John H. 2006. *Empires of the Atlantic World. Britain and Spain in America, 1492–1830*. New Haven, CT: Yale University Press.

Goodman, David. 1997. *Spanish Naval Power: 1589–1665. Reconstruction and Defeat*. Cambridge: Cambridge University Press.

Kamen, Henry. 2002. *Spain's Road to Empire: The Making of a World Power*. London: Allen Lane.

O'Flanagan, Patrick. 2008. *Port Cities of Atlantic Iberia, c. 1500–1900*. Aldershot: Ashgate Publishing.

Parry, J. H. 1990. *The Spanish Seaborne Empire*. Berkeley: University of California Press.

Stein, Stanley J., and Barbara H. Stein. 2000. *Silver, Trade, and War: Spain and America in the Making of Early Modern Europe*. Baltimore: Johns Hopkins University Press.

Columbian Exchange

About 12,000 years ago the global climate became warmer, melting most of the massive ice sheets that had formed on the lower latitudes of the earth's surface. Water that had been locked away in glaciers gushed into the world's oceans and seas, raising sea-levels everywhere and submerging the terrestrial bridge across the Bering Strait that humans had used to cross from the Afro-Eurasian landmass to the Americas. In this new aquatic configuration, the two continental islands inhabited by *Homo sapiens* evolved almost entirely independently of one another, buffered by the vast expanse of the Pacific and Atlantic Oceans. The arrival of Christopher Columbus and his crew in the Caribbean shattered this isolation in

1492 CE, and inaugurated the sustained transfer of biota from one major landmass to the other, a continuing process historians call the Columbian Exchange.

Columbus famously set out from the Iberian Peninsula to find a transatlantic route to the spice-rich lands of Southeast Asia, not anticipating the obstructive presence of the American continent. The wherewithal of European sailors to face the Atlantic in 1492 CE was forged in the late 14th and early 15th centuries, when the Portuguese, French, and Spanish crowns invaded the Madeiran and Canary archipelagos, Atlantic islands off the coast of Morocco. In their regular voyages to these islands, navigators learned the cyclical movement of oceanic winds. More specifically, they discovered that at latitudes south of the Tropic of Cancer, trade winds will drive a ship westward, and westerlies north of that point will drive a ship eastward. Combined with improvements in vessels and navigational technology, knowledge of how to reliably harness Atlantic winds propelled Columbus and other profit-minded European sailors to attempt blue-water journeys into the great unknown.

Reuniting the divergent trajectories of life in Afro-Eurasia and the Americas, the Columbian Exchange had explosive consequences. To begin, the pathogens carried by Columbus and his crews had a particularly devastating impact on the indigenous Americans, possibly killing as much as 95 percent of that population over the course of a century. The lethality of humanity's reunion stemmed from evolutionary differences between the two landmasses during their separation. An early agricultural inclination in Afro-Eurasia resulted in a preponderance of dense settlements with a range of domestic animals, the perfect conditions for opportunist microbes, like smallpox, anthrax, and typhus, to jump from animal to human hosts. In the Americas, conversely, neither the social nor biological context presented the same level of parasitical opportunity, an epidemiological innocence whose rupture shaped the trajectory of the Columbian Exchange.

With much of the indigenous American population cut down by disease, Europeans exploited the Americas for their economic potential. Indeed, some of the most significant flora carried from Afro-Eurasia to the Americas during the early phases of the Columbian Exchange were luxury crops whose cultivation had been limited by climate or labor constraints. Sugarcane was one of the earliest and most influential of the transfers. A majority of southern Europeans had tasted the crystalized sweetness of processed cane by the end of the first millennium CE, thanks to the medieval diffusion of the plant across the Mediterranean by Arab agronomists. Finding European ecologies to expand the range of the tropical plant, however, proved difficult until the conquest of Madeira and the Canary Islands at the beginning of the 15th century. Columbus's voyages opened a vast new frontier for European sugar-cane production, as virtually the entire Atlantic coast of the Americas between the tropics supported the plant's growth. More importantly, the first profitable cane harvests attained by the Spanish were followed swiftly by shipments of African slaves, whose fettered labor enabled the creation and expansion of commercially oriented plantations as early as 1526 CE. The diffusion of sugarcane and other luxury crops, such as cotton, tobacco, and coffee, played a central role in the development of the horrific Atlantic slave trade over the next three centuries.

The legacy of the Columbian Exchange also can be read in local and regional adoptions of alien biota. The friable soils of Ireland, for instance, proved a hospitable home for the Andean-born potato. Stalks of maize, a grass plant domesticated in Mexico, shot up with unprecedented haste in the warm sun of Sub-Saharan Africa. After hanging around Europe for a few centuries as an ornamental and medicinal plant, Peruvian tomatoes found a prominent place in Mediterranean diets. The absence of large, domesticated ruminants in the Americas, on the other hand, meant that Afro-Eurasian faunal exports thrived in the grasslands of the western hemisphere. Furthermore, the introduction of the horse and ox to the Americas provided that continent with its first beasts of burden, whose swift and strong bodies made possible herding of cattle and other domesticated animals or pulling a heavy plow through the twisted roots of switchgrass, respectively.

By 1492 CE, most of the favorable areas for raising staple crops including wheat, barley, and rice in Afro-Eurasia had been fully exploited, leaving little room for increasing food production. The introduction of new plants and animals from the Americas as a result of the Columbian Exchange, however, enabled people to utilize soils and seasons that previously had been unsuitable to traditional practices. Potatoes and maize were not simply replacements for pre-Columbian staples in Ireland and Sub-Saharan Africa, but agricultural augmentations that brought unused land or fallow-cycles online. In this way, the Columbian Exchange added so much food to global agricultural regimes that something exceedingly rare happened in the centuries that followed—human population levels, despite the epidemic catastrophe in the Americas, increased sharply, a trajectory matched only by the demographic bump provided by the Neolithic transition from hunting and gathering to agriculture 10,000 years previously. Judged in these terms, the importance of the Columbian Exchange can be measured alongside the agricultural revolution as pre-industrial human developments with truly global implications.

Benjamin Graham

Further Reading

Cook, Noble David. 1998. *Born to Die: Disease and New World Conquest, 1492–1650.* Cambridge: Cambridge University Press.

Crosby, Alfred. 1972. *The Columbian Exchange: Biological and Cultural Consequences of 1492.* Westport, Connecticut: Greenwood Publishing Company.

Crosby, Alfred. 2009. *Ecological Imperialism: The Biological Expansion of Europe, 900–1900*, 2nd ed. Cambridge, Cambridge University Press.

Diamond, Jared. 1999. *Guns, Germs, and Steel: The Fates of Human Societies.* New York: W.W. Norton & Company.

Gentilcore, David. 2010. *Pomodoro! A History of the Tomato in Italy*. New York: Columbia University Press.

Mintz, Sidney. 1985. *Sweetness and Power: The Place of Sugar in Modern History*. New York: Penguin.

Nunn, Nathan, and Nancy Qian. 2010. "The Columbian Exchange: A History of Disease, Food, and Ideas." *The Journal of Economic Perspectives* 24(2): 163–88.

Columbus, Christopher, 1451–1506 CE

Christopher Columbus was an Italian explorer who proposed reaching Asia by means of a westward route across the Atlantic Ocean, and instead discovered and explored the Caribbean, as well as parts of Central and South America. Sponsored by King Ferdinand II (1452–1516 CE) and Queen Isabella I (1451–1504 CE) of Spain, Columbus and the members of his three-ship expedition became the first Europeans to cross the Atlantic and reach the Americas since the long-forgotten voyages of the Vikings, and so were credited with discovering the "New World" of the Americas.

Tales of great civilizations in the East, carried to Europe along the Silk Roads and by travelers such as Marco Polo, and the wealth to be made in the spice trade encouraged European maritime exploration in the hopes of finding new routes to the East. Contrary to popular opinion today, people in Columbus's day did not believe that the Earth was flat. That notion was popularized by novelist Washington Irving (1783–1859 CE) and later writers. Columbus, like other educated people of his day, knew the Earth was round, an understanding dating to classical Greek civilization. The dispute revolved around the size of the Earth. Columbus was among those who dramatically underestimated the Earth's size, and it was this misunderstanding of the distance involved that encouraged him to sail west to reach Asia. He expected to reach the East Indies, Japan, and China, in several weeks—rather than the months such a voyage actually required—and return with ships laden with spices and other riches.

Such a voyage required financial backing, and Columbus first proposed his plan to the King of Portugal who rejected it. Discouraged, he turned his attention to Spain, but was rebuffed for seven years. King Ferdinand II (1452–1516 CE) and Queen Isabella I (1451–1504 CE), rulers of recently united Spain, agreed to fund his voyage in January 1492 CE. A few months later, they conquered the Emirate of Granada, the last remaining Muslim state in Spain, and ordered the expulsion of all Jews from their territory unless they converted to Christianity. The conquest and expulsions enriched the crown, and on April 17 Ferdinand and Isabella signed an agreement with Columbus naming him Admiral of the Ocean and appointing him viceroy of any territories he discovered, which would be claimed by Spain, as well as one-tenth of any profits from his voyage. Columbus secured three ships for his voyage, the *Niña*, *Pinta*, and *Santa Maria* (the largest of the three).

First Voyage, 1492–1493 CE

Columbus sailed on August 3, 1492, but they soon stopped in the Canary Islands to repair the *Pinta's* rudder. Afterwards, the squadron sailed west. Although some members of the expedition became discouraged over time, Columbus persevered. Sightings of birds and wooden debris in the water in October indicated that land was near, but following a false sighting of land on October 7, sailors became increasingly restless. Fortunately for Columbus, his determination that land lay to the southwest proved correct and on October 12 they arrived in the Bahamas.

Columbus, who first thought they had landed in Japan, but later concluded that it was India, named the Taino people they encountered "Indians." Columbus and his men explored the Bahamas, Cuba, and Hispaniola, where the *Santa Maria* grounded and was abandoned. They used the material from the ship to establish a small settlement that Columbus named "La Navidad" on the island. On January 13, the expedition fought a small skirmish with Ciguayos warriors, the only violent encounter with local peoples. They sailed for Spain in the *Niña* and *Pinta*, shortly afterward arriving separately due to a storm. They returned with a small amount of gold, samples of the local flora, and various items they procured by trade, along with seven or eight indigenous Caribbean people who survived the voyage. Perhaps a dozen others died on the trip. Warmly welcomed by Ferdinand and Isabella, Columbus began planning his return to the New World with a larger expedition.

Second and Later Voyages

Columbus departed on his second voyage on September 24, 1493, with 17 ships, more than 1,200 men, and supplies to establish a permanent settlement. They sighted land on November 3, and Columbus again explored, locating many additional islands including Puerto Rico and the Virgin Islands. On November 22, they returned to La Navidad and found it burned to the ground and 11 of the 39 men left dead; the others were missing. Columbus and his men founded a new settlement on the north coast of Hispaniola, "Isabella," and spent five months there before sailing to Cuba. They resumed their explorations for a time, but Columbus spent much of the next year and a half establishing settlements and securing a foothold for Spain in this New World. Although a superb navigator, Columbus proved a poor governor and he compounded his mismanagement by enslaving local peoples, some of whom he brought back to Spain, inaugurating the transatlantic slave trade.

Columbus returned to the Caribbean in a third voyage (1498–1500 CE) and explored the cost of Central America, but was afterward arrested and charged with mismanaging Spain's colonial enterprise in the Caribbean. Pardoned by Ferdinand, he returned for a fourth and final voyage (1502–1504 CE), which explored the Central American coast. A hurricane damaged his ships, which were also plagued with rot and shipworms. Their poor state stranded Columbus in Jamaica, and he had to await rescue to return to Spain. There, he discovered that his patron, Queen Isabella, had died. Columbus himself died two years later.

Columbus's four transatlantic voyages opened the Americas to European exploitation and colonization, as well as the slave trade. They marked an important turning point in world history with long-term ramifications for Europe, the Americas, and the rest of the world. Animals, plants, ideas, technologies, and people spread back and forth from the New World to the Old dramatically changing the environment and societies. The discovery of the Americas stimulated competition and war among Europe's powers, but also encouraged Europeans to seek a greater understanding of the world. Columbus, himself, remains a much-debated figure, lauded for his achievement in reaching the Americas, but criticized for his behavior once there.

Walter Stucke

Further Reading

Axtell, James. 1992. *Beyond 1492: Encounters in Colonial North America*. New York and Oxford: Oxford University Press.

Catz, Rebecca. 1993. *Christopher Columbus and the Portuguese, 1476–1498*. Santa Barbara, CA: Praeger Publishers.

Columbus, Christopher. 1992. *The Four Voyages*. J. M. Cohen (trans.). New York: Penguin Classics.

Columbus, Ferdinand. 1992. *The Life of the Admiral Christopher Columbus by His Son Ferdinand*. Benjamin Keen (trans.). New Brunswick, NJ: Rutgers University Press.

Granzotto, Gianni. 1986. *Christopher Columbus*. Stephen Sartarelli (trans.). London: Collins.

Irving, Washington. 1829: *The Life and Voyages of Christopher Columbus*. New York: G. & G. & H. Carvill.

Morison, Samuel Eliot. 1991. *Admiral of the Ocean Sea: A Life of Christopher Columbus*. New York: Little, Brown and Co.

Phillips, Jr. William D., and Carla Rahn Phillips. 1993. *The Worlds of Christopher Columbus*. New York: Cambridge University Press.

Magellan, Ferdinand, 1480–1521 CE

Ferdinand Magellan (Fernão de Magalhães) was a Portuguese sailor, explorer, and navigator. He explored first for Portugal (1505–1513 CE) and then for Spain

(1519–1521 CE) for which he led the first expedition to successfully circumnavigate the world, though he died before it completed its voyage. Until his trip around the world he was one of several Portuguese captains involved in early commercial and colonizing voyages to South East Asia.

Born to Rui de Magalhães and Alda de Mesquita, a wealthy family in northern Portugal, Ferdinand became a page to Eleanor of Viseu (1458–1525 CE), Portugal's queen, following the death of his parents when he was only 10 years old. Fifteen years later, he enlisted in the fleet of Francisco de Almeida, Portugal's first Viceroy of India, which sailed in 1505 CE. Magellan spent the next eight years in Asia. He took part in numerous Portuguese endeavors and campaigns including the Battle of Diu (2–3 February 1509 CE) and the conquest of Malacca (1511 CE). He married an Indonesian woman, and amassed considerable wealth from the spice trade. In 1513 CE, having returned to Portugal, he participated in an expedition to Morocco in which he was wounded, but afterward failed to secure additional postings from King Manuel I (1469–1521 CE).

Rejected at home, Magellan offered his services to Spain's King Charles I (1500–1558 CE) along with Rui Faleiro, a Portuguese astronomer. They proposed sailing west to seek a passage south of the Americas to reach the Spice Islands, because the Treaty of Tordesillas reserved the passage around Africa to the Portuguese. The king accepted their plan, appointed them captains general of the expedition, and promised them a 10-year monopoly on any routes they discovered and appointment as governors of the newly discovered lands, which entitled them to a 5 percent share of the profits extracted from them. Repeatedly delayed, the expedition did not sail until September 20, 1519, and without Faleiro and many other Portuguese sailors who were replaced with Spaniards to quell suspicions about Magellan's intentions. Financed by the Spanish court and Christopher de Haro, a wealthy merchant, it consisted of five ships: the *Trinidad* (Magellan's flagship), *San Antonio*, *Concepción*, *Victoria*, and *Santiago* and about 270 men, mainly Spanish and Portuguese, but also some from other nations, including Antonio Pigafetta (ca. 1491–1531 CE), a Venetian who wrote a detailed account of the expedition, and Enrique, a servant Magellan had recruited in 1511 CE in Malacca who would prove invaluable as interpreter once the expedition reached Southeast Asia.

Magellan's ships avoided a Portuguese fleet sent to halt them, passed the Canary Islands, and sailed for Brazil. Crossing the equator on November 27, they anchored near today's Rio de Janeiro on December 13 where they took on supplies and water before departing to seek a passage south of the continent, working their way along the coast. They reached Port San Julian (today in Argentina) on March 30. There, they celebrated Easter and Magellan also crushed a mutiny led by two of his Spanish ship captains. Magellan executed one of the captains and marooned the other on an island, but forgave the mutinous sailors, as they were vital to the expedition's success.

Afterward, the painstaking voyage continued. The *Santiago*, scouting ahead of the expedition, was wrecked by a storm, although its crew survived and was rescued. On October 21, 1520, the expedition's remaining four ships reached 52-degrees South latitude and rounded the Cape of the Virgenes at the southeastern tip of South America, which they correctly concluded—due to its depth and salinity—marked the passage to the Pacific. Carefully navigating the 373-mile passage, three of Magellan's ships reached the Pacific Ocean (so named by Magellan for its calm waters) on November 28. The captain of the fourth, the *San Antonio*, abandoned the mission a week earlier, and sailed his ship home to Spain, claiming on arrival that the expedition had failed.

Magellan led his three ships along the shores of modern Chile and in mid-December turned his ships out to sea, uncertain of the breadth of the Pacific Ocean, which they incorrectly expected to be roughly the size of the Atlantic Ocean. After 99 days at sea, running short of food and water, the ships sighted and landed at Guam in the Mariana Islands on March 6, 1521. There, they obtained fresh water, fruit, vegetables, and other food. Three days later, they returned to sea, continuing their voyage and reaching the Philippines on March 16, an archipelago previously visited by Portuguese sailors. Magellan landed on the uninhabited island of Homonhon, where his men gathered food and water. Moving on, they made contact with indigenous peoples on the islands of Limasawa and Cebu, established friendly relations, and worked to convert them to Christianity. Encouraged by these new friends, on April 27, Magellan led a small expedition against their enemies on Mactan Island. Magellan hoped to convert their leader, Lapu-Lapu, but they instead encountered fierce resistance. Overwhelmed by perhaps 1,500 warriors, Magellan and several of his men fell in battle. The survivors fled to their ships.

The expedition continued after Magellan's death, the reduced crews sailing two ships, which reached the Moluccas. There, one of the ships proved too damaged to continue, and its crew was imprisoned by the Portuguese. The last ship, *Victoria*, commanded of Juan Sebastian Elcano, continued and arrived in Spain on September 8, 1522. Elcano and the 17 surviving members of his crew became the first sailors to circumnavigate the globe.

Jakub Basista

Further Reading

Bergreen, Laurence. 2003. *Over the Edge of the World: Magellan's Terrifying Circumnavigation of the Globe*. New York: William Morrow & Company.

Pigafetta, Antonio. 1969. *Magellan's Voyage: A Narrative Account of the First Circumnavigation* (R. A. Skelton trans.). New Haven: Yale University Press.

Zweig, Stefan. 2011. *Magellan*. London: Pushkin Press.

Ponce de León, Juan, 1460–1521 CE

Juan Ponce de León, born in 1460 CE in San Sérvas de Campos, Spain, was a Spanish conquistador and explorer. He established his military reputation fighting Muslim Moors in Granada during the early 1490s and then served in Christopher Columbus's second expedition to the Americas in 1493–1494 CE. He led the expedition that conquered Puerto Rico in 1508 CE, but is best known for his explorations of Florida and search for a "fountain of youth."

After serving with Columbus, León settled in Hispaniola, where he received a substantial land grant. He successfully led Spanish troops against the indigenous Tainos, for which he was rewarded in 1504 CE with the governorship of Higuey, the island's eastern province. In 1508 CE, León led an expedition that conquered Puerto Rico. There, he enslaved the surviving Tainos and parceled out their land to his men. Already one of the richest men in the Caribbean, León obtained approval from Spain's King Ferdinand to explore and capture additional Caribbean islands.

On April 2, 1513, León's three ships landed on what he thought was an island, named it "Pascua Florida" ("Flowery Easter"), and began explorations, searching for gold and, according to later tradition, a fabled "fountain of youth." On April 21, the expedition's ships encountered the Atlantic Ocean's Gulf Stream, a clockwise-rotating warm current that passes along parts of the Caribbean and the Southeastern United States and then moves out into the Atlantic. Two ships successfully anchored after discovering they were being drawn out to sea despite having the wind in their sails. The third ship, drawn away by the current, was lost for two days. This accidental discovery proved fortuitous, as the Gulf Stream became the primary route for transporting gold and other goods from the Americas to Spain.

León, still thinking Florida an island, never having reached its northern extremes, returned to Spain to report his discoveries to King Ferdinand who promoted him to Captain General and governor of Florida. In 1521 CE, he returned to Florida with 200 men and settled near present-day Charlotte Harbor. Soon attacked by the local Calusas, whom the Spanish had antagonized on their previous expedition, they abandoned the settlement and sailed for Havana, Cuba. There León, struck by an arrow in the fighting, died from infection.

John R. Burch

Further Reading

Weber, David J. 1992. *The Spanish Frontier in North America*. New Haven: Yale University Press.

Weddle, Robert. 1985. *Spanish Sea: The Gulf of Mexico in North American Discovery, 1500–1685*. College Station, TX: Texas A&M University Press.

Spanish Armada

The Spanish Armada, one of the largest fleets of the era, sailed from Spain in 1588 CE, commanded by the Duke of Medina-Sidonia. Forty large warships escorted about 90 transports for a planned invasion of England, but were defeated and driven off by a smaller English force. The Armada's defeat marked the emergence of England as an important sea power.

In the late 16th century, a Spanish army fought to suppress a revolution in the Netherlands sparked by the spread of Protestantism and political differences. Similar disputes, compounded by English piracy, worsened relations between Spain and England. When England offered assistance to the Dutch in 1585 CE, Spanish King Philip II ordered ships readied for an invasion of England.

Learning of Philip's decision, England dispatched a force under Francis Drake in 1587 CE to disrupt Spanish preparations. Drake's attack destroyed or captured two dozen ships. As a consequence, Spain's Armada did not sail until May 1588, only to be delayed again when unfavorable conditions forced it to divert into port.

The Spanish Armada finally appeared off the southwestern English coast on July 29, 1588, and three encounters named for nearby geography—Plymouth, Portland Bill, and Isle of Wight—took place between July 30 and August 4 as the Armada advanced. (Dates are from the Julian calendar in use in England; Spain used the newer Gregorian calendar.)

The swift English ships under the Baron of Effingham quickly gained the tactical advantage called the "weather gage" that allowed them to harass the Spanish with their heavier, long-range guns. The Spanish, expecting to close and board the English warships using infantry, could not do so with their slower ships.

On August 6, the Armada anchored near the port of Calais. English warships continued to harass the fleet, and after midnight on August 8, favorable winds and tides carried English fire ships into the Spanish formation. Many armada captains cut their anchor cables and fled from the danger, scattering the fleet.

The following morning near Gravelines, the English attacked the disorganized Spaniards again. Combined with contrary winds, these attacks forced Medina-Sidonia to abandon the invasion and escape north. The Armada was still largely intact, and Medina-Sidonia hoped to sail around Scotland Britain and return home. Instead, the voyage proved fatal to most of his ships. Navigational errors and storms overwhelmed many ships—particularly those which had cut their anchors and thus could not anchor safely to ride out storms. Only 67 of the original 130 ships returned to Spain, along with about only 10,000 of the nearly 30,000 men who sailed with the Armada.

England's adoption and skillful use of fast ships armed with heavy guns mounted in carriages, which permitted rapid reloading, gave its ships a decisive advantage. The Armada's defeat marks the beginning of the preeminence in naval warfare of gun-armed warships. Yet, it was the weather more than English gunnery that destroyed the Armada.

Larry A. Grant

Further Reading

Barratt, John. 2005. *Armada 1588: The Spanish Assault on England*. Barnsley: Pen & Sword Military.

Hutchinson, Robert. 2014. *The Spanish Armada*. New York: Thomas Dunne Books, St. Martin's Press.

Martin, Colin, and Geoffrey Parker. 2002. *The Spanish Armada*. Manchester: Manchester University Press.

Matthews, Rupert. 2009. *The Spanish Armada: A Campaign in Context*. Stroud: Spellmount.

Treaty of Tordesillas

Concluded on June 7, 1494, the Treaty of Tordesillas was a treaty between King John II of Portugal (1455–1495 CE) and King Ferdinand (1452–1516 CE) and Queen Isabella (1451–1501 CE) of Castile and Aragon that divided the Atlantic Ocean into two separate spheres of influence. Setting a boundary line at 370 leagues west of the Cape Verde Islands, the treaty allowed Portugal to retain its claims to the lands and oceans east of this line. It granted Castile rights over lands and oceans to the west of it.

An agreement between Castile and Portugal became necessary after the return of Christopher Columbus (ca. 1451–1506 CE) from his first voyage on March 4, 1493. Ferdinand and Isabella had funded Columbus's voyage in an attempt to find a western route to Asia and its lucrative trade routes. Portugal had attempted to reach them in the later 15th century by sailing down the western coast of Africa. When Columbus landed in Portugal, claiming to have reached Japan and some other islands off the coast of the Asian mainland, Ferdinand and Isabella as well as John II maneuvered to secure access to the sea routes to Asia for themselves and their subjects and to deny it to those from other kingdoms. Drawing on precedent set by previous Portuguese kings, Isabella and Ferdinand petitioned Pope Alexander VI (1431–1503 CE) to grant them and their subjects the disputed lands and routes, which he largely did in a series of four papal bulls in 1493 CE. Failing to win the ear of the Spanish pope, John II threatened to arm a fleet and attack any Spanish ships sailing the Atlantic. At this point, Ferdinand, Isabella, and John II resolved to negotiate their differences to avoid war, resulting in the Treaty of Tordesillas.

Though meant to apply only to the Atlantic Ocean, the treaty soon became the basis on which Spanish and Portuguese monarchs extended their claims over undiscovered lands and peoples in Africa, Asia, and the Americas. It also was used to deny Europeans from other kingdoms access to these territories. For the first time in European history, the ocean became a politicized space—a space that European monarchs continued to fight over throughout the period of European colonial expansion (Newitt 2005, 57).

Lindsay J. Starkey

Further Reading

Brown, Stephen R. 2011. *1494: How a Family Feud in Medieval Spain Divided the World in Half.* New York: St. Martin's Press.

Dawson, Samuel Edward. 1899. "The Lines of Demarcation of Pope Alexander VI and the Treaty of Tordesillas A.D. 1493 and 1494." *The Transactions of the Royal Society of Canada*, vol. V, sec. II. Ottawa: J. Hope & Sons.

Newitt, Malyn. 2005. *A History of Portuguese Overseas Expansion 1400–1668.* London: Routledge.

Nowell, Charles Edward. 1945. "The Treaty of Tordesillas and the Diplomatic Background of American History." Adele Ogden and Engel Suiter (eds.). *Greater America: Essays in Honor of Herbert Eugene Bolton*, 1–18. Berkeley: University of California Press.

Zacuto, Abraham ben, ca. 1452–1515 CE

An astronomer and historian, Abraham ben Zacuto is best known for improving the mariner's astrolabe and developing navigation charts. His contributions facilitated the sea voyages of Portuguese and Spanish explorers to the Americas and around Africa to the Indian Ocean.

Zacuto was born in Salamanca, Spain, to parents of French-Jewish ancestry. At the age of 20, he began his most important work, *Ha-Hibur ha-Gadol* ("*Perpetual Almanac of the Heavenly Bodies*"), which he completed in 1478 CE. It was subsequently translated from Hebrew into Spanish, Arabic, and Latin. His friend and patron, Bishop Gonzalo de Vivero, arranged for Zacuto to become professor of astronomy at the prestigious University of Salamanca where he designed the first astrolabe specifically suited to use at sea. Smaller and more accurate, it helped seafarers determine their latitude. More importantly, the 65 detailed charts of his Almanac tracked the positions of the Sun, Moon, and five planets. Easy to use, Zacuto's charts facilitated Portuguese and Spanish exploration, particularly near the equator where the Pole Star was not visible.

In 1492 CE, Zacuto met and advised Christopher Columbus, who set out on his voyage with Zacuto's astronomical tables. Stranded on Jamaica during his last journey to the Americas, Zacuto's tables enabled Columbus to predict a lunar eclipse, which he used to convince the reluctant natives to aid him with provisions.

The same year that Columbus set out on his first journey, Ferdinand and Isabella of Spain issued the Edict of Expulsion ordering Jews out of the country. Zacuto immigrated to Portugal, which accepted Jews providing they paid a fee. King John II (1455–1495 CE) appointed Zacuto astronomer to the Portuguese court. In 1496 CE, the king consulted Zacuto for guidance concerning Vasco da Gama's voyage to India and Da Gama's ships were equipped with Zacuto's astrolabes. Portuguese explorers also used Zacuto's tools and charts on their voyages to Brazil.

Despite his contributions to Portuguese exploration, Zacuto fell prey to anti-Semitism following King John's death and fled Portugal to escape forced conversion. He lived for a time in North Africa, where he wrote several historical works, before traveling to Jerusalem where he likely died in 1515 CE.

Jonathan Henderson

Further Reading

Chabás, José, and Bernard R. Goldstein. 2000. *Astronomy in the Iberian Peninsula: Abraham Zacut and the Transition from Manuscript to Print*, Volume 90, Part 2. American Philosophical Society.

Goldstein, Bernard R. 1998. "Abraham Zacut and the Medieval Hebrew Astronomical Tradition." *Journal for the History of Astronomy* 29.2: 177.

Randles, W. G. L. 1985. "Portuguese and Spanish Attempts to Measure Longitude in the 16th Century." *Vistas in Astronomy* 28: 235–41.

PRIMARY DOCUMENTS

First Voyage of Vasco da Gama, ca. 1460–1524 CE

Vasco da Gama (ca. 1460–1524 CE) commanded the first Portuguese expedition to reach India. A journal of this voyage was published anonymously by a member of the crew, possibly Alvaro Velho, though some scholars favor João de Sá (d. 1514 CE) who traveled aboard the São Rafael, *commanded by da Gama's brother Paulo (d. 1499 CE). Unfortunately, little is known about either man. The journal, however, provides a detailed account of the expedition. The selections below describe some of the Arab ships they encountered, their arrival at the port of Calicut in India, and their terrifying experience with scurvy—the first reported occurrence of this nutritional deficiency—on the voyage home.*

[After rounding the Cape of Good Hope and sailing north, the expedition encountered Arab ships off the coast of modern Mozambique.] The vessels of this country are of good size and decked. There are no nails, and the planks are held together by cords as are also those of their boats. The sails are made of palm matting. Their mariners have Genoese needles [compasses], by which they steer, quadrants, and navigating charts.

[Arriving in India, we] anchored two leagues from the city of Calecut and we did so because our pilot mistook Capua, a town at that place, for Calecut. . . . After we were at anchor, four boats approached us from the land, who asked of what nation we were. We told them, and they then pointed out Calecut to us.

On the following day [May 21] these same boats came again alongside, when the captain-major sent one of the convicts [several convicted criminals sailed with da Gama in exchange for pardons] to Calecut, and those with whom he went took him to two Moors from Tunis, who could speak Castilian and Genoese. The first greeting he received was in these words: "May the Devil take thee! What brought you hither?" They asked what he sought so far away from home, and he told them that he came in search of Christians and spices. . . . After this conversation they took him to their lodgings and gave him bread and honey. When he had eaten he returned to the ships accompanied by one of these Moors, who was no sooner on board, than he said these words: "A lucky venture, a lucky venture! Plenty of rubies, plenty of emeralds! You owe great thanks to God for having brought you to country holding such riches!" We were greatly astonished to hear his talk, for we never expected to hear our language spoken so far away from Portugal.

[They proved unable to establish friendly trading relations with Calecut's ruler, but they did learn a lot about local trade.]

From this country of Calecut . . . come the spices, which are consumed in the East and the West in Portugal, as in all other countries of the world, as also precious stones of every description. The following spices are to be found . . . much ginger and pepper and cinnamon, although the last is not so fine in quality as that brought from an island called Cillan [Ceylon, Sri Lanka today], which is eight days journey from Calecut. . . . Cloves are brought to this city from an island called Melequa [Malacca]. The Mecca [Arab] vessels carry these spices from these to city in Mecca [Arabia] called Judea [Jidda] . . . a voyage of 50 days sailing before the wind, for the vessels of this country cannot tack. At Judea [Jidda] they discharge their cargoes paying customs duties to the Grand Sultan. The merchandise is then transshipped to smaller vessels, which carry it through the Red Sea to . . . Tuuz, where customs duties are paid once more. From that place the merchants carry the spices on the backs of camels . . . to Cairo, a journey occupying 10 days. At Cairo duties are paid again. On this road to Cairo they are frequently robbed by thieves who live in that country, such as Bedouins and others.

At Cairo the spices are embarked on the river Nile . . . and descending the river for days they reach a place called Roxette [Rosetta], where duties have to be paid once more. There they are placed on camels, and are conveyed in one day to a city called Alexandria, which is a seaport. This city is visited by the galleys of Venice and Genoa, in search of these spices, which yield the Grand Sultan a revenue of 600,000 cuzados [a Portuguese gold coin] in customs duties.

[Voyaging home, da Gama successfully found other ports to trade with, but the crew suffered from scurvy on the long voyage, a result of sailing against the Monsoons.]

87. Owing to frequent calms and foul winds it took us three months less three days to cross this gulf [the Arabian Sea], and all our people again suffered from

their gums, which grew over their teeth, so that they could not eat. Their legs also swelled, and other parts of the body, and these swellings spread until the suffered died, without exhibiting symptoms of any other disease. Thirty of our men died in this manner—an equal number having died previously—and those able to navigate each ship were only seven or eight, and even these were not as well as they ought to have been . . . if this state of affairs had continued for another fortnight, there would have been no men at all to navigate the ships. [The captains considered returning to India, but] it pleased God in his mercy to send us a wind, which in the course of six days carried us within sight of land, and at this we rejoiced. . . .

Source: Anonymous, E. G. Ravenstein (ed.). 1898. *A Journal of the First Voyage of Vasco da Gama.* London: Hakluyt Society, pp. 26, 48–49, 77–78, 87.

The Treaty of Tordesillas, June 7, 1494 CE

Spain and Portugal both explored west into the Atlantic and settled the islands they discovered. They disputed control of the Canary Islands in the 1420s and 1430s until the pope (Eugene IV) confirmed Spain's claim. Three papal bulls in the 1450s secured Portugal's claims in West Africa. Continued Portuguese exploration into the South Atlantic and Indian Ocean and Columbus's explorations of the Americas appeared likely to ignite further disputes between Portugal and Spain. Wishing to maintain harmony between these Catholic powers, the papacy again helped negotiate a settlement. The Treaty of Tordesillas preserved Columbus's discoveries for Spain, but secured Portuguese control over the only known route from Europe to India, around the Cape of Good Hope, which Vasco da Gama (1460–1524 CE) would soon sail, and left open the possibility of further Portuguese exploration of the South Atlantic.

Don Ferdinand and Dona Isabella, by the grace of God king and queen of Castile, Leon, Aragon, Sicily, Granada . . . treated . . . with the most serene Dom John, by the grace of God, king of Portugal . . . in regard to the controversy over what part belongs to us and what part to the said Most Serene King . . . agreed . . . as follows:

[I.] That, whereas a certain controversy exists between the said lords, their constituents, as to what lands, of all those discovered in the ocean sea up to the present day, the date of this treaty, pertain to each one of the said parts respectively; therefore, for the sake of peace and concord, and for the preservation of the relationship and love of the said King of Portugal for the said King and Queen of Castile, Aragon, etc., it being the pleasure of their Highnesses, they . . . agreed that a boundary or straight line be determined and drawn north and south, from pole to pole, on the said ocean sea, from the Arctic to the Antarctic pole. This boundary or line shall be drawn straight, as aforesaid, at a distance of three hundred and seventy leagues west of the

Cape Verde Islands, being calculated by degrees, or by any other manner as may be considered the best and readiest, provided the distance shall be no greater than abovesaid. And all lands, both islands and mainlands, found and discovered already, or to be found and discovered hereafter, by the said King of Portugal and by his vessels on this side of the said line and bound determined as above, toward the east, in either north or south latitude, on the eastern side of the said bound provided the said bound is not crossed, shall belong to, and remain in the possession of, and pertain forever to, the said King of Portugal and his successors. And all other lands, both islands and mainlands, found or to be found hereafter, discovered or to be discovered hereafter, which have been discovered or shall be discovered by the said King and Queen of Castile, Aragon, etc., and by their vessels, on the western side of the said bound, determined as above, after having passed the said bound toward the west, in either its north or south latitude, shall belong to, and remain in the possession of, and pertain forever to, the said King and Queen of Castile, Leon, etc., and to their successors.

[2.] Item, the said representatives promise and affirm by virtue of the powers aforesaid, that from this date no ships shall be despatched—namely as follows: the said King and Queen of Castile, Leon, Aragon, etc., for this part of the bound, and its eastern side, on this side the said bound, which pertains to the said King of Portugal and the Algarves, etc.; nor the said King of Portugal to the other part of the said bound which pertains to the said King and Queen of Castile, Aragon, etc.-for the purpose of discovering and seeking any mainlands or islands, or for the purpose of trade, barter, or conquest of any kind. . . .

[3.] Item, in order that the said line . . . may be made straight and as nearly as possible the said distance of three hundred and seventy leagues west of the Cape Verde Islands, . . . within the ten months immediately following the date of this treaty their said constituent lords shall dispatch two or four caravels, namely, one or two by each one of them, a greater or less number, as they may mutually consider necessary. These vessels shall meet at the Grand Canary Island during this time, and each one of the said parties shall send certain persons in them, to wit, pilots, astrologers, sailors, and any others they may deem desirable . . . so that they may jointly study and examine to better advantage the sea, courses, winds, and the degrees of the sun or of north latitude, and lay out the leagues aforesaid, in order that, in determining the line and boundary, all sent and empowered by both the said parties in the said vessels, shall jointly concur. . . .

[4.] Item, inasmuch as the said ships of the said King and Queen of Castile, Leon, Aragon, etc., sailing as before declared, from their kingdoms and seigniories to their said possessions on the other side of the said line, must cross the seas on this side of the line, pertaining to the said King of Portugal, it is therefore concerted and agreed that the said ships of the said King and Queen of Castile, Leon, Aragon, etc., shall, at any time and without any hindrance, sail in either direction, freely, securely, and peacefully, over the said seas of the said King of Portugal. . . .

. . .

Source: Davenport, Frances Gardiner. 1917. *European Treaties Bearing on the History of the United States to 1648.* Washington, DC: The Carnegie Institution of Washington.

Magellan's Round-the-World Voyage, ca. 1491–1535 CE

Ferdinand Magellan (ca. 1480–1521 CE), believing that the Pacific Ocean was much smaller than it actually is, contracted with King Charles I of Spain (1500–1558 CE) to sail west across the Atlantic and from there seek a passage to Asia and the Spice Islands. Among Magellan's five ships and 280 officers and sailors was Antonio Pigafetta (ca. 1491–ca. 1535 CE) who published an admiring account of the voyage and Magellan on his return. Magellan encountered a host of dangers on the voyage, including storms, scurvy, and mutiny by several of his captains. Magellan died in battle on Samar in the Philippines, having been drawn into a local conflict. Only one of the expedition's ships, that captained by Juan Sebastián Elcano (1476–1526 CE), completed the round-the-world voyage and returned to Spain. Pigafetta, still looking for adventure joined the Knights of St. John at Malta and is believed to have died fighting the Turks in 1535 CE. The passages below describe the discovery of what was later named the Strait of Magellan, the expedition's experience with starvation and scurvy, and one of their many encounters with the native inhabitants of the lands they explored.

[O]n the day of the Eleven Thousand Virgins [October 21], we found, by a miracle, a strait, which we called the Cape of the Eleven Thousand Virgins [today's Cape Virgenes, the entrance to the Strait of Magellan]. This strait is a hundred and ten leagues long, which are four hundred and forty miles, and almost as wide as less than half a league, and it issues in another sea, which is called the peaceful sea [the Pacific Ocean]. . . . This strait was a round place surrounded by mountains . . . and the greater number of the sailors thought that there was no place by which to go out thence to enter into the peaceful sea. . . . The captain [Magellan] sent two of his ships, one named *St. Anthony* and the other the *Conception*, to seek for and discover the outlet of this strait. . . . The other two ships met with such a head wind that they could not weather a cape which the bay made almost at its extremity; wishing to come to us, they were near being driven to beach the ships. But, on approaching the extremity of the bay, and whilst expecting to be lost, they saw a small mouth . . . they threw themselves into it, so that by force they discovered the strait. . . .

After having entered inside this strait we found that there were two mouths, of which one trended to the Sirocco (S.E.), and the other to the Garbin (S.W.). On that account the captain again sent the two ships, *St. Anthony* and *Conception*, to see if the mouth which was towards Sirocco had an outlet beyond into the said peaceful sea. [The officers of the *San Antonio* mutinied against their captain, Magellan's brother.] *The*

Conception, not being able to follow that one, was always waiting for it, and fluttered hither and thither. . . . So we remained there four days to wait for the other two ships. A short time after we sent a boat well supplied with men and provisions to discover the cape of the other sea: these remained three days in going and coming. They told us that they had found the cape, and the sea great and wide. At the joy which the captain-general had at this he began to cry. . . .

. . .

Wednesday, the twenty-eighth of November, 1520, we . . . entered into the Pacific sea, where we remained three months and twenty days without taking in provisions or other refreshments, and we only ate old biscuit reduced to powder, and full of grubs, and stinking from the dirt which the rats had made on it when eating the good biscuit, and we drank water that was yellow and stinking. We also ate the ox hides which [protected some of the rigging]. They were very hard on account of the sun, rain, and wind, and we left them for four or five days in the sea, and then we put them a little on the embers, and so ate them; also the sawdust of wood, and rats which cost half-a-crown each . . . the upper and lower gums of most of our men grew so muchthat they could not eat, and in this way so many suffered, that nineteen died, and . . . twenty-five or thirty fell ill of diverse sicknesses, both in the arms and legs, and other places, in such manner that very few remained healthy. However, thanks be to the Lord, I had no sickness. During those three months and twenty days we went in an open sea, while we ran fully four thousand leagues in the Pacific sea. This was well named Pacific, for during this same time we met with no storm, and saw no land except two small uninhabited islands, in which we found only birds and trees. . . .

. . .

[O]n Wednesday, the 6th of March, we discovered a small island in the north-west direction, and two others lying to the south-west. One of these islands was larger and higher than the other two [probably Guam]. The captain-general wished to touch at the largest of these three islands to get refreshments of provisions; but it was not possible because the people of these islands entered into the ships and robbed us, in such a way that it was impossible to preserve oneself from them. Whilst we were striking and lowering the sails to go ashore, they stole away with . . . the skiff, which was made fast to the poop of the captain's ship, at which he was much irritated, and went on shore with forty armed men, burned forty or fifty houses, with several small boats, and killed seven men of the island; they recovered their skiff. After this we set sail suddenly, following the same course.

Source: Lord Stanley of Alderley. 1874. *The First Voyage Around the World by Magellan, Translated from the Accounts of Pigafetta (1536).* London: Hakluyt Society, pp. 57–59, 64, 67.

Suma Oriental of Tomé Pires, ca. 1516 CE

A Portuguese apothecary from Lisbon, Tomé Pires (ca. 1465–1524 CE) traveled east and lived in Malacca between 1512–1515 CE. There he became involved in the spice trade and wrote the Suma Oriental, *which described the region and local trade. Possibly written as a report to King Manuel of Portugal (1469–1521 CE), it was not published until 1944 CE when scholars discovered it in an archive. Pires traveled to China in 1516 CE as part of a Portuguese embassy. Never received by the emperor—who regarded Portugal with suspicion—they found themselves trapped in China where many of them died, including Pires who probably died in 1524 CE, but perhaps lived until 1540 CE. In the passages below, Pires describes regional trade in India and Malacca.*

I now come to the trade of Cambay [modern-day Gujarat, India]. The [Gujaratis] are [like] Italians in their knowledge of and dealings in merchandise . . . [they] have the cream of the trade. . . . There are also some Cairo merchants settled in Cambay, and many Khorasans and Guilans from Aden and Ormuz, all of whom do a great trade in the seaport towns of Cambay; but none of these count in comparison with the heathens [Gujaratis], especially in knowledge. Those of our people who want to be clerks and factors ought to go there and learn, because the business of trade is a science in itself, which does not hinder any other noble exercise, but helps a great deal.

And so both the Gujaratis and the [foreign] merchants who have settled in Cambay . . . sail many ships to all parts, to Aden, Ormuz, the kingdom of the Deccan, Goa, Bhatkal, and all over Malabar, Ceylon, Bengal, Pegu, Siam, Pedir, Pase, Malacca, where they take quantities of merchandise, bringing other kinds back, thus making Cambay rich and important. Cambay chiefly stretches out two arms, her right arm out towards Aden and with the other towards Malacca, as the most important places to sail to. . . .

The merchants from Cairo bring the merchandise which comes from Italy and Greece and Damascus to Aden, such as gold, silver, quicksilver, vermilion, copper, rosewater, camlets, scarlet-in-grain [a dye], colored woolen cloth, glass beads, weapons and things of that kind.

[The merchants of] Aden bring the abovementioned goods with the addition of madder, raisins, opium, rosewater, quantities of gold and silver and horses that Aden gets from Zeila and Berbera and the islands of Suakin, in the Strait, and from Arabia, and they come to do business in Cambay. They take back with them all the products of Malacca: cloves, nutmeg, porcelain, and other things . . . as well as the following from the country itself: rice, wheat, soap, indigo, butter . . . oils, carnelians, coarse pottery live from Seville [Spain], and all kinds of cloth, for trading in Zeila, Berbera, Sokotra, Kilwa, Malindi, Mogadishu, and other places in Arabia. And this trade is carried out by ships from Aden and ships from Cambay. . . .

. . .

Finally, in the port of Malacca very often eighty-four languages have been found spoken, every one distinct, as the inhabitants of Malacca affirm; and this in Malacca alone, because in the archipelago which begins at Singapore and Karimun up to the Moluccas, there are forty known languages for the islands are countless.

Because those from Cairo and Mecca and Aden cannot reach Malacca in a single monsoon, as well as the Parsees and those from Ormuz . . . Turks and similar peoples such as Armenians, at their own time they go to the kingdom of Gujarat, bringing large quantities of valuable merchandise. . . . Those from Cairo take their merchandise to Tor, and from Tor to Jidda, and from Jidda to Aden, and from Aden to Cambay, where they sell in the land things which are valued there, and the others they bring to Malacca. . . .

Those from Cairo bring the merchandise brought by the galleasses of Venice, to wit, many arms, scarlet-in-grain, colored woolen cloths, coral, copper, quicksilver, vermillion, nails, silver, glass and other beads, and golden glassware.

Those from Mecca bring a great quantity of opium, rosewater and such like merchandise, and much liquid storax [a fragrance and medicine].

Those from Aden bring to Gujarat a great quantity of opium, raisins, madder, indigo, rosewater, silver, seed-pearls, and other dyes, which are of value in Cambay.

In these companies go Parsees, Turks, Turkomans and Armenians, and they come and take up their companies for their cargo in Gujarat, and from there they embark in March and sail direct for Malacca; and on the return journey they call at the Maldive Islands.

Four ships come every year from Gujarat to Malacca. The merchandise of each ship is worth fifteen, twenty, or thirty thousand *crusados,* nothing less than fifteen thousand. And from the city of Cambay one ship comes every year; and this is worth seventy or eighty thousand *crusados,* without any doubt.

The merchandise they bring is cloths of thirty kinds, which are of value in these parts; they also bring pachak, which is a root like rampion, and catechu, which looks like earth; they bring rosewater and opium; from Cambay and Aden they bring seeds, grains, tapestries and much incense; they bring forty kinds of merchandise. . . .

Source: Armando Cortesao (trans.). 1944. *The Suma Oriental of Tomé Pires and the Book of Francisco Rodrigues.* London: Hakluyt Society, I: 41–43 and II: 268–270. Used by permission.

Gottlieb Mittelberger's Journey to Pennsylvania, 1754 CE

One of more than a million immigrants who traveled to North America in the 18th century, Gottlieb Mittelberger describes the arduous voyage from Europe and

harsh conditions at sea, as well as the practice of selling indentures—people ar-
ranging to work for several years after arrival to pay the costs of their voyage.
Mittelberger found work as an organist and schoolmaster for the German St.
Augustine's Church in New Providence, a small German community near Phil-
adelphia, but he returned to Germany after four years. Mittelberger wrote this
account to warn people about the difficulties they would face and to expose the
poor conditions of indentured servants.

In the month of May 1750, I departed from Enzweihingen, Vaihingen County, my native place, for Heilbronn, where an organ stood ready to be shipped and sent to Pennsylvania. With this organ, I sailed the usual way, down the Neckar and Rhine to Rotterdam in Holland. From Rotterdam I sailed with a transport of about 400 souls . . . across the North Sea to Kaupp [Cowes] in England, and [then] across the great ocean, until I landed in Philadelphia. . . . From home to Rotterdam, including my sojourn there, I spent 7 weeks, caused by the many stoppages down the Rhine and in Holland, whereas this journey could otherwise be made swifter; but from Rotterdam to Philadelphia the voyage lasted 15 weeks. . . .

[T]he most important occasion for publishing this little book was the wretched and grievous condition of those who travel from Germany to this new land, and the outrageous and merciless proceeding of the Dutch man-dealers and their man-stealing emissaries . . . to reveal to the people of Germany the pure truth about it. . . . When all this will have been read, I do not doubt that those who may still desire to go there, will remain in their fatherland, and carefully avoid this long and tedious journey and the fatalities connected with it. . . .

. . . This journey lasts from the beginning of May to the end of October, fully half a year, amid such hardships as no one is able to describe adequately with their misery.

[T]he Rhine-boats from Heilbronn to Holland have to pass by 36 custom-houses, at all of which the ships are examined, which is done when it suits the convenience of the custom-house officials. In the meantime the ships with the people are detained long, so that the passengers have to spend much money. The trip down the Rhine alone lasts therefore 4, 5 and even 6 weeks.

When the ships . . . come to Holland, they are detained there likewise for 6 weeks. . . . Both in Rotterdam and in Amsterdam the people are packed densely, like herrings so to say, in the large sea-vessels. One person receives a place of scarcely 2 feet width and 6 feet length in the bedstead, while many a ship carries four to six hundred souls; not to mention the innumerable implements, tools, provisions, water-barrels and other things which like wise occupy much space.

On account of contrary winds it takes the ships sometimes 2, 3 and 4 weeks to make the trip from Holland to . . . England. . . . Everything is examined there and the custom-duties paid, whence it comes that the ships ride there 8 to 14 days and even longer at anchor, till they have taken in their full cargoes. During that time every one is compelled to spend his last remaining money and to consume his little stock of provisions which had been reserved for the sea; so that most passengers, finding themselves on the ocean where they would be in greater need of them, must greatly suffer from hunger and want. . . .

[From England] the ships, unless they have good wind, must often sail 8, 9, 10 to 12 weeks before they reach Philadelphia. But even with the best wind the voyage lasts 7 weeks. But during the voyage there is on board these ships terrible misery, stench, fumes, horror, vomiting, many kinds of seasickness, fever, dysentery, head-ache, heat, constipation, boils, scurvy, cancer, mouth-rot, and the like, all of which come from old and sharply salted food and meat, also from very bad and foul water, so that many die miserably.

Add to this want of provisions, hunger, thirst, frost, heat, dampness, anxiety, want, afflictions and lamentations . . . the lice abound so frightfully, especially on sick people, that they can be scraped off the body. . . . Children from 1 to 7 years rarely survive the voyage. . . .

. . .

That most people get sick is not surprising, because, in addition to all other trials and hardships, warm food is served only three times a week, the rations being very poor and very little. Such meals can hardly be eaten, on account of being so unclean. The water which is served out on the ships is often very black, thick and full of worms, so that one cannot drink it without loathing, even with the greatest thirst. . . .

When the ships have landed at Philadelphia after their long voyage, no one is permitted to leave them except those who pay for their passage or can give good se-curity; the others, who cannot pay, must remain on board the ships till they are pur-chased, and are released from the ships by their purchasers. . . .

. . . Every day Englishmen, Dutchmen and High-German people come from the city of Philadelphia and other places . . . and go on board . . . and select among the healthy persons such as they deem suitable for their business, and bargain with them . . . adult persons bind themselves in writing to serve 3, 4, 5 or 6 years for the amount due by them, according to their age and strength. But very young people, from 10 to 15 years, must serve till they are 21 years old.

Source: Eben, Carl Theo. (trans.). 1898. *Gottlieb Mittelberger's Journey to Pennsyl-vania in the Year 1750 and Return to Germany in the Year 1754*. Philadelphia: John Jos. McVey. From the Historical Society of Pennsylvania, http://hsp.org/sites/default /files/legacy_files migrated/mittelberger.pdf. Accessed November 24, 2016.

Olaudah Equiano Describes a Slave Ship; Excerpt from *The Interesting Narrative of the Life of Olaudah Equiano, Or Gustavus Vassa, The African, Written by Himself,* 1789 CE

Olaudah Equiano (ca. 1745–1797 CE) was kidnapped at age 11 in West Africa and sold to slave traders. Transported across the Atlantic and sold in Virginia, he had several owners until purchased at age 20 by Robert King, a Quaker merchant in

Philadelphia. King taught Equiano to read and allowed him to earn money to pur-
chase his freedom for 40 pounds, the price King paid for him. Although King of-
fered to make him his business partner, Equiano feared life in the colonies and the
constant threat of kidnapping and re-enslavement and moved to England. There,
he found work, married, raised two daughters, and became active in the abolition-
ist movement. His book helped influence England's decision to ban the slave trade
in 1807 CE. Below he describes the slave ship that brought him to America.

The first object which saluted my eyes when I arrived on the coast was the sea, and a slave ship, which was then riding at anchor, and waiting for its cargo. These filled me with astonishment, which was soon converted into terror when I was carried on board. I was immediately handled and tossed up to see if I were sound by some of the crew; and I was now persuaded that I had gotten into a world of bad spirits, and that they were going to kill me. Their complexions too differing so much from ours, their long hair, and the language they spoke (which was very different from any I had ever heard) united to confirm me in this belief. Indeed such were the horrors of my views and fears at the moment, that, if ten thousand worlds had been my own, I would have freely parted with them all to have exchanged my condition with that of the meanest slave in my own country. When I looked round the ship too and saw a large furnace or copper boiling, and a multitude of black people of every description chained together, every one of their countenances expressing dejection and sorrow, I no longer doubted of my fate; and, quite overpowered with horror and anguish, I fell motionless on the deck and fainted. When I recovered a little I found some black people about me, who I believed were some of those who brought me on board, and had been receiving their pay; they talked to me in order to cheer me, but all in vain. I asked them if we were not to be eaten by those white men with horrible looks, red faces, and loose hair. They told me I was not; and one of the crew brought me a small portion of spirituous liquor in a wine glass; but, being afraid of him, I would not take it out of his hand. One of the blacks therefore took it from him and gave it to me, and I took a little down my palate, which, instead of reviving me, as they thought it would, threw me into the greatest consternation at the strange feeling it produced, having never tasted any such liquor before. Soon after this the blacks who brought me on board went off, and left me abandoned to despair. I now saw myself deprived of all chance of returning to my native country, or even the least glimpse of hope of gaining the shore, which I now considered as friendly; and I even wished for my former slavery in preference to my present situation, which was filled with horrors of every kind, still heightened by my ignorance of what I was to undergo. I was not long suffered to indulge my grief; I was soon put down under the decks, and there I received such a salutation in my nostrils as I had never experienced in my life: so that, with the loathsomeness of the stench, and crying together, I became so sick and low that I was not able to eat, nor had I the least desire to taste any thing. I now wished for the last friend, death, to relieve me; but soon, to my grief, two of the white men offered me eatables; and, on my refusing to eat, one of them held me fast by the hands, and laid me across I think the windlass, and tied my feet, while the other flogged me severely. I had never experienced any thing of this kind before; and although, not being used to the water, I naturally feared that element the first time I saw it, yet nevertheless, could I have got over the nettings, I would have jumped over the side, but I could not; and, besides, the crew used to watch us very closely who were not chained down to the decks, lest we should leap into the water: and I have seen some of these poor African prisoners most severely cut for attempting to do so, and hourly whipped for not eating. This indeed was often the case with myself. In a little time after, amongst the poor chained men, I found some of my own nation, which in a small degree gave ease to my mind. I inquired of these what was to be done with us; they gave me to understand we were to be carried to these white people's country to work for them.

Source: Olaudah Equiano. 1789. *The Interesting Narrative of the Life of Olaudah Equiano, or Gustavus Vassa, The African, Written by Himself.* London, pp. 71–75.